INTRODUCTION
TO CRIMINAL JUSTICE

Robert D. Pursley
Associate Professor
University of Arkansas at Little Rock

GLENCOE PRESS
A division of Benziger Bruce & Glencoe, Inc.
Encino, California

Glencoe Press
A division of Benziger Bruce & Glencoe, Inc.
17337 Ventura Boulevard
Encino, California 91316
Collier Macmillan Canada, Ltd.

Library of Congress Catalog Card Number: 76-4033

ISBN 0-02-477540-1

1 2 3 4 5 6 7 8 9   80 79 78 77

Contents

GLENCOE PRESS CRIMINAL JUSTICE SERIES

General Editor:

G. DOUGLAS GOURLEY
Chairman, Department of Criminal Justice
California State University at Los Angeles
Los Angeles, California

Preface

This book is intended for use in introductory courses dealing with the processes, institutions, and administration of criminal justice in the United States. It was written with three objectives in mind: first, to provide students majoring in criminal justice with the background necessary for more advanced studies; second, to give general students a fundamental understanding of the criminal justice system, since they will be helping to shape its future; and third, to satisfy my need and that of my colleagues for a basic text with broad coverage and a reasonable balance between descriptive and conceptual material. The result, hopefully, is a comprehensive text that examines both the functions of criminal justice agencies and the way these agencies interact with each other and with society.

Although I consulted many people about the material to be included, the final selection is my own. Part 1 provides an overview of our criminal justice system and describes the environment in which specific agencies carry out their tasks. Part 2 covers the history of law enforcement in the United States, including its origins in Great Britain; discusses the range of police services offered at federal, state, and local levels; and analyzes developing trends with regard to delivery of these services. Part 3 examines the role played by courts in administering criminal justice and outlines the responsibilities of each "actor" in the courtroom drama, from judge to witness to court reporter. Part 4 takes a close look at corrections in America, tracing the changing correctional philosophy from its foundations in seventeenth-century Britain to the modern emphasis on community-based methods. The facilities, programs, administrative structure, and problems that constitute the American correctional system are studied in detail. In addition, the book's final part is devoted to the special problems inherent in the juvenile justice system.

As the summary above suggests, throughout the text the strengths and weaknesses of today's criminal justice system are explored in the context of related historical, social, and political developments. By gaining a sound understanding of the link between past events and current practices, students can perceive not only how criminal justice agencies operate, but also why they function as they do.

I am deeply indebted to William Bryden, criminal justice editor at Glencoe Press, for encouragement and assistance in shaping this book; to Kevin L. Parsons for research assistance and critical insight concerning the choice of subject matter; and to Claire Trazenfeld and Jenny Alkire for editorial help. I also want to thank my colleagues for their many valuable suggestions, which I have tried to incorporate in the final product.

Part 1

THE CRIMINAL JUSTICE PROCESS: OVERVIEW AND ISSUES

UNITED STATES
COURT HOUSE

Chapter 1

Introduction to the Criminal Justice System in Contemporary America

The administration of criminal justice in America is characterized by the complex relationships of the agencies to society and each other. In fact, these relationships are so intricate that the student of criminal justice must first understand a great deal about society if he or she is to understand the criminal justice process. This understanding can come only after long years of study, reflection, and experience. To the beginning student, one word of caution. The criminal justice system can never be understood as an isolated entity; nor can it be understood merely by studying legal texts and court decisions or by memorizing theories of crime causation, juvenile delinquency, or principles of police or correctional management. The challenge, and the reward, lie in comprehending, extracting, and applying knowledge gathered from many disparate sources.

The agencies of criminal justice must be seen as interrelated parts of a total system. Our system of criminal justice can be compared to an atom, with its nucleus surrounded by electrons, the arrangement and behavior of which determine the interactive process of the whole. In our system of criminal justice, society is the nucleus and the individual agencies of criminal justice are the electrons. Both are highly interactive, yet have distinct characteristics. Society, for example, has an impact on the administration of criminal justice as it defines the operations and nature of the agencies and develops certain expected standards of performance. In the same way, individual agencies interact and influence the policies and operations of other agencies. Together these patterns of interaction and influence determine in no small way how the overall administration of criminal justice is carried out in the United States.

In an elementary sense, the criminal justice agencies and the administration of justice are the visible embodiment of collective society's mechanism for social control. The criminal justice system is usually thought of as our primary *formalized* means of controlling aberrant behavior for the collective protection of society. This idea, however true it may be, unfortunately tends to over-simplify the complexity of the nature and roles of the overall process. It is the less visible roles which have in recent years attracted legal scholars, political scientists, sociologists, anthropologists, and economists to the study of crime and the administration of justice. Their efforts point out how thought-provoking and rewarding criminal justice as a field of academic inquiry can be. Since it is not constrained by the more well-defined boundaries of older and established disciplines, the serious student is constantly stimulated and quickly realizes that a firm foundation in other disciplines is necessary to understand the administration of criminal justice.

For example, from the political scientist comes the declaration that definitions of crime and the criminal justice system are created and maintained by the dominant class in society;[1] from sociologists comes the idea that crime is one of the most obvious manifestations of class conflict and that determinants of crime are applied by the social class that has the power to shape the enforcement and administration of criminal law.[2] From the economist comes the pronouncement that crime is less a result of economic or cultural deprivation or lack of socialization than simply a business-oriented economic opportunity in which the offender "rationally" weighs the costs versus the benefits before committing the criminal act.[3]

Assuming that the primary goal of criminal justice is to protect society (without entering into the argument at this point as to whether it protects the dominant interests at the expense of other groups), we find that it attempts to accomplish its task through a number of subgoals, such as:

- Crime prevention
- Apprehension of offenders
- The adjudicatory determination of guilt or innocence
- Disposition of those who transgress the existing legal codes
- Correction of inappropriate behavior by socially approved means

Although each of these may seem to be the sole responsibility of a certain agency, in fact these are common goals of the overall system. For example, the police may have a preeminent role in preventing crime and apprehending offenders, but they must rely upon the other agencies of justice to accomplish that objective. By determining who should be sentenced to prison and under what circumstances, the courts may (or may not) be assisting the police in their crime prevention efforts. If the courts are too lenient, they do not effectively remove criminal offenders from the community, nor do they deter potential violators. On the other hand, if the courts arbitrarily sentence offenders to prison, they may be breeding incipient hostility that hampers attempts to reform offenders.

The correctional agency is also involved in crime prevention. This agency's policies of release and programs of rehabilitation contribute directly to the crime prevention efforts of the police as well as to the workload of law enforcement agencies and the courts, which must deal with offenders who have been released from prison and return to crime. Since 99 percent of all imprisoned offenders will ultimately be released, we can see that should they choose to continue in their criminal ways, the crime preventive efforts of the police will probably have little impact and the courts will again be called upon to pass sentence on those the police are successful in apprehending.

Similarly, the police and the courts can affect correctional efforts by their practices of arrest, adjudication, and sentencing. An offender who perceives, rightly or wrongly, that he has been "railroaded" by the police or courts will not be very receptive to the reform efforts of correctional agencies. By the same token, an offender who sees a discrepancy in the sentence he receives compared with those received by similar offenders is not going to have much regard for such "justice" and those agencies and officials who administer it.

THE SYSTEM OF CRIMINAL JUSTICE

Although the administration of criminal justice has been referred to so far as a system, there are many who argue that it is, in fact, not a system.[4] This proposition needs to be examined a little more closely. The major argument put forth by those who do not think that criminal justice administration is a system is that the overall administration of the process is disjointed, that the individual agencies involved often neither share nor perceive common goals, philosophies, or methods of operation and as a result do not engage in cooperative and mutually complementary behavior. Unfortunately, the agencies of criminal justice often do *not* work together, and much of their uncooperative behavior is purposeful, brought about by jealousy, misunderstanding, lack of communications, and similar problems. For instance, law enforcement continually criticizes the courts, and both criticize corrections, and vice versa.

However, this turmoil and disagreement may be an essential element of our system of law and government. It should not be surprising that each agency of criminal justice sees the commission of crime, the needed remedies, and the process of justice from a different perspective. The perceptions and the values of the individuals involved are determined by life-long experiences, education, environment, peers, and a host of other factors. Are we to expect, for example, that a judge or an attorney from an upper-middle-class background with seven years of college and professional legal training, who is apt to see the administration of criminal justice from the perspective of the legal application of the law in the imposing decorum of the courtroom, will have perceptions and attitudes similar to those of a police officer on the street who comes from a working-class background with a high school education or less? In the same way, can we expect a caseworker in a correctional facility or a probation or parole agent trained in social work who sees his or her "client" in situations far different than does the police officer, who may have made the arrest during the commission of the crime, to think of the offender in the way that the police do?

It may well be that these differences in attitudes and perceptions actually strengthen rather than weaken the administration of justice and that the clash of different philosophies in fact illuminates and tempers the concept of justice. The actors in the criminal justice process should not suffer from "groupthink," for their lack of common perceptions, values, and attitudes can serve as an internal system of check and balances. Only thus can we approach dispensing justice in this nation and yet retain our fundamental considerations of fairness and equity.

Let's see how this might apply. In many cases the police—either because they caught the offender in the act or because of their investigative efforts—may be thoroughly convinced of the offender's guilt and express this attitude openly. However, should we expect our judges to harbor the same opinion without first testing the facts and evidence in the courtroom? The judge and the administrative process of criminal justice thus act as a check on other agencies. Admittedly, understanding among agencies of criminal justice may suffer, but this is a cost we as a free people must be willing to pay for higher standards of fairness and equity.

The naturally competitive relationship that exists among agencies and personnel in criminal justice also contributes to their lack of cooperation. For example, these agencies must compete with one another for budget appropriations. Therefore, each tries to demonstrate that it is doing a better job in dealing with the crime problem than other agencies competing for resources. Now there are two strategies that can be employed: First, one can demonstrate beyond any question that a particular agency is doing a better job than another agency. However, this would require having available measures which would permit one to make and prove such statements, and there are no such measures. Second, one can employ the strategy of seeking scapegoats. Each agency can say that it is doing the job as well as ever—the problem is that other components are to blame. Since the first strategy is not attainable, agencies naturally employ the second. This certainly does not create harmony and cooperation in the system.

In spite of these limitations on cooperative and joint behavior, the argument that the administration of criminal justice is a nonsystem cannot be easily supported. First of all, we have to understand what a system is and then examine whether or not the overall administration of criminal justice fulfills that definition. If we accept the definition that a system is a group of related processes in which the actions of one part of the process will have a direct impact upon the other parts, then the administration of justice certainly constitutes an overall system made up of mutually related parts.[5] For example, if we were to provide the police with an even larger share of the total criminal justice resources because we felt that they had the most important role in crime suppression, the other agencies would immediately become more ineffective, and their ineffectiveness would diminish the effectiveness of the police. Say that we drastically increased the resources of the police at the expense of the courts and corrections. There would probably be only a marginal improvement in the crime detection and apprehension rates of the police, but a significant reduction in the capabilities of the courts and corrections to perform their functions. We would see a tremendous backlog of cases pending disposition in our courts and a lack of institutional facilities and prisons to handle offenders. Under these circumstances, the courts would be forced to release more offenders because there would be no prisons to handle them; what inmates the prisons did receive would experience less corrective efforts; crime rates would continue to soar; and the police would become increasingly less able to cope with the situation. Thus, the weaknesses of any single component decreases the efficiency of others. The administration of criminal justice is therefore clearly seen to be a group of related processes, and the mere problem of integrating the elements does not qualify it to be referred to as a nonsystem.

CRIMINAL JUSTICE AGENCIES

Figure 1-1 depicts the formal agencies of justice which constitute the criminal justice system as well as the usual sequence of steps in the overall process.

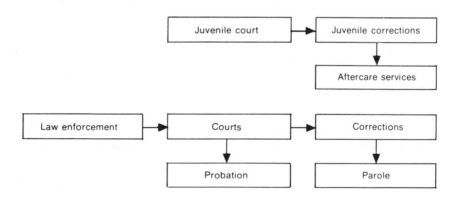

Figure 1-1 Agencies of Criminal Justice in the United States

The criminal justice system consists of three major components—law enforcement, the courts, and corrections—and the specialized auxiliary services of the juvenile justice process, probation, and parole. (Probation and parole agencies are usually classified within the general category of corrections. Similarly, juvenile corrections is often considered as a part of corrections, and juvenile courts are often considered with courts in general). Each of these units is responsible for performing highly specialized tasks as well as those general tasks which complement the objectives of the overall process. These complementary objectives can be seen by examining the functions of the six components of criminal justice.

Functions of the Major Components

Law Enforcement

This component consists of all police agencies at the federal, state, county, and municipal levels that, as members of the executive branch of government, serve the following functions:

1. *Prevention of criminal behavior.* Efforts directed toward reducing the causes of crime (delinquency prevention programs; citizen education programs).

2. *Repression of crime.* Efforts to eliminate or reduce the opportunities for criminal behavior (preventive and conspicuous patrol activity; intelligence and information gathering; crowd control; target-hardening strategies in an effort to make certain physical sites less vulnerable to criminals).

3. *Apprehension and arrest of offenders.* Criminal investigation; gathering of evidence; presentation before the courts of those who violate the criminal law.

4. *Protection of life and property.* All the strategies of crime prevention, crime repression, and apprehension designed to protect society and the provision of specialized services to assure public safety.

5. *Regulation of noncriminal conduct.* Police efforts to ensure compliance through regulatory means in an effort to maintain public safety and security.

Courts

This component includes those judicial agencies at all levels of government which perform the following functions of criminal justice administration:

1. *Determining by all available legal evidence whether a person is to be convicted of a crime.* Review of all evidence presented by the police or private citizens to determine its relevance and admissibility. Examination of the circumstances surrounding the crime.

2. *Protection of the rights of the accused.* Review of the actions of enforcement agencies of the executive branch to ensure that the police have not violated the rights of the accused.

3. *Proper disposition of those convicted.* Examination of the background of the accused, consideration of possible sentencing alternatives, and selection of the most proper form of disposition.

4. *Protection of society.* Removal from society of those who pose a threat to the safety of life and property.

5. *Prevention and repression of criminal behavior.* The task of imposing proper penalties which should take into consideration the circumstances of the crime, the characteristics of the offender, and the threat to public safety. This should be done in a manner so as to act as a deterrent to future criminal acts by the accused and others who would threaten public safety.

Corrections

This component comprises those executive agencies of federal, state, and local government which are responsible both directly and indirectly for the following functions:

1. *Maintaining institutions.* Maintaining prisons, jails, halfway houses, etc., to receive convicted offenders sentenced by the courts.

2. *Protection of law-abiding members of society.* Providing custody and security over offenders in order to prevent them from committing further crimes in society.

3. *Offender reform.* Providing those services that will assist offenders to be released and returned to society to lead noncriminal lives.

4. *Crime deterrence.* Encouraging incarcerated and potential offenders to lead law-abiding lives through the experience of incarceration and the deprivation liberty.

Functions of the Auxiliary Components

Juvenile Justice System

Specialized juvenile agencies of an adjudicatory and treatment nature adjudicate cases of delinquency involving minors and cases involving adults who have committed crimes against minors. This component of the system includes agencies and services that provide predelinquency, delinquency, and post-delinquency services to youth and society. Its functions are:

1. *Provision of needed care to the child.* Examining and determining the needs of the child and providing appropriate services.

2. *The determination of whether the child is to be adjudicated a delinquent.* Examining the facts surrounding the offense and examining admissible evidence.

3. *The proper disposition of the delinquent.* Examining the facts of the situation and the needs of the child to determine the proper disposition of the youthful offender.

4. *Deterrence of criminal acts.* Assisting in the correction of deviant attitudes and deterring those youths who would commit delinquent acts by the provision of appropriate services and the use of proper sanctions.

5. *The protection of public safety.* If warranted by the circumstances, institutionalizing the child for the protection of society.

6. *The protection of the child.* Adjudication and proper disposition of adults who encourage and contribute to delinquent behavior.

Probation

This auxiliary court-related component provides services at all levels of government to supervise an offender who has been found guilty. It is responsible for the following:

1. *Provision of a sentencing alternative other than commitment to a correctional institution.* Providing a means to divert the offender who has been found guilty of a crime from the corrections process by maintaining supervisory authority over the individual while permitting him to remain in the community.
2. *Deterrence and regulation of potential criminal conduct.* Helping the offender lead a noncriminal life by means of direct supervision and assistance.
3. *Provision of reports for the courts.* By an investigation of the offender's background, assisting the court in determining the proper disposition of an offender who has been found guilty.

Parole

The last auxiliary component is responsible for providing services to an offender who has been conditionally released from a correctional facility prior to the statutory expiration of his or her sentence. These services include:

1. *Provision of an alternative to maintaining an offender in custody.* Providing a means to release an offender to the supervision of a parole agency so that the offender can be assisted in readjusting to life outside the institution.
2. *Provision of needed services to an ex-offender.* Assisting the ex-offender in obtaining employment and providing counsel and guidance.
3. *Deterrence and regulation of potential criminal conduct.* Assisting in the prevention of criminal conduct by the individual by means of supervision to regulate the behavior of the parolee.

THE CRIMINAL JUSTICE SYSTEM IN OPERATION

Figure 1-1 seems to indicate that the justice system operates in a linear and interrelated fashion. Although it does, to a degree, it doesn't do so to the extent many people imagine. If the justice system operated in this linear and interrelated way, we could conceive of the process as follows: The police charged with the responsibility for investigating violations of the law would, if sufficient evidence existed, arrest the violator and bring the accused before the courts. After determination of the defendant's guilt, the court would sentence the convicted offender to a form of community supervision such as probation or to an institution which serves as a means of punishment and as a deterrent to further offenses. The offender might be released on parole before the sentence expired or released completely without parole supervision if the full sentence was

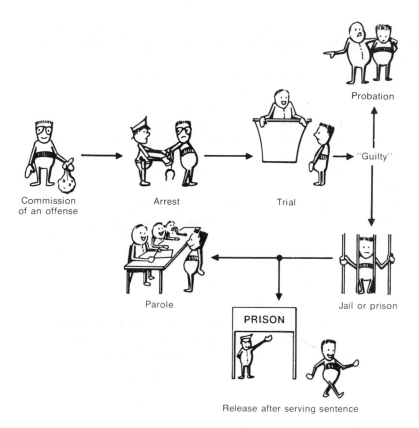

Figure 1-2   Hypothetical Sequence of Steps in the Criminal Justice
Process

served. In this model, the offender would be processed through each successive
stage in the process from arrest to conviction to final disposition. Figure 1-2
shows this hypothetical sequence of steps.

This model showing the agencies of justice operating in a series of highly
visible procedures and sequential steps is a very simple and inaccurate view of
how justice is dispensed. It does not indicate the complexities of the process or
the nonvisible areas of discretion that are a real part of the procedure.

To understand the justice system in the United States, one has to understand
the relationships between justice and certain sociopolitical characteristics of
American society. The administration of criminal justice, like all human social
institutions, is not perfect. There is a great deal of "slippage" within the
system. Due process of law and equal treatment, embodied in such lofty principles as propounded in the Bill of Rights, often fall short of the ideal in actual
practice. In addition, the system itself presents numerous obstacles to effective crime control, and it is often criticized for the threats it poses to the very

ideals it was designed to preserve and promote. Knowledgeable critics are contending that instead of preventing crime, the justice process through its agencies of law enforcement, courts, and corrections may be actually contributing to the serious crime problem which exists today.[6] For example, if the police disregard the rights of the accused, they are themselves contributing to a greater disrespect for our laws. The courts, in their leniency toward such white-collar crimes as price-fixing by corporations and in dealing lightly with offenses committed by political elites, are also contributing to a general distrust of our laws and the agencies and personnel of justice that are charged with enforcing them. Finally, correctional methods, in failing to reform those sentenced to institutions and often increasing their bitterness, are playing an effective role in the suppression of crime. The same can be said for conditional release programs such as parole, probation, and bond. For example, in a study of 7,057 felony arrests in Washington, D.C., in 1974, 26 percent of those arrested were out on some form of conditional release at the time of their arrests. Table 1-1 indicates the results of that study.

TABLE 1-1   Proportion of Felony Arrests during 1974 in Washington, D.C., in Which the Person Arrested Was Free on Some Form of Conditional Release Such as Parole, Probation, or Bond

Arrest Charge	Percentage of Arrestees on Conditional Release at Time of Arrest
Murder	28
Rape	19
Robbery	31
Burglary	32
Assault	11
Average for all felony arrests	26

Source: Institute for Law and Social Research, California Bureau of Statistics, *Felony Justice* (Boston: Little, Brown, to be published).

To understand just how far the administration of justice in the United States departs from any idealized model or system, we need to examine how the process actually operates. In effect, it works like a complex filter, screening out offenders at various points in the system. Consider the report of the President's Commission on Law Enforcement and Administration of Justice, which related serious offenses known to the police to the number of arrests made and the disposition of offenders through the justice process for the year 1965 (see Figure 1-3). In that year, nearly 2,800,000 serious offenses were brought to the

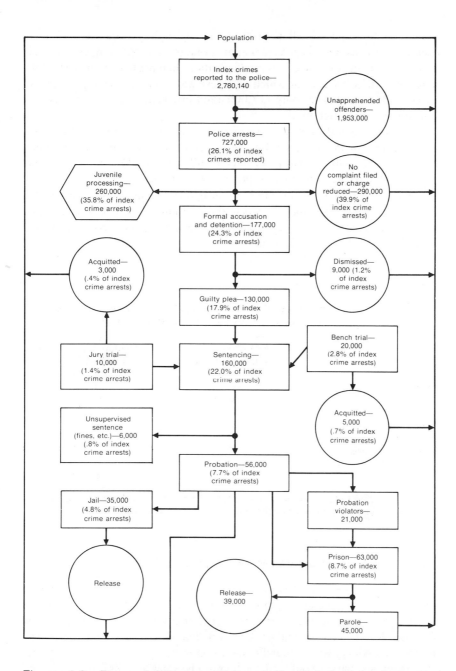

Figure 1-3   Flow of Offenders through the Criminal Justice
            System

Source: Adapted from the President's Commision on Law Enforcement and Administration of Justice, *The Challenge of Crime in a Free Society* (Washington: U.S. Government Printing Office, 1967) pp. 262–263.

attention of the police. Of all these offenses, only slightly more than 26 percent resulted in arrests. Of this percentage, over one-third were juveniles who were turned over to the juvenile courts for disposition. In more than 60 percent of the remaining 467,000 cases in which an arrest was made, the charges were reduced or dismissed. Thus only 177,000 adult offenders were even accused or placed in pretrial detention.[7]

The picture is just as bleak if we take the process of criminal justice a few steps further. Of the relatively few felony cases that end up in our criminal courts for trial, only a small percentage result in conviction, and even fewer convicted felons are sent to jail or prison for their crimes. A study conducted recently in six large American cities or metropolitan counties indicates that the average conviction rate for arrested felons in these jurisdictions is approximately 40 percent, of whom only 20 percent are sent to jail or prison. Table 1-2 shows the record in these six areas.

TABLE 1-2   Percentage of Persons Arrested on Felony Charges Who Are Convicted and Sent to Jail or Prison

Jurisdiction	Percentage of Arrestees Convicted	Percentage of Convicted Felons Sent to Jail or Prison
Washington, D.C.	33	18
Chicago	26	15
Baltimore	44	28
Detroit	58	20
Los Angeles County	46	28
San Diego County	34	14
Average	40	20

Source: Institute for Law and Social Research, California Bureau of Statistics, *Felony Justice* (Boston: Little, Brown, to be published).

Low Percentage of Arrests Made in Serious Crimes

These facts raise a number of questions: First, why are law enforcement agencies able to make arrests in only about one-fourth of all *serious* crimes which are reported to them. This is an extremely low success rate by any standard. It should be pointed out, however, that in some cases the police may arrest an individual who is found to have committed two, three, or even more serious crimes, which would reduce the ratio between serious crimes reported to the police and the number of offenders arrested. Even so, the police arrest only a small percentage of the offenders who commit serious crimes in this country. A part of the answer almost certainly lies in the traditional inefficiency of the police in solving crimes. However, this inefficiency cannot be considered simply as ineptness. Our criminal justice processes and the powers of the police are severely curtailed by our expressed concern for the rights of the individual and our unwillingness to permit the police a great deal of autonomous authority. Consequently, a free society, it would seem, must be willing to forgo greater police efficiency for the assurance that police powers will not be used to curtail the rights we cherish in the United States. A very precarious balance exists between police power and a free society—one which requires constant vigilance, as history has repeatedly demonstrated.

Another part of the answer lies in the very nature of most crimes. Much criminal behavior is of a covert nature, with the odds drastically in favor of the offender. The police, because of limitations in resources, personnel, and operating strategies, are naturally placed in a defensive role in trying to curtail crime. They usually must wait until a crime occurs before they can take action. This gives a tremendous advantage to the criminal, who can take the initiative by choosing the time, place, and method of attack. Even a police agency with the most highly qualified and dedicated police personnel, using the most modern technological crime-solving advances, would probably be only slightly more efficient than one with only mediocre personnel and resources. Although many people place great stock in the ability of ''more qualified'' police personnel to make an appreciable difference in crime levels, this relationship has never been demonstrated (and probably never will be).

High Percentage of Juveniles Arrested

A second question raised by the statistics shown in Figure 1-3 is: Why are the police more successful in arresting juveniles than adults for serious offenses? At first glance, one might think that it is because juveniles commit a higher proportion of serious offenses than do adults. However, several factors argue against making this conclusion: First, to make such a judgment, one would need to know the total number of serious crimes committed (including those not reported to the authorities) what percentage were committed by juveniles, and what percentage of the total population consists of juveniles. Of course, we'll never know the total number of serious crimes committed, and even if we did, we would not know in many cases whether the crime was committed by a juvenile or an adult because the offender will never be arrested.

Another problem is that states have set age limits within which an individual can be considered as a juvenile for the purpose of criminal prosecution. A person over these statutory ages (usually seventeen or eighteen) is considered an adult.[8] Thus, the period of time when a child is perhaps psychologically and physically most capable of committing crimes is limited to four or five years. If the arrest statistics are interpreted literally, juveniles would have to be extremely active in their preadolescent and adolescent years in the commission of serious offenses. Although juveniles from the ages of twelve to seventeen may, in fact, be committing more serious crimes in proportion to their numbers than say those in the age bracket of twenty-five to thirty-two, we should not be willing on the basis of what little we know to say that they are committing over one-third of all serious crime!

The more probable reason that they are so overrepresented in the arrest statistics is that juveniles are more likely to be caught. Their crimes are less sophisticated and covert than those committed by adults. Crimes requiring a high degree of specialized knowledge, skills, and organization are not those normally entered into by juveniles. Instead, they are more likely to engage in the more crude street crimes, which are precisely the types of crimes that police departments are most capable of dealing with.

High Percentage of Charges Reduced or Dismissed

A third question raised by the data concerns the large percentage of arrests in which either no complaint is filed or the charges are reduced. This would indicate that something of importance for understanding the criminal justice process is occurring at this stage. Why is it that so many offenders do not complete the preliminary steps in the judicial process and even less ultimately wind up in jail?

The reason that so many arrestees do not have complaints filed against them may be a result of a number of factors: The first obvious reason is that the police may be arresting individuals without enough evidence to warrant prosecution of the offender; thus the charges are dismissed. However, there may be other factors as well: For example, in crimes committed by one spouse against the other, it is not at all unusual for the victim to refuse to file charges. In other instances, witnesses and even victims out of fear of retaliation, because of the inconvenience, or because they have moved from the jurisdiction cannot or will not testify; without this crucial testimony, the state has no case.

Why do so many of those arrested have their charges reduced and never end up being sentenced to jail or a penitentiary? For example, of those offenders who admitted their guilt to serious crimes, Figure 1-3 shows that only slightly more than 61 percent (98,000) were sentenced to either jail or prison, with only 39 percent (63,000) being sent specifically to penitentiaries for longer-term incarceration. A probable clue to this can be found in the fact that for all defendants whose cases were not dismissed at the formal accusation stage (168,000), 77 percent (130,000) entered guilty pleas at the guilty plea stage in Figure 1-3.

The number of individuals who plead guilty to a serious offense and ultimately end up serving time for their admitted offenses is often reduced by the process of *plea bargaining* which is a form of negotiation between the defendant's attorney and the prosecutor in which the accused agrees to plead guilty in exchange for a reduction in the charge, probation, or a reduced sentence.

One of the major functions of our judicial process is to determine the guilt or innocence of those accused of crimes. This goal in itself serves to divert offenders out of the system. Our system of justice operates on two principles of criminal law that are very important for understanding the overall process. The first of these is the presumption of innocence. Those accused of crimes are considered innocent until proved guilty. The second principle is the burden of proof, which in criminal cases is guilt beyond a reasonable doubt. The state must prove its accusations against the accused in such a manner that there is no reasonable doubt as to his guilt—if reasonable doubt exists, the accused must be acquitted.

Theoretically, this determination is the result of adjudicating the issues of fact or law in the particular case; in actual practice, however, this seldom happens. In many cases, the existence of guilt is supported by sufficient evidence; in others where the issues of fact are such that the accused may or may not be found guilty beyond a reasonable doubt, concessions are worked out which may result in reducing the charge if the accused agrees to plead guilty.[9] Thus, a form of calculated gamesmanship is a feature of many criminal prosecutions. The question becomes: Is there enough evidence to convict? This question concerns both the prosecution and the defense. Obviously, if there is ample evidence to convict, the prosecution is not interested in bargaining; by the same token, if there is not possibly enough evidence to convict, there is no need for the accused to bargain away certain acquittal. It is in the gray area between certain guilt and probable innocence that bargaining takes place. The accused may agree to plead guilty to a reduced charge rather than take the chance that the state can prove its case. If this is acceptable to the prosecution, the accused will often be given probation and thus avoid sentencing to jail or a penitentiary.

Another basic purpose of the criminal justice system which serves to divert offenders is that of *determining the consequences to be imposed on the accused after he has been determined to have committed the crime.* It involves determining the specific offense with which to charge the accused as well as the proper dispositon of the offender who has been found guilty. It also involves determining whether or not to convict at all since some cases are dismissed by the judge or prosecutor in spite of sufficient evidence to convict. This usually occurs because the police, the prosecutor, or even the trial court has made some form of legal error.

In the criminal justice systems of most states, alternative dispositions are available to the court that are more lenient than those specified by statute. Many of these alternative dispositions are made because massive case loads glut the criminal courts, which lack sufficient prosecutorial, judicial, and staff personnel to handle each case to its ultimate (and perhaps, just) conclusion.

Dispositions are arrived at by an interaction of the parties in the criminal case, which include the criminal justice officials, particularly the prosecutors, police, and judges, as well as the defendant and his attorney.[10] Their actions are influenced by a number of considerations, including the nature of the crime, the characteristics of the accused and of the victim, the dispositions available, the strength of the case, the amount of time that overburdened officials can devote to the case, and public attitudes and policies toward the type of offense or the offender.

There exists among criminal justice officials some consensus as to the relative seriousness of various crimes. First, crimes against property which involve no physical threats are thought to be less serious than violent crimes against persons or those crimes that have the inherent potential for violence. Second, the relationship of offender to victim may play an important role. For example, crimes committed by one spouse on another in which no serious harm has occurred are considered less serious than those involving strangers.[11] Third, the relative magnitude of the offense is important. Although the possession for sale of narcotics is considered a serious offense, the possession of a few ounces of marijuana is not as serious as the possession of several pounds of the substance.

The characteristics of the offender also play an important role. Young defendants with minor records are often seen as less serious offenders and therefore more entitled to the leniency of the court than older persons who commit the same type of offense. For the same reason, first-time adult offenders are treated much more leniently by the courts than are adult offenders with extensive prior criminal records.

Another factor which will influence how officials perceive and react to a particular circumstance is the victim. The age, race, and relationship of the victim to the accused all will play some part, as may the attitude of the victim. If the victim insists that the accused be prosecuted, and evidence is sufficient, the chances are that this will occur. Conversely, if the victim does not desire to have the state prosecute the case, the state is likely to dismiss charges unless there are overriding policy considerations. The attitude of the victim may be also influential in other ways. If the victim is so insistent that the state has little choice but to prosecute, the judge may be less severe or in some cases, more severe than would ordinarily be the case.

The tactics and skill of defense counsel also affect the nature of the disposition. In some cases, the defense may use issues of law such as those pertaining to evidence to obtain an acquittal by the court. Or the defense may persuade the court that the probability of a successful prosecution of the case is very low or that the nature of the crime, perhaps because of extenuating circumstances, does not justify the time required to conduct a trial. By threatening to force a trial on the merits of the case and the existing evidence or by portraying the facts so as to lessen the perceived severity of the offense, the defense may persuade the prosecutor or judge to lessen the severity of the disposition.

Because of the inability of the police to arrest criminal violators, and because of the inability or unwillingness of the courts to convict offenders or sentence them to imprisonment once they are convicted, only slightly more than *3 percent* of all serious crimes *which come to the attention of the police* result in the offender being found guilty and sentenced to jail or a penitentiary!

So far, we have been concerned only with the attrition rate of cases which come to the attention of the police. If we were to look at the attrition process for

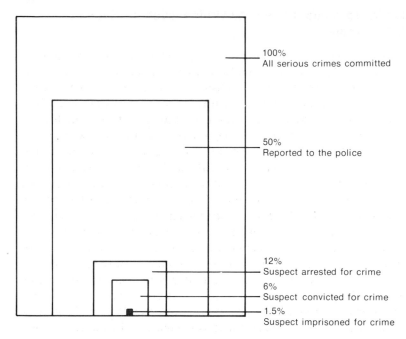

100%
All serious crimes committed

50%
Reported to the police

12%
Suspect arrested for crime

6%
Suspect convicted for crime

1.5%
Suspect imprisoned for crime

Figure 1-4   Serious Crimes in the United States and
Percentage of Suspects Imprisoned
for These Crimes

Source: Adapted from National Commission on the Causes and Prevention of Violence, *Final Report* (Washington, D.C.:
U.S. Government Printing Office, December 1969), p. xviii.

all estimated serious crimes which are committed *regardless of whether they
are reported to the police or not,* the picture is even more bleak. In these cases,
only *1 1/2 percent* of all serious crimes occurring are concluded by a suspect
being found guilty and sentenced to a jail or penitentiary (see Figure 1-4).

All these facts tell us that the criminal justice process departs drastically from
the sequence of offense-arrest-conviction-punishment that is theoretically associated with the administration of criminal justice. How and under what conditions arrested individuals are being diverted from the system has been given
careful examination in recent years by those who are attempting to shed some
light on how the system actually operates.

THE RELATIONSHIP OF LAW AND POLITICS TO JUSTICE

So far in this chapter we have been concentrating on the interactive processes
among the agencies and actors *within* the criminal justice system. Looking back
at our analogy of the atom, it is now appropriate to examine the relationship of
society to the administration of criminal justice.

Conflicting Ideas about How the Criminal Justice System Should Operate

As a point of departure, it should be recognized that the administration of criminal justice serves both as a formulator of public policy and as a reflection of policy which has been broadly established and defined by society. In the latter case, society provides the criminal justice system with certain guidelines by which it is supposed to operate. These guidelines are often contradictory. For example, choices must be made among such competing values as the rights of the accused and the protection of society. This means that the administration of justice must rest on some implicit idea of what justice involves. However, society itself interprets the meaning of justice and how it is to be accomplished very differently and often inconsistently. People simply have different ideas and expectations of how the process should be administered. As a consequence, the machinery of criminal justice has no consensual guidelines in the way it is supposed to operate. Nobody will argue with the fact that the primary purpose of the system is to protect society; however, differences of opinion over the manner in which this protection is to be afforded subject individual agencies and the entire administrative process to criticism by one group or another. This problem has been neatly placed into perspective by Herbert Packer. He suggests that the administration of criminal justice is complicated by the competition between two opposing value systems which are expressed by society and which underlie the process. These values he refers to as *crime control* and *due process*. [12]

According to Packer, underlying the crime control model is the idea that the most important function of the criminal justice system is the repression of criminal conduct. The rationale for this model rests on the idea that the failure of law enforcement and other agencies of criminal justice to bring criminal conduct under tight control leads to the breakdown of public order and, as a result, the disappearance of social tranquillity, which is an important condition of human freedom. In order to guarantee the maintenance of the existing social order, the administration of criminal justice must stress "efficiency," that is, the increased capacity to apprehend, try, convict, and dispose of a high proportion of criminal offenders, with a premium placed on speed and finality in dealing with offenders.

The assumption of this model is that the offender is guilty, an assumption that contradicts the basic presumption of innocence that is supposed to surround the accused under our system of criminal jurisprudence. However, it should be pointed out that Packer's crime control model sees this presumption of guilt as qualified; it occurs only after extensive fact-finding procedures are employed by the police and prosecutors. In this way, all cases that probably would not result in a successful conviction are screened out at preliminary stages, leaving only those where the offender is almost certainly guilty. Thus, all fact finding is accomplished before the trial rather than during it. In this model the trial and disposition process resemble an assembly line.

The *due process* model is the opposite of the crime control model. Whereas the crime control model resembles an assembly-line at the judicial stage, the due process model has the features of an obstacle course for judicial authorities. Under this model, each stage of the criminal justice process from arrest through the court's disposition of the accused is designed to present formidable impediments to carrying the accused any further along in the process. A basic distinction between the two is that the crime control model tends to rely more heavily on the preliminary screening of the police and the prosecutor to determine the merits of the case in terms of its potential for successful prosecution. The due process model rejects this role for the police and prosecutors on the grounds that it is not compatible with our system of laws and government; instead, it places the screening burden on the court, which should subject the merits of the case to scrutiny in the courtroom.

Interestingly, the crime control model is very similar to the criminal justice process that exists in Great Britain and many West European countries, where the prevailing philosophy is that the accused is guilty until proved innocent. The American ideal of criminal jurisprudence requires us to consider the accused as innocent until proved guilty. Packer views both systems as striving for quality control, but with the due process model emphasizing "reliability" (i.e., we must be willing to live with the fact that some guilty offenders will in fact be found innocent of their crime in order to ensure that innocent persons are not unjustly convicted) and the crime control model placing greater emphasis on "efficiency" and "productivity" (i.e., we would be more willing to accept a few mistakes in convicting and disposing of offenders, but the overall improvement in the administration of justice to deal with problems of crime and disorder would more than compensate for the mistakes).

The public often expresses attitudes about the way the criminal laws in our nation should be administered which are very similar to the underlying ideas of these two models, a fact that indicates the fundamental difference in philosophy that besets the administration of criminal justice in our nation and the range of feelings people have as to how the system of criminal justice should deal with offender.

Decentralization of Criminal Justice Operations

Other factors also have an impact upon the process of criminal justice in the United States. One is that the administration of criminal justice is decentralized in operation with over 41,000 local agencies of criminal justice alone.[13] This number represents 87 percent of all criminal justice agencies in the United States.[14] This decentralization has tremendous implications for the way in which criminal justice is administered in this country, for it is at the local level of government where agencies of justice can most readily be influenced by political considerations.[15] This fact was recognized by such notables as James Madison, who, in *The Federalist* No. 10, perceived local government as a ready-made means by which dominant interests could have an inordinate amount of influence over governmental policies and affairs to the exclusion of others in the community. What would seem to compound this problem is the fact that many laws are ambiguous and lack public consensus and support for their enforcement. This permits arbitrary and capricious enforcement, in which the police, the prosecutor, and the courts are given a wide range of discretionary powers to determine who will be arrested, what charges will be prosecuted, and how the accused will be disposed of.[16] Since those decisions are made on a daily basis within the context of the local community, the political ramifications of the system are heightened, and the conflict that marks the quest for justice is one of the characteristics that makes the administration of justice an element of the political arena.

Besides the general pervasiveness of politics in the administration of justice, there are other ways in which political influences enter the legal system. Political considerations and partisan politics play an important role in the recruitment of judges, prosecutors, and other legal personnel. Likewise, even in "reform" cities employing civil service systems, the police are often tainted, with political decisions being made for job assignments, promotions, and other considerations. In many cities, the road to a judgeship is paved by the practice of performing deeds for the successful political party. Prosecuting attorneys are also actively engaged in partisan politics, and they rely on the party machinery for nomination and election. Studies of the police in local communities are replete with instances of political considerations being made in determining enforcement policies, including the decision as who is arrestable and who is not and what laws are subject to enforcement or nonenforcement. In fact, one researcher has suggested that the environment of a community (which would necessarily include its politics) is associated with the very "style" of law enforcement it receives.[17]

Now this is not to suggest that certain more "serious" crimes such as homicide or armed robberies are highly susceptible to political influence. They probably are not for a number of reasons: First, those likely to commit such crimes are not politically influential. Secondly, there is a greater consensus among citizens that these crimes are inherently dangerous to the security of society. But what about other less visible crimes whose economic consequences may in fact be even greater? For example, an unscrupulous merchant may steal far more from unsuspecting customers by overcharging or selling inferior merchandise than the burglar who breaks into a gas station and escapes with $20. However, who is more likely to receive the attention of the police and the criminal justice system? It is in these areas of low visibility that the administration of criminal justice is most vulnerable to manipulation. Recently, a famous political figure died in Texas. After his death, the state police decided to conduct an investigation into his "empire." They are finding that over the years he had appropriated to his own use hundreds of thousands of dollars from the government treasury. Yet many people are asking why the police waited until after his death to conduct their investigation when his operations had been widely publicized for years?

One of the most visible impacts of political influence on local criminal justice systems is on the passage of local ordinances and their enforcement by the local police and courts. These local ordinances provide us the best window to view how local influentials and political interests distribute and make applicable to the citizens of the particular community certain values. The legislation and enforcement of laws concerning gambling, prostitution, liquor sales, pornography, consumer fraud, and loitering and such concerns as zoning ordinances and licensing regulations are typical extensions of certain values held in the community.

Invariably then, community values are related to the creation and enforcement of local laws. This same relation exists in the making and enforcement of laws at all levels of governments, but it is much more difficult to pinpoint when the law is more encompassing at higher levels of government. How important the culture of a community is to the administration of criminal justice can be demonstrated by the recent experience some communities have had with decriminalization of marijuana offenses. For example, in 1973, the city of Ann Arbor, Michigan, which is the site of the University of Michigan, passed a local ordinance which called for the imposition of a $5 fine for the use of marijuana. The values of that particular community were such that the use of marijuana was almost an acceptable practice that did not warrant the imposition of the much more severe sanctions that existed in the laws of neighboring communities.

In the final analysis, then, a society's system of criminal justice—the making, interpretation, imposition, and administration of criminal law—both reflects and defines the environment that surrounds it. Probably no other formalized social institution can provide a clearer insight into the character of a people and their attitudes, values, prejudices, and concerns. Given the nature of our own criminal justice system, we as Americans should feel a sense of pride, and a sense of shame as well. This combination of feelings is essential if we hope to improve that system.

SUMMARY

The criminal justice system is an institution designed to protect society. It consists of six specialized yet interrelated agencies: police, courts, corrections, juvenile justice system, probation, and parole. These agencies share complementary goals and objectives. The administration of justice is often thought of as operating in a linear fashion from arrest to incarceration; in fact, the process is more complex because of diversionary practices which are the result of many factors.

The criminal justice system is a very complicated extension of an even more complicated social system that provides it with conflicting guidelines by which to operate. Since the largest segment of the criminal justice system is found in local governments, it mirrors the conflict and accommodation that occur at the local level.

Suggested Additional Readings

Advisory Committee on Intergovernmental Relations. *State-Local Relations in the Criminal Justice System*. Washington, D.C.: U.S. Government Printing Office, 1971.

Bent, Allen E. *The Politics of Law Enforcement*. Lexington, Mass.: Lexington Books, 1974.

Cole, George F. *Politics and the Administration of Justice*. Beverly Hills, Calif.: Sage, 1973.

Cole, George F. ed. *Criminal Justice: Law and Politics*. North Scituate, Mass.: Duxbury Press, 1972.

Committee for Economic Development. *Reducing Crime and Assuring Justice*. New York: CED, June 1972.

Klonoski, James, and Robert Mendelsohn, eds. *The Politics of Local Justice*. Boston: Little, Brown, 1970.

Neubauer, David. *Criminal Justice in Middle America*. Morristown, N.J.: Gerneral Learning Press, 1974.

Oaks, Dallin, and Warren Lehman. *A Criminal Justice System and the Indigent*. Chicago: University of Chicago Press, 1967.

Parsons, Talcott. "The Law and Social Control." In William Evan, ed., *Law and Sociology*. New York: Free Press, 1962, pp. 56–72.

Sanders, William B., and Howard C. Daudistel, eds. *The Criminal Justice Process*. New York: Praeger, 1976.

Vines, Kenneth. "Courts as Political and Governmental Agencies," in Herbert Jacob and Kenneth Vines, eds., *Politics in the American States*. Boston: Little, Brown, 1965, pp. 239–287.

Watson, Richard, and Ronald Downing. *The Politics of the Bench and Bar*. New York: Wiley, 1969.

Notes

1. See William J. Chambliss and Robert B. Seidman, *Law, Order and Power* (Reading, Mass.: Addison-Wesley, 1971); and George Rusche and Otto Kirchheimer, *Punishment and Social Structure* (New York: Columbia University Press, 1969).

2. See Richard Quinney, "The Social Reality of Crime," in Abraham Blumberg, ed. *Current Perspectives in Criminal Behavior* (New York: Knopf, 1974), pp. 35–45.

3. See Simon Rottenberg, *The Economics of Crime and Punishment* (Washington, D.C.: The American Enterprise Institute for Public Policy Research, 1973); and Gary J. Becker, "Crime and Punishment: An Economic Approach," *Journal of Political Economy* 76 (1966): 169–217.

4. See Harry W. More, *Principles and Procedures in the Administration of Justice* (New York: Wiley, 1975), pp. 10–11; and the National Advisory Commission on the Causes and Prevention of Violence, *Law and Order Reconsidered* (New York: Bantam, 1969), especially chap. 13.

5. For a brief insight into how a system is defined, see Basil S. Georgopoulos, "An Open-Systems Theory Model for Organizational Research," in A. R. Negandhi, ed., *Modern Organizational Theory* (Kent, Ohio: Kent State University Press, 1973), pp. 102–131. For a review of how systems theory can be applied to examine the criminal justice process, see Jim L. Munro, "Toward a Theory of Criminal Justice Administration: A General Systems Perspective," *Public Administration Review* 31 (November/December 1971): 621–631.

6. National Advisory Commission on Criminal Justice Standards and Goals, *Corrections* (Washington, D.C.: U.S. Government Printing Office, 1973), p. 1.

7. President's Commission on Law Enforcement and Administration of Justice, *The Challenge of Crime in a Free Society* (Washington, D.C.: U.S. Government Printing office, 1967), pp. 262–263.

8. There are some exceptions to this. For example, some states have youthful offender statutes which, in some cases, may extend the jurisdiction of the juvenile court over a youth beyond the statutorily prescribed age of seventeen or eighteen.

9. Frank W. Miller, *Prosecution: The Decision to Charge a Suspect with a Crime* (Boston: Little, Brown, 1969).

10. See Herbert Jacob, *Urban Justice* (Englewood Cliffs, N.J.: Prentice-Hall, 1973), especially chap. 6.

11. Edward Green, "Sentencing Practices of Criminal Court Judges," *American Journal of Corrections* 32 (July-August 1960); P. Greenwood, et al., *Prosecution of Adult Felony defendants in Los Angeles County: A Police Perspective* (Santa Monica, Calif.: Rand 1973).

12. Herbert L Packer, *The Limits of the Criminal Sanction* (Stanford, Calif.: Stanford University Press, 1968).

13. Michael J. Hindeland, et al., *Sourcebook of Criminal Justice Statistics* (Washington D.C.: Law Enforcement Assistance Administration, August 1973), p. 23.

14. Ibid.

15. For example, see Anwar Syed, *The Political Theory of American Local Government* (New York: Random House, 1966); Paul Ylvisaker, "Some Criteria for a 'Proper' Areal Division of Governmental Powers," in Arthur Mass, ed., *Area and Power* (New York: Free Press, 1959), pp. 34–54.

16. For example, see Joseph Goldstein, "Police Discretion Not to Invoke the Criminal Process: Low-Visibility Decisions in the Administration of Justice," in Jack Foster, ed., *Readings in Criminal Justice* (Berkeley, Calif.: McCutchan, 1969), pp. 153–169.

17. James Q. Wilson, *Varieties of Police Behavior* (Cambridge, Mass.: Harvard University Press, 1968), p. 227.

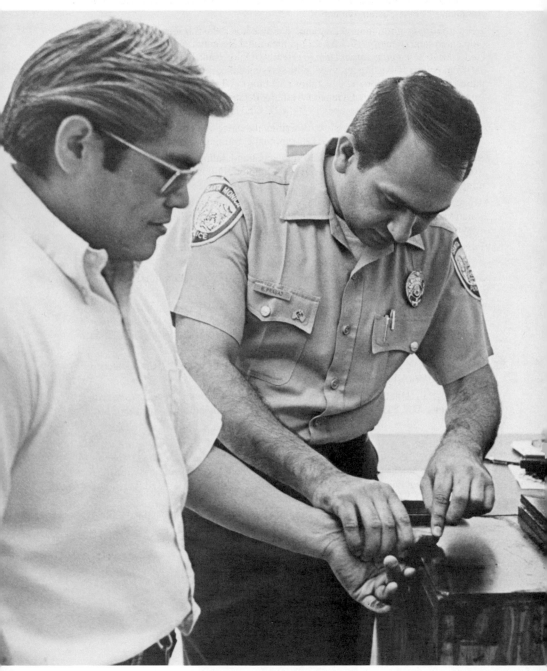

Chapter 2

The Classification of Crimes and Introductory Legal Terminology

In this chapter, we shall examine the elements that make certain acts crimes and explain how some important crimes are classified in the criminal law. We shall also define some basic legal terms and describe a few legal documents commonly employed in the administration of criminal justice.

ELEMENTS OF CRIME

A crime has been defined as a voluntary and intentional violation by commission or omission, by a legally competent person, of a legal duty that commands or prohibits an act for the protection of society, and which is punishable by judicial proceedings in the name of the state.[1] From this legal definition of a crime, a number of things are apparent. First, the act must be voluntary. Thus, if the particular behavior which constitutes the criminal act can be shown to be involuntary, as where an individual is forced to commit a criminal act against his or her will, the person cannot be guilty of the crime charged. The question that must be addressed in such circumstances is: Did the offender actually act involuntarily and what circumstances forced this involuntary act? If, for example, one was forced to participate in a crime at gunpoint or in fear of one's life or safety or the life or safety of one's family, one committed the act involuntarily and is not guilty of the crime. In this case, it must be demonstrated that the fear was justified and because of it the individual committed the crime.

For an act to be a crime, it must also be intentional. This would excuse otherwise criminal acts that occur by accident.

The act, if it is to constitute a crime, must also be committed by a legally competent person. In the law, certain categories of people are considered incompetent to commit crimes, for example, someone who was "insane" at the time of the act or someone of very tender age. The law will view the acts committed by such persons as not fulfilling the requirements of being voluntary and intentional because their mental state is such that they do not comprehend the nature of their behavior.

The definition of a crime also shows us that behavior which constitutes a crime can be either an act of commission or an act of omission. We are guilty of committing a crime by doing something that the law says we should not do as well as not doing what the law says we must. At this point, we should discuss a fundamental requirement of criminal law as it exists in the United States. Any act of commission or omission, before it can constitute a crime, must be an act that is unlawful by statute *at the time of the act*. For example, if you were to commit an act today, which at the time of its commission was not illegal, you could not be later arrested for the act if it were later to be enacted into law as a crime. This is called an *ex post facto* (after the fact) law, and such laws are forbidden by the U.S. Constitution.[2] Thus, the criminal law cannot be applied retroactively to charge persons for criminal acts when at the time of their act there was no law prohibiting such behavior.

Finally, a crime is an act which threatens the protection of society and which is punishable by judicial proceedings in the name of the state. In this way, crime is considered to be an act against the collective public safety, welfare, and well-being of society. In a theoretical and legal sense, the act which constitutes a crime is more than merely the act of an offender directed against an innocent victim; the victim exists as an appendage of society itself. This is one of the major distinctions in the law between criminal law and civil law. In civil law, in which someone brings a lawsuit against another for damages, both parties in the case are viewed as private citizens. The party alleging damages and bringing suit is called the *plaintiff,* and the one from whom the damages are sought is called the *defendant*. The case is referred to by the names of the plaintiff and defendant, respectively, as in *Smith* v. *Brown*. In criminal cases, the government is referred to as the *prosecution* and the accused as the *defendant*. In criminal cases, the prosecution represents the people, and the case name reflects this, as in *United States* v. *Brown, People* v. *Smith,* or *Colorado* v. *Green*.

In the law, every crime contains what are called *elements* of the offense. These elements can be thought of as the specific legal definition of the crime. Before anyone can be convicted of a crime, each of these elements must be proved by the state. The elements that constitute a crime are:

1. The act
2. The intent
3. The concurrence of act and intent
4. The causation
5. The result[3]

For example, looking at the legal definition of a crime given earlier, we can see that before the government could convict someone of committing a crime, it must show: (1) that there was committed an act which, at the time of its commission, was prohibited, or that the accused failed to do something commanded by the law (the act); (2) that the accused did the act voluntarily and with full knowledge of what he or she was doing (the intent); (3) that the act resulted from the intent (the concurrence of act and intent); (4) that the act and the intent caused something to occur which was offensive to the law (causation); and (5) that it resulted in some harm to society (result).

Criminal Intent

Most of these elements of the law are rather straightforward. For example, since every crime involves the commission or omission of an act, before the defendant in a criminal case can be found guilty of theft, there must be the actual taking of an object. It is, however, in the area of proving intent as an essential element of each crime that we enter into the gray area of the criminal law. The idea of intent in the criminal law is more complicated because it bears on an evaluation of the psychological motives of the offender. The idea behind intent is found in the Latin phrase *mens rea,* which means roughly that the law will consider that the offender possessed the necessary intent as shown by his actions and by the common experience of mankind.[4] For example, if a man commits a crime, it will be assumed that he did so voluntarily, and since he did so voluntarily, he must have also possessed the required intent. The law will then even go one step further. Since it is presumed by his actions and our common experience that he committed the crime voluntarily, which we then assume he did intentionally and of his own free will, these factors together lead us to the natural assumption that he also committed the act *knowingly.* Figure 2-1 shows the legal reasoning behind showing intent as a necessary element of each crime.

Of course, the defendant in a criminal case can overturn this natural presumption of intent in any number of ways. The state may be able to show, for example, that the accused participated in a criminal act, but the accused may be able to demonstrate that by virtue of decreased mental reasoning capacity (e.g., insanity), he or she had no knowledge of the act. In some states, the defendant may be able to show that because of insanity he or she was the victim of an "irresistible impulse" which destroyed all ability to exercise free will (voluntariness) in the commission of the act. In these cases, intent could not be proved as a necessary element of the crime and the defendant could not be found guilty of the crime charged.

This idea of intent and the necessary conditions of voluntariness and knowledge are embodied in the two types of intent known as *general intent* and *specific intent* which exist in our system of law.

General Intent

General intent is thought of as a state of mind bent on the commission of any offense or any deviation from standard conduct which, without regard for

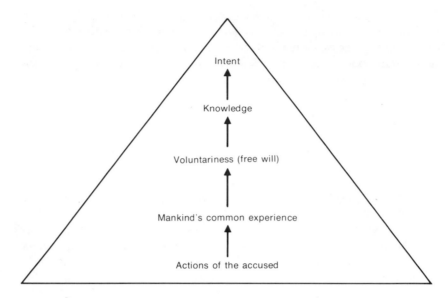

Figure 2-1. The Concept of *Mens Rea* in Proving Intent

others, may expose anybody to harm, even without any specific intent as to the object or consequences of such conduct.[5] In other words, someone who does not conform to legal conduct is assumed to intend harmful consequences whether he or she does intend harmful consequences or not. The most common example is drunk driving. Let us say a woman operating an automobile while intoxicated strikes and kills a pedestrian or another motorist. Certainly, she did not "intend" the consequences of her act. However, even though the motorist had no actual intent to kill another party, she would be charged with manslaughter or vehicular homicide under the principle of general intent. Her general criminal intent is implied from the circumstances surrounding her behavior leading up to the act itself. The law assumes that she voluntarily became intoxicated; she then operated her automobile, which exposed others to harm; and there was forseeable knowledge based upon the human experience of mankind that the voluntary state of intoxication and the driving of an automobile in such a physical condition could conceivably result in injury or death to others. Thus, there exists general criminal intent, and the state does not have to prove that the individual formed the actual intent to kill the victim.

Specific Intent

This type of intent forms the basis for most crimes. Specific intent indicates that the individual determined before the commission of the act to commit the offense. This specific intent exists as an element of all crimes except those requiring only a showing of general intent. In the offense of rape, for example, the specific intent is to have carnal knowledge of a female, not one's wife, against her will; in the case of theft, it is to take something of value from the true owner in order to permanently deprive the owner of his or her possession.

CLASSIFICATION OF CRIMES

Crimes are classified according to their seriousness and the type of penalty that they carry. This modern distinction among classes of crimes developed in early England and was incorporated into the common law. It was brought to the Colonies and exists relatively unchanged today.

At the common law, crimes fell into three categories. These were:

- Treason
- Felonies
- Misdemeanors

Treason

In the early common law, treason was the most serious crime. At one time, it was more a crime of a personal nature directed toward the sovereign; later it was to become an act which threatened the institutions of government and a nation's security.[6] Today, some legal scholars consider treason as merely the most serious felony rather than a separate classification.

Felonies and Misdemeanors

For students of criminal justice, the distinction between felony and misdemeanor crimes is the most important in modern law. Generally, the various state penal codes distinguish between the two by the nature and extent of the punishment that can be imposed. A felony is usually defined as a criminal act which may be punishable by death or imprisonment in a penitentiary for more than one year. A misdemeanor, on the other hand, is usually an offense which is punishable by fine or imprisonment for less than one year. In those few states that do not differentiate between felonies and misdemeanors according to the period of incarceration, the distinction between the two is the place of incarceration. If the crime carries the possibility of confinement in a penitentiary, it is considered a felony; if not, it is considered a misdemeanor. A few states classify certain offenses as *high misdemeanors*. In terms of seriousness, these offenses fall between felonies and misdemeanors. Although still technically misdemeanors, they often provide for penalties in excess of one year in the penitentiary.

Specific Criminal Offenses

Typically, state criminal codes list crimes by specific categories or types of offenses. Although state codes generally use the same categories to classify crimes, the elements or definitions of crimes may vary somewhat from state to state, and you should be aware of the particular differences in your own state. In spite of this limitation, there is enough similarity between state penal codes to warrant an examination of specific offenses. The categorization of crime in most penal codes is usually as follows:

- Inchoate offenses
- Crimes against the person
- Crimes against property
- Crimes against public morality and decency
- Crimes against the public order and administration of justice

Inchoate Offenses

Inchoate offenses are those criminal acts which are only partially completed; that is, circumstances intervene which preclude them from being carried out to their conclusion. They are, nonetheless, considered crimes because their design and purpose is criminal in nature and, except for intervening factors, would constitute a completed crime. The major inchoate offenses are *attempts, conspiracy,* and the crimes relating to what are called *principals* and *accessories*. The reason for making these inchoate offenses crimes is to protect society by deterring those who, without laws prohibiting these acts, might undertake the commission of a crime.

Attempt

An attempt is the committing of an act which of itself is a substantial step toward the commission of a specific crime, but the criminal act falls short of completion. Merely preparing to commit a criminal act is usually not enough to be charged with attempt. A substantial portion of the act must be completed, but the act must still fall short of a completed crime.[7] For example, a man enters a supermarket and at gunpoint demands the cash receipts, but at that moment is surprised and arrested. This would constitute an attempted robbery.

Conspiracy

Conspiracy is the crime of unlawfully entering into agreement with one or more other persons to commit a specific offense. At the common law, the state had only to show that two or more persons merely entered into an agreement to commit a crime. Today, most modern statutes require additional proof beyond the mere agreement—now there must be some overt act toward the completion of the crime itself.[8] Under conspiracy statutes, each member of the conspiracy, once entering into a common agreement, is equally liable for the acts of all other conspirators whether that person was part of the subsequent acts or not if these acts were done in the furtherance of a common enterprise agreed upon by the conspirators.[9]

Principals and Accessories

Common law established the idea that parties to the commission of a felony should be considered either principals or accessories to the crime, depending upon their involvement. Today, many states do not distinguish between the two, but consider all accessories as principals in the crime. These states, however, usually cite two categories of principals. A *principal in the first degree* is one who is actually or constructively present during the commission of a crime. A person is actually present if he or she participates in the perpetration of the crime; a person is constructively present if he or she engineered the crime, but it was committed through an innocent agent. A *principal in the second degree* is one who might be actually or constructively present, but is involved only in aiding or encouraging the commission of the crime.

Those states which have retained the distinction between principals and accessories consider the principal as someone who in some manner participates in the actual commission of the crime. One who has in some way helped the principals is known as an *accessory*. An *accessory before the fact* is someone who, although not actually or constructively present at the time of commission, has procured, counseled, commanded, or encouraged someone to commit the criminal act before its actual commission. An *accessory after the fact* is one who knowingly receives, hides, shelters, or in some way assists, either personally or through the agency of others, one who has committed a felony. The law views the accessory after the fact as someone whose purpose and intent is to assist the felon in escaping justice. The elements of proof that the state must demonstrate before someone can be convicted of this crime are the following: (1) a felony has been committed and completed; (2) the individual being helped committed the felony; (3) the one helping the felon must reasonably believe that a felony has been committed and that the person being helped committed it; and (4) the accessory must personally or through the agency of another, have harbored, concealed, or otherwise helped the felon to escape.[10]

Crimes against the Person

There are seven major crimes against the person that the reader should have some familiarity with. Although there are other crimes against the person, these seven are considered the most serious felonies: *homicide, manslaughter, assault, rape, kidnapping,* and *robbery.* The subdivisions within these categories are outlined below.

Homicide and Manslaughter

Homicides fall into the two major categories of *criminal* and *noncriminal* homicide. The crime of homicide is defined as the killing of one human being by another human being who can be shown to be mentally competent. At the common law, there were only two distinctions of criminal homicide—murder and manslaughter. Murder under the common law was considered to be any homicide that was committed with "malice aforethought."[11] The penalty for murder was death. Many states over the years have modified the common law classification of homicide because the two categories were too restrictive. It was their experience that certain forms of murder did not warrant the death penalty because of mitigating circumstances surrounding the commission of the crime. Thus, many states have by statute divided the crime of murder into degrees, requiring different penalties and elements depending upon the particular degree of murder committed.

Criminal homicide includes the following:

1. *First-degree murder* requires that the act be committed by willful, deliberate, and premeditated means with malice aforethought. The key to murder in the first degree is the presence of sufficient premeditation to warrant it as a cold-blooded and calculated killing. In some states, first-degree murders are also those murders which fall into the category of *felony-murder,* or murders which are committed during the commission of such serious crimes as rape, robbery, kidnapping, arson, or burglary. Even though there is not a strict element of premeditation involved, the courts have held that participation in these types of criminal acts creates "a foreseeable risk of death."[12] Other states also consider the killing of a law enforcement officer or a prison guard as first-degree murder.

2. *Second-degree murder* is usually defined as any murder which is not murder in the first degree as determined by a jury. Usually, the element of premeditation and deliberation is not present to the point which must be demonstrated in first-degree murder. The death of a student who was beaten in a fight is an instance when the survivor might be charged with murder in the second degree.

3. Manslaughter differs from murder in that there is no malice aforethought, but there is still an unjustifiable and inexcusable taking of a human life. In manslaughter, the degree of ill will is less and there is no premeditated design to kill. In some states, the crime of manslaughter is broken down into two subcategories of *voluntary manslaughter* and *involuntary manslaughter.* In those states which make this distinction, voluntary manslaughter is the intentional killing of another due to adequate provocation, but in the sudden heat of passion. The important feature of this crime is the question of the rage or sudden heat of passion which must be of "an intensity sufficient to obscure the reason of the actor."[13] Involuntary manslaughter is an unintentional homicide in which the death of the victim is not intended nor contemplated by the one performing the act, but the act itself was done in such a reckless manner that it

cannot be considered an innocent act or accidental. Closely related to this is the crime of *negligent homicide,* which applies primarily to death as a result of the reckless operation of a motor vehicle. (The vehicle must be operated in a careless or negligent manner and the death must not be willful or deliberate). Negligent homicide can also be charged, however, in other types of cases. The killing of a friend with a gun that the accused "didn't know was loaded" is a rather common example.[14]

Noncriminal homicide stems from the common-law idea that under certain circumstances, homicide was not a crime. There are two types of noncriminal homicide: justifiable homicide and excusable homicide.

1. *Justifiable homicide* exonerates the one who commits the homicide because the act itself was justified and sometimes even ordered by the law. Some examples of justifiable homicide are the execution of a death sentence, lawful acts of war, prevention of the commission of a felony or atrocious crime, and the killing of a dangerous and known felon who is escaping.

2. *Excusable homicide* is an act which causes death, but is tolerated because of its nature or because of the circumstances. This includes self-defense and homicide where the killing is accidental or is simply a negligent and unintentional killing. In this instance, negligence is to be distinguished from "recklessness," which is an element of involuntary manslaughter.[15]

Assault and Battery

This felony also includes two categories: aggravated and simple assault.

1. The crime of deliberately attacking another through force or violence for the purpose of doing severe bodily injury to the victim is called *aggravated assault.* Before the charge of aggravated assault can be made, there must be apparent or present ability to carry out the threat, such as a weapon or superior physical strength, and the threat and possibility of rendering physical violence must be immediate and not in the future.

Mere threats do not usually constitute aggravated assault, but it is not necessary for there to be actual physical contact. For example, raising a fist in anger as if to strike another person is sufficient in some jurisdictions to constitute an aggravated assault. This is based on the idea that as long as physical force is set in motion and the victim has reasonable apprehension of being personally injured, aggravated assault has occurred. Closely associated with aggravated assault are what some states call *felonious assaults.* These are specific types of aggravated assault which are classified according to intent. For example, assault with intent to commit murder; assault with intent to commit great bodily harm less than murder; assault with intent to commit rape or ravish; and assault with attempt to rob.

2. In most states, *simple assault* is defined as an assault committed without a weapon and without intent to commit great bodily harm or to commit a felony. In almost all instances, this crime is only a misdemeanor.

3. *Battery* is nothing more than the completed assault.[16] Whereas a threatening gesture is enough to constitute an assault, the actual unlawful touching of another person with intent to inflict injury constitutes battery. This points up the fact that more serious offenses include other and less serious crimes which are separate offenses. For example, assault is included in battery, and assault and battery are naturally included in violent crimes against the person such as murder, manslaughter, robbery, and rape. Usually, however, most jurisdictions will merge the assault and battery with the higher offense and charge the accused only with the more serious crime.

Rape

The two categories of rape are forcible and statutory rape.

1. *Forcible rape* is generally defined as the carnal knowledge of a female above a certain age by a male who is not her husband. The crime of forcible rape includes the following elements: it must be an act of sexual intercourse and carnal knowledge with any slight degree of penetration by the male organ as sufficient; the victim must be female; the use of force must be actual or implied, and the victim must perceive herself in danger of great bodily harm. Lastly, the act of willing consent must be absent.

The crime of forcible rape has undergone some statutory revisions in many states in the last few years. Until recently, a number of states required that before a man could be convicted of forcible rape it had to be shown as a condition of nonconsent that the victim "resisted to her utmost" the advances of her attacker. This degree of proof has been made more reasonable in most states. In the past, a favorite tactic of many lawyers for the accused has been to attack the credibility of the victim by trying to show the court that she is an unchaste or sexually promiscuous woman. In many cases, it became the victim who was on trial rather than the accused. Because of the rape victim's vulnerability to such questionable tactics by the defense counsel, it was not at all unusual for forcible rape victims simply to not report the crime to the police or to refuse to go through with the trial. Now, a number of states have set limits on the employment of such strategy by the defense.

The last few years have also seen other changes in rape laws by some states. Where, at one time, rape was considered as an offense that could be committed only against a female, some states now recognize that males can also be raped and provide equal protection for that sex.

2. *Statutory rape* involves all the usual elements of rape with the exception that it is not necessary to show that force was used or that it was accomplished without the willing consent of the female. In fact, statutory rape is the act of engaging in *voluntary* sexual intercourse with a female under the statutory age of consent by an adult male. This crime exists to protect the virtue and chastity of young females who, because of their tender years, are more vulnerable to the sexual advances of adult males.

Kidnapping

Kidnapping statutes usually define this crime as falsely imprisoning someone with intent to secrete the victim within the state or forcibly and fraudulently taking a person from his or her place of residence without lawful authority.[17] The best-known kidnapping statute is the federal government's famous Lindbergh Act, which was passed by Congress after the ill-fated kidnapping of the Charles Lindbergh baby. This act reads:

1. Whoever knowingly transports in interstate commerce, any person who has been unlawfully seized, confined, inveigled, decoyed, kidnapped, abducted or carried away and held for ransom or reward or otherwise, except in the case of a minor by a parent, therefore, shall be punished:
   A. By death if the kidnapped person has not been liberated unharmed and if the verdict of the jury shall so recommend, or
   B. By imprisonment for any term of years or for life, if the death penalty is not imposed.
2. The failure to release the victim within 24 hours after having been unlawfully seized, confined, inveigled, decoyed, kidnapped, abducted or carried away shall create a rebuttable presumption that such person has been transported in interstate or foreign commerce. [Author's note: This makes the offense a federal crime. When a citizen of a state is kidnapped, it is strictly a state crime until 24 hours have elapsed. After the 24-hour period, the victim is assumed to have been transported in interstate commerce and the Lindbergh Act is invoked to give the FBI the jurisdiction to enter the case.]
3. If two or more persons conspire to violate this section and one or more such persons do not avert or act to affect the object of conspiracy, each shall be punished as provided in subsection A.[18]

Robbery and Extortion

Robbery usually falls into the categories of armed and unarmed robbery; extortion, while similar to robbery, is a separate category in itself.

1. Robbery is defined as the taking of personal property or things of value from another in his or her presence and against his or her will, by force or fear, violence or threat. The key element of robbery is the use of force or fear directed toward the victim that causes the victim to give up the property. To merely steal the property of another without confronting the owner and without the use of force or fear is not robbery. Even in such crimes as purse snatching or pocket-picking, this force or fear is not present, and as a result these crimes are generally considered larcenies (thefts).

2. A number of states categorize robbery into *armed* and *unarmed,* with the latter being a less serious offense. In these states, armed robbery usually entails the use of a dangerous weapon or an instrumentality which would lead the victim to believe that it is, in fact, a dangerous weapon. Unarmed robbery involves the use of physical force with no weapon.

3. The difference between *extortion* and robbery is that while extortion is an attempt to obtain property or money by means of actual or implied threat, the threat is less defined and is more of a threat to use force in the future. Thus, extortion does not quite contain the element of force or its immediate application required by robbery statutes, but at the same time it is more than a larceny since the element of force is still present.

Crimes against Property

Although all crimes against property are also crimes against the person of the victim because he or she suffers a loss, a distinction between the two is made primarily for purposes of classification. Since in certain types of crimes there is no direct confrontation between the offender and the victim which theoretically would place the victim in greater personal peril, these crimes against property are often considered by the law as less serious than those committed against the person. Even so, the more serious of these property crimes are still felonies. The major crimes against property are *burglary, larceny, auto theft, embezzlement, receiving stolen goods, arson,* and *malicious destruction of property.*

Burglary

At the common law, burglary consisted of the following elements: (1) breaking and entering with specific intent to do so (2) into the dwelling house of another (3) at nighttime (4) with the intent to commit a felony therein.

These elements were rather restrictive, and many states have therefore enacted various degrees of burglary. The degree of seriousness is determined by the presence or absence of certain of the elements. For example, if the structure is not a dwelling house, the crime may be considered a less serious offense; if the crime is committed during the daylight hours, it is considered less serious, and so on. Other states, rather than specifying degrees of burglary, have retained the common law doctrine of burglary, but have added the additional crime of *breaking and entering* as a form of burglary. In these states, breaking and entering does not have to occur to a dwelling house, in the night, or with the intent to commit a felony within; thus the burglary of a building in the daylight hours would constitute breaking and entering. Although a lesser offense than burglary or burglary in the first degree, breaking and entering is nonetheless almost invariably a felony.

Larceny

Larceny, the legal term for theft, is the taking and carrying away of the personal property of another with the intent to permanently deprive the true owner and to convert the property to one's own use. It is usually necessary that all these elements be present before the crime can be larceny. However, the courts have some latitude in determining whether their requirements have been met. For example, the necessary element of carrying away the property has been interpreted to mean any slight removal regardless of the distance the object was actually moved as long as the thief has successfully taken the property into his or her control.[19]

States have divided the crime of larceny into *grand larceny* and *petit larceny* on the basis of the value of the property taken. In Michigan, for example, if the value of the property stolen exceeds $100, the crime is grand larceny; below that amount, the crime is petit larceny. Grand larceny is a felony, and petit larceny is, in most instances, a misdemeanor. If someone stole over a period of time a number of items whose total value constituted grand larceny, that person could be prosecuted accordingly. The test the courts apply in such cases is "whether the entire taking was governed by a single intent and a general illegal design."[20]

Larceny usually involves the idea of stealth and not of force, and as such it is considered a "crime of opportunity."[21] There are different forms of larceny, which may be separate crimes. An example is *larceny by deception* (or false pretenses), where the accused obtains the personal property of the true owner by trickery, fraud, or some form of misrepresentation. In this case, if the owner had known the real identity or purpose of the taker, he or she would not have parted voluntarily with the property. Another form of larceny is *conversion,* where there is no fraud or misrepresentation involved. Rather, the taker knowingly and with intent to permanently deprive converts to his or her own use property that has come into the taker's possession legally.

A separate form of larceny is the crime of *pocket-picking.* It may be prosecuted under the existing larceny laws of the state or as a separate offense. Either way, the elements are basically the same, with perhaps the additional requirement of actually taking from the concealed person of another. The crime of *shoplifting* is also a form of larceny. It also may be prosecuted under the general larceny statute of the state or it may exist as a separate offense. It may constitute grand or petit larceny, depending on the value of the merchandise stolen, and it may therefore be a felony or misdemeanor.

Auto Theft

Auto theft, while a form of larceny, is not held to the same requirements of proof as most larcenies. For example, it is often defined as the willful taking away of a motor vehicle belonging to another without the true owner's permission. The requirement of showing intent to permanently deprive is absent since many automobile thefts are committed by adolescents who take the vehicle for a "joy ride" and then abandon it.

Embezzlement

Another crime closely associated with larceny is the offense of embezzlement. Unlike the crime of larceny, which is a trespassory invasion of the property of another in which the criminal has no right to the property, a person who has, in fact, the lawful possession of somebody else's property cannot be guilty of the crime of larceny if he or she wrongfully converts the property to his or her own use.[22] Therefore, to deal with such matters as the theft of the master's property by the servant, the specific crime of embezzlement was enacted. Under embezzlement statutes, the following elements exist: (1) the fraudulent appropriation or conversion (2) of personal property of another (3) by a person having lawful possession by virtue of a relationship of trust and confidence (4) with intent to feloniously convert or use as not intended by the nature of the possession. The important feature of this offense is the nature of the confidence and trust that exists between the offender and the victim. It usually applies when an employee entrusted with the lawful possession of an employer's property steals it and converts it to his or her own use. The relationship and degree of trust involved determines whether the crime is embezzlement or not. If, for example, you were to steal and convert to your own use a friend's property which was entrusted to your care, you would more likely be guilty of *larceny by conversion* rather than embezzlement.

Receiving Stolen Goods

A final larceny-related offense is the crime of receiving stolen goods. In some jurisdictions, this exists as a separate and specific offense. In other states, the one who receives or conceals stolen goods with the knowledge of their nature and with intent to permanently deprive will be considered as either an accessory after the fact or as a principal in the original crime in which the stolen goods were obtained.

Arson

Under the common law arson was the "malicious burning of the house or outhouse of another man,"[23] and it applied to dwellings that were inhabited. Under modern arson statutes, this requirement has been dropped or there have been added degrees of arson depending upon whether or not the structure was used for habitation. Committing arson to a dwelling is still considered the most serious violation of the arson law because of the obvious danger to the inhabitants. Nonetheless, arson now generally applies to the destruction of any permanent building or structure. In some instances, it also applies to personal property such as automobiles.

Malicious Destruction of Real and Personal Property

This crime involves the deliberate, willful, and malicious destruction of land, structures, and other forms of real property. In the offense of malicious destruction of personal property, the same elements exist, but the target is personal property. In both cases, whether the crime is considered a felony or a misdemeanor will be determined by the value of the property damaged or destroyed.

Crimes against Public Morality

The law recognizes that certain acts are offensive to the public morality and need to be regulated by prescribing criminal penalties for their commission. Many of our so-called vice laws fall into this category. These crimes are usually thought of in the law as *malum prohibitum* offenses, that is, considered wrong because society prohibits them rather than *malum in se* crimes, such as murder, rape or robbery, which are wrong in and of themselves. Since Chapter 4 will discuss some of these crimes against public morality in terms of the focus of modern thought, only brief attention will be given them here. Some of the more common crimes which might fall into this category are *incest, seduction, indecent liberties with a child, adultery, bigamy, prostitution, homosexuality, obscenity,* and *pornography.*

Incest

This crime is committed when someone has sexual intercourse or performs an act of deviant sexual conduct with someone who is too closely related to marry legally. Incest covers sexual acts between father and daughter, mother and son, or brother and sister. The usual case involves a parent charged with taking sexual liberties with his or her minor child. In some instances, both parties can be charged if they are both of age. The courts, however, usually look at the total circumstances in determining whether to charge one, both, or neither. This crime is very rarely prosecuted today. The courts are often more likely to resolve the matter by removing the child from the parent and placing the child in a foster home.

Seduction

Seduction is still a crime in a few states and at the common law. It is the performing of an act of sexual intercourse with a chaste woman under the false pretext of marriage. Because of the problems of proof required in the prosecution of this offense and the more liberal view toward premarital sex in the United States, this crime is of little significance today.

Indecent Liberties with a Child

This crime is the act of lewd fondling or touching in a sexual manner the body of a child below the age of consent. The law refers to this type of an act as *pedophilia* and adults who engage in this conduct as *pedophiles*.

Adultery

Adultery is the crime of having sexual intercourse with either an unmarried person or a married person who is not one's spouse. A married person commits this offense by having sexual intercourse with a person who is not his or her spouse. An unmarried person who has sexual intercourse with a married person, knowing that person to be married, is also guilty of adultery. Like so many other crimes of a private sexual nature, this offense today has little standing in the criminal courts. It still serves an important function, however, in certain civil cases such as divorce proceedings, but even this is rapidly changing because of the adoption of uncontested divorce proceedings in which grounds such as adultery are no longer required.

Prostitution

This crime is committed by someone who performs or agrees to perform for money an act of sexual intercourse or an act of deviant sexual conduct. In most cases, it is a crime in which females are charged with the offense, but it applies to males as well. The offense of prostitution also involves some other related crimes. *Solicitation* is the offense of soliciting for a prostitute by encouraging, arranging, or offering a meeting of persons for the purpose of prostitution. The crime of compelling a female to become a prostitute or offering or arranging a situation in which a female may practice prostitution is known as *pandering*. The crime of *pimping* is the act of receiving money or property from a prostitute, knowing that it was earned by engaging in prostitution. *Patronizing a prostitute* is committed when a male engages in an act of sexual intercourse or deviant sexual conduct with a prostitute or enters and remains in a place of prostitution with intent to engage in an act of sexual conduct.

Homosexuality

Homosexuality is the crime of performing an "unnatural" sex act involving only males. When a sex act is performed which involves only females, it is called *lesbianism*. Modern statutes in many states have now removed these as offenses, or at least states have not encouraged the prosecution of these offenses as long as they are done in private and involve consenting adults. In the case of an adult and a child, the offender is usually charged with contributing to the sexual delinquency of a minor.

Obscenity and Pornography

Chapter 4 will examine recent changes dealing with these crimes. At this point, it is sufficient to say that one commits the crimes of obscenity and pornography when, with knowledge of the content, one sells, delivers, provides, or agrees to sell, offer for sale, or deliver any obscene writing, picture, record, or other representation of obscene material.[24]

Crimes against the Public Order and the Administration of Justice

These types of offenses are prohibited because they are considered by their nature to subvert and destroy the very institutions of government and the processes that contribute to the stability, continuance, and effectiveness of a government to protect the safety and well-being of its citizens. Some of the offenses in this category are *treason, sedition, espionage, forgery, bribery of a public official, perjury, contempt of a duly prescribed governmental function,* and *embracery.*

Treason

This crime is considered the most serious offense against the public order and is viewed as an attack against a nation's people, collectively, and its government. It goes beyond the mere act of rebellion against authority in that it threatens the very existence of the nation and its form of government.

In the United States, the crime of treason is a constitutional offense and is proscribed in the U.S. Constitution. Most state constitutions also make treason against the state government a crime for the same reasons it is a crime against the national government.

The U.S. Constitution provides that treason is the commission of any of the following acts: (1) levying war against the United States or (2) aiding, comforting, and supporting an enemy of the United States.[25] The courts have held that there must be some overt act beyond a mere conspiracy in order to constitute the crime of treason, which employs force, violence, or some violent means through or with an assembly of people.[26]

Regarding the element of proof to convict someone for the crime of treason, the U.S. Constitution is quite specific. It provides that ''no person shall be convicted of treason unless upon the testimony of two witnesses to the same overt act, or a confession [by the accused] in open court."[27]

Other treason-related crimes, proscribed by act of Congress, cover treasonous conduct not specified in the Constitution. One of these is the crime of *the attempted overthrow of the United States government,* which makes it a crime to conspire or attempt to overthrow the government of the United States. This criminal offense applies to attempted acts of treason or conspiracy to commit treason which do not satisfy the elements of treason as they are spelled out in the Constitution. Congress has also passed *misprision of treason* laws, which make it a crime for a U.S. citizen not to report an instance of treason when the citizen knows or has reasonable grounds to believe that treason or treasonable acts have occurred.

Sedition

This crime involves the intent to subvert the Constitution and the U.S. form of government by means of open violence. It is not considered as serious as treason because it involves only the subversion of the government and is not an open attack upon the nation. Under federal law, there also exists a distinction between seditious acts in wartime and those in peacetime.

Espionage

Congress has passed espionage or spying legislation which makes it a crime to gather or transmit information which affects or is in regard to the national defense with intent, knowledge, or foreseeability that such information or data might be used against the United States or to the military advantage of any foreign government.[28]

Forgery

Although it may at first seem strange that this crime is classified as one directed against the public order, after a little thought the reason should be quite obvious. Forgery is considered as a crime against the public order because of the potential effects of this offense on the economic well-being of society. In fact, as Loewy says, "Forgery is generally punished more severely than other nonviolent theft crimes. The rationale for this appears to be the impact that a forged instrument has on the entire commercial system as well as the impact on the person whose name is forged."[29]

Specifically, forgery is the crime of falsely making or materially altering a document or writing which, if genuine, would have legal efficacy, or be the basis for legal liability, with intent to defraud.[30] At the common law, forgery was considered a misdemeanor. Under modern statutes, it is often a felony, and only in certain instances a misdemeanor, depending upon the type of instrument that was forged and the value of the property involved.

When the forgery is actually offered with the statement by words or actions that the forged document is valid, a separate offense called *uttering* is involved. It is not necessary that someone believe the forged document to be valid; the mere offering of the forged document constitutes the offense.[31] This fact, coupled with there being no petit forgery in most jurisdictions, means that a person who forges and cashes five $10 checks can be convicted of ten separate felonies.[32]

Bribery of a Public Official

Among the crimes against the administration of justice is bribery of a public official, which is the offering, promising, giving, or soliciting of something of value with the corrupt intent to influence the actions of a public official. The key elements of this offense are the corrupt intent and the attempt to influence a public official to perform his or her duties in an improper manner.[33]

Perjury

Perjury is the act of making an intentional statement under oath or affirmation in a judicial or nonjudicial proceeding with the knowledge that the statement is false. *Subornation of perjury* is the crime that occurs when one unlawfully procures a person to commit perjury with the preconceived knowledge and intent that perjury be committed. The witness does not have to perjure himself or herself on the witness stand for this crime to be completed. The crime is considered complete when there is a false taking of the oath or affirmation by the procured witness.[34]

Contempt

Many times you will hear of someone being cited in contempt. There are actually two types of contempt offenses. The first of these is *civil contempt,* which is the refusal to obey the lawful decision of a competent court which has ordered something done. This is considered contempt because it has the affect of hindering the process of justice. *Criminal contempt,* on the other hand, is unreverent and disrespectful conduct toward the court which damages the dignity and authority of the court. An important distinction between the two is that although the offender can be fined and imprisoned after being found guilty of civil contempt, the punishment is not meant to be punitive as such, but rather, executive, that is, necessary for the court to carry out its proper functions. In the case of criminal contempt the punishment is considered punitive because it punishes the one held in contempt for impugning the solemn power of the court.

Refusal to testify before a legislative body may be regarded as *contempt of a legislative body*. This offense is based on the idea that legislative bodies must be informed if they are to effectively carry out their objectives.[35] State legislatures rarely cite an individual for refusal to testify, but the U.S. Congress has done so on occasion. Congress, however, cannot punish someone for contempt who rightfully exercises his or her constitutional rights against self-incrimination.

Embracery

Another offense that strikes at the very nerve center of the administration of justice is the crime of embracery. This is the act of attempting by unlawful means to corrupt or influence a juror with respect to a verdict. To those concerned with the equitable administration of criminal justice in the United States, this is a base offense because, in the words of the Supreme Court, it "saps the very foundation of the jury system."[36]

BASIC LEGAL TERMINOLOGY

Criminal justice students and citizens in general should have some familiarity with basic legal terms and documents. All of us have heard the terms *arrest, arrest warrant, search warrant, subpoena, writ of habeas corpus, bail,* and *extradition,* but do we really know the legal definitions and requirements of each? The remainder of this chapter will attempt to explain these legal terms and show the reader what some of these documents look like.

Arrest

An arrest is the taking of a person into custody in a case and in the manner authorized by law. Just as a specific offense has elements, so does the act of arrest. First, there must be an intention to arrest; second, this intention to arrest must be communicated to the person arrested; third, the one arresting must have the one being arrested under his or her control; last, there must be an understanding by the person arrested that he or she is being arrested.[37] However, if one or more elements are missing, the arrest may not be invalid. For example, an intoxicated man may be unconscious and not understand that he is being placed under arrest.

In most states, a police officer can arrest without a warrant on the following conditions: (1) if a felony has been committed in the officer's presence, (2) if there is probable cause (reasonable grounds) to believe a felony has been committed and the person being arrested committed the felony, or (3) if a misdemeanor has been committed in the officer's presence. An arrest by a citizen, normally referred to as a "citizen's arrest," is restricted in most states to instances in which felonies have been committed in the citizen's presence or in which the citizen has probable cause to believe a felony has been committed and the person being arrested committed the felony. Citizens are generally prohibited from making arrests for misdemeanors.

Arrest Warrant

An arrest warrant is an order signed by a magistrate or judge which commands the person addressed or anyone authorized to execute the warrant to take a named person into custody and to bring that person before the court to answer for the crime specified in the warrant. In the event that the name of the offender is not known and therefore cannot be entered on the face of the warrant, a "John Doe" warrant can be issued which does not name the individual.

There are several ways in which an arrest warrant is issued: The victim or complaining witness may go directly to the prosecutor (district attorney) with the information about the crime. The prosecutor then prepares a supporting affidavit (a form of sworn statement) which the complainant swears to and signs. The prosecutor and the complainant then go before a magistrate who is authorized to issue an arrest warrant for the particular offense. (In some states, complaints for minor misdemeanors may be sworn to before the prosecutor or the clerk of courts.) The magistrate questions the complainant thoroughly to determine if there is probable cause to believe a crime has been committed and if the one named in the complaint is the probable offender.[38] If the magistrate is satisfied on these facts, the warrant will be signed and turned over to the police to serve.

Police officers may also initiate complaints. The police officer goes before the magistrate or in some cases the prosecutor to file the complaint. In these circumstances, the police officer becomes the complainant and has to swear to the facts. Figure 2-2 is an arrest warrant issued by a federal magistrate.

Search Warrant

A search warrant, like an arrest warrant, is an order issued by a magistrate which commands and authorizes a law enforcement officer to search the premises described on the warrant for those articles listed on the warrant itself. The procedure and substance of search warrants are defined by no less authority than the U.S. Constitution, the Fourth Amendment of which reads:

> The right of the people to be secure in their persons, houses, papers and effects, against unreasonable searches and seizures, shall not be violated and no Warrants shall issue, but upon probable cause, supported by oath or affirmation, and particularly describing the place to be searched and the persons or things to be seized.

Warrant for Arrest of Defendant (Rev. 7-52) Cr. Form No. 12

United States District Court

FOR THE

EASTERN DISTRICT OF PENNSYLVANIA

UNITED STATES OF AMERICA

v.

JAMES ADAM TROJANOWICZ

No. P-76-226 Cr.5

To [1] any Special Agent of the Federal Bureau of Investigation

You are hereby commanded to arrest James Adam Trojanowicz and bring him forthwith before the United States District Court for the Eastern District of Pennsylvania in the city of Philadelphia to answer to an Indictment charging him with

Bank robbery and bank robbery with assault by use of a dangerous weapon.

in violation of

18 USC 2113(a) and 18 USC 2113(d)

Dated at Philadelphia, Pennsylvania Robert A. Lorinskas, Clerk.

on October 24 1976.

By J. P. Thelen, Deputy Clerk.

Bail fixed at $50,000.00 cash or approved surety.

RETURN

District of ss

Received the within warrant the 10 th day of November 1976 and executed same.

Special Agent, FBI,

By Conrad A. Veltema,

[1] Insert designation of officer to whom the warrant is issued, e. g., "any United States Marshal or any other authorized officer"; or "United States Marshal for .... District of ...."; or "any United States Marshal"; or "any Special Agent of the Federal Bureau of Investigation"; or "any United States Marshal or any Special Agent of the Federal Bureau of Investigation"; or "any agent of the Alcohol Tax Unit."

Figure 2-2 Warrant for Arrest of Defendant

In order to obtain a search warrant, a police officer must go before a magistrate and file a sworn affidavit indicating the *particular place* to be searched and the *particular things* to be seized (see Figure 2-3). Police officers are forbidden from searching any other place than that described on the face of the warrant. However, police officers can seize those items which are not listed on the face of the warrant as long as they are offensive to the law and their search did not exceed the scope of the warrant.[39] The magistrate must examine the affidavit in which the police officer has stated the reasons that he or she believes illegal objects are to be found in the place to be searched. After examination of the facts contained in the affidavit, and perhaps some additional questions of the officer, the magistrate must determine whether probable cause exists to believe that illegal objects or persons are present on the premises. If the magistrate is satisfied that there is probable cause, the warrant will be issued (see Figure 2-4).

When the search warrant is executed, the law enforcement officers must leave a copy of the warrant with the person occupying the premises searched. In the event that no one is there when the search is conducted, a copy must still be left in plain view. In addition, the police must leave an itemized inventory of all property seized and return a copy of the inventory and notice that the warrant has been served to the authorizing magistrate. Figure 2-5 shows the return and inventory portion of a search warrant. Once the search warrant has been issued, it is common for statutes or court rules to require that it must be executed within a fixed period of time, such as ten days.[40]

Subpoena

A subpoena is merely an order from a court which compels someone to appear and provide testimony concerning a particular matter which he or she is supposed to have knowledge of (see Figure 2-6). One form of subpoena is a *subpoena deuces tecum,* which directs the person named to appear with certain specified documents (see Figure 2-7). In this manner, the court can compel the production of certain records and documents. The federal government and all states provide by law that anyone issued a subpoena and failing to appear or testify (in the absence of self-incrimination) be charged with contempt of court.[41]

Writ of Habeas Corpus

Another important legal document is the writ of habeas corpus, which provides the remedy when a person is held in restraint by the state. It is a court order directed to the police or penal authorities who have a particular person in custody commanding them to ''produce the body'' at a time and place specified in the writ and show why the person is held in custody or restraint.[42] After a hearing of the facts, the court may place the person back into custody, release the person on bail, or discharge the person. This is accomplished by a written

United States District Court

FOR THE

WESTERN DISTRICT OF TENNESSEE

UNITED STATES OF AMERICA

vs.

A HOUSE LOCATED AT
646 CROSBY STREET
MEMPHIS, TENNESSEE

Docket No.

Case No. 724(p)

**AFFIDAVIT FOR
SEARCH WARRANT**

BEFORE HONORABLE NORMAN A. SPENCER, Chief Judge, United States District Court
    Name of Magistrate or Judge   Address of Magistrate or Judge
Memphis, Tennessee
The undersigned being duly sworn deposes and says:

That he has reason to believe that XXXXXXXXXXXXXX (on the premises known as)

646 Crosby Street
Memphis, Tennessee

which is a one-story, ranch style, yellow brick house, with black shutters, and
a detached garage

in the **Western** District of **Tennessee**

there is now being concealed certain property, namely two (2) red ceramic plaques which contain
a white powdered substance believed to be cocaine.
    here describe property

which are in violation of Title 21, United States Code, Sections 841 (a) (1) and
952(a) (1).
    here insert alleged grounds for search and seizure

And that the facts tending to establish the foregoing grounds for issuance of a Search Warrant
are as follows: On April 18, 1976, Inspectors T.O. Bryan and R. Jones, U.S. Customs
Service, while inspecting incoming merchandise from Mexico at Metro Airport routinely inspected
two plaques shipped from Mexico to a Memphis address. In the plaques a white powdered substance
was discovered. Inspector Bryan conducted a field test which indicated the white powdered
substance was cocaine. On April 19, 1976 at approximately 1:30 P.M., a white male described
as 6'0", medium build, 175 lbs., identified himself as Tony Carano and claimed the plaques. He
was observed placing the plaques into a 1975 tan Chrysler (Ohio LC-197). He then was followed
by U.S. Customs Agents and Drug Enforcement Administration Agents to 646 Crosby Street, Memphis,
Tennessee where he entered the house with the plaques.

Material witnesses will be Inspectors T.O. Bryan and R. Jones, United
States Customs Service Agents; Michael Wornica and William Foster, Special Agents of Drug
Enforcement Administration.

Michael Wornica
              Signature of Affiant.
Special Agent, DEA
              Official Title, if any.

Sworn to before me, and subscribed in my presence,   April 19 , 19 76

Norman Q. Spencer
              Judge or Federal Magistrate.

* If the warrant is to authorize execution pursuant to 21 U.S.C. § 879 without prior notice of authority or purpose, indicate the circumstances
creating the need for such a warrant.

FPI LC 3-73-90M-6990

Figure 2-3 Affidavit for Search Warrant

United States District Court

FOR THE

WESTERN DISTRICT OF TENNESSEE

UNITED STATES OF AMERICA

vs.

A HOUSE LOCATED AT
646 CROSBY STREET
MEMPHIS, TENNESSEE

Docket No.

Case No. 724(p)

SEARCH WARRANT

To   UNITED STATES MARSHAL OR ANY DULY AUTHORIZED OFFICER

Affidavit(s) having been made before me by Michael Wornica, Special Agent, Drug Enforcement Administration

that he has reason to believe that { ~~on the person of~~
on the premises known as } 646 Crosby Street,
Memphis, Tennessee, which is a one-story, ranch style, yellow brick house, with black shutters, and a detached garage

in the Western   District of Tennessee

there is now being concealed certain property, namely   two (2) red ceramic plaques which
here describe property
contain a white powdered substance believed to be cocaine.

and as I am satisfied that there is probable cause to believe that the property so described is being concealed on the person or premises above described and that the foregoing grounds for application for issuance of the search warrant exist.

You are hereby commanded to search within a period of __two days__ (not to exceed 10 days) the person or place named for the property specified, serving this warrant and making the search { ~~in the daytime—6:00 A.M. to 10:00 P.M.~~
at anytime in the day or night[1] } and if the property be found there to seize it, leaving a copy of this warrant and a receipt for the property taken, and prepare a written inventory of the property seized and promptly return this warrant and bring the property before me as required by law.

Dated this 19th day of   April,   , 19 76

Norman O Spence
Judge or Federal Magistrate.

[1] The Federal Rules of Criminal Procedure provide: "The warrant shall be served in the daytime, unless the issuing authority, by appropriate provision in the warrant, and for reasonable cause shown, authorizes its execution at times other than daytime." (Rule 41(C))

Figure 2-4   Search Warrant

RETURN

I received the attached search warrant   April 19,   , 1976   , and have executed it as follows:

On April 20,   , 1976 at 11:30 o'clock P M, I searched the person or premises described in the warrant and

I left a copy of the warrant with ____ANTHONY MARTIN CARANO_____
name of person searched or owner or "at the place of search"

together with a receipt for the items seized.

The following is an inventory of property taken pursuant to the warrant:

Two red ceramic plaques depicting oriental scenes of a pagoda.

This inventory was made in the presence of Special Agent James Moore, Drug Enforcement Administration
                              and

I swear that this Inventory is a true and detailed account of all the property taken by me on the warrant.

Michael Wonica

Subscribed and sworn to and returned before me this 21st   day of April   , 19 76 .

Norman A. Spenor
                                        Judge or Federal Magistrate.

Figure 2-5   Search Warrant Return

Subpoena to Testify Cr. Form No. 20 (Rev. 5-68)

United States District Court

FOR THE

Southern District of Louisiana

UNITED STATES OF AMERICA v. Paul J. Clifton	}	No. N75-251 Cr.

To Eugene A. McCoy, 1121 Sunshine Lane, Wadsworth, Mississippi

You are hereby commanded to appear in the United States District Court for the Southern District of Louisiana at 544 Federal Building in the city of New Orleans on the 20th day of January 1976 at 11:00 o'clock A.M. to testify in the above-entitled case.

This subpoena is issued on application of the[1] United States of America

January 12, 1976.

Kenneth A. Selby
Attorney for United States
544 Federal Building
Address New Orleans, LA 63217
Phone 492-412-8040

Bernard F. Toman, *Clerk.*

By Parker J. Meredith, *Deputy Clerk.*

RETURN

Received this subpoena at on and on at I served it on the within named by delivering a copy to and tendering[2] to the fee for one day's attendance and the mileage allowed by law.

________________________,

By ________________________,

Service Fees

Travel ______________ $
Services ______________
Total ______________ $

[1] Insert "United States," or "defendant" as the case may be.
[2] Fees and mileage need not be tendered to the witness upon service of a subpoena issued in behalf of the United States or an officer or agency thereof. 28 USC 1825, or on behalf of a defendant who is financially unable to pay such costs (Rule 17(b), Federal Rules Criminal Procedure).

FPI MI—4-18-72-2400 PADS-7544

Figure 2-6 Subpoena to Testify

United States District Court

FOR THE

EASTERN DISTRICT OF MICHIGAN

UNITED STATES OF AMERICA

v.

No.

GUY WILLIAM FOSTER, and
To   KENNETH A. BERISKO

Mr. Frank S. Horvath, 22 Elm Lane, Napoleon, Ohio

You are hereby commanded to appear in the United States District Court for the   Eastern
Clerk's Office

District of   Michigan   at   Federal Building   in the city of
410 W. Cass Avenue

Detroit   on the 7th   day of   January   1976 at 1:30 o'clock P M.

to testify in the case of United States v. G.W. Foster and K.A. Berisko   and bring with you
all proof of ownership of the following: Case Backhoe, Serial Number 5198756;
Case Loader, Serial Number 5432670; Case Tractor, Model T460A, Serial Number
5674397; and a Case Bulldozer, Model 210AE, Serial Number 245673, all stolen
on or about September 3, 1975.

This subpoena is issued upon application of the[1] United States of America

December 28 _____, 19 75 .

Frank K. Gibson
    Attorney for the United States   ,
544 Federal Building   *Clerk.*
    Address Detroit, Michigan   By _____ ,
                                                                      Deputy Clerk.
    [1] Insert "United States" or "defendant" as the case may be.

RETURN

Received this subpoena at Detroit, Michigan   on January 2, 1976
and on January 3, 1976   at Napoleon, Ohio
served it on the within named Frank S. Horvath
by delivering a copy to him   and tendering to h im   the fee for one day's attendance and the mileage
allowed by law.[2]

Dated: January 3, 1976

_____, 19____   _____ , U.S. Marshal   ,

Service Fees   By _____   ,
        Travel   _____$
        Services _____

        Total   _____$

_____
    [2] Fees and mileage need not be tendered to the witness upon service of a subpoena issued in behalf of the United States
    or an officer or agency thereof. 28 USC 1825.

Figure 2-7   Subpoena to Produce Document or Object

order of the court which must be obeyed. Figure 2-8 is the form of a federal habeas corpus writ.

The courts have called the writ of habeas corpus the ''great writ of liberty.''[43] The first Habeas Corpus Act was enacted in the reign of Caroline II of England (1689) and was regarded as a great constitutional guarantee of personal liberty. The writ of habeas corpus was provided for in the U.S. Constitution and in the constitution of all the states. Among the powers denied Congress in Article I of the Constitution is the right to suspend the privilege of the writ except in cases of rebellion and invasion.[44]

Other Writs

There are a few more writs that students in criminal justice should be familiar with. A *writ of mandamus* is an order from a higher court to an inferior court or other agency such as the police or prosecutor compelling performance of a certain act as required by law. A *writ of injunction* is an order from a higher court to a lower court or to some other governmental agency or private citizen to ''cease and desist'' from performing a certain act. Finally, a *writ of coram nobis* is a writ of review directed to the trial court by the accused which petitions the court to set aside its judgment in the case against the accused because certain facts existed which, through no negligence on the part of the accused, were not brought out at the trial and which, if presented, would likely have changed the court's ruling in the case.

Other Terms

Venue is simply the geographical location of the crime and the jurisdiction of the court to try a particular case.

Bail is a procedure in the administration of justice for obtaining temporary liberty after arrest or conviction by means of a written promise to appear in court as required. To obtain bail, it may be necessary to deposit cash bail, a surety bond, or evidence of ownership or equity in real property. In recent years, the practice of releasing on one's *own recognizance* has developed. In these cases, the individual is released without having to post any form of financial security.

Extradition is merely the legal process of initiating and requesting another state (or nation) to surrender persons who have committed crimes and are fugitives from justice in the requesting jurisdiction. The procedure by which one sovereign state yields or returns the individual to the state initiating the request is called *rendition*.

SUMMARY

The basic elements of a crime are the act, the intent, the concurrence of act and intent, the causation, and the result. Each crime has specific elements which must be proved before an accused can be convicted.

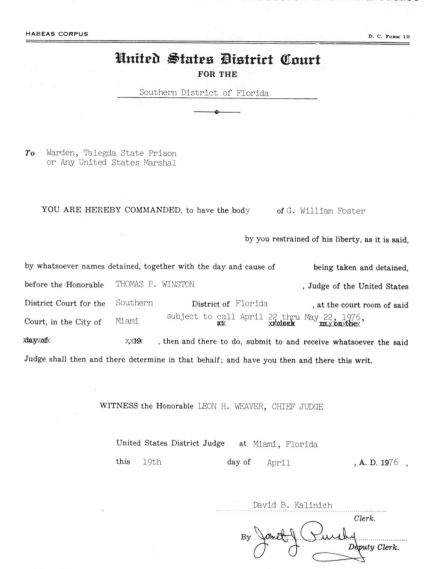

HABEAS CORPUS   D. C. Form 10

United States District Court
FOR THE

Southern District of Florida

To   Warden, Talegda State Prison
       or Any United States Marshal

YOU ARE HEREBY COMMANDED, to have the body   of G. William Foster

by you restrained of his liberty, as it is said,

by whatsoever names detained, together with the day and cause of   being taken and detained,

before the Honorable   THOMAS P. WINSTON   , Judge of the United States

District Court for the   Southern   District of   Florida   , at the court room of said

Court, in the City of   Miami   subject to call April 22 thru May 22, 1976,
                                   at   o'clock   m, on the

day of   xx19x   , then and there to do, submit to and receive whatsoever the said

Judge shall then and there determine in that behalf; and have you then and there this writ.

WITNESS the Honorable LEON H. WEAVER, CHIEF JUDGE

United States District Judge   at Miami, Florida

this   19th   day of   April   , A. D. 1976 ,

David B. Kalinich
                                                            Clerk.

By   *Deputy Clerk.*

Figure 2-8   Writ of Habeas Corpus

Crimes are classified into misdemeanors, felonies, and treasonous acts. These three broad categories are further divided into inchoate offenses, crimes against the person, crimes against property, crimes against public morality and decency, and finally crimes against the public order and administration of justice.

An understanding of some important legal procedures and a familiarity with basic legal documents are essential for the beginning student of criminal justice.

Suggested Additional Readings

American Bar Association. *Tentative Drafts on ABA Project on Standards for Criminal Justice.* New York: Institute of Judicial Administration, 1968.

Bureau of National Affairs. *The Criminal Law Revolution and Its Aftermath, 1960–72.* Washington, D.C.: Bureau of National Affairs, 1973.

Chamelin, Neil C., and Kenneth R. Evans. *Criminal Law for Policemen.* Englewood Cliffs, N.J.: Prentice-Hall, 1971.

Hall, Jerome. *Theft, Law and Society.* 2d ed. Indianapolis, Ind.: Bobbs-Merrill, 1952.

Leonard, V. A. *The Police, the Judiciary and the Criminal.* Springfield, Ill.: Charles C. Thomas, 1969.

Nelson, William E. "Emergency Notions of Modern Criminal Law in the Revolutionary Era: A Historical Perspective." *New York University Law Review* 42 (May 1967): 453–468.

Rich, Vernon. *Law and the Administration of Justice.* New York: Wiley, 1975.

Wells, Paul W. *Basic Law for the Law Enforcement Officer.* Philadelphia: Saunders, 1976.

Notes

1. M. Cherif Bassiouni, *Criminal Law and Its Processes* (Springfield, Ill.: Charles C Thomas, 1969), p. 50.
2. U.S. Constitution, Art. 1, sec. 9.
3. Bassiouni, op. cit., p. 50.
4. See Arnold H. Loewy, *Criminal Law* (St. Paul, Minn.: West, 1975), pp. 115–118.
5. Bassiouni, op. cit., p. 66.
6. R. T. Prudhoe, *England's Great Common Law* (London: Cambridge University Press, 1922), p. 49.
7. H. Sayre, "Criminal Attempts," *Harvard Law Review* 41 (1928).
8. *State v. Carbone,* 10 N.J., 329, 91 A.2d 571 (1961).
9. Bassiouni, op. cit., p. 168.
10. Ibid., pp. 170–171.
11. Loewy, op. cit., p. 25.
12. *State v. Jenkins,* 230 A.2d, 262 (Del. 1967).
13. *Lang v. State,* 6 Md. App. 128, 250 A.2d, 276 (1969).
14. A. F. Brandstatter and Alan A. Hyman, *Fundamentals of Law Enforcement* (Beverly Hills, Calif.: Glencoe Press, 1971), p. 103.
15. Bassiouni, op. cit., p. 178.
16. See Rollin M. Perkins, *Criminal Law and Procedure* (Brooklyn, N.Y.: Foundation Press, 1966), p. 345.
17. *Vandiver v. State,* 97 Okla. Crim. 217, 261 P.2d 617 (1953).
18. 18 U.S.C.A., § 1201.

19. *People v. Lardner,* 300 Ill. 264, 133 N.E. 375 (1921); *People v. Baker,* 365 Ill., 328, 6 N.E. 2d 667 (1937).

20. *People v. Cox,* N.Y. 137, 36 N.E. 2d 84 (1941).

21. Brandstatter and Hyman, op. cit., p. 109.

22. Bassiouni, op. cit., p. 259.

23. Blackstone, *Commentaries,* 254.

24. Bassiouni, op. cit., p. 245.

25. U.S. Constitution, Art. 3, sec. 3; see also *Kawakita v. United States,* 342 U.S. 717, 72 S. Ct. 950 (1952).

26. See *Cramer v. United States,* 355 U.S. 1, 65 S. Ct. 918 (1945); and Bassiouni, op. cit., p. 287.

27. U.S. Constitution, Art. 3, sec. 3.

28. See 18 U.S.C.A.

29. Loewy, op. cit., p. 102.

30. *People v. Adams,* 300 Ill. 20 132 N.E. 765 (1921).

31. *Murphy v. State,* 17 R.I. 698 24 Atl. 473 (1892).

32. See *Barker v. Ohio,* 328 F.2d 582 (6th Cir. 1964).

33. *Randall v. Evening News Association,* 97 Mich. 136, 56 N.W. 361.

34. Bassiouni, op. cit., p. 300.

35. *Giancana v. United States,* 352 F.3d 921.

36. *Hoffa v. United States,* 385 U.S. 293, 87 S. Ct. 408 (1966).

37. It is commonly believed that certain formal words and an actual touching of the arrestee are required. This is not true.

38. See Lloyd L. Weinreb, *Criminal Process* (Mineola, N.Y.: Foundation Press, 1969), pp. 17–22.

39. See *Bostwick v. State,* 124 Ga. App. 113, 182 S.E.2d 925 (1971).

40. See *Federal Rules of Criminal Procedure* 41 (d); and Yale Kamisar, Wayne R. La Fave, and Jerold H. Israel, *Basic Criminal Procedure* (St. Paul, Minn.: West, 1974).

41. For example, see *Mich. Stats. Ann.* 8 279 23 C.L. (1948).

42. Hazel B. Kerper, *Introduction to the Criminal Justice System* (St. Paul, Minn.: West, 1972), p. 404.

43. *Ex Parte Kelly,* 123 N.J. EQ 489, 198 A. 203 (1938).

44. Kerper, op. cit., p. 403.

Chapter 3

Crime in the United States

Crime is a perennial problem for society. During the 1960s, it became a major public issue in the United States. By 1970, several public opinion polls indicated that the public viewed crime as a problem unsurpassed in seriousness by any other issue—including race, inflation, and the war in Vietnam.[1] The media have dramatized the problem with examples of criminal acts that confirm official statistics indicating rising crime rates. *Life* magazine described a six-story building in New York in which seventeen of twenty-four apartments had been burglarized. One resident even purchased a German shepherd watchdog to protect himself, but it too was stolen.[2] *Life* followed up this story with a questionnaire exploring individual experiences with crime. The 43,000 responses, which were not necessarily representative of the general population of the United States, indicated that at least 70 percent of those responding were afraid to go out on the streets after dark, were occasionally afraid of crime even while at home, and were prepared to pay more for improved protection.[3]

Perhaps because crime is so publicized in our nation it is often felt that of all the industrialized and urban societies in the world, the United States has one of the highest crime rates, if not the highest.[4] The average American usually thinks of crime in terms of such violent offenses as homicide, forcible rape, and robbery. The serious student of criminal justice must approach the inflammatory rhetoric surrounding crime with a great deal of caution. When we examine crime and certain aspects of the types of human behaviors considered to be crimes, how crime figures are calculated, and the lack of solid research evidence, we must conclude that we cannot make many of the statements we commonly hear with any degree of certainty.

In the first place, we have no evidence that crime is any greater in the United States than in other nations because we have no ways to precisely measure our own crime rates, let alone the crime rates of other countries. We do know that serious crime is certainly not confined to the United States. Large foreign cities are also experiencing what seems to be an increase in violent crime. In Britain, crimes of violence increased from 26,716 to 41,088 between 1966 and 1970, with London experiencing more violent crimes in the first half of 1971 than in the whole of 1970. Similar trends are observable in continental Europe and Latin America.[5] In Africa, a serious wave of violence, accompanied by demands for public execution, struck Nigeria following its civil war. When such so-called crime waves are added to continuing violence in Northern Ireland and the recent surge of international terrorism, the crime situation in the United States appears a little less impressive.

For example, what little data are available on international crime rates may be somewhat surprising. The United Nations compared the homicide rates in various countries from 1960 to 1962, and although incomplete data were available in some nations, the following picture emerged (numbers given are per 100,000 population):[6]

Colombia	36.5
Mexico	31.9
South Africa	21.8
United States	4.8
Japan	1.5
Canada	1.4
Federal Republic of Germany	1.2
England/Wales	0.7
Ireland	0.4

To obtain a picture of crime in this country, we must know what types of behavior constitute the reported crimes. Table 3-1 indicates the most frequently reported crimes handled by the police in 1973. The violent offenses of homicide, forcible rape, and robbery make up only a very small fraction of all known crimes committed. In the year 1973, for example, those particular

TABLE 3-1   Seven Most Frequent Crimes Coming to the
Attention of the Police (1973)

Rank	Offense	Number	Percentage of all reported crimes
1	Drunkenness	1,599,000	17.7
2	Driving under the influence	946,800	10.5
3	Larceny	858,900	9.5
4	Burglary	434,000	4.8
5	Possession of marijuana	420,700	4.7
6	Simple assault	383,700	4.2
7	Violation of liquor laws	272,000	3.0
	TOTAL		54.4

Source: Based on FBI, Uniform Crime Reports, 1973 (Washington, D.C.: U.S. Government Printing Office, 1974).

offenses constituted less than 2 percent of the crimes reported to the police. The vast majority of crimes being handled by the criminal justice system and appearing as official statistics in crime summaries are much less serious offenses, such as drunkenness, driving under the influence, larceny, burglary, possession of marijuana, simple assaults, and liquor law violations. Add to this the vast number of traffic cases and other misdemeanors which are being processed by the police, courts, and jails, and a different picture of crime emerges. This is not meant to imply that we should not be concerned with the incidence of crime in this country or that we should devote less resources to understanding and preventing such behaviors; however, as the remainder of this chapter will demonstrate, we need to analyze crime more rationally if we are to understand this social problem.

THE UNIFORM CRIME REPORTING PROGRAM

During the 1920s, the International Association of Chiefs of Police (IACP) saw the need to develop a national system for gathering and publishing crime statistics. It was able to convince the federal government, and in 1930 Congress authorized a national and uniform system of compiling crime statistics known as the Uniform Crime Reporting Program. Congress vested the Federal Bureau of Investigation with the responsibility to develop the program and authorized that agency to be the national clearinghouse for statistical information on crime. Under this program, crime reports were to be voluntarily submitted to the FBI by city, county, state, and other federal law enforcement agencies throughout the country. To provide for uniformity in reporting crimes by various jurisdictions, national standardized definitions of crimes and the method of reporting them were adopted. Although there still remain a few police agencies which do not routinely report crimes to the FBI, by 1973 almost 11,000 city, county, state, and federal police agencies were voluntarily supplying crime data to the FBI. From these data, the FBI publishes annual *Uniform Crime Reports* (UCR), statistical summaries of those crimes coming to the attention of the police as reported by all the police agencies participating in the program. In the past few years, twenty-two states have developed their own uniform crime reporting programs. In these states, a central agency (often the state police) collects the data from all local governmental jurisdictions which maintain law enforcement services and forwards the statistics for the state to the FBI.

Offenses in the Uniform Crime Reporting Program are broken down into two categories. Part I of the UCR consists of seven major crimes or "index offenses," viewed by the FBI as indicators of national and regional crime trends. Extensive data are gathered on these index offenses, dealing with such factors as crime trends by age and sex, population groups, suburban and nonsuburban counties, arrest rates, and clearances. Part II consists of twenty-two other offense categories for which data are not as complete. Table 3-2 indicates the twenty-nine offenses covered in the *Uniform Crime Reports.*

TABLE 3-2   Uniform Crime Report Offenses

Part I (Index Offenses)	Part II (Other Offenses)	
1. Criminal homicide	8. Simple assaults	19. Gambling
2. Forcible rape	9. Arson	20. Offenses against the
3. Robbery	10. Forgery and counter-	family and children
4. Aggravated assault	feiting	21. Driving under the
5. Burglary	11. Fraud	influence
6. Larceny-theft	12. Embezzlement	22. Violation of liquor
7. Auto theft	13. Buying, receiving, or	laws
	possessing stolen	23. Drunkenness
	property	24. Disorderly conduct
	14. Vandalism	25. Vagrancy
	15. Weapons (carrying,	26. All other offenses
	possession, etc.)	(excluding traffic)
	16. Prostitution and com-	27. Suspicion
	mercialized vice	28. Curfew and loitering
	17. Other sex offenses	(juveniles)
	18. Violation of narcotic	29. Runaway (juveniles)
	drug laws	

CRIME AS A SOCIAL PROBLEM

Ultimately, crime must be considered as a social problem which will entail massive efforts on the part of society if it is ever to be reasonably controlled. In fact, many authorities doubt that crime can ever be brought under control, given the nature of the factors that seem to be associated with it. Wilson, for example, sees crime as the result of three very broad social factors; (1) the numbers of youth in society at a particular time, (2) the disruptive nature of our society on the family unit, and (3) the urbanized society in which we live, which presents many new opportunities for the successful commission of crime.[7] Whether or not we accept these ideas, these forces probably do, in some way, play a role. Crime is not a problem that can be left to the meager resources of the criminal justice system, for the issues which underlie crime in any society transcend the ability of the police, courts, or corrections to deal with this complex phenomenon in any meaningful way.

Historical Background

It should be realized that crime is not a recent phenomenon of the American experience. Virtually every generation in America has felt threatened by rising crime and violence. In the 1860s, the accounts of San Francisco told of extensive areas of that young city where "no decent man was in safety to walk the street after dark; while at all hours, both night and day, his property was jeopardized by incendiarism and burglary."[8] In New York, roving teenage

M. Licht/Stockmarket, Los Angeles

street gangs who "preyed upon innocent victims" gave rise to the word "hoodlum" in 1877.[9] Even before the American Revolution, "alarming" increases in robbery and violent crimes were reported in the cities of New York, Boston, and Philadelphia, leading some citizens to complain that municipal governance with its laws was a failure and that citizens should fall back on the law of self-preservation and self-action if individual safety was to be preserved.[10]

Many instances of crime and violence occurred in our early history. During the great railway strike of 1877, hundreds of persons were killed in outbreaks of violence and terrorism that swept the country and culminated in a massive confrontation and ensuing violence between strikers and company police and militia; scores were killed or injured, and almost two miles of buildings and railway property was laid waste.[11] The looting and takeover of New York for three days by mobs in the 1863 draft riots equalled the major disturbances that racked our cities in the 1960s. Racial disturbances have long plagued our major cities, as seen by the race riots that took place in Atlanta in 1907, in Chicago, Washington, and East St. Louis in 1919, and Detroit in 1943.[12] Al Capone, "Pretty Boy" Floyd, and the Barkers are all examples of our heritage of crime and violence in America. It would seem that urban disorders, student demon-strations, and other acts which many consider to be the beginnings of the ultimate destruction of our nation have been with us for a long period of our history; yet our nation still exists, and as a result of our experiences may, in some respects, be even stronger.

Although we do not know which specific variables produce crime or how these various factors may interrelate with each other, we have been able to identify what we think are some of the more important factors. Among these might be the following:

Social Characteristics:
- Density and size of the community
- Social composition of the community in terms of age, sex, and race
- Existing cultural mores of society which control behavior
- Economic conditions present
- Relative stability of the population
- Educational, religious, and recreational characteristics

Individual Characteristics:
- Attitudes conducive to criminal behavior
- Perceived value and meaningfulness of legitimate behavior
- Self-esteem; perceived abilities to compete in the legitimate world

Specific Characteristics of the Criminal Justice System:
- Effective strength of the police force
- Quality of police personnel
- Policies of the prosecuting officials and courts
- Attitude of the public toward the police and other criminal justice agencies
- Administration and investigative efficiency of the local police

The measurement of crime and a better understanding of what causes such behavior depends upon those quantitative and qualitative tools that we have available for analysis. We are handicapped in understanding crime because we do not have adequate measuring instruments, nor do we have the knowledge to account properly for the multitude of factors which might have some relation-ship to criminal behavior. As a result of these limitations, any analysis of our existing crime statistics and therefore any conclusions must always be suspect. These limitations also present significant problems in measuring the impact and results of many of the programs being undertaken to reduce crime in this country.

CRIME TRENDS AND CHARACTERISTICS

At this point, we should examine some of the data provided by the *Uniform Crime Reports*. Although the UCR is far from being an accurate reflection of crime in our nation, as we shall see later, let us analyze what trends and characteristics of crime it purports to show. First, the UCR indicates that crimes seem to be increasing at an alarming rate in the United States. Table 3-3 shows the national crime rate and the percentage change in the reported seven index crimes from 1960 to 1973.

TABLE 3-3   National Crime Rate and Percent Change
for Index Offenses from 1960 to 1973)

Offense	Rate per 100,000 inhabitants (1973)	Percent change over 1960
Murder	9.3	+ 86.0
Forcible rape	24.3	+ 155.8
Robbery	182.4	+ 204.5
Aggravated assault	198.4	+ 132.9
Burglary	1,210.8	+ 140.3
Larceny-theft	2,051.2	+ 100.3
Auto theft	440.1	+ 141.8

Source: FBI, *Uniform Crime Reports, 1973* (Washington, D.C.: U.S. Government Printing Office, 1974), p. 1.

What is particularly disturbing about these relative crime trends is the apparent disproportionate increase in crimes which involve personal violence. Such offenses as murder, forcible rape, robbery, and assault fall into this category. Many observers feel that the increase in these types of crimes is an indication of the malaise that underlies the social fabric in America today.[13] Certainly the publicity given these types of offenses contributes to considerable fear and concern among Americans.

In recent years, the threat of violence has been incorporated into the political campaign rhetoric of "law and order" and "safe streets" advocates, who call for repressive measures to deal with this situation—a cure which may be more damaging to individual freedom in the United States than the cause.

Crime Clocks

Situated conspicuously in the FBI's Washington headquarters are clocks which ominously tick off the occurrence of the seven index offenses in the United States. Every day, crowds of visitors gather before this visual display of the awesome extent of crime in the United States. In 1973, sixteen serious crimes came to the attention of the police every minute, and the violent crime of murder, forcible rape, robbery, aggravated assault was recorded every thirty-six seconds. These statistics are frightening, but what may be more meaningful is a comparison of the relative frequency of these crimes in 1970 and 1973.

Crime Clocks

SERIOUS CRIMES
1973—16 each minute
1970—11 each minute

VIOLENT CRIMES
Murder, forcible rape
Robbery or assault to kill
1973—one every 36 seconds
1970—one every 43 seconds

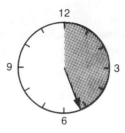

MURDER
1973—one every 27 minutes
1970—one every 33 minutes

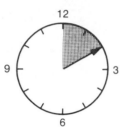

FORCIBLE RAPE
1973—one every 10 minutes
1970—one every 14 minutes

AGGRAVATED ASSAULT
1973—one every 76 seconds
1970—one every 96 seconds

ROBBERY
1973—one every 82 seconds
1970—one every 91 seconds

BURGLARY
1973—one every 12 seconds
1970—one every 15 seconds

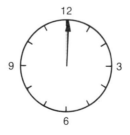

LARCENY THEFT
1973—one every 7 seconds
1970—one every 18 seconds

AUTO THEFT
1973—one every 34 seconds
1970—one every 34 seconds

Figure 3-1 Comparison of the Incidence of Serious Crimes in the United States: 1970 and 1973

Source: Federal Bureau of Investigation, *Uniform Crime Report,* 1973 and 1970 (Washington, D.C.: U.S. Government Printing Office, 1973 and 1970).

Figure 3-1 compares crime frequency rates as shown by the clocks in 1970 and 1973. Note that only the reported crime of auto theft has remained the same; all other offenses show a significant increase.

Crime Cycles

Seasonal Variations in Crime

The relationships between seasons of the year and the occurrence of crime has fascinated criminologists for many years, and a great deal of research has examined this relationship. A number of nineteenth century studies concluded that sexual crimes occurred more frequently in the summer months and that crimes against property were more likely to be committed in winter.[14] Pioneering criminologist Cesare Lombroso provided the first definitive study of seasonal crime rates in 1911.[15] By examining statistical data on sexual crimes, murders, and political crimes of rebellion, he concluded that they occur in their greatest frequency during the hottest months.[16] Von Mayr also arrived at a similar conclusion. From the analysis of criminal statistics in Germany from 1883 to 1892, he concluded that there was a characteristic rise and fall in types of crimes depending upon the seasons of the year; that is, offenses against the person reached their maximum in August and their minimum in December, while offenses against property reached their maximum in December and their minimum in April.[17]

Cohen, analyzing the UCR over a five-year period, also found some seasonal crime trends in the United States. Murder was generally more frequent in the summer than in the winter, but there were variations in the relative frequencies of these offenses by month in different geographical regions. The crimes of aggravated assault and forcible rape were generally lowest in January and then began to rise until they reached their peak in midsummer. December was the peak month for robbery, which then declined until July, at which time it began its upswing. The property offenses of burglary, larceny-theft, and automobile theft were less uniform than robbery in their patterns of occurrence. Nonetheless, Cohen believes that these property crimes also reflect seasonal influences, with a slight rise from January through March, a lower but relatively constant level to August, and a gradual upswing to a peak in either November or December. Overall, he concluded that crimes against the persons increase in the summer months, while property crimes are most frequent during the winter.[18] The reason given by criminologists for these seasonal differences is that the warm summer months find more people in daily contact with each other, while the winter months provide shorter days and the cover of darkness for the commission of property crimes requiring stealth.[19]

TABLE 3-4   Percentage Distribution of Index Crimes by Day of Week and Hour of Day—Kansas City, Mo., 1972

Day of Week	Percentage of Weekly Crimes	Midnight to 4 A.M.	4 A.M. to 8 A.M.	8 A.M. to noon	noon to 4 P.M.	4 P.M. to 8 P.M.	8 P.M. to midnight
Monday	13.8	12.9	5.8	12.4	20.8	22.3	25.8
Tuesday	12.1	11.6	4.3	13.4	22.5	23.1	25.1
Wednesday	13.4	11.9	4.0	13.3	21.9	21.3	27.4
Thursday	13.9	12.5	5.9	12.8	20.4	22.8	25.9
Friday	15.1	10.7	4.3	10.7	19.7	21.5	33.1
Saturday	17.6	18.3	6.5	7.3	15.6	20.0	32.3
Sunday	14.1	21.5	7.3	7.1	14.3	21.8	28.0

Source: *Comprehensive Law Enforcement Plan,* Missouri Law Enforcement Assistance Council, 1972.

Daily Variations in Crime

Most data indicate that major crimes are most likely to be committed on weekends, with the peak coming on Saturday and then declining from Sunday through Tuesday, after which crime begins to climb toward the Saturday peak.[20] Table 3-4 provides data from Kansas City which would indicate, in that city at least, such is the case.

Hourly Variations in Crime

Analyses by the Kansas City Police Department, which has an excellent research unit, indicate that the incidence of index crimes is highest during the hours from 8:00 P.M. to midnight; on the average a little over 28 percent of the crimes committed during any twenty-four hour period occur during those four hours. This phenomenon is documented by similar studies done by other law enforcement agencies.[21]

The Geography of Crime

Crime by Regions

Data indicate that there are regional differences in both the rates of total crimes and the relative frequency of occurrence of certain index offenses in the United States. These data should not be interpreted to mean that physical geography is a major factor in and of itself—at most, they may hint at the relationship between geographical areas and their sociological characteristics.

For example, geographical areas of the country differ in the distribution and characteristics of their population. Although these differences are not as great as in the past, they still exist. Regions differ in the relative distributions of their populations according to such characteristics as age, sex, race, life styles (urban versus rural), educational attainment, customs, residential mobility, occupation, and other factors. These characteristics are recognized as factors which determine what crimes are likely to be committed, what particular opportunities for certain types of offenses exist, the likelihood of reporting crimes to the authorities, and those crimes which are most likely to be handled by official intervention by the criminal justice system.

Table 3-5 indicates some striking geographical differences in the distribution of index crimes. For each index offense in the table, the regions with the highest and lowest number of the specific offenses are shown. The total indicates the average number of these offenses per 100,000 population for the entire nation. The Pacific states seem to have the highest incidence of index offenses, while the West North Central states record the lowest. Looking at specific crimes, we see that the Northeast states record the most auto thefts. Although the table does not show the figures, the Northeast states, in 1973, ranked near the bottom in the crime of forcible rape. In 1973, the Middle Atlantic states recorded the highest frequency of robbery, followed very closely by the Northeast states, while the East South Central region recorded the fewest number of robberies. The Pacific states have the distinction of leading the rest of the country in the crimes of forcible rape, aggravated assault, burglary, and larceny.

The states in the South rank first in the numbers of homicides which come to the attention of the police. They also follow very closely the lead of the Pacific states in the number of aggravated assaults. It would seem that crimes of personal violence are particularly characteristic of the Southern states. On the other hand, the Southern states report relatively fewer property crimes, such as burglary, larceny-theft, and auto theft, than do most other regions of the country.

Although the data reflect only the crimes recorded for 1973, a number of studies conducted earlier show similar geographical distributions of crime. For example, the high rates of homicide and aggravated assault seem to be a long-standing characteristic of the Southern states.[22] A number of criminologists have tried to explain this phenomenon in terms of the cultural and social stratification which has existed in the South.[23] Similarly, the high number of index offenses occurring in the Pacific states would also seem to have been with us for a few years at least. Keith Harries found in his 1968 and 1971 examinations of the geographical occurrence of crime that the Pacific states were in the forefront in the number of robberies, aggravated assaults, forcible rapes, and burglaries and second only to the South in number of homicides committed.[24]

A recent and excellent analysis of crime in the United States done by Harries indicated that the larger the metropolitan area, the higher the relative crime rate;

TABLE 3-5 UCR Index Crimes Known to the Police per 100,000 Population by Geographic Regions, 1973

Regions	Murder, non-negligent manslaughter	Forcible rape	Robbery	Aggravated assault	Burglary	Larceny-theft	Auto theft
Northeast							581.6
Middle Atlantic			297.3			1,520.3	
North Central							
W. North Central	5.0	18.3		107.5	933.6		
South	12.9						
E. South Central			91.1				239.4
W. South Central							
West							
Pacific		37.3		242.8	1,871.3	3,073.0	
Total							
United States	9.3	24.3	182.4	198.4	1,210.8	2,051.2	440.1

Source: FBI, *Uniform Crime Report, 1973* (Washington, D.C.: U.S. Government Printing Office, 1974).

that the larger the black population, the higher the rates of homicide and assault; that major violent crimes except rape are much more likely to occur on the street than in any inside location; and that the higher the number of aggravated assaults in a community, the higher also the number of the other six index crimes.[25]

Crime by Type of Community

Another characteristic of crime which should not be particularly surprising is that official crime rates show the cities recording a much higher rate than rural areas. However, some trends seem to be developing which indicate a possible narrowing of this gap. In 1973, the UCR indicated that index crimes in small towns of less than 50,000 population and suburban communities are increasing at alarming rates. Table 3-6 indicates the percentage increase of the index crimes by size and type of community. It would seem that small American towns and suburban areas are experiencing an increase in these crimes much greater than that occurring in larger cities. While our large cities show a steady increase in all crimes except robbery for the year 1973, only the crime of forcible rape increased more in our major cities than in the suburbs, smaller cities, or rural areas.

How can we account for these drastic increases in reported crimes in small town and suburban areas, which have often been thought of as havens of tranquillity and security? Probably, part of the answer is simply that more of these offenses are indeed being committed in small towns and suburban communities than in the past. For years the movement of large shopping centers and commercial establishments to the suburbs has increased opportunities for crime and the vulnerability of these establishments to criminal attack. Suburban and rural banks are an excellent example. Minimum security and the proximity of arterial routes make them a favorite target of opportunity for robbery. For example, a study done by the DeKalb County Police Department, which is adjacent to the city of Atlanta, Georgia, indicated that a high percentage of crimes committed in that county were by individuals residing in Atlanta. Criminals in Atlanta would select sites to commit burglaries, robberies, larceny, and auto theft in the county and then, with the help of the excellent freeway and interstate highway system, return to the city of Atlanta and disappear.[26]

Another factor which may be contributing to the increases of reported crimes in small towns and suburban communities is the actions of the local police departments in these areas. Police agencies in these areas are becoming more sophisticated in their detection of crimes, recording techniques, and reporting of crimes. Just a few years ago, only a handful of the larger local police departments employed advanced techniques in these areas. Now some of the smaller cities have even surpassed metropolitan police departments in levels of service and the use of advanced techniques which, because of better reporting methods, send more complete data to the FBI.

TABLE 3-6

Crimes Known to the Police:
Percentage Rates of Increase from 1972 to 1973

	Murder and nonnegligent manslaughter	Forcible rape	Robbery	Aggravated assault	Burglary	Larceny	Auto theft
Total increase for all cities	+ 6.9	+ 10.3	+ 0.9	+ 5.8	+ 6.6	+ 14.0	+ 2.3
Cities over 250,000	+ 5.3	+ 13.2	− 1.7	+ 1.1	+ 3.7	+ 4.0	+ 0.9
Cities of 50,000 and less	+ 18.5	+ 12.0	+ 10.9	+ 10.1	+ 11.5	+ 25.4	+ 9.7
Suburban areas	+ 8.7	+ 7.2	+ 9.8	+ 13.7	+ 10.5	+ 23.9	+ 9.6
Rural areas	+ 0.2	+ 5.5	+ 6.3	+ 4.5	+ 8.5	+ 28.2	+ 14.7

Adapted from: *FBI, Uniform Crime Report, 1973* (Washington, D.C.: U.S. Government Printing Office, 1974), pp. 98–107.

THE CONTROVERSY OVER THE UNIFORM
CRIME REPORTS AND CRIME RATES

So far, we have relied upon data published in the UCR to examine such things as the increase in crime in the United States, the relative frequency of the occurrence of the index crimes, geographical patterns of criminal activity, and changes in the relative incidence of crimes by types of communities. At this point, we should examine the UCR itself and how it measures up as an effective and meaningful indicator of crime in this nation. After all, most of the published facts and figures about the increase or decrease of crime in the United States are based on this instrument.

The Center for Studies of Crime and Delinquency of the National Institute of Mental Health has indicated that criminal statistics if they are to be meaningful must fulfill certain requirements. The Center believes that statistics pertaining to the criminal justice system should:

1. Provide information about the types of crimes committed.
2. Indicate something of the circumstances surrounding the crime.
3. Provide some information about the kinds of persons involved.
4. Indicate the forms of disposal decided on by the courts or other authorities.
5. Separate first offenders (or first convictions) according to age, sex and other social and psychological data.
6. Provide data on the cost of maintaining the services connected with the detection and prevention of crime and the treatment of offenders and relate these to some measures of effectiveness.[27]

The fact that the UCR does not meet any of these requirements satisfactorily has led to its widespread repudiation by most knowledgeable people who have studied problems of crime in this country. The noted criminologist Lloyd Ohlin has said that the UCR index, which is repeatedly quoted by newspapers, law enforcement agents and politicians as the official summary of crime, is *almost worthless* (emphasis added).[28] Sellin, another eminent scholar in the study of crime, has said that the United States "has the worst crime statistics of any major country in the western world."[29] Why does the FBI's *Uniform Crime Reports* receive so much criticism?

Unreported Crimes Not Included

One criticism of the UCR as a crime index is that it reflects only those crimes which are known to the police and which the police agencies themselves report. Thus, all crimes do not end up in the statistics because victims quite frequently do not report them to the police. For example, the University of Chicago's National Opinion Research Center (NORC) asked 10,000 households in Chicago, Boston, and Washington, D.C., whether any member of the household had been a victim of crime during the past year and whether the crime had been reported.[30] The surveys revealed that the amount of crime in the United States is several times that reported in the UCR. The NORC survey found that forcible rapes were 3½ times the reported rate, burglaries three times greater, aggravated assaults and larcenies of $50 and over more than double, and robbery 50 percent greater than the reported rate. The number of crimes against the person reported to NORC was almost twice the UCR rate, and the number of property crimes more than twice as much. For certain specific offenses, the Washington survey showed from three to ten times as many crimes as the numbers indicated by police statistics.[31]

Reliance on Voluntary Submission of Data

The second criticism of the UCR is that it relies upon the voluntary submission of crime data by police agencies. This has led to some notorious instances of falsification in cities like Chicago and New York, whose police agencies had manipulated the data that they reported to the FBI. Often for political reasons, the police have not accurately recorded all the crimes coming to their attention in order to appear to be doing a better job of controlling crime in the community.[32] An opposite phenomenon may now be occurring. With federal monies being made available to police agencies, there may be an incentive to increase the recording of crimes so as to demonstrate a need for additional federal monies to help in the so-called war on crime.[33] By the same token, police administrators are aware of widespread public acknowledgment that the police cannot be solely responsible for crime—it is a social problem beyond their control. Under these circumstances, showing a dramatic crime increase in a community may be an advantage when requesting more resources at budget time.

Number of Reported Crimes Influenced by Numerous Factors

Crime rates may seem to be increasing because of the increasing professionalism and bureaucratization of the police, who may be resorting to the use of more formal actions, more formal records, and less informal disposition of cases that come to their attention.[34] In this way, some police agencies may be officially recording more crimes than they have in the past.

Recent changes in reporting systems have also resulted in apparent increases in UCR index offenses from one year to the next, ranging from 26.2 percent for Miami to 202 percent for Kansas City. A classic example of the effect of procedural changes can be seen in New York City, where in 1950 a central reporting system was installed: the following year, increases amounted to 400 percent for robberies and 1,300 percent for burglaries.

The reporting of crimes and official crime rates is also affected by the increasing availability and use of theft insurance. Most insurance companies require that a police report be made for any theft claims. In the absence of such insurance, many thefts might not come to the attention of the police. It should also be mentioned that the availability of insurance may also lead to unknown numbers of fraud cases. A businessman may report a theft, burglary, or robbery to the police although it never occurred in order to collect from the insurance company for the ''loss.'' This loss would then become an official crime statistic.

Another circumstance that may be having a bearing on the number of crimes reported is the rising expectations of the poor and segregated minority groups.[35] In the past, the police were more prone to overlook crimes committed in minority areas in the city as ''natural'' occurrences in these neighborhoods that did not warrant much attention. Many of these groups were likely inhibited from reporting their victimization to the police. Today, minority groups may feel that they too are entitled to equal treatment by the police and as a result are more likely to report crimes to the police when they are victimized.

Changes in ''classifications'' also affect reporting. For years, the UCR included larceny of *over* $50 as one of the seven index crimes. Because of inflation, misreporting (e.g., police departments placing a value of less than $50 on items stolen so as not to register an index crime), and general criticisms of the $50 figure as an arbitrary one, the FBI in 1973 classified *all larcenies regardless of the value of the property stolen* as an index crime. As might be imagined, this caused the index crime rate to jump upward significantly.

Data Not Meaningful

Another criticism of the UCR is that it provides mostly summaries of the number of crimes reported and does not tell us anything meaningful about the crimes. If we are ever to understand the causes of crime in this country so that we can develop strategies to reduce its incidence, we need to know the circumstances surrounding the commission of these acts. The police, particularly, could improve their efficiency if they had more data upon which they could rely, such as crime data related to age, sex, race, and economic status;[36] the rate of population mobility as a basis for the measurement of crime rates;[37] occurrence data which indicate the extent to which different kinds of neighborhoods are subjected to different kinds of index crimes;[38] data on unreported offenses; and victim surveys to supplement the UCR.[39]

Data Based on Inconsistent Definitions of Crimes

Although the UCR definitions of crimes and classifications of offenses try to be specific, jurisdictional differences between states in how they define and classify various offenses cause serious problems for accurate reporting. Again, the President's Commission on Law Enforcement on Administration of Justice found this to be a widespread problem, and even the best police statistical departments were found to have made mistakes in the way they classified crimes before they sent their data off to the FBI to be included in the *Uniform Crime Reports*.

Poor Classification

A fifth criticism of the UCR is the manner in which it determines the "seriousness" of crimes and whether a specific crime is a Part I (index) crime or a less serious Part II offense. For example, many critics argue that auto theft does not belong as an index crime. Most stolen vehicles are taken by youths for joyriding, and nine out of every ten cars are returned to their owners within a short time after they have been stolen.[40]

What we would seem to need and what the UCR does not give us are more precise and probably different kinds of definitions that can identify crimes that are serious and distinguish them from those which are less serious. Are we to consider, for example, that larceny and auto theft are more serious than kidnapping, the sale of "hard" narcotics, arson, or embezzlement? Until better measures are devised of what should be really considered serious index crimes, the UCR will continue to be a less than useful measurement of crime.

Distortion of Facts

A sixth criticism of the UCR is that the FBI does not present its crime figures honestly to the public. Graham, for example, charges that when the FBI publishes the UCR, it slices off those years that show a downward trend when it makes multiyear comparisons, showing only those years in which crime increased so as to bear out its claim of "record highs" in crime.[41] Former U.S. Attorney General Ramsey Clark indicates that an even more flagrant distortion is created by the FBI crime clocks, which each year show a progressively smaller time period between the commission of index crimes. In a nation that is now growing by almost 3 million persons a year, the interval between crimes is necessarily smaller this year than it was last year even though the relative crime rate may have remained the same. Clark feels that the FBI, rather than publicizing the fact that a homicide occurs every so many minutes, could tell the public that the average citizen's chances of becoming a victim of homicide on a given day are about one in almost 7 million or that the chance of being a victim of any crime of violence is one in 146,000 per day.[42]

Overemphasis on Crime Control as a Measure of Police Effectiveness

Another criticism of the UCR is that the use of this instrument places too great an emphasis upon crime as the measure of whether a police agency is or is not effectively fulfilling its role in society. Are we to say that because a certain community experiences an increase in crime, its police department is not doing its job? Just the opposite might be true. A department may report a high rate of crime because it is efficiently managed, has developed an accurate and sophisticated records system, and is administered with integrity. A less professional police organization may have none of these characteristics and thus actually give the impression on paper that it is doing a better job of dealing with crime.

Also, if we use published crime data as an indicator of police effectiveness, we are almost certainly forcing police agencies to commit more of their resources to crime control than may be warranted. The police perform many other services than merely crime control activities, as we shall see later in the section on law enforcement. If we overemphasize crime control, we forgo the use of police resources in other and perhaps more important functions. Since in any organization, resources are always limited, their use in one activity reduces the opportunity to use them in other areas. Economists refer to this phenomenon as "lost opportunity costs" of management. As long as we continue to use and interpret UCR crime data as an indicator of how well a police department is doing, police managers under political pressure and by virtue of their own instincts for survival will continue to stress crime, probably completely out of proportion to the time the agency is actually involved in dealing with it.

Lack of Baseline Data

An eighth criticism of the UCR and of the measurement of crime in America generally is that we really have no accurate baseline data for analysis. For example, although we record a UCR "crime increase" of a certain percentage over last year, the last ten years, or the last thirty years for that matter, what does it really tell us? First of all, as has been pointed out, the increase may simply be due in large part to more complete reporting, better police work at uncovering crimes, or any combination of factors other than the relative growth in crime itself. The UCR, with its dramatic pronouncements that crime has increased a certain percentage, would tend to lead the average American into feeling we are being engulfed by an unprecedented crime wave. If we had meaningful baseline data in which accurate statistics for, say, the years since 1876 had been gathered, we could compare them with present statistics and reach meaningful conclusions.

Are we, in fact, being engulfed by an unprecedented crime wave? A number of studies cast some doubt. A study was made in Buffalo, New York, covering a period of 100 years from 1864 to 1964. It found that the years following World War II evidenced a lower relative crime rate than the turbulent period following the Civil War. The crime trend in Buffalo based on all forms of crime actually decreased between 1946 and 1964; and the number of bookings for assault was larger in the 1870s when the city was one-fifth its present size than in the 1960s.[43]

The findings of the Buffalo study are similar to those of a study made of the annual arrest rates of the Boston police from 1849 to 1951 for the seven major crimes of murder, manslaughter, forcible rape, assault, robbery, burglary, and larceny. When the rates of these crimes were examined collectively, they showed a distinct downward trend, almost uninterrupted from a peak in 1875-1878 to the present. Since that time, the relative per capita crime rate in Boston has declined steadily to a level of about one-third the 1875-1878 rate. Murder, assault, and larceny have shown a clear decline during the 100-year period, while robbery and burglary have shown a downward tendency, the periodic upswings being accounted for by wars and depressions.[44]

By now, it should be apparent that the question of whether crime in the United States is increasing, decreasing, or remaining stable cannot be answered with any degree of certainty. Again, this is not to say that crime and the factors that cause it should be of any less concern to us as a nation. We must continue to examine it, but in ways more meaningful than we have used in the past. The next section will examine a major step that has been taken to better measure the incidence of crime in the United States today.

THE NATIONAL CRIME PANEL

In 1973, the UCR indicated that nearly 8.75 million offenses were recorded by the police. This was slightly over four offenses for every 100 citizens in the United States. However, as we have seen from the earlier National Opinion Research Center study, this underrepresents the actual amount as many crimes are not reported. In an attempt to develop a more accurate picture of unreported crime in the nation, a new crime analysis program has been created and is beginning to compile data.

This new program has been developed by the Law Enforcement Assistance Administration (LEAA) of the U.S. Department of Justice, which has initiated a $12 million per year survey of individuals and businesses to obtain statistical data on the incidence of crime, its cost, and the characteristics of its victims and of various criminal events. LEAA has contracted with the U.S. Bureau of the Census to conduct the surveys and compile the data. In the words of LEAA:

> (The National Crime Panel) is one of the most ambitious efforts yet undertaken for filling some of the gaps in crime data; victimization surveys are expected to supply criminal justice officials with new insights into crime and its victims, complementing data resources already on hand (i.e., the UCR) for purposes of planning, evaluation and analysis. The surveys subsume many of the so-called hidden crimes that, for a variety of reasons, are never brought to police attention. They also furnish a means for developing victim typologies and, for identifiable sectors of society, yield information necessary to compute the relative risk of being victimized.[45]

Using scientific sampling procedures, the Panel began in 1973 to survey crime victimization among individuals, households, and commercial estab-

lishments, concentrating on the crimes of forcible rape, robbery, assault, larceny, burglary, and auto theft.[46] The idea behind the project is to select a
random sample of citizens who are representative of all the city's residents.
Researchers interview the citizens in the sample to see whether they have been
victims of crimes, and if so, what types of crimes, how they were committed,
and whether they reported their victimization to the police. These studies are
often referred to as *victimization studies*. From the sample, researchers project
data for the city's entire population. The initial surveys are being conducted in
our five largest cities of New York, Chicago, Los Angeles, Philadelphia, and
Detroit. Another similar study is also being conducted in thirteen other large
cities in the nation.

The preliminary data gathered from the survey during the first half of 1973
indicated broad discrepancies between the number of serious offenses committed and the number reported in the UCR. It appeared that the problem was
not only the failure of citizens to report their victimization to the police, but
also the fact that many incidents which were reported were not listed by the
police in their official statistics. It should be recognized, however, that in some
instances the police do not record crimes when reported because the reports
prove to be unfounded. In any event, the data from this first survey of
serious crime added fuel to the controversy surrounding the validity of the
Uniform Crime Report. Table 3-7 examines the preliminary findings of the
victimization survey.

TABLE 3-7   Incidents from the National Crime Panel Preliminary Report

Type of Crime	Total Incidents	Incidents Reported to the Police	Incidents from the Uniform Crime Reports
Rape	81,600	35,900	23,409
Robbery	600,600	318,100	179,478
Aggravated Assault	637,200	314,500	198,560
Burglary	3,691,300	1,863,300	1,171,358
Larceny	11,085,800	2,406,500	1,980,007
Motor Vehicle Theft	586,100	381,700	429,492
Total	16,682,600	5,320,000	3,982,304

Source: Law Enforcement Assistance Administration, *Newsletter* 4, No. 6 (December,
        1974), p. 5.

The first complete findings from these preliminary surveys were finally compiled and released in 1975. With the development of improved methodology in
conducting the surveys, these completed findings indicated that the UCR discrepancies were not quite as large as the preliminary survey data indicated.
Even so, the 1975 report found that the incidence of the six crimes examined
was approximately twice that reported to the police in the eighteen cities
studied.

The first complete findings were released in 1975. The Crime Panel found that the incidence of the six crimes they were concentrating on was approximately twice that reported to the police in the eighteen cities they studied. In other words, if the police were accurately recording and reporting all crimes to the UCR that came to their attention, the UCR would, on the average, still reflect only one-half the crimes being committed. Table 3-8 shows the average percentage of crimes that were reported to the police in these cities.

TABLE 3-8   Percentage of Specific Crimes Reported to the Police in Eighteen Major Cities

Type of Crime	Percent of Victims Reporting the Crime to Police
1. Forcible rape	48.5
2. Robbery	52.9
3. Assault	39.9
4. Larceny	33.1
5. Household larceny	25.4
6. Household burglary	54.9
7. Auto theft	75.4
8. Commercial burglary	76.2
9. Commercial robbery	83.8
Average	54.6

Source: Law Enforcement Assistance Administration, *Criminal Victimization Surveys in 13 American Cities* (Washington, D.C.: U.S. Government Printing Office, June 1975), and Law Enforcement Assistance Administration, *Crime in the Nation's Five Largest Cities* (Washington, D.C.: U.S. Government Printing Office, April 1974).

Among the crimes examined, those against commercial establishments were most frequently reported. Of the crimes not directed at businesses, auto theft was most frequently reported, while assault and larceny were reported only about one-third of the time they occurred.

Interestingly, the Crime Panel studies have produced some unexpected findings. In the first place, serious crime is being reported to the police more frequently than had been thought. Where the earlier NORC victimization studies indicated that overall the amount of unreported crime was nearly three times the amount being reported to the police, the Crime Panel data indicates that the amount of unreported serious crime is slightly less than one-half of the offenses being committed.[47] Even in the case of forcible rape, nearly one-half of the victims notified the police, a figure much higher than expected for this crime. The Crime Panel surveys also reported that in at least three-fourths of the personal incidents involving violence or the threat of violence, the confrontation was between strangers, that is, between the victim or victims and one or more unknown assailants. This finding conflicts with the often expressed belief that a large percentage of such crime involves people who are in some way acquainted. For example, the NORC studies in 1966 came to that conclusion.[48]

The Crime Panel surveys found that victimization rates produced common patterns in each of the eighteen major cities studied.[49] Males were much more likely to be victims of crimes than females, and persons under age thirty-five were much more likely to be victims of crimes than older persons. It was also found that members of minority races had significantly higher rates of victimization throughout all comparable age levels than whites, particularly for the offenses of robbery and aggravated assault. Single persons were much more likely to be assaulted than were persons who were married, widowed, divorced, or separated. Persons with family incomes of less than $3,000 were much more frequently victims of the violent crimes of rape, robbery, and aggravated assault. Those with higher incomes were more likely to be the victims of larceny without contact than were citizens with lower incomes. From these data, it is obvious that the more serious forms of crime particularly affect members of minority groups and low-income citizens. This is especially true of crimes against the person and crimes of a violent nature.

Among the respondents sampled, an effort was made to determine what types and specific characteristics of crimes were more likely to be reported to the police and which were not. Generally, nonviolent crimes against the person were most likely not to be reported. If the crime involved violence to the victim, it was more likely to be reported. Crimes against the household including auto theft were more often reported than were crimes against the person.

Those interested in the study of crime have long been puzzled by the question of why people do not report the fact that they have been victimized to the police. One reason may be that they do not trust the police or they view the police as a threatening symbol. In order to shed some light on this question, Crime Panel researchers in each city attempted to determine why those who indicated they had been the victims of crimes did not notify the authorities. The most frequent reason given was that the victims felt ''nothing could be done.'' About one-third of the victims felt that it ''wasn't important enough.''[50] There was no direct indication that they did not trust the police.

Although we cannot tell why the victims felt so strongly that nothing could be done, we must wonder what is behind such an attitude. It may demonstrate a significant lack of confidence by citizens in the ability of the police to bring the offender to justice. It may, in fact, be a general lack of confidence in the entire criminal justice system to perform its role in society.

APPLICATION OF COMPUTERS

In the past few years, a great deal of attention has focused on the application of computers to the study of crime and offenders. Criminal justice agencies, particularly the police, see the storage and retrieval capabilities of the modern computer as a means to classify known criminals, store information on stolen property, and maintain and cross-index *modus operandi* (method of operation) files of particular crimes and criminals. For example, a few police agencies enter into the computer characteristics of certain crimes, including method of commission, description of suspect(s), property stolen, and any other clues available. When a new crime is committed, they crosscheck all the characteristics of the offense to see whether these characteristics match up with prior unsolved crimes. In this way, they try to develop a composite work-up of similar offenses, that is, a composite set of clues from a number of crimes having similar characteristics. Thus the investigating officer can have a great deal more information than would otherwise be available. Without the computer to compile and store the information, each investigating officer would have only the information from one crime to work with and might not know that similar crimes were being investigated by other police personnel.

Researchers also see the computer as a tremendous aid in the study of crime and criminals. First, the computer could help in classifying criminals according to specific individual characteristics that can be analyzed. For example, by feeding computers with enough information on the background and psychological and other characteristics of types of offenders, a profile of offenders who commit certain types of crimes might be developed. Such a profile would be an important aid in identifying such persons and bringing them to justice or developing programs to treat them once they are institutionalized.

Researchers also envision the computer as an important tool to study the effects of different treatment and rehabilitation programs. For example, case histories and personal characteristics of the offenders could be examined in relation to the particular treatment programs the offenders were exposed to. In this way, researchers hope to discover what specific types of programs seem to work best given the identified characteristics of an offender. This matching of the needs and characteristics of the offender with appropriate treatment techniques has long been a goal of rehabilitative programs.

Although such uses of the computer are not yet a reality, there have been some prototype demonstration projects of more meaningful application of computer technology to criminal justice. One of the most highly publicized endeavors was the development of the System for Electronic Analysis and Retrieval of Criminal Histories (SEARCH). This was a federally funded effort to gather crime data and related information in a fifteen state network. A master computer system was set up to gather the crime data of all the participating states. Such important data as information on offenders and their criminal histories was to be included. A unique feature of SEARCH was that it would provide a means to examine the relationship between characteristics of offenders and the types of crimes they committed as well as the type of treatment they had been exposed to if they had previously been imprisoned.[51]

SEARCH was never made fully operational because of congressional concern and the withdrawal of appropriation needed to develop it. A few states have continued efforts to develop state systems based upon the SEARCH model, such as Michigan's Criminal Case History (CCH) computer system. However, these efforts are comparatively small-scale, in terms of both the computer hardware system and the data base or records which they intend to use and keep on file.

A recent effort to link modern computer technology to the study of crime, offenders, and the administration of justice has been the development and study of transaction statistics. This new system, now being developed in California, is appropriately titled offender-based transaction statistics (OBTS). It is a state-wide data-gathering and analysis system which examines the transactions, or contacts, an arrestee has with the various agencies of the criminal justice system. The unit of analysis is the offender. Each offender constitutes a single file, and as he or she moves through the various processing stages of the criminal justice system, data is collected on matters such as the most serious charge brought against the offender, the disposition of the charge, and the correctional action taken.[52]

In this way, the operations of the various agencies of criminal justice can be studied in a total systems-like manner from the moment the offender is arrested by the police until he or she is eventually released from the process. Among the questions that may be answered by this type of research are:

- What is the relationship between police charges and those pressed by the prosecutor? In what way is plea bargaining reflected in the charges? In what types of cases are the reduction of charges most significant?

- What is the relative frequency of guilty pleas, jury trials, and bench trials, and how do they relate to offense and offender characteristics?

- What are the conviction rates by offense type, by trial type, and by defendant characteristics? What is the gap between original and final charges, and what are the most typical forms of reduction in charges?

- What is the relationship between sentences imposed and offense and offender characteristics? What is the relationship between sentences and plea or trial convictions, and between sentences and offenders freed on bail or detained?

- What are the practices of correctional agencies in granting parole, training or treatment programs, types of probation, work release, and admission to halfway houses?

- How does recidivism (defined as rearrest, or reconviction) relate to actions taken against an individual as recorded in previous OBTS cycles? For example, was the individual convicted in his or her previous case(s)? incarcerated? treated?

- What is the average (median) time lapse between steps in the process for all cases —misdemeanors or felonies, violent offenses or property offenses, etc.? What parts of the system are more time-consuming than others?

- How does the total number of cases for a given period—and the resulting case-load—affect the quantity of cases prosecuted, pled, and convicted? How does this number affect the type of dispositions made?

- What is the attrition rate of cases at each phase? What types of crimes are most likely to drop out? How are these factors related to caseloads at each agency?

- Is there a clear and consistent interagency policy to apply more resources in certain types of cases? For example, is more police work, special prosecution, or a speedier trial obtained for violent crimes, recidivists, major misdemeanors, etc.?[53]

Although the value of the computer is unquestioned, its use has certain other implications that should be mentioned. Of great concern is the question of individual freedom and the right of privacy. The centralization and ready availability of criminal case histories may pose a grave threat to the right of privacy and the dignity of the individual which, in the long run, may be more threatening to our society than is the problem of crime. It was because of this concern that Congress withdrew funding for SEARCH. In recent years, we hear increasingly of instances when agents of the government, particularly law enforcement agencies, through the use of newly developed technology, have been able to spy on private citizens and gather enormous files on their everyday lives. Although it may seem warranted when dealing with organized crime figures and others involved in the commission of serious crime, there is always the danger that this technology could be employed to gather information on those who express views which are merely not in line with the existing political ideology. Such use would be a direct strike at the very precepts of American democracy.

In the last few years, Congress and many groups of concerned Americans have expressed this fear. Because of the public sensitivity to the potential threat that computer systems represent, it is doubtful that such systems will ever be fully used in criminal justice. This is particularly unfortunate for science, but it is a price that must be paid. In the final analysis, the development and use of computer systems in criminal justice will probably be limited to the gathering of specific data that can be used in such limited ways as helping to identify suspects, to suggest ways to reduce court delays, and to make decisions on whether to grant or deny probation and parole; such systems will be of little help in explaining crime or criminal behavior.

SUMMARY

We often hear that the United States has the highest crime rate in the world. The fact is that we have no way to prove or disprove this statement. What little we do know about crime comes mostly from official accounts published annually in the *Uniform Crime Reports*. The *Uniform Crime Reports* indicate that certain characteristics appear to be associated with crime in this country; for example, some geographical areas have a higher relative incidence of certain types of offenses than other areas.

However, we still know very little about crime in this country, particularly how much crime there is and whether it is really increasing. The problem is that we have no effective way to measure crime. Recently, the federal government has tried to provide a more accurate picture of the extent of crime in the United States through the use of victimization surveys conducted by the National Crime Panel.

The computer could be used to study crime and criminal behavior, but will probably be limited in its usefulness to science because of concerns over the perverted use of such technology.

Suggested Additional Readings

Ferdinand, Theodore N. "Demographic Shifts and Criminality: An Inquiry." *British Journal of Criminology* 10 (1970): 165–178.

Gibbons, Don C., Joseph F. Jones, and Peter G. Garabedian: "Gauging Public Opinion about the Crime Problem." *Crime and Delinquency* 18 (April 1973): 134–146.

Graham, Fred P. "A Contemporary History of American Crime," In H. D. Graham and Ted R. Gurr, (eds.), *Violence in America*. New York: Bantam, 1970, pp. 485–504.

Hawkins, E. R., and Willard Waller: "Critical Notes on the Cost of Crime." *Journal of Criminal Law, Criminology and Police Science* 46 (January-February 1956): 657–672.

Kitsuse, John T., and Aaron V. Cicourel: "A Note on the Uses of Official Statistics." *Social Problems* 11 (Fall 1963): 131–139.

Lottier, Stuart: "Distribution of Criminal Offenses in Sectional Regions," *Journal of Criminal Law, Criminology and Police Science* 29 (1938): 1038–1045.

President's Commission on Law Enforcement and Administration of Justice: *Task Force Report: Crime and Its Impact—An Assessment*. Washington, D.C.: U.S. Government Printing Office, 1967.

Robison, Sophia M. "A Critical Review of the Uniform Crime Report." *Michigan Law Review* 64 (April 1966): 1031–1054.

Sellin, Thorsten, and Marvin E. Wolfgang: *The Measurement of Delinquency*. New York: Wiley, 1964.

Turk, Austin F. "The Mythology of Crime in America." *Criminology* 8 (February 1971): 397–411.

U.S. Department of Justice: *National Crime Panel Survey of Chicago, Detroit, Los Angeles, New York and Philadelphia*. Washington, D.C.: U.S. Government Printing Office, April 1975.

Winslow, Robert W. *Crime in a Free Society*. Belmont, Calif.: Dickenson, 1968.

Wolfgang, Marvin E. "Urban Crime." In James Q. Wilson (ed.), *The Metropolitan Enigma*. Cambridge, Mass.: Harvard University Press, 1968, pp. 246–251.

Notes

1. Frank F. Furstenberg, Jr., "Public Reaction to Crime in the Streets," *American Scholar* 40 (1971): 601.

2. "Fortress on 78th Street", *Life* (Nov. 19, 1971): 26–36.

3. "Are You Personally Afraid of Crime?" *Life* (Jan. 14, 1972): 28.

4. National Commission on the Causes and Prevention of Violence, *To Establish Justice, To Ensure Domestic Tranquility* (New York: Bantam, 1970), p. xxv.

5. David Lawrence, "Why Is Crime Now a Worldwide Epidemic?" *U.S. News and World Report* (Sept. 6, 1971): 84.

6. Edwin M. Schur, *Our Criminal Society* (Englewood Cliffs, N.J.: Prentice-Hall, 1969, p. 34.

7. James Q. Wilson, "A Long Look at Crime," *FBI Law Enforcement Bulletin* 44 (Feb. 1, 1975): 1-6.

8. Daniel Bell, *The End of Ideology* (New York: Collier Books, 1962), p. 172.

9. Robert V. Bruce, *1877: The Year of Violence* (New York: Bobbs-Merrill, 1969), p. 13.

10. Bell, op. cit., p. 165.

11. Bruce, op. cit., pp. 138–158.

12. Robert M. Fogelson, "The 1960s Riots: Interpretations and Recommendations," a report to the President's Commission on Law Enforcement and Administration of Justice, 1966 (mimeo).

13. For example, see Marvin E. Wolfgang (ed.) *Annals of American Academy of Political and Social Science,* 364 (March 1966).

14. Hugo Herz, *Verbrechen and Verbrechertum in Osterreich* (Tubingen: Laupp, 1908).

15. Cesare Lombroso, *Crime, Its Causes and Remedies* (Boston: Little, Brown, 1912).

16. Ibid., p. 7.

17. Georg Von Mayr, *Statistik and Gesellschaftslehere* (Tubingen: Mohr, 1917), p. 608.

18. Joseph Cohen, "The Geography of Crime," *Annals of the American Academy of Political and Social Science,* 217 (September 1941): 30.

19. Elmer H. Johnson, *Crime, Correction and Society* (Homewood, Ill.: Dorsey, 1968), p. 45.

20. Ibid.

21. See "Crime Distribution in Los Angeles," research report, Los Angeles Police Department, 1972.

22. For example, see Stuart Lottier, "Distribution of Criminal Offenses in Sectional Regions," *Journal of Criminal Law, Criminology and Police Science,* 29 (1938): 336; Lyle W. Shannon, "The Spatial Distribution of Criminal Offenses by States," *Journal of Criminal Law, Criminology and Police Science,* 45 (1954): 270; and Keith D. Harries, "The Geography of American Crime, 1968," *Journal of Geography,* 70 (1971): 204–213.

23. Raymond D. Gastil, "Homicide and a Regional Culture of Violence," *American Sociological Review,* 36 (1971): 414.

24. Keith D. Harries, *The Geography of Crime and Justice* (New York: McGraw-Hill, 1974), pp. 16–36.

25. Ibid.

26. Discussion with the chief of the DeKalb County Police Department, December 1972.

27. National Institute of Mental Health, *Criminal Statistics* (Washington, D.C.: U.S. Government Printing Office, 1972), p. 1.

28. "Crime Statistics Often Numbers Game," *The New York Times,* Feb. 4, 1968, p. 58.

29. National Commission on the Causes and Prevention of Violence, *Violence in America: Historical and Comparative Perspectives* (Washington, D.C.: U.S. Government Printing Office, 1969), p. 372.

30. President's Commission on Law Enforcement and Administration of Justice, *Criminal Victimization in the United States: A Report of a National Survey* (Washington: U.S. Government Printing Office, 1967), pp. 36–44.

31. President's Commission on Law Enforcement and Administration of Justice, *Report on a Pilot Study in the District of Columbia on Victimization and Attitudes toward Law Enforcement* (Washington, D.C.: U.S. Government Printing Office, 1967).

32. For example, see Will Sparks, "Terror in the Streets," *Commonweal,* 82 (11): 345-348; and U.S. National Commission on the Causes and Prevention of Violence, *To Establish Justice, to Ensure Domestic Tranquility.*

33. See Michael E. Milakovich and Kurt Weis, "Politics and Measures of Success in the War on Crime," *Crime and Delinquency,* 21 (January 1975): 1–10.

34. President's Commission on Law Enforcement and Administration of Justice, *Criminal Victimization in the United States.*

35. Johnson, op. cit.

36. David J. Pittman and William F. Handy, "Uniform Crime Reporting: Suggested Improvements," in Alvin Gouldner and S. M. Miller, eds., *Applied Sociology (New York: Free Press, 1965), pp. 180–188.*

37. *Hugo O. Englemann and Kirby Throckmorton, "Interaction Frequency and Crime Rates," Wisconsin Sociologist* 5 (1967): 33–36.

38. Sarah Lee Boggs, "The Ecology of Crime Occurrence in St. Louis: A Reconceptualization of Crime Rates and Patterns," unpublished Ph.D. dissertation, St. Louis: Washington University, 1964.

39. Philip H. Ennis, "Crime, Victims and the Police," *Transaction* 4 (1967): 36–44.

40. Sophia M. Robison, "A Critical View of the Uniform Crime Reports," *Michigan Law Review* 64 (1966): 1031–1054.

41. National Commission on the Causes and Prevention of Violence, *Violence in America,* pp. 371–385.

42. Ramsey Clark, *Crime in America* (New York: Simon & Schuster, 1970), p. 49.

43. Elwin H. Powell, "Crime as a Function of Anomie," *Journal of Criminal Law, Criminology and Police Science* 57 (June 1966): 161–171.

44. National Institute of Mental Health, op. cit., pp. 14–15; Theodore N. Ferdinand, "The Criminal Patterns of Boston since 1849," *American Journal of Sociology* 73 (July 1967): 84–99; and Roger Lane, "Urbanization and Criminal Violence in the Nineteenth Century," *Journal of Social History* 2 (December 1968): 156–163 [reprinted in Alexander B. Callow, Jr., ed., *American Urban History,* 2d ed. (New York: Oxford University Press, 1973)].

45. Law Enforcement Assistance Administration, *Criminal Victimization Surveys in the Nation's Five Largest Cities* (Washington, D.C.: U.S. Government Printing Office, April 1975), p. 1.

46. Law Enforcement Assistance Administration, *Crime in the Nation's Five Largest Cities*—Advance Report (Washington, D.C.: U.S. Government Printing Office, April 1974).

47. President's Commission on Law Enforcement and Administration of Justice, *Criminal Victimization in the United States.*

48. Johnson, op cit., pp. 31–32.

49. See Law Enforcement Assistance Administration, *Criminal Victimization in the United States* (Washington, D.C.: U.S. Government Printing Office, May 1975).

50. Law Enforcement Assistance Administration, *Crime in the Nation's Five Largest Cities*.

51. Paul K. Worneli, "Project SEARCH: System for Electronic Analysis and Retrieval of Criminal Histories," *National Symposium on Criminal Justice Information and Statistics System* (Washington, D.C.: U.S. Government Printing Office, 1970), p. 17.

52. Carl E. Pope, *Offender-Based Transaction Statistics: New Directions in Data Collection and Reporting* (Washington, D.C.: U.S. Government Printing Office, 1975), p. 12.

53. Susan Katzenelson, "Analysis of the Criminal Justice System with Offender-Based Transaction Statistics," in Leonard Oberlander, ed. *Quantitative Tools for Criminal Justice Planning* (Washington, D.C.: U.S. Government Printing Office, 1975): 86–87.

Chapter 4

Law and Moral Values: Victimless Crime Problems in Criminal Justice

No subject in the administration of justice has been debated more than the question of the enforcement or nonenforcement of victimless crimes. The argument rages on both sides. Some noted authorities, such as Kadish, see the enforcement of laws against victimless crimes as an attempt to enforce morals, resulting in the "crisis of overcriminalization" which threatens the very administration of criminal justice.[1] On the other hand, there are those who strongly defend not only government's right to enforce these laws, but its duty to do so. Lord Devlin, a great English jurist, has urged the legitimacy of the enforcement of victimless crime statutes on the ground that "society cannot ignore the morality of the individual any more than it can his loyalty; it flourishes on both and without either it dies."[2]

In recent years, most scholars in the areas of criminal justice have sided with those opposed to enforcing such laws. This is not to imply that they are any more right than those who argue for enforcement. However, the weight of public opinion and the "new morality" we are experiencing in the United States seems to be swinging the pendulum toward greater toleration of conduct which used to be considered deviant—and along with this, more libertarian attitudes toward certain forms of moral behavior.

In this chapter, we will examine these controversial areas of the law carefully and explore the issues from both viewpoints whenever possible. In some instances, it may seem that this author favors striking offenses against morals from our criminal codes. This is not the author's purpose, nor is it his judgment to make—it is the reader's. However, those who oppose enforcement of laws against victimless crimes have done their homework better; while those who support such laws continue to base their arguments on moral sentiments, those who oppose them are gathering data to support their argument. Any discussion of this subject must include these facts.

THE CONCEPT OF VICTIMLESS CRIMES

To consider homosexuality, prostitution, fornication, adultery, drunkenness, obscenity and pornography, gambling, and narcotics use as crimes is to imply that anyone who participates in these acts offends the whole of society. To many, this form of legal reasoning presents the difficult problem of trying to reconcile the traditional definition of crime with the true nature of these particular offenses. The first problem is trying to connect the prohibited behavior with meaningful harm done to society. Critics of the statutory criminalization of these acts point to the fact that many of these offenses are private acts among consenting adults and, in some cases, involve only the individual and are not harmful to others not directly engaged. They contend that if the acts are harmful, the harm is inflicted only on the participants themselves.[3]

The traditional relationship between perpetrator and victim is also absent. There is no unwilling victim because for the most part the acts are *voluntarily* and *mutually* entered into by *both* parties, neither of whom views himself or herself as a "victim" under the traditional relationship which exists in other types of crimes. Thus, these offenses are referred to as victimless crimes. At most, these acts are crimes of mutual perpetration and involvement, willingly committed.

Those who advocate the decriminalization of such acts are able to offer some rather convincing evidence that the laws against them, which were originally enacted to control and deter such behavior, have had little effect upon preventing their occurrence.[4] As a matter of public policy or official disregard by the authorities (which are often synonymous), the laws on homosexuality, prostitution, drunkenness, obscenity, and pornography are, in many communities, disregarded openly. When these laws are enforced, it is often not done with uniformity and fairness, but with caprice. This serves to destroy the concept of equal application of the criminal law, which further undermines citizen respect for the administration of justice.[5]

If the criminal justice system is also to be held responsible for the reformation of offenders, it fails miserably in dealing with individuals who violate these victimless crime statutes. Our crowded prisons and jails, already understaffed with rehabilitative personnel, are further taxed in trying to deal with these offenders. Herein lies a major paradox of the entire system of justice: The arrest and incarceration of these individuals often results in their leaving the institution more embittered than when they entered. Now for the first time they view themselves as "victims"—not of the crime for which they have been tried and found guilty, but of a hypocritical and unjust system of justice which, in a discriminatory manner, penalizes *them* for their deviant behavior. What they may often correctly perceive is that similar behavior by others is often overlooked and sometimes even engaged in by their very accusers. We must ask ourselves whether the system of criminal justice may unwittingly be guilty of abetting the formulation of procriminal attitudes among these individuals and whether present enforcement practices will result in future diminishment of these behaviors.

There are other considerations as well. The most frequent charge leveled at enforcement of victimless crime laws is that it places an inordinate strain upon the resources of the criminal justice system. We must consider the police and court personnel and other resources spent on the enforcement of such laws—resources that many feel could better be devoted to dealing with more serious offenses and offenders.[6] When we examine the costs of enforcing these laws and consider that the behaviors show no indication of being diminished in absolute numbers, we must pause to reflect a moment about the utility of our past efforts to deal with this problem.

COSTS OF ENFORCING VICTIMLESS CRIME LAWS

Direct Costs

Nobody really knows the costs to the criminal justice system of enforcing these laws. In recent years, some states have begun dealing with these offenders in special programs outside of the criminal justice process, but as late as 1970 nearly 50 percent of all arrests fell into the victimless crime category. By 1975, the proportion had dropped to about one-third of all arrests. But even with this decline, we can conservatively place the cost of prosecuting these crimes in terms of billions of dollars when we consider the costs of law enforcement, the courts, and incarceration. And this is probably a substantial underestimate. Not figured in this calculation is the category of "all other offenses" (a large miscellany of 1,196,600 arrests in 1973), many of which would fall into the victimless crimes category, but are excluded from our calculations because they cannot be specifically identified from the published FBI data.

Indirect Costs

There is another associated "cost" to society that will never appear in the ledger sheets of any governmental agency. One very serious consequence of the laws relating to victimless crimes is that they have often provided the basis for a network of organized crime operations. Organized crime is an excellent study in economic market strategy—it exists and flourishes because it provides the goods and services people want and cannot obtain legally. Such commodities and services as narcotics, gambling, and prostitution provide crime syndicates with operating and investment capital. Ironically, the state, in effect, gives organized crime a virtual monopoly on the provision of these illicit goods and services. Crime syndicates invest their huge profits in ways which assure that they can continue to provide their services to the consuming public. In recent years, they have also mounted a massive infiltration into legitimate businesses, financed by the profits obtained from supplying illegal commodities and services.

An excellent example of how this process occurs and how difficult it is to legislate morals can be found in our nation's experience with the passage of the Eighteenth Amendment. This amendment, which prohibited the manufacture, sale, or transportation of intoxicating liquors, ushered in prohibition. In the fourteen years that passed before this amendment was repealed, it provided the foundation for many of the criminal cartels that still exist today. It also indicated to many criminologists how absurd it was to try to legislate behavior in this area and how damaging such legislation could be on the administration of criminal justice.

Furthermore, victimless crime laws often serve as the basis for official corruption. Because the offender wants what is illegal, those who provide it must continually bribe the police, courts, and other officials to permit their profitable enterprise to continue with a minimum of interruption. According to authorities on organized crime, gambling and large-scale distribution of drugs could not exist unless public officials were bribed. One estimate puts the graft at more than $2 billion a year.[7]

The police appear to be particularly vulnerable to organized crime's efforts to assure that their supply of vice services will continue uninterrupted, especially in terms of organized narcotic trafficking, gambling, and prostitution. This fact was first documented thoroughly in 1931, when the federal government released a fourteen-volume study of crime in America known as the *Wickersham Commission Reports*. Commenting on the problem of organized crime and police and judicial corruption, the reports said:

> Those criminal octopus organizations have now grown so audacious, owing to their long immunity from prosecutions for their crimes, that they seek to make bargains with law enforcing officers and even with judges of our courts to be allowed for a price to continue their criminal activities unmolested by the law.[8]

The years since the release of these reports seem not to have diminished this problem in some of the larger municipal police departments in this country. Periodic scandals involving police and judicial corruption in enforcing victimless crime laws have broken out all over the country. Down through the years, Detroit, Kansas City, Cleveland, Atlanta, Miami, and a host of other cities have experienced such scandals. During the 1950s and 1960s, Chicago's police department suffered scandals involving narcotics payoffs; in the 1960s, Buffalo, New York, was rocked with scandals of police and judicial involvement in organized gambling and prostitution. The latest and perhaps most extensive documentation of police corruption occurred in New York City in 1972, when the Knapp Commission released a devastating report of widespread police involvement in narcotics, gambling, and prostitution which had been going on for many years. Understandably, citizens seem to have become rather blasé about police corruption. Yet the majority of police agencies and individuals uphold their integrity in spite of the corruption around them and in spite of organized crime's efforts to the contrary.

The crime of narcotics use is particularly pernicious in the contribution it makes to total crime pictures. In the United States, the heroin addict cannot obtain the drug legally but must pay a high price to obtain it illegally. Patrick Murphy, former police commissioner of New York, contends that half the crime committed in that city is by addicts stealing and robbing to obtain money to support their addiction. Although we cannot confirm or deny Murphy's statement, we do know that narcotic addicts are involved in a great deal of crime. For example, addicts polled in a New Jersey study averaged nearly six previous arrests. Although a number of arrests were for narcotics-related charges such as the sale and abuse of drugs, the vast majority were for other types of crime, such as burglary or robbery.[9]

Finally, there is one last unanticipated consequence of the enforcement of victimless crime laws that also bears on the indirect costs of this type of legislation. Since these laws are by their very nature discriminatory, in theory, enforcement, and application, they have alienated large segments of our population not only from the criminal justice system itself, but from the institutions of government which are represented by the agencies of justice. This is particularly true among young people in all socioeconomic strata. The youth of today see instances of official corruption where the police and courts invoke sanctions against the more vulnerable poor and young, yet tolerate flagrant abuses among the rich and powerful. The issue, it would seem, is not the inherent wrongness of these types of offenses as much as it is the inherent wrong brought about by the seemingly selective enforcement of laws against these crimes. At a time when popular opinion is already indicating that many Americans no longer trust public officials and governmental agencies, this may well be the most serious charge leveled at the continued efforts to enforce these laws. The agencies of criminal justice, because they are the most highly visible extension of government authority, must be symbols of public respect and confidence and serve as an example of the precepts of equity and justice. As long as they are required to handle the problems associated with the enforcement of victimless crime laws, it would seem that these agencies cannot gain public respect and confidence.

Under the circumstances, it is not difficult to understand why many noted criminal justice authorities have called for the revocation of most statutes pertaining to victimless crimes. Among them are James Vorenberg, director of the President's Commission on Law Enforcement and Administration of Justice; Dr. Norval Morris, director of the University of Chicago's Criminal Justice Center; Patrick Murphy, now director of the Police Foundation; and Arlen Spector, former district attorney of Philadelphia. Such prestigious organizations as the National Council on Crime and Delinquency and the American Bar Association have also recommended the repeal of many of these statutes.

Most of these efforts at repeal have developed around efforts to reclassify crimes based upon an examination of their seriousness as a threat to the well-being of society. Thus, victimless crimes are at least being examined in terms of the offense itself and the penalties attached. Among the suggested new legislation to deal with these types of offenses are the provisions contained in the Model Penal Code proposed by the American Law Institute, the suggestions contained in the Sentencing Alternatives of the American Bar Association and the Model Sentencing Act of the National Council on Crime and Delinquency. Each of these proposals calls for either the abolishment of these victimless crimes as offenses or a significant reduction in the penalties attached. A number of states and the federal government have already revised, or are in the process of revising, their criminal codes to reflect these suggestions.

ARGUMENTS FOR THE RETENTION OF THESE ACTS AS CRIMES

Many groups and individuals actively oppose the decriminalization of these acts or the lessening of penalties for these crimes. Much of their argument centers on the theme of the moral well-being of society, and they reject the idea that these acts are "victimless." For example, they maintain with some justification that harm is indeed done to the individuals participating in such acts regardless of the fact that it is voluntarily inflicted harm. Physical harm is certainly associated with the use of marijuana or the opiates, and venereal disease could very well be a greater problem if prostitution were widespread and tolerated.

However, they are even more concerned about what the tolerance of these forms of behavior portends for society in general. Many people in the United States would be offended by the tolerated presence of these activities. The question then becomes whether or not citizens who do not participate in these acts should be subjected to what they perceive as the offensive behavior of others. These citizens could certainly be considered as "victims."

Some of the groups that oppose the abolition of these acts as crimes are found within the criminal justice system itself. Opposition is particularly strong among law enforcement agencies to the decriminalization of narcotics use, gambling, prostitution, and to a lesser extent, pornography and obscenity.[10] Their concerns are usually expressed in terms of the moral implications, the disruptiveness of such acts to general law and order, and the encouragement and attraction their abolition as crimes would afford to other forms of crime. They should not be discounted out of hand, for it is the police who may be nearest the problem and may have a better insight than the rest of us. At this time, the verdict is not in. The fact remains that there is little evidence that would conclusively support either side in the argument.

What all the polemics surrounding this issue does show us is that the criminal law is an evolving human instrumentality that serves as an important indicator of basic human behavior. The fact that mankind has progressed at all is often displayed in the different attitudes toward what constitutes "crime" and what is "good" or "bad" by changing standards of judgment.

At this point, we need to examine each of these victimless crimes in an effort to see how they mirror social and legal trends. Particular attention will be paid to the nature of these acts, changes in the law that have occurred, and special concerns surrounding the enforcement or nonenforcement of each of these offenses.

GAMBLING

It is almost unanimously agreed that gambling is the greatest source of revenue for organized crime.[11] The major concern of most law enforcement officials in the United States today centers on five kinds of gambling operations: (1) the numbers, sometimes known as "policy," "bolita," "the figures," or the "the digits" (one purchases a slip with certain numbers on it; winners are those individuals who hold the right combination of numbers as determined by various selection means); (2) casino-style gambling; (3) lotteries; (4) parimutuel betting at race tracks and off-track betting; and (5) large dice and card games. Anyone whose independent operation becomes successful is likely to receive a visit from an organized crime group that convinces the independent operator, by means of fear or the promise of greater profit and protection, to share his revenue with the organization.[12]

The extent of illegal gambling in the United States is considered by the President's Task Force on Organized Crime to be in the area of $7 billion to $50 billion annually, with the amount probably closer to the larger sum.[13] Gambling by its very characteristics lends itself to organized crime activities. It is necessary to develop large-scale organizations in order to prevent severe losses, since a small operator may take more bets on one horse or one number than the operator could pay off if that horse or number should win. The operator has to cover these sums by laying off bets. This so-called layoff betting is accomplished through a network of local, regional, and national layoff men who take bets from gambling operations.[14]

Illicit gambling also encourages other offenses. One of these is the practice of loan sharking, which is the lending of money at usurious interest rates. Money is loaned to pay for the incurred gambling debts with interest rates varying from 1 to 150 percent a week according to the relationship between the lender and borrower, the intended use of the money, the size of the loan, and the repayment potential.[15] A 6-for-5 loan, that is, interest at 20 percent a week, is common with small borrowers. Understandably, the lender is more interested in continuing the exorbitant interest payments than in collecting the principal. This leads to a second area of criminal activity associated with gambling, that of extortion by use of force or threats of force of the most brutal kind. Interest rates are paid, protests are eliminated, and the borrower is coerced by fear into not reporting the activity to enforcement officials.[16] Although no reliable estimates exist of the gross revenue from organized loan sharking, it is known that profit margins are even higher than for gambling operations, and many officials consider the profits to be in the billions.[17]

Those who propose the decriminalization of gambling are concerned for more than the welfare of those who fall prey to the efforts of organized crime. Many citizens have asked why the authorities do not recognize that the imposition of criminal sanctions for gambling offenses is no deterrent. Since people will continue to gamble regardless of whether it is a crime or not, many citizens feel that gambling should be made "respectable" by governmental regulation and the monies used to support governmental projects, thereby relieving the burden on the taxpayer. They contend that Nevada, where casino gambling is legal, has been able to accomplish just that. In recent years, a number of states have, in fact, begun state lotteries, and New York City, in 1971, approved off-track betting. There is a great deal of logic behind such arguments, but unfortunately, little research to substantiate the claim that government-sponsored gambling has appreciably curtailed organized and illicit gambling activities in these areas.

The argument that the present statutes prohibiting gambling are a corruptive influence on public officials is based on our nation's past experience with the relationship between organized gambling and official corruption and is much more plausible because of adequate documentation of the relationship.

On the other hand, there are those who feel just as strongly that not only should the gambling laws remain on the books, they should be more vigorously enforced. They reason that by means of strict and persistent enforcement, those who are susceptible to gambling will not be able to locate gambling activities and, therefore, will be saved from themselves. Whenever there is a proposal to legalize certain forms of gambling in various jurisdictions, there will invariably arise opposition groups, such as the antigambling league that formed in New York a few years ago. This particular group ran ads depicting a woman and four small children, with the caption, "Who will feed the children when my husband gambles his paycheck away?" Viewed in light of the widespread availability of existing illegal gambling operations, this campaign points up the fact that the public is either misinformed or unaware of the complexities of the problem.

Into this argument in recent years have come certain behavioral scientists who at least tacitly imply that the very act of gambling has some positive benefits to those who gamble aside from the strictly financial reward of winning. Zola, for example, has pointed out that in the lower classes gambling serves as a means by which people are able to achieve recognition for their accomplishments by demonstrating ability in the selection of horses, skill at cards, or some other form of gambling.[18] Others contend that such gambling activities as numbers satisfy the emotional needs of ghetto dwellers as well as give them the feeling that if they "win big," they will increase their chances for upward social mobility.[19] Other researchers have claimed to find that many residents consider numbers as an integral part of neighborhood life and that residents defend its existence on the grounds that it is crucial to the economic security of the community because of the jobs it provides.[20]

Regardless of the arguments for and against the decriminalization of gambling, one thing is apparent. It is time that we reappraised some of our past attempts and repeated failures to deal with this problem. One of our first priorities would seem to be to determine whether more strict and uniform enforcement of the law is warranted or whether we should sanction open gambling and in this manner try to destroy the corruptive influences of covert operations on the justice system while minimizing the psychic and financial costs to individuals and society as a whole.

DRUNKENNESS

In 1973, nearly 1.2 million arrests were made by the police for the offense of being drunk in public. This figure does not include the more serious related offenses such as driving under the influence or the often related offense of disorderly conduct or vagrancy. The great volume of these arrests places an extremely heavy burden on the operations of the criminal justice system. In the words of the President's Commission, "It burdens police, clogs lower criminal courts and crowds penal institutions throughout the United States."[21]

Drunkenness is punishable under a wide variety of laws which usually describe the offense as being drunk in a public place. The failure of many of these laws is that they do not provide a precise definition of what constitutes the act of being intoxicated. Consequently, the police often use the pretext that they could smell liquor on a person's breath or that the person's eyes were "glassy" to arrest someone for this crime because they felt the person was not cooperative or did not display the proper respect.

Although public intoxication is considered a crime in almost every jurisdiction, there have been some recent changes in dealing with the public inebriate. Approximately twenty states have abolished their drunkenness statutes and are rewriting their legislation to reflect some significant changes in dealing with public inebriates. Michigan's new statute (effective January 1, 1977) is indicative of similar legislation in other states. Under the new Michigan law, a local government is prohibited from adopting or enforcing a law, ordinance, resolution, or rule which imposes a civil or criminal penalty for public intoxication, being a common drunkard, or being incapacitated. This prohibition does not apply to laws concerning drunken driving and similar offenses or the sale, purchase, or possession of alcoholic beverages at stated times. Minnesota not only revoked its laws pertaining to public intoxication, but went one step further by ordering that twenty-five health districts set up special facilities to handle persons who have problems with alcohol and come to the attention of the authorities.

This deemphasis on drunkenness as a crime seems to be reflected in the *Uniform Crime Reports*. For example, in 1965 there were over 2 million arrests for this offense. The number would be expected to be quite high during this period, however, because several cities experienced urban disorders in which a particularly high rate of arrests for this offense were made. To clean up and control an area, the police were often likely to arrest many persons found on the streets for being intoxicated. By 1971, the number of arrests had dropped to 1.8 million, and by 1973 it was down to 1.2 million. However, arrest data for the last few years seem to indicate that a new phenomenon is developing. Many of the states that passed legislation to deemphasize drunkenness as a crime are experiencing increased arrests for the offense of disorderly conduct. It may be that some police are now using this offense to deal with the public inebriate.

Costs to the Taxpayer

The costs to the taxpayer of dealing with drunkenness are unknown, but conservative estimates put the sum at over $2 billion annually. The costs involved in the arrest of the public inebriate alone are staggering. For example, the St. Louis Detoxification and Diagnostic Evaluation Center made a rather exhaustive study of the handling of drunkenness arrests by the St. Louis Police Department. It found that the arrest of an individual on the charge of intoxication required the arresting officer(s) to spend an average of 95.8 minutes in arresting, transporting, and processing the arrestee.[22] This drain on law enforcement resources indicates that we need to think of better means of dealing with this problem. The time of police personnel could be better utilized in other enforcement and crime preventive functions.

This same argument could be applied to the costs of prosecution, courts, and incarceration as well. Costs will increase further if the courts hold that these types of offenders are entitled to representation by court-appointed counsel, which may be likely if present trends continue. For example, in 1972 in *Argersinger* v. *Hamlin*, the U.S. Supreme Court held that no person could be imprisoned as the result of a criminal prosecution in which the defendant was not accorded the right to public representation.[23] The language of this decision implies that indigent drunks who are arrested for this offense are entitled to taxpayer-supported legal representation at their trials. Indeed, some local and state courts are moving in this direction.

Costs to Society and the Process of Justice

In addition to the economic costs involved in enforcing drunkenness laws, there are other important considerations. A large percentage of those arrested, convicted, and incarcerated or fined for public intoxication are later rearrested and the cycle begins anew. Anyone who has witnessed the trials of these offenders cannot but be aware that the concept of due process for these individuals is being blatantly disregarded. At best, the "trial" consists of a few minutes spent before the magistrate before sentencing. It is almost an assembly-line operation as the defendants are paraded through the courtroom, found guilty, and fined or incarcerated. The only thing absent is the clang of the cash register as "justice" is dispensed.

In addition, the process has absolutely no deterrent effect on the vast majority of individuals arrested for this offense. The criminal justice system has neither the resources nor the ability to deal with this problem. The irony of the situation, however, is that dealing with the problem is precisely what society expects. The police, courts, and corrections are supposed to solve the problem of the public nuisance whose presence is offensive to citizens who want such unsightly members of humanity removed and warehoused out of sight. The emphasis then, is not on helping people, but on merely removing a social eyesore from view.

The enforcement of laws against drunkenness is particularly discriminatory in application. Although the National Institute on Alcohol Abuse and Alcoholism of the National Institute of Mental Health has repeatedly pointed out that alcoholics or persons with serious drinking problems number in the millions in the United States and come from all socioeconomic strata, lower-class persons account for a disproportionate number of all arrests. The more affluent citizens may be just as publicly intoxicated as the poor wino in the ghetto, but because of the social circles in which they move as well as the greater reluctance of the police to arrest them, they are not likely to appear in court on a charge of drunkenness unless more serious behavior is involved.

It must be mentioned, however, that the arrest of certain chronic alcoholics does in a strange way perform one humanitarian role. Our jails, as pitiful as they are, provide, in many cases, a better home for many derelict alcoholics than they would find on the street. At least jails provide shelter from the weather and some security from those criminals who would prey upon the alcoholics in their helpless condition.

Current Needs and New Directions

As has been pointed out, the laws are changing. People are beginning to realize that chronic alcoholism is a disease that requires appropriate treatment which cannot be provided by the criminal justice system. Following the release of the 1967 President's Crime Commission recommendations on public intoxication, alternative solutions were sought. As a result, the American Bar Association and the American Medical Association Joint Committee on Alcoholism began to study this problem. In August 1971, they published a model act, which they encouraged the states to adopt. Under the ABA-AMA model act, the laws against public intoxication would be repealed except in cases where the individual could be considered a disorderly intoxicant. All intoxicated persons who were not actually disorderly would be handled under civil detoxification inpatient and outpatient procedures in hospitals and clinics.[24]

The most significant development in the area of model legislation occurred in 1971. In August of that year, the National Conference of Commissioners, representing the governors of all fifty states, adopted a Uniform Alcoholism and Intoxification Treatment Act. As a result of this meeting, the representatives of the various states agreed to work with their respective state legislative bodies in getting the Uniform Act adopted in their states.

Section 1 of the Uniform Act enunciates the following policy:

> It is the policy of this state that alcoholics and intoxicated persons may not be subjected to criminal prosecution because of their consumption of alcoholic beverages, but rather should be afforded a continuum of treatment in order that they may lead normal lives as productive members of society.[25]

The Uniform Act requires, among other things, that:

1. The states establish programs for the treatment of intoxicated persons and alcoholics

2. Intoxicated persons and those incapacitated by alcohol be assisted to their homes or to treatment facilities by the police or emergency service patrols in protective custody under civil law

3. Political subdivisions of any state be prohibited from adopting any law making public intoxication or any related behavior or conditions (except drunken driving) an offense or the subject of any sanction of any kind

Work is just beginning to obtain enactment of the Uniform Act throughout the country. The Secretary of the Department of Health, Education, and Welfare is working very closely with the governor of each state, endorsing the Uniform Act and urging its early enactment.[26]

The courts are also taking a more active role in the decriminalization of public intoxication. On September 23, 1964, Dewitt Easter, a homeless derelict alcoholic was arrested for public intoxication. At his trial, it was brought out that he had been arrested approximately seventy times since 1937 for public intoxication and other minor offenses related to his alcoholism. This aroused the curiosity of the media, and Easter's plight received a great deal of publicity. In the Easter case, the argument of the defense was unique. It was contended that since Easter was an alcoholic, his drinking was an illness, and because of this, his actions were involuntary, and he, therefore, could not be held criminally responsible for his actions.

Following the national publicity surrounding the Easter case and his defense, another test case was started by one Joe Driver, who filed a habeas corpus petition in the U.S. District Court for the Eastern District of North Carolina. Driver was appealing from a two-year jail sentence for public intoxication which had been upheld by the North Carolina Supreme Court.[27] Driver's record showed over 200 arrests for public intoxication and other minor offenses related to his alcoholism. As a result, he had spent at least two-thirds of his adult life in jail for nothing more than being drunk in public.

Like Easter, Driver challenged his conviction on the fundamental principle of criminal responsibility—that criminal sanctions may be applied only to voluntary action—and a chronic alcoholic does not drink voluntarily. It was also argued that since Driver was a homeless derelict alcoholic, his appearance in public was not of his own choice.

After adverse decisions from the lower courts in both cases, the federal courts returned unanimous favorable decisions. In the Easter case, the District of Columbia Court of Appeals agreed that a chronic alcoholic's public intoxication is involuntary and, therefore, not punishable.[28] In Driver's case, the court held that the Eighth Amendment, which prohibits cruel and unusual punishment, prevents the conviction of a chronic alcoholic for public intoxication.[29]

Since these two important decisions, numerous state and federal courts have wrestled with the problem. In 1968, a similar case went before the U.S. Supreme Court. In the case of *Powell v. Texas,* the Supreme Court upheld the Texas trial court conviction of Powell for the crime of public intoxication, but expressed agreement with the principles and philosophy enunciated by the lower federal courts in the Easter and Driver cases.[30] This has created some confusion in the lower courts. A number of states, however, have tried to comply with the rulings in the Easter and Driver cases and have struck down their public intoxication statutes and ordinances. The issue is, unfortunately, still not clear, and there are certain to be more court tests of the constitutionality of public intoxication laws in future years.

Detoxification centers to treat public alcoholism and drunkenness have grown in recent years. These special centers, which may be either publicly or privately supported, are shelters for the initial placement of public inebriates. In lieu of being placed into jail, the individual is brought by the police or a special service unit to a center where he or she remains until sober. Many of these units have established a network of coordinated facilities to treat the individual. Both inpatient and outpatient services are provided as well as hospital referral programs, Alcoholics Anonymous programs, mental health agency services, counseling services, and assistance in obtaining employment. Special provisions are also being made in the more progressive programs for self-referral programs and residential treatment facilities so that the alcoholic does not have to return to the streets upon release.

The years to come will probably see the growth of similar programs in many communities across the country. The major problem now seems to be one of obtaining adequate financial support for such centers and support programs.

NARCOTICS AND DRUG USE

Probably no area of the criminal law is involved in greater public controversy today than the laws concerned with the voluntary *use* of illegal drugs, ranging from the opiates such as heroin to cocaine through hallucinogens such as LSD to milder forms of narcotics such as marijuana, amphetamines, and barbiturates. The *sale* of illegal drugs falls outside our consideration and is not included in the category of victimless crimes.

Opiates and Other Narcotics

The history of our current drug laws dates from 1914, when Congress passed the Harrison Narcotic Control Act, which regulated the sale and distribution of narcotics and provided the legislation for criminal enforcement at the federal level. In recent years, the problems associated with addiction to these types of drugs have led to increased efforts by the criminal justice system to deal with the problem of narcotics use and related offenses. Public opinion in this area varies widely. Some people favor tougher penalties against both users and sellers of opiates, particularly against the latter. Responding to this, a number of states in recent years have introduced legislation which would carry the penalty of life imprisonment for those convicted of the sale of "hard" drugs. Other people favor incarcerating drug users under existing criminal penalties and requiring them to submit to treatment during their incarceration. There are also those who believe that the only acceptable national policy is to follow the example of Great Britain. Under the system adopted in Britain, which began as a result of the *Rolliston Committee Report* in 1926, it is possible for addicts to receive drugs legally as long as they are registered as addicts. However, recent years have seen some problems develop with this approach. Because of a large increase in the number of addicts in that country, the Dangerous Drugs Act of 1967 was passed. This act established treatment centers where only specially authorized and licensed physicians were permitted to dispense drugs to addicts. Efforts are thus being made to cut down on the supply of drugs which were being diverted by some unscrupulous physicians to a growing black market in drugs in that country.[31]

This idea of supplying the known addict with heroin has frequently been discussed in the United States. One experimental project was proposed by the Vera Institute of Justice in New York City. Under this proposed plan, 300 adult addicts, who had demonstrated resistance to other forms of treatment for narcotics addiction, would be maintained on heroin for six months. They would also be offered a full range of medical, psychological, and social services. The Vera Institute believes that many questions about heroin maintenance could be answered through such an approach. One question they hope to answer is whether a program could be developed that would attract heroin addicts who, for physical and psychological reasons, could not shake their addiction, yet wanted to function satisfactorily in a job and as socially adjusted individuals.[32]

Although such heroin maintenance programs have been discussed, critics are quick to point out that such distribution programs are not likely to work. Their reasoning is based on the fact that heroin effects last only four to six hours and narcotic addicts with well-established habits must take the drug six times a day to avoid withdrawal symptoms. Under these circumstances, it is not likely that many addicts would be effectively served by such distribution programs. It is more likely that it would be necessary to give them supplies which they could take home, and as a result, diversion to unregistered and experimental users would surely occur.[33]

Another recommendation calls for the establishment of methadone treatment centers for addicts. Methadone, itself a drug, is an inexpensive substitute for heroin. It can be given orally and its effects last up to thirty-six hours. Addicts maintained on this drug do not experience the severe withdrawal symptoms associated with giving up heroin or some other addictive narcotic, nor do they have to be involved in the illegal traffic in drugs or crimes to support their habit. They simply stop by the treatment center whenever they feel the need for the drug. Periodic tests are made to ensure that they have not reverted to heroin use.

The results of methadone treatment are mixed. Some programs seem to have been quite successful, but others have enjoyed only marginal success.[34] As might be imagined, the problem often has been one of trying to keep the addict from reverting to the use of illegal drugs. In addition, the methadone programs have come under attack from various critics who contend that all they accomplish is the substituting of one dependence-forming drug for another.[35]

In 1972 Massachusetts adopted a statute pertaining to the pretrial diversion of drug offenders as a possible alternative to the use of the criminal justice system in dealing with these individuals.[36] Under the provisions of its Comprehensive Drug Abuse Rehabilitation and Treatment Act, any person charged with a drug offense is notified at his or her first court appearance of the right to an examination to determine if he or she is a drug-dependent person who would benefit by treatment. A person who elects to be examined and is found to be drug-dependent, may request commitment to a treatment facility in lieu of prosecution. If it is a first drug offense not involving sale, the judge must commit the accused to the drug treatment facility. If the defendant is charged with the sale of drugs or has previously been found guilty of the use of drugs, the judge has complete discretion to refuse a treatment commitment. A defendant is treated at either inpatient or outpatient facilities, with a minimum treatment period of two years for addicts and one year for drug-dependent nonaddicts. Compliance with the treatment order, whether or not the individual is in fact "cured," leads to dismissal of the charges. The consent of the defendant is required for both examination and commitment.[37] California has also passed similar diversion legislation for first-time drug users.[38]

Solutions to this most vexing problem are still unclear. Somehow, the United States must address this problem in ways other than the traditional method of trying to legislate and enforce the problem out of existence. No one at this time can say with any degree of validity that enforcement is the solution. All that enforcement seems to have accomplished is to drive up the cost of obtaining narcotics, and as a result, addicts commit other crimes to support their habit. On the other hand, to legalize the use and distribution of these drugs might encourage more widespread addiction.

Marijuana

Most states have had laws prohibiting the use of marijuana for fifty years, but the widespread use of this drug is a relatively recent phenomenon. The National Commission on Marijuana and Drug Abuse estimates that at least 24 million Americans have been involved in marijuana use at one time or another.[39] One of the most comprehensive surveys of marijuana use in the United States was conducted in the junior and senior high schools of San Mateo, California, from 1967 to 1970. It was found that 50.9 percent of the senior high school students had used marijuana at least once during the previous twelve months.[40]

Marijuana arrests as a percentage of all arrests for the use of narcotics has grown rapidly in recent years. For example, in 1965 of the total drug arrests only 31.1 percent was for marijuana.[41] By 1970, the percentage had increased to 45.4 percent, and by 1973 this figure was up to 66.9 percent.[42] Not only has the incidence of marijuana use increased substantially, its users have been found in new demographic sectors identified by age, sex, region, education, and occupation.

These facts have generated considerable critical comment about the deterrent value of statutes which prohibit its use as well as concern with the operation of the criminal justice system. Whether marijuana statutes can be enforced by the present law enforcement system in a manner consistent with constitutional definitions of fairness and legitimacy raises serious issues. As examples, concern has been expressed about the extent to which current marijuana statutes encourage police misconduct, particularly in the area of search-and-seizure procedure.[43] Another question concerns the selective enforcement of marijuana statutes and the consequence of law bearing unequally on age, racial, and occupational groups.[44] Finally, questions have been raised about whether the criminal processing of marijuana offenses is an appropriate way of handling the population involved. It has been argued that both the stigma and the severe penalties associated with marijuana offenses are not only undesirable, but damage the credibility, integrity, and effectiveness of the criminal law and its enforcement system.[45]

The major argument against legalizing marijuana use or reducing the penalty for marijuana offenses centers on the claim that marijuana use leads to the use of hard drugs and addiction. There is some conflicting evidence in this area. Some studies show that a large percentage of addicts also used marijuana early in their lives, while other studies show that there appears to be no relationship between marijuana usage and criminality and eventual addiction.[46]

The argument has also been raised that the frequent use of marijuana leads to serious psychological disturbance, and in a few research endeavors this relationship has been claimed to exist.[47] Again, the evidence appears inconclusive. The research studies that have indicated this relationship have been refuted by many other scientists on grounds of faulty research procedures or similar studies which drew different conclusions.

Another frequent argument is that marijuana use can impair the sensory functions and cause the user to place in jeopardy other members of society by operation of an automobile, etc. This argument is usually repudiated on the grounds that the use of alcohol is well documented to cause similar effects, yet is readily available. Many reputable medical groups consider that in terms of potential harm, the consumption of alcohol has more negative consequences for the individual and society than does the use of marijuana.[48]

Whatever comes out of the heated debates surrounding the decriminalization of marijuana use, certain facts are quite clear. Punitive policies toward the use of marijuana have resulted in a number of consequences

1. The penal code automatically turns at least one-third of the younger generation who have used marijuana into criminals.

2. Hostility and disrespect for the criminal justice system and particularly the police have increased in relation to the growth in the use of marijuana.

3. Many citizens see in the enforcement of the marijuana laws and the statements issued by some governmental agencies a great deal of hypocrisy and outright lies. This further alienates citizens from their government and decreases the government's credibility.

4. Tremendous expense is associated with our futile attempts to enforce the marijuana laws and to control marijuana distribution. In California alone, the cost is estimated to be $72 million each year.[49]

5. Enforcement efforts have resulted in a flourishing and lucrative traffic in marijuana. This has encouraged the exploitation of this market by members of organized crime or the drug culture.

6. Enforcement has further widened the generation gap between adult members of society and youth.

Society must now arrive at some clear idea of what must be done. Certainly, use of marijuana should be no more encouraged than is the use of alcohol or tobacco. Perhaps the answer lies with some youthful members of our society.

Recently, a very insightful and persuasive argument was published by a group of University of Virginia law students who in the *Virginia Law Review* made the following statutory recommendations for dealing with marijuana:

1. Prohibit possession of marijuana over four ounces unless the defendant can show that it was possessed solely for personal use.
2. Prohibit public use of the drug.
3. Prohibit driving or operation of any dangerous machine while under the influence of the drug.
4. Prohibit transfer to any one party of more than four ounces of marijuana.
5. Prohibit transfer of any amount of marijuana to children under sixteen.
6. Punish all violators as misdemeanants.[50]

OBSCENITY AND PORNOGRAPHY

The terms *obscenity* and *pornography* are used synonymously. In the most general sense, obscenity means simply that which is offensive to chastity.[51] Pornography is the depiction in some way of offensive, obscene materials. In the discussion that follows, these two terms will be used interchangeably, as they normally are in the law.

The creation and enforcement of obscenity and pornography laws raises the question of whether the state should have the power to prohibit conduct solely on the ground that it is considered harmful to the morality of the actor. Those opposed to relaxation of obscenity and pornography laws claim that permissiveness in this area will undermine the moral fabric of our nation and will make its impact felt most notably on the vulnerable members of society, such as the young or those with deviant sexual desires. To date, research has been somewhat inconclusive in this regard. Although the research efforts of Kinsey and the Commission on Obscenity and Pornography and the experience of the Scandinavian countries would tend to discount this argument, further research is needed in this area before we can be more definitive in our statements.

Those who advocate the legalization of obscene material argue that adults should have the right to choose the books they read, the movies they see, and the plays they attend. They claim along with other civil libertarians that this right is granted them under the First Amendment's guaranties of freedom of speech, press, and assembly.

The merits of both these positions have been frequently argued before the courts. Unfortunately, the criminal justice system has been no more able to resolve this question than any similar victimless crime issues. The immediate future shows very little promise of improvement.

The History of Obscenity Laws

The offense of obscenity as we now know it did not exist in either England or the United States until the nineteenth century. Although ''obscenity'' was made a crime in England in the sixteenth century, only seditious or heretical writings or plays which attacked the state or the church were considered obscene. In 1797, a man named Curl was prosecuted for "obscene libel" for publishing the book *Venus in the Cloister or the Nun in Her Smock*. This case developed the common law crime of obscenity.[52] The court was not so concerned with the explicitness of the book as with the fact that it discredited established religion or its servants.[53]

Most historians are of the opinion that there was little concern over obscenity in colonial New England because the colonists felt little need for legal prohibitions. By the early nineteenth century, a number of books were banned in England and America. One of these books, *Fanny Hill,* brought the first obscenity case dealing with a book to the attention of the courts in 1821. The publisher was found guilty under the common law doctrine established in the Curl case in England. That same year, Vermont passed the first state statute to prohibit obscenity. The test of obscenity was first applied by a Massachusetts statute of 1835 which held that the test was whether the work was "manifestly tending to the corruption of the morals of youth."[54] Thus it was the state legislatures which took the most active role in dealing with obscenity during this period. It would be many years before the courts would become the primary actors in dealing with this offense, as they are today.

Although antiobscenity laws appeared on the books during the first half of the nineteenth century, they were not often enforced. It was only after the Civil War that citizen groups began to agitate for stronger enforcement. In 1868, the New York legislature passed a bill to suppress obscene literature.[55] At this time, a grocery store clerk in New York, named Anthony Comstock, took it upon himself to track down, on his own time and at his own expense, the sellers of obscene publications and to have them prosecuted under the 1868 act. Comstock, however, felt limited in this pastime to local sellers because of the lack of a federal obscenity statute. So, Comstock joined efforts with the YMCA to work for national antiobscenity legislation that would make possible prosecution of publishers as well as local dealers. Together, they formed the Committee for the Suppression of Vice, and with Comstock leading them, the committee set about lobbying Congress to pass laws prohibiting the sale and distribution of obscene matter. In response to this lobbying, Congress in 1873 passed an act governing the passage of obscene material through the mail.[56]

In 1933, the first major modification of early statutes and court decisions was made by the federal courts. Up until this time, material was considered obscene if it could be judged corruptive to the morals of youth or corruptive to those whose minds might be open to such immoral influences. In that year, the federal courts were called upon to examine James Joyce's famous novel *Ulysses* and pass judgment on whether it was obscene. The U.S. Court of Appeals ruled that it was not. In this case, the court refuted the established tests that a book was to be considered obscene by its "corruptive influence on the morals of youth" or "those whose minds might be open to such immoral influences" and established a new test. This new test said that obscenity was to be judged by "its effect on the average person.''[57] Thus, obscenity was to be judged on the basis of its effect on the average individual rather than on those individuals who because of certain characteristics might be more susceptible to sexual arousal.

In 1957, the Supreme Court was first called upon to examine the relationship between obscenity and the guarantees of the freedom of expression granted by the First Amendment and the due process provision of the Fourteenth Amendment. In the case of *Roth* v. *United States,* the court ruled that obscenity was not protected by the First Amendment, as not every form of speech or protection is guaranteed by the Constitution. It reaffirmed the decision handed down by the court in the *Ulysses* case that the ''average person'' standard should apply, and added two additional tests. These were ''whether the dominant theme as a whole appeals to prurient interests; and whether it is without redeeming social importance.''[58]

In 1961, another test standard was added. In the case of *Manual Enterprises* v. *Day,* the court expanded the already existing tests under the Roth case to include the concept of ''patent offensiveness'' of the material.[59]

Three years later, in *Jocobellis* v. *Ohio,* the court faced the question of whether local standards were to prevail in applying the tests developed. The court replied that the constitutional status of an allegedly obscene work must be determined on the basis of a national standard.[60]

In 1966, the Supreme Court decided the cases of *Ginzberg* v. *United States* and *Mishkin* v. *New York.* In these cases, the test of whether the work was without redeeming social value was employed as well as a modification of the ''average person'' test in that ''when the material in question is designed and primarily disseminated to a clearly defined group, it is to be judged by the standards of that group.''[61]

Whether something was obscene was now to be determined by the following tests: (1) the appeal of the dominant theme of the material to prurient interest, (2) the ''patent offensiveness'' of the material in its description or representation of sexual matters, and (3) the material's utter lack of redeeming social value. The standard for determining the prurient appeal and the offensiveness to the community in sexual description is that of the national contemporary community as applied to the average person. The exception is where deviant groups are involved.[62]

In trying to formulate vague tests and have these tests apply nationwide, the Supreme Court was sinking further into the quagmire of confusion. Beginning in the late 1960s, the Court began reassessing its role in trying to determine what is or is not obscene or pornographic. This reassessment has had some far-reaching effects on obscenity and pornography laws in this country.

In 1971, the National Commission on Obscenity and Pornography released its much-publicized report.[63] After a great deal of research on the subject, the commission found no significant relation between exposure to erotic materials and antisocial behavior. Twelve of the eighteen members of the commission recommended repeal of all state and federal statutes prohibiting the sale, exhibition, or distribution of sexual materials to consenting adults.[64]

Important Recent Decisions

Two recent Court decisions have had a significant impact on obscenity laws. In 1969 in the case of *Stanley* v. *Georgia*, the Supreme Court overturned the ruling of the Georgia Supreme Court which upheld the conviction of Stanley for possession in his home of three pornographic films. The Court ruled that the First and Fourteenth Amendments prohibit making mere private possession of obscene material a crime. Under this ruling, an individual has the right to read or observe what he or she pleases in the privacy of his or her own home.[65] In 1971, the Court also upheld lower-court decisions that set limits on the power of the postal authorities to prohibit the mailing of obscene materials on the basis that consenting adults should have the right to choose their own moral standards as long as they do not directly offend others.

The most recent decision of the Supreme Court in the 1973 case of *Miller* v. *California* seems to be another landmark decision. The Court in this notable case let it be known that it was unable to formulate a meaningful definition of obscenity that could be applied nationwide. Instead of continually trying to accomplish this task over the years, as it had done in the past, it was going to formulate a few guidelines and leave the ultimate decision of what is obscene or pornographic to local communities. It now became the responsibility of local governments to make the determination.[66]

However, states and local communities are finding themselves unable to find any more effective solution to the problem than did the Supreme Court. Numerous state legislatures are trying to develop some kind of uniform standards, but local communities that have adopted ordinances prohibiting pornography are finding they are unenforceable in state courts. It would appear that an ultimate solution is still to be found.

SEX OFFENSES

The sex offenses of prostitution, homosexuality, fornication, and adultery are classified as victimless crimes. The original purpose of laws against these offenses was to deter acts considered morally harmful to the basic fabric of society. However, these laws have had no demonstrated deterrent effect except perhaps to drive such behavior underground.

In recent years, society has become much more tolerant of these acts and those who engage in them. This is particularly true with the crimes of fornication and adultery and, in some instances, certain forms of homosexual behavior and prostitution. The offenses of fornication and adultery, for instance, are widely tolerated in our society, and the laws against them are most certainly unenforceable by today's moral standards. Florida, for example, has prosecuted only one case of adultery in the last 100 years.

Prostitution

While some states, such as Nevada, permit counties to license and regulate houses of prostitution, the laws against prostitution are still zealously enforced by many local police agencies. Perhaps because prostitution is more directly offensive to certain members of the community than the more covert forms of ''deviant'' sexual behavior, the police are forced to take periodic steps to remove prostitutes—at least those who openly solicit customers.

What can we say about the enforcement of prostitution laws? In the first place, in spite of the enforcement efforts of the police, it is a very large business. Winick and Kinsie, in their comprehensive study of prostitution, suggest that it is nationwide in scope and involves over a billion dollars annually. They estimate that this ''oldest profession'' involves between 100,000 and 500,000 women in the United States alone.[67]

Those who favor strict enforcement of laws against prostitution argue as follows: First, the existence of prostitution in a community encourages the growth of other criminal activities such as drug abuse, assaults, and homicides, often involving the customer, the prostitute, and her pimp, or other vicious crimes as pimps try to obtain the services of girls working for other procurers. It also leads to greater incidence of venereal disease and to the corruption and demoralization of law enforcement. The existence of prostitution in a community also corrupts the morals of youth and leads young girls into this form of behavior as a livelihood. Finally, by sanctioning prostitution the community encourages moral decay and sexual promiscuity among its members which destroys familial relationships and the sanctity of marriage.

Others who feel that it would be far more prudent to legalize and regulate such behavior argue that prostitution cannot be enforced out of existence— instead, the best we can hope to accomplish is to control it through regulation. They often suggest that cities which have perennial problems with prostitution establish licensed brothels in designated areas of the city where they would be least offensive to the citizenry. Such a policy is thought to have certain advantages: It would better contain this behavior to certain locations in the community rather than having such operations widely dispersed. Through careful licensing and periodic medical examinations of prostitutes, the rates of venereal disease associated with prostitution could be reduced. It is also felt that close police supervision of regulated brothels would reduce many of the problems associated with illegal prostitution. Such problems as the activities of pimps whom the women must turn to for protection and the violence that surrounds this arrangement would be eliminated, and narcotics trafficking, blackmail, robberies, assaults, and other forms of criminal activity could be curtailed. Finally, there are those who look upon the regulation of prostitution as a method for communities to obtain additional revenues through licensing fees and taxes.

It would seem that countries that have tried to legalize prostitution have found it to be a mixed blessing.[68] The mere fact that the activity is licensed and regulated has not eliminated many of the traditional problems associated with prostitution. Nevada, on the other hand, in which prostitution is legal in fifteen of the seventeen counties, claims that it has been able to control the dispersion of prostitution in that state as well as the other criminal problems associated with it by means of licensed brothels regulated by the police or the local district attorney's office.[69]

Some local communities have recently adopted new strategies to deal with problems of prostitution. One is to arrest the prostitute's customer as well as the prostitute. Another is to have female police officers operate in areas frequented by streetwalkers; when a male approaches the policewoman and propositions her, he is arrested. Both of these enforcement strategies rely upon the fact that it is a crime to participate in a sexual act with a prostitute or to solicit a woman's services for prostitution.

Homosexual Behavior

Another problem area in the law is the crime of homosexual behavior. As of 1975, the laws of forty-three states and the District of Columbia imposed criminal penalties on consenting adults who engage in private homosexual conduct. Most of these laws are sodomy statutes which also prohibit oral and anal intercourse between humans and sexual acts with animals.[70] It is necessary to make a distinction at this point between homosexual activities involving consenting adults and similar activities directed at children or other nonconsenting individuals. It is only the statutes prohibiting this sort of behavior between consenting adults that many people are advocating be removed from the statute books.

The existence of such laws has had a significant impact upon homosexuals in at least three ways. First, laws prohibiting homosexual contact may inhibit persons who seek sexual satisfaction in this manner. Second, such laws may encourage blackmail by providing a means whereby homosexuals can be threatened with exposure or prosecution, and this may discourage employers from hiring homosexuals for fear that their vulnerability to blackmail might pose security risks.[71] Finally, such laws indirectly sanction discrimination against homosexuals in employment, housing, and public accommodations.[72]

The most reliable and most often quoted figures on the extent of homosexuality in the United States are those reported in the studies by Alfred Kinsey and his research associates. Their studies found that 4 percent of the American white males are "exclusively homosexual throughout their lives after the onset of adolescence."[73] They further found that over 37 percent of the total male population had sometime during their lives engaged in homosexual activity.[74]

The enforcement of the criminal statutes prohibiting homosexual conduct has often been the subject of abuse. While working with the police in a number of cities, the author witnessed numerous instances when police personnel with nothing better to do engaged in the harassment and intimidation of known "gays."

Some nations are a little more enlightened in their approach to dealing with this form of sexual behavior. In 1957, the Wolfenden Committee in Great Britain, after exhaustive study, concluded that it found no evidence which supported the view that homosexuality is "a cause of the demoralization and decay of civilizations."[75] In short, the committee considered that private, adult consensual homosexuality was "not the law's business."[76] In 1966, Parliament approved recommendations made by the Wolfenden Committee, agreeing that consensual homosexuality in private would no longer be a criminal offense provided that someone under age sixteen was not involved.[77]

In the United States in the past few years, there has been a growing trend among the states to liberalize laws regarding certain forms of homosexual behavior. In 1969, a Task Force on Homosexuality sponsored by the National Institute of Mental Health released a report which urged that the United States follow the example of Great Britain and abolish laws prohibiting private homosexual conduct among consenting adults. The report put the issue in perspective when it said:

> Homosexuality presents a major problem for society largely because of the amount of injustice and suffering in it, not only for the homosexual, but also for those concerned about him.[78]

In the past few years, admitted homosexuals have been taking an active and public role in the repeal of such statutes. Organizations such as the Gay Liberation Front and others are openly challenging the constitutionality of laws prohibiting such acts among consenting adults. As a result, the police and the courts are more and more reluctant to enforce these laws. If present trends continue, it would seem that this form of adult sexual behavior will soon be decriminalized completely.

SUMMARY

Gambling, drunkenness, narcotics use, obscenity and pornography, fornication, adultery, prostitution, and homosexuality are often referred to as victimless crimes because the usual relationship between the offender and the victim is absent. Increasingly, large segments of our society are calling for new methods of dealing with those who engage in such behaviors, and the laws governing these crimes have undergone major changes in recent years. These changes are reflected in new institutions and processes and increased efforts to divert offenders from the criminal justice system.

Victimless crimes are of particular interest to students of criminal justice because they demonstrate most graphically how such institutions and groups as the courts, other agencies of criminal justice, professional associations, interest groups, and others affect our system of law and government.

Suggested Additional Readings

Callahan, Daniel. *Abortion: Law, Choice, and Morality*. New York: Macmillan, 1970.

Cressey, Donald R. *Criminal Organization*. New York: Harper & Row, 1972.

——*Theft of the Nation: The Structure and Operations of Organized Crime in America*. New York: Harper & Row, 1969.

Duster, Troy. *The Legislation of Morality: Laws, Drugs and Moral Judgement*. New York: Free Press, 1970.

Esselstyn, T. C. "Prostitution in the United States." *The Annals* 376 (March 1968): 123–135.

The National Council on Crime and Delinquency. *The Alcoholic Offender*. New York: NCCD, August 1964.

Pittman, David J., and C. Wayne Gordon. *Revolving Door*. New York: Free Press, 1958.

Plascowe, Morris. "Sex Offenses: The American Legal Context." *Law and Contemporary Problems* 25 (Spring 1960): 217–225.

President's Commission on Law Enforcement and Administration of Justice. *Task Force Report: Drunkenness*. Washington, D.C.: U.S. Government Printing Office, 1967.

Regush, Nicholas M. *The Drug Addiction Business*. New York: Dial Press, 1971.

Rubington, Earl. "The Chronic Drunkenness Offender." *Annals of the American Academy of Political and Social Science* 315 (January 1958): 65–72.

Schur, Edwin M. *Crimes without Victims*. Englewood Cliffs, N.J.: Prentice-Hall, 1965.

Notes

1. Sanford B. Kadish, "The Crisis of Overcriminalization," *The Annals of the American Academy of Political and Social Science* 374 (November 1967): 157–170.

2. Lord Devlin, *The Enforcement of Morals* (London: Oxford University Press, 1965), p.23.

3. For example, see Herbert L. Parker, *The Limits of the Criminal Sanction* (Stanford, Calif: Stanford University Press, 1968), p. 266.

4. Gilbert Geis, *Not the Law's Business?* (Washington D.C.: U.S. Government Printing Office, 1969), pp. III–IV.

5. See Eugene Doleschal, "Victimless Crime," *Crime and Delinquency Literature Abstracts* (June 1971): 254–269.

6. Kadish, op. cit.

7. Milton G. Rector, "Victimless Crime: Whose Responsibility?" *Trends* (July-August 1972): 6–9.

8. National Commission on Law Observance and Enforcement, *Wickersham Commission Reports,* vol. 1, p. 149.

9. George Nash, *The Impact of Drug Abuse Treatment upon Criminality: A Look at 19 Programs* (Montclair, N.J.: Drug Abuse Treatment Information Project, December 1973), p. 1.2.

10. See Edward M. Davis, "Victimless Crime: The Case for Continued Enforcement," *Journal of Police Science and Administration* 1 (March 1973): 11–20.

11. See Kefauver Commission, *2d Interim Report*, no. 141, 82d Cong., 1st Sess., 11 (1951).

12. Statement by former inspector, Arthur C. Grubert, New York City Police Department, Apr. 19, 1965, New York.

13. President's Commission on Law Enforcement and Administration of Justice, *Task Force Report: Organized Crime* (Washington, D.C.: U.S. Government Printing Office, 1967), p. 3.

14. Donald R. Cressey, "The Functions and Structure of Criminal Syndicates," in ibid., pp. 35–36.

15. See MacClellan Committee, *Final Report*, S. Rep. No. 1139, 86th Cong., 2d Sess., pt. 4 at 722 (1960).

16. President's Commission on Law Enforcement and Administration of Justice, *Task Force Report: Organized Crime*, p. 3.

17. New York Commission of Investigation, *The Loan Shark Report*, 17 (1965).

18. Irving K. Zola, "Observations on Gambling in a Lower-Class Setting," *Social Problems*, 10 (Spring 1963): 360.

19. Thomas J. Johnson, "Numbers Called Harlem's Balm," *The New York Times*, Mar. 1, 1971.

20. St. Clair Drake and Horace R. Clayton, *Black Metropolis: A Study of Negro Life in a Northern City* (New York: Harcourt Brace, 1945), pp. 493–494.

21. President's Commission on Law Enforcement and Administration of Justice, *The Challenge of Crime in a Free Society* (Washington, D.C.: U.S. Government Printing Office, 1967), p. 233.

22. The St. Louis Detoxification and Diagnostic Evaluation Center, Alternative Disposition of the Public Inebriate (Washington, D.C.: U.S. Government Printing Office, 1969), p. 16

23. *Argersinger v. Hamlin*, 407 U.S. 25 (1972).

24. U.S. Department of Health, Education, and Welfare, *First Special Report to the U.S. Congress on Alcohol and Health*, (Washington, D.C.: U.S. Government Printing Office, 1972), p. 92.

25. National Institute of Mental Health, *Alcoholism and the Law* (Rockville, Md.: January 1973), p. 14.

26. U.S. Department of Health, Education, and Welfare, op. cit., p. 93.

27. *State v. Driver*, 262 N.C. 92, 136 S.E. 2d 208 (1964).

28. *Easter v. District of Columbia*, 361 F. 2d (D.C. Cir. 1966).

29. *Driver v. Hinnant*, 356 F. 2d 761 (4th Cir. 1966).

30. *Powell v. Texas*, 392 U.S. 514 (1968).

31. Carl M. Liebemann and Jack D. Blaine, "The British System of Drug Control," *Drug Dependence* (Washington, D.C.: U.S. Government Printing Office, 1970), pp. 12–16.

32. Vera Institute of Justice, "Heroin Research and Rehabilitation Program" (New York: Vera Institute, May 1971).

33. National Advisory Commission on Criminal Justice Standards and Goals, Community Crime Prevention (Washington, D.C.: U.S. Government Printing Office, 1973), p. 101.

34. For example, see V.P. Dole and M. E. Nyswander, *New York State Journal of Medicine* 66 (1965): 645; Methadone Maintenance Evaluation Committee, *First National Conference on Methadone Treatment* (New York: The Rockefeller University, 1968); Vernon D. Patch, A. E. Raynes and Alan Fisch, "Methadone Maintenance and Crime Reduction in Boston—Variables Compounded," paper presented at the Annual Meeting of the American Psychiatric Association, May 1973; and S. B. Sells (ed.), *The Effectiveness of Drug Abuse Treatment, Volume I: Evaluation of Treatments* (Cambridge, Mass.: Ballinger Publishing Company, 1974).

35. *Governor's Report on Narcotic Addiction Programs in New York* (Albany, 1969).

36. Mass. Gen. Laws Ann., ch. 123, §38–55 (supp. 1972).

37. John A. Robertson and Phyllis Teitelbaun, "Pre-Trial Diversion of Drug Offenders: A Statutory Approach," *Boston University Law Review,* 52 (2) (Spring 1972).

38. See Robert Berke and Michael I. Dillard, *Drug Offender Diversion in California: The First Year of Penal Code 1000,* a report of the State Drug Abuse Prevention Advisory Council, January 1974.

39. National Commission on Marijuana and Drug Abuse, *Marijuana: A Signal of Misunderstanding,* vol. II (Washington, D.C.: U.S. Government Printing Office).

40. San Mateo County, Department of Public Health, Research and Statistics Section. *Five Mind-Altering Drugs (Plus One),* 1970, p. 5.

41. National Commission on Marijuana and Drug Abuse, op. cit., p. 612.

42. Federal Bureau of Investigation, Uniform Crime Report, 1973 (Washington, D.C.: U.S. Government Printing Office, 1974), p. 34.

43. R. Bonnie and C. Whisenand, "The Forbidden Fruit and the Tree of Knowledge: History of American Marijuana Prohibition," *Virginia Law Review,* 56 (1970): 971–1003.

44. San Mateo County, op. cit.

45. J. Kaplan, *Marijuana: The New Prohibition* (New York: World Publishing, 1970)

46. National Commission on Marijuana and Drug Abuse, op. cit., p. 620.

47. For example, see Harold Kolansky and William T. Moore, "Effect of Marijuana on Adolescents and Young Adults," *Journal of the American Medical Association,* 216 (Apr. 19, 1971): 486–492.

48. R. S. Weingarter, "Fact and Fiction Surrounding Marijuana," *Journal of Mental Health* 5 (June 1973): 61–78.

49. Geis, op. cit., p. 169.

50. Bonnie and Whitebread, op. cit., pp. 1177–1178.

51. Rollin M. Perkins, *Criminal Law and Procedure* (Brooklyn, N. Y.: Foundation Press, 1966), p. 206.

52. A. Schroeder, "Obscene Literature at Common Law," *Albany Law Journal,* 69 (1907): 146.

53. *Technical Report of the Commission on Obscenity and Pornography,* vol. II (Washington, D.C.: U. S. Government Printing Office, 1971), p. 69.

54. Ibid., p. 76.

55. New York State, 309.

56. L. Broun and E. P. Leech, *Anthony Comstock: Roundsman of the Lord* (New York: Boni & Liveright, 1925).

57. *United States v. One Book Called "Ulysses,"* 5F, Supp. 182 (1933).

58. 354, U.S. 476 (1956).

59. 370, U.S. 478 (1962).

60. 378, U.S. 184 (1964).

61 383, U.S. 412 (1965).

62. M. Cherif Bassiouni, *Criminal Law and Its Process* (Springfield, Ill.: Charles C Thomas, 1969), p. 247.

63. *The Report of the Commission on Obscenity and Pornography* (Washington, D.C.: U.S. Government Printing Office, 1971).

64. Ibid., pp. 51-52.

65. 394, U.S. 557 (1969).

66. 413, U.S. 15 (1973).

67. Charles Winick and Paul M. Kinsie, *The Lively Commerce: Prostitution in the United States* (Chicago: Quadrangle, 1971).

68. Geis, op. cit., pp. 172–221.

69. *The New York Times,* Jan. 13, 1974, p. 9, col. 3.

70. "The Constitutionality of Laws Forbidding Private Homosexual Conduct," *Michigan Law Review* 72 (August 1974): 1613.

71. "Security Clearances for Homosexuals," *Stanford Law Review* 25 (June 1973): 409–411.

72. *The New York Times* (Dec. 23, 1973), p. 5, col. 1.

73. Alfred C. Kinsey, Wardell B. Pomeroy, and Clyde E. Martin, *Sexual Behavior in the Human Male* (Philadelphia: Saunders, 1948), pp. 650–651.

74. Ibid, p. 651.

75. Great Britain Committee on Homosexual Offenses and Prostitution (CMND 247, 1957), p. 22.

76. Ibid., p. 24.

77. The Sexual Offenses Act, 1967 (1967, c. 60), Halsbury, 3d ed. vol. VIII, pp. 577–582.

78. National Institute of Mental Health, Task Force on Homosexuality, *Final Report (Washington, D.C.: U.S. Government Printing Office, Oct. 10, 1969), p. 4.*

Part 2

LAW ENFORCEMENT

Chapter 5

Law Enforcement: Its History and Political Organization Within the States

THE POLICE IN A DEMOCRATIC SOCIETY

The police are the gatekeepers of the system of criminal justice. In most cases, it is their action of arrest which initiates the justice process. Because of their key role in the overall administration of justice, they are the official agency most able to affect the process and, strangely enough, the one most affected by it.

For example, a very popular political theme of recent years, which has the potential of impacting forcefully upon the police, has been the issue of "law and order." Unfortunately, the complexity of this issue is not understood completely by most Americans. Too often, those who rather flippantly employ this term, as well as those who unthinkingly support it, fail to recognize that it incorporates two rather distinct concepts.

In our democratic society, we profess to believe very strongly in the rights of individual freedom. Fundamental to this belief is the requirement that certain patterns of behavior and conduct be tolerated to a degree that would not (and probably could not) be acceptable in countries where the heritage and concerns for the rights of the individual in relation to the state were less. This presents a basic dilemma to all free societies: If we want "order" in a society to the degree that some suggest, it would seem that we must forgo some of the present protections we receive from our laws. If the police were given the necessary resources (including increased enforcement power through important mod-ifications in our legal structure), it would be possible to maintain a high level of order in our society, but at a cost in freedom we may very well not be will-ing to pay. Although there are those who profess that we can have both, the history of mankind indicates otherwise. In today's complex society, it would seem that such "order" would require a policy of increased enforcement which would threaten to make life intolerable for those who responsibly cherish the freedom we enjoy.

Although our laws are written as if total enforcement were expected, the police determine the outer limits of actual enforcement.[1] Decisions are daily made by the police to enforce certain laws but not others because of a number of factors: the difficulty of making arrests, the resources needed to obtain evidence, disagreements in the community as to whether certain acts should be considered unlawful, and pressure from persons with influence who desire that some laws not be enforced. As Cole points out: "These 'low visibility' choices by police administrators are one of the political ingredients in the criminal justice system. Law enforcement agencies are faced with fulfilling their obligations under the law, yet with doing so in ways which will maintain community support."[2]

Most of us do not realize how complex the functions of the police are: Not only are they given responsibility to maintain order, enforce the law, and provide a broad range of social services, but their enforcement policies also determine who is to be labeled deviant. Society generally agrees that certain acts, such as vicious street crimes, are criminal acts and that the police should deal with them appropriately. However, there are other acts which are not so universally accepted as criminal. Victimless crimes, of course, are the most notable, but, there are other crimes as well, for example, white-collar crimes such as fraud or embezzlement committed by "respectable" citizens and price-fixing conspiracies among corporate giants. Although the local police usually lack the authority, resources, or design to enforce these latter offenses, the fact that they are often not enforced by federal police agencies or regulatory commissions indicates that our society (or at least our officials) attaches different priorities to criminal behavior. These priorities are then translated into enforcement decisions.

Let's face the facts squarely: the police are aware that their image is more greatly enhanced by arresting narcotics pushers, burglars, and rapists than by cracking down on white-collar crime. There may be some justification for this attitude, as narcotics dealers and rapists may pose a graver threat to society than unscrupulous merchants, but the fact remains that the police by virtue of their enforcement discretion and the actions they take probably reinforce the conception of what should be considered "important" crimes and who should be labeled as "criminal" in terms of our value system.

POLICE FUNCTIONS

At this point, we should examine certain roles that are important in understanding the function of the police in our society. Some observers see the police function in terms of two important roles: law enforcement and order maintenance.[3] Law enforcement concerns a violation of law when only guilt must be assessed. Order maintenance, on the other hand, usually involves a legal infraction, but there may be a dispute about the interpretation of right conduct and the assignment of blame.[4] Although we normally think of the police in terms of obvious law enforcement activities such as arresting offenders, it has been argued by many observers that their principal function is to maintain peace in the community.[5]

This is particularly apparent when we study the role of the officers patrolling a beat. Such officers are primarily concerned with behavior that either disturbs or threatens the peace. They confront the public in ambiguous circumstances and are given some discretion in their own actions. They may be required to help persons in trouble, control crowds, supervise certain licensed services, and assist those who are not fully accountable for what they do.[6]

In our society the police are increasingly called upon to perform non-crime-related functions. One study of a metropolitan police department indicated that more than half the calls that the police received were for help or support in connection with personal and interpersonal problems.[7] In Detroit, one researcher found that only 16 percent of the calls to the police were crime-related.[8] Because the police are often the only representatives of local government readily available on a twenty-four hour basis, they are the agency to which people turn in times of trouble. In our cities, the poor and the ignorant often seek help from the police in place of perhaps more appropriate sources.

In order to better understand the present role of the police, one must be familiar with their historical development. It is no accident of fate that American police agencies are organized and operate the way they do. They have evolved by a long process that mirrors basic changes in the social relationships of Western people and in the role of the police in controlling these relationships. This chapter and the next will examine the history and development of local and state law enforcement and the composition and authority of major federal enforcement agencies.

EARLY DEVELOPMENT OF LAW ENFORCEMENT

Historians have not provided us with much insight into the development of law enforcement. Although ancient civilizations probably had some type of organized law enforcement, the first recorded police organization occurred during the reign of Egyptian Pharoah Hur Moheb (circa 1340 B.C.).[9] This Egyptian king established a river security unit equipped with strong boats to ensure navigational safety along the Nile. These river police were responsible for preventing piracy, searching suspect ships, and guarding commerce activities on the river.

Around 500 B.C., Rome created the first detectives, who were called *quaestores* or "trackers of murder." These individuals were given the responsibility of investigating murder and searching for the culprit. During the reign of Augustus Caesar (27 B.C. to A.D. 14), the city of Rome was divided into four quarters which were to serve as areas of police administration in that city. These areas were patrolled during the day by *curatores*, the equivalent of superintendents of police in those areas. At night, their place was taken by *vigiles*, whose responsibility it was to make their rounds and search out criminals.[10] Interestingly, other principles of modern law enforcement were also developed

at this time. Throughout the provinces of ancient Rome were posted detachments of policelike organizations whose members were distributed in stations
dotted about the countryside and in villages. Thus, these organizations fore-
shadowed the modern idea of geographical police deployment throughout
large jurisdictions.

With the end of the Roman Empire, Western civilization and the kind of a
government that could foster a more centralized form of administration of
criminal justice came to an end. Western Europe then became enveloped in
what some historians refer to as the "Dark Ages." Gradually, the feudal system
began to evolve out of the chaotic state of affairs in Western Europe at that time.
By the eleventh century, the feudal system had developed certain laws which
were based much more on the idea of the individual than on the more abstract
concepts of state, justice, or the public good.[11]

Power to envoke sanctions for the commission of crimes rested in the hands
of the noblemen and small landowners. In fact, they even decided what types of
behavior constituted a crime. Although the church had some influence in de-
fining certain types of conduct as criminal, this was a period when "might was
right" and powerful feudal lords could act with impunity toward God's
laws—or the king's—provided they possessed the required force of arms.

The concepts of high justice and low justice developed at this time. The
invoking of high justice was the prerogative of the wealthy lord, who could deal
with crimes punishable by death or mutilation. Small landowners were entitled
to dispense low justice for crimes involving penalties of corporal punishment
or fines.[12] There is no indication that there were specific police officials of a
strictly civil nature at this time. Police powers were vested in the lord's men-
at-arms, who acted under his direction.

DEVELOPMENT OF THE POLICE IN GREAT BRITAIN

Because the police model developed in Great Britain has had such a strong
impact on the structure of law enforcement in the United States, the development and history of English law enforcement needs to be examined in order that
we might understand how modern concepts of police organization have developed to their present state.

By conquering Britain, Rome not only brought to the British Isles highly
developed laws, but succeeded in establishing a police system, particularly in
the villages, similar to that which existed in Rome and the other urban areas of
the empire. In the rural areas, however, law enforcement was in the hands of the
military or was left to be handled by existing tribal customs. However, historians point out that the Roman system of law and its administration and enforcement had little impact on these early Gallic Celts who inhabited the British
Isles. They bitterly resisted attempts by their Roman overlords to impose their
system of laws and justice and clung tenaciously to their ancient tribal customs.[13]

By the fifth century, Rome was beginning to lose its grip on Britain as peoples of Germania began to migrate westward, causing the Roman army to abandon many of its outposts in the area. The Germanic tribes brought with them their traditional custom of employing a form of kin-police which decreed that every man was not only responsible for the misdeeds of others in his community, but was also permitted to avenge wrongs done to him. This system was called the "peace of the folk." The laws were not written, but had come down by tradition over the years. The first written laws have been attributed to King Aethelbert of Kent, who was reigning when the mission under St. Augustine arrived in England in A.D. 597. His laws imposed a tariff or payment for injuries done to one of his subjects. This detailed tariff went so far as to state the amount of compensation for the loss of a toenail! The laws also related to the punishment of slaves and freemen for crimes, offenses against the king and noblemen and wrongs committed against the church and its clergy.[14]

Around the year 690, the king of Wessex extended the criminal law to provide for a financial penalty for anyone hiding a thief or letting him go. Thus, we can infer that a form of *citizens arrest* was enacted. In this case, the individual was held responsible for the safeguarding of a prisoner until the offender made restitution to the victim or was punished.

During the reign of King Alfred the Great (872-901), major steps were taken to provide a more systematic and organized form of law enforcement. He decreed that every freeman was to be a member of a group called a *tithing*. A tithing was a group of about ten families. Every member of the tithing was bound by his pledge or oath to be answerable for the good behavior of others in his group. Each tithing was organized in a district or township, and strangers in the area were kept under surveillance to ensure that they did not break the law. The tithings were grouped into unions of ten, and this large group was known as a hundred. The hundred met frequently, and at these meetings offenders were dealt with and local problems discussed and corrected. The whole country was divided into shires or counties, and a shire reeve (sheriff) was responsible to his earl for the peace of the county.[15]

After the Norman conquest in 1066, William the Conqueror continued the existing tithing system. The only change that he made was to require that only persons of good character be permitted to be members of the tithing. If a man was dishonest, he could neither belong to the group nor live in the area. If such a person was found in the area, the tithing was punished. Consequently, the only course of action left for such an "outlaw" was to flee the district and live in some outlying area of the country or hide in the forests.

In 1285, the Statute of Winchester prescribed that the old Saxon *hue and cry* would be strictly complied with in order to capture and bring to justice felons throughout the countryside. The hue and cry was the pursuance of a criminal "with horn and voice" from town to town until the offender was arrested or cut down. Everyone was required to join the chase or be fined once the words "Stop thief!" rang out. The individual responsible for organizing the hue and cry and maintaining order in the town was called a *constable*. The statute also directed that in the walled towns, the gates were to be closed at night, watches were to be kept, and any suspicious-looking individuals wandering about the streets were to be arrested. Because highwaymen were a particular problem, special citizen patrols were established to patrol the highways and to clear all underbrush on each side of the highway to a distance of at least 200 feet so that highway robbers could not lie in concealment, awaiting a victim.

This system of law enforcement prevailed relatively unchanged until the seventeenth century. In these years, the responsibility for ensuring law and order in the cities, towns, villages, and manors increasingly evolved upon the constables. They were selected on a rotating basis and were required to perform their police functions for at least a year. They were neither paid for their services nor provided with uniforms. A fee system, however, developed by which they were compensated for arresting people, flogging criminals, carrying the hue and cry to neighboring towns, and performing other minor duties related to their law enforcement functions. By the beginning of the seventeenth century, this system of law enforcement was beginning to break down. A policy had developed over the years whereby an individual could avoid service as a constable by paying a substitute to act for him. As a consequence, able-bodied men began turning these responsibilities over to the ill, the infirm, beggars, and even thieves and other criminals in some cases. These practices brought a general breakdown in law and order and an outcry for a more effective form of local policing.

The forces of history intervened at this point. During the reign of Charles I (1625-1645), civil war developed in England over the absolutist rule of this monarch. Charles used the existing machinery of criminal justice as a means of punishing those who disagreed with his policies. This was a period when English citizens began to question the absolute right of the Crown to invoke its will upon them. After the execution of Charles in 1649, Oliver Cromwell assumed the leadership of the country under the title of lord protector. In an effort to bring order out of chaos, he immediately placed the country under martial law. He divided the nation into twelve districts and appointed a military general known as a *provost marshal* over each district. Under tight military control, law and order was reestablished and crime was curbed drastically. However, Cromwell and his appointed provost marshals were not above invoking the use of the criminal justice system and force to maintain order. Ostensibly to restore order and rid the countryside of criminals, Cromwell suspended the rights of English freemen. Citizens were subject to arrest and their property confiscated almost at will. Trials were suspended, and courts of justice became a mockery. In effect, a police state under Cromwell had been substituted for one imposed by Charles I. A prime instrument of both was the use of the authority of the military in the role of the police and the complete perversion of the system of justice. Because of the experience of the English people with these two despotic authorities, a deep-seated fear of the abuses inherent in a centralized police was established in the minds of the English people. This fear would later reemerge when efforts were undertaken to create a more uniform and systematic civil police service. In ways, this ideological legacy is still important in England and the United States.

After the civil strife had ended and a new monarch, Charles II, had been restored to the Crown, law enforcement, which at least had enjoyed some stability under Cromwell, reverted to the constable system. Chaos and internal disorder again became widespread. Conditions in London became so bad that Charles II formed a special group of a thousand night watchmen called bellmen or "Charlies." Their responsibilities were to patrol the streets of London in an effort to suppress the gangs of criminals and thugs that preyed upon law-abiding citizens. Each was issued a bell which he rang to announce his presence and to arouse the honest citizens in the event of trouble. The conditions in other parts of the kingdom were no better than in London. The highways were so fraught with peril from robbers, murderers, and thieves that the king was forced to dispatch troops to patrol them. The patrols failed to suppress the highwaymen, however, and the government then attempted to restore law and order by instituting a system of money rewards together with pardons to anyone who gave assistance or information which led to the arrest of highwaymen. This system was soon extended to aid officials in curtailing the thieves and robbers in London.[16]

The immediate consequence of this system was the creation of an army of blackmailers, false accusers, and "framers" of trials, whose activities confounded the rapidly growing criminal confusion of London and the countryside. Constables and city marshals were almost totally impotent. The government tried to remedy the situation by creating more constables, but found itself frustrated by loudly voiced protests from citizens who were not happy with the burden and unpleasantness of having to serve in that capacity. Again, those pressed into police service were allowed to provide and pay deputies to act for them. These deputies quickly became professionals, serving one household after another for twelve months at a time and creating yet another branch of the immense industry of crime which by the eighteenth century had become a leading and appalling feature of the economic activities of London.[17]

The early eighteenth century saw the complete breakdown of the existing apparatus of law enforcement in London. By the end of the century, owing to the lack of foresight and understanding on the part of the government and the people, this breakdown had spread with steadily increasing momentum to and through the provinces and, especially, in the new industrial towns. There, the experiences of London were repeated in detail: in increase of uncontrollable crime and in frequency of outbreaks of uncontrollable riot and disorder.[18]

Beginnings of the Modern Era of Law Enforcement

The British police system and the influence it has had in America were not because of the British people, but in spite of them. In the words of Reith, a noted historian on the development of the police, "It is almost solely the product of personalities; those of five individuals whose single-mindedness in vision, ideals and purposes was eventually brought by the last of them to practical adaptation in the shape of the police as we know them today.''[19]

The first of the five creators of modern police concepts was the novelist Henry Fielding. Although he is most widely remembered for his plays and novels, his achievements as a magistrate working to achieve social and police reform are certainly no less significant in terms of lasting value to humanity. He conceived of the idea that police action should be directed at the *prevention* of crime instead of seeking to control it, as was the custom at the time, solely by waiting for its occurrence and then attempting to repress it by means of violence or through the brutal savagery of criminal punishments.

Fielding was a perceptive observer of the nature and causes of crime in London. He saw that crime and criminals had become so open in the city that the constables of the time were powerless to intervene and completely at the mercy of the criminal elements. So bad had the situation become that no constable dared to arrest many of the criminals. Fielding also observed that the law-abiding citizens of London did not grasp the possibilities or value of collective security against the criminal. Fielding alone conceived the idea that there was another method of dealing with crime and disorder besides that of waiting helplessly for its manifestations and then attempting to meet violence with violence. He realized that citizens might combine together collectively and go out into the streets, trace the criminals to their haunts, and arrest them. To test this theory, he selected six citizens of integrity and physical prowess and under his leadership swept the criminal elements from the Bow Street area of London. Many criminals were arrested. Others fled. The work of these men and the simplicity of their results caused a sensation. So astonishing were the results of his Bow Street Amateur Volunteer Force that the government provided him with a salary and asked him to extend the idea into other areas of London. Before he could accomplish this, he died in 1754, and for a few years his efforts were carried on by his brother. Soon, however, his original group degenerated into a motley band known as the Bow Street Runners, and it would be thirty years before Henry Fielding's values and ideas would receive the recognition they deserved.

The next reformer was Patrick Colquhoun, a prosperous Glasgow businessman who expressed a deep interest in social and criminal reform. He was appointed as a magistrate in London and began to study the significant social problems of the day and their relationship to crime. He worked diligently to help bring about needed social reforms for the poor. Intrigued by Fielding's earlier work, he crystallized the novelist's ideas into the ''new science of preventive police.''[20] He proposed that a large police force should be organized for London under the direction of a board of control. Although his plan was ultimately rejected, in 1789 he formed a special river police force patterned after Fielding's idea that proved to be a success and pointed to a solution to a citywide and nationwide problem. Unfortunately, his ideas were still too advanced for the times, as the English people still harbored a great deal of mistrust toward any form of organized police that would have broad enforcement authority.

The next significant reformer was Sir Robert Peel, the home secretary of England. Although many writers give credit to Peel as the most instrumental of police reformers, some historians who have thoroughly researched the history of the English police credit him only with the handling of the bill that provided for the creation of the Metropolitan Constabulary and the foresight to choose wisely the first two commissioners of the new agency who actually planned, organized and directed the establishment.[21]

Whatever Peel's contribution, the Metropolitan Constabulary for the city of London was created in 1829. Among its principles that are still an integral part of professional police service today are:

1. The police must be under governmental control.

2. The police must be stable, efficient, and organized along military lines.

3. The efficiency of the police will be determined by the absence of crime.

4. The deployment of police strength both by time and area is essential.

5. Applicants for the police force should be judged on their own merits.

6. A perfect command of temper is an indispensable trait of a policemen.

7. Policemen should be hired on a probationary basis.

8. Police records are necessary to the proper distribution of police strength.

9. Training of police officers assures greater efficiency.

Although these were the enunciated principles of the new London Metropolitan Constabulary, they were nothing more than ideas when the first two police commissioners, Charles Rowan and Richard Moyne, were appointed in 1849. It was the combined efforts of these two men that established the concepts of modern policing and left an indelible mark on the functions of the British police even today. The Metropolitan Constabulary was almost disbanded before the principles could be tested. Parliament was being widely criticized by angry groups of citizens calling for the repeal of the act. Members of Parliament were engaged in acrimonious debate, and the fate of the new department hung in the balance. Wisely, these two brilliant, dedicated, and capable administrators began the task of assembling the agency while denunciations swirled about them and Parliament was locked in prolonged debate. The first task was to screen personnel for positions in the new department. Rowan and Moyne realized that this was perhaps the most critical concern, for public approval would depend a great deal on the type of personnel they obtained. The applicants were offered a career for life if they satisfied the standards and could produce accordingly. Out of 12,000 initial applicants, 1,000 were chosen and placed into six divisions. They first concentrated their efforts in the high-crime areas of the city. During their probationary period, the new constables were supervised quite extensively. During the first three years of the department's operation, there were 5,000 dismissals and 6,000 required resignations. Such use of the probationary period was a forceful indication of the seriousness of these two commissioners.[22]

The success of the new department was almost phenomenal. Crime and disorder sharply declined, yet without loss of individual freedom to the law-abiding. So successful were the commissioners in their efforts to organize, recruit, and train a professional police agency that within ten years the people considered Peel as a sort of folk hero, and the constables of the London Metropolitan Constabulary became known to the English people and the world as "Bobbies" out of respect for Sir Robert Peel. With this success, the idea of a centralized, trained, and well-organized permanent group of police constables soon spread throughout the urban centers of England and eventually to the rural areas as well.

DEVELOPMENT OF LAW ENFORCEMENT IN AMERICA

If the history of law enforcement up to the nineteenth century in England can be considered shameful, the American experience must be considered a disgrace. We Americans, it would seem, are uniquely adept at ignoring the facts and lessons of history. During the 200 years of our existence, we have overlooked the constantly repeated lesson of history that laws are meaningless in the absence of authority that can secure *observance* of those laws. During the years of our nation's creation and early growth, we contented ourselves with the making of laws and the structuring of elaborate procedural machinery, while ignoring the need to provide effective means by which the laws could be enforced.

Although we patterned our police forces after the British model, we often adopted only those features that had already proved to be ineffective at best. We adopted the weak and defective constable system of rural England and transplanted it to America. The elected constables of England became the elected sheriffs and deputy sheriffs of the counties within our states and the elected marshals of our towns and cities. The lack of concern displayed by Americans for the necessity of law enforcement must, in part, be attributed to our heritage of disdain for strong central government and the Jeffersonian ideal of the "little republics." Jefferson believed very strongly in the idea of local self-government, by which each citizen was afforded the opportunity to be involved actively and personally in the conduct of government. It was Jefferson's belief, adopted from the writings of John Locke and later supported by Alexis de Tocqueville in his celebrated work *Democracy in America,* that local government should have "preeminent authority over such responsibilities as the care of the poor, roads, police, administration of justice in minor cases, and elementary exercises for the militia."[23] These ideas received strong support from the American people and remain an ideological legacy today.

This conception of the locus, authority, and rights of local government has had a significant impact on the development and patterning of law enforcement services throughout the United States. Past estimates have placed the number of law enforcement agencies at between 32,000 and 40,000.[24] A more recent survey places the figure at over 39,785, but only slightly over 20,000 of these agencies can be considered primarily law enforcement agencies; the remainder are various public agencies that have quasi-law enforcement roles in very specialized areas.[25] These figures indicate that law enforcement in this nation is extremely fragmented and decentralized. Table 5-1 indicates the number and types of police or quasi-police agencies that exist.

**TABLE 5-1   Publicly Funded Law Enforcement Agencies
in the United States (1974)**

Types of Law Enforcement Agencies	Number
State police/patrol agencies	49
State law enforcement agencies	355*
Sheriff's departments	3,033
County law enforcement agencies	3,333†
Municipal police departments	14,301
District/municipal/local agencies	15,983‡
Campus police organizations	406
Federal law enforcement organizations	37
Miscellaneous and quasi-law enforcement agencies	2,288§
Total	39,785

*Includes various boards and agencies with limited law enforcement responsibilities (alcoholic beverage control boards, state game and fish departments, state fire marshals, state dock authorities, etc.).
†Includes agencies with limited and specific law enforcement authority (county coroners, county detectives, county attorneys, probation and parole officers, etc.).
‡Included in this category are constable and borough police, transit district agencies, harbor police, regional crime squads in Connecticut, etc.
§Miscellaneous agencies not falling into the other categories.

Excerpted from article by John P. Granfield published in the July 1975 issue of *The Police Chief* with permission from the International Association of Chiefs of Police.

Many of these agencies consist of one person or a few persons in villages or small towns, but all are ideologically organized and function in a manner similar to the early Germanic kin-police system. That is, the police are viewed as representatives of the people or, in this case, the local community, from which they receive their authority. According to Reith, this has presented almost insuperable problems for the development of police organizations in the United States. Reith goes on to say:

> The weakness of law enforcement machinery in the United States is because of the fact that, as the people's choice, the police were allowed to become corruptly the instruments and servants not of the law, but of policy and of local and corrupt

controllers of policy. By her solution of the problem of the breakdown of the
Constable system, England was able to abolish the old system entirely, and under
the new system which she created in 1829, her police were made, entirely and
exclusively, instruments of law and not of policy and servants of the public. By
the fact of having secured independence, the United States lost the benefit of this
conception, and the development of the American police has suffered ever
since.[26]

The development of local law enforcement in the United States was often
conditioned by predisposing factors and local conditions. For example, in the
North the primary unit of local government was the town. At first, settlers in
these areas banded together in small communities for mutual protection from
Indian attacks. Later as the Industrial Revolution made its impact, these towns
grew, and so did the need for law enforcement. Since these were primarily
urban settlements, the English urban police model of the town constable or
watchman developed. As some of the cities grew even larger, more elaborate
systems were developed in which groups of night watchmen were given the
responsibility to maintain law and order and to suppress crime.

In the South, the agrarian nature of this region led to the adoption of strong
county government as the primary unit of local government. Just as the sheriff
was the primary law enforcement official in rural areas in England so did this
office become one of the most, if not the most, influential in county government
throughout the Southern states. Even today, although his authority has diminished somewhat over time, the office of the county sheriff is one of considerable importance and power in the South.

Law enforcement services in the Western United States are an amalgam of
organizational arrangements which predominated in the North and the South.
Settlers migrating westward tended to adopt police organizations like those in
the areas from which they came. Many of the same factors that led to the
creation of towns in the Northeast were also experienced in the westward
movement. For example, the necessity to form protective communities against
hostile Indian attacks resulted in the establishment of towns and the adoption of
constables or town marshals. At the same time, the vastness of the area encouraged an agrarian and livestock economy more suited to the adoption of the
county sheriff form of law enforcement. As a result of these patterns, law
enforcement services in the various regions of the country still have a somewhat
distinctive difference today. In the Northern states, municipal police are more
prevalent, while the South retains a great deal of authority in the county sheriff.
In the Western states, more of a balance is struck between the jurisdictional
authority of municipal police and the sheriff.

Municipal Police

The development of city police in the United States is inextricably a part of
the changing social, economic, and political forces that left their imprint upon

the history of municipal governance. In the early seventeenth century, major reliance was placed upon the use of military forces, perhaps assisted by a constable or night watchman. Later, the constable system replaced the military in this role. Still later, a separate day watch was established, and finally the day and night watches were combined into a single police organization.

The first night watch was established by Boston in 1636. In 1658, the city of New York added a similar unit, followed by Philadelphia in 1700. New York's night watch was referred to at the time of its creation as the ''Shiver and Shakers'' or the rattle watch, because the night watchmen used rattles to announce their presence and to communicate with each other as they made their rounds. Like their counterparts in England at the time, these watchmen were often lazy, inept, and not too reputable or honest. In a number of cases, minor offenders were sentenced to serve on the watch as punishment for their crimes. Just as in England, citizens called to serve on the watch could hire substitutes. Such was the state of the art of policing at this time. For about the next 100 years, there were no major changes in methods of providing law enforcement services. When cities grew large enough to warrant a form of law enforcement, they adopted the night watch system of Boston, New York, and Philadelphia and incorporated all their negative features.

In 1833, Philadelphia passed a city ordinance that was to prove to be a major innovation. It established the first daytime police force consisting of salaried men working under the direction of a captain appointed by the mayor. In 1854, the day police were consolidated with the night watch into one department, under the leadership of a marshal who was elected for a two-year term. During this period, the city of New York also developed a daytime police service, when the New York State legislature, in 1844, authorized communities to organize police forces and appropriated special funds that could be given to cities to provide around-the-clock police protection. By the outbreak of the Civil War, a number of other cities, such as Chicago, New Orleans, Cincinnati, Baltimore, and Newark, had adopted similar police operations, and the foundation of today's municipal police departments had been laid.

The following years were very difficult ones for the establishment of law enforcement, as the police were dominated by political interests and corruption. Departmental reports of the time indicate a condition of utter lawlessness on the part of the police themselves. For example, in 1852, documents of the New York Board of Aldermen reported such acts as assaulting superior officers, refusing to go on patrol, forcibly releasing prisoners from the custody of other policemen, drunkenness, theft, pimping, and extorting money from prisoners. These acts were daily occurrences which the police committed with impunity under the protection of their political overlords.[27] In Baltimore, Cincinnati, Boston, St. Louis, and other major cities, control of the police was vested in a patronage system, controlled by the dominant political party. In many documented cases, such as in Baltimore, the police were employed principally as an instrument of the political faction in power to control elections.[28] In nothing was the undisciplined attitude of the police more clearly shown than in their refusal to wear uniforms. The police considered it a form of degradation and servitude. Gradually, they began to wear distinctive apparel, but this was brought about more by their identification with a particular precinct or ward or group of politicians than by anything else. For example, in Philadelphia the police in one ward would wear felt hats to identify their source of patronage while those in another ward would wear white duck suits as their badge of political identification.[29]

A number of cities and states, spurred on by reform groups, tried various means to bring about change. A few states tried to take the control of local police forces in certain large cities out of the hands of the local politicians by putting the departments under state control. This attempt met with great hostility and resentment and except in a very few cities proved to be unworkable. In other cities, special supposedly nonpartisan police boards or commissions were established, and some cities still retain this arrangement.

Today, significant reform has occurred among most municipal police departments. The reasons underlying this reform are varied; the major reason, however, is that municipal government itself has come under the influence of reform, and changes in police departments are part of an overall change. In the late nineteenth and early twentieth centuries, such reform groups as the National Municipal League, the League of Women Voters, and others began developing and implementing certain programs of municipal reform with the goal of eliminating corruption, increasing efficiency of city government, and making local government more responsive to the will of the public. Although it is not possible to examine all the features of municipal reform and their interrelationships, such characteristics as the adoption of civil service systems; nomination by petition; the initiative, recall, and referendum; the short ballot; the council-manager form of government; nonpartisan elections; and certain sociological and demographic phenomena have brought significant changes to city governance and as a direct consequence to the provision of municipal police services.[30]

The State Police

In comparison with municipal police, state police agencies are of relatively recent origin. The impetus for the development of state police agencies came from a number of circumstances. One was the realization that in a number of instances corrupt and inefficient municipal law enforcement agencies and sheriff's departments were unable to provide adequate law enforcement services in their respective jurisdictions. With the failure of state governments to impose state governing boards over the operations of local law enforcement services, some states chose to create special police agencies that would have the power to enforce all state laws.

Another factor was the introduction of the automobile, which provided criminal offenders with mobility. It became increasingly difficult for local and county police agencies to apprehend criminals who could easily flee their jurisdiction. In addition, the automobile provided some unique enforcement problems of its own. As the number of automobiles increased, so did state highway systems. As a consequence, increasing attention had to be devoted to traffic regulation and control upon these highways—a type of regulation and control that had to be multijurisdictional in nature and could not be handled satisfactorily by the local police and sheriff's departments.

Finally, state governments came to the realization that they did not have an agency that could enforce the criminal code of the state or certain regulatory legislation. As it was, the state had to rely completely upon the municipal or county law enforcement officials to carry out the state's sanctions. If a particular law or regulation was unpopular or was not being enforced for whatever reason by the political subdivisions in the state, the state was powerless to compel local compliance or to force local police officials to take enforcement action.

The first state police-type agency was the Texas Rangers. This agency was established by the Texas Provisional Government in 1835 when Texas was still a republic.[31] It was originally established as a purely military unit for use on the Texas borders. Later, it began work in the area of criminal investigation and gradually developed into a state police force which proved to be effective in controlling sporadic outbreaks of anarchy caused by the absence of any law enforcement machinery in the new state. Today it is primarily concerned with the conduct of criminal investigations and rendering technical assistance to other law enforcement agencies in Texas.

Massachusetts was the next state to recognize the need for a statewide enforcement agency. In 1865, responding to the problem of uncontrolled vice in certain communities, the state legislature gave the governor authority to create a small group of state constables whose primary purpose was to investigate organized vice activities. In 1879, because of official corruption in this unit, it was reorganized into a new state investigative unit called the Massachusetts District Police, which ultimately became the Massachusetts State Police in 1920.

In 1903, Connecticut established a state investigative unit patterned after the Massachusetts District Police. Like the earlier Massachusetts constables, this unit was set up primarily to investigate vice, which had become rampant in certain communities and which local police agencies were powerless to take enforcement action against because of police corruption and political collusion. This unit also proved to be incapable of solving the problem and later was absorbed into a more effective organization known as the Connecticut State Police.

The credit for establishing the first truly professional and modern state police organization belongs to Pennsylvania. In 1905, the Pennsylvania State Constabulary was formed. It is considered the first true state police organization because the state law enforcement agencies that preceded it were created in response to limited needs, such as frontier problems or the enforcement of vice laws. This agency was established largely because local police forces in a number of areas of the state were unable to control the riots which had become a feature of the coal mining regions. Armies of coal miners fought bloody labor disputes with mercenary forces hired by mine owners and management.

It was also hoped that the new agency would improve law enforcement services in the rural areas of the state where county officials were unable to provide adequate protection. A last reason for the agency's creation, and one which is invariably cited by many who oppose the creation of state police forces today, was that Governor Pennypacker realized that he needed some assistance in carrying out the responsibilities and mandates of his office. Pennypacker issued the following statement when he created the agency:

> In the year 1903 when I assumed the office of chief executive of the state, I found myself thereby invested with supreme executive authority. I found that no power existed to interfere with me in my duty to enforce the laws of the state, and that by the same token, no condition could release me from my duty to do so. I then looked about me to see what instruments I possessed wherewith to accomplish this bounded obligation—what instruments on whose loyalty and obedience I could truly rely. I perceived three such instruments—my private secretary, a very small man; my woman stenographer; and the janitor. So, I made the state police.[32]

Other characteristics which entitle the Pennsylvania State Police to be considered the first such agency were organizational and jurisdictional in nature. In terms of organization, this agency was under the administrative control of a superintendent appointed by the governor. Troop detachments and substations were situated throughout the state so that protection was afforded in even the most remote areas.[33] This organizational arrangement and deployment of personnel served as the model for other state police agencies. In terms of jurisdiction, this agency was empowered to enforce all state laws throughout Pennsylvania.

Today, some states have bona fide state police departments and others have primarily traffic enforcement agencies, commonly referred to as *highway patrols*. There are some basic distinctions between the two. State police agencies have full jurisdiction and authority to enforce all state laws anywhere in the state. Their responsibilities are quite broad. For example, state police agencies in Pennsylvania, New York, and Michigan provide a full range of police services and support activities. In addition to performing routine patrol and traffic enforcement activities, they have investigative units that investigate major crimes, intelligence units that investigate organized crime activities, juvenile units, crime lab services, statewide computer facilities that compile crime data for the state, and other related functions.

Highway patrol organizations, on the other hand, such as those in Florida, Georgia, Ohio, and California, are mainly specialists in traffic regulation and enforcement. For the most part, their responsibilities are to enforce traffic laws on state and interstate highway systems. In some cases, they have the responsibility to investigate crimes that occur in specific locations or under specific circumstances, such as on state highways or state property or involving the use of public carriers. For the most part, their investigative resources and functions are quite limited, and their support and technical services relate specifically to traffic. States having such units usually have separate small investigative agencies that assist the highway patrol organizations and other local and county police agencies, but operate under very limited jurisdictional authority. For example, Georgia has a state investigative bureau under its department of public safety, but the bureau is not permitted to conduct investigations in the political subdivisions of that state without the approval of the local county sheriff.

Many state legislative bodies, faced with the growing volume of automobile traffic on state highways, recognized the need for a statewide regulatory police agency but were reluctant to create anything but a traffic control agency. As a consequence, the legislation which created highway patrol agencies was purposely designed to ensure that these bodies would be little more than traffic enforcement units. The reluctance to give these agencies full state police authority was the result of several factors: First, traditionally in our nation's history there has been a mistrust of the executive. Many legislators were afraid that a state police under the control of the governor would become an instrument of oppression that the governor could control at will and could easily use against his political opposition. The early use of such organizations as the Pennsylvania State Police in strike-breaking activities engendered a great deal of hostility among supporters of organized labor, who campaigned vigorously in a number of states against establishment of state police forces. This opposition combined with the legislator's traditional hostility for increasing in any way the power of the chief executive proved to be decisive.

Finally, the strong political connections of local law enforcement officials, particularly the county sheriffs, were brought to bear. These officials perceived the creation of a state police system as a direct threat to their own enforcement responsibilities and authority. Today, strong sheriff associations exist in almost every state and at the national level. Suggestions that highway patrol agencies be expanded into state police organizations are met with furious opposition from these organizations, which have become quite adept and powerful in local political circles and in state capitals.

The fact that these fears have never materialized in those states that have given their state police full police authority seems to be of no concern to those interests opposed to the concept of a state police.[34] Similarly, the fact that the state police have reached, in many states, a level of professionalism and detachment from control of political interests far beyond those of county and municipal police agencies seems to also have had little bearing. In many ways, the lack of a state police organization is an unfortunate and costly disservice to the citizenry of these states, who deserve and pay for far better law enforcement than they often receive from their local departments.

County Law Enforcement

In most areas, the law enforcement services in rural and unincorporated portions of a county are handled by the sheriff's department, while municipal police forces serve their respective cities.

As we have seen, the office of the sheriff has a very ancient lineage which dates back to eighth-century England. Under the tithing system, a reeve was given the responsibility for coordinating and directing the activities of the tithing members throughout the shire (county). Appointed by the local earl, the shire reeve was the earl's chief ministerial representative in the shire.

These shire reeves were very powerful and influential local officials. Among their responsibilities were to protect and oversee the earl's property and the property of the king which the earl was obligated to protect. In addition, they were responsible for the collection of taxes, overseeing the conduct of local tribunals while serving as chief magistrate of these courts, the apprehension and prosecution of those who violated the king's law, and other minor administrative tasks. Thus, unlike today's sheriffs these early shire reeves were not only responsible for the law enforcement or executive tasks of governance, but the judicial responsibilities as well—their role was to apprehend, try, and punish the offender in a very simplified and seemingly crude and perverted form of justice.[35] The American Colonies adopted the idea of sheriff as an important county office, but by the time of the settlement of the Colonies, the sheriff had become primarily a law enforcement and custodial officer with no direct judicial powers.

Because of a combination of historical and political reasons, the sheriffs in many states have broad authority and power. In thirty-three states, the sheriff is a constitutional officer and is regarded as the chief law enforcement officer in the county. This authority stems from early English law which invested the sheriff with the power of *posse comitatus,* that is, authority to coordinate the activities of all other local police agencies. The sheriff's political power is derived from the fact that the office is part of the county's plural executive. The sheriff's political status and the visibility of the police function make the sheriff a key political figure. Historically, the argument for retaining the sheriff's constitutional powers has been based on the need to protect the independence of the office. Politically, the office has retained this status because of its pivotal place in local party politics.

Today, the office of the sheriff has three primary responsibilities. The first is to provide law enforcement services in the county. Whether the sheriff will provide law enforcement services to municipalities in the county is contingent upon a number of factors. Some states, by virtue of home rule and other statutory provisions, have given the authority to cities to provide their own police departments. In some states, when this grant of authority is given, the city police department has primary jurisdiction over all offenses committed therein, and the sheriff's department has authority and jurisdiction only outside the municipality except in a few instances. However, many states still recognize the chief law enforcement function of this official throughout the entire county and give the sheriff full authority and jurisdiction within communities. Often an agreement is reached between cities and the sheriff's department whereby the latter will not enforce the criminal laws within the community except to take specific action in cases such as official police corruption, civil strife, or other conditions which might warrant his department's intervention.

The other two responsibilities of this office are to maintain the county jail and care for the prisoners and to serve as an officer of the county courts. The sheriff often receives many of the prisoners who have been arrested in the county. In some cases, particularly where there are larger cities within the county, the city police retain arrestees in city jails, pending trial. Even where cities have their own jail facilities, however, they often transfer more serious offenders to the county jail before trial because of the presence of greater security measures and other facilities that city jails do not provide. Even a serious felon who has been retained in city jail will usually be transferred to the county jail after the trial to await transportation to a state institution.

As an officer of the county courts, the sheriff has numerous responsibilities. Often, this office provides personnel to serve as court bailiffs, transports prisoners to and from the courts, transports juveniles that have been adjudicated as delinquents and sentenced to institutions, and transports mental patients who have been remanded to state mental health facilities. The sheriff's department is also responsible for certain civil process matters such as court-ordered liens, service of forfeiture and eviction notices, divorce papers, the sale of confiscated property, administration and sale of foreclosed property, and related civil judgments as directed by the courts. Figure 5-1 shows the typical organizational arrangement of a medium-sized sheriff's department.

In recent years, the enforcement responsibilities of the sheriff's department have come under a great deal of attack from such prestigious groups as the Committee for Economic Development and the Advisory Commission on Intergovernmental Relations.[36] These and other groups argue that too many sheriff's departments are infused with self-serving political interests that detract from their professional law enforcement role. On balance, many of these criticisms are probably justified when one examines the characteristics of these agencies on a national scale. In too many documented cases, these agencies become patronage empires for the sheriff and other elected county officials who use this office to reward their political followers. As a consequence, personnel not being afforded civil service protection in most of these agencies constantly change and are replaced. Modern law enforcement requires extensive training

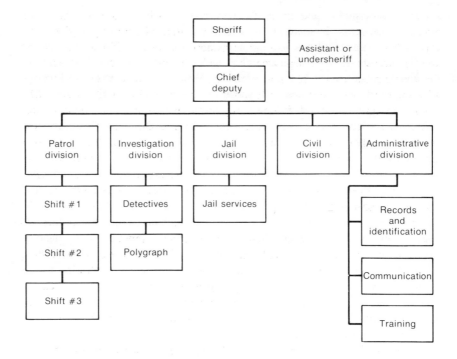

Figure 5-1   Administrative Organization of a Medium-size
              Sheriff's Department

and knowledge that personnel in these agencies do not have when hired and do not acquire on the job. In many instances, the sheriff is more a politician than a professional in law enforcement.

Although sheriff's departments are often particularly susceptible to criticism because of their poor selection standards, lack of training, and quality of service, there are certainly exceptions. In fact, a number of these departments, particularly in California, are among the finest law enforcement organizations in the United States. The Los Angeles County Sheriff's Department is one of the most professionally well-equipped and trained police agencies in the nation. The Multnomah County (Oregon) Sheriff's Department was one of the first agencies to require a four-year college degree as a condition of employment. The unfortunate fact is that too often such standards among sheriff's departments are the exception rather than the rule.

In recent years, a number of recommendations have been made to improve county law enforcement. One suggestion has been to abolish the constitutional authority of the sheriff and invest the office only with statutory powers. This idea is in line with county reform efforts designed to replace the plural executive organization of county government with centralized county administration represented by a county chief executive or county board of commissioners. This type of county reorganization seeks to increase the accountability of county agencies. As long as the sheriff retains constitutional status, however, it is nearly impossible for county officials to maintain meaningful control and accountability over the actions of the sheriff's department.

Another recommendation is that states provide, through appropriate legislation, the option of assigning basic responsibility for countywide police services to an independent county police force under the control of the county chief executive or county board of commissioners. Today, there are about sixty such county police departments throughout the United States. Many counties which have adopted the county police department have given this agency full authority and responsibility to perform all law enforcement functions. In many cases, the sheriff's department has been retained, but its responsibilities have been limited to maintenance of the jail and providing the usual services to the county courts.

Unfortunately, these reorganizations have created a vexatious problem for some communities. Much of the problem is brought about by the legal and political traditions inherent in the sheriff's office. Georgia, for example, recognizes the sheriff as a constitutional officer, yet permits counties to establish independent police agencies. As a consequence, a few counties in that state not satisfied with the quality of service provided by the sheriff have created county police departments, yet are forced to retain the sheriff, who still has the same full responsibilities. Thus, two police agencies have responsibility for law enforcement services outside municipalities in those counties. This duplication is costly, and citizens do not know whether to call the sheriff's department or the county police. A great deal of political acrimony has also been apparent between the heads of these two agencies as well as among political supporters and elected officials who side with the sheriff or with the county police. This results in charges and countercharges of incompetence, poor service, corruption, and a host of other claims being leveled at one agency by supporters of the other.

There would seem to be an immediate need to reappraise the office of the sheriff and its enforcement responsibilities. The Advisory Commission on Intergovernmental Relations recommended that states give metropolitan counties the option of assigning basic responsibility for countywide police services to an independent county police force under the control of the county chief executives or county board of commissioners. As part of this arrangement, the sheriff's department would turn over all court and jail duties to the appropriate court and correctional agencies.[37] Although this recommendation might have some merit, it is impractical. What may be a more valid solution is for the states to begin enacting legislation to force sheriff's agencies to become more professional. Such legislation would place sheriff's department personnel under civil service, require them to be compensated solely on a salary basis, provide them with adequate retirement benefits, and require them to undergo a specified period of training.

In the years to come, many states will probably begin to require that sheriff's departments measure up to the challenges before them. Already, a number of states have begun to take a closer look at these agencies and are at least thinking about enacting legislation that would require some fundamental changes in the traditional operations and policies of this office.

SUMMARY

The police are the gatekeepers of the system of criminal justice. Although we usually think of the police in their role as law enforcers, they also provide a great many services that are not directly associated with this role. In fact, the police spend more of their time in providing non-enforcement-related services than in enforcing laws.

The organization of police service as we know it is less than 150 years old. During the history of Western civilization, various organizational arrangements were employed to enforce laws. As society became more complex, methods for providing police services were modified and improved. The fear that a centralized and full-time police service could be employed to restrict individual liberties was particularly apparent in England, which eventually developed a law enforcement service that was to be copied in the United States.

The history of law enforcement in America, particularly in our cities, is not a proud one. Early city police departments were often corrupt organizations that served the interests of political factions more than they did the community. Gradually, as municipal reform became a reality in the late nineteenth and early twentieth centuries, the improvement of law enforcement began and continues to this day.

In a number of states, vice conditions, poor local law enforcement services, and the advent of the automobile made it necessary to create statewide police agencies. These agencies are of two types: state police and highway patrol organizations. Usually, the distinction between the two is the enforcement authority they possess.

Most sheriff's departments have responsibilities beyond merely providing law enforcement services to rural areas. The enforcement responsibilities of sheriffs' departments have come under a great deal of criticism in recent years. Although a few states have tried to limit these responsibilities, sheriff's departments continue to provide a broad range of services in most states.

Suggested Additional Readings

Ahern, James R. *Police in Trouble*. New York: Hawthorn, 1972.
Banton, Michael. *The Policeman in the Community*. New York: Basic Books, 1964.

Berkeley, George. *The Democratic Policeman*. Boston: Beacon Press, 1969.

Black, Algernon D. *The People and the Police*. New York: McGraw-Hill, 1968.

Blumberg, Abraham. *Law and Order: The Scales of Justice*. New York: Aldine, 1970.

Chapman, Brian. *Police State*. New York: Praeger, 1970.

Germann, A. C., Frank D. Day, and Robert R. J. Gallati. *Introduction to Law Enforcement and Criminal Justice*. Springfield, Ill.: Charles C. Thomas, 1973.

Maas, Peter. *Serpico*. New York: Bantam, 1973.

Niederhoffer, Arthur. *Behind the Shield: The Police in Urban Society*. Garden City, N.Y.: Doubleday, 1967.

———— and Abraham Blumberg. *The Ambivalent Force: Perspectives on the Police*. Lexington, Mass.: Ginn, 1970.

Reiss, Albert J. *The Police and the Public*. New Haven, Conn.: Yale University Press, 1971.

Skolnick, Jerome. *Justice without Trial: Law Enforcement in a Democratic Society*. New York: Wiley, 1966.

———— *The Politics of Protest*. New York: Simon & Schuster, 1968.

Westley, William A. *Violence and the Police*. Cambridge, Mass.: M.I.T. Press, 1971.

Notes

1. For example, see: Joseph Goldstein, "Police Discretion Not to Invoke the Criminal Process: Low-Visibility Decisions in the Administration of Justice," *Yale Law Journal* 69 (March 1960): 543–594; and Wayne LaFave, "The Police and Nonenforcement of the Law," *Wisconsin Law Review,* Part 1 (January 1962): 104–137; Part 2 (March 1962): 179–239.

2. George F. Cole, *Politics and the Administration of Justice* (Beverly Hills, Calif.: Sage, 1973), p. 76.

3. James Q. Wilson, *Varieties of Police Behavior* (Cambridge, Mass.: Harvard, 1968), p. 16.

4. Cole, op. cit., p. 78.

5. Ibid.

6. For example, see Egan Bittner, "The Police on Skid Row: A Study of Peace Keeping," *American Sociological Review* 32 (October 1967): 699–715.

7. Elaine Cumming, et al., "Policeman as Philosopher, Guide and Friend," *Social Problems* 12 (1965): 267–286.

8. Thomas E. Bercal, "Calls for Police Assistance: Consumer Demands for Governmental Service," *American Behavioral Scientist* 13 (1970): 681–691.

9. James Cramer, *The World's Police* (London: Cassel, 1964), p. 5.

10. Ibid., pp. 8–9.

11. Zoe Oldenbourg, *The Crusades* (New York: Random House, 1966), p. 11.

12. Ibid., p. 16.

13. Michael A. Saint-Mont, *History of English Civil Law* (London: Carthington, 1916), p. 20.

14. Cramer, op. cit., p. 12.

15. Ibid., p. 14.

16. Charles Reith, *The Blind Eye of History: A Study of the Origins of the Present Police Era* (London: Faber, 1912), p. 31.

17. Ibid., p. 31.

18. Ibid.

19. Ibid.

20. Ibid., p. 137.

21. For example, see Patrick Pringle, *Hue and Cry: The Birth of the British Police* (London: Museum Press, 1955); Charles Reith, op. cit., pp. 148-149; and Albert Lieck, *Justice and Police in England* (London: Butterworth, 1936).

22. A. C. Germann, Frank Day, and Robert Gallati, *Introduction to Law Enforcement and Criminal Justice*, (Springfield, Ill: Charles C Thomas, 1973), pp. 61–62.

23. Anwar Syed, *The Political Theory of American Local Government* (New York: Random House, 1966), p. 38.

24. See, for example Bruce Smith, *Police Systems in the United States*, 2d rev. ed. (New York: Harper, 1960), p. 22; and Committee for Economic Development, *Reducing Crime and Assuring Justice* (New York: CED, 1972), p. 30.

25. John P. Granfield, "Publicly Funded Law Enforcement Agencies in the U.S.," *Police Chief* 42 (7) (July 1975): 26.

26. Reith, op. cit., pp. 82–83.

27. Documents of the New York Board of Aldermen, Document No. 53, pp. 1047ff.

28. Raymond B. Fosdick, *American Police Systems* (New York: Century, 1920), p. 68.

29. James T. Allison and Robert T. Penrose, *Philadelphia, 1681-1887, A History of Municipal Development* (Baltimore: Johns Hopkins Studies in Historical and Political Science, vol. II, 1887), pp. 37–41.

30. For an excellent analysis of the reform movement in municipal government, see Edward C. Banfield and James Q. Wilson, *City Politics* (New York: Random House, 1966); Richard Hofstadter, *The Age of Reform* (New York: Knopf, 1955), especially chap. IV; Lorin Petersen, *The Day of the Mugwump* (New York: Random House, 1961); Frank M. Steward, *A Half Century of Municipal Reform: The History of the National Municipal League* (Berkeley: University of California Press, 1950); and T. R. Mason, "Reform Politics in Boston" (unpublished dissertation) Department of Government, Harvard University, 1963.

31. Vern L. Folley, *American Law Enforcement* (Boston: Holbrook Press, 1973), p. 64.

32. Katherine Mayo, *Justice to All: The Story of the Pennsylvania State Police* (New York: Putnam, 1917), pp. 5–6.

33. Folley, op. cit., p. 67.

34. Committee for Economic Development, op. cit., p. 31.

35. T. A. Tobias, *The History of English Law* (London: Westholver and Westholver, 1920), pp. 109–110.

36. See Advisory Commission on Intergovernmental Relations, *State-Local Relations in the Criminal Justice System* (Washington, D.C.: U.S. Government Printing Office, 1971); and Committee for Economic Development, op. cit.

37. Advisory Commission on Intergovernmental Relations, op. cit., p. 27.

UMMONS IN A CIVIL ACTION

United States District Court

FOR THE

District of Columbia

1593-73

CIVIL ACTION FILE NO

SENATE SELECT COMMITTEE ON PRESIDENTIAL
CAMPAIGN ACTIVITIES, suing in its own
name and in the name of the UNITED STATES,
et al

Plaintiff s

v.

SUMMONS

RICHARD M. NIXON, individually and as
President of the United States

Defendant

To the above named Defendant :

You are hereby summoned and required to serve upon

SAMUEL DASH
Chief Counsel

plaintiff's attorney , whose address   is   United States Senate
Washington, D. C. 20510

an answer to the complaint which is herewith served upon you, within 60 days after service of this
summons upon you, exclusive of the day of service. If you fail to do so, judgment by default will be
taken against you for the relief demanded in the complaint.

JAMES F. DAVEY

Clerk of Court.

Deputy Clerk.

Date: August 9, 1973   [Seal of Court]

NOTE:—This summons is issued pursuant to Rule 4 of the Federal Rules of Civil Procedure.

Chapter 6

Law Enforcement Efforts of the Federal Government

Law enforcement at the federal level is characterized by certain distinctive features. In the first place, most federal enforcement agencies are highly specialized units which concentrate only on certain specific offenses as contained in the U.S. Criminal Code. Because of this, the jurisdictional authority of most of these agencies is quite limited. Since Congress has been reluctant to expand the enforcement responsibilities of existing agencies, the number of separate agencies scattered throughout the executive branch has proliferated. For example, the Departments of Agriculture, Labor, Justice, Defense, Treasury, Interior, and others have developed law enforcement or quasi-enforcement agencies to deal with criminal and regulatory functions. In addition, a number of independent regulatory bodies, such as the Interstate Commerce Commission, the Securities and Exchange Commission, and the Federal Trade Commission, perform certain regulatory and compliance functions requiring enforcement and quasi-enforcement units.

In many instances, the enforcement problems of local and state governments are mirrored in the operations of federal law enforcement agencies. Jurisdictional disputes, lack of coordination among different agencies, agency rivalries, lack of communication, and failure to share intelligence information and other resources have created some very serious problems for the effective enforcement of federal laws. And, given the nature of the federal bureaucracy, the problems seem even less amenable to solution than similar problems among the political subdivision in our states.

In 1789, when the Constitution was finally ratified, the "police" provisions of the federal government were quite specific and narrow. The framers of the Constitution wanted to form a stronger central government than had existed under the Articles of Confederation, but they were aware that the new states would not accept too strong a national government. As a consequence, they vested only certain powers in the national government and reserved the rest for the states.[1] Among the important specific police powers originally vested in the federal government were those given to Congress to "lay and collect taxes," "to regulate commerce," "to establish post offices and post roads," and "to provide for the punishment of counterfeiting."[2] These powers have played a very important role in the creation of federal police agencies, as much of the enforcement authority of federal agencies hinges on the power of taxation and the regulation of interstate commerce. With the expansion of taxation legislation and the interpretation of Congress and the federal courts as to what can be considered interstate commerce, the law enforcement authority of the federal government has grown substantially. Federal law enforcement authority has also derived from the power of Congress to enact all "necessary and proper" laws and from the federal judiciary's interpretation of the Fourteenth Amendment, and from the immediate need of the federal government to enforce new laws and court rulings.

Although the beginning student of criminal justice should be aware that there are many agencies of the federal government that provide specialized law enforcement careers for young men and women, it is not possible to examine each of them. Instead, only the major agencies can be examined in any meaningful way. Since a large share of enforcement activities of the federal government are centered in the Departments of Justice, Treasury, and Defense and in the Postal Service, each of these will be examined closely. In addition, a few specialized agencies will be considered briefly.

DEPARTMENT OF JUSTICE

The Department of Justice is responsible for the major enforcement functions of the federal government. To accomplish its broad enforcement responsibilities, it incorporates such agencies as the Federal Bureau of Investigation, the Immigration and Naturalization Service, the Drug Enforcement Administration, the U.S. Marshal Service, and the Organized Crime and Racketeering Section. It also includes the Law Enforcement Assistance Administration, which (though not an enforcement agency) has in recent years played a significant national role in the administration of criminal justice.

The Federal Bureau of Investigation

The FBI is the chief investigative arm of the Department of Justice. Although the office of attorney general was established in 1789, the Department of Justice was not created until 1870, when the problems of post-Civil War reconstruction and the need to centralize and coordinate the federal government's legal activities led to its formation. Before that time, the prosecution of federal violators was handled separately by the various governmental departments. By an act of Congress in 1870, the attorney general was given this responsibility, and with the help of one "special agent," the use of U.S. marshals, borrowed

Secret Service agents, or hired private detectives, the enforcement activities of the Department of Justice began.[3]

Although a number of later attorneys general tried to persuade Congress to appropriate funds for a special group of investigators for the Department of Justice, Congress adamantly refused. In 1907, Attorney General Charles S. Bonaparte again tried to persuade Congress to create a small group of investigative personnel that were to be employed solely by the Department of Justice. As in the past, opposition from Congress was immediate. Many members of Congress and private citizens feared that the creation of such a unit would develop into a federal secret police. Members of Congress pointed out that there was no need to establish an additional police force since there already existed the Treasury Department's Secret Service and the Post Office inspectors.

Many of the nation's leading newspapers were also opposed to the idea. Again, the fear of a centralized police agency came to the forefront. Among the allegations that the newspapers expressed was that such an idea was contrary to democratic principles, that there was no need for a national police organization, and even that it would make Attorney General Bonaparte, grandnephew of Napoleon I, a possible dictator.

In 1908, Congress responded by prohibiting the use of Secret Service agents by the Justice Department. It was felt that this would ensure that the Department of Justice would not become too powerful.

Undaunted, Bonaparte continued his efforts. In June of 1908, he requested that the chief of the Secret Service give him a list of men who had worked with the Justice Department. From the list he then selected nine men who were immediately transferred to the Department of Justice to become investigators. As this was done, President Theodore Roosevelt issued an executive order which established a small law enforcement unit as a permanent subdivision of the Department of Justice. This force consisted of the nine former Secret Service agents and fourteen previously hired special agents.[4]

When Congress reconvened, it summoned Bonaparte to a special hearing and sought to bring him to task for his action. He argued that the unit was so small that it could not possibly be considered a threat to national governance and that Congress had forced him to establish such a unit when it prohibited the use of Secret Service agents from the Treasury Department. Roosevelt also intervened in behalf of the new unit. The President pointed out that the commission of federal crimes was rising at an alarming rate and that such an investigative unit was desperately needed.

Still, Congress refused to pass legislation authorizing a permanent investigative agency in the Department of Justice. For several months, congressional inquiry and debates continued. Finally, a compromise that carefully restricted the investigative authority of the unit was proposed. Congress accepted this proposal and authorized the establishment of the Bureau of Investigation in 1909. The authority of the new agency was limited to investigations of treason, murder on Indian reservations and government properties, opium smuggling, impersonation of a federal officer, and a few other federal crimes.[5]

In 1910, Congress passed the Mann Act, which prohibited the transportation of females in interstate commerce for purposes of prostitution and other crimes involving interstate commerce. Enforcement of this law was turned over to the Bureau of Investigation. During World War I, espionage and selective service violations were added to its jurisdiction, and in 1919 Congress passed the National Motor Vehicle Theft Act, which increased the scope of its authority.

Although the Bureau of Investigation can be credited with some noteworthy achievements during this time, especially with recovering large areas of public lands that had been illegally taken over by private citizens, these accomplishments were clouded over by serious defects. The agency was poorly managed and organized and was itself often engaged in extralegal activities for corrupt politicians. Men with criminal records were sometimes appointed, and the bureau conducted brutal raids, illegal searches, and massive dragnet operations aimed at locating draft dodgers or aliens accused of sabotage. Innocent citizens were frequently arrested during these operations. As a result, there was serious talk about disbanding the bureau and transferring its jurisdiction to other federal agencies.[6]

In 1924, a young government attorney by the name of J. Edgar Hoover was given the task of restructuring the agency and weeding out the corruption. Hoover agreed to accept the directorship only if the attorney general would assure him that the bureau would be free of politics and all appointments and promotions would be based on merit. These conditions were accepted, and he was appointed director. He immediately set to work reorganizing the bureau, establishing new administrative procedures, and initiating a general clean-up campaign. He removed incompetent and unreliable personnel, and all applicants were thoroughly investigated as to their character and ability before appointment. In 1935, Congress changed the name of the Bureau of Investigation to the now familiar Federal Bureau of Investigation.[7]

The FBI Today

Although the image of Hoover, and indeed of the entire agency, has been besmirched in recent years because of its alleged preoccupation with internal communism, the Nixon appointment of Patrick Grey as Hoover's successor, and alleged abuses in connection with the domestic surveillance of private citizens, the bureau overall still has a tradition of excellence unequaled by any other American law enforcement agency.

Today, the legal jurisdiction of this agency has been extended over all federal crimes not specifically the responsibility of another federal law enforcement agency. At the present time, this numbers about 185 offenses. Among the more significant crimes that come under FBI jurisdiction are kidnapping; robbery, burglary, or embezzlement of funds from any member bank of the Federal Reserve System or any bank insured by the Federal Deposit Insurance Corporation; theft, embezzlement, or robbery of federal property; piracy of aircraft and other crimes aboard aircraft; interstate flight of a person to avoid prosecution, custody, or confinement after conviction for a felony or to avoid giving testimony in any felony proceedings; violation of the Civil Rights Act that indicates racial discrimination in public accommodations, facilities, public education, and certain areas of private employment; and interstate gambling and organized crime. In addition, although the protection of the president falls under the jurisdictional authority of the Secret Service, an assault upon, kidnapping of, or killing of any federal officer, including the president, or any conspiracy or attempt to do so, would be an investigative responsibility of the FBI.[8]

The FBI is organized into ten operating divisions under a director, an associate director, deputy associate director, and two assistants to the director. These ten divisions are:

Identification Division

This division was created in 1924 to provide a national repository and clearinghouse for fingerprints. The division began by consolidating the criminal records of the International Association of Chiefs of Police (IACP) and those maintained by the military authorities at Leavenworth Penitentiary. Today, this division maintains in excess of 2 million fingerprints, which are classified into civil and criminal categories and which it receives from other agencies of criminal justice, the armed services, and civilian government agencies. Access to these records is strictly limited to appropriate governmental agencies.

An important component of this division is the Disaster Squad, which is available to state and local police agencies to assist them in identifying victims of major tragedies such as airline crashes. In 1974, nearly 30,000 fingerprints were submitted daily to this division and over 40,000 fugitives were identified.[9] The division also exchanges fingerprint information with eighty-seven noncommunist nations.

Training Division

This unit maintains and conducts the FBI training program for newly appointed agents at Quantico, Virginia. It also conducts the National Academy Program at this site for selected state and local law enforcement officers throughout the United States and police officials from friendly nations. An additional responsibility is to develop training programs and resource personnel among the FBI special agents, who then conduct in-service training programs at various locations throughout the country for state and local police personnel.

Administrative Division

This division is concerned with fiscal and budgetary matters required to administer the bureau.

Files and Communications Division

This division controls and maintains FBI files and the teletype, telephone, and radio network of the FBI which links the Washington headquarters of the bureau to all field offices.

Special Investigative Division

This division deals with organized crime and criminal intelligence in that area; security of government employees; and apprehension of escaped federal prisoners, fugitives from justice, and deserters from the armed forces.[10]

Crime Records Division

This unit gathers, compiles, and studies the great volume of information on crime and subversion which pours in every day from the field offices and other federal, state, and local police agencies.

In 1967, the FBI implemented a computerized crime information gathering and dissemination service known as the National Crime Information Center (NCIC). Under this arrangement, each state has a number of computer terminals that interface with the FBI master computer in Washington. On file in the computer records in Washington are records of stolen property and persons wanted for major crimes. This information is fed into the NCIC computer network by state, local, and other federal law enforcement agencies throughout the nation. In this way, a police officer in Colorado, for example, who is following a car with Tennessee plates that he or she believes to be stolen can contact the police dispatcher by radio, and the dispatcher in turn will relay the inquiry to an NCIC computer terminal in Colorado, which then makes a direct inquiry to Washington. In a matter of seconds, the officer will be notified whether the automobile bearing the Tennessee plates is listed with NCIC as stolen.

Laboratory Division

This division, founded in 1932, provides a wide range of scientific skills as an aid in the investigation of crimes. The services of the laboratory are available without charge to local and state law enforcement agencies. The FBI will even provide the court and testimony services of laboratory specialists who have examined the evidence submitted by a local or state police agency. The laboratory is divided into four sections: (1) the Document Section, which deals with

United Press International

the examination of handwriting, hand printing, typewriting, forgeries, fraudulent checks, paper, inks, printing, shoe prints, tire treads, and related matters;
(2) the Physics and Chemistry Section, which makes scientific examinations
through chemistry, toxicology, metallurgy, spectrography, etc., on such items
of evidence as firearms, fibers, glass, blood, hairs, and many others; (3) the
Radio Engineering Section, which develops new communications equipment
for field use and establishes and maintains a network of radio stations for
emergency use; and (4) the Cryptanalysis-Translation Section, which is primarily responsible for examining cipher messages and codes and translating documents.

Domestic Intelligence Division

This section investigates matters involving espionage, sabotage, and subversion and gathers evidence for use in legal proceedings.

General Investigation Division

This division supervises the investigation of most of the federal crimes that fall under the jurisdiction of the FBI but are not the express responsibilities of other specialized divisions, for example, bank robbery, burglary, larceny, theft of government property, interstate transportation of stolen vehicles, interstate travel in aid of racketeering, civil rights violations, and the assaulting or killing of a federal officer.

Inspection Division

This division oversees the operations of the FBI in order to improve them and to ensure that its policies and procedures develop the administrative, supervisory, and investigative resources of the entire agency to their full potential.

Immigration and Naturalization Service

This agency, created in 1891, is responsible for administering the immigration and naturalization laws, which relate to the admission, exclusion, deportation, and naturalization of aliens. Under the Immigration and Nationality Act, the INS screens applicants for admission to this country in an effort to exclude thirty-one categories of persons deemed to be "undesirable aliens" because of criminal histories, moral turpitude, or other related reasons. The agency also investigates aliens in order to identify those engaged in various types of criminal activity and is responsible for the detention and deportation of those illegally entering the United States. The service maintains records of all persons granted or denied admission. Its Border Patrol works to prevent the illegal entry of aliens and the smuggling of illegal goods or contraband.

The Border Patrol was created in 1924, when Congress allocated funds for the establishment of a border patrol unit within the then existing Bureau of Immigration; a group of 450 officers were assigned to the unit.[11] Today, the Border Patrol is divided into twenty-two sectors, each headed by a chief Border Patrol agent. In each sector there are usually two assistant chief Border Patrol agents, one intelligence officer, a Border Patrol pilot, and any number of Border Patrol stations. The Border Patrol is most active on our borders with Canada and Mexico. Its primary responsibility is to deter entry of illegal aliens and goods. In recent years, a great deal of its efforts have centered on our common border with Mexico in an attempt to intercept and arrest those involved in smuggling narcotics. In many instances, the Border Patrol is involved in joint investigations with other federal and local police agencies in these areas as well as with the Mexican police. Since the traffic in drugs along our borders has become such a serious problem, investigation and efforts to stem this flow have required massive and cooperative efforts by various federal and local agencies as well as international cooperation.

Drug Enforcement Administration

This agency was created in 1973, when Congress approved consolidation of the former Bureau of Narcotics and Dangerous Drugs, the Office of National Narcotics Intelligence, the Office for Drug Abuse Law Enforcement, and the drug investigation and drug intelligence operation of the U.S. Customs Service into one major federal agency with overall responsibility to enforce the federal narcotics and dangerous drug laws. This major reorganization occurred after previous attempts to stem the problem of narcotics had failed owing partly to the fragmentation among various federal agencies of jurisdictional authority relating to illegal narcotics.[12] Ever since the Hoover Commission's Report on Governmental Reorganization in 1949, various commissions had recommended such consolidation of federal enforcement agencies. Finally, the seriousness of the narcotics problem forced Congress to act and create a consolidated federal agency to deal with this specific problem.

The basic responsibility of the DEA is the control of the distribution and use of narcotics and dangerous drugs. Its major targets are those organized groups that deal in the growth, distribution, and marketing of these drugs. Its enforcement efforts are therefore directed at national and international cartels that control the manufacturing and distribution networks. It operates its own network of enforcement personnel and regional laboratories throughout the United States and in thirty-one foreign countries. Often, this agency also conducts investigations with local and state police in which major drug traffickers are involved.

To assist state and local governments to combat illicit drugs, it has developed specialized training programs which attract state and local police department members from throughout the country. It also conducts specialized narcotics training programs for police personnel of foreign countries in such diverse places as Mexico, Peru, Australia, and the Philippines. As does the FBI, the DEA makes available to other police agencies the scientific expertise of its crime labs and provides expert scientific testimony on evidence these labs receive and analyze for local and state police agencies. This agency is also authorized to regulate and inspect nearly 5,000 licensed drug manufacturing and distribution firms to prevent possible diversion of legally manufactured drugs to illicit sources.

U.S. Marshal Service

The office of marshal appeared in England shortly after the Norman conquest. As this ancient office developed, the marshal became the court officer whose duty it was to escort into the courts the offender, the victim, and the witnesses to the crime. Today, there are two types of marshals in the United States. Some small communities which are not large enough to require a municipal police department have a town marshal who is the equivalent of a chief of police. In some instances, the town marshall may hire deputies to assist in providing law enforcement services in these communities, but usually the position is a part-time one. Town marshals are also usually responsible for serving the local municipal or mayor's court. In this capacity, they may be called upon to serve subpoenas and arrest warrants and escort prisoners to trial.

The other type of marshal is the U.S. marshal, a federal law enforcement officer who serves the federal courts under the jurisdiction of the U.S. attorney general. Although the Colonies had marshals who performed law enforcement services, it was not until the passage of the Judiciary Act of 1789 that this office became a federal one. This act prescribed the judicial structure of the federal government and authorized the appointment of a U.S. marshal for each state and territory to service these newly created federal courts.

The first U.S. marshals were appointed by President Washington for four-year terms. In 1801, this appointive power of the president was recognized by law. These early U.S. marshals performed a wide variety of assignments for the federal government. They were directed by Congress to take the census, hire and supervise jails for federal prisoners, take into custody all vessels and goods seized by revenue officers, sell lands possessed by the United States, serve as fiscal agents of the courts, and perform other miscellaneous tasks as directed.[13]

We all know that U.S. marshals played a very important role as law enforcement officers in the Old West. In many instances, they were the only federal law enforcement personnel in the Western states and territories.[14] Although the federal government had Post Office inspectors and later Secret Service agents in these areas, these two groups were too small in numbers and had too limited jurisdiction to be of much help in maintaining law and order. As a result, the responsibility of enforcing most federal laws fell to the U.S. marshals.[15]

The modern office of U.S. marshal has undergone two major reorganizations in recent years. The last major reorganization occurred in 1969, when the United States Marshal Service was created. The service was placed under the authority of a director supervised by the deputy attorney general, the second in command in the Department of Justice. The director of the U.S. Marshal Service supervises ninety-four U.S. marshals in districts covering the fifty states, the District of Columbia, the Canal Zone, Guam, the Virgin Islands, and Puerto Rico. All U.S. marshals (except the U.S. marshal for the Virgin Islands) are appointed by the president with the consent of the Senate for four-year terms.

In each of the federal judicial districts then, there is a U.S. marshal, who is authorized by the attorney general to appoint the necessary number of deputy marshals and clerical assistants. These deputies are appointed on the basis of competitive examination and must possess certain minimum qualifications which indicate that they can perform general law enforcement functions and deal with the public. However, their appointments can at any time be canceled by the U.S. marshal as the "public interest" may require.[16]

The authority of U.S. marshals and their deputies is fairly broad. In most cases, their authority at the federal level is very similar to that of the sheriff within the states. Generally, a U.S. marshal has the power to enforce all federal laws except those which have been specifically delegated by law to other federal agencies and is responsible for serving legal documents issued by the federal courts, congressional committees, and governmental agencies. Although the Marshal Service has law enforcement authority, its work today is mainly in assisting the courts. Basically, the responsibilities of this office fall into four major categories:

1. The U.S. marshal or a deputy marshal is required to attend the sessions of the federal courts and to maintain the decorum of the courtroom, to handle juries, to protect witnesses and judges, and to perform duties in the courtroom as the judge may direct.

2. The U.S. marshal is responsible for seizing, guarding, selling, or otherwise disposing of personal or real property according to federal court orders. He or she is responsible for making arrests and placing federal prisoners in jail, transporting federal prisoners between jails and courtrooms during the course of trials, and transporting convicted prisoners to a penitentiary or similar institution.

3. The U.S. marshal performs service of process for the federal courts. This includes handling of a subpoena or summons, seizure of goods and chattels, storage of seized articles, publication of notices, and sale of property.

4. The U.S. marshal is a disbursing officer for the Department of Justice and the federal courts; he or she is responsible for paying the salaries of Department of Justice and federal court personnel, disbursing witness and juror fees, and making associated court payments.[17]

Organized Crime and Racketeering Section

In 1951, the Kefauver committee, a congressional committee investigating organized crime, concluded after an exhaustive study: "There is a sinister criminal organization known as the Mafia operating throughout the country."[18] In the intervening twenty-five years, the existence of organized crime has become generally acknowledged.[19] Numerous congressional committees have examined the problem, but organized crime thrives today more than ever.[20]

One of the major problems of dealing with organized crime is that the activities of large criminal cartels encompass geographically and statutorily the entire spectrum of enforcement and prosecutorial jurisdiction.[21] American law enforcement is too decentralized to handle the problem at the local and state level. The Organized Crime and Racketeering Section (OCR) of the Department of Justice was established in 1954 to spearhead and coordinate investigations of organized crime. Its specified functions were to:

> Coordinate, generally, enforcement activities directed against organized crime and racketeering and to accumulate and correlate data related to organized crime and racketeering, . . . initiate and supervise investigations, formulate general prosecutive policies and assist U.S. Attorneys in preparing indictments and conducting trials in the field.[22]

By 1957, there were only ten attorneys in OCR. Its inability to grow and become effective during this period has been attributed to a "lack of coordination and interest by some Federal investigative agencies."[23] Following the famous meeting of leading organized crime figures in Apalachin, New York, the Special Group on Organized Crime was established within the Justice Department in 1958. The function of this office was to establish regional offices from which intelligence could be gathered and federal grand jury proceedings conducted regarding the activities of the organized crime figures who met at Apalachin. Spurred on by congressional investigations of organized crime into labor unions, the FBI and Treasury enforcement agencies began supplying OCR with regular intelligence reports on leading Cosa Nostra figures. However, efforts were still on a small scale, and only minimal criminal intelligence information from other law enforcement agencies was available.

In 1961, Attorney General Robert Kennedy took an active interest in the Department of Justice's investigations and prosecution of organized crime figures. Under his leadership, the number of attorneys and federal investigators assigned to OCR grew dramatically, as did efforts to coordinate intelligence activities. Whereas in 1961 only 49 organized crime figures were convicted, by the time of Kennedy's departure from the Department of Justice in 1965, this number had increased to 468.[24]

Strike Forces

After Kennedy's departure, the momentum of the organized crime efforts slowed owing to a number of problems of a coordinative and organizational nature. In an attempt to reinvigorate the organized crime drive, President Johnson in 1966 issued a memorandum calling for increased federal efforts.[25] Johnson followed this in 1968 with a special executive order which provided that the attorney general was to coordinate the criminal law enforcement activities against organized crime of all federal agencies. This executive order was the basis for the creation of organized crime strike forces within the Organized Crime and Racketeering Section. Today, the OCR coordinates its strike force efforts through three groups: (1) the Administrative Unit, (2) the Intelligence and Special Services Unit, and (3) the Special Operations Unit.[26]

The Administrative Unit consists of the chief of the OCR and four deputy chiefs. This group manages the efforts of OCR, coordinating field activities and investigations among the various federal agencies involved. Each deputy chief is responsible for the operation of strike forces in one geographical area. There is almost daily contact between each local strike force and the OCR in Washington with respect to the status of pending investigations.

Before the strike force takes any prosecutive action, it submits to the OCR a prosecution memorandum setting forth the evidence obtained as a result of field investigation. The memorandum contains the strike force attorney's recommendations on whether or not a prosecution should be initiated. Unless the OCR approves, no criminal prosecution is begun.

The Intelligence and Special Services Unit provides a comprehensive, centralized intelligence file devoted exclusively to organized crime. Over the years, this unit has compiled a computer-based index with the names of thousands of individuals who have some association with organized crime. It also maintains a special "racketeer profile" on about 30,000 individuals who are in some way importantly involved in organized crime. The bulk of the intelligence contained in this special file has been supplied by federal investigative agencies and includes such items as the names of known racketeers, their criminal activities, associates, place of employment or legitimate business activities, residence, telephone numbers, and automobile license numbers.[27]

The files are utilized in a number of ways. The unit handles an average of fifty information requests a day from strike force personnel, federal investigative and regulatory agencies, and local and state law enforcement agencies.[28] An additional function of the system is to provide a data source for the preparation of comprehensive surveys of particular problems. One such use is to determine if a strike force should be established in a given area. The files are constantly reviewed to ascertain the activities of organized crime figures around the country. In addition, in order to keep the files as current as possible, a list of 3,700 principal organized crime leaders is periodically circulated to various federal agencies for updating.[29]

The Special Operations Unit performs four major functions: review of applications for electronic surveillance under federal statutes,[30] preparation of recommendations with regard to granting immunity from prosecution for witnesses, analysis of correspondence, and legal research in the conduct of investigations and case preparation.

As of late 1975, there were seventeen strike forces operating throughout the country, usually in metropolitan areas where there are particular organized crime problems. The OCR designates the areas these strike forces will operate in. Strike force teams can be pulled in or out of a geographical area, depending upon the perceived need. Each strike force has an attorney-in-charge who is directly responsible for the work of other U.S. Department of Justice attorneys assigned to the strike force. The attorney-in-charge supervises the work of the strike force attorneys and investigators and coordinates the efforts of the team with the U.S. attorney in the jurisdiction where the strike force is working and with the OCR in Washington.

A strike force usually consists of eight to ten federal investigators who receive special training in this type of investigation. Most investigators are assigned from the Justice and the Treasury Departments and represent the FBI; Drug Enforcement Administration; Secret Service; IRS Intelligence; Customs; and the Bureau of Alcohol, Tobacco and Firearms. However, in certain cases, the Postal Service or the Securities and Exchange Commission will also provide investigative personnel.

An important component of the strike force concept is the utilization of special federal grand juries. In the jurisdiction where a strike force is operating, a special federal grand jury is empaneled to deal with organized crime activities. The grand jury deliberates on the evidence gathered by the strike force to determine whether prosecution is warranted.

Law Enforcement Assistance Administration (LEAA)

Although this is not a federal law enforcement agency, it deserves attention because it may be the single most important development that has affected criminal justice in the United States. This agency grew out of the Office of Law Enforcement Assistance (OLEA), which was created in 1965 to make federal funds available to states, localities, and private organizations to improve methods of law enforcement, court administration, and prison operation.[31] The act creating this agency was the first federal law giving money to local government for improvement of criminal justice.

In 1968, the Omnibus Crime Control and Safe Streets Act became effective. This act repealed the Law Enforcement Act of 1965 and replaced the Office of Law Enforcement Assistance with a new agency known as the *Law Enforcement Assistance Administration*. The Safe Streets Act was a milestone for the nation and expressed a fundamental philosophy about crime in the United States, namely, that it is a problem of national dimensions, but it is most appropriately addressed at the state and local levels through the support of federal monies. This was a drastic departure from the past. State and local law enforcement and other criminal justice activities have traditionally not brought about federal involvement. Like public assistance activities in general, this area had not been traditionally regarded as belonging to the federal government's natural sphere of interest. As we have seen, American law enforcement and criminal justice activities were considered to be responsibilities of state and local governments and were dependent upon them for both their authority and their funds.[32]

Under the provisions of the act, as administered by LEAA, a number of funding programs are available to all fifty states, Guam, Puerto Rico, American Samoa, the Virgin Islands, and the District of Columbia. Each is awarded a block grant based on its population. The block grants are to be used to develop crime-related programs and to assist and improve local and state agencies of criminal justice. In addition, LEAA awards action and discretionary grants to foster the development of state and local planning capabilities that would improve the administration of justice and to aid research activities directed at crime or the improvement of agencies of justice.

LEAA requires states to develop centralized state planning agencies (SPAs) as well as local planning units. These SPAs are responsible for allocating to local units of government much of the money that states receive from LEAA. Overseeing the operations of these SPAs, as well as the local planning units in the states, are supervisory boards whose members represent state and local criminal justice agencies, other public agencies, and citizen groups.[33] New legislation was written in 1973 which requires that a state must develop a comprehensive master plan that is multiyear in nature in order to be eligible to receive federal funds from LEAA. Thus, each SPA was required to coordinate the activities of local planning agencies into a single master plan of how the problem of crime was to be handled in the particular state.

In its early years of existence, the programs that LEAA funded as well as its priorities came under a great deal of criticism from members of Congress and many large city mayors. Much of the money earmarked for local governments and distributed to the states went to regional planning councils instead of the major cities where the problems of crime are most acute.[34] As a consequence, the act was amended in 1971 to provide for direct assistance to local units of government having a population of 250,000 or more.[35] Other criticism of LEAA has been its past emphasis upon funding money to law enforcement agencies at the expense of other components of the criminal justice system and its funding of "hardware" items such as riot equipment, radios, automobiles, etc.

In spite of these criticisms, many of the programs sponsored by LEAA are meritorious. One of its major efforts was to designate and develop Pilot Cities Programs in eight medium-sized communities throughout the United States. The idea behind this project was to utilize university-based interdisciplinary teams and criminal justice specialists to develop planning, training, and research capabilities that would upgrade the agencies of criminal justice in these cities as well as provide a means by which the delivery of criminal justice services in these communities could be better systematized. LEAA has also developed the Law Enforcement Education Program (LEEP), which in the years from 1971 to 1974 alone provided over $40 million in college tuition assistance to people employed in the criminal justice system or students contemplating a career in criminal justice. To date, this program has provided thousands of individuals with an opportunity to receive a college education.

LEAA has created within its overall organization the National Institute of Law Enforcement and Criminal Justice. This unit serves as the research and evaluation arm of the agency. Its purpose is to monitor some of the major grant programs engaged in by LEAA and to conduct empirical and applied research in the criminal justice area. This unit contracts with individuals, universities, and private technical firms to develop new concepts and approaches and to conduct independent evaluation of projects. One of the most significant undertakings by this unit is its Exemplary Projects Program. The specific goal of the Exemplary Projects Program is to encourage widespread use of advanced criminal justice practices by systematically identifying outstanding criminal justice programs throughout the country, verifying their achievements, and publicizing them widely so that other communities and agencies of criminal justice can adopt similar programs.[36] A few of the Exemplary Project Programs to date are the volunteer Probation Counselor Program, Lincoln, Nebraska; Prosecutor Management Information Center, Washington, D.C.; Street Crime Unit, New York City Police; and the Neighborhood Youth Resources Center, Philadelphia.

The National Institute of Law Enforcement and Criminal Justice has also developed the National Criminal Justice Reference Service and the National Criminal Justice Statistics Center. The reference service compiles and disseminates information concerning current research and publications in the field of criminal justice. Persons engaged in activities related to criminal justice are provided annotated bibliographies of publications that may be of interest to them. In addition, the service maintains a reference library of selected publications available to all its users through a document interlibrary loan program as well as a microfiche distribution source in which certain materials not readily available through other sources are distributed free of charge to users of the service. Recently, a loan and referral program for films and other media materials was developed.

The National Criminal Justice Statistics Center gathers criminal justice statistics to promote a better understanding of the processes of justice and renders technical assistance to states that are also engaged in developing statistical centers. The center publishes and distributes a number of reference sources and monographs dealing with national statistics such as the *Annual Expenditure and Employment Data for the Criminal Justice System*, *Directory of Criminal Justice Agencies*, *National Prisoner Statistics*, and *National Jail Census*. The systems analysis unit of the center has primary interest in identifying application of systems analysis techniques which might be useful in improving the administration of criminal justice. The center also maintains various information systems at the national level which are used to support the administration of LEAA programs and extends technical assistance to state and local governments in applying computer technology to automated records systems.

In spite of this agency's many contributions to the improvement of criminal justice, its continued existence at this time is in doubt. The U.S. House of Representatives has recently indicated that it wants to discontinue appropriations to the agency in the near future. Congress feels that in spite of all the monies made available LEAA has failed to demonstrate that it has been instrumental in reducing crime.

Some of this criticism is justified. In addition to LEAA's earlier policies of overfunding law enforcement and spending large sums on police "hardware" items, the agency constantly has been plagued by its failure to fully evaluate the way in which program monies are spent. Its most glaring failure was its funding of the High Impact Anticrime Program. This program had as its goal the reduction by 20 percent of burglary and stranger-to-stranger street crimes over a five-year period in eight major cities. From 1972 to 1975, LEAA spent some $160 million on this program in these cities. The program was finally abandoned after only three years of operation when it was generally recognized as a massive failure. Some of the factors leading to this failure were a lack of initial planning, the inability of local law enforcement and criminal justice agencies in the eight cities to implement effective planning, and local inability to resolve differences over how the program objectives could be achieved.

Whether or not Congress agrees to authorize the continued existence of LEAA, there are certain facts which bear directly on the question of federal support to local and state criminal justice efforts. Evidence would seem to indicate that federal subsidies for criminal justice improvement beyond those subsidies provided through general revenue sharing funds are necessary. State and local units of government simply do not have the financial resources necessary to support improvement programs.

It is also doubtful that state and local governments possess human resources with the necessary knowledge and skills to plan, develop, and evaluate methods to improve the administration of justice at the state and local levels. Our experience of leaving the administration of justice to local efforts has not produced an admirable record of dealing with problems of crime. At the very least, federal involvement in this area during the past decade has brought about greater coordinating efforts and overall program direction as well as a greater understanding of how complex the problem of crime abatement really is.

The experiences of LEAA and of federal involvement in the attempt to improve the administration of justice and reduce crime have demonstrated another important fact. Money alone cannot solve the problem. The agencies of criminal justice cannot be expected to make a major impact alone. Associated efforts have to be directed toward the elimination of crime-producing factors in society itself.

TREASURY DEPARTMENT

Another very important department with law enforcement responsibilities at the federal level is the Treasury Department. The law enforcement agencies of this department are specialists in certain types of federal crimes that fall under the authority of the secretary of the treasury. The primary law enforcement agencies of the Treasury Department are the Secret Service; the Bureau of Alcohol, Tobacco and Firearms; the Customs Service; and the Intelligence and

Inspection and Internal Security units of the Internal Revenue Service. In addition, the Treasury Department enforcement agencies are assisted by various support systems and serve as the United States liaison with Interpol.

Secret Service

The counterfeiting of currency has been a problem in the United States since the country's inception. During the Revolutionary War, Britain tried to destroy the economic base of the Colonies by printing vast quantities of currency that appeared to be issued by the Continental Congress. The English felt that if it could destroy the Colonies' economic foundation it could destroy their ability to wage war. The effort nearly succeeded. Owing to the presence of vast quantities of spurious currency, our young country was hard pressed to purchase needed war materials from European nations, and because of this we came closer to losing the War of Independence than most people realize.[37]

After the Revolutionary War, the problem of dealing with counterfeiting continued. This was a period when the greater part of American currency was issued by private banks that were licensed by states to print money. Operating without adequate regulation, they designed their own currency, and it was validated by the signatures of their own officials.[38] "Wildcat banks," having nothing more than a charter and a printing shop, became common in many states. The tactic of these banks was to print and sell a huge amount of currency as quickly as possible and then leave town. A book published in 1839 maintained that there were ninety-seven such banks whose currency, though legal, was worthless. It also listed 254 more banks whose currency had become the object of successful and widespread counterfeiting.[39]

In response to this situation and because it became necessary to raise large sums of money during the Civil War, Congress passed the National Currency Act of 1863, which established a national banking system and a uniform national currency, called "greenbacks." The market value of these greenbacks, which were not backed by gold reserves, began to depreciate almost as soon as they were issued, and a sharp inflation affected the entire economy. Counterfeiters had a heyday circulating imitation greenbacks extensively. The only enforcement authority against counterfeiters was in the hands of the local police, and they were practically helpless. The secretary of the Treasury then set up a system of rewards for the detection of counterfeit currency, but the situation was so bad that the counterfeiters themselves were collecting the rewards. Finally, in 1865, the Secret Service was created as a federal investigative agency with authority to enforce the laws against counterfeiting.

When this agency was created, it was estimated that nearly one-third of all paper money in circulation was counterfeit. The agency immediately began the task of curtailing the problem. In its first year of existence alone, it arrested over 200 counterfeiters.[40] In 1974, special agents of the Secret Service seized over $19 million in counterfeit bills.[41]

Today, the Secret Service is best known for its protective assignment to the president and his family. Originally, there had been little concern for the safety of United States presidents. The attempted assassination of President Jackson and the successful assassinations of Presidents Lincoln in 1865 and Garfield in 1881 failed to prompt Congress to pass legislation to assign special bodyguards for presidents of the United States. In 1901, President McKinley was assassinated in spite of the security provided by local police and soldiers. Informed of the assassination, the secretary of the Treasury promptly assigned the Secret Service the duty of protecting presidents, and in 1906 Congress appropriated the funds and officially assigned the Secret Service its protective role.

After the tragic assassination of John F. Kennedy in 1963, Congress increased the scope and responsibilities of the Secret Service as a result of recommendations by the Warren Commission. Among the recommendations implemented were an increase in the amount of training and number of Secret Service agents assigned to presidential protection, enlargement of the protective intelligence function, increased liaison with other law enforcement agencies, and acquisition of sophisticated technical security equipment, computer systems, and communications.

Following President Kennedy's assassination, Congress passed legislation authorizing the Secret Service to protect the widow and minor children of a former president and making the assassination of the president a federal crime. In 1965, the Secret Service was authorized to protect a former president and his wife during his lifetime, and minor children of a former president. This responsibility was extended in 1968 to provide protection for the widow of a former president until her death or remarriage and protection of minor children of a former president until the age of sixteen.

After the assassination of Senator Robert F. Kennedy in 1968, Congress authorized the Secret Service to protect major presidential and vice-presidential candidates and nominees. Since that time, the Secret Service has also been given the responsibility to protect foreign dignitaries visiting the United States.

Today, the Secret Service is organized into five main divisions. The Administrative Division deals with such concerns as administrative operations, management, finance, personnel, and training. The Inspection Division is responsible for inspection of field offices located throughout the United States and its possessions and for rendering advice on special problems. The Division of Investigation investigates violations of laws relating to the Treasury Department. It has four sections:

- An investigation unit, which coordinates and directs the organized crime activities of the agency
- A counterfeit unit, which directs the investigations against counterfeiting, develops technical aids, and provides training to bank and commercial personnel in the detection of counterfeiting

- A forgery unit, which investigates forgeries of U.S. checks, bonds, and federal food stamps
- A special unit to supervise the uniformed guards that provide security for the Treasury and Treasury Annex buildings

The fourth division is the Office of Protective Services. The units in this division provide permanent protective security to government officials. For example, included are the Executive Protection Service, Presidential Protection Division, Vice-Presidential Protection Division, and special units for any residences that the president might maintain. The Executive Protection Service consists of the uniformed police personnel who guard the White House and any other buildings that might house a presidential office. Agents of the Presidential Protection Division accompany the president and protect him wherever he resides or travels, and this division coordinates the various field offices of the Secret Service in providing protection should he visit a city in their geographical area.

The fifth division of the Secret Service is the Office of Protective Intelligence. This unit compiles intelligence information on individuals who might try to harm any of the officials who are protected by the Secret Service. In addition, it is responsible for developing and installing technical security devices, communication and computer systems, and other scientific equipment needed to provide protection.

The Secret Service also offers limited training programs to other law enforcement personnel. A few police officers from other jurisdictions are trained to study and analyze handwriting and typewriting found on questioned and disputed documents, such as forged checks or bonds and anonymous letters. A special one-week course on protective operations is available to state and local police officers who have protective responsibilities. Finally, a limited number of police officers are accepted in the Secret Service Firearms Instructor course, which is an intensive two-week course in all phases of firearms proficiency.

The Bureau of Alcohol, Tobacco and Firearms

The Bureau of Alcohol, Tobacco and Firearms (ATF) has undergone a number of important alterations since its inception. This agency was created in 1862, when a tax was imposed upon liquors and tobacco. The act that imposed this tax also created the office of commissioner of internal revenue, who was authorized to hire three detectives to suppress the illegal manufacturing of distilled spirits. A few years later, an additional twenty-two agents were hired, and the agency continued to grow at a slow pace until 1919.

In 1919, the Eighteenth Amendment to the Constitution was ratified and prohibition was ushered in. Under the provisions of the National Prohibition

Act, the manufacture, sale, transportation, and importation of intoxicating liquors became a federal crime. The responsibility for the enforcement of this act came under the authority of the commissioner of the Bureau of Internal Revenue (now the Internal Revenue Service). Operating under the commissioner was a prohibition commissioner whose authority included the direct enforcement of the National Prohibition Act and the imposition of taxes on alcohol produced legally for medicinal and industrial purposes.

The prohibition commissioner established eighteen districts throughout the United States. Each district had a director who supervised prohibition agents. The prohibition agents were authorized to investigate all violations of the Prohibition Act and report these violations to the U.S. attorneys for prosecution. During the next fifteen years, more reorganizations came about as attempts were made to streamline the organization and to lessen some problems of enforcement and graft that periodically shook the agency with scandal.

In 1934, the Alcohol Tax Unit (ATU) was created under the authority of the secretary of the Treasury. The idea was to centralize the enforcement efforts of all federal agencies engaged in the enforcement of Internal Revenue laws dealing with alcoholic beverages. In 1951, the Alcohol Tax Unit was replaced by a new agency with expanded duties, the Alcohol and Tobacco Tax Division.

During the mid and late 1960s, increasing congressional and citizen concern was focused on the relationship between guns and rising crime in the United States. It began with the assassination of President Kennedy in 1963 and was renewed with the killing of Martin Luther King in 1968. After King's assassination, a gun bill was passed in Congress as part of the Omnibus Crime Control and Safe Streets Act. However, before the Omnibus Crime Bill was signed into law, Senator Robert Kennedy was killed in Los Angeles in June 1968. The assassination aroused so much antigun sentiment in Congress that a flurry of bills was introduced in both the House and Senate to control guns, ammunition, and explosives. These efforts resulted in the passage of the Gun Control Act of 1968.

Responsibility for enforcing the Gun Control Act was given to the Alcohol and Tobacco Tax Division of the Internal Revenue Service. With this responsibility, the name of this agency was changed to the Alcohol, Tobacco and Firearms Division. In 1972, the secretary of the Treasury removed the Alcohol, Tobacco and Firearms Division from the authority of the Internal Revenue Service and made it a separate bureau. Since then, the laws relating to alcohol, tobacco, firearms, and explosives have been withdrawn from the Internal Revenue Service.[42]

Since ATF's enforcement responsibilities in the area of distilled spirits and tobacco have changed very little, we need not concentrate on their enforcement powers in these areas. It is in the area of gun control and explosives that much of their current investigative efforts are concentrated. Among other responsibilities, ATF regulates businesses that deal in the importing or selling of firearms and prohibits the possession of certain firearms such as machine guns or sawed-off rifles and shotguns, silencers, and destructive devices. It is responsible for the control and investigation of interstate commerce that transports firearms and explosives. It conducts investigations of the possession and use of firearms and explosives by certain categories of people such as aliens, convicted felons, those who have been discharged from the armed forces under dishonorable conditions, and mental incompetents. It also investigates all thefts of firearms and explosives and all criminal detonations of explosives and bomb threats or the use of explosives during the commission of a felony. Because of its jurisdiction in these areas, it is also involved in extensive intelligence-gathering activities involving militant extremist groups that might resort to the illegal use of firearms and explosives.

The ATF works very closely with state and local police in dealing with firearms and explosives. It has established a National Firearms Tracing Center which traces firearms ownership from manufacturer to retailer to purchaser. It is also currently involved in a gun violence profile program in seventeen major metropolitan areas in conjunction with local police in an effort to determine the types and sources of guns used in street crimes. In addition, the ATF helps other police agencies investigate actual or attempted bombings and conducts extensive training programs under a 1974 LEAA grant for local and state police personnel in an effort to familiarize them with federal gun control legislation, bomb scene investigative techniques, and organized crime operations.

Customs Service

This agency assesses and collects duties, internal revenue taxes, fines, penalties, and other fees associated with the importation of merchandise. It examines persons, carriers, cargo, and mail entering the United States and carriers and cargo leaving. The Customs Service is also responsible for detecting and preventing all forms of smuggling designed to defraud the government of revenues or gain illicit entry of prohibited articles and contraband. It uses such means as high-speed aircraft with infrared scanning devices to intercept the flow of illicit contraband entering our borders. When narcotics or dangerous drugs are found, Customs contacts the DEA, which handles the investigation if warranted or turns it over to a local law enforcement agency for disposition. Customs officers made some 14,300 drug seizures and arrested 10,000 persons during 1973. The value of these drug seizures, which included over 1,200 pounds of hard narcotics, was more than $1 billion.[43]

The Customs Service is made up of two groups of personnel. The majority are inspectors, who are usually uniformed and are likely to be stationed at the various ports of entry to search for smuggled goods. There are also investigators, whose primary responsibilities are to conduct on-going investigations in which the service is involved. To assist its inspectors and investigative personnel, the Customs Service maintains eight regional laboratories in major cities across the nation. Their broad mission is to supply scientific knowledge to customs import specialists, particularly in identifying and classifying commercial imports. They also help local police agencies with testing unidentified substances such as narcotics.

Internal Revenue Service

The Internal Revenue Service performs a number of law enforcement functions through its Intelligence, Audit, and Inspection and Internal Security Divisions.

Its primary criminal investigative unit is the Intelligence Division. This unit investigates possible criminal violations of federal tax laws, particularly those statutes dealing with personal and corporate income tax and excise, estate, and gift taxes. The offenses with which this division must deal most frequently are willful nonfiling of returns and attempts to evade full payment of taxes. The Intelligence Division works very closely with the Audit Division. This latter unit seeks to promote the highest possible level of voluntary compliance with tax laws. To accomplish this, it conducts an extensive audit of tax returns. Issues may arise in the conduct of these tax audits which are civil concerns, or the audits may turn up deliberate attempts to defraud the federal government of tax revenues. When criminal violations are uncovered, the case is turned over to the Intelligence Division for investigation and possible prosecution.

Today, the Intelligence Division conducts two major enforcement operations: the General Enforcement Program, which is directed at cases involving legitimate persons and businesses, and the Special Enforcement Program, which focuses upon those who obtain unreported income from illegal activities, including bribery, extortion, and the sale of narcotics. In recent years, agents of the Special Enforcement Program have played a significant role in the investigation of organized crime activities in the United States by virtue of the fact that much of the income from such activities is not reported.

The Inspection and Internal Security Division was created in 1952 to serve as a watchdog over IRS activities after a serious scandal indicated that alarming numbers of IRS employees were involved in accepting bribes for not reporting income tax violators. The primary function of this unit is to investigate all allegations of bribery and serious misconduct by IRS employees and to arrest employees who accept bribes as well as citizens who through such actions attempt to corrupt the integrity of the IRS. This unit also conducts extensive background investigations of persons applying for sensitive positions within IRS and certain federal agencies.

The Intelligence Division operates a few limited training programs for state and local police personnel. These training programs are designed to instruct in methods of financial investigative techniques, such as rules of evidence as they apply to financial documents, tracing and records examination, and indirect methods of proving personal and corporate income.

Support Systems

In the last few years, the enforcement agencies of the U.S. Treasury Department have expanded their technical capabilities in communications and data processing. Indicative of this has been the creation of the Treasury Enforcement Communications System (TECS). A computer-based index file for use by Treasury enforcement agencies, TECS consists of a central data bank in San Diego, California, and about 500 access terminals at Treasury facilities throughout the country. Systems users include the Customs Service; Bureau of Alcohol, Tobacco and Firearms; IRS Inspection and Internal Security Division; IRS Intelligence Division; and Interpol. This system contains intelligence information on individuals sought by the Treasury agencies. The system also connects with the National Law Enforcement Telecommunications System (NLETS), which provides administrative message capability between TECS and law enforcement agencies in all the states on vehicle registrations and drivers' licenses. It also interfaces with the computer facilities of the National Crime Information Center (NCIC) for instant access to information from this source.[44]

Interpol

The International Criminal Police Organization (Interpol), although not an agency of the United States, nonetheless has a very close working relationship with the enforcement units of the U.S. Treasury Department. Its American liaison office is staffed by federal law enforcement personnel in the U.S. National Central Bureau, located in the Treasury Department. Any federal, state, or local law enforcement agencies requesting information from any of Interpol's 120 member nations must forward their requests through the National Central Bureau of the Treasury Department, which since 1958 has been designated as our representative to this international organization.

There are a great many misconceptions about the role of Interpol. This organization, which has its headquarters in St. Cloud, France, is not an investigative unit; its sole purpose is to coordinate investigative efforts among member nations by serving as a clearinghouse and depository for intelligence information. Its massive computer banks contain data on wanted criminals, stolen items, and other related information supplied by user nations. Other Interpol services include transferring requests from one nation to another to conduct investigations leading to arrest or extradition, conducting criminal history and license plate or operator's license checks, issuing an international wanted circular and all points bulletin in any or all of the member nations, and tracing weapons and motor vehicles.[45]

POSTAL INSPECTION SERVICE

The American postal service was created on July 26, 1775, when Benjamin Franklin was appointed provisional postmaster general by the Continental Congress. In the early years of the American postal service, serious crimes involving the U.S. mail were quite commonplace. Part of the problem was the use of dishonest mail carriers who absconded with the mail. Another serious problem was robbery of the mails. Highwaymen infested the post roads, where they ambushed post coaches. It became such a serious problem that Congress, in 1794, passed a law which called for the death penalty for stealing mail.

The early postmasters general were authorized to appoint assistants who surveyed mail routes, examined post offices to see that the mails were being handled properly and that postal revenues were not stolen by employees, and investigated robberies of the mails. The law enforcement authority of the post office changed very little until 1872, when Congress passed a law prohibiting the usage of the postal service to defraud. In 1873, Congress also passed a law which prohibited the use of the mails to transport obscene materials. To enforce these laws, Congress authorized the hiring of additional special agents, and the investigative authority of the postal service came of age. In 1879, Congress changed the title of special agent to inspector; in 1954, the title was changed to postal inspector.

Today, postal inspectors perform a broad range of activities. A sizeable portion of their workload involves in-service investigations in which they conduct periodic audits and inspections of postal facilities as well as special investigations of alleged criminal theft or misuse of postal service property by employees. However, the largest percentage of their work involves criminal investigations of both employees and those outside the service.

The Postal Inspection Service is divided into four special offices, two of which are of particular importance to law enforcement. The first of these is the Office of Security, which is further specialized into three branches: Security Requirements, Security Force and Personnel Suitability, and Security Programs. The other is the Office of Criminal Investigation, which has two divisions. The first of these is the Organized Crime Division, which conducts investigations of the use of the mails by organized crime and maintains liaison with other federal, state, and local law enforcement agencies involved in these types of investigations. The other is its Operating Programs Division, which has four specialized subunits: Internal Thefts, Burglary-External Thefts, Fraud, and Prohibited Mailings Branch.

The postal inspectors are responsible for investigating all burglaries and holdups committed against postal installations, equipment, and employees; mail frauds; all thefts from house letter boxes; obscene and prohibited mailings; and all financial irregularities committed by postal employees against the service. In addition, postal inspectors conduct an extensive program of personnel security investigations, including field investigations of employees occupying or being considered for sensitive positions.

FEDERAL LAW ENFORCEMENT TRAINING CENTER

The federal government has approximately fifty law enforcement agencies, which do not include security or guard services at various civilian agencies such as federal hospitals. Many of these agencies have been unable to provide adequate training programs and facilities for their enforcement personnel. In 1967, the Bureau of the Budget (now the Office of Management and Budget) conducted an extensive study of this problem. It found that the training of many of these employees was worse than imagined and that local and state police training facilities and programs were inadequate for the purpose of training federal law enforcement personnel.

In 1968, it was proposed that a modern law enforcement center be established to train most federal law enforcement personnel.[46] The most important points of the proposal were:

1. The training center could be jointly sponsored and controlled on a cooperative basis by the participating agencies.

2. The training center should be designed to provide the necessary facilities and equipment for conducting recruit, advanced, specialized and refresher training for Federal law enforcement personnel of the participating agencies.

3. The facility would consist of a campus-like training center with modern classrooms, firing ranges, specialized training areas and equipment, dormitories, support facilities and services to accommodate about 700 resident students.[47]

With the Department of the Treasury as the prime agency, the Consolidated Law Enforcement Training Center was formally established in 1970 to fulfill the need for an interagency training facility. The supervision of the new facility was to rest with a seven-member board of directors, including representatives of the Departments of Treasury, Interior, and Justice, the Postal Service and three other members. The initial training sessions were conducted in Washington, D.C., and a large tract of land was purchased in Beltsville, Maryland, which was to become the future site of the training center. Before construction could begin on the new site, legal problems developed, and in 1975 the training center was transferred to the site of the naval air station in Brunswick, Georgia.

At the present time, a number of federal departments and their law enforcement units utilize the center for basic, specialized, or advanced training. Among the participating agencies are:

The Department of Justice for its U.S. Marshals, Border Patrol Inspectors and Immigration Investigators.

The Treasury Department for its Secret Service Special Agents, Executive Protective Service Agents, Customs Agents, and the Internal Revenue's Special Investigators, Intelligence Special Agents and Internal Security Inspectors.

The Department of the Interior for its U.S. Park Rangers, U.S. Park Policemen, the Bureau of Indian Affairs' Investigators and Indian Policemen and the Sport Fisheries and Wildlife's Game Management Agents and Visitor Protection Specialist.

The U.S. Postal Service for its Postal Inspectors.

The Department of State for its Security Agents.

The Smithsonian Institution for its Zoo Police.

The Department of Commerce for its National Oceanic and Atmospheric Administration and Commercial Fisheries Agents.

The security force for the Bureau of Engraving and Printing; miscellaneous security forces such as those at Walter Reed Army Hospital, Bethesda Naval Hospital and other veterans' hospitals.[48]

The training center has two directors. One is in charge of the police training program, which trains such personnel as U.S. park rangers and police, Indian police, game management agents, the District of Columbia Transit Police, and various security personnel at federal civilian institutions. The police training program runs from five to eight weeks. The second director is in charge of the investigation program, which runs for twelve weeks and trains investigative personnel of federal agencies. Among the groups that attend this program are Secret Service agents; special investigators for IRS; Alcohol, Tobacco and Firearms investigators; Customs agents; immigration investigators; postal inspectors; and security agents for the Department of State.

In addition to providing academic training, the center has facilities for training in weapons, pursuit driving, physical training, and related areas.

ARMED FORCES POLICE

Army Military Police Corps

During the Revolutionary War, George Washington, in 1776, established the "provost marshal" as an appointed aide to enforce the rules and regulations of the Continental Army, to apprehend deserters, and to perform other military police duties. After the war, this position was discontinued. In the years that followed, when our country was involved in war, the office of provost marshal and the corps of military police were reactivated, but at the end of each war this position was discontinued and the military police units were again disbanded.

As a precautionary measure, the office of provost marshal general was established in the War Department in July 1941, and two months later the Military Police Corps was activated under the provost marshal general's supervision.[49] After the conclusion of World War II, the office of the provost marshal general was retained along with Military Police Corps, and in 1950 Congress made the corps a permanent operating branch of the U.S. Army.

Today, the provost marshal general's office is in Washington, D.C., where he reports directly to the deputy chief of staff for personnel. He is responsible for provost marshal and military police activities; criminal investigations and crime prevention; traffic control and enforcement; search for army personnel who have unwarranted absences; army correctional facilities; and prisoners of war and civilian internees.[50]

Directly under the provost marshal general are the provost marshals, who supervise the military police units at army installations. These provost marshals advise the facility commander and his staff concerning military police matters under their command and coordinate the activities of the military police at the army base.

During peacetime, military police perform all law enforcement services on army property and involving army personnel. During wartime and in a combat area, military police also assemble and segregate prisoners of war, inspect and maintain war prisoner compound areas, maintain security of facilities and prisoners, and perform similar responsibilities.

The Criminal Investigations Division (CID) is a special branch of the military police. This unit of highly trained investigative specialists conducts the army's major on-going criminal investigations. In many instances, a CID investigator may be in civilian clothes or posing in an undercover capacity as a member of a regular army unit.

Navy Shore Patrol

The Navy Shore Patrol operates out of the eighteen naval districts in the United States and its possessions. In charge of all shore patrols in a naval district is the commandant of the naval district. Under his command is a senior shore patrol officer who establishes the shore patrol headquarters for the naval district and coordinates the activities of the shore patrol with other military and civilian law enforcement agencies in the area.

The Navy Shore Patrol is not as organizationally sophisticated as the Army Military Police Corps nor does it provide the varied types of law enforcement services. For the most part, it maintains basic patrol functions in civilian areas frequented by naval, Marine Corps, and Coast Guard personnel. Even its security function is less, because much of the guarding of naval installations is handled by a special detachment of Marine Corps personnel. The shore patrol also has limited training programs for its personnel and must rely upon the Army Military Police School for much of its formalized training.

Major crimes committed by naval personnel are investigated by the Naval Investigative Service, which until recently was known as the Office of Naval Intelligence. When the shore patrol is informed of any offense involving naval property or personnel, a specialist from the Naval Investigative Service is assigned to the case. These investigation specialists perform both peacetime and wartime services for the Navy very similar to those performed by the CID.

Air Force Security Police

In 1947, when Congress established the United States Air Force as a separate branch of the armed forces, military police serving with the Army Air Corps were transferred to the new Air Force and were redesignated as Air Police.

During the Korean War, air bases were frequently overrun by the enemy. In many cases, the Air Police were the only armed fighting force on the base. Consequently, the Air Force developed a more extensive base defense system. As a result, the Air Police School redesignated the Air Base Defense School, trained its candidates in two major areas, law enforcement and base defense. In addition, in 1960 the air provost marshal became the director of security and law enforcement, and in 1966, the name of the Air Police was changed to Air Force Security Police. Its mission can be summarized as (1) the security of the combat capacity of the Air Force, (2) enforcement of law and order, (3) protection of the resources of the Air Force, and (4) assistance in the correction of Air Force prisoners.[51]

Under the director of security and law enforcement are chiefs of security police, who are the commanders of the base security police forces at each air base. Under each chief are an operations branch and an administration branch. The operations branch has four important sections—security, law enforcement, dogs and equipment—each of which is headed by a junior officer. Security police are given six weeks of basic law enforcement training at Lackland Air Force Base in Texas. All candidates must take competitive examinations and meet certain qualifications. Once they have completed their basic training, they can apply for special advanced training. Like the Army's Military Police Corps, they provide a broad range of enforcement and security services both on military installations and off base where there are likely to be found significant numbers of Air Force personnel.

Within a security police unit, a separate investigative section may be established which consists of a noncommissioned officer in charge, some investigators, and clerical staff. These investigative sections, however, are concerned only with very minor incidents such as traffic accidents and minor thefts.

If the crime is a major one or specialists are needed, the Office of Special Investigation (OSI) is notified. Like their counterparts in the CID and Naval Investigative Service, these are highly trained specialists in criminal investigation. Security police can apply to become special agents of the OSI. Special qualifying examinations and experience are required to be considered for this position, and those selected are appointed to the OSI for intensive advanced training in criminal investigation.

The Air Force Security Police also maintain all confinement centers for Air Force personnel sentenced to correctional institutions. Personnel sent to provide security at these facilities are given extensive training in corrections.

SUMMARY

Law enforcement agencies at the federal level are highly specialized in terms of the crimes they deal with since most have very limited jurisdiction. Jurisdictional disputes and lack of coordination have led to problems which may be even more serious than similar problems at the local or state level

The major investigative arm of the federal government is the Department of Justice. Among its enforcement agencies are the FBI, the Immigration and Naturalization Service, the Drug Enforcement Administration, the U.S. Marshal Service, and the Organized Crime and Racketeering Section. The Department of Justice also contains the Law Enforcement Assistance Administration, which, since its inception in 1968, has been a significant federal agency for dealing with problems associated with the agencies of criminal justice at all levels of government.

Another major enforcement effort is conducted by the Treasury Department. This department supervises the efforts of the U.S. Secret Service; the Bureau of Alcohol, Tobacco and Firearms; the Customs Service; and the enforcement agencies of the Internal Revenue Service. Treasury Department personnel also staff the U.S. liaison office to Interpol and have been instrumental in the development of the Consolidated Law Enforcement Training Center.

Other major enforcement agencies are the Postal Inspection Service and the military law enforcement agencies of the Army, Navy, and Air Force.

Suggested Additional Readings

Adams, Thomas F. *Law Enforcement*. Englewood Cliffs, N.J.: Prentice-Hall, 1968.

Baughman, U. E. *Secret Service Chief*. New York: Harper & Row, 1962.

Cook, Fred J. *The FBI Nobody Knows*. New York: Macmillan, 1964.

Daxe, Arnold, Jr. "Military Police Training." *Military Police Journal* (October 1970).

Dorman, Michael. *The Secret Service Story*. New York: Dekarte Press, 1967.

Federal Bureau of Investigation. *Know Your FBI*. Washington, D.C.: U.S. Government Printing Office, 1972.

―――. *The Story of the FBI National Academy*. Washington, D.C.: U.S. Government Printing Office, 1967.

Kuhn, Ferdinand. *The Story of the Secret Service*. New York: Random House, 1965.

Markis, John N. *The Silent Investigator*. New York: Dutton, 1959.

Ottenberg, Miriam. *The Federal Investigation*. Englewood Cliffs, N.J.: Prentice-Hall, 1962.

Overstreet, Harry. *The FBI in Our Open Society*. New York: W. W. Norton, 1969.

Schmeckebier, Laurence F., and Francis X. Eble. *The Bureau of Internal Revenue: Its History, Activities and Organization*. Baltimore, Md.: Johns Hopkins, 1923.

Turner, William W. *Hoover's FBI—The Men and the Myth*. Los Angeles: Sherbourne, 1970.

U.S. Bureau of Customs. *Your Career with Customs*. Washington, D.C.: U.S. Government Printing Office, 1968.

U.S. Department of the Army. *The Military Policemen.* Washington, D.C.: U.S. Department of Defense, 1969.

U.S. Department of Justice. *Authority of Officers of the Immigration and Naturalization Service.* Washington, D.C.: U.S. Government Printing Office, 1972.

————. *The Border Patrol.* Washington, D.C.: U.S. Government Printing Office, 1972.

————. *Outline of the Office of United States Marshal.* Washington, D.C.: Executive Office for United States Marshal, 1973.

U.S. Post Office Department: *History of the Inspection Service.* Washington, D.C.: U.S. Government Printing Office, n.d.

U.S. Treasury Department. *The Alcohol and Tobacco Tax Division.* Publication no. 425, n.d.

Whitehead, Donald F. *The FBI Story.* New York: Random House, 1956.

Notes

1. James M. Burns and J. W. Peltason, *Government by the People* (Englewood Cliffs, N.J.: Prentice-Hall, 1966), p. 63.
2. Art. 1, sec. 8.
3. Vern L. Folley, *American Law Enforcement* (Boston: Holbrook Press, 1973) pp. 72–73.
4. Bela Rektor, *Federal Law Enforcement Agencies* (Astor, Fla.: Danubian Press, 1975), p. 34.
5. Harry Overstreet and Bonaro Overstreet, *The FBI in Our Open Society* (New York: Norton, 1969), pp. 26–73.
6. Donald F. Whitehead, *The FBI Story* (New York: Random House, 1956), pp. 66–68.
7. Rektor, op. cit., p. 36.
8. See 18 U.S.C. § 1073.
9. Federal Bureau of Investigation, *FBI Annual Report—1974* (Washington, D.C.: U.S. Government Printing Office, 1975).
10. Federal Bureau of Investigation, *Know Your FBI* (Washington, D.C.: U.S. Government Printing Office, 1972), pp. 4–5.
11. U.S. Department of Justice, *The Border Patrol* (Washington, D.C.: U.S. Government Printing Office, 1972), p. 2.
12. Vernon D. Acree, "This Is Customs," *Drug Enforcement,* 1(3) (Spring 1974): p. 10.
13. Thomas F. Adams, *Law Enforcement* (Englewood Cliffs, N.J.: Prentice-Hall, 1968), p. 88.
14. Rektor, op. cit., p. 103.
15. Department of Justice, "Outline of the Office of the United States Marshal," (Washington, D.C.: Executive Office for United States Marshal, 1973), p. 2.
16. 28 U.S.C. §§ 541–542.

17. Rektor, op. cit., p. 113.

18. *Senate Special Committee to Investigate Organized Crime in Interstate Commerce, 3d Interim Report,* S. Rept. 307, 82d Cong., 1st Sess. 2 (1951).

19. See, for example, *Senate Select Committee on Improper Activities in the Labor or Management Field, 1st Interim Report,* S. Rept. 1417, 85th Cong., 2d Sess. (1958); *Permanent Subcommittee on Investigations of the Senate Committee on Government Operations, Organized Crime and Illicit Traffic in Narcotics,* S. Rept. 72, 87th Cong., 1st Sess. (1965); *House Committee on Government Operations, Federal Effort against Organized Crime,* House Rept. 1574, 90th Cong., 2d Sess. (1968).

20. Former Attorney General John Mitchell stated that $50 billion per year is a conservative estimate of gross profits of organized crime (*The New York Times,* Mar. 9, 1969, p. 1, col. 2.).

21. P. Johnson, "Organized Crime: Challenge to the American Legal System," part 1, *Journal of Criminal Law, Criminology and Police Science,* 53 (1962): 418.

22. "The Strike Force: Organized Law Enforcement v. Organized Crime," *Columbia Journal of Law and Social Problems,* 496 (1970): 502.

23. President's Commission on Law Enforcement and Administration of Justice: *Organized Crime* (Washington, D.C.: U.S. Government Printing Office, 1967), p. 11.

24. *Ibid.*

25. "The Strike Force," op. cit., p. 504.

26. Interview with Edward T. Joyce, deputy chief, Organized Crime and Racketeering Section, July 17, 1975.

27. Ibid.

28. "The Strike Force," op. cit.

29. Ibid.

30. Specifically, Title III of the Omnibus Crime Control and Safe Streets Act (1968).

31. Folley, op. cit., p. 83.

32. Eleanor Chelinsky, "A Primary-Source Examination of the Law Enforcement Assistance Administration (LEAA), and Some Reflections on Crime Control Policy," *Journal of Police Science and Administration* 3 (June 1975): 203–221.

33. National Advisory Commission on Criminal Justice Standards and Goals, *Criminal Justice System* (Washington, D.C.: U.S. Government Printing Office, 1973), p. 7.

34. National League of Cities and United States Conference of Mayors, *Criminal Justice Coordinating Council* (Washington, D.C.: National League of Cities, 1971), p. 3.

35. Pub. L. 91–644, Title I-4(2), Jan. 2, 1971.

36. National Institute of Law Enforcement and Criminal Justice, *Exemplary Programs* (monograph), April 1975, p. 3.

37. James M. Thoreabeau, *The History of the American Revolution* (New York: Crittendon, 1912), p. 69.

38. Rektor, op. cit., p. 178.

39. Miriam Ottenburg, *The Federal Investigator* (Englewood Cliffs, N.J.: Prentice-Hall, 1962), p. 228.

40. Walter S. Bowen and Harry F. Neal, *The United States Secret Service* (Philadelphia: Clifton, 1960), p. 20.

41. H. Stuart Knight, "The United States Secret Service: Ten Years Since," *Police Chief,* 42 (July 1975): 32.

42. Treasury Department Order No. 221, *Federal Register,* June 10, 1972, 11696.

43. Acree, op. cit., p. 11.

44. Vernon D. Acree, "U.S. Customs Assistance Programs," *Police Chief,* 42 (7) (July 1975): 36.

45. David R. MacDonald, "Treasury Department Assistance Programs to State and Local Law Enforcement Agencies," *Police Chief,* 42 (7) (July 1975): 30.

46. The FBI maintains its own separate training facility at Quantico, Virginia.

47. Department of the Treasury, "Consolidated Law Enforcement Training Center" (mimeo), Mar. 25, 1971, p. 3.

48. Rektor, op. cit., p. 382.

49. Department of the Army, *The Military Policeman* (Washington, D.C.: U.S. Government Printing Office, 1969), pp. 18–20.

50. General Services Administration, *United States Government Organizational Manual, 1973–74* (Washington, D.C.: U.S. Government Printing Office, 1973).

51. Department of the Air Force, *Security Police Handbook,* (Washington, D.C.: Air Training Command, 1971), p. 14.

Chapter 7

Delivery of Police Services: the Internal Organization of Police Agencies

The delivery of service by local police agencies is no small task. The demands made upon police agencies, particularly at the local level, are greater than those made on any other agency of city government. In municipalities, the importance of providing police services can be seen by the fact that police budgets are often the single largest expenditure of city governments.[1] This is particularly true in our largest cities. Similarly, police budgets also consume a great deal of all monies earmarked for criminal justice at all levels of government. Figure 7-1 shows the distribution of expenditures for criminal justice by all levels of government for the years 1972 and 1973. The data indicate that over 84 percent of the monies spent by cities for maintaining the local justice system goes to the police. Note the differences in how the various governmental levels apportion their spending among the agencies and services of criminal justice. After the police, the counties spend large percentages on the courts and corrections, which reflects their emphasis on providing these services. States, on the other hand, spend far more for correctional services because of their maintenance of prison systems. The federal government, which maintains an extensive network of courts and correctional systems, still spends approximately one-half of all criminal justice expenditures on law enforcement activities.

Because municipalities are the most numerous form of government in the United States, and since they expend nearly 68 percent of all monies spent on law enforcement service in the United States, this level of police service needs to be examined quite closely.[2] Municipal police agencies can be broken down into *management, line, staff,* and *auxiliary* services. In many smaller communities there will be no need for such specialization, but in medium to large cities extensive specialization is a characteristic of the organization of police services. Figure 7-2 shows the typical internal organization of a fairly large municipal police department. Although management is incorporated in line,

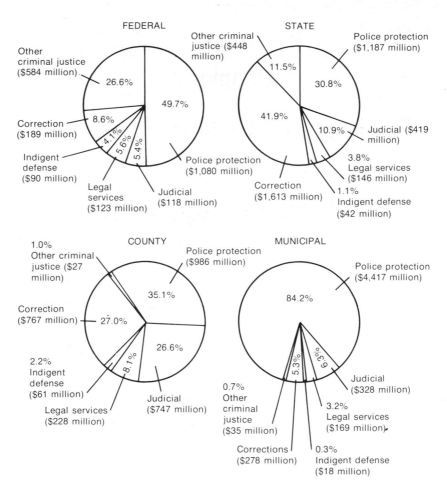

Figure 7.1   Total Government Expenditure for Criminal Justice
by Levels of Government (1972–1973)

From: U.S. Department of Justice, *Expenditure and Data for the Criminal Justice System,* 1972–73 (Washington: U.S. Government Printing Office, February 1975) pp. 9–14.

staff, and auxiliary services, we are treating it separately in order to better analyze it.

POLICE MANAGEMENT

The problems facing law enforcement today have a particularly strong impact on the police administrator. Although police management is an exacting

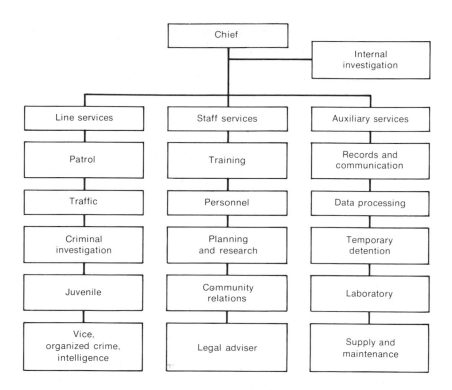

Figure 7.2   The Internal Organization of a Large Municipal
Police Department

responsibility that in all but the smallest cities requires highly developed managerial abilities, many police administrators lack the in-depth training and preparation necessary to develop the required administrative skills. Traditionally, promotions to the positions of chief or director of police have been from within the ranks of the particular department. Thus, an officer who has served twenty or thirty years in the department and has risen through the ranks becomes the chief of police.

This is not to say that loyalty and service should not be important considerations for appointment as the police administrator; however, there are serious limitations in this traditional practice. Under this system, too many individuals are appointed who do not have the requisite skills to manage such a complex organization as a modern police agency. For example, the typical career path of a police chief has been in the various operational areas of patrol, traffic, or investigation. Although experience in these areas may make a very proficient patrol or detective commander, they often do not provide the specific managerial skills needed by a top administrator. Skills in budgeting and fiscal management, labor negotiations, and departmental planning, and the ability to represent the department effectively before legislative and community groups are frequently necessary.

V. A. Leonard and Harry W. More, two noted authorities on police management, point out this paradox of effective police administration:

> Too frequently, it is assumed that the man who has the longest service, or if several are approximately equal on this point, then the man with the best record as a policeman may confidently be expected to be successful in the management of the department as its chief. The fallacy of this procedure is demonstrated by its failure in many American cities. The administration of a police department is a technical undertaking, requiring not only successful experience as a policeman, but also special talent and a number of peculiar skills that are not acquired in the course of ordinary police training and experience.[3]

This problem has become acute in recent years as police agencies have become more technically sophisticated and as greater demands have been made upon law enforcement agencies and police executives. For example, the growing political power of minority groups and their widespread demands for greater police responsiveness to their needs has added additional concerns for police management. As these groups have been able to register their dissatisfaction with the traditional methods of providing police services in minority neighborhoods, police administrators have had to make many changes in the deployment of police personnel and create specialized units to deal with the problems created by often hostile minority attitudes toward the police.

Likewise, the growing activism of Congress and the courts in the area of affirmative action programs has caused the police manager to reassess many long-standing police personnel practices in hiring and promotion of racial and ethnic minorities and women. At the same time, the police administrator has often faced increased militancy within the department from those opposed to the inroads made by minority groups in the operation of the department and to recent court-imposed guidelines on minority hiring and promotional policies. Thus the police executive must often deal with two opposing forces: those external to the department who demand change and those within the department who want to maintain the status quo.[4]

Another recent concern of police managers has been the issue of police productivity. As cities are finding themselves unable to meet the demands for increased services, municipal officials prodded by irate taxpayers are forcing city department heads to take an accounting of how well their alloted tax dollars have been spent. Since police departments spend such a high percentage of a community's available tax resources, they are coming under particularly close scrutiny.[5] In fact, Detroit and New York have been forced to cut back drastically on police services and personnel, and the situation is often no better in many smaller cities throughout the nation.

Increasingly, more communities are seeking to conserve tax dollars by more efficient utilization of police resources and at the same time to upgrade police executive talent. Four approaches are receiving attention by cities across the nation. These are (1) the creation of public safety departments and the appointment of a professional public safety director, (2) integration of police and fire services, (3) appointment of a professional police manager from outside the department, and (4) improvement of the management capabilities of present and future police administrators.

The Creation of Public Safety Departments

The public safety department centralizes all the community's public safety activities. For example, the police and fire services, civil defense, ambulance service, certain licensing and regulatory activities, and animal control are placed in a single department of public safety. Figure 7-3 shows the typical organizational arrangement of a city with a public safety department.

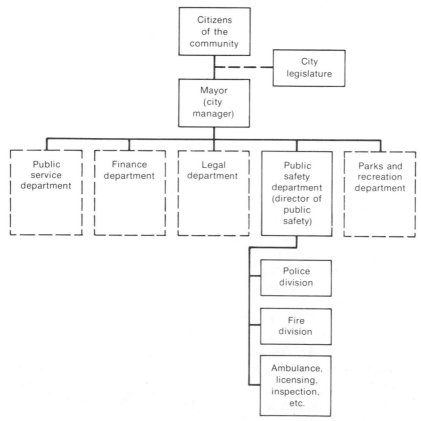

Figure 7.3   Typical Organizational Arrangement of Cities Having a Public Safety Department

The idea of the public safety department is not new. The city charter of Pittsburgh, Pennsylvania, authorized such a department and the position of director of public safety in 1901. A professional public safety director is often hired from outside the community and given the responsibility to direct and coordinate all the various safety services included in the agency. In many instances the public safety director is a qualified professional public administrator with experience in public safety agencies as well as in management.

Often, communities have adopted this type of arrangement as a means of bringing effective management to poorly run police and fire departments. Cities sometimes find that they cannot remove police and fire chiefs because these officials are under the protection of civil service.[6] Faced with this problem, some cities have consolidated all safety services under the management of a public safety director who reports directly to the mayor or city manager.

The Integration of Police and Fire Services

This concept calls for the merger of police and fire services into one integrated unit. Public safety officers provide both police and fire services; thus, an individual working in a city which utilizes this idea is both a police officer and a fire fighter.

This organizational arrangement has been most successful in medium-sized suburban communities. Its lack of success in some communities has often been due to the opposition of police and fire personnel who perceive it as a direct threat to their job security.

The strongest argument for its adoption is based simply on economics. Maintaining separate police and fire departments is more costly than maintaining an integrated department that performs both functions. Some who have argued for the adoption of integrated police and fire agencies point out that actual fire fighting accounts for only approximately 1 percent of a fire fighter's time.[7] Although a number of more progressive departments also conduct fire inspection and public education programs, and all fire departments require extensive equipment maintenance, fire fighters could be trained in law enforcement so that they could provide police services during their uncommitted time. Under the integrated police-fire concept, public safety officers spend most of their time providing police services but are available to respond to a fire if the need arises.[8] To accomplish this, they carry their fire fighting equipment in the trunks of the police cruisers.

In Sunnyvale, California, which has had a combined department since 1957, the city manager estimated that the unification was saving that city more than $300,000 per year. Although most of the savings comes from greater efficiency in the use of the work force, some of it is a result of not having to maintain two communication systems, two sets of buildings, two record facilities, and other duplicate services.[9]

Once the integrated department has been implemented, it seems to be very successful.[10] Under this arrangement communities realizing a significant reduction in costs of operation have been generally able to provide higher salaries to public safety personnel than they would have received as fire fighters or police officers. This has helped these communities attract more qualified and highly educated personnel as well as providing them with up-to-date equipment and training in both law enforcement and fire-fighting techniques.

Although the integrated police-fire service would be ideal for many smaller communities, its growth has been limited by the increasing opposition of organized police and fire labor organizations. Even in the absence of these formal labor groups, police and fire personnel have lobbied strongly in communities that have considered adopting such an arrangement.[11] Faced with increasing militant actions among police and fire labor groups, city officials have often been reluctant to implement this type of program. Yet as fiscal problems mount, the feasibility of this concept is being considered by growing numbers of municipal officials.

The Appointment of a Professional Police Manager From Outside the Department

There appears to be a definite trend among more and more cities to forsake the traditional method of appointing a police chief from within the ranks of the department. Increasingly, cities are recruiting top administrative talent from the outside. In many instances cities recruit throughout the nation by advertising in professional journals and holding open, competitive examinations for the position of police chief. Many of the most progressive police departments in the country are managed by such professional police administrators.

In many cases these professional police managers have extensive management experience in other city, state, or federal police agencies, and nearly all possess undergraduate and graduate training in police administration, business, or public management.[12] In an effort to further this type of professional development, organizations such as the International Association of Chiefs of Police (IACP) have developed a special registry service that contains the qualifications of police management personnel. This service, through a process of screening and testing, tries to match up the qualifications of the members of this registry with the requirements of cities seeking police managerial personnel.

The appointment of professional police executives does have some drawbacks. In many cases the appointment of an "outsider" is resented by members of the department, particularly the chief administrator's immediate subordinates who feel they have been passed over. In addition, sometimes outsiders are not aware of the particular social conditions in a certain community which are reflected in developed styles of law enforcement. The outsider who implements policies that are at variance with community attitudes may arouse both personal hostility and opposition toward the new policies.[14]

Another inhibiting factor is the problem of pension portability. A police manager in one community would lose pension rights if he or she accepted a job as police chief in another community. Some states, such as Ohio, have created a state-administered retirement system for police employers so that pension benefits are not lost when an individual transfers to another police agency in that state. Unfortunately, many states do not provide for similar pension transfers.

In spite of these limitations, professional police management will surely continue to grow. Many college students in criminal justice programs today will find increasing opportunities in the future provided they have the necessary educational preparation and acquire the necessary experience. Probably no other public occupation is as challenging as a career in police management.

Improvement of the Management Capabilities of Present and Future Police Administrators

The last eight or ten years have witnessed tremendous attempts to upgrade the skills of police managers and to prepare young men and women for future administrative responsibilities in law enforcement. Not only are increasing numbers of today's police administrators enrolled in undergraduate and graduate degree programs, but many are involved in intensive nondegree programs sponsored by universities and colleges. Such programs as those conducted by the Police Science Division of the Institute of Government at the University of Georgia are examples of the commitment of higher education to the training of police executives. This program brings together top police executive talent from across the country as well as teachers and researchers in the areas of management for various workshops, colloquia, and training programs. Teams of police executives and management experts conduct these programs for police management personnel, who attend from every state in the nation and from some foreign countries.

In addition, the FBI has recently constructed new facilities in Quantico, Virginia, to increase the training of police supervisory and management personnel. California and Florida have also sponsored supervisory and management programs in an effort to better develop police executive resources.

Recent years have also seen a tremendous proliferation of academic programs in colleges and universities that award degrees in the area of criminal justice management. In 1960, there were only 15 baccalaureate and graduate degree programs available to students in this country; by 1973, 515 institutions were offering degrees in criminal justice ranging from the associate degree to the Ph.D.[14] These programs are now developing the talent that will be managing criminal justice agencies of the future. In spite of this impressive growth, only a small beginning has been made in assuring that there will be available enough qualified police executives for the years to come.

LINE SERVICES

Line services are the direct operational components of the police service which have the responsibility to perform the basic overall police task. Depending upon the size of the police agency, the line units one might find are the following: *patrol; traffic; criminal investigation; juvenile or youth bureau;* and *vice, organized crime,* and *intelligence.*

Patrol

Every police agency has a patrol unit. The patrol force is the foundation of the police department and its largest operating unit. In large departments about 50 percent of all sworn personnel serve in this unit; in small departments the patrol force is, in effect, the department. Its personnel, who serve in uniform, are distributed throughout the city and perform most directly all the major functions required of modern law enforcement.

Thus, the patrol force is the action arm of the police department. Its field functions range from crime deterrence, prevention, and apprehension to such tasks as responding to sudden disasters, arbitrating domestic disturbances, and transporting and counseling citizens with whom they come in contact. Since the functions and responsibilities of the police officer assigned to the patrol unit are so broad and demanding, only police officers of the highest demonstrated competence and knowledge should be assigned to this unit. Eastman says of the work of the patrol force:

> With the patrol force deployed throughout a community and able to respond rapidly to calls for service, one or more of these men usually arrive first at the scene of a crime or disaster. But merely reaching the scene of an incident does not mark the end of a patrolman's mission; it is just the beginning. The measures a patrolman takes to confront a situation, the discretionary decisions he makes, the way he interacts with citizens, the skill and imagination he applies to conducting investigations, questioning suspects, interviewing complainants and witnesses, and the techniques he follows in searching crime scenes, and preserving physical evidence are the hallmarks of his job. Hence, the work of a patrolman is of far reaching importance and the quality of service rendered by the whole department is largely dependent upon his competence.[15]

Unfortunately, too many police departments still consider the patrol unit and its personnel to be inferior to other specialized units, notably the investigations or detective bureau. As a result of this narrow and erroneous view, many young men and women eagerly look forward to the day when they can be "promoted" to the supposedly more meaningful tasks and assignments of a specialized bureau.

Increasingly, however, with better police leadership developing in many agencies, the functions of the patrol unit are receiving greater attention and credit. Some police managers are now saying that only the most capable people in the department should be performing the generalist functions of patrol operations. Certainly the more effective the patrol unit is, the less pressure there is on the specialized operating units such as detectives, traffic, vice, etc., and the less need there is to have these specialized units. It is only when the patrol force cannot perform effectively in the traditional areas of police work that there is a need to create specialized units to support the functions of patrol.

Concepts of how best to provide patrol services to citizens have been changing in recent years. Years ago, the officer walking the beat was the visible symbol of police authority. In more recent years and particularly since World War II, police officers have been pulled off walking beats and assigned to multifrequency radio-equipped cars. The reasoning behind this change was that the police would be able to cover more territory and react to crimes a lot more quickly—and do them both at far less cost. Police management thinking also underwent changes after the war. Departments were organized much more like the military. Police administrators emphasized centralized control, close supervision, instant communications, and motorization. Individual officers were not allowed to stay in one neighborhood very long. The emphasis was on internal mobility under the dual theories that a mobile department is a "clean" department and that the mobile policeman became a "well-rounded" officer. The whole concept was called "professionalism."[16]

Today, the trend is reversing itself. Cincinnati, Oakland, Los Angeles, and many other cities are bringing back the idea of the beat cop. Cincinnati, for example, under a program called Com-Sec, assigns the same police officers regularly to a specific neighborhood, where they are encouraged to develop local contacts and rapport with residents—an obvious return to the oldtime beat idea. The Com-Sec experimental area is a 4-mile square section that includes the downtown business complex, which embodies only 5 percent of the city's total area, but accounts for 25 percent of its crime. Com-Sec divides that area into six neighborhoods, each with its own particular social and criminal complexion. The plan calls for each neighborhood to have its own mini-police department, supervised by a lieutenant and three sergeants, who command a team of from eighteen to eighty personnel, depending upon the sector. The idea behind Com-Sec and similar programs is to make the small neighborhood patrol unit a part of the neighborhood and to develop community assistance and support for the police task.

Patrol by Aircraft

Increasingly, police agencies are employing aircraft in an effort to improve the effectiveness of their patrol forces. VTOL (vertical take off and landing) aircraft such as helicopters, which have been used by the New York City Police since 1947, have in the past few years been adopted by more and more police agencies.

The use of helicopters by the police is often justified on the grounds that it (1) improves preventive patrol capabilities, (2) increases the probabilities of apprehension, (3) improves riot and disaster control operations, and (4) enhances

Monkmeyer

community support and service by increasing the visibility of the police.[17] The high-speed chase of fleeing felons through congested streets by automobile, an extremely hazardous undertaking to both police officers and innocent citizens, can be eliminated to a great extent with the availability of aircraft.

   The acquisition of a fixed-wing or helicopter patrol program is not limited to larger cities and counties. Adjacent communities are finding that cooperative arrangements can be made to purchase and utilize such aircraft. Sheriff's departments are in a particularly advantageous position to provide fixed-wing and helicopter services to local communities in the county.

Computer-Assisted Dispatching and Car Locators

A group of communities on the suburban fringe of Chicago is employing a unique computer-assisted dispatching and records maintenance system know as Automated Interactive Dispatch (AID).[18] The location and status of all patrol units are indexed in a centralized computer. When a patrol unit is dispatched to a call, all information is automatically transcribed, including type of incident, caller, victim, address, phone number, unit and officers assigned, time assigned, time of arrival of the police unit, and upon completion of the call, the disposition of the case. The system also provides for direct field unit access to national, state, regional, and local law enforcement computer networks for instantaneous checks on wanted persons, stolen property, and related information usually contained in such computer systems. The system has proved to be extremely useful in providing rapid dispatching capabilities and minimizing the time required for a police unit to respond to the scene of a call.

Another technological development that promises to be of great assistance to patrol operations is the Automatic Car Locator System. This system employs special sensors that are located throughout a community and tuned to be activated by passing police patrol vehicles. The activated signal is then transmitted to a master control map of the city. Police dispatchers are then able by a series of lights to monitor the location of police vehicles. When an emergency call is received, the police dispatcher can tell by a glance at the monitor panel which car is nearest the scene.

Crime-Specific Enforcement Units

As mentioned in Chapter 6 on federal law enforcement, LEAA's Impact Program was designed to attack the problem of violent street crimes in eight large American cities. It also sought to encourage local law enforcement agencies to counteract the surge in these types of offenses by concentrating their efforts on certain major crimes, such as robbery, burglary, grand larceny (including auto theft), rape, and other violent stranger-to-stranger street crimes.

The special police units that are assigned to concentrate on these specific offenses are known by a number of names. Detroit calls its crime-specific unit STRESS. Chicago refers to its as the Tactical Unit; Oakland, California, created a special Burglary Prevention and Control Coordination Group. Other jurisdictions might refer to them as selective enforcement units or metropolitan squads. These units employ various techniques. Atlanta, for example, was particularly concerned with a breakout of armed robberies in liquor stores and similar places of business. To counteract this, special teams of undercover stake-out officers were positioned in selected places of business that past experience indicated were most likely to be victimized. In other cases, decoy squads of police personnel dressed as civilians walk the streets to cut down on mugging or rape attempts.

Many of the more meaningful crime-specific enforcement programs incorporate similar features: first, police personnel chosen for these assignments are specially trained in combating specific offenses. Often, as in the case of the crime of burglary, special efforts are made to make citizens aware of how they can help the police and lessen their own chances of victimization. Typically, antiburglary information is distributed through mass mailings and presentations before citizen's groups. In a special form of citizen education called target hardening, police personnel advise business people and homeowners how to make their businesses and residences less vulnerable to crime.

Another important component of crime-specific enforcement programs is evaluation. As in any study, careful attention must be given to the gathering and interpretation of data to measure the program's effectiveness as well as to point out weaknesses in the particular strategy employed. The California Council on Criminal Justice, which is responsible for criminal justice planning and coordination throughout the state, developed one of the most comprehensive crime-specific plans involving the four largest cities and the two largest county police agencies in California. One of the most crucial features of the plan was the built-in provision for evaluation that was developed before the plan was implemented.[19]

Traffic

The traffic unit of a police department is responsible for developing and maintaining police-related traffic programs with responsibility for (1) enforcement, (2) citizen education, (3) investigation, (4) parking, and (5) engineering. A great deal of police effort is devoted to the general concept of traffic safety, which involves (1) gathering statistical facts about accidents, so that preventive action can be taken; (2) assisting accident victims by appropriate first aid and the transportation of injured parties; (3) offering public education and awareness programs dealing with the safe operation of motor vehicles and inspecting vehicles to ensure compliance with established safety standards; (4) assisting the traffic engineer and traffic safety education agencies by providing them with information useful in their accident prevention work; (5) serving as city government's inspection, investigative, and reporting unit to uncover problems and suggest improvements to expedite vehicular and pedestrian movement and parking; and (6) determining facts about accident occurrence as a basis for both accident prevention and service to involved citizens who need objective evidence to obtain justice in civil settlements of accident losses.[20]

Usually the traffic unit operates as a support and backup unit to the patrol force. Often it handles major traffic accidents where there is serious bodily injury or extensive property damage, conducts preliminary investigations of hit-skip cases, prepares evidence in traffic-related cases for criminal or civil court cases, and compiles and disseminates all traffic-related data to other police units and municipal agencies such as the traffic engineer.

The job of a traffic specialist requires special skills in accident investigation, alcohol testing equipment, traffic engineering support, and related areas. A number of highly regarded and extensive training programs such as Northwestern University's Traffic Institute and various programs sponsored by the National Safety Council have been developed to increase the skills of police traffic specialists in all areas of traffic enforcement and services.

Criminal Investigation

The criminal investigator (detective) is a police specialist who concentrates on the apprehension and conviction of adult criminal offenders. Unlike most other police units, this specialist group has as its primary goal the apprehension of the offender rather than prevention of a crime. The primary responsibilities of this unit are (1) identification, location, and arrest of criminal offenders; (2) collection and preservation of physical evidence; (3) location of witnesses; and (4) recovery and return of stolen property.[21]

The criminal investigative unit is necessary because continuing investigations involving weeks and even months of sustained effort cannot be accomplished by the patrol force without seriously depleting that units manpower. Often the patrol unit conducts preliminary investigations and even complete investigations when feasible. However, given the present operating characteristics of most municipal police departments, the detectives must take over most sustained investigations.

In smaller departments, a single investigative generalist will handle almost all the investigations; in larger departments the detective unit is subdivided into specialized subunits. The administrative recommendation in recent years has been to divide the detective unit into three specialist groups that handle most routine offenses.[22] These are (1) the crimes-against-persons unit, (2) the crimes-against-property unit, (3) the general assignment section.

The crimes-against-persons unit would conduct investigations where a person is the victim of a crime—e.g., murder, forcible rape, robbery, or assault. The crimes-against-property unit would conduct investigations involving loss of property. Such crimes as burglaries, larcenies, and auto theft would fall in this category. The general assignment section would conduct all investigations not handled by the other two units, such as fraud cases or general "con" games, embezzlement, and bad checks. Although this is the recommended organizational arrangement for many of the medium to large city police departments in the United States, in the very largest cities a far greater degree of specialization may be needed. For example, New York City has special units that handle nothing but burglaries, homicides, and similar crimes. Even burglaries may be further broken down into business/commercial and residential. Detroit has a special homicide squad called "Squad Six" which handles only drug-related homicides.

In recent years many police departments have undertaken a number of organizational charges that have somewhat modified the traditional operations of the criminal investigation unit. In the first place, detectives are more often generalists who no longer are assigned to investigate only certain offenses, but are required to be proficient investigators in a wider range of crimes. Secondly, especially with the advent of team policing, which will be discussed in the next chapter, patrol personnel and neighborhood team units are performing more and more of the investigative functions formerly assigned to the detective unit.

Juvenile or Youth Bureau

Since a great percentage of the problems that the police encounter involve juveniles, many police departments have created specialized juvenile units or youth bureaus to deal specifically with youth activities that directly affect the police.[23]

The responsibilities of the juvenile unit are quite broad and require special skills of the personnel assigned to this unit. This unit is responsible for performing not only law enforcement services, but many other related activities. The Children's Bureau of the U.S. Department of Health, Education, and Welfare sees the broad service role of this unit as consisting of the following:

1. Assisting the chief administrator in forming and implementing policy for dealing with juveniles.
2. Reviewing nonaction complaints and following up on action situations after initial contact by other police personnel.
3. Reviewing all reports dealing with police contact with juveniles.
4. Promoting liaison with other community agencies dealing with children, such as community welfare councils, juvenile courts, the school system voluntary social and welfare agencies, and other concerned institutions.
5. Completing follow-up investigations of specific types of complaints against children.
6. Adjusting cases when the best interest of the child and community can be served without resorting to court action.
7. Processing youths who are a danger to themselves or the community.
8. Working closely with the investigations unit in the examination of major offenses committed by children.
9. Providing for prevention and repression of delinquent behavior by youth.[24]

In recent years police juvenile units have slowly begun to adopt policies that will place them in line with the overall change in philosophy that characterizes all criminal justice agencies. This new philosophy is reflected in a concerted

Owen Franken/Stock, Boston

effort to divert youth away from the juvenile justice system so that their problems will be defined and handled outside the context of delinquency and official sanctions. Some far-sighted police departments are encouraging *proactive* rather than *reactive* strategies for dealing with youth. In other words, they seek to prevent and deter delinquent behavior rather than wait until a delinquent act has been committed and then arrest the child and process him or her through the courts.

Although this proactive approach has been criticized by many police personnel as "social work rather than police work" and a form of "coddling" the child, there are some very sound arguments for the adoption of this role by the police. Probably the best one is that the police and the schools are the first public agencies to come in contact with the delinquent or predelinquent child. If quick intervention is a partial solution to the problems of delinquency in this country, the police are in a position to intervene effectively. Unlike the schools, which have the primary function of education, the police (1) already have a general preventive role to play, (2) have a greater understanding of crime and its causes, and (3) are available with resources on a twenty-four hour basis.

Vice, Organized Crime, and Intelligence

In some larger agencies, the problems and responsibilities of enforcing vice laws, dealing with organized crime, and gathering intelligence in these areas is handled by specialized units. Vice is often the responsibility of a small group of investigative specialists, with organized crime and intelligence gathering the responsibility of another group. However, many police agencies and police managers have come to the realization that there is often a direct relationship between vice activities in a community and organized crime so that these formerly separate functions have been made the responsibility of a single unit.

The effectiveness of any police department, particularly a small specialist subunit, in these areas is questionable. Local police must overcome formidable problems in these type of crimes. The first problem is that local police departments just do not have the trained personnel, investigative equipment, or jurisdictional authority to counteract organized crime efforts. The federal agencies have demonstrated that to be successful organized crime investigations require extensive manpower commitments, the availability and use of technical and legal investigative resources, and a sizeable operating budget. Local police departments have none of these to the extent they are required.[25] In addition, organized crime efforts transcend local jurisdictional boundaries, and therefore local law enforcement is hampered in conducting the necessary multijurisdictional investigations.[26]

Another major problem area that one must forthrightly address when considering the problems of local efforts against organized crime is corruption among police and other local public officials. This has long hampered effective local investigations and prosecutions of organized crimes.[27] A final impediment is the traditional organization of local police departments and a general police reluctance to exchange intelligence between departments or even share it among members of the same police agency. The President's Commission points this out when it says:

> The apparent versatility exhibited by professional criminals suggests that the traditional organization of police agencies into specialized squads such as robbery, burglary, auto theft and bunco requires reconsideration. It suggests also the need for a much greater degree of communication between law enforcement agents with information on professional criminals. Detectives tend to be too reluctant to share their information sources with other detectives or to supply information to any centralized intelligence unit which may exist. Also the traditional complaint orientation of police departments is not appropriate for dealing with persons who are engaged continuously, rather than episodically in criminal activities.[28]

As a consequence, most vice, organized crime, and intelligence units in local police departments are relegated to making isolated and unimportant arrests of small-time narcotics dealers, prostitutes, and other low-level criminal operatives.

STAFF SERVICES

The staff units of a police department are support units whose primary function is to assist the line services in their task of carrying out the basic police responsibilities. The staff units in police agencies have come into their own in recent years. With the demands placed on police agencies for more and better services, there has been an increased emphasis on upgrading staff services, which in turn has improved the operational capabilities of the line units. There are six basic staff units that may be found in municipal police departments: *training, personnel, planning and research, community relations, legal, and internal investigations*.

Training

Until the past few years most police agencies in cities of medium size and larger had a training unit. The recent trend has been to turn recruit training over to regional training academies operated by the state. There have been two reasons for this: first, it was recognized that unless recruit training was available to all newly hired police personnel from *all* communities in the state, the same old problems would continue to exist; namely, the small cities would not offer any training for their personnel, and even the larger cities would provide only mediocre training because of their lack of resources and qualified personnel to conduct the necessary training.[29] Secondly, states have passed legislation that requires all newly appointed police personnel to undergo a stipulated minimum number of hours of training in approved police training programs before they can be certified as police officers anywhere in the state. New Jersey, Michigan,

Texas, Florida, Idaho, Georgia and California have this type of legislation and have established regional training centers.

However, a number of larger departments still maintain their own training programs. Whether given at the department or regionally sponsored, a typical recruit training program covers the following subjects:

1. Classroom Notetaking.
2. The Role of Law Enforcement.
3. Police-Community Relations.
4. Police Ethics.
5. Racial and Minority Groups.
6. Laws of Arrest, Search and Seizure, Constitutional Guarantees.
7. Code of Criminal Procedure, Criminal Law.
8. Vehicle and Traffic Law.
9. Traffic Control.
10. Traffic Accident Investigation.
11. Laws of Evidence.
12. Evidence Resources in a Criminal Case, including the Crime Scene Search.
13. Collection, Care, Identification and Preservation of Evidence.
14. Court Organization and Procedure.
15. Courtroom Demeanor and Testifying.
16. Basic Criminal Investigation.
17. Notetaking and Report Writing.
18. Interviews, Interrogation, Admissions, Statements.
19. The Patrol Function.
20. Care and Use of Firearms.
21. Defensive Tactics.
22. Techniques and Mechanics of Arrest.
23. Emergency Aid to Persons.
24. Recognition and Handling of Abnormal Persons.[30]

In the past, police training programs traditionally emphasized firearms proficiency, physical training, and defensive tactics; recent emphasis has been more on subjects that examine the psychological and sociological environment in which a police officer must work so that he or she can better relate to citizens and to the job of a police officer.[31]

In addition to recruit training, police training personnel are responsible for developing special *in-service training programs*, which deal with specific subject areas. Some departments, as in New Haven, Connecticut, have introduced special taped spot lectures which are periodically broadcast over the police radio to all units in the field.[32] This innovative extension of the in-service training program covers such topics as interpersonal relations with members of the community, legal issues, and operational techniques, such as how to properly stop vehicles carrying possible suspects. Another method of in-service training used by a number of police training units is *roll call training*. The idea was originally developed in the Los Angeles Police Department. Under this system, training is presented for fifteen to thirty minutes during the roll call period at the beginning of a shift and just before the officers go out on duty.

Those police agencies which still operate their own training programs often use some of their best college-educated personnel as members of the training unit. This seems to be a logical choice of assignment because these individuals are often eager and bright men and women who consider keeping up with new developments in the field as part of their professional responsibility.

Personnel

This specialist function is typically found only in the largest police departments. In most cases, police personnel functions are handled by the city's central personnel office which performs the *personnel function* for all city employees.

Where they do exist, police personnel units are concerned with such matters as (1) the selection, recruitment, assignment, and promotion of personnel; (2) the evaluation of performance and accomplishments of personnel so that individuals with certain talents can be used most advantageously in assignment and promotion; (3) coordinating functions with training personnel so that unsuitable performance will be recognized and remedial programs instituted to maintain a suitable level of service; (4) paying careful attention to such matters as whether there is effective supervision, complaints against officers investigated or turned over to the specialist personnel assigned this function, and suitable disciplinary measures applied when needed; and (5) rendering attention to the welfare of police personnel. Also included are such duties as checking on whether conditions of employment are satisfactory, whether provisions for pension plans and retirement are implemented, and whether there are desirable relations among supervisory and subordinate personnel in the department.

Planning and Research

Every police agency is involved in planning activities. However, some departments are much more sophisticated and deliberate in the planning process than others and have created special supporting staff units to assist police management in this endeavor. As police management has become more sophisticated in recent years, the need for this type of activity has been increasingly recognized. The planning and research unit of a police department is responsible for assisting management in the following areas:

1. The establishment of written policy which will determine specific agency goals and the means to measure the attainment of these goals.
2. The development and suggestion of plans that will improve police service.
3. The gathering and organizing of data needed for agency planning. This includes such areas as: a) administrative planning; b) tactical/operations plans; c) fiscal and management plans; and d) extradepartmental plans.
4. The conduct of research and development and the gathering of appropriate data that will be useful to police management in making decisions.[33]

The increased emphasis on planning has created the need for new skills among police personnel and has led to greater use of civilians. Such areas as statistics and research methodology, systems analysis and computer technology, grant-writing skills and evaluative program techniques, and budget preparation are responsibilities of the planning unit. As a consequence of this new emphasis, many universities offering four-year and graduate programs in criminal justice are emphasizing these skills in their academic course offerings. For example, the School of Criminal Justice at Michigan State University in addition to basic courses in police administration requires course work in systems development, fiscal administration, information systems, and quantitative methods at the master's level.

An important component of the overall planning and research activity is *operations analysis*, which looks at such things as reports of serious crime in order to determine the location, time, special characteristics, similarities to other criminal attacks, and various significant facts that may help to identify patterns of criminal behavior so that the department may take appropriate action through preventive and apprehension strategies, manpower deployment, etc. Similarly, traffic patterns and problems are analyzed so that corrective action may be taken. Research and development (R&D) activities are also undertaken to improve the capabilities and use of existing police equipment. R&D activities focus on examining the capabilities and limitations of existing equipment and making recommendations for improvement or the purchase of different equipment. These recommendations guide the administrator in developing the budget and making purchases for the agency.

Community Relations

The issue of police-community relations (PCR) has assumed particular importance for the police in recent years. Until the 1950's the concept of a formal community relations unit was virtually unknown in police departments, but by the late 1960's some far-reaching changes had been made. During the tumultuous 1960's social unrest became a fact of American life. Racial concerns, an unwanted war, and the affluence that permitted young people to engage in civil protest almost as a career were the forces that by 1968 caused the police response to social unrest to become a matter of broad public concern. It attracted the attention of four presidential and numerous local commissions; it was the subject of countless studies, articles, books, and speeches. As a result of this pressure, police departments began to adopt community relations programs on a wholesale basis. They established the appropriate bureaucracies, opened storefront offices to reach the public, trained their people in community relations, and generally tried to accommodate their critics.[34]

Although most police departments still consider the PCR unit as a staff support unit, knowledgeable critics argue vehemently (1) that it should more appropriately be a line unit operating directly out of the office of the police chief or (2) that it should not exist as a specialized unit—the primary responsibility of PCR should rest with all line units and personnel.[35] The argument usually is that the chief administrator should demonstrate total commitment to PCR programs and set the example for the department and that the creation of a specialized unit will give the impression to line personnel that PCR is a function only of the special unit and that line personnel need not be concerned.

Although it is not possible to list all the activities that an effective PCR unit is engaged in, broad areas of concern can be mentioned. Table 7-1 indicates three general areas and the specific programs that might fall into each. The serious student might also wish to review some of the published bibliographies on the subject.

TABLE 7-1
Areas of Concern for PCR Programs

Public Relations	Personal cleanliness and good grooming (wearing uniform smartly, having shoes polished, etc.)
	General politeness, courtesy, and good manners
	Telephone etiquette
	Car cleanliness (keeping cars washed, etc.)
	Modifications in the military-type uniform (redesigned blazers, jackets, etc.; inconspicuous carrying of weapons)
	Speaker's bureau activities, skill demonstrations, equipment exhibits, etc.
	Open houses at police stations
	Dog shows, water safety shows, etc.
	Displays on bumper stickers, car cards, billboards
	Awards and citations for outstanding police officers and citizens

Liaison for press personnel and facilities
Cooperation between the chief and media executives
Tidiness and good order in administrative facilities
American flag insignia worn

Community Service Service	Informational or interpretive newspaper or magazine features, newsletters, and door knob hangers; radio and television presentations (e.g., education on drugs, auto safety, auto theft, house burglaries)
	Safety instruction for operating autos, bicycles, and other vehicles
	Youth programs (e.g., Police Athletic League, summer camping)
	Store-front centers in neighborhoods
	Annual or periodic reports, *if* designed for public understanding
	Complaint procedure
	Public fund raising for tuition to help improve the education of police officers (by a citizens' organization)
	Ride-in-a-patrol-car programs.
	Sponsorship of scouting units (e.g., Explorers)
	Police junior band or drum-and-bugle corps
	Law enforcement career clinics in high schools
	Policeman Bill and *Officer Friendly* types of programs in elementary schools
	Police aid and advice for parades, demonstrations, etc.
	Emergency facilities for demonstrations
	Police assignments to job opportunity centers
	Assistance to crisis-intervention agencies
	Crime prevention literature
	Helping Hand programs
	Distribution of information to new residents
	Tire-changing assistance
	Checks on vacationers' residences
	Ambulance service
	Lost-and-found auctions (e.g., bicycles)
	School counseling assistance
	Social service referrals
Community Participation	Councils of social agencies (e.g., United Fund, Community Chest)
	Family and neighborhood stabilization councils
	Coordinating councils on community relations
	Councils on police-community relations
	Precinct or district police-citizens committees or workshops
	Councils on crime and delinquency
	Interdenominational clergy-police councils
	Police-community relations seminars
	Community or neighborhood councils

Source: Louis A. Radelet, *The Police and the Community,* 2nd ed., © 1977, p. 28. Reprinted by permission of Glencoe Press.

Unfortunately, the PCR programs adopted in recent years have not reached nearly their potential. There are a number of reasons for this: Many of these programs and units were created in an atmosphere of crisis, and commitment was maintained only as long as the crisis was remembered. Too often police and other city officials have regarded community relations efforts as attempts to relieve immediate pressures, and this lack of commitment has been clearly communicated to the ranks at which the programs must be carried out. Low budgets, a large proportion of black officers, training projects divorced from the rest of the police training curriculum, the employment of civilians, and other characteristics have communicated to the police department that community relations is not a serious activity.

Most community relations programs have also been established as a function separate from patrol, crime prevention, investigations, and other traditional aspects of policing. Because the separateness of community relations has been emphasized, it has tended to be marginal to the operations of the police department. PCR programs have also suffered from unclear objectives and almost no meaningful evaluation. Often goals were defined in such broad generalities as "improving the relationship between the police department and citizens" or "giving citizens a greater appreciation of the police department and increasing their willingness to cooperate in attaining its objectives."[36]

Many authorities appear to be less than optimistic that PCR will continue even as a marginally viable special goal of police departments for all of the above reasons as well as because the urban disorders which were the initial precipitant are no longer a major issue in the 1970s. The fact that the police are already deemphasizing PCR is truly unfortunate.

Legal Adviser

The office of legal adviser is a relatively new one. A 1965 survey conducted by the National League of Cities of 276 police departments indicated that only 14 employed legal advisers and 6 of these were part-time.[37] Although there have been no recent surveys, the present number is certainly larger.

The duties of a police legal adviser are to advise the chief administrator on disciplinary matters and prosecution of cases before internal trial boards; to interpret court decisions for police personnel and assist in the legal presentation of police cases to the prosecutor; to act as liaison between the police and the prosecutor's office; to advise the police chief in order to protect the chief executive's management interest when collective bargaining negotiations are being undertaken; and to evaluate the effect of legislative proposals at the level of enforcement and draft requests for legislative amendments or other statutes needed by the department. Legal units can also be useful by meeting with the local judiciary to learn the extent of proof that individual judges require from officers in specific cases and by working closely with the training unit in developing in-service legal courses for police personnel.

Even though a community might not be large enough to support the services of a legal adviser, the National Advisory Commission recommends that legal counsel be available to all police departments. A legal adviser might serve all police agencies in a district, or this function could be incorporated in the existing prosecutor's office, with additional assistant prosecutors assigned to work with the police as advisers when they are not in court. Another possibility would be to employ part-time or contractual advisers. This might be an appropriate alternative for medium-sized agencies that cannot afford a full-time legal adviser.[38]

Columbus, Ohio, has taken a unique approach to the problem that is expected to save costs in the long run. The police in that city are training experienced police officers as paraprofessional legal advisers.[39] Four police officers have been selected to attend a three-year-program of special law courses given at a local law school. Upon completion of their studies, they will become full-time legal advisers to the department. As experienced police officers, these paraprofessionals are expected to be highly effective as advisers to other police officers.[39]

Internal Investigations

Since the 1960s many persons outside law enforcement have urged establishment of civilian review boards which would investigate complaints against police personnel. Undoubtedly, this demand has been prompted by feelings that the police have avoided making fair and vigorous investigations of wrong-doing within their ranks.

The function of an internal investigations unit is to investigate complaints against police personnel or other actions which may bring disrepute to the agency. This includes interviewing the complainant, any witnesses, and the police officer(s) involved and presenting all the evidence to the police internal trial board or the prosecutor if the investigation reveals that the allegation of police misconduct is justified. Specifically, the responsibilities of such a unit include making appropriate inquiry of:

1. Any allegation or complaint of misconduct made by a citizen or other person against the department or any of its members.
2. Any alleged or suspected breach of integrity or case of moral turpitude from whatever source it may be reported or developed.
3. Any situation where an officer has been killed or injured by the deliberate or willful act of another person.

4. Any situation in which a citizen has been injured or killed by an officer either on or off duty.

5. Any situation involving the discharge of firearms by an officer.

6. In addition, other delegated responsibilities might include: *a*) assisting in any disciplinary case when requested by police management personnel; *b*) assisting any member of the department by investigating cases of harassment, threats, or false accusations against the officer; and, *c*) fully advising citizen complainants of the decisions and actions taken following receipt of complaints. [40]

In larger agencies, the internal investigations unit usually consists of a small group of carefully chosen and experienced personnel who should possess the highest principles of professionalism and personal integrity. In smaller departments, the task of inquiry may be turned over to a trusted investigator when any allegations are made. In some small agencies, the chief of police personally conducts such inquiries.

The organizational chart of a police department in Figure 7-2 shows this unit as being directly under the office of the police chief. This indicates that in most instances it is administratively recommended that this unit report directly to the chief. The rationale for this is quite obvious. Because of the importance of such activity to the department and the sensitive nature of this unit's work in terms of the attitudes and perceptions of citizens and police personnel, the unit should have direct and frequent access to the chief. The full authority of the chief's office should stand behind the responsibilities of this unit.

AUXILIARY SERVICES

The auxiliary services are support units other than staff services which assist the line units in performing the police function. We will briefly examine five typical auxiliary services: *records and communications, data processing, temporary detention, laboratory,* and *supply and maintenance*.

Records and Communication

The central records and communication unit in a modern police agency is responsible for storing, indexing, retrieving, and disseminating to police operations personnel and management all pertinent information of a police nature. The records section, however, deals more with crime-related information than with management-related information. For example, the records section gathers data on crimes committed, wanted persons, case histories of known offenders, stolen property, *modus operandi* (method of operation) information, and other similar data.

The functions of records and communication are, of necessity, integrated processes, and as agencies adopt rapid access on-line computer capabilities, data processing of crime-related information is also tied into this unit. Central records and communications systems provide the means by which law enforcement agencies can gather information about crimes quickly and efficiently, store this information when not needed, yet instantly retrieve and communicate pertinent information when requested by the field units.

The records and communication unit often provides the following specific services to line units in the field: (1) receiving personal and telephone complaints; (2) receiving and dispatching radio messages to police mobile units in the field; (3) monitoring adjoining county and municipal police and fire departments, state law enforcement agencies, and other public safety radio systems; (4) receiving and transmitting teletype messages; (5) upon requests from field units, making inquiries from regional, state, and national computerized records systems; (6) controlling the movement of unauthorized personnel within the building; and (7) in some cases providing booking, personal identification, and jail security assistance.[41]

Data Processing

Only the largest police departments have data processing units. The very large agencies often have their own computer facilities and supporting software components. Medium-sized departments often use existing municipal computer facilities on a time-sharing basis. The data processing unit assists line and staff operation and police management personnel in a number of ways. It can be used for processing uniform crime-reporting information on a monthly basis; gathering intelligence and compiling budgeting information and other information of administrative value, such as fleet operating costs and personnel records. Many departments are using computer-assisted work force deployment programs; by gathering and analyzing data pertaining to crime patterns in terms of both geographical areas and hours of occurrence, police patrol personnel can be assigned to the areas and at the specific times when the data indicate that the majority of crimes occur or the workload is heaviest.

The data processing unit is also responsible for developing real time, on-line computer capabilities for the operations units. Real-time, on-line computer systems are designed so that information stored in the computer can be immediately accessed and retrieved for immediate dissemination to requesting units. Such a system would normally contain the following information:

1. Wanted persons
    a. Persons with warrants outstanding
    b. Persons wanted for questioning
    c. Missing persons
    d. Persons under investigation or surveillance
    e. Revoked and suspended driver's license data

2. Persons: criminal history information
    a. Arrest data
    b. Conviction data

    c. Parole and probation data
    d. Aliases and nicknames
    e. Personal and physical characteristics
    f. Method-of-operation patterns

3. Vehicles
    a. Stolen vehicles
    b. Stolen license plates or tags
    c. Vehicles wanted in connection with crimes
    d. Other vehicle status, such as repossessed, impounded, or abandoned
    e. Vehicles under surveillance

4. Property
    a. Stolen property
    b. Lost property
    c. Recovered property

5. Miscellaneous
    a. Parking tickets
    b. Schedule of court cases

Temporary Detention

Police agencies that operate their own jail facilities have a temporary detention or jail unit. Unfortunately, many small police departments often turn this job over to the dispatcher or some other individual who usually is neither concerned nor qualified to handle the responsibilities of prisoner care.[42]

The jail unit is usually responsible for the following functions:

1. The search and control of prisoners during the booking process.
2. The booking of prisoners.
3. Fingerprinting and photographing of prisoners.
4. Compliance with legal requirements that the prisoner have access to an attorney, etc.
5. The custody and return of prisoners' property.
6. The inspection, supervision and care of prisoners and jail facilities.
7. The transfer of prisoners to court or to some other jail or institution.[43]

In addition to these routine responsibilities, the jail unit may supervise prisoners engaged in work details or treatment programs. In some jurisdictions the detention staff may also serve as court officers.

Laboratory

Only very large police departments maintain crime laboratory facilities. Staffing such a unit with scientific and technical personnel and providing the required equipment is too costly for all but a few large agencies that can justify it on the basis of demonstrated need to conduct frequent scientific analyses. Typically, the laboratory equipment in a medium-sized agency is limited to such things as special cameras, photographic darkroom, latent fingerprint analysis capabilities, and perhaps some infrared equipment, such as night vision devices. Thus, most of it can be mastered by a police technical expert in a relatively short time.

In many states a central laboratory services the needs of local and county police agencies. For example, Michigan has established regional crime labs throughout that state under the auspices of the Michigan State Police. Often the state laboratories have mobile crime vans that can be dispatched to the scene of a crime or major disaster to make scientific analyses on the spot. These laboratories also provide various scientific experts from their staffs who work closely with local police agencies in field investigations and members are available as expert witnesses to testify at trials. Such federal agencies as the FBI, DEA, and others also provide laboratory services to local police agencies upon request.

The police laboratory typically performs scientific analyses in the following areas:*

- Chemical examinations:
  Narcotics
  Alcohol
  Explosives
  Incendiary materials
  Toxic substances
  Analysis of unknown specimens—for identification and tracing
  Analysis for comparison—the evidence specimen is compared with specimens of known origin

- Physical examinations:
  Automobile parts—broken ornaments, lenses, and other parts
  Broken windows—and other glass problems
  Electrical appliances
  Locks and keys
  Tool marks and other impressions
  Etching deleted numbers

- Personal markings for identification purposes:
  Fingerprints
  Foot and shoe impressions
  Laundry and dry-cleaning marks

- Documentary examinations:
  Questioned handwriting
  Typewriting
  Erasures and obliterations
  Paper, ink, and pencil problems

*   Harry Sodermann and John J. O'Connell, *Modern Criminal Investigation*, 5th ed., Copyright © 1962; previous copyrights 1935, 1940, 1952 by Funk & Wagnalls Publishing Company, Inc. Used by permission of the publisher.

- Firearms problems:
  Identification of bullets and cartridges
  Firearms examination
  Trajectories
- Biological examinations:
  Blood
  Semen
  Hair and fibers
- Photography:
  Contrast and filter photography
  Infrared and ultraviolet photography
  Photomicrography
  Radiography

There are many opportunities today for young men and women who are interested in becoming criminalists, that is, specialists who apply the physical sciences to the solution of crimes. Preparation for a career in this field requires a strong background in such scientific areas as physics, chemistry, and biology together with an adequate foundation in criminal investigation, criminal law, and evidence and a knowledge of the criminal justice system. A number of universities offer specialized undergraduate and graduate degree programs in criminalistics.

Supply and Maintenance

This unit, which exists in only the very largest police departments, incorporates such services as building and automotive maintenance, radio service, tailor shop, and the police armorer. More commonly, city maintenance personnel maintain the police facility, although some cities use prisoners from the city jail to provide most of the routine maintenance. Responsibility for vehicle and radio maintenance is most often let out on bid to private contractors.

SUMMARY

Municipal police departments are the most numerous law enforcement agencies in the United States, and they are costly services to maintain. The police receive almost 85 percent of all municipal monies spent on the administration of justice.

In recent years cities have been examining alternative organizational arrangements in an effort to improve local law enforcement. Some of the more common are the appointment of a professional public safety director who manages a consolidated department of public safety; the even more controversial integrated police-fire concept; and the appointment of a professional police manager from outside the police department.

Municipal police departments are patterned after military organizations. Thus, operational units in police departments are broken down into line, staff and auxiliary services. The line units, which perform the basic overall police task, are patrol; traffic; criminal investigation; juvenile; and vice, organized crime, and intelligence.

The staff services, which are specialized support units that assist the line units in carrying out their basic police tasks, are training, personnel, planning and research, community relations, legal, and internal investigations.

The auxiliary services, which are support units other than staff services, are records and communication, data processing, temporary detention, laboratory, and supply and maintenance.

Suggested Additional Readings

American Bar Association. *Standards Relating to the Urban Police Function*. Chicago: American Bar Association, 1972.

Bopp, William J. *Police Personnel Administration*. Boston: Holbrook Press, 1972.

Butler, Alan J. *The Law Enforcement Process*. Port Washington, N.Y.: Alfred, 1976.

Gourley, G. Douglas, and Allen F. Bristow, *Patrol Administration*. Springfield, Ill.: Charles C. Thomas, 1961.

International City Management Association. *Municipal Police Administration*. Washington, D.C.: International City Management Association, 1969.

Munro, Jim L. *Administrative Behavior and Police Organization*. Cincinnati: W. H. Anderson, 1974.

Saunders, Charles B. *Upgrading the American Police*. Washington, D.C.: Brookings, 1970.

Shanahan, Donald T. *Patrol Administration—Management by Objectives*. Boston: Holbrook Press, 1975.

Stahl, O. Glenn, and Richard A. Staufenberger (eds.). *Police Personnel Administration*. North Scituate, Mass.: Duxbury Press, 1974.

Weston, Paul B. *Police Organization and Management*. Pacific Palisades, Calif.: Goodyear, 1976.

Whisenand, Paul M., and Fred R. Ferguson. *The Managing of Police Organizations*. Englewood Cliffs, N.J.: Prentice-Hall, 1973.

Wilson, O. W. *Police Administration*. New York: McGraw-Hill, 1963.

———— and Roy C. McLaren. *Police Administration*. 3d ed. New York: McGraw-Hill, 1972.

Notes

1. The one possible exception to this is found in those cities which have an unusually extensive capital development program involving large construction undertakings or the retirement of bonds used to finance capital improvement.

2. Committee for Economic Development, *Reducing Crime and Assuring Justice* (New York: Committee for Economic Development, 1972), p. 84.

3. V. A. Leonard and Harry W. Moore, *Police Organization and Management,* 4th ed. (Mineola, N.Y.: Foundation Press, 1974), p. 40.

4. For example, see Hervey A. Juris and Peter Feville, *Police Unionism: Power and Impact in Public Sector Bargaining* (Lexington, Mass.: Heath, 1973).

5. See John A. Grimes, "The Police, the Union and the Productivity Imperative," in Joan L. Wolfe and John F. Heaphy (eds.), *Readings on Productivity in Policing* (Washington, D.C.: Police Foundation, 1975), pp. 47–85.

6. O. W. Wilson and Roy C. McLaren, *Police Administration,* 3d ed. (New York: McGraw-Hill, 1972), p. 21.

7. Ibid., p. 191.

8. On the question of a police officer's uncommitted time, see George L. Kelling, et al., *The Kansas City Preventive Patrol Project* (Washington, D.C.: Police Foundation, 1974).

9. Wilson and McLaren, op. cit., p. 190.

10. See Harry W. More, *The New Era of Public Safety* (Springfield, Ill.: Charles C Thomas, 1970).

11. See James A. Edwards, "A Survey of Police-Fire Consolidation Attempts in California," unpublished thesis (Los Angeles: University of California Press, 1963).

12. See Robert D. Pursley, "Leadership and Local-Cosmopolitan Attitudes among a National Sample of Traditionalist and Non-Traditionalist Police Chiefs," unpublished dissertations (Athens: University of Georgia, 1974).

13. Frank Sherwood, "A City Manager Tries to Fire His Police Chief," monograph (Indianapolis: Bobbs-Merrill, 1955).

14. International Association of Chiefs of Police, *1972–73 Directory of Law Enforcement and Criminal Justice Education* (Gaithersburg, Md.: IACP, 1972).

15. George D. Eastman (ed.), *Municipal Police Administration* (Washington, D.C.: International City Management Association, 1969), p. 77.

16. Richard Baker, "Remember Your Friendly Neighborhood Cop?" *Sky Magazine* 3(7) (July 1974): 21.

17. See Paul M. Whisenand and George M. Medak, "Police Helicopter Patrol," *Management Information Service Bulletin* (Washington, D.C.: International City Management Association, October 1971); and the Law Enforcement Assistance Administration, *Project Skynight: A Demonstration of Aerial Surveillance and Crime Control* (Washington, D.C.: U.S. Government Printing Office, 1968).

18. For a description of this system, see Arthur B. Carroll, et al., "Computer Aided Dispatching for Law Enforcement Agencies," *Community Technology* (mimeo.), 1975.

19. See JoAnne W. Rockwell, "Crime Specific . . . An Answer?" *Police Chief,* 39 (September 1972): 38–43.

20. Eastman (ed.), op. cit., p. 106.

21. N. C. Chamelin et al., *Introduction to Criminal Justice* (Englewood Cliffs, N.J.: Prentice-Hall, 1975), p. 120.

22. For example, see International City Management Association, op. cit., pp. 130–133; and Wilson and McLaren, op. cit., pp. 386–389.

23. For a good insight into the role of the police in problems involving juveniles, see Robert C. Trojanowicz, *Juvenile Delinquency: Concepts and Control* (Englewood Cliffs, N.J.: Prentice-Hall, 1973), especially chap. 7.

24. U.S. Department of Health, Education, and Welfare, Children's Bureau, *Police Work with Children: Perspectives and Principles,* Children's Bureau Pub. No. 399 (Washington, D.C.: U.S. Government Printing Office, 1962), pp. 9–10, 44.

25. Hank Messick, *The Silent Syndicate* (New York: Macmillan, 1967), p. 43.

26. Gus Tyler (ed.), "Combating Organized Crime," a special issue of *The Annals of the American Academy of Political and Social Science,* 347 (May 1963).

27. For example, see Donald R. Cressey, "Corruption of the Law Enforcement and Political Systems," in John E. Conklin (ed.), *The Crime Establishment* (Englewood Cliffs, N.J.: Prentice-Hall, 1973), pp. 131–145.

28. President's Commission on Law Enforcement and Administration of Justice, *Crime and Its Impact—An Assessment* (Washington, D.C.: U.S. Government Printing Office, 1967), p. 101.

29. For example, a 1965 survey of 4,000 police departments conducted by the International Association of Chiefs of Police revealed that 85 percent of the officers appointed were sent into the field prior to their recruit training. President's Commission on Law Enforcement and Administration of Justice, *Police* (Washington, D.C.: U.S. Government Printing Office, 1967), p. 138.

30. Leonard and More, op. cit., p. 251.

31. See James E. Cavanaugh, "A New Emphasis in Recruit Training," *Police* (January–February 1968): 32–36; and statement by G. L. Kuchel, "Number One Problem," *Police Chief,* 37 (August 1970): 17.

32. See Harold Berg, "Training on Patrol—A Top Program," *Police Chief,* 41 (November 1974): 28.

33. National Advisory Commission on Criminal Justice Standards and Goals, *Police* (Washington, D.C.: U.S. Government Printing Office, 1973), p. 117.

34. Robert Wasserman, Michael P. Gardner, and Alana S. Cohen, *Improving Police Community Relations* (Washington, D.C.: U.S. Government Printing Office, June 1973), p. 1.

35. For example, see Louis A. Radelet, *The Police and the Community* (Beverly Hills, Calif.: Glencoe Press, 1973), p. 615; and Wasserman, Gardner, and Cohen, op. cit., p. 9.

36. Wasserman, Gardner, and Cohen, op. cit., pp. 3–4.

37. Raymond L. Bancroft, "Municipal Law Enforcement, 1966," *Nation's Cities* 4(24) (February 1966): 13.

38. National Advisory Commission, op. cit., p. 286.

39. See John W. Palmer, "An Alternative to the Police Legal Advisor," *Police Chief,* 50 (December 1973): 56–57.

40. Eastman (ed.), op. cit., pp. 203–204.

41. Ibid., p. 25.

42. See U.S. Bureau of Prisons, *The Jail: Its Operation and Management* (Washington, D.C.: U.S. Government Printing Office, n.d.).

43. Wilson and McLaren, op. cit., p. 531.

Chapter 8

Current Issues and Trends in Law Enforcement and the Nature of Private Policing

The decade from 1966 to 1976 probably witnessed more fundamental and far-reaching changes for the police service in America than were seen in the entire preceding century. The magnitude of the changes and the brief span of time in which they took place are particularly noteworthy. In the past, change in law enforcement operations and philosophy was very slow—so slow in fact as to be almost imperceptible to close observers.

In the past the police would point to such examples of innovation and change as the adoption of the automobile or two-way communications systems. These, however, were merely technological advances superimposed on old traditions, practices, and philosophies. Today it is these traditions, practices, and philosophies that are the immediate targets of change. Perhaps, but just perhaps, we are entering an era of meaningful change. However, we must be cautious in making any appraisals at this point. The police have traditionally been reluctant to adopt alternative approaches and change is usually made only under pressures from various social groups, the courts, or other significant sources of influence. That change must in most cases be forced upon the police from the outside is one of the major problems in law enforcement. Consequently, we might expect that once external pressures relax, change will decelerate rapidly. At the present time, however, these pressures do not seem to be diminishing. What we are seeing is a shift in emphasis. The demand for more effective community relations has been largely replaced by greater demands for minority rights and increased interest in police cost effectiveness in terms of productivity. As one pressure for change subsides, another appears ready to make its impact felt.

The beginning student of criminal justice should realize that change in criminal justice agencies, and indeed in many public agencies, is often temporary and situational in nature; as issues and pressures change, so do police strategies. By the process of accommodation, the police try to relieve the pressure by modifying their programs and operations so that their critics are at least somewhat appeased and thus less critical. However, as these issues and critics are dealt with, new issues and critics arise which the police must then accommodate. Thus, it is extremely difficult to forecast what issues will be of concern a few years from now. In spite of this limitation, there are probably a number of important concerns that will continue to involve the police in the future. Some of these more important issues now need to be examined.

CHANGING POLICE ORGANIZATIONS

The Traditional Military Model

Traditionally the police have relied upon a military model of organization. There are many logical reasons why this has occurred. The military model, with its emphasis upon superior-subordinate relationships, rank structure, defined areas of accountability, and discipline, was supposed to provide the necessary close control and supervision over the practices of the police by the ranking command personnel in the department. Like the military, the police also have a practical monopoly on the legal use of force in our society.[1] If we remember that two of the major problems the police faced when they were first created were (1) the widespread fear that if the police themselves were not controlled they might threaten the civil liberties of citizens and (2) the actions of police in some of our large cities, where police personnel were little more than undisciplined rabble who with impunity disregarded the directions of their superiors, we can understand why the control features of the military model were universally adopted.

Whatever advantages the military model may have had in bringing some form of order and control to the police service, recent years have increasingly demonstrated that it may no longer be appropriate. History has shown us that the military model and the internal controls that it is supposed to provide have not been nearly as effective as such externally imposed controls as the courts, citizen complaints, and other sources. Now increasingly, more and more observers of the police service in America are calling for the abandonment of the military model because it is becoming counterproductive.[2]

This traditional model of police organization may also be too limited in the opportunities it provides to the growing numbers of college-educated police officers. While the military services have created complex career-ladder systems based on specialized occupation and professional skill levels, most police departments still expect police officers to perform unspecialized and nonprofessional tasks. Today's police officers may be required to direct traffic, drive a van full of alcoholics, fingerprint offenders, and perform a large variety of essentially menial tasks. The result has been that many young, well-educated, and highly motivated men and women have found police work to be unchallenging and are leaving police departments.

To counteract this costly waste of potential talent, a number of police agencies are experimenting with possible alternatives. One such strategy is referred to as job enlargement. Under job-enlargement opportunities such as exist in Baltimore, Cincinnati, and Kansas City, police officers in the patrol unit are given the chance to conduct criminal investigations and participate in the organization and development of community crime prevention and other programs which under traditional police organization would be the province of specialist units. Baltimore, for example, has a police agent program in which college-educated police personnel can expect to become police agents after a couple of years of experience performing the routine patrol work. The police agent is kind of a "supercop" who is expected to handle difficult investigations, perform operations research and planning, and be involved in the development of community programs and other more demanding (and rewarding) aspects of police work.

Neighborhood Team Policing

Another major police organizational change has been the development of neighborhood team policing. This concept developed in England and Scotland a few years after World War II but has only recently become widely known among American police administrators. Neighborhood team policing aims to decentralize police departments so that police personnel can become more responsive to neighborhood concerns.[3] Although the traditional precinct or district stations are also a form of police decentralization, they are significantly different from neighborhood team policing, which breaks up relatively large divisions or precincts into teams of twenty to forty police officers and police command personnel. A team commander is responsible and accountable for the effectiveness of the team. The team is assigned a neighborhood containing from 12,000 to 35,000 residents and business people, where its duties are to control crime, improve community relations, and provide all routine police services on a twenty-four hour basis.

The neighborhood team is given a number of specific responsibilities and a unique method of organization to carry out its duties. The first emphasis is on indigenous planning; that is, both the entire team and the community are encouraged to participate in planning. Team commanders are urged to be innovative in developing specific programs and police strategies for the neighborhood. This form of planning is far different from that found in traditional police organizations.

In developing its methods of operation, the team first surveys the area in order to get to know the neighborhood and its residents and what neighborhood resources are available to assist them. The police try to get neighborhood residents involved in police programs, the planning process, and crime control efforts—to identify with the team as "our police." As greater rapport between the police and the community is established, traditional hostilities and suspicion are lessened. When this occurs, the residents become the "eyes and ears" of the police team. This community involvement is absolutely essential; without such help the police cannot be as nearly effective in their crime prevention, crime control, and apprehension strategies.

Another feature of team policing is this idea of job enlargement and specialist integration. The team is responsible for carrying out most of the police tasks that traditionally have been given to specialized units. For example, the team performs all traffic functions within its neighborhood and conducts and follows up on most crime investigations. This permits team members to gain experience in a full-range of police activities. Normally, when this program is implemented, former specialists (detectives, traffic investigators, analysts, etc.) are assigned as members of the team. By working within the team and interacting closely with other team members, the specialists can pass on their expertise. In most typical police agencies this exchange of skills among specialized units is almost nonexistent.

In the final analysis, team policing attempts to offer the usual advantages of small town law enforcement services while capitalizing on the available resources in a large police department. It is usually most applicable to larger cities or medium-sized communities which have identifiable ethnic and minority group neighborhoods. To date, this concept, or some version of it, has been or is being utilized in Albany, New York; St. Petersburg, Florida; the Venice division of the Los Angeles Police Department; Oxnard, California; Cincinnati, Ohio; and other cities.

THE AFFIRMATIVE ACTION ISSUE

The issue of discrimination in the personnel policies of police departments and the affirmative action programs that have been employed to attract minorities have created a great deal of concern the past few years. Increasingly, police agencies are finding themselves involved in litigation over their traditional hiring, promotion, and dismissal policies. It is particularly in the area of police personnel selection and promotion that the courts and legislative bodies have begun to exert their influence. The basic issue is whether police agencies have practiced discrimination in their personnel policies of the past and are continuing to do so.

A logical starting point to understand the history of what are referred to as affirmative action programs is the Civil Rights Act of 1964.[4] Title VII of this act prohibits discriminatory employment practices. On March 8, 1971, the U.S. Supreme Court issued a landmark decision in *Griggs v. Duke Power Company.*[5] This was a suit brought by a group of minority employees of Duke Power Company who alleged that this firm was in violation of the Civil Rights Act of 1964 because the company by requiring high school diplomas and the passing of a standard intelligence test for employment and promotion was discriminating against minorities. The court held that intelligence tests and requirements were discriminatory *unless they could be shown to measure the attributes needed to perform the specific job.*

The Equal Employment Opportunity Act of 1972 supersedes the 1964 Civil Rights Act, ánd this legislation has been extended to state and local governments.[6] The federal Equal Employment Opportunities Commission (EEOC) was created to oversee the enforcement of the act, and various states have created their own fair employment practices commissions.

In recent years, suits and countersuits involving the police have sprung up all over the country. In a number of court cases minority groups have been successful in having police employment examinations ruled discriminatory. In addition, such long-standing police requirements for employment as age, height, weight, sex, arrest record, and other factors have also been successfully challenged in the courts.[7] Unfortunately, the effects on personnel selection have sometimes been negative. For example, the EEOC recently ruled that the preemployment requirement of a college education by the Arlington, Virginia, police department was discriminatory.[8] The Connecticut State Police, along with many other police agencies, has been forced to lower the minimum age to eighteen, change the height and weight requirements, and eliminate the need for a high school diploma.

How discriminatory have police practices been in the past in regard to the hiring of minority males and all females? Some indication can be obtained from a 1973 study of police personnel practices conducted by the International Association of Chiefs of Police and the Police Foundation.[9] In this study, 493 of the largest state, county, and city police departments in the country were contacted about their personnel policies. Overall, minority males (Blacks, Spanish-surnames, Orientals, Indians, etc.) together with all women totaled about 4 percent of all sworn police personnel in these departments.[10]

The situation, however, is improving. Much of the argument against women, for example, has centered on the idea that they are physically incapable of performing the physical tasks that are from time to time required in police work. A study by the Police Foundation of women working in the patrol unit of the Washington, D.C., police department found some very interesting facts: Generally, women performed as well as men even when dealing with citizens who were dangerous, angry, upset, drunk, or violent. Men were likely to be slightly more aggressive in their work, which resulted in more arrests and traffic citations. Women, on the other hand, were less likely to be involved in behavior that resulted in departmental disciplinary action being taken. In most of the other measures used to judge their performance they performed similarly.[11]

Turning to the issue of promotional opportunities for minority males and all females, the picture is worse. Of the 493 agencies surveyed, in the 1973 study, 243 indicated that they employed sworn minority male police officers in command or supervisory positions. Table 8-1 shows the distribution of minority male command or supervisory personnel in these 243 large police agencies. Only 94 of the 493 agencies surveyed indicated that they employed sworn

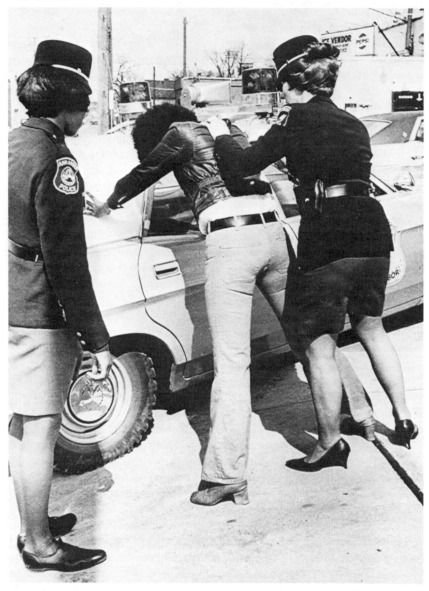

United Press International

females in command or supervisory positions. Table 8-2 indicates their distribution among the 94 police agencies. Minority males and all women seem to have enjoyed limited promotional opportunities in law enforcement in the past, particularly at the higher command levels.

TABLE 8-1   Distribution of Minority Male Command or Supervisory Personnel in 243 Large State, County, and Local Police Agencies

Rank	Total Number	Per Agency
Corporal	131	.5
Sergeant	855	3.6
Detective	613	2.6
Lieutenant	230	1.0
Captain	92	.4
Major	20	.1
Deputy/Director	20	.1
Chief	7	.0
Other	18	.1
Total	1,986	8.4

Source: Terry Eisenberg, Deborah A. Kent and Charles R. Wall, *Police Personnel Practices in State and Local Governments* (Washington, D.C.: Police Foundation, December 1973):34. (adopted with permission)

The issue of the appropriate criteria for promotions is a troublesome one. Typically in the police service, scores on written examinations, proficiency scores, oral interviews, and in some cases "politics" play a role in determining who will be promoted. Particularly strong emphasis has been placed on the score one receives on a written promotional examination, yet too often this measures one's academic knowledge and test-taking abilities rather than one's applied supervisory or managerial talents.[12]

Recently, police departments in a number of cities such as New York City and Los Angeles have been attempting to develop alternative assessment programs modeled after promotional procedures developed by the Office of Strategic Services during World War II and used by a number of large private corporations in their search for managerial talent. These assessment programs rely on extensive analyses of the job to be performed, psychological tests to measure the qualities needed as a supervisor or manager, and situational tests. In situational tests, conducted and evaluated by high-level police managerial personnel and management specialists, the applicant for promotion is given a number of hypothetical management problems related to police work and is judged by how well he or she handles the problems. These tests are structured to test such managerial requirements as decision-making skills, planning and organizing abilities, knowledge, initiative, and other important considerations.[13]

This entire area of personnel practices, particularly in relation to employment, is far from settled. Many police agencies are making significant efforts to recruit minority personnel with varying degrees of success. Some of the major problems the police have faced in these recruiting efforts are brought about by the general hostility of many minorities toward the police. Another problem

TABLE 8-2   Distribution of Females in Command or Supervisory Ranks Among 94 Large State, County and Local Police Agencies Employing Females in Command Ranks

Rank	Total Number	Per Agency Average
Corporal	7	.1
Sergeant	139	1.5
Detective	118	1.3
Lieutenant	28	.3
Captain	6	.1
Major	0	.0
Chief	0	.0
Other	6	.1
Total	304	3.4

Source: Terry Eisenberg, Deborah Kent and Charles Wall, *Police Personnel in State and Local Governments,* © 1973, p. 36. Reprinted by permission of the International Association of Chiefs of Police and Police Foundation.

faced by state and to a lesser degree some county police agencies is the reluctance of qualified minorities to leave their homes in urban areas to serve in rural state police or county posts. There is also the problem of attracting and retaining qualified minority personnel, because such people are also in demand by private firms that can offer higher salaries and other considerations as an inducement. Furthermore, these recruiting efforts are often opposed by existing police officers who do not feel that women are capable of becoming police personnel and who view affirmative action programs as operating under a dual standard which accepts less-qualified minorities at the exclusion of whites. How these issues are going to be settled, nobody knows. What is obvious is that women and racial minorities will almost certainly enjoy increasing opportunities for careers in law enforcement in the years ahead.

CRISIS INTERVENTION

By the very nature of their occupation, police personnel are called upon to intervene in situations of actual or potential violence. In 1974, 22 percent of all police officers killed in the line of duty died while responding to disturbance complaints; 41 percent of the assaults on police officers occurred on such assignments.[14]

The management of interpersonal conflict is not only one of the most hazardous assignments but also probably the most time-consuming aspect of the police function. For example, one study monitored telephone calls to the Syracuse, New York, Police Department and found that almost 20 percent of them concerned disputes in public and private places and among family members, neighbors, and total strangers.[15] The police departments of Kansas City, Missouri; Dallas, Texas; Cambridge, Massachusetts; and New York City report similarly high percentages of time allocated to situations involving interpersonal conflict.

In the last few years large numbers of police agencies have sought ways to alleviate this problem by training their personnel in techniques of crisis intervention both to protect themselves and to prevent violence from becoming destructive and injuring others. Social scientists trained in techniques of behavior analysis and control have been conducting intensive programs for police personnel so that the latter may be better able to recognize, diagnose, and control potentially violent situations.[16]

Crisis-management services usually take two forms. The first is referred to as a *generalist-specialist* model and the other as a *generalist* model.[17] In the generalist-specialist model, employed by a number of very large municipal police agencies, a selected group of general patrol officers handle all family disturbance and related calls in a specified area. These officers operate in uniform and on all tours of duty on a twenty-four hour basis. When not engaged in the management of disturbances, they provide general patrol services in an assigned area. This model has some noted advantages. The special group of police officers who handle crisis calls can be trained extensively in conflict-management techniques, a practice which would not be feasible for all personnel in the department. The special group also can develop greater awareness of existing social agencies and their programs and thus can refer citizens who need help to such agencies. Lastly, these specialists can be chosen because of their demonstrated abilities and willingness to handle conflict situations.

The generalist model is more suited to small police agencies that cannot support specialists in this area. In this model, all patrol personnel are given at least limited training in handling potentially dangerous encounters and they all handle these situations along with their other responsibilities.

ECOLOGICAL (PHYSICAL) DETERRENCE OF CRIME

It is no secret that the police are losing their struggle to control the incidence of crime. For years the phenomenon of crime was based on the premise that criminal behavior is the result of various social, psychological, and economic factors. From this followed the idea that crime prevention should therefore be directed at understanding and eliminating these causes before they could channel an individual into acts of criminal behavior. Social scientists have cited such factors as economic instability, a history of family problems, limited opportunity for participation in the accepted life style of society, and personal susceptibility to narcotics addiction as just some of the factors underlying crime in this country.

This recitation of factors demonstrates a number of things: first we have not been able to isolate and identify the specific factor(s) responsible for crime. Those who have tried offer varied explanations, none of which is very satisfactory. Secondly, even if we could identify one or all of these factors as important, the correction of these "social ills" is far beyond the present ability of our society to remedy. Thirdly, the police themselves have very little impact on the broad social problems that may underlie crime. Although we may consider them as our first line of defense, they cannot deal with the problem in any effective way at the present time.

What we then are faced with are certain conditions that are so broad and encompassing that they reject any meaningful solution short of drastic social steps and repression that are intolerable in a free society. In the last few years, a great deal of discussion has been given to what might be called the ecological deterrence of crime in our large urban cities. This concept is based on the idea that the act of committing a crime results from two things: one's *desire* to commit the crime and one's *opportunity* to do so. Since we cannot in many cases remove the desire, we should concentrate on limiting the opportunity for its successful conclusion. By limiting the opportunity, we may have a better chance to reduce crime, and the police will undoubtedly play a larger and more meaningful role in this strategy in the years ahead.

Ecological deterrence strategies use city planning and architectural design to limit the opportunities for criminals to victimize innocent citizens.[18] The expertise of physical planning experts, architects, social scientists, and the police is drawn upon in developing designs of residential complexes so that crime and vandalism will be reduced. The idea is to design residential areas, particularly multifamily apartment complexes, so that the positioning of apartment units and buildings and the placement of paths, windows, stairwells, doors, and elevators are such that the opportunities to an offender are limited. Social scientists are also demonstrating how the structural design of housing can create a more community-centered feeling rather than the present house-centered feeling that predominates among urban dwellers today.[19] Thus, the planners are seeking to create a neighborhood atmosphere similar to that which existed in many ethnic neighborhoods of years gone by in our large cities.

Another strategy is being tried in Portland, Oregon, where a federally supported crime prevention program for commercial areas is being designed for a section of that city. The program—called Crime Prevention through Environmental Design—will focus on a 20-block commercial area that has a high rate of robbery, burglary, assault, and purse snatching. The idea is to revitalize the area by making it safer for pedestrians at night and improving it physically, socially and economically. So-called safe-passage corridors along existing streets will link commercial areas and transit stops to residential areas. Those corridors will receive supplemental street lighting, demolition and clearing of abandoned structures and property, selective screening and fencing of dark enclaves, and added trees and shrubs to improve the appearance of the streets. Also planned are minimalls and miniplazas to increase personal security, new bus shelters to increase security at transit stops, and toll-free telephones for summoning emergency assistance.[20]

The police are just beginning to play more active roles as consultants in urban planning. For example, in New York City and St. Louis, the police have periodically met to discuss crime prevention and security arrangements for the construction of new public housing facilities. The police need to take an active role in such considerations. Perhaps one approach, suggested by a police planner in Detroit, is for the police to become active spokesmen for developing licensing and building code ordinances designed to make homes, streets, parks, and other physical sites less vulnerable to crime.[21] Such codes now exist in terms of fire prevention measures, so why not crime prevention? Indications are that the police will increasingly be called upon to provide expertise in such crime prevention strategies.

THE POLICE CONSOLIDATION/DECENTRALIZATION ISSUE

Since World War II, certain developments have taken place among local governments throughout the United States, particularly in metropolitan areas. First, urbanization has occurred at a phenomenal rate, creating unusual problems in governmental management, increased demand for urban services, and problems in social adjustment. Second, numerous communities have incorporated to avoid annexation to central cities, provide tax relief, or achieve other purposes, thus creating significant problems such as overlapping and fragmented jurisdictions. Third, because of financial limitations, many of these cities have found themselves unable to provide adequate urban services. Finally, the antiquated governmental framework found in most counties does not allow for effective responses by counties to urban problems. For example, metropolitan areas in the Midwest and the Far West often contain more than 100 separate governments; in some of our largest metropolitan areas, the picture is even worse. The metropolitan area of Chicago has 1,113 governments, Philadelphia has 876, Pittsburgh has 704, and New York has 551.[22]

Many of these local units of government in metropolitan areas maintain their own police departments. For example, Figure 8-1 depicts the overlapping and fragmentation of police departments in metropolitan Detroit, where there are 85 police departments. Almost 78 percent of these local departments have less than fifty members and nearly one-third have less than twenty members. The Detroit Police Department, which has 4,682 members, has more police personnel than all the rest of the eighty-four surrounding jurisdictions combined.

This fragmentation of police services has caused many study commissions, consultant groups, and scholars to recommend that police services in metropolitan areas be combined.[23] The President's Commission on Law Enforcement

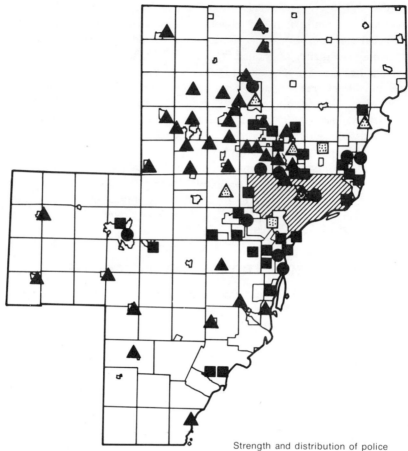

Strength and distribution of police
agencies in Detroit metropolitan region

Number of men	Departments	Code
0–20	40	▲
21–50	27	■
51–100	10	●
101–150	5	◬
151–200	2	▦
201–5000	1	▨

Figure 8.1   Fragmentation of Urban Police Departments in the
Detroit Metropolitan Area

Source: President's Commission on Law Enforcement and Administration of Justice, *Task Force Report: The Police*
(Washington, D.C.: U.S. Government Printing Office, 1967), p. 69.

and the Administration of Justice states: "Each metropolitan area and each county should take action directed toward the pooling, or consolidation, of police services through the particular technique that will provide the most satisfactory law enforcement service and protection at the lowest cost."[24]

Those who would reform police services in metropolitan areas by consolidating them point out that a large police department would be able to provide better police service at a far lower cost than is required to maintain many small independent departments.

Since local governments are facing problems of financing police services, consolidation of police services will be a major proposed reform in the years ahead. But is total consolidation of police services the answer? There is evidence that it has not always lived up to the promises of the reformers. For example, research of consolidated government in Nashville-Davidson County, Tennessee, indicates that consolidation of Nashville with its contiguous suburbs actually increased drastically the costs of providing local governmental services.[25] When residents of the suburbs were also asked if they perceived any difference in police services after the consolidation, 58 percent said that services were the same and 8 percent thought that services were worse.[26] Others who have studied this question have concluded similarly. Citizens living in the suburbs of Cleveland and Detroit were very well satisfied with the services of their small, suburban police departments.[27]

In recent years many community attempts to consolidate suburban police departments have been soundly defeated by the voters at the polls. A proposal to make the Erie County (Pennsylvania) Police Department the single law enforcement agency in the county was defeated by suburban residents in twenty-four out of twenty-five suburbs and all sixteen villages in the surrounding area.[28] Suburban voters in Dade County, Florida, recently voted against further consolidation of the police departments serving that area. Suburban residents in Marion County, Indiana, strongly opposed merging their smaller police forces with the Indianapolis Police Department.[29]

Given these facts, it would seem that the consolidation of local police departments (and governments) in the forseeable future is not as likely to occur as some of its advocates indicate. As some researchers such as Ostrom and Canfield have shown, many communities want to maintain their own individual police departments.[30]

Consolidation of Support Services

Citizens' desire to maintain their own police agencies probably will not preclude some forms of consolidation, such as consolidation of staff and auxiliary services on a metropolitan or regional basis. For example, such services as centralized communication operations in a metropolitan area will continue to grow. In these types of operations, a central dispatcher receives all calls for police assistance in a particular geographical area and dispatches units from the various cities participating. This system has been demonstrated to be a very effective form of consolidation in Genesee County, Michigan, where Flint and twenty surrounding cities participate in a centralized communication network.

Similarly, records, laboratories, training, and jail services lend themselves to consolidation efforts. For example, areawide records centers and communications centers are needed for effective and coordinated police operations in metropolitan areas where many police agencies serve essentially a common area. If certain basic police information is collected on an areawide basis according to common standards and forms and then integrated into an areawide records center, several advantages will result. First, inquiring jurisdictions need check only one source rather than several. This should eliminate duplication of effort and of physical facilities and greatly increase the speed with which an inquiry or search may be handled. Second, detailed crime analysis and planning studies may be conducted which may suggest, for example, more effective deployment of personnel in high-crime areas.[31]

Laboratory, training, and jail facilities might also be more appropriately handled on an areawide basis because of the prohibitive costs to individual units of government of providing and maintaining these services. Now that the states have enacted legislation requiring certain hours of training for police officers and have established legislation dealing with the maintenance and custody of jail facilities and prisoners, small cities must in many cases pool their resources to comply with these new standards.

Contract Law Enforcement

Another form of consolidation that has received a great deal of attention in recent years is contract law enforcement. Under this arrangement, small communities enter into contractual agreements with the county or an adjacent city for police services. This relieves the local community from having to maintain its own police department. The most notable example of this kind of arrangement is the Lakewood Plan, in which the Los Angeles County Sheriff's Department provides police services to twenty-nine incorporated cities within the county.[32] Under the Lakewood Plan, the city receiving the police service agrees to pay the jurisdiction providing the service an annual sum depending upon the police services wanted. Connecticut has also experimented with this idea through its Resident State Trooper Program; under this arrangement, small towns can contract with the state police for a resident trooper to carry out all of the functions of police service.[33] However, like consolidation attempts in general, contract law enforcement has still not been widely adopted.

Special Squads

Another type of agreement that is becoming more common is one that provides for what have been called metropolitan squads, major case squads, or metropolitan strike forces. Such agreements are made between police departments, and in many instances, are just informal agreements among police administrators to participate in a joint cooperative venture dealing with certain types of offenses. Since organized crime efforts, particularly in the area of vice, recognize no jurisdictional boundaries, many communities in a metropolitan area participate in an areawide investigative and intelligence-gathering group. Usually this special group is made up of representatives from each of the cooperating departments and it concentrates on certain crimes and offenders. In some cases, the county prosecutor's office is responsible for supervising and coordinating the activities of the group; in other cases, a command officer from one of the participating police departments is placed in charge. In many instances, this arrangement has worked quite well; in other areas, political problems over who will have control of the group, who is responsible to whom, and similar problems have limited the effectiveness of such joint efforts.

THE RISING CONCERN OVER POLICE PRODUCTIVITY

Increasingly, police departments are coming under pressure to produce evidence to justify the costs of their fearfully expensive services. Many citizens cannot accept police excuses for not being more effective in controlling crime nor their demands for more personnel and other resources so long as police are unable to demonstrate that the phenomenal increase in the cost of police services has had any impact whatsoever. At the municipal level of government alone, costs of police services increased from $5.5 billion in 1972 to an estimated $8.1 billion in 1975.[34] It would seem that a day of public reckoning is fast arriving. For example, in August 1975, the mayor of San Francisco without the approval of the city council capitulated to police salary demands that would cost the city an additional $21 million. According to the *Washington Post*, "the police merely walked off the job, then violated a court order to return to work, allegedly performed acts of sabotage, and walked picket lines armed with revolvers."[35] This same paper called it "a major skirmish in the nationwide struggle by cities for financial survival." The result of this action has been to alienate the taxpayers of this city, who now view the police with increased hostility.

The problem is not whether we need to develop some ways to measure police productivity, but how do we measure police service in any meaningful and quantifiable way. Traditionally, the police have relied on official crime statistics as their indicator of efficiency. We know by now that these are a completely inappropriate measure because such statistics are unreliable and do not reflect other more time consuming tasks that the police perform. In spite of these limitations, it is reported that former President Nixon used to summon the chief of the Washington, D. C., police to the Oval Office to review the previous month's crime reports as an index of that department's performance.[36]

Special research institutes such as the Police Foundation and the Urban Institute are now studying ways that might be used to measure police productivity. They have identified certain "levels of concern," among which are:

- The productivity of an individual police officer.
- The productivity of police units (e.g., shifts, police districts, neighborhood team policing units, or precincts).
- The productivity of particular kinds of units, such as motorized police, foot patrols, investigative units, tactical forces, canine corps, etc.
- The productivity of the police department as a whole.
- The productivity of the crime control system, including both police activities and private activities to reduce crime.
- The productivity of the total community criminal justice system, including the police, the courts, the prosecutor's office, corrections and social service agencies, and private sector crime prevention activities (such as use of locks, watchdogs, etc.)[37]

Although it is not possible to examine all the measures that are being developed to measure police productivity, Table 8-3 indicates some that might be developed. The effective measurement of police services, however, will not occur overnight. Like other public service agencies, the police perform functions that almost defy quantitative measurement. This problem is compounded by the fact that where public safety is the issue at stake, tolerances for misjudgments are very limited and the case for an insurance margin most compelling.

COLLEGE-BASED POLICE TRAINING

A few states, notably California and Florida, have developed training programs for all police personnel in cooperation with their state junior college systems. Florida, for example, rests training responsibilities in certified community colleges, and a police recruit must complete a stipulated period of training at one of these regional academic centers. Such cooperative undertakings permit the state to draw upon the resources available in community colleges. For example, these colleges have faculty trained in such areas as curriculum development, testing, and the behavioral sciences, as well as extensive access to various teaching aids such as audio-visual equipment, closed-circuit instructional TV, learning laboratories, and other resources.

This approach also has the potential of alleviating a traditional police problem—isolation. In years past, the police taught other police either formally in training programs or informally while on the job. Because of this, the police were often not exposed to different ideas or required to examine and analyze their own thinking or the way they traditionally have operated. Even today, some old-time police officers will say, "What can citizens who have no experience in police work tell me about policing?" The answer is: A great deal. In too

Table 8-3   Some Recommended Measures of Police Productivity

Police Function Being Measured	Measure Employed
1. Police Patrol Operations	a. Number of patrol officers assigned to street patrol in terms of total patrol officers b. Work-hours of patrol time spent on activities contributing to patrol objectives in terms of total patrol work-hours c. Number of calls of a given type and response time for answering these calls d. Arrests resulting from patrol which survive the first judicial screening e. Felony arrests from patrol surviving the first judicial screening f. Arrests (felonies and misdemeanors) which result in convictions
2. Provision of Noncrime Services	a. Number of noncrime calls for service which are satisfactorily responded to in terms of work-hours devoted to noncrime service calls b. Medical emergency calls that emergency room personnel evaluate as having received appropriate first aid
3. Human Resource Management	a. Number of disciplinary charges filed and number substantiated in terms of total departmental personnel b. Number of work-hours lost during the year due to illness, injury, or disciplinary action
4. Miscellaneous Considerations	a. Population served per police employee and per dollar b. Crime rates and changes in crime rates for reported crimes (relative to dollars or employees per capita) c. Clearance rates of reported crimes (relative to dollars or employees per capita) d. Arrests per police department employee and per dollar e. Crime rates including estimates of unreported crimes based on victimization studies f. Clearance rates including estimates of unreported crimes based on victimization studies g. Percent of crimes solved in less than x days h. Percent of population indicating a lack of feeling of security i. Percent of population expressing dissatisfaction with police services

Sources: The National Commission on Productivity, *Opportunities for Improving Productivity in Police Services* (Washington, D.C.: National Commission on Productivity, 1973), pp. 14–28, 49–52; and The Urban Institute, *The Challenge of Productivity Diversity: Improving Local Government Productivity Measurement and Evaluation, Part III, Measuring Police-Crime Control Productivity* (Washington, D.C.: The Urban Institute, June 1972).

many instances, the police officer sees situations only from his or her own viewpoint and does not understand how citizens perceive police action. The police and citizens need to discuss their attitudes about the police so that both groups have a better understanding of the concerns and attitudes of the other. Cooperative training ventures try to accomplish just that.

There is another advantage that states might realize in encouraging such college-based police training programs. Many community colleges offer associate degree programs in police science or criminal justice, and faculty members in these programs often have extensive experience in law enforcement or other areas of the criminal justice system. These individuals can coordinate efforts of faculty specialists so that the educational experience can be more enriching for the student. In addition, they can develop contacts with resource people in the community who, as guest lecturers, can strengthen both the training program itself and the degree program offered by the college. Finally, it is hoped that these college-based training programs will encourage police personnel who participate in them to continue in their educational endeavors and some day obtain a degree themselves.

This writer's discussions with training directors in Florida seem to indicate that many of the advantages discussed are being realized. Now, additional states are beginning to adopt such an approach. It would appear that the future will see increasing use of the college or university as an important component of recruit, in-service, supervisory, and managerial training programs for the police as well as for other agencies of the criminal justice system.

These are just some of the trends that point the way law enforcement agencies of the future are going. Other trends in such areas as collective bargaining, methods of recruitment and selection, career development, communication and information systems, lateral entry, and a host of other areas have potentially important consequences for the newly emerging police service in the United States. A career in law enforcement in the years ahead promises to be both challenging and stimulating for young men and women who possess intelligence and sensitivity, who are willing to work hard and learn, and who prepare themselves adequately with a sound educational foundation.

PRIVATE SECURITY

Private security incorporates much more than physical security services to industry. Security services fall into two general categories: (1) crime-related public and private security services and (2) noncrime-related services such as privately sponsored fire and general safety programs and personnel-administration technology.[38] Fire and general safety programs provide preventive fire and safety services to private and public firms in light of such federal legislation as the Occupational Safety and Health Act, which requires that employers provide certain standards of health and safety for their employees.

The area of personnel-administration technology refers to programs designed to screen personnel to ensure their integrity and trustworthiness. From this we can see that uniformed private guards providing physical security are just one aspect of the security industry. The remainder of this section will concentrate on both crime-related and noncrime-related public and private security services.

The Extent and Growth of Security Forces

Crime-related public and private security services absorb considerable resources. The most thorough examination of security forces in the United States arose from a five-volume study of the industry conducted by the Rand Corporation beginning in 1969 and sponsored by the National Institute of Law Enforcement and Criminal Justice of the Law Enforcement Assistance Administration. In 1969, over 800,000 people were security workers, and well over $8 billion was devoted to security services and equipment. One in every 100 persons in the civilian labor force was employed in security work, and over $40 per capita was spent on security.[39] About 36 percent of all security personnel were employed in the private sector and the remainder in governmental agencies at all levels of government. Between the years 1960 and 1969, it is estimated that expenditures for private security increased approximately 150 percent.[40] This is a phenomenal growth rate, and it probably has not abated.

What has led to this tremendous increase in the growth of security forces? One of the most common explanations is that increasingly the public feels that public law enforcement agencies are just not capable of providing the kinds of services required. Thus, citizens, business, industry, and even governments have turned to other sources for supplementary security services and devices.

Although this may be part of the reason, other underlying factors must be considered. Most knowledgeable observers would include some or all of the following:

- Increasing business losses to crime ($20.3 billion in 1974). [This U.S. Commerce estimate is based on estimates of loss from *conventional* crimes only (e.g., robbery and burglary); it does not include such crimes as white-collar crime, shoplifting, and bad checks.]

- Insurers raising rates or refusing coverage so that security measures are used increasingly as a substitute for insurance.

- Insurers requiring the use of certain private security systems or granting premium discounts when certain private security measures are used.

- The federal government's need for security in its space and defense activities during the past decade and more recently, the need for security against air hijackings, violent demonstrations, and bombings of federal, state, and local government facilities.

- The basic business trend toward purchases of specialized services, which may contribute to the growth of the contract security forces.

- The nations's growth and advancing state of the art in electronics and other scientific areas, which has sparked new and distinct manufacturing branches of several protection companies, providing greatly improved security devices, especially for intrusion detection.

- The general increase in corporate and private income, which has resulted in more property to protect and, at the same time, more income to pay for protection.[41]

Areas of Specialization

There are basically six areas of security specialization, with of course, some overlapping of functions and responsibilities.

Plant Protection

Plant protection protects the physical integrity of the property and the safety of employees in a particular industrial plant. It is concerned with such things as reducing operating costs of the firm by employing safety and theft-control measures, such as on-site inspection of company property, visible patrol and guardianship of property boundaries, inspection of employees as they leave the premises, and other similar activities.

It protects the safety of employees by programs of inspection of fire and safety equipment, lights, and fences, and by preventing access to the facility of persons or objects that are potentially hazardous from either a general safety or a crime-control viewpoint. Up until World War II, this specialty constituted almost the entire security industry.

Security of Classified Information

The safeguarding of classified information which developed as a specialty during World War II, has become of great concern in recent years. As technology has developed, the government has increasingly turned to private firms for contract work in research and development. This has increased the need for security in these firms. For example, the development of atomic resources for use in nuclear reactors has tremendous implications. It is entirely conceivable that certain radical groups could obtain enough scientific data to construct crude yet effective atomic bombs which they could employ in terrorist activities against the U.S. government and the civilian populace.

Classified information security specialists are also increasingly being employed by firms concerned with protecting industrial intelligence. Firms wishing to protect their trade secrets have to be increasingly concerned that their own employees or persons infiltrating their organization from the outside are not supplying their competitors with information that could seriously jeopardize their market position.

A very sensitive area of concern in industrial intelligence is computer security. As more and more firms employ data processing to store trade secrets, compile payroll information, and process credit accounts, the potential for theft, fraud, and sabotage of the computer system and all the firm's important records is very real.[42] One knowledgeable computer security specialist considers the threat so grievous "that if the facts were known how vulnerable business (and government) secrets are by virtue of the adoption and use of computers, corporation and government officials might even conceivably not employ their usage."[43]

Physical Security

This specialty is concerned with certain technical and managerial questions. For example, physical security specialists survey and inspect facilities and make recommendations for ways to improve security measures. Is it more economical, for instance, to use electronic intrusion devices such as alarm systems, closed-circuit TV and scanners to provide physical security rather than to employ a uniformed guard force? Because technical developments in the field of electronic intrusion devices are very rapid and the operation of such devices requires increasing technical knowledge, the physical security specialist is expected to have a broad knowledge of the applications of these devices and their operating technologies.

Personnel Security

This specialty deals with the question of quality control over personnel selections, promotions, and similar personnel matters. This is an extremely sensitive issue in our society today. The use of such standard techniques as lie-detector screening, background investigations, and similar inquiries creates concern. On the one hand, employers increasingly need to be assured that the people they employ are loyal and trustworthy—particularly those people in positions of trust that have access to sensitive information. On the other hand, individuals demand the right of privacy. Somehow, the rights of the individual must be judiciously balanced with the need to maintain appropriate security.

At the present time, there are no clear guidelines or appropriate safeguards in these areas. Although some states and the federal government have adopted legislation that prohibits the use of lie detectors for employment and the federal Fair Credit Reporting Act imposes standards of accuracy upon private firms that regularly investigate and prepare preemployment, credit, and insurance reports, these provisions do not adequately cover the possible abuses of surreptitious electronic eavesdropping or questionable methods of investigating the backgrounds and habits of employees or candidates for positions of employment. In many cases, the aggrieved party has no recourse but to sue under the general tort law of the state.[44] Even these tort remedies are far from effective, and often the aggrieved party cannot afford the costs of such a suit.

Fire and Safety Security

Fire and safety security is concerned with the inspection and engineering of fire and safety security measures. This, too, is a somewhat technical field that incorporates such areas as structural design and architecture, safety systems design, inspection, and testing. Fire and safety security specialists work closely with engineers, architects, and systems design personnel to develop, implement, and refine existing security devices. Since there are so few qualified individuals in this area, they often serve as consultants to private and governmental insitutions concerned with fire and safety hazards.

Disaster Control and Defense Planning

This last security specialty is responsible for developing disaster and defense plans for firms or governmental agencies. These specialists are concerned with both natural disasters and acts of war or sabotage directed at key industries or governmental complexes. World War II demonstrated that the destruction of military-related industrial concerns can severely hamper and even preclude the ability of a country to continue to wage war. As a consequence, contingency plans must be made to continue the production of necessary goods and services under the most extreme adverse situations. Protection must extend not merely over the machinery and equipment, but also to the human beings upon which the continued operations of industrial concerns and the government ultimately depend.

Education and Careers in Security

In 1974 the American Society for Industrial Security, a professional organization of security specialists, conducted a survey of institutions of higher education and found that 100 colleges and universities throughout the nation offered either a degree or course work in industrial security.[45] Some of the more typical courses in an industrial security program are:

- Introduction to security.
- Protection of classified government information and business assets
- Civil disturbance and emergency planning
- Traffic and access control
- Security Management
- Loss Prevention in business, industry, and institutions
- Criminal evidence and procedure

- Issues and concerns in security law
- Investigative techniques

Students majoring in security are also encouraged to take courses in business organization and management, accounting, data processing and business and administrative law, as well as relevant courses in criminal justice.

Careers in the security industry appear to be very favorable for young men and women who prepare themselves adequately. As the security industry has grown rapidly in recent years, so has the need for qualified people. Often graduates can expect to enter as security management trainees. After gaining experience in such areas as physical security and fire and safety, those who have demonstrated ability can in many cases advance rather rapidly.

SUMMARY

The police service in America has undergone some major changes in the past decade. For the most part these changes have come about because of external pressures which have forced the police to reassess their traditional methods of organization and their policies. These changes have occurred in a patchwork pattern and are far from universal.

Some of the police-related issues which have assumed increasing importance in recent years are the recommendations to demilitarize the police; the adoption of new organizational models such as the neighborhood team policing concept; the affirmative action issue; crisis intervention as a police strategy; the growing role of the police in ecological (physical) deterrence and other crime preventive measures; the issue of consolidation of small local police departments; the meaningful measurement of police productivity; and the development of college-based police training programs.

The security and private police industry in the United States has developed six areas of specialization: plant protection, security of classified information, physical security, personnel security, fire and safety security, and disaster control and defense planning.

Suggested Additional Readings

Bittner, Egon. *The Functions of the Police in Modern Society.* Washington, D.C., U.S. Government Printing Office, 1970.

Ishak, S. T. *Consumer's Perception of Police Performance: Consolidation vs. Decentralization: The Case of Grand Rapids, Michigan Metropolitan Area.* Bloomington: Indiana University Press, 1972.

Jeffrey, C. Ray. *Crime Prevention through Environmental Design.* Beverly Hills, Calif.: Sage, 1971.

Juris, Hervey A., and Peter Feville. *Police Unionism*. Lexington, Mass.:
    Lexington Books, 1973.
Kakalik, James, and S. Wildhorn. *The Private Police Industry*. Vols. 1–5.
    Washington, D.C.: U.S. Government Printing Office, February 1972.
Measuring Police-Crime Control Productivity. Part III of *The Challenge of
    Productivity Diversity—Improving Local Government Productivity Mea-
    surement and Evaluation*, prepared for the National Commission on Pro-
    ductivity by the Urban Institute. Washington, D.C.: National Technical In-
    formation Service, U.S. Department of Commerce (Document no.
    PB223117), 1972.
Ostrom, Elinor, and Roger B. Parks. "Suburban Police Departments: Too
    Many, Too Small?" *Urban Affairs Annual Reviews*. Vol. 7. Beverly Hills,
    Calif.: Sage, 1973.
The Police Foundation. *Team Policing: Seven Case Studies*, Washington,
    D.C.: The Police Foundation, 1973.
U.S. Department of Justice: *Innovation in Law Enforcement*. Washington,
    D.C.: U.S. Government Printing Office, June 1973.
The Urban Institute: "Neighborhood Team Policing." Project report to LEAA.
    Washington, D.C.: The Urban Institute, 1973.
Washington, Brenda E. *Deployment of Female Police Officers in the United
    States*. Gaithersburg, Md.: International Association of Chiefs of Police,
    1974.
Weisbord, Marvin R., Howard Lamb, and Allan Drexler. *Improving Police
    Department Management through Problem-Solving Task Forces*. Reading,
    Mass.: Addison-Wesley, 1974.

Notes

1. Jerome H. Skolnick and Thomas C. Gray, *Police in America* (Boston: Educational
   Associates, 1975), p. 213.

2. For example, see Robert D. Pursley, "Traditional Police Organization: A Portent of
   Failure?" in William Bopp (ed.), *Police Administration* (Boston: Holbrook Press,
   1975), pp. 83–86; and Egon Bittner, *The Functions of the Police in Modern Society*
   (Washington, D.C.: U.S. Government Printing Office, 1970), especially chap.
   VIII.

3. The description of team policing that follows was adapted from Peter B. Bloch and
   David Specht, *Neighborhood Team Policing* (Washington, D.C.: Law Enforcement Assistance Administration, December 1973).

4. 42 U.S.C.A. § 2000 et seq.

5. *Griggs v. Duke Power Company*, 915 Sup. Ct. 849 (1971).

6. Pub. L. No. 92–261.

7. For example, see *Morrow v. Crisler*, Civil Action No. 4716, U.S. Dist. Ct., S.
   Miss. (1971); *Smith v. East Cleveland*, 363 F. Supp. 1131 (1973); *Guardian
   Association* v. *Civil Service Commission*, 490 F.2d. 400 (1973); *Wilson* v. *City of
   Torrance*, Civil Action No. 74–963, U.S. Dist. Ct., E. Ca. (1974).

8. Memo from the *Washington Post,* Jan. 27, 1975.

9. Terry Eisenberg et al., *Police Personnel Practices in State and Local Government* (Washington, D.C.: Police Foundation, 1973).

10. Ibid., p. 35.

11. See Peter B. Bloch and Deborah Anderson, *Policewomen on Patrol: Final Report* (Washington, D.C.: Police Foundation, 1974).

12. See Benjamin Shimberg and Robert J. DiGrazia, "Promotion," in O. Glenn Stahl and Richard A. Staufenberger (eds.), *Police Personnel Administration* (Washington, D.C.: Police Foundation: 1974), pp. 101–124.

13. See Paul F. D'Arcy, "Assessment Center Program Helps Test Managerial Competence," *Police Chief* 41 (December 1974):52–53.

14. Federal Bureau of Investigation, *Uniform Crime Reports, 1974* (Washington, D.C.: U.S. Government Printing Office, 1975).

15. E. Cumming, *Systems of Social Regulation* (New York: Atherton Press, 1968).

16. See Morton Bard: *Family Crisis Intervention: From Concept to Implementation* (Washington, D.C.: Law Enforcement Assistance Administration, December 1973).

17. Ibid., p. 9.

18. See Oscar Newman, *Architectural Design for Crime Prevention* (Washington, D.C.: Law Enforcement Assistance Administration, 1971).

19. For example, see William Michelson, *Man and His Urban Environment: A Sociological Approach* (Reading, Mass.: Addison-Wesley, 1970); and Anas Aleksandros, "A Dynamic Disequilibrium Model of Residential Location," *Environment and Planning* 5 (1973).

20. "Portland Tests Crime Prevention through Environmental Design," *LEAA Newsletter* 5 (August 1975):4.

21. Speech given by Captain Anthony Hopfinger, Symposium on Crime Prevention and the Police, at Wayne State University, Detroit, Mich., Aug. 16, 1975.

22. Advisory Commission on Intergovernmental Relations, *Urban America and the Federal System* (Washington, D.C.: U.S. Government Printing Office, 1969), pp. 75 and 117.

23. For example, see David L. Noorgard, *Regional Law Enforcement* (Chicago: Public Administration Service, 1969); Advisory Commission on Intergovernmental Relations, *State-Local Relations in the Criminal Justice System* (Washington, D.C.: U.S. Government Printing Office, 1971); Committee for Economic Development, *Reducing Crime and Assuring Justice* (New York: Committee for Economic Development, June 1972).

24. President's Commission on Law Enforcement and Administration of Justice, *Task Force Report: The Police* (Washington, D.C.: U.S. Government Printing Office, 1967), p. 308.

25. Elinor Ostrom and Roger B. Parks, "Suburban Police Departments: Too Many and Too Small?" in Louis H. Masotti and Jeffrey K. Hadden (eds.), *The Urbanization of the Suburbs* (Beverly Hills, Calif.: Sage, 1973), chap. XIV. An increase in the per capita costs of municipal services also occurred after the Ontario legislature created Toronto Metro; see H. Kaplan, *Urban Political Systems: A Functional Analysis of Metro Toronto* (New York: Columbia University Press, 1967).

26. Robert E. McArthur, *Impact of City-County Consolidation of the Rural-Urban Fringe: Nashville-Davidson County Tennessee* (Washington, D.C.: U.S. Government Printing Office, 1971), pp. 19–22.

27. See Adam Campbell and H. Schuman, "A Comparison of Black and White Attitudes and Experiences in the City," in C. H. Harr (ed.), *The End of Innocence: A Suburban Reader* (Glenview, Ill.: Scott, Foresman, 1972), p. 109.

28. David L. Skoler and J. M. Hetler, "Government Restructuring and Criminal Administration: The Challenge of Consolidation," in *Crisis in Urban Government: A Symposium on Restructuring Metropolitan Urban Government* (Silver Spring, Md.: Thomas Jefferson Publishing, 1970), pp. 53–75.

29. Elinor R. Ostrom, Roger B. Parks, and Gordon P. Whitaker, "Do We Really Want to Consolidate Urban Police Forces? A Reappraisal of Some Old Assertions," *Public Administration Review* (October/November 1974):423–432.

30. For example, see Elinor R. Ostrom, "Community Public Services and Responsiveness: On the Design of Institutional Arrangements for the Provision of Police Services," paper presented at the American Political Science Association annual meeting, Chicago, Ill.: Aug. 29–Sept. 2, 1974; and Roger B. Canfield, "Citizen Satisfaction and Police Effectiveness: Perspectives beyond Productivity and Social Equity," paper presented at the 1974 National Conference of the American Society for Public Administration, Syracuse, N.Y., Mar. 17–21, 1974.

31. Noorgard, op. cit., p. 24.

32. Letter from Gilbert E. Schollen, Los Angeles County Sheriff's Department, Dec. 17, 1975.

33. James H. Ellis, "The Connecticut Resident State Police System," *Police*, 5 (September–October 1960):69–72.

34. U.S. Commerce Department, *Economic Indicators in Government Services* (mimeo) (Washington, D.C.: U.S. Department of Commerce, August 1975).

35. Leroy F. Aarons, "Police Fire Strike Unnerves Other Cities" (*Washington Post* synd.), *The State Journal*, Lansing, Mich., Tuesday, Aug. 26, 1975, A11.

36. Reported in Edward K. Hamilton, "Police Productivity: The View from City Hall," in Joan L. Wolfe and John F. Heaphy (eds.), *Readings on Productivity in Policing* (Washington, D.C.: Police Foundation, 1975), p. 13.

37. Harry P. Hatry, "Wrestling with Police Crime Control Productivity Measurement," in ibid., p. 90.

38. The term "personnel-administration technology" is taken from Leon H. Weaver, "Security and Protection Systems," *Encyclopedia Britannica*, 15th ed. (New York: Encyclopedia Britannica, 1974), p. 454.

39. James S. Kakalik and Sorrel Wildhorn, *Private Police in the United States: Findings and Recommendations* (Washington, D.C.: U.S. Department of Justice, February 1972), p. 10.

40. Ibid., p. 13.

41. Ibid., p. 15.

42. For example, see Robert L. Taylor and Robert S. Feingold, "Computer Data Protection, *Industrial Security* (August 1970); Leonard J. Krauss, "Safe Security Audit and Field Evaluation for Computer Facilities," *Amacom*, 3(1)(January 1972):8–11; William F. Brown, *AMR's Guide to Computer and Software Security* (New York: AMR International, 1972).

43. William E. Nye: "Computers: Our Achilles Heel?" *Business Automation* (August 1973):23.

44. Tort law is the law that defines the general duties of citizens to each other and allows lawsuits to recover damages for the injury caused by one citizen's breach of such a duty.

45. Arthur A. Kingsbury, "Security Education," *Security Management* (September 1974).

Part 3

THE COURTS

Chapter 9

The Courts in the Administration of Criminal Justice

The American courts are the most important institutional setting for the administration of the criminal law. Situated between the police and their powers of arrest and the corrections component of the criminal justice system, they play perhaps the most important role in the administration of American justice—a role which they have often been criticized for not effectively fulfilling. When one examines all the agencies of criminal justice and the progress they have made in recent years, the courts would probably remain in the unenviable position of having demonstrated the least progress and the least willingness or ability to improve their particular responsibilities.

This section will first examine certain characteristics of our system of courts, their development, and present structure. Then the trial process, institutional arrangements, and court personnel will be considered. Finally, an examination will be made of the particular changes the courts are undergoing and what recommendations are being made to improve the handling and disposition of criminal cases by our courts.

ORGANIZATIONAL FEATURES

Certain features of organization characterize the American judiciary. These are (1) a dual system of courts, (2) absence of supervisory control, (3) specialization, and (4) geographical organization.[1]

A Dual System of Courts

The court system in the United States is organized on the principle of political federalism. Although the first Congress, acting under the authority of the Constitution, established the federal court system, the states were permitted to establish their own court structures. In fact, most legal matters were left to the state courts. Only in recent years have the federal government and the federal courts begun to exercise increasing jurisdiction over crimes and civil matters. As a result of new federal legislation and broad interpretation of the power to regulate interstate commerce, the federal courts now have authority over 2,800 federal crimes.

Thus, a dual system of state and federal courts exists. In many instances, the state and federal courts have *concurrent jurisdiction* over specific crimes. For example, the federal government has enacted special legislation to prohibit bank robbery, kidnapping, and fraud cases, as have the various states. Under these circumstances, an individual who robs a bank has committed both a state and a federal crime and could be brought to trial in either a state court or a federal court.

The implications of this dual legal system and court structure have had some impact on the administration of criminal justice in America. For example, in 1914 in the case of *Weeks v. United States*[2] the U.S. Supreme Court established the Federal Exclusionary Rule. Weeks was charged by federal agents with conducting a lottery in interstate commerce by use of the mails. Weeks was arrested at his place of employment, and his residence was searched without the authority of a search warrant. During this search, incriminating evidence was found and introduced at his federal trial. On appeal to the U.S. Supreme Court, he alleged that this search was unlawful under the provisions of the Fourth Amendment. The Supreme Court agreed and established the Federal Exclusionary Rule, which held that evidence unlawfully obtained by federal agents in violation of one's constitutional rights could no longer be introduced into federal prosecutions. The Supreme Court, however, made it quite clear that this decision applied only to federal agents and federal courts and not to police officers or courts at the state level. This led to the famous "Silver Platter Doctrine." Since the Federal Exclusionary Rule prohibited only federal officers from illegally seizing evidence and introducing it into federal trials, nothing was to prevent state police officers from illegally searching for and seizing evidence and turning it over to the federal authorities on a "silver platter" for introduction into the federal courts. It was not until 1961 that the U.S. Supreme Court finally imposed the Federal Exclusionary Rule on state courts.[3]

The jurisdiction of federal courts and the laws that guide their actions are often shaped by different political interests than are the laws and court actions of the state level. This is seen by the enforcement of certain laws at the national level. Minority groups that have received no consideration from their state courts have often sought help from Congress in having the jurisdiction of the federal courts enlarged so that they may obtain redress for their grievances through the federal judiciary. For example, with the passage of the Civil Rights Act of 1964 and subsequent legislation federal law enforcement officials were empowered to investigate and bring to trial individuals who interfere with the exercise of civil rights. This legislation has been used in many cases where state agents such as law enforcement personnel have violated the civil rights of citizens within their states.

Absence of Supervisory Control

The second most notable characteristic of American courts is that they perform their adjudicatory function with little or no supervisory control. The U.S. Supreme Court and the state supreme courts are usually supreme courts only in the sense that they serve as appellate courts from the lower judiciary, and they establish certain procedures for the lower courts.

In the case of the U.S. Supreme Court, for instance, most citizens believe that there exists an automatic right to appeal to the Supreme Court and that in this way the Supreme Court exercises authority over the lower federal courts and the state courts. Nothing could be further from the truth. The number of cases heard by the U.S. Supreme Court is only an infinitesimal part of the number of cases heard by the lower courts. There are a number of reasons for this: First, before someone who is tried for a crime on a state level can appeal to the Supreme Court, that person must have exhausted every appellate process available in the particular state. Secondly, the case must involve a substantial federal question and/or constitutional issue. Third, the issue must be of significant social importance to warrant a Supreme Court hearing. Fourth, the process is extremely costly and time-consuming, which, in itself, is often a major inhibiting factor.

This absence of supervisory control over the courts is also manifest in other ways. No single authority has the power to control the assignment of court personnel, the formulation of the budget, or the distribution of supplies and facilities among the courts or the flow of cases through each court. In many states, the legislature is required by state constitutions or statutes to ensure the necessary operating budget for the judiciary. Since most of our state judges are elected, they are theoretically responsible only to the people, which makes it nearly impossible to supervise them or remove them from office except through the ballot box.

This absence of supervisory control is even extended to the support personnel in these courts. Court bailiffs, probation officers, clerks, and other functionaries in many instances are appointed by the court, and these positions are often patronage appointments for faithful political support in the state or local political arena.

Specialization

Another important structural feature of courts, particularly at the state and local levels, is their arrangement according to specialized areas. For example, the lower courts at the local and municipal levels are often courts of limited jurisdiction that can try only misdemeanor cases. If a felony is committed, the trial is conducted by a court of original and general jurisdiction at the county, district, regional, or state level. In recent years, specialized juvenile courts have been established to handle crimes committed by youth, and in some larger municipalities, specialized branches of local courts handle traffic offenses or vice crimes. This same procedure is also carried over into civil law, where different courts have been established to handle claims, wills and estates, and civil suits, based upon the amount of money sought for damages.

Geographical Organization

Our courts are also organized according to geographical considerations. The states and the federal government are divided into judicial districts, with various levels of courts situated in each area.

This areal organization of courts has implications for the administration of criminal justice. The particular location of a court influences its responsiveness to political interests. Rural courts are less likely to be as understanding of certain criminal violations as are urban courts. The judges in these rural areas often perceive that their constituents are less likely to sanction offenses against blue laws, which prohibit certain businesses from operating on Sundays, liquor and drug offenses, gambling, and other normative vice offenses. In Michigan, for example, the courts in the Upper Peninsula, a rather isolated rural area, are notoriously more stringent in the application of penalties against drug offenses than are similar courts in the Detroit area.

Numerous studies have been made of how courts and individual judges differ in terms of the sentences they impose in different locales. In one study of the federal system, the average length of prison sentences for narcotics violations was eighty-three months in the Tenth Circuit, but only forty-four months in the Third Circuit.[4] Another study some years ago found that the average sentence for forgery ranged from a high of sixty-eight months in the Northern District of Mississippi to a low of seven months in the Southern District of that state; the highest average sentence for auto theft was forty-seven months in the Southern District of Iowa, and the lowest was fourteen months in the Northern District of New York.[5]

This is not to imply that differences in sentences imposed by courts in different areas necessarily reflect different social values and attitudes. No research has ever conclusively established such a relationship, though any given local culture clearly must have some impact on the operation of the courts in that region.

HISTORY AND DEVELOPMENT OF STATE COURT SYSTEMS

The Colonial Period

During the early years of the American colonies, courts were simple institutions with little authority or jurisdiction. Power rested in the hands of the colonial governors, who were appointed by the king as overseers to the crown's domain in the New World. For the most part, what few courts did exist served in an advisory capacity to the governors. Members of these courts were appointed by the governor and served at his pleasure. The judicial officials of these courts were given the limited authority to settle matters too trivial to warrant the time and effort of the governor.

This was a period when the tasks of governing were relatively simple and routine. Because the population was small and scattered throughout small settlements, there existed no need for extensive political institutions. Just as there existed no courts as we know them today, there also existed no legislative bodies. In their place, an assembly of advisers advised the governor on matters pertaining to the administration of the colony. As the population of the colonies grew and social relations became more complex, town and county courts began to develop to provide a local authority for settling conflicts. The establishment of courts in the county seats was an idea which had been developing in the shires of England. Each county seat was so situated that a rider on horseback could reach the county seat and return home in one day. Town courts, which had developed in medieval England, were also adopted by the colonies as the population grew and the need for this type of court developed. In medieval England, the settlement of local, minor squabbles demanded a mode of judicial administration unhampered by the inconveniences of a highly centralized system. To meet this problem, there was developed the office of *justice of the peace,* an appointive official with authority to settle petty civil cases and try minor criminal offenses. The justice usually was a respected townsman without legal training, but blessed with common sense. The system of local justices became a permanent part of the English system and was transported virtually unchanged to American soil, where it has remained in use in some states for over 300 years.[6]

Appeals from these courts usually could be taken to the governor and the assembly and, ultimately, to the courts of England. Rarely, however, were the decisions of these local and county courts ever appealed to the governor or the assembly and even less frequently to the English courts. Since these courts had such limited jurisdiction, the issues before them usually did not warrant the time and expense of an appeal.

The early colonies were often settled by different groups—Maryland by Roman Catholics, Pennsylvania by Quakers—and thus the judicial and legal systems developed differently in each colony, depending upon local beliefs and customs. With but a few exceptions, the English common law tradition and English court structures were adopted. However, the individual colonies soon modified these somewhat to suit the requirements of local demands. The commercial development in each colony also contributed to different rulings and court arrangements.[7] In a number of ways, these early variations among the colonies are still reflected in the variety of court systems in the states.

Glick and Vines consider that the lack of legal experts in the colonies was an important feature in the early development of colonial court systems.[8] There are a number of reasons why legal and judicial talent was not available to assist in the creation of colonial courts. In the first place, the king's law and those who administered to it were held in disrepute by many of the colonists. As a result, very few professionally trained lawyers and jurists were attracted to the colonies from England and Europe. In addition, lawyers and judges were not welcomed by the colonial merchant class and wealthy land-owners, who were concerned that the development of a professional class of attorneys would renew the persecution by the law they had experienced in the past as well as create competition for the general social, economic, and political control they enjoyed in the colonies.[9]

As a consequence, these early courts came under the domain of prestigious laymen in the towns and counties. The judges were usually wealthy merchants, planters, or landowners, who, without benefit of legal training, settled the local disputes that arose. As might be imagined, these courts often served the interests of the wealthy, and in terms of political control, judicial, economic, and financial interests became interlocked.

As the population grew, courts were added to the judicial system in order to respond to increased litigation and the need for court intervention in settling disputes. The major impetus behind the expansion of colonial courts, however, was the economic growth of the colonies. As commerce increased, so did the need for courts to settle differences between economic interests. As early as the late seventeenth century, the colonies of Massachusetts, Pennsylvania, and Connecticut began to divide cases between existing courts. In this way, specialized jurisdictions of courts began to be established, and the early development of a higher court for appeal began to appear. In 1698, Connecticut, for example, established a few special courts to deal with wills and estates, which until this time had been handled by the county courts. These new courts were called probate courts, and the idea of this type of specialized court spread to other colonies.[10] The spread of these specialized courts encouraged the development of legal experts and judges to service these courts. This, in turn, fostered the growth of rules and procedures to process the growing litigation.

State Court Development in the Postrevolutionary Period

After America gained its independence, the powers of the governors of the new states were drastically reduced, and the state legislatures became the focus of authoritative power. The courts that existed in the states at this time were purposely kept very weak. The legislative bodies, and indeed the citizens of the new nation, were quite content with this arrangement. The citizens still remembered the courts as extensions of the authority of the colonial governors, and they did not relish the possibility that the courts might serve the same function for the governors of the new states. This fear that the executive branch and the judiciary might wield too much power at the expense of the states' legislative bodies prevented the development at that time of an independent state judiciary.

The state legislatures scrutinized quite closely the actions of the state courts, and they freely appointed and removed judges and even abolished courts that did not agree with their policies.[11]

Beginning in the early 1800s, distrust of the judiciary became even more pronounced as some courts began to rule that the actions of legislative bodies were unconstitutional. This power of the courts to declare the actions of the legislature or executive branches to be in violation of constitutional provisions is known as the power of *judicial review*. In 1803, in the famous case of *Marbury v. Madison*[12] the U.S. Supreme Court authoritatively established this power for the nation's highest tribunal. This power of judicial review of legislative action is largely an American creation. Before the Revolution, it had been used on a few occasions to justify opposition to the crown's edicts, but it did not become an important instrument of authority until the early nineteenth century. Exercise of the power of judicial review often led to a struggle for political power between the judiciary and the legislative branches of the states. Despite the efforts of the state legislatures to curtail the power of the courts by removing judges and eliminating certain courts, the state courts became more assertive and openly declared, in a number of instances, that state legislative action, particularly in the area of economic interests, violated state constitutions.

These struggles were instrumental in developing state court organization, for they nurtured the idea that an independent judiciary was necessary to maintain an equal and meaningful separation of powers between the branches of state government. Although certain state legislatures continued to perform an appellate function for a number of years, by the beginning of the Civil War the power of state legislatures to serve as an appellate body from judicial decisions had been abolished in all states.

The Development of the State Courts from 1850 to the Present

The rapid growth of our nation in the mid to late 1800s had pronounced effects on the growth of state court systems. This was a period of rapid industrial expansion and massive immigrations from Southern and Eastern Europe. As American society pressed forward into its "golden age" of technology, life styles changed and new attitudes, structures, and expectations became the order of the day. Like all other institutions of that period, the courts were affected by the fundamental changes that society was undergoing.

The growth of industry and commerce led to new conflicts that had to be resolved; rules had to be imposed, and legislative bodies had to enact new laws to regulate the changing character of American society. As these changes occurred, states devised new statutes, and local governments enacted ordinances controlling human behavior. The advent of the automobile alone contributed enormously to the workload of the courts. As people clustered together in large cities, the incidence of crime increased, and the courts were called upon to adjudicate more and more criminal matters. While this was occurring at the state level, similar problems and developments were happening at the federal level. Congress, through its express powers to regulate commerce between the states, coin money, lay and collect taxes, and make all laws "which shall be necessary and proper," was passing increasing legislation and enacting criminal penalties for noncompliance. Thus, the criminal (and civil) workloads of the federal courts increased drastically as the need to enforce these laws grew apace.

As the existing courts found themselves inundated with litigation, specialized branches began to appear. For a time, existing city courts, primarily justices of the peace, dealt with much of the new litigation, but since most of these justices and lower-level magistrates had little or no training in the law, they were unable to deal with the complex legal questions involved in many of the cases that came before them. As a result, new court systems were created. Small claims courts were added in a number of states to simplify legal procedures so that small debts could be collected at minimal cost. Juvenile and family relations courts were also developed to handle cases involving juvenile offenders and the troubled family. Many communities also created special courts to handle motor vehicle offenses. As these courts developed, so did the need for specialists such as social workers, psychiatrists, and other treatment personnel assigned to juvenile courts. The adult criminal courts expanded their staffs and added probation officers to supervise the offender after adjudication of guilt. Figure 9-1 depicts the growth of state court systems in America.

This rapid growth of state court systems did not occur without cost. The sheer numbers of these courts and the complexity of the judicial system has had a significant impact upon the administration of justice. Lepawsky, in a study of Chicago during the 1930s, found that this one city had 556 independent courts, 505 of which were justice of the peace courts.[13] The remaining courts were divided up between various state and local courts and included municipal courts, circuit courts, a superior court, a county court, a probate court, a juvenile court, and a criminal court. The jurisdiction of these courts was not exclusive. A single case could be brought before any number of courts, depending upon the legal and political advantages that each one offered. As a consequence, "courtroom shopping" prevailed, and the alternatives open to attorneys were vast.[14]

For example, a prosecutor, depending upon the value of the particular criminal case to the state, would consider the reputation of the judge for handing down lenient or stiff sentences, how difficult or easy it was to get evidence introduced, and how quickly the particular courts could dispose of a case, and choose accordingly. Often attorneys would "shop" for a court whose procedures were such that the sheer confusion, red tape, and delay would frustrate the opposition or where the particular magistrate, who was paid on a fee basis, might be eager to trade a favorable decision for a lawyer's client for the assurance that he would get the particular attorney's business in the future.[15]

Figure 9.1 Historical Development of State Courts

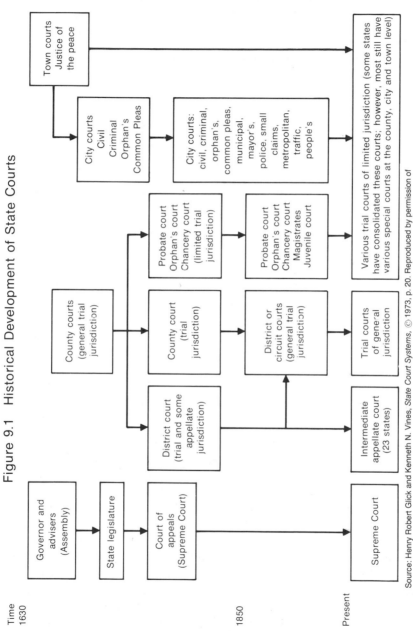

Source: Henry Robert Glick and Kenneth N. Vines, *State Court Systems*, © 1973, p. 20. Reproduced by permission of Prentice-Hall, Inc., Englewood Cliffs, NJ.

Time
1630

1850

Present

Governor and advisers (Assembly)

State legislature

Court of appeals (Supreme Court)

Town courts Justice of the peace

County courts (general trial jurisdiction)

District court (trial and some appellate jurisdiction)

Probate court Orphan's court Chancery court (limited trial jurisdiction)

County court (trial jurisdiction)

City courts Civil Criminal Orphan's Common Pleas

City courts: civil, criminal, orphan's, common pleas, municipal, mayor's, police, small claims, metropolitan, traffic, people's

Probate court Orphan's court Chancery court Magistrates Juvenile court

District or circuit courts (general trial jurisdiction)

Intermediate appellate court (23 states)

Supreme Court

Trial courts of general jurisdiction

Various trial courts of limited jurisdiction (some states have consolidated these courts; however, most still have various special courts at the county, city and town level)

Unfortunately, the proliferation of state courts and the complexity of their jurisdictions is still confusing, even to lawyers. A report released a few years ago on the nature of Maryland's judicial system points this out:

> Maryland's court system is very complex. There are no less than 16 different types of courts, with little uniformity from one community to another. A lawyer from one county venturing into another is likely to feel almost as bewildered as if he had gone into another state with an entirely different system of courts.[16]

Despite their numbers, there are not enough courts to go around. Because of a lack of administrative resources and a host of other problems, the lower courts in many states, particularly in densely populated areas, must cope with an enormous volume of cases. It was estimated by the President's Task Force on the Courts that in 1965 over 4½ million misdemeanor cases were brought before the lower courts of the United States.

Data from various cities illustrate the seriousness of this problem. Washington, D.C., in 1972 had eight judges in the District of Columbia Court of General Sessions to process the preliminary stages of more than 2,400 felony cases and to hear and determine 9,300 serious misdemeanor cases, 41,000 petty offenses, and nearly 44,000 traffic offenses.[17] In 1969, the courts which handle the criminal cases in Milwaukee disposed of 11,078 cases; thirty judges handled most of these cases in addition to 95,000 civil cases. Jacob reports that if each judge in Milwaukee shared this workload equally and worked 255 days a year, he would have to dispose of thirteen cases every day.[18] In Detroit, over 20,000 misdemeanor and nontraffic petty offenses must be handled by the single judge sitting in the Early Sessions Division.[19] In Atlanta in 1964, three judges of the municipal court disposed of more than 70,000 cases.[20] The situation is not a great deal better in the federal courts. In fiscal 1970, the then existing eighty-nine federal district courts saw their workload of cases increase 18 percent from fiscal 1969 and 172 percent from fiscal 1960. In eleven districts, over one-third of the cases had been pending for a year or more.[21]

These criminal court delays can have drastic consequences. This was demonstrated in 1970, when approximately 4,500 prisoners, incarcerated in New York City's House of Detention known as the "Tombs" and four other local jails, rioted and seized hostages in an effort to express their grievances. One of their major complaints concerned delays in the city courts which prevented them from receiving speedy trials. Because many of them were unable to afford to obtain bond for their release, they were forced to remain in jail until their cases were called. A survey indicated that on the average, prisoners were detained in these facilities for ninety-one days before coming to trial. Some had been waiting six months or a year in jail. Because of this, many state and local officials called for reforms to speed up the work of the courts. Few specific proposals were made, however, and some judges suggested that what was

Table 9-1   Structure of State Court Systems

Supreme Court

All states have one supreme court. In some states this court is termed the supreme judicial court or court of appeals.

Intermediate Appellate Courts

23 states have intermediate courts of appeals. California has 5 such courts and Oklahoma, Tennessee, and Texas have 2 intermediate courts of appeals, 1 each for civil and criminal cases. Intermediate appellate courts have various names: superior court, court of appeals, or appellate division of supreme court.

Trial Courts of General Jurisdiction

38 states have 1 type of trial court of general jurisdiction, 9 states have 2, 2 states have 3, and 1 state has 4. The names of the courts vary widely: circuit court, court of general sessions, superior court, district court, common pleas, and in New York, the supreme court.

Trial Courts of Limited or Special Jurisdiction

8 states have only 1 or 2 of these kinds of trial courts; 10 states have different kinds; 20 states have 4 or 5; 12 states have 6 or more different kinds. The names and functions of these courts vary widely. They include probate courts, police courts, small claims courts, city and town courts, juvenile courts, orphan's courts, courts of oyer and terminer, and courts of chancery.

Source: Henry R. Glick and Kenneth N. Vines, *State Court Systems* (Englewood Cliffs, N.J.: Prentice-Hall, 1973) p. 28.

needed was not additional judgeships and more administrative efficiency in the court system, but simply more jails in order that the overcrowding could be relieved.[22]

State Court Systems Today

All fifty states have at least three levels of courts. The highest level consists of the appellate courts. At this level is the state court of last resort as well as intermediate appellate courts in the most densely populated states. The main function of these appellate courts is to review the decisions of the lower courts. The middle level is made up of those courts of general jurisdiction which usually handle felony criminal trials and major civil cases. The lowest level consists of courts of limited and special jurisdiction that have original jurisdiction to try misdemeanor cases, conduct preliminary hearings for felony offenses, try traffic cases, adjudicate civil matters involving small amounts of money, and handle wills and estates.

Although the basic structure of state court systems is similar, the specific number, names, and functions of state courts vary widely. Glick and Vine break state court systems down into four categories, as depicted in Table 9-1.

The major differences among the states are in the presence or absence of intermediate appellate courts and the great variation in the number of trial courts of limited or special jurisdiction. Most states have only one or two types of trial courts of general jurisdiction. State court systems vary from the very simple, with jurisdictions clearly defined, to highly complex systems having numerous trial courts of limited jurisdiction whose functions frequently are unclear and may overlap with one another.[23]

Justice of the Peace

The office of justice of the peace represents the lowest rung in the judicial pattern of organization in a number of states. Although it boasts an honorable tradition dating back to the fourteenth century, today this office is often the object of scorn. In the early years of our nation's history, this was an appointive office, but since the days of Andrew Jackson this post has usually been an elective one. With few exceptions, legal training is not required. A survey conducted in the late 1960s in Oregon and Pennsylvania indicated that less than 2 percent of the justices of the peace in those two states possessed a law degree.[24] Compensation is often in the form of fees collected from litigants, a system which has led to a great deal of abuse. The term of office is short, usually two years. While the office was at one time found in virtually all localities, it is fast disappearing in urban areas.

The jurisdiction of justices of the peace varies among the states, but in all instances it is very limited. Their criminal jurisdiction is usually limited to minor misdemeanors and traffic offenses. In a few states that retain crimes constituting high misdemeanors, this court is empowered in some instances to hold preliminary hearings on these offenses. The justice ordinarily has authority to settle civil disputes involving very small sums of money—usually not over a few hundred dollars. Other duties might include providing notary services, performing marriage ceremonies, and issuing minor warrants. Decisions of the justice are commonly appealable to higher courts, where the case may be tried *de novo;* that is, a completely new trial will be held. In most instances, there are no provisions for jury trials in justices of the peace courts.

Years ago, when travel was difficult and communications were slow, justices of the peace served a useful purpose. They were able to handle petty cases without the expense and loss of time involved in carrying grievances to higher courts. In modern society, these same conditions do not prevail, and many states have eliminated these particular courts. The major criticism of justice of the peace courts is that since legal training is generally not required, this office is frequently occupied by individuals totally unfit to administer the law. There have been instances when illiterates were elected to this post, and often the office is filled by small-time politicians more interested in the political opportunities of the office than in its legal responsibilities. In most instances, the justices also operate without a courtroom, with the result that proceedings may be, and usually are, conducted in any kind of setting. The justices are forced to keep their own records, since no clerical assistance is provided, and thus frequently no permanent records are maintained. Another major criticism is that this court operates for the most part completely unsupervised by any other judicial or court regulatory authority. In the words of one state's attorney general: "They are a form of justice unto themselves."

Because of these weaknesses, a number of states have adopted drastic reforms or abolished the office outright. States that have purposely set about to unify the structure of their state courts usually absorb the functions of these courts by transferring their jurisdiction to local courts of record. In other instances, their jurisdiction has been sharply curtailed. A few states have provided for their gradual elimination, and still others have undertaken various reforms, such as requiring the maintenance of records, abolishing the fee system, and requiring that justices have law degrees and be licensed to practice in that particular state or that they be certified and licensed by completing formal training programs. There are, of course, many justices of the peace who execute their duties honestly and efficiently, but there are still too many who contribute to an already bad system of justice at this level and continue to perpetuate the fact that this particular court, overall, is the weakest link in the judicial chain.

Magistrate's Courts

Magistrate's courts are the urban counterpart of rural justices of the peace. These courts are sometimes referred to as police, mayor's, and in some states, recorder's courts. Usually, their jurisdiction is similar to that of the justice of the peace. The major difference between the two is brought about by the settings in which they are found. This is reflected in the types of cases that each handles. Typically, in large urban areas magistrate's courts handle the bulk of all criminal matters involving misdemeanors and the like. In some instances, depending upon whether the city maintains special courts for traffic violations, small claims, and minor civil matters, the magistrate's courts will also handle these.

Magistrate's courts are often criticized as having the same weaknesses as the justice of the peace courts. In fact, the situation may be even worse in these urban tribunals because of the pressures and influences exerted upon them by unscrupulous politicians and lawyers. In a notable public statement, former Philadelphia District Attorney Arlen Specter, long a foe of the entire magistrate system in that city, declared that "the only difference between Chief Magistrate Walsh and his 27 cohorts and Ali Baba and the 40 Thieves is that one group is somewhat larger."[25] The history of judicial corruption and venality in these courts has certainly contributed to this feeling and is indicative of the need for reform of many of these tribunals.

Municipal Courts

Because of the volume of cases to be tried, many more populous cities have established municipal courts. The first municipal court was established in Chicago in 1906. The jurisdictions of these courts is sufficiently broad to include many cases that might be heard by magistrates or the general trial courts of the state. These courts are usually authorized to try misdemeanor cases and civil cases involving amounts up to a few thousand dollars, to serve as preliminary hearing tribunals in cases of felony offenses, and to hear appeals from magistrates' courts if such courts are retained after the creation of the municipal courts.

The municipal court is typically much better equipped and staffed than are the courts presided over by magistrates and justices of the peace, and the decorum of the court is more typical of what citizens expect to see in courtrooms. The judges must be trained in the law, are usually elected to longer terms of office, and are provided with clerical assistance. Because of these factors, it can usually be expected that more capable individuals are attracted to serve as municipal judges.

Municipal courts are often part of a unified state court structure and must adhere to certain uniform policies and procedures imposed on them by law. Still, in spite of the recommendations of many judicial reform groups, a number of states have retained a nonunified state judiciary and have imposed only minimal requirements on these courts. In large cities the municipal court is often broken down into specialized sections which hear certain types of cases. For example, one section may hear traffic cases, another small claims, and a third domestic relations or civil matters. In this type of arrangement, a chief judge, either appointed or elected, has the responsibility for the overall administration of the court, which usually includes the authority to assign or transfer judges within the court as case dockets require or depending upon the particular talents or predilections of the judges.

Miscellaneous Local Courts

Some cities have created special courts to handle specific types of cases. Thus a city or county may create a special court for small claims, probate and estate matters, or juvenile delinquency cases. Michigan, for example, has created special local courts on the county level in each of that state's eighty-three counties to handle probate matters and all juvenile delinquency cases as well as cases involving neglected or dependent children.

Many states also have distinct county courts which exist as tribunals midway between justices of the peace and the general trial courts. The jurisdiction of these county courts varies widely from state to state. In some states, they exercise a great deal of authority, and in others they play a very limited role in the judicial process. Often, their jurisdiction overlaps with that of the justice of the peace courts and the general trial courts. Usually, these county courts are presided over by judges trained in the law, and they have many of the features of the municipal courts which are their urban counterparts.

General Trial Courts

All fifty states are divided into judicial districts, with each district usually composed of one or more counties, depending upon population. In each district, there exists a general trial court. States use a variety of titles to identify this court. For example, in Michigan, general trial courts are called circuit courts; in California, superior courts; in South Carolina, courts of general sessions; and in Ohio, common pleas courts. General trial courts are usually presided over by a single judge or in more populated districts, a number of judges. The judge, who must be a member of the bar, presides over scheduled sessions held in courtrooms usually located in the county courthouses.

Persons accused of felonies are prosecuted in these general trial courts. The attorney who prosecutes in the name of the state is the locally elected prosecutor, known in different states as the district attorney, county prosecutor, solicitor, or county attorney. Trials are heard only after formal accusation either by grand jury indictment or the filing of an information and are conducted before juries. Violations of state criminal laws are as a rule tried in these courts unless some other court is specifically directed or empowered to hear these cases.

General trial courts have what is referred to in the law as *original jurisdiction* over felony cases; that is, all felony trials are initiated and held in these courts. Most states specify that their lower courts of limited jurisdiction have original jurisdiction in misdemeanor cases (crimes punishable by sentences of up to one year in jail).

Many states also authorize general trial courts to exercise *appellate jurisdiction* as well. Under these provisions, a misdemeanor tried under the original jurisdiction of the lower courts can be appealed to the general trial court in instances where someone is dissatisfied with the legal rulings of a lower court. When an appeal is made to a general trial court, there will be a trial *de novo,* or completely new trial. This procedure differs significantly from that in intermediate courts of appeal or the state supreme court, where only the particular legal points in question will be reviewed.

Intermediate State Appellate Courts

In order to reduce the number of cases that must be reviewed by the state supreme court, the most heavily populated states have formed intermediate appellate courts. Twenty-three such states now have such courts. These courts are composed of three or more judges, who are usually elected to this office.

Usually, their terms of office are longer than the terms of office of lower-court judges in the state system. In addition, many states employ a rotational system of electing these jurists. For example, if a state elects judges to eight-year terms of office on this bench and there are eight judges on the appellate court, every two years there would be new elections to fill two judgeships.

These courts, like the federal courts of appeal, have basically only appellate jurisdiction. Only in some states, in cases of disputed elections, do these courts have original jurisdiction in which they actually try cases. In both civil and criminal appeals, the usual procedure is for the attorneys of the parties to submit briefs to the court and present oral arguments before the judges. The judges examine these briefs, hear the oral arguments, and examine the record of the case in the lower court. The judges then, in consultation with each other, reach a decision by means of majority vote. Ordinarily, an appeals court does not concern itself with the facts of a particular case, but bases its decisions upon whether the law has been correctly interpreted and applied by the lower court.

State Supreme Courts

Just as in the federal judiciary, every state court system has an appellate court of last resort, usually called the state supreme court. These courts are established by the respective constitutions of the states. In most states, justices are elected to the bench, but in a few states, the governor or the legislature appoints individuals to this court. The chief justice of this court is usually the senior member of the court, although the court itself may select one of its members for this post or, less commonly, the chief justice may be chosen by the state legislature. Terms of office for the chief justice range from a few years to a lifetime appointment in a few cases.

Just as with the U.S. Supreme Court, decisions are written and published in an official series of volumes called a *reporter*. In most cases, decisions by a state supreme court marks the end of litigation. Review by the U.S. Supreme Court is restricted to those cases involving a federal question, that is, an issue of federal law. When review is sought on the grounds that state action has resulted in a denial of due process of law as guaranteed by the Fourteenth Amendment, the Supreme Court must then decide whether the federal question is important enough to warrant a review of the case.

A special agreement or judicial courtesy known as *comity* has developed between the federal and state courts. This is an understanding that federal courts will accept and apply the interpretations of state law as it pertains to state statutes and state constitutions. If no significant federal question is involved or state law does not conflict with federal law, the decisions of the state courts will not be reviewed by the federal courts.

These then are the courts one might typically find at the state level. The number of courts, their names, and their respective jurisdictions vary considerably from state to state. Table 9-2 indicates how the court organizations of three

Table 9-2   A Comparison of the Judicial Structure in Three States

CALIFORNIA	MICHIGAN	GEORGIA
	Appellate Courts	
Supreme Court (1)	Supreme Court (1)	Supreme Court (1)
Court of Appeals (5)	Court of Appeals (1)	Court of Appeals (1)
	Courts of General Jurisdiction	
Superior Courts (58)	Circuit Courts (45)	Superior Courts (41)
	Recorder's Court -	
	Detroit (1)	
	Courts of Limited and Special Jurisdiction	
Municipal Courts (77)	Common Pleas Court	Courts of Ordinary (159)
Justice Courts (229)	(Detroit) (1)	State Courts (60)
	Court of Claims (1)	Small Claims Courts (31)
	District Courts (100)	Special Municipal Courts (5)
	Municipal Courts (31)	Miscellaneous Municipal Courts, Re-
	Probate Courts (83)	corder's Courts, Mayor's Courts, City
		Courts, Police Courts (137)
		Magistrate's Courts (2)
		Justice of the Peace Courts (*)

*Data not available.

Source: U.S. Department of Justice, *National Survey of Court Organization* (Washington, D.C.: U.S. Government Printing Office, 1973).

states differ. California, although the most populous state in the nation, has consolidated and streamlined its system so that only five types of courts exist in that entire state. California has been the leader in centralizing the state judiciary and making it more efficient.

Michigan provides an example of intermediate court consolidation and centralization. In spite of a relatively recent reorganization act aimed at consolidating existing courts, that state retains a number of courts of limited and special jurisdiction. Particularly noticeable is the continued existence of specialized courts which operate only in Detroit.

Georgia illustrates a decentralized and fragmented state judiciary. In that state, there exist eleven different kinds of local courts of limited and special jurisdiction. In spite of periodic efforts to abolish this system, Georgia has, for various political reasons, been unable to restructure the state judiciary and bring it in line with some of the more progressive state court systems.

THE FEDERAL JUDICIARY

In many respects, the federal court system is far less diversified than the various state systems. However, even in the federal system, these are more

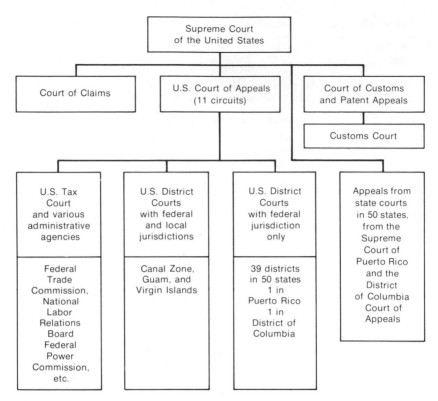

Figure 9.2   The United States Court System

Source: *The United States Courts—Their Jurisdiction and Work* (Washington, D.C.: U.S. Government Printing Office, 1975) p. 3.

courts than most people realize. Figure 9-2 indicates the federal court system. There are two major types of courts at the federal level in terms of both their creation and their functions: the *legislative courts* and the *constitutional courts*. The power to establish legislative courts is vested in Congress from Article 1 of the Constitution, which gives Congress "the power to create tribunals inferior to the Supreme Court" and the power to make all laws "necessary and proper" for executing its powers.

These legislative courts are courts of special jurisdiction, such as the Court of Customs and Patent Appeals or the Tax Court, which has jurisdiction over controversies involving taxpayers and the Internal Revenue Service. Also included are some territorial courts in the Canal Zone, Guam, and the Virgin Islands. Finally, there are district and appellate courts in the District of Columbia which were created by Congress through its constitutional power to govern the nation's capital. Since legislative courts have only a limited relationship to the administration of criminal justice, they need not be examined here.

Table 9-3 Appellate and Original Jurisdiction of the Federal Courts

Court	Original Jurisdiction	Appellate Jurisdiction
U.S. Supreme Court (1)	Cases between the United States and a state Cases between two or more states Cases involving foreign ambassadors, ministers, and consuls Cases between a state and a citizen of another state or country	All lower federal constitutional courts and some legislative and territorial courts The highest state court in cases of a substantial federal question
U.S. courts of appeals (11)		U.S. district courts U.S. territorial courts, Tax Court, and some District of Columbia courts U.S. regulatory commissions and certain administrative agencies
U.S. district courts (94)	All federal crimes All civil actions under the constitution, laws, and treaties of the United States when the matter in controversy exceeds $10,000 Cases involving citizens of different states or aliens if the matter in controversy exceeds $10,000 Review and enforcement of orders and actions of certain administrative agencies and departments	Limited appellate jurisdiction involving certain actions tried before U.S. magistrate's courts
U.S. magistrate's courts	Very minor misdemeanors Preliminary hearing Setting bond Issuance of warrants	

The Constitutional Courts

Although Article III of the Constitution provided for a Supreme Court, the entire organization of the lower federal judiciary has been left to Congress to create. With the exception of the specialized District of Columbia courts, four constitutional courts handle federal criminal cases and, in some instances, state criminal cases on appeal. These are U.S. Magistrate's Courts, U.S. District Courts, Courts of Appeal, and, of course, the U.S. Supreme Court. Table 9-3 shows the appellate and original jurisdiction of the Federal courts.

U.S. Magistrate's Courts

These are the lowest courts in the federal judicial structure. Presided over by U.S. magistrates (formerly called U.S. commissioners), they used to occupy a place in the federal system similar to that of the justice of the peace in the state judicial system. Since the passage of the Federal Magistrate's Act of 1968, their authority has changed somewhat. They now have the authority to try federal cases involving minor offenses where the possible penalty is less than $1,000 and less than one year incarceration. They are empowered to issue search and arrest warrants, conduct preliminary hearings, review habeas corpus petitions, conduct pretrial conferences in both civil and criminal hearings, and handle special assignments delegated by a federal district court judge which does not conflict with any constitutional questions of authority.

Until the 1968 legislation, U.S. magistrates were part-time judicial personnel who were paid on a fee basis and were not required to be attorneys. To qualify as a U.S. magistrate today, an individual must be an attorney with considerable practical experience. Most of the full-time appointees are former state and county judges, assistant U.S. attorneys, public defenders, or trial lawyers with many years of criminal and civil experience. The term of appointment for a full-time magistrate is eight years, and appointments are made by district court judges. Full-time magistrates earn an annual salary of $30,000 and are not permitted to engage in the private practice of law. Part-time magistrates receive up to $15,000 in salary and may practice law, but not in federal courts handling federal criminal cases.

U.S. District Courts

At the present time, there are ninety-four districts courts, with at least one in each state. The more populous states, such as California, New York, and Illinois, are divided into districts with a U.S. district court in each. For example, there is a U.S. judicial district for northern Illinois and a U.S. judicial district for southern Illinois. A district may be divided into divisions and may have several locales where the court hears cases. Each district has from one to twenty-seven judges, depending upon the volume of cases which must be decided. By law, 400 district judgeships are authorized, and the salary of each is $40,000 a year. In districts having two or more judges, the judge who is senior in service and who has not reached seventy years of age is the chief judge.

These courts are the workhorses of the federal judiciary. In 1974, they heard over 320,000 cases, including civil, criminal, and bankruptcy cases.[26] District courts in the Canal Zone, Guam, and the Virgin Islands have jurisdiction over local cases as well as those arising under federal laws. Since the courts in these three places are not limited to the types of cases defined in the Constitution as part of the federal judicial power, they are legislative rather than constitutional courts.

U.S. district courts have original jurisdiction over almost all criminal cases arising under federal criminal law. These courts are similar to the courts of general jurisdiction in the state systems. Although the district courts, for the most part, have original jurisdiction only, when necessary, they do have the obligation and authority to review actions and orders tried before U.S. magistrates.

The criminal workload of these district courts during the year ending June 30, 1974, was 37,667 cases. Of this number, 4,685 involved embezzlement or fraud; 4,360, forgery and counterfeiting; 1,790, interstate transportation of a stolen motor vehicle; 641, failure to pay the tax on alcoholic beverages; and 1,008, violation of the selective service laws. The remainder involved the violation of a host of other laws.[27]

Each district has a number of important officers for the court. The first of these is the U.S. attorney, an officer comparable to the local prosecutor or district attorney in the states. A U.S. marshal's office is also located in each district. Both of these officers are appointed by the president with the advice and consent of the Senate. The U.S. attorney is the criminal prosecutor for the federal government. He or she appoints a number of assistant U.S. attorneys, often in conjunction with the wishes of influential members of the president's political party. The U.S. attorney is not supervised by the federal district court judges, but functions under the authority of the U.S. attorney general and the U.S. Department of Justice.

In addition, in each district are U.S. magistrates, probation officers, court reporters, and one or more bankruptcy judges. Each district court also has a plan under which lawyers are provided for poor defendants in criminal cases. To assure adequate service, full-time public defenders are appointed in those courts where criminal cases are numerous.

Courts of Appeals

Standing immediately above the U.S. district courts in the federal court system are the U.S. courts of appeals. There are eleven circuits wherein a court of appeals is located; each includes three or more states except the District of Columbia Circuit. U.S. courts of appeals are essentially what the name implies—appellate courts only. Criminal appeals may be taken from a U.S. district court to the court of appeals of the circuit where the trial is situated. For example, someone tried in Miami for a federal crime would have his or her case heard in the U.S. District Court for Miami (Florida Southern U.S. Judicial District). If the individual appealed, the case, would go to the Court of Appeals for the Fifth Circuit, which is located in New Orleans, since the Fifth Circuit includes Florida.

The courts of appeals hear cases that are appealed from the lower federal courts. In only three instances will a case that has been tried in the lower federal

Table 9-4   U.S. Courts of Appeals Circuits

Courts of Appeals	Number of Authorized Judgeships	Location
First Circuit (Main, Massachusetts, New Hampshire, Rhode Island, Puerto Rico)	3	Boston
Second Circuit (Connecticut, New York, Vermont)	9	New York
Third Circuit (Delaware, New Jersey, Pennsylvania, Virgin Islands)	9	Philadelphia
Fourth Circuit (Maryland, North Carolina, South Carolina, Virginia, West Virginia)	7	Richmond
Fifth Circuit (Alabama, Florida, Georgia, Louisiana, Mississippi, Texas, Canal Zones)	15	New Orleans
Sixth Circuit (Kentucky, Michigan, Ohio, Tennessee)	9	Cincinnati
Seventh Circuit (Illinois, Indiana, Wisconsin)	8	Chicago
Eighth Circuit (Arkansas, Iowa, Minnesota, Missouri, Nebraska, North Dakota, South Dakota)	8	St. Louis
Ninth Circuit (Alaska, Arizona, California, Hawaii, Idaho, Montana, Nevada, Oregon, Washington, Guam)	13	San Francisco
Tenth Circuit (Colorado, Kansas, New Mexico, Oklahoma, Utah, Wyoming)	7	Denver
Eleventh Circuit (District of Columbia)	9	Washington, D.C.

courts bypass the particular court of appeals and go straight to the Supreme Court: (1) if the case has been decided by a special three-judge district court, (2) if it is a case where a federal statute has been held unconstitutional by a U.S. district court and the United States is a litigant in the case, or (3) it can be shown that the case is "of such imperative public importance . . . as to require immediate settlement."

The eleven U.S. courts of appeals currently are receiving about 16,500 cases every year. They hear cases *en banc;* that is, from three to nine judges sit together and hear a particular case. The appeals court may affirm the decision of the district court or reverse it and send it back for a new trial. Criminal appeals to the U.S. Supreme Court from the courts of appeals may be taken in certain cases involving federal constitutional questions or where the constitutionality of a statute is being called into question. However, cases appealed from state supreme courts are not heard by the federal courts of appeals. Table 9-4 indicates the various circuits of the U.S. courts of appeals.

U.S. Supreme Court

This court stands at the apex of the federal judiciary. It consists of nine justices, appointed for life by the president with the advice and consent of the

Senate. One justice is designated as the chief justice. The officers appointed by the Court include a clerk to keep the records, a marshal to maintain order and supervise the administrative affairs of the Court, a reporter to publish its opinions, and a librarian to serve the justices and the lawyers of the Supreme Court bar. The chief justice is also authorized to appoint an administrative assistant.

The Court meets on the first Monday of October of each year. It usually continues in session until June and receives and disposes of about 5,000 cases each year. Most of these cases are disposed of by the brief decision that the subject matter is either not proper or not of sufficient importance to warrant full court review. But, each year between 200 and 250 cases of great importance and interest are decided on the merits. About one-half of these decisions are announced in full published opinions.

The Constitution does not spell out the Supreme Court's appellate jurisdiction, but leaves this question to Congress. In an effort to relieve the Court from an intolerable burden of cases, Congress passed a law in 1925 which permits the Court to exercise its own discretion in deciding what cases that are appealed to it will be heard. This is called its *certiorari power* and comes from a special *writ of certiorari,* which is a writ of review that the Court issues. The writ of certiorari commands a lower court to "forward up the record" of a case which it has tried so that the Supreme Court can review it.

A defendant who has been found guilty in a criminal trial in a state court and who has exhausted all judicial appellate remedies available in the particular state may petition the Supreme Court for a writ of certiorari. The Supreme Court may grant or deny the petition. If the Court decides to hear the case, it will send down to the highest state court (or, when applicable, to the particular court of appeals) a demand that all proceedings in the case be immediately forwarded to the Supreme Court for review. The Supreme Court will not try the case de novo, but will decide upon the particular point of law involved and render its decision.

The U.S. Supreme Court does not have the right to review all decisions of state courts in criminal matters. It has authority to review only those cases where a federal statute has been interpreted or a federal constitutional right of the defendant has allegedly been violated, that is, where there is a substantial federal question.

In a state trial for a criminal offense, before the defendant can have the case reviewed by the U.S. Supreme Court, he or she must invoke the rights to due process and dual citizenship under the Fourteenth Amendment as well as the particular constitutional right that has been violated. The Fourteenth Amendment reads in part:

All persons born or naturalized in the United States, and subject to the jurisdiction thereof, are citizens of the United States and of the State wherein they reside. No State shall make or enforce any law which shall abridge the privileges or immunities of citizens of the United States; nor shall any State deprive any person of

life, liberty or property, without due process of law; nor deny to any person within
its jurisdiction the equal protection of the laws. . . .

This amendment prohibits the states from depriving citizens of the due
process of law and grants to state citizens dual citizenship as citizens of both
their respective state and the United States. These two clauses permit the
Supreme Court to intervene in state criminal trials. Getting back to our example, let us assume that an individual that was convicted in a state court alleges
that his or her Fourth Amendment rights regarding search and seizure have been
violated. The defendant cannot merely petition the Supreme Court to grant
certiorari based upon the violation of the Fourth Amendment. Instead, the
appeal would have to be framed in a manner similar to this: Since my Fourth
Amendment rights have been violated, and since this is a violation of my right
to due process, and since I am also a citizen of the United States (Fourteenth
Amendment), I am petitioning the Supreme Court for review of my case. Thus,
the Fourteenth Amendment acts as the "carrier amendment"; that is, it must
accompany the particular Bill of Rights violation (in this case, the Fourth
Amendment) before it can come before the Supreme Court. The defendant on
trial in a federal court for a federal crime would need merely to show that his or
her Fourth Amendment rights were violated and would not have to invoke the
Fourteenth Amendment to appeal the case.

Because of its vested constitutional power, the only federal court whose
decisions are binding on state courts is the U.S. Supreme Court. This means
that in criminal cases, the final word as to whether the accused in a case before it
has been accorded all his or her due process rights is the Supreme Court. When
the Supreme Court decides a case, the ruling is usually not retroactive. For
example, if the court should overturn the conviction of a defendant on a legal
technicality, all other persons convicted under the same set of circumstances
prior to the decision in this particular case would not have their convictions set
aside because of the present ruling. In most situations, the new rule would be
applied only from the date of decision forward. Whether a decision will have a
retroactive effect is determined by the Supreme Court, based upon the nature of
the right, the extent to which the previous rule has been relied upon, the possible
consequences that such a change in the rule would have upon the administration
of justice, and other considerations.[28]

It is important that students of criminal justice, along with students in other
disciplines who take their obligation of knowledgeable citizenship seriously,
understand the organization of the judiciary in their own states and at the federal
level. It is also important that they correctly understand what specific powers
are delegated to what courts, what limitations on jurisdictional authority exist,
and the degree to which the pronouncements of one court are binding upon other
courts in the system. It should be remembered that not even the U.S. Supreme
Court has absolute authority and jurisdiction over all litigative matters.

SUMMARY

The American judicial system has a dual system of courts, with one system operating at the state level and the other at the federal level. Both systems are organized geographically. Since external supervision is not imposed, the courts can, in many instances, operate more autonomously than the executive or legislative branches of government. Our courts are highly specialized. This specialization is usually determined by their limited jurisdiction.

The historical development of court systems reflects the general cultural, demographic, and political trends that have been a part of our history as a nation. As American society became more complex, the need increased for laws to regulate human behavior and for courts to enforce these laws. The state court systems reflect the particular social forces within each state. In recent years, a number of states have attempted to streamline their judiciary and to consolidate the random proliferation of courts. While some states have been able to accomplish this, many others have not.

State and federal courts have similar organizational characteristics. Both systems maintain courts of special and limited jurisdiction at the lowest level in the judicial hierarchy. Next are the courts of general jurisdiction, which handle major criminal and civil cases, and above them are the appellate courts. About one-half of the states and the federal government have a court of last resort at the pinnacle of the judiciary. In the federal system, this court is the Supreme Court.

Suggested Additional Readings

Abraham, Henry J. *The Judicial Process*. London: Oxford University Press, 1968.

American Judicature Society. *Intermediate Appellate Courts*. Report no. 20. Chicago: American Judicature Society, 1968.

Aumann, Francis R. *The Changing American Legal System*. Columbus: Ohio State University Press, 1940.

Becker, Theodore L. *Political Behavioralism and Modern Jurisprudence*. Chicago: Rand McNally, 1961.

Jahnige, Thomas P., and Sheldon Goldman. *The Federal Judicial System*. New York: Holt, 1968.

President's Commission on Law Enforcement and Administration of Justice. *Task Force Report: The Courts*. Washington, D.C.: U.S. Government Printing Office, 1967.

Vanderbilt, Arthur T. The *Challenge of Law Reform*. Princeton, N.J.: Princeton University Press, 1956.

Vanlandingham, T. "The Decline of the Justice of the Peace." *Kansas Law Review* 389 (1964):380-397.

Notes

1. Herbert Jacob, *Urban Justice: Law and Order in American Cities* (Englewood Cliffs, N.J.: Prentice-Hall, 1973), pp. 80-91.

2. 232 U.S. 383 (1914).

3. See *Mapp v. Ohio,* 367 U.S. 643 (1961).

4. Federal Bureau of Prisons, *Statistical Tables* (Washington, D.C.: U.S. Government Printing Office, 1965), pp. 26-27. At the time of the study, the Tenth Circuit consisted of Colorado, Kansas, New Mexico, Utah, Oklahoma, and Wyoming; the Third Circuit was made up of Delaware, New Jersey, Pennsylvania, and the Virgin Islands.

5. A. Youngdahl, "Sentencing Disparities in U.S. District Courts," *Report of the Institute for Judicial Administration* (Washington, 1965), pp. 33-41.

6. Russell W. Maddox and Robert F. Fuquay, *State and Local Government* (Princeton, N.J.: Van Nostrand, 1962), p. 208.

7. Francis R. Aumann, *The Changing American Legal System* (Columbus: Ohio State University Press, 1940), p. 6.

8. H. R. Glick and K. N. Vines, *State Court Systems* (Englewood Cliffs, N.J.: Prentice-Hall, 1973), p. 19.

9. Charles Warren, *A History of the American Bar* (Boston: Little, Brown, 1911), p. 8.

10. David Mars and Fred Kort, *Administration of Justice in Connecticut* (Storrs: Institute of Public Service, University of Connecticut, 1963), p. 22.

11. Herbert Jacob, "The Courts as Political Agencies," in Herbert Jacob and Kenneth N. Vines (eds.), *Studies in Judicial Politics* (New Orleans: Tulane University Press, 1962), p. 17.

12. U.S. (1 Cranch) 137 (1803).

13. Albert Lepawsky, *The Judicial System of Metropolitan Chicago* (Chicago: University of Chicago Press, 1932), pp. 19-23.

14. Ibid., pp. 43-62.

15. Ibid., p. 61.

16. *Survey of the Judicial System of Maryland* (New York: Institute of Judicial Administration, 1967), pp. 11-12.

17. *Report on the District of Columbia Courts* (Washington, D.C.: U.S. Government Printing Office, 1973), p. 2.

18. Jacob, *Urban Justice,* p. 105.

19. President's Commission on Law Enforcement and Administration of Justice, *The Courts* (Washington, D.C.: U.S. Government Printing Office, 1967), p. 31.

20. Atlanta Commission on Crime and Juvenile Delinquency, *Opportunity for Urban Excellence* 184 (1966).

21. Committee for Economic Development, *Reducing Crime and Assuring Justice* (New York: Committee for Economic Development, 1972), p. 19.

22. *The New York Times,* Oct. 7, 1970, p. 1, col. 2.

23. Glick and Vines, op. cit., pp. 28-29.

24. *The Christian Science Monitor,* May 9, 1967, p. 5. Note: Pennsylvania now requires its justices of the peace either to be licensed attorneys or to complete a course of training and instruction in the duties of that office.

25. Public statement, Dec. 1, 1966.

26. *The United States Courts–Their Jurisdiction and Work* (Washington, D.C.: U.S. Government Printing Office, 1975), p. 7.

27. Ibid., p. 13.

28. Hazel B. Kerper, *Introduction to the Criminal Justice System* (St. Paul, Minn.: West, 1972), p. 226.

JUDGES
CHAMBERS

PRIVATE

Chapter 10

The Criminal Pretrial, Trial, and Post-Trial Process

This chapter will examine in detail the various steps in the conduct of a criminal trial. Before beginning this chapter, the student should become familiar with the basic criminal processes for a misdemeanor and a felony, as shown in Figures 10-1 and 10-2.

PRELIMINARY TRIAL PROCEEDINGS

To begin the prosecution of an accused, a complaint is filed before a magistrate or judge, usually of a court of limited jurisdiction. Although these courts have original jurisdiction only in misdemeanor cases, they often conduct many of the pretrial processes in a felony case.

The purpose of filing a complaint is to determine whether an arrest warrant should be issued. The existing evidence and, in some cases, the testimony of the complainant is presented to demonstrate that there is probable cause to believe that the accused has committed a crime. If the judge or magistrate determines that probable cause exists, he or she will issue the arrest warrant. If the accused is in custody, the warrant authorizes that individual's detention pending initial appearance; if the accused is not in custody, the warrant will direct the police to arrest the individual and bring him before a magistrate.

THE CONDUCT OF MISDEMEANOR CASES

The conduct of a misdemeanor trial and the steps in the process are much less elaborate than those for a felony. An accused arrested for a misdemeanor is brought before the particular court of limited jurisdiction which has the authority to try such cases. When the defendant appears before the court, the offense complaint is read and explained. The defendant is then asked whether he understands the charge. Depending upon the particular nature of the case, the

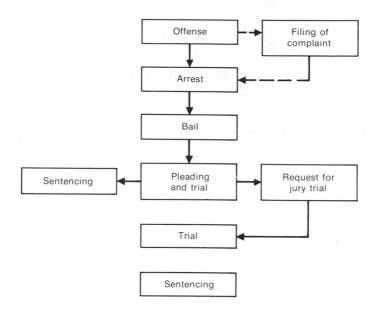

Figure 10.1   Basic Criminal Process for a Misdemeanor

judge may ask the defendant whether he wants court-appointed counsel to assist him if he cannot afford to retain his own.

If the defendant pleads guilty, the magistrate, after a limited inquiry of the circumstances and the possible testimony of the accused and others concerning the circumstances of the case and the characteristics of the offender, will impose a fine, a limited jail sentence, or both as prescribed by the particular statute or ordinance that was violated.

If the defendant pleads not guilty, the judge has several alternatives. The judge may immediately conduct the trial, which is typically what occurs when the defendant is charged with a minor traffic infraction or public drunkenness. If the defendant indicates that he wishes to postpone the trial until a later date so that he can obtain an attorney, if the defendant wants a jury trial in those jurisdictions where it is permissible,[1] or if he needs time to prepare his case and obtain witnesses, the judge will set a date for a later trial and establish bail or release the individual on his own recognizance without requiring the posting of a cash bond.

Most misdemeanor cases of a minor nature are disposed of by guilty pleas. In many jurisdictions, the state is not represented by a prosecuting attorney. In these cases the only parties usually present are the defendant, the arresting officer, and the judge. In many misdemeanor courts it is only in cases where the defendant pleads not guilty and a subsequent trial is arranged or where the

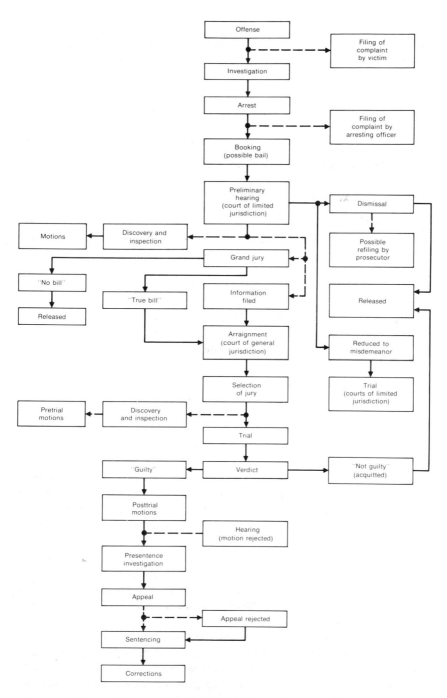

Figure 10.2 Basic Criminal Process for a Felony

defendant retains counsel or requests a jury trial that a prosecutor appears to represent the state. However, even in those jurisdictions which normally assign an assistant prosecutor to such cases, there are usually some significant differences in the conduct of misdemeanor trials. The proceedings are less adversarial in nature and are conducted with greater courtroom and legal informality than are the more serious felony cases in the courts of general jurisdiction.

THE CONDUCT OF FELONY CASES

Preliminary Examination (Hearing)

An individual arrested for a felony first appears for a preliminary examination or hearing. Although a few jurisdictions still conduct an initial appearance hearing prior to the preliminary examination, most states have abolished that extra procedural step.

It is not necessary that the accused have a preliminary hearing. He can waive this right and proceed to the next step in the judicial process. In many cases, however, if the accused has by this time retained an attorney, his lawyer will insist on the right to a preliminary hearing. It is often a tactical advantage to the defense to have a preliminary hearing. The defense attorney will try by means of the preliminary hearing to obtain as much insight as possible into the strengths and weaknesses of the state's case and thus will be better able to prepare the defendant's case should it eventually go to trial.

The preliminary examination is normally conducted before a lower-level court of limited and special jurisdiction, such as a municipal or magistrate's court at the state level or a U.S. magistrate's court if the individual is accused of a federal felony. In theory, the preliminary hearing in federal courts is essentially the same as in state courts. However, the standards are often applied differently. The Federal Rules of Criminal Procedure command federal officers to take the arrestee before a federal magistrate ''without unnecessary delay.'' This emphasis on conducting a prompt inquiry arose from two U.S. Supreme Court rulings in which that court, exercising its supervisory authority over standards in federal courts, held under the *McNabb-Mallory* rule and the *Upshaw v. United States* decision that a delay which is unjustified is unreasonable and sufficient to presume that all statements made by the arrestee between the arrest and the delayed hearing are inadmissible in evidence as the product of an unlawful detention.[2]

Although many states have similar provisions calling for a preliminary hearing without unnecessary delay, most state courts consider the delay to be a mere factor in the totality of circumstances surrounding the case. In fact, even the National Advisory Commission on Criminal Justice Standards and Goals recommends that state courts establish standards that guarantee that the arrestee will be afforded a preliminary hearing within two weeks following arrest.[3]

At the preliminary examination, the individual is advised by the judge of the charges against him and the formal complaint is read to him. In many jurisdictions, the accused is provided with a copy of the complaint. The basic purposes of the preliminary examination are (1) to determine whether a crime has been committed, (2) to determine whether the evidence establishes probable cause to believe that the defendant committed it, (3) to determine the existence of probable cause for which a warrant was issued for the defendant's arrest, (4) to inquire into the reasonableness of the arrest and search and the compliance of the executing officer with the requirements of the warrant, and (5) to determine the appropriate bail for the accused. The preliminary examination is not a trial to determine guilt or innocence, and so a plea will not be asked for by the court.

At this examination, the court will inquire whether the defendant has counsel. The judge will explain to the defendant that he has the right to counsel. If the defendant indicates that he wants to retain counsel, the judge, in most jurisdictions, will postpose the examination until legal assistance is obtained. If the individual wants counsel but is indigent, the court will provide him with an attorney.

The state and the defendant have the right to produce witnesses who testify under oath. The state will attempt to introduce only enough evidence to make a *prima facie* case, that is, to show probable cause to believe that a crime has been committed and that the defendant committed it. The state need not (and most experienced prosecutors will not) introduce all their evidence at this time. The full range of witnesses and evidence will be saved for the later trial. This tactic prevents the defense from knowing all the facts of the state's case and thus gaining too much insight at this time into its possible weaknesses. Both the prosecutor and the defense counsel have the right to cross-examine the witnesses introduced by the opposing side. The testimony of all witnesses is transcribed, and since the testimony is under oath, it can be used to impeach the credibility of a witness if it is inconsistent with later testimony given at the trial.

Since preliminary hearings are conducted on an inquiry basis, they are not limited by the rules of evidence which apply to trials. If the state fails to show probable cause, the defendant will be dismissed by the magistrate, who will order his release. The preliminary hearing only assures the individual that he will not be incarcerated without the existence of valid probable cause and gives the accused the opportunity to be released on bail. A release by a magistrate on a preliminary hearing or a dismissal of the charges is not, however, binding upon the state. Since the defendant has not stood trial and has not been placed in jeopardy, the prosecutor in most states can file another complaint on the same offense, having the individual rearrested and brought again before the courts for another preliminary hearing. In recent years, some states have required that the prosecutor provide additional evidence which was not known to the state at the time of the first preliminary examination before the accused can be rearrested and brought back before the court for another preliminary hearing on the same charge.

If the state satisfies the court that it has met its burden of proof, the judge will issue an order binding over the defendant to the next step in the judicial process. The judge will also be required to certify that a preliminary examination has been held and that the evidence presented has established probable cause to believe that a crime has been committed and that the accused committed it. This certification confers jurisdiction upon the grand jury or the trial court and authorizes the prosecutor to continue to the next step in the judicial process.

The defendant, at this time, will also be advised of his right to waive grand jury examination if he so requests. This right, of course, exists only in federal courts and those states which still use the grand jury. If the defendant knowingly and intelligently waives these rights, the court will bypass the grand jury and transfer the case to the court which has jurisdiction over the conduct of felony cases.

Lastly, the court will determine the proper bail bond that should be imposed on the accused, pending his release prior to trial. This practice of requiring some form of bond to obtain the release of an accused gives some assurance to the court that he will return for trial. During the period of release on bail, the accused is under the authority of the court and must comply with any conditions established by the judge who authorizes the bail. The terms "bail" and "bond" are often used interchangeably, but there is a distinction. Bail is the process by which a bond can be posted for someone's release. The bond is the posting of a surety or some other valuable consideration such as money that will give the court some assurance that the accused will be available at the time of the trial. If he is not, the particular surety is forfeited to the court. In some instances, a bond may be merely the accused's word that he will not absent himself from trial. This is usually referred to as a recognizance bond.

The philosophy behind the development of bail is an ancient idea. Bail was first established in England by the Statute of Westminister in 1275. The original purpose of the law was to regulate the discretion that the sheriffs of that time had in determining who was eligible for release before trial and who was not.[4] As a consequence of this law, two forms of bail were established: *special bail* or "bail below," which was given to the sheriff upon the arrest of the accused to guarantee his appearance in court, and *bail to the action* or "bail above," which a defendant had to deposit with the court to ensure that if the plaintiff (victim) won the judgment at the trial, he would be able to collect from the defendant.[5] The first is the basis for modern bail procedure; the second is no longer used.

Generally, the court has discretion in setting the pretrial bail in all but the most serious capital offenses (e.g., murder). Although an offense may warrant bail, the judge in most jurisdictions can refuse to authorize bail and the posting of bond if there is evidence that the release of the accused would jeopardize his own safety or the safety of others. The basic premise underlying the granting of bail is the fundamental principle of American criminal justice that all persons accused of crime are presumed innocent until proved guilty. This idea is a cornerstone of our system of justice and was so important to our way of life that it became an implicit guarantee, reinforced by the Eighth Amendment to the U.S. Constitution, which provides that "excessive bail shall not be required."

Discovery and Inspection

Once the preliminary hearing has been conducted and the accused has been bound over to the next stage in the judicial process, many jurisdictions provide that discovery and inspection procedures come into play. In recent years expanded rights of discovery and inspection have developed, particularly in the federal court system. States are now adopting similar procedures to guide the conduct of criminal trials in their courts. The idea behind discovery and inspection is to ensure that each party has the opportunity to test the evidence submitted by the other side. It is contended that advance knowledge of the evidence to be used is essential to prepare for the cross-examination of a witness or to gather evidence to refute testimony.[6] The reader will recall that in the preliminary examination, the prosecutor often does not disclose all the state's evidence; those states that have expanded the scope of pretrial discovery and inspection have limited the ability of the prosecutor to withhold evidence. However, this right to discovery and inspection is a two-way street; just as the evidence of the state is made more readily available to the accused, so is the evidence that the defendant might have more readily accessible for examination by the prosecutor.

The possible extent of pretrial discovery and inspection rights for both sides is indicated by the following suggestions on this matter by the National Advisory Commission on Criminal Justice Standards and Goals:

> The prosecution should disclose to the defendant all available evidence that will be used against him at trial. Such disclosure should take place within five days of the preliminary hearing or apprehension or service of summons following indictment, whichever form the initiation of prosecution takes in the particular case. The evidence disclosed should include, but should not be limited to the following:
>
> 1. The names and addresses of persons whom the prosecutor intends to call as witnesses at the trial;
> 2. Written, recorded or oral statements made by witnesses whom the prosecutor intends to call at the trial of the accused or of any codefendant;
> 3. Results of physical or mental examinations, scientific tests and any analyses of physical evidence and any reports or statements of experts relating to such examinations, tests or analyses; and
> 4. Physical evidence belonging to the defendant or which the prosecutor intends to introduce at trial.[7]

The commission also recommends that the defense supply the prosecution with certain evidence. Similar recommendations have been made by the American Bar Association Project on Minimum Standards for Criminal Justice in its

Standards Relating to Discovery and Procedure before Trial.[8] This defense-supplied evidence would require disclosure of such facts as intent to rely on an alibi or an insanity defense; any reports or results, or testimony thereto; physical or mental examinations or scientific tests, experiments, or comparisons, or any other reports or statements of experts which defense counsel intends to use at a hearing or trial.[9]

Of course, these standards are careful to exclude such information as statements made by the witness (which might be incriminating) or whether the defendant will testify at the trial.[10] Those who advocate the liberalization of discovery and inspection do so on the grounds that it will maximize the early resolution of issues regarding the admissibility of evidence and will encourage administrative disposition of cases with no significant increased danger of conviction of innocent defendants and no unjustifiable infringements upon the right of guilty defendants to be treated with dignity.[11]

The Grand Jury

As we have seen, after the preliminary hearing, the case may be bound over to the grand jury. The grand jury originated in 1166 at the Assize of Clarendon. An assize at that time was a court sitting or session which had developed earlier in France and was brought to England by the Norman conquerors. The original purpose of the grand jury was to empanel twelve individuals who personally knew the accused. These jurors would then question witnesses in order to determine whether the accused appeared to be guilty of the alleged crime. Since they knew the accused and often the accusor as well, these grand jurors were in a good position to screen out unfounded accusations. In these earlier times, the grand jury had considerable authority, and it provided a significant opportunity for direct community involvement in the local system of criminal justice.

Historically, the grand jury served two important functions: (1) determining whether an accused should stand trial by virtue of the fact that there is probable cause to believe that he has committed a felony and (2) protecting the innocent from false accusations and harassment by the state where there is no reason to believe a felony has been perpetrated. In recent years, the grand jury system has been widely criticized for failing to accomplish either task and in some cases of actually contributing to the circumstances it was designed to prevent.

The idea of the grand jury was incorporated in the U.S. Constitution and the constitutions of most states. The Fifth Amendment to the U.S. Constitution provides that ''no person shall be held to answer for a capital, or otherwise infamous crime, unless on presentment or indictment of a grand jury.'' From this, it would appear that the Constitution clearly requires that persons accused of major crimes be accused by a grand jury, yet less than half the states use the grand jury today. The reason is that the U.S. Supreme Court has not seen fit to require that the grand jury requirement be made applicable to the states through the due process clause of the Fourteenth Amendment.

The grand jury does not determine the guilt or innocence of the accused, but only whether the individual should be brought to trial. In those states which do not routinely use the grand jury, an individual is usually brought to trial after the preliminary hearing by the filing of an *information* by the prosecutor. This information must state the charges, the statute that was violated, and the approximate time and place of the occurrence of the crime, and the accused must be served with the notice of these facts and specifications. In recent years, those states which still employ the grand jury are increasingly bypassing the grand jury by using the information. In many other instances, the accused is waiving this right to grand jury and thereby also bypassing it.

Although the grand jury is an extension of the court, it has the authority to act independently of the court. Neither the court nor the state may limit the scope of grand jury investigations. It has the power to subpoena witnesses and documents, to grant immunity to witnesses who testify before it, and to proceed in independent criminal investigations. These investigations may be of public officials as well as private citizens. The grand jury is charged by statute to inquire into matters relating to crime and corruption within its jurisdiction and to bring to trial those whom it feels the state has been derelict in not prosecuting. In addition, many jurisdictions require that the grand jury periodically investigate certain functions or governmental operations within the jurisdiction, such as jail facilities or law enforcement agencies, and publicly report its findings and recommendations. These particular functions are called its *investigatory responsibilities;* however, most of the work of the grand jury in dealing with routine criminal cases falls under its *hearing responsibilities,* which will be the focus of attention for the remainder of the examination of the grand jury in this section.

The grand jury is usually composed of sixteen to twenty-three citizens of the judicial district who are chosen by a statutorily prescribed selection process and summoned by a court with general jurisdiction over criminal cases.[12] After the grand jurors are selected and before they commence their activities, the court selects a foreman from among them. The responsibility of the foreman is to verify that a quorum of grand jurors is always available when evidence is being presented and that there are a sufficient number of votes to return an indictment. In many jurisdictions, the foreman also administers the oath to witnesses who testify before this body and performs related administrative tasks required to handle the grand jury proceedings.

The decisions of the grand jury need not be unanimous. Most state statutes prescribe that a two-thirds or three-fourths majority is all that is necessary to return or refuse to return an indictment. An indictment is a formal accusation by the grand jury that is arrived at after consideration of the evidence against the accused. In order to indict someone, the foreman writes on the indictment "A True Bill" and attests to this with his or her signature. For example, let us assume that in a particular state there are eighteen grand jurors, of which twelve must concur for an indictment. After hearing all the evidence, thirteen grand jurors believe that there is sufficient evidence to believe a crime has been committed and that the accused committed it. Thus, the thirteen would vote for indictment and a true bill would be signed. The accused would then be bound over for trial. If the required two-thirds majority could not be reached, the foreman would write ''No Bill'' on the indictment, and the accused would be released.

The indictment is a very important legal document that must carefully set forth a number of facts. It must:

1. State the type and nature of the offense
2. Cite the specific statute alleged to have been violated
3. Set forth the nature and elements of the offense charged
4. State as definitively as possible the time and place of the occurrence of the crime
5. State the name and address of the accused if known, and if not known, provide a description sufficient to identify the accused with reasonable certainty
6. Bear the signature of the foreman showing that it has been returned as a true bill
7. Indicate the names of all co-defendants in the offense charged as well as the number of counts against them[13]

The proceedings of the grand jury have some important characteristics. In the first place, it is what is called in the law an *ex parte* (one-party) proceeding. This means that the accused and his attorney are not permitted to be present during the conduct of the grand jury hearing. Under these circumstances, the accused does not have the opportunity to cross-examine the witnesses against him or object to their testimony or to the introduction of evidence. Only the state or representatives of the state such as police officers and their witnesses are authorized to be present during the conduct of the hearing. The hearings are presided over by the prosecutor, who, in essence, runs the grand jury. He controls the introduction of witnesses and the presentation of evidence and sets the general framework for the questioning by the members of the grand jury.

Witnesses are usually not permitted to be represented by counsel during the grand jury hearing. The conduct of these hearings is very informal in comparison to that of a trial. Usually, the witness is brought in, the oath is administered, and the witness relates what he or she knows in response to questions from the prosecutor or grand jurors. The rules of evidence do not apply. As an example, hearsay evidence is admissible. In a trial, a witness, except under a few limited circumstances, could not testify to what he or she heard someone say because the witness does not have direct knowledge of the facts and the truth of the matter; no such prohibition applies to witnesses before the grand jury.

The grand jury has the right to compel witnesses to testify except in cases where the witness is subject to the right against self-incrimination. However, the grand jury has the right to extend immunity to a witness. This is a guarantee that even though the testimony is self-incriminating, the witness will be immune from later prosecution for testifying.[14] Since the grand jury has this right,

UNITED STATES OF AMERICA

IN THE UNITED STATES DISTRICT COURT FOR THE

WESTERN DISTRICT OF MICHIGAN, SOUTHERN DIVISION

- - - - - - - - - -

UNITED STATES OF AMERICA,)
        Plaintiff,)
  vs.)
EUGENE JOHN McCOY,)
        Defendant.)
	No. 76-223 Cr.7
	
	INDICTMENT

The Grand Jury charges:

Timothy J. Ott

Timothy J. Ott
CHIEF JUDGE
UNITED STATES DISTRICT COURT

That on or about the 12th day of July, 1976, at Emmettsville, in Ingham County, in the Southern Division of the Western District of Michigan,

EUGENE JOHN McCOY

by force and violence and by intimidation did take from the person and presence of Carol Ann Drucker approximately Fourteen Thousand Five Hundred Twenty-two and no/100 ($14,522.00) Dollars in money belonging to and in the care, custody, control, management and possession of the Exchange National Bank, Emmettsville Branch, 279 East Robinson Avenue, Emmettsville, Michigan, the deposits of which were then insured by the Federal Deposit Insurance Corporation. 18 U.S.C. S 2113(a)

A TRUE BILL

Charles E. Eckenrode

Charles E. Eckenrode
United States Attorney

James T. Hardmann

FOREMAN

it also has the authority to jail for contempt those witnesses who will not cooperate unless they claim self-incrimination and immunity is not given.

The proceedings of grand juries are secret, as are the actual deliberations. Any testimony given by a witness to the grand jury is considered a privileged communication and cannot be revealed. Grand jurors are required to adhere to the strict rules of secrecy during their term of appointment. They are also told to disregard all information they hear outside of the grand jury room which may have a bearing on the case and to concentrate solely on the testimony and evidence presented to them in the conduct of the hearing.

Preliminary Proceedings in the Trial Court

Arraignment

After an indictment has been returned as a "true-bill" by the grand jury or an information has been filed by the prosecutor, the accused is arraigned before a court of general jurisdiction which has the authority to try the case. The arraignment is the procedure whereby the accused is called into court to answer the charge against him. It is not a trial, and the court will not at this time examine any matters pertaining to the accused's guilt or innocence. If the defendant has not previously been given a copy of the indictment or information, he is now given one. The contents of the indictment or information are also read to him. In this way, the state informs the defendant that it is ready to proceed with the charges against him.

If the defendant still does not have counsel, the court must assure him that he has this right, and if he is indigent, the court will appoint legal assistance for him. The court will point out that counsel is advisable so that the accused knows and understands the nature of the charges against him and the implications of the plea that the accused might make. In the event that the accused does not have counsel and indicates that he wants one, the court will temporarily suspend arraignment until the defendant has had reasonable time to obtain an attorney.

Pleas

During the arraignment, the accused will be asked to enter a plea to the charge. Basically, depending upon the statutory provisions of the particular jurisdiction, the defendant may enter a plea of *not guilty, nolo contendere,* or *guilty* or he may merely stand mute.

If the defendant pleads not guilty, he denies every material allegation contained in the accusation by the state and requires the state to establish these allegations beyond a reasonable doubt. In those states that permit the practice, the accused will, after entering a plea of not guilty, be advised of his right to trial by jury or before a judge without a jury. Once the defendant indicates this choice, his case will be placed on the court calendar or docket and scheduled for future trial.

The plea of nolo contendere literally means "I will not contest it." This plea technically means that the individual does not wish to contest or argue the issue of guilt or innocence. Such a plea, in a number of jurisdictions, has to be approved by the prosecutor and the judge. In essence, it is a guilty plea and has the same effect. It authorizes the court to enter judgment and sentence upon the plea. This plea has some legal significance in that in subsequent criminal or civil proceedings, the admission of guilt is not present as it would be if the accused had entered a plea of guilty to the charge. Under these circumstances, the acknowledgment of guilt could not be introduced into a later trial. Since it serves no useful purpose other than to protect the individual from the consequences of his conviction, some states do not feel it serves the purpose of justice and have abolished it.

If the defendant remains mute when asked how he pleads to the charge, an automatic plea of not guilty will be entered by the court. The major advantage of standing mute is that in some jurisdictions a plea is the same as saying that the defendant accepts the jurisdiction of the trial court and, as a result, waives the right to protest any irregularities or defects which may have occurred in the preliminary examination or grand jury.[15]

If the defendant pleads guilty, the judge will immediately inquire whether the plea is made with full understanding of its ramifications and whether it is voluntarily made. The courts have held that a guilty plea must be free from coercion or promises and must not be otherwise unfairly obtained or the result of ignorance or fear.[16] If the court is not thoroughly convinced that these requirements have been met, it cannot accept the plea. Nor is the court supposed to assume that these requirements are fully met merely because the defendant is represented by an attorney. Since a guilty plea is the same as a waiver of the defendant's right to require the prosecution to prove his guilt beyond a reasonable doubt, the judge is under a strict responsibility to be certain that such a plea is voluntary and knowingly given. If it should later be proved that this is not the case, there will exist grounds for reversal of the conviction.

If the defendant pleads guilty, the court may immediately sentence him. A number of states require that a presentence investigation be conducted of the defendant and his background so that the judge can be guided in determining the particular sentence to impose.

Pretrial Motions

After the indictment or information has been filed, the defendant may, prior to the arraignment or before the trial, employ a number of motions in an effort to have the case dismissed or to gain a particular legal advantage in the preparation of his case or the introduction of evidence at the trial. A motion is a request that the court make an examination of a particular legal point that the defense contends is an error in the state's case. In filing the motion, the defense asks the court to rule on the particular legal point in hopes that the ruling will be in behalf of the accused. Although it is not possible to review all the motions that the defense might raise, some of the more frequently encountered and important motions will be examined briefly.

Motion to discharge or dismiss the case. This is probably the most important of the various pretrial motions. It is initiated upon written request of the defendant prior to the beginning of the trial, but usually after the plea has been entered. The defendant asks the court to dismiss the indictment, information, or complaint for any of a number of reasons. Some of these reasons might be that the grand jury that returned the indictment was illegally selected and empanelled, that the grand jury permitted the presence of unauthorized individuals during their deliberations, that the charge brought against the defendant does not state an offense punishable under the laws of the state, that there has been a fundamental denial of the defendant's constitutional rights, such as the denial of the right of defense counsel to have the opportunity to cross-examine witnesses at the preliminary hearing or failure to advise the defendant of his rights against self-incrimination.

Motions may also be directed at the indictment or information, contending that these documents are not technically correct in that they fail to specify clearly the charges, the elements of the offense, or the specific offense violated or that the foreman of the grand jury did not certify in writing a true bill. The defendant may also allege that the statute of limitations has run out on the particular offense of which he is accused. Most states require that in felony crimes, prosecution must begin within seven years after the commission of the offense, except in capital cases, which have no statute of limitations. This means that the prosecution cannot initiate charges against the individual after that time.[17] Lastly, the defendant may allege that he has been granted immunity from the courts for the offense for which he is charged.

In reality, many of these motions serve no useful purpose to the accused other than to delay the start of the trial. Often, the judge will merely direct the prosecutor or the grand jury to correct the deficiencies in the documents that are found to be incorrect. Only in such cases as former grants of immunity or the expiration of the statute of limitations will the motions result in a dismissal of the charges.

Motion for a bill of particulars. This is a motion by the defense requesting the state to provide additional facts in the indictment or information so that the accused can develop his defense. This motion must be filed within a specified time after the arraignment but before the commencement of the trial. If this motion is upheld by the court, it will order the prosecutor to clarify the charges by adding the necessary facts to the original indictment or information in the form of an amendment. For example, if a bookstore owner was being charged with the possession and sale of pornographic material, the defense would want to know which of the confiscated reading materials the prosecutor intends to use as the basis for the case.

Motion to suppress or quash evidence. This is an attempt to have evidence that the state has gathered excluded from consideration. This motion may be brought before or after the arraignment or during the trial when there is an objection to the admission into evidence of certain items or testimony.

This motion will contend that the particular evidence that the state plans to use was illegally obtained by means of a violation of the defendant's rights and is, therefore, not admissible. Often, this motion is filed by the defense to exclude evidence that has been obtained as a result of an illegal search and seizure or wiretap or to challenge the validity of a confession.

In determining whether to grant this motion and thereby exclude the evidence, the judge will conduct a special hearing, at which witnesses who have relevant testimony will be examined. In these hearings, the burden of proving that the evidence was not illegally obtained rests with the state. Under these circumstances, the prosecutor is permitted to cross-examine the defense witnesses as well as to introduce the state's witnesses. When the hearing is concluded, the judge, based upon all the testimony presented, will rule whether or not the evidence can be used against the defendant. If the judge rules that it cannot, the state will not be able to use the evidence against the accused and may then be forced to ask the court to dismiss the case if it cannot possibly win without the evidence.

If the defense, during the conduct of the trial, objects to evidence which the state introduces and files a motion to suppress, the trial will immediately stop, and there will be a similar special hearing on the motion. However, in order for the defense to file this motion during the trial, it must show that it did not have the opportunity to do so before the trial began. The hearing on the motion will then be conducted in a special session from which the jury is excluded.

Motion for change of venue. The defendant may also introduce a motion to move the trial to another jurisdiction. This motion is based on the defendant's contention that because of prejudice against him, he cannot obtain a fair trial in the particular locale of the court. Often, in cases of more sensational crimes which have received considerable publicity in the local media, the defense will contend that an impartial trial is impossible. In most cases, the state will be permitted to file counterarguments against a change of venue. After hearing the evidence, the court decides whether, in the best interests of justice, the trial should be moved elsewhere.

Motion for continuance. States have enacted statutes specifying various conditions under which a trial date can be postponed. Both the defense and the prosecution can apply for a continuance. Some of the more common reasons for which a continuance can be granted are that counsel for the defense or the prosecution is ill, has died, or is engaged in the trial of another case; that the defendant is ill; that a material witness for the defense or the state is unavailable at the time; or that the bill of particulars which amended the original indictment or information has introduced new facts or allegations which require more time to present an adequate defense.

Some of the other pretrial motions that might be introduced are motion for discontinuance, motion for a list of witnesses, motion for a joinder of related prosecutions, motion for a severance of joint prosecutions, and motion for a change of judge.

Selection of the Jury

After the hearing of any motions, the judge will ask for the plea. If the accused pleads not guilty or nolo contendere, the court will ask whether the defendant wants a jury trial. If he indicates that he does, the case will be placed on the general trial court's criminal docket, and the next step in the trial process will be the selection of jurors.

The right to trial by jury has historically existed at the common law. In 1215 when the Magna Carta was signed, there was a special provision made that no freeholder would be deprived of his life or property except by judgment of his peers. This right was incorporated into the U.S. Constitution, where Article III, Section 2 states: "The trial of all crimes, except in cases of impeachment, shall be by jury." Likewise, the Sixth Amendment provides that "in all criminal prosecutions, the accused shall enjoy the right to a speedy and public trial by an impartial jury of the State and district wherein the crime shall have been committed."

While we consider the right to a jury trial as a fundamental constitutional guarantee, the fact of the matter is that until 1968, in the case of *Duncan v. Louisiana,* the U.S. Supreme Court did not guarantee this right to defendants in state courts.[18] In that case, the Supreme Court overruled one of its earlier decisions and applied the right to jury trial to defendants in state courts by virtue of the Fourteenth Amendment.

The trial jury in a felony case usually consists of twelve jurors. Why the courts have settled on twelve jurors, nobody really seems to know. Some believe it is based on the fact that Christ had twelve disciples. The Constitution does not specify the number of jurors required, and many states use less than twelve jurors in misdemeanor cases. Under the early common law, jurors were witnesses who were summoned to testify for the state or the defense. Today jurors are impartial persons who will render a decision on the facts presented them during the trial.

The prospective jurors are chosen by means specified in the particular legislation of the state. Usually, names of prospective jurors are compiled by the designated official (jury commissioner, clerks of courts, sheriff, etc.) from voter registration lists of the jurisdiction. The names are placed on slips of paper and drawn at random by some means. These prospective jurors constitute what is known as the jury panel or *venire*. The number of individuals ultimately selected at the beginning of each term of court depends on the number of cases pending and their nature. If cases have received notoriety, more individuals may need to be selected in order to find unbiased jurors.

The selection of jurors must satisfy minimum standards of due process in that they must be a representative sample of the community, and there can be no discrimination based upon race, religion, or national origin. All states prescribe that certain characteristics of an individual will exclude that person from jury service. Some of the more common are inability to read, write, or understand the English language; mental deficiency or some disabling physical defect such as deafness or blindness; blood relationship to the defendant; prior conviction of a felony; and service on the grand jury that returned the indictment. Certain individuals are exempt from jury duty by virtue of their occupation or particular status. Some examples are physicians, dentists, attorneys, and, in some jurisdictions, military personnel on active service and mothers whose absence from the home would create a particular hardship.

After these exclusions, the prospective jurors are drawn, and the process known as the *voir dire examination* begins. This is the process of examining and questioning each prospective juror under oath to see if he or she is acceptable to both the prosecution and the defense. In some states, the examination is conducted by the attorneys for the prosecution and defense; in other states, the judge does the questioning, with the counsel for the state and the accused indicating specific questions that they want the judge to ask. Both sides may challenge prospective jurors that they want removed from serving on the particular trial jury. When it can be shown that the juror is biased, prejudiced, has formed an opinion, or is otherwise unable to perform the duties of a juror fairly and impartially, the challenge is called a *challenge for cause*. Both the prosecution and defense can exclude an unlimited number of jurors for cause, and the voir dire examination will continue until a full panel of jurors is found qualified. In many sensational cases with a lot of attendant publicity, this can be a very time-consuming process. For example, in December 1970, when Black Panthers Bobby Seale and Ericka Huggins were put on trial in New Haven in connection with the murder of another Black Panther, it took over four months to conduct the voir dire, and over 1,000 prospective jurors were excluded for cause.

The second way jurors can be excluded is through a *peremptory challenge*. A peremptory challenge, as its name implies, is a challenge which requires no reasons or explanation, and its use is wholly discretionary.[19] The number of peremptory challenges is strictly limited by statute and varies from state to state and according to the seriousness of the crime. Usually, the number is greater for felonies than for misdemeanors and even greater for capital offenses. For example, Michigan permits the prosecution and defense to exclude five jurors each by means of peremptory challenges in offenses not punishable by death or life imprisonment. In cases where the possible penalty is death or life imprisonment, that state provides that the defense can exercise twenty peremptory challenges and the prosecution fifteen. Attorneys use these peremptory challenges where there is something about the prospective juror that the attorney is unsure of or does not like.

From one to four alternate jurors are also chosen, depending upon the particular state. These alternate jurors substitute for primary jurors who become ill during the trial or the deliberations of the jury. These alternate jurors sit in on the trial, but do not vote unless they have replaced one of the original twelve.

The Trial

Once the jury has been selected and sworn in, the trial process begins. The indictment or information is read, and the state makes its *opening statements*. In its opening statement, the prosecutor outlines the state's case to the jury. The prosecutor usually explains how the state plans to introduce witnesses and physical evidence to show beyond a reasonable doubt that the defendant committed the crime for which he is now being tried. In the opening statement, the prosecutor is required to stick to the facts of the charges and the manner in which the state plans to prove its case.

Next, the defense is permitted to make its opening statement. The defense does not have to make an opening statement, and may waive this right if it desires. If the defense elects to make an opening statement, it will also explain to the jury how it plans to introduce and develop its own evidence to show that the defendant did not commit the alleged crime.

Once the opening statements have been concluded, the *state's case* is presented. At this point, the state calls its first witness. Usually, the first witnesses establish the elements of the crime, and then witnesses introduce any physical evidence that the state may have. The prosecutor begins with a *direct examination* of the witness. Usually this direct examination consists only of eliciting facts in some chronological order from the witness. After this direct examination, the prosecution rests, and the defense is permitted to *cross-examine* the witness.

In this defense cross-examination, most states apply what is referred to as the restrictive rule. Under this rule, the defense counsel must restrict questions to those facts brought out by the prosecutor in the direct examination. After the cross-examination, the defense rests, and the prosecutor is given the opportunity to conduct a *redirect examination* of the witness. Often, the prosecutor may question the witness on only those new facts brought out in the defense cross-examination. After the redirect examination, the defense is then given the opportunity to conduct a *recross-examination* of those new facts brought out in the redirect examination. After the state has concluded its case, it rests.

The *defense case* is the next stage of the trial. Sometimes the defense at this stage will make a motion for dismissal on the grounds that the state did not prove the defendant guilty "beyond a reasonable doubt." If the judge concurs, the case is dismissed, and the accused is released. If the judge does not accept the motion, the defense then begins its case, following the steps outlined above. After the defense has concluded its case, it rests.

The next phase of the trial is called the *prosecutor's rebuttal*. The prosecutor may elect to introduce new witnesses or evidence in an effort to strengthen the state's case. The same format of direct examination, cross-examination, redirect, and recross-examination is followed. At the conclusion of the prosecutor's rebuttal, the defense can again make a motion for dismissal of the charges, which is usually referred to as requesting a directed verdict or verdict of acquittal. If the motion is denied, the defense is entitled to the *defense surrebuttal,* and alternating examinations by both sides are again conducted.

Finally, both sides present their *closing arguments* to the jury. In most states, the prosecutor makes the state's closing argument first. Both the state and the defense usually have broad latitude in their range of discussion, the use of illustration, and the employment of persuasions, so long as they confine themselves to discussion of the evidence presented and normal deductions that one might make from the evidence.[20]

Instructions to the Jury

At the conclusion of the closing arguments to the jury, the judge charges the jury to retire to the jury room and consider the facts of the case and the testimony presented and from their deliberations to return a just verdict. The judge's charge to the jury includes instructions as to the possible verdicts. The jurors are given a written form for each verdict. The foreman is instructed to sign the appropriate one and return it to the court after the jury has reached agreement. The typical forms of verdict in a criminal case are "guilty" or "not guilty." The jury in certain types of cases, however, may have the option of determining the particular degree of the offense, for example, murder in the first degree, murder in the second degree, and manslaughter. In certain cases, the verdict of "not guilty by reason of insanity" may also be a possible verdict.

After the jurors have been charged by the judge, they are placed in the custody of the court bailiff, who sees that they are sequestered (isolated from nonmembers of the jury) during their period of deliberation. Normally, they retire to a jury room to deliberate the verdict. The jurors take with them the pleadings in the case, the judge's instructions, and sometimes any evidence that has been introduced at the trial. No juror is permitted to leave the jury room until the jury has returned the verdict and the members are discharged or unless they have to be put up in accommodations for the night when they are still deliberating. The bailiff has the responsibility of maintaining complete security over the jury deliberations. This means that this court officer ensures that the jurors are not approached by any person not a juror and that they do not receive any communications that might influence their vote.

If during the course of their deliberations, they want to refresh their memories about the testimony of a witness or want further explanation of the instructions given by the court, they contact the bailiff. If necessary, the court clerk will provide them with the transcript of the testimony and the judge and the attorneys will send new instructions to them by way of the bailiff.

Jury Deliberations and Return of the Verdict

The foreman of the jury, who is usually chosen by the jury itself, often begins the deliberations by taking a vote of the jury. In some cases, the first vote results in a unanimous verdict. Usually, however, the first vote indicates that the jury is divided. The jurors then discuss the case in an attempt to resolve their differences and reach unanimity.

If after a prolonged period they cannot reach a unanimous verdict, they report this fact to the court. A jury that cannot reach a verdict is called a "hung jury" and is dismissed by the judge in open court. A hung jury does not automatically result in the acquittal of the defendant. The accused can be retried with a new jury, but the fact that a jury cannot reach a unanimous verdict sometimes results in the state deciding not to conduct another trial. The state may reason that since it could not convict the defendant in the first trial, there is little reason to believe that it could do so in a second trial.

In recent years, some states have passed laws that permit defendants to be convicted with less than unanimous verdicts. Oregon, for example, requires a minimum requisite vote of ten to two. When this law was challenged by a convicted defendant, the U.S. Supreme Court upheld it. The Court ruled that a verdict that is less than unanimous does not violate the Sixth Amendment right to a trial by jury.[21]

Once the jury has reached a verdict, the jury is brought back into the courtroom, where are present the defendant, the judge, and the attorneys for the prosecution and defense. The judge inquires whether the jurors have reached a verdict. When they reply that they have, the bailiff takes from the foreman the written verdict which the foreman has signed and attested to. The verdict is then handed to the judge, who reads it and then hands it back to the bailiff to read aloud in court. The verdict is usually phrased in the following language: "We, the jury, duly empaneled and sworn, find the defendant guilty (or not guilty) as charged."

The prosecutor or defense counsel may request that the jurors be *polled*. When a jury is polled, the judge or perhaps the bailiff or even the clerk of courts asks each juror individually if the verdict announced is his or her individual verdict. This is done to determine whether each juror is in accord with the verdict rendered and has not been pressured into voting a particular way by the other jurors.

Post-Trial Motions

If the verdict is not guilty, the defendant is immediately released from custody. If a guilty verdict is returned by the jury, most jurisdictions permit the accused the right to file for a motion for a new trial or to set the judgment of the jury aside. Usually, the defense has ten days or so to file this motion. The grounds are usually one of the following: (1) that the state failed to charge an offense in the indictment or the court lacked proper jurisdiction in the case[22]; (2) that the jury was guilty of misconduct in its deliberation (e.g., a juror was in contact with an outsider who influenced her or him); (3) that the court made a mistake in judgment in permitting some evidence to be introduced or in overruling an objection, etc.; or (4) that the instructions that the judge gave to the jury were improper.

The trial judge may grant or deny any of these post-trial motions. Again, a hearing on the motion is held, and the judge, after listening to the arguments, issues a ruling. Most motions are denied. In some instances, these motions permit the judge to review the case before the accused files for an appeal by the appellate courts. In this way, an error can often be corrected at this level without having to go to the higher courts.

The Presentence Investigation

After the conclusion of the hearing on any post-trial motions which do not change the guilty verdict of the jury, the judge in most jurisdictions has a presentence investigation conducted. About half the states now make a presentence report mandatory in all felony cases. These reports are usually conducted by the probation officers assigned to the court. The purposes of a presentence investigation are fivefold:

1. To aid the court in determining the appropriate sentence,
2. To aid the probation officer in the rehabilitative efforts during probation and parole supervision where probation, and later parole, are warranted,
3. To assist the Department of Corrections in their classification and treatment programs and in their release planning,
4. To furnish the parole board with information pertinent to its consideration of parole,
5. To serve as a source of information for systematic research.[23]

The United States Probation Office has developed a model presentence investigation report which is employed by federal probation officers in the U.S. district courts. Figure 10-3 shows the face sheet of this report, while Figure 10-4 indicates the narrative summary that accompanies it.

The Sentence

Once the presentence investigation is completed and reviewed by the trial court judge, the accused is brought back into court for the imposition of sentence. The state legislatures and the U.S. Congress provide by statute the sentences that state and federal judges can impose for various crimes. However, many state legislatures prescribe that in capital cases the determination of the sentence rests with the jury rather than the judge. This practice is widely disavowed by reformers who would abolish the authority of the jury to render sentence. In recent years, there has been a trend in a few states to turn the sentencing authority over to an administrative body. One such administrative body is the California Adult Authority. Under this system, a defendant is merely sentenced by the court to be imprisoned in a state penitentiary. The individual is then turned over to the director of corrections, and the department of corrections fixes the particular term of imprisonment.

One form of sentence is the *definite sentence,* which is for a stated number of years. For example, confinement in the state penitentiary for twenty years is a definite sentence. An *indeterminate sentence,* which most states employ, has a minimum and a maximum length. Thus, an individual may be sentenced to imprisonment for two to five years.[24] A *truly indeterminate sentence* is one that theoretically has no maximum and no minimum. Thus, the individual could be incarcerated from one day to life.

Many states also have *habitual-offender statutes.* These statutes call for an increased period of incarceration for someone who has previously been convicted of two or more felonies or two or more felonies of a certain type. Under certain circumstances, then, someone could be sentenced to life imprisonment upon the conviction of a third felony. However, habitual offenders statutes are rarely invoked by the courts.

In the last few years, a number of states have passed *mandatory sentencing acts.* These acts impose an *additional* mandatory penalty for certain circumstances pertaining to the crime. For example, if the convicted offender used a dangerous weapon in the commission of the crime, he or she would be sentenced to a period of incarceration in excess of that received for committing the crime itself.

Another characteristic of sentences is that they may be imposed on either a *concurrent* or a *consecutive* basis. An offender may be tried for more than one offense at the same time or may be tried for more than one count. For example, an individual who is apprehended and charged with the commission of three robberies could be tried separately for each offense or charged in one trial on three counts. If found guilty, most states permit the judge to run the sentences concurrently or consecutively. If the sentences run concurrently, they all run simultaneously; if they run consecutively, the individual will serve one after the other.

Appeals and Postconviction Reviews

The right of appeal, as prescribed by modern American statutes, is not found in the common law.[25] The early English courts began to permit very limited

```
PROBATION        UNITED STATES DISTRICT COURT
FORM 2              Central District of New York
  FEB 65                PRESENTENCE REPORT

NAME                          DATE
   John Jones                    January 4, 1974
ADDRESS                       DOCKET NO.
   1234 Astoria Blvd.             74-103
   New York City              OFFENSE
LEGAL RESIDENCE                  Theft of Mail by Postal
   Same                          Employee (18 U.S.C.
AGE      DATE OF BIRTH 2-8-40    Sec. 1709) 2 counts
   33           New York City  PENALTY
SEX        RACE                  Count 2: 5 years and/or
                                 $2,000 fine
   Male       Caucasian       PLEA
CITIZENSHIP                      Guilty on 12-16-73 to Count 2
   U.S. (Birth)                  Count 1 pending
EDUCATION                     VERDICT
   10th grade
MARITAL STATUS                CUSTODY
   Married                       Released on own
DEPENDENTS                       recognizance. No time in
   Three (wife and 2 children)   custody.
SOC. SEC. NO.                 ASST. U.S. ATTY
   112-03-9559                   Samuel Hayman
FBI NO.                       DEFENSE COUNSEL
   256 1126                      Thomas Lincoln
DETAINERS OR CHARGES PENDING:    Federal Public
   None                          Defender
CODEFENDANTS (Disposition)
                              Drug/Alcohol Involvement:
   None                          Attributes offense to
                                 need for drinking money

DISPOSITION


DATE


SENTENCING JUDGE
```

Figure 10-3 Face Sheet for Model Selective Presentence Investigation
Report

Source: "The Selective Presentence Investigation Report," *Federal Probation* (December 1974): 53. Reprinted by permission.

Offense: Official Version.—Official sources reveal that during the course of routine observations on December 4, 1973, within the Postal Office Center, Long Island, New York, postal inspectors observed the defendant paying particular attention to various packages. Since the defendant was seen to mishandle and tamper with several parcels, test parcels were prepared for his handling on December 5, 1973. The defendant was observed to mishandle one of the test parcels by tossing it to one side into a canvas tub. He then placed his jacket into the tub and leaned over the tub for a period of time. At this time the defendant left the area and went to the men's room. While he was gone the inspectors examined the mail tub and found that the test parcel had been rifled and that the contents, a watch, was missing.

The defendant returned to his work and picked up his jacket. He then left the building. The defendant was stopped by the inspectors across the street from the post office. He was questioned about his activities and on his person he had the wristwatch from the test parcel. He was taken to the postal inspector's office where he admitted the offense.

Defendant's Version of Offense.—The defendant admits that he rifled the package in question and took the watch. He states that he intended to sell the watch at a later date. He admits that he has been drinking too much lately and needed extra cash for "drinking money." He exhibits remorse and is concerned about the possibility of incarceration and the effect that it would have on his family.

PRIOR RECORD

Date	Offense	Place	Disposition
5-7-66 (age 26)	Possession of Policy Slips	Manhattan CR. CT. N.Y., N.Y.	$25.00 Fine 7-11-66
3-21-72 (age 32)	Intoxication	Manhattan CR. CT. N.Y., N.Y.	4-17-72 Nolle

Personal History.—The defendant was born in New York City on February 8, 1940, the oldest of three children. He attended the public school, completed the 10th grade and left school and was active in sports, especially basketball and baseball.

The defendant's father, John, died of a heart attack in 1968, at the age of 53 years. He had an elementary school education and worked as a construction laborer most of his life.

The defendant's mother, Mary Smith Jones, is 55 years of age and is employed as a seamstress. She had an elementary school education and married defendant's father when she was 20 years of age. Three sons were issue of the marriage. She presently resides in New York City, and is in good health.

Defendant's brother, Paul, age 32 years, completed 2½ years of high school. He is employed as a bus driver and resides with his wife and two children in New York City.

Defendant's brother, Lawrence, age 30 years, completed three semesters of college. He is employed as a New York City firefighter. He resides with his wife and one child in Dutch Point, Long Island.

The defendant after leaving high school worked as a delivery boy for a retail supermarket chain then served 2 years in the U.S. Army as an infantryman (ASN 123 456 78). He received an honorable discharge and attained the rank of corporal serving from 2-10-58 to 2-1-60. After service he held a number of jobs of the laboring type.

The defendant was employed as a truck driver for the City of New York when he married Ann Sweeny on 6-15-63. Two children were issue of this marriage, John, age 8, and Mary, age 6. The family has resided at the same address (which is a four-room apartment) since their marriage.

The defendant has been in good health all of his life but he admits he has been drinking to excess the past 18 months which has resulted in some domestic strife. The wife stated that she loved her husband and will stand by him. She is amenable to a referral for family counseling.

Defendant has worked for the Postal Service since 12-1-65 and resigned on 12-5-73 as a result of the present arrest. His work ratings by his supervisors were always "excellent."

Evaluative Summary.—The defendant is a 33-year-old male who entered a plea of guilty to mail theft. While an employee of the U.S. Postal Service he rifled and stole a watch from a test package. He admitted that he planned on selling the watch to finance his drinking which has become a problem resulting in domestic strife.

Defendant is a married man with two children with no prior serious record. He completed 10 years of schooling, had an honorable military record, and has a good work history. He expresses remorse for his present offense and is concerned over the loss of his job and the shame to his family.

Recommendation.—It is respectfully recommended that the defendant be admitted to probation. If placed on probation the defendant expresses willingness to seek counseling for his domestic problems. He will require increased motivation if there is to be a significant change in his drinking pattern.

Respectfully submitted,

Donald M. Fredericks
U.S. Probation Officer

Figure 10-4 Narrative Section of a Model Selective Presentence Investigation Report

Source: "The Selective Presentence Investigation Report," Federal Probation (December 1974): 54. Reprinted by permission.

rights of appeal around the fifteenth century. Most of the rights of appeal, as we know them today, began to develop in the nineteenth century. Since then, there have developed extensive procedural rights for an accused to obtain a review of his case.

Rights of review from the decisions of state trial courts of general jurisdiction are to either the state supreme court or the state court of appeals if the state has adopted an intermediate-level appellate court. In an appeal, the defendant alleges that the trial court in some manner erred in interpreting or applying the law in the specific case.

Appeals are based on the written record of what transpired in the trial at the lower-court level. Thus, the appellate court concerns itself only with the particular errors that the defendant alleges. The appellate court does not conduct a new trial but merely examines the transcript of the case and any supporting briefs by the attorneys for both sides, hears oral arguments that are presented, and rules accordingly. However, if a defendant is appealing a case from a court of limited or special jurisdiction (e.g., magistrate's or municipal court) to a general trial court for review, the general trial court usually holds a completely new trial.

Before the higher courts accept an appeal from a lower-court ruling, they usually require that the party appealing show that the particular point upon which the appeal is based had been appropriately objected to during the course of the trial. The higher court must be convinced that the rights of the defendant were so violated as to adversely affect the course of the trial and its results.

In most cases, appeal is not automatic; that is, the aggrieved party must apply for appellate review. However, some states provide for automatic appellate review of a trial court's decision in the case where the defendant has been sentenced to death and in a few cases where he has received life imprisonment. The individual appealing the case must show the higher court that he has exhausted all remedies such as writs, motions, etc., with the lower trial court.

In most cases, the rights of appeal of the state are very limited; thus, the prosecutor can very rarely appeal an adverse ruling. Such a practice would constitute a form of double jeopardy and would also put a burden upon the defendant in having to defend himself again, particularly in terms of financial costs and psychological anguish.

Most appeals from state trial courts of general jurisdiction never get past the state intermediate court of appeals or the state supreme court. The number of cases heard in state trial courts that eventually get to the U.S. Supreme Court is almost infinitesimal. In most cases the state appellate courts refuse to grant a review. In a few instances, if the defendant alleges that his constitutional rights have been violated, the defendant may file a petition for a writ of certiorari with the U.S. Supreme Court for review.

The petition for a writ of certiorari indicates the particular nature of the case, the errors alleged, and the previous court dispositions of the case.[26] The writ is granted by the Supreme Court when four justices feel that the issues raised are of sufficient public importance to merit consideration. Petitions for writs of certiorari are filed in accordance with prescribed forms, the petitioner stating why the Court should grant the writ. The opposing party also may file a brief, outlining why the case should not be reviewed by the Court on certiorari. According to the revised rules of the Supreme Court, "a review on writ of certiorari is not a matter of right, but of sound judicial discretion, and will be granted only where there are special important reasons therefore."

If the writ of certiorari is not granted, the defendant may resort to a collateral attack upon the judgment. Although various post-appeal remedies are available in different states, the most universal method of collateral attack is by petition for a writ of habeas corpus.[27] This writ, which has its origin in the ancient common law, has been incorporated as a right in state constitutions and in Article I, Section 9, of the U.S. Constitution. A petition for a writ of habeas corpus questions the legality of the detention of the petitioner and requests that the court issue an order directing the state or the person who has custody of the petitioner to bring the individual before the court to see whether the person is being held illegally.

If, upon hearing, the court determines that there is no legal authority to detain the petitioner, the court must order his discharge, and the individual holding the petitioner must release him. The petition for habeas corpus can be granted even after the final judgment by the highest court of competent jurisdiction.[28] Generally, the petition may be filed with the trial court, but in some states the state supreme court has original jurisdiction in such matters. These petitions may also be filed in federal court and in the U.S. Supreme Court from an individual incarcerated in a state. Federal judges may grant writs of habeas corpus whenever it appears that a petitioner is being detained in violation of his constitutional rights by either federal or state authorities.

Review by the Chief Executive

The president of the United States and the governors of each state have the power to pardon an individual convicted of a crime, to commute the sentence to a less severe one, or to grant a reprieve in some cases. A *pardon* is a forgiveness for the crime committed and acts as a bar to subsequent prosecution for the crime. It has the effect of legally erasing the conviction of the defendant. A *commutation* does not remove the defendant's guilt, but does mitigate the punishment imposed. It has usually been employed to reduce the penalty from death to life imprisonment without requiring any demonstration or condition of future behavior. A *reprieve* is a delay in the execution of a sentence and has no effect on the defendant's guilt or punishment. It is most likely to be used in postponing execution of the death sentence so that the accused may have additional time to file a motion for relief in judgment.

These powers are usually vested exclusively in the chief executive and may be exercised at his or her discretion. A few states, however, require that petitions for executive clemency be first filed with a clemency board or committee for review. This board or committee reviews the petition, in some cases holds public hearings on the matter, and makes its recommendations to the governor accordingly. In a couple of states, the clemency board may only have to agree in the affirmative before the governor can exercise executive prerogative in this area.

SUMMARY

The judicial process in misdemeanor cases is very simple compared with the procedure in felony cases. In a felony case, the arrestee is first brought before a court of limited or special jurisdiction for a preliminary hearing. If there is reasonable grounds to believe that a felony has been committed and that the accused committed it, the defendant's case may be bound over to a grand jury, which issues an indictment if it believes a trial is warranted. More commonly, the case is brought to trial by the prosecutor's filing an information.

Once the accused is bound over to a court of general jurisdiction for trial, the next step is an arraignment. At this stage of the judicial process, the accused is asked to enter a plea to the charge(s). If he pleads not guilty and wishes a jury trial, the selection of the jury will take place. Once the jury has been chosen and empaneled, the trial begins. Evidence is presented in a very formalized manner.

After receiving its instructions from the judge, the jury retires and deliberates. If the jury returns a verdict of guilty, most jurisdictions require that a presentence investigation be conducted before the judge imposes sentence. Following the imposition of sentence, the offender can employ a number of postconviction remedies and appeals.

Suggested Additional Readings

American Bar Association. *Law and Courts*. Chicago: American Bar Association, 1960.

Deming, R. *Man and Society: Criminal Law at Work*. New York: Hawthorn, 1970.

Felkenes, George. *The Criminal Justice System: Its Function and Personnel*. Englewood Cliffs, N.J.: Prentice-Hall, 1973.

Graham, Kenneth, and Leon Letwin. "The Preliminary Hearing in Los Angeles." *UCLA Law Review* 18 (1971):635–757.

Inbau, Fred E., and James R. Thompson. *Administration of Criminal Justice*. New York: Foundation Press, 1970.

Newman, Edwin S. *Police, the Law, and Personal Freedom*. Dobbs Ferry, N.Y.: Oceana Publications, 1964.

Uviller, H. Richard. *Adjudication*. St. Paul, Minn.: West, 1975.

Vetter, Harold J., and Clifford E. Simonsen. *Criminal Justice in America*. Philadelphia: Saunders, 1976.

Notes

1. Some minor courts have no provision for a jury trial. In these instances, if the accused demands a jury trial, the case will usually be transferred to another court which is set up to routinely empanel juries for cases.
2. See: *McNabb v. United States*, 318 U.S. 332, 63 S. Ct. 608 (1943); *Mallory v. United States*, 354 U.S. 499, 77 S. Ct. 1356 (1957); *Upshaw v. United States*, 355 U.S. 410, 69 S. Ct. 170 (1948).

Herwig/Stock, Boston

3. National Advisory Commission on Criminal Justice Standards and Goals, *Courts* (Washington, D.C.: U.S. Government Printing Office, 1973), p. 87.

4. Edw. 1.C. 150.

5. M. Cherif Bassiouni, *Criminal Law and Its Processes* (Springfield, Ill.: Charles C. Thomas, 1969), p. 440.

6. President's Commission on Law Enforcement and Administration of Justice, *Task Force Report: The Courts* (Washington, D.C.: U.S. Government Printing Office, 1967), pp. 43-44.

7. National Advisory Commission, op. cit., p. 89.

8. American Bar Association Project on Minimum Standards for Criminal Justice, *Standards Relating to Discovery and Procedure before Trial*, approved draft (Chicago: American Bar Association, 1970).

9. National Advisory Commission, op. cit., pp. 89-91.

10. In criminal cases, the accused cannot be compelled to take the stand and testify.

11. National Advisory Commission, op. cit., p. 91.

12. James L. LeGrande, *The Basic Processes of Criminal Justice* (Beverly Hills, Calif: Glencoe Press, 1973), p. 98.

13. Bassiouni, op. cit., p. 454.

14. This immunity is often granted by the court and bars the use against the witness of any statements or evidence derived from these statements in any legal proceedings against him.

15. LeGrande, op. cit., p. 102.

16. *Kercheval v. United States,* 274 U.S. 220, 47 S. Ct. 348 (1927).

17. The statute of limitations normally begins when the crime is committed, not when it is discovered. The statute of limitations can be ''tolled,'' or stopped from running, when a formal complaint has been issued, an indictment returned, or an arrest warrant issued.

18. 390 U.S. 145, 88 S. Ct. 1444 (1968).

19. See Paul B. Weston and Kenneth M. Wells, *The Administration of Justice* (Englewood Cliffs, N.J.: Prentice-Hall, 1967), pp. 193-196.

20. LeGrande, op. cit., p. 132.

21. *Apodaca* v. *Oregon,* 406 U.S. 404, 92 S. Ct. 1628, 32 L. Ed. 2d 184 (1972).

22. These grounds may serve the same purpose as a pretrial motion to dismiss the indictment. However, there are some distinguishing differences. A reason sufficient to sustain dismissal of an indictment may be insufficient to sustain a motion in arrest of judgment. It must be shown that the defect in the indictment or information was such that it affected the legal basis of the offense charged and the proof of guilt. See Bassiouni, op. cit., pp. 506-507.

23. Administrative Office of the United States Courts, ''The Selective Presentence Investigation Report,'' *Federal Probation* 38 (December 1974): 48.

24. Although this example seems to imply that the individual must serve a minimum of two years, this is often not what happens. For example, states and the federal government employ ''good time'' to reduce the period of imprisonment. This ''good time'' is usually computed on the basis of three months for every year served. Thus, the inmate serving a two to five-year sentence could be released on parole after only eighteen months. The time might even be less than eighteen months if the state credits the inmate with the time served in jail before trial.

25. J. O'Halloran, ''Development of the Right of Appeal in England in Criminal Cases,'' *Canadian Bar Review* 27 (1949): 153.

26. LeGrande, op. cit., 152.

27. Ibid.

28. See Hazel B. Kerper and Janeen Kerper, *Legal Rights of the Convicted* (St. Paul, Minn.: West, 1974), pp. 207-238.

NONPARTISAN

JUDICIAL

Judge of the Superior Court Office No. 1 **Vote for One**	ELANA SULLIVAN Workers' Compensation Judge	58 →	◯
	S. S. SCHWARTZ Attorney at Law	59 →	◯
	EMIL GUMPERT Incumbent, Judge of the Superior Court	60 →	◯

| Judge of the Superior Court Office No. 2 **Vote for One** | ARTHUR STANLEY KATZ
Attorney at Law | 62 → | ◯ |
| | LAURENCE J. RITTENBAND
Incumbent-Judge of the Superior Court | 63 → | ◯ |

| Judge of the Superior Court Office No. 15 **Vote for One** | AARON H. STOVITZ
Deputy District Attorney | 65 → | ◯ |
| | ELISABETH EBERHARD ZEIGLER
Incumbent, Judge of the Superior Court | 66 → | ◯ |

Judge of the Superior Court Office No. 28 **Vote for One**	WILLIAM P. KENNEDY Judge of the Superior Court-Incumbent	68 →	◯
	BYRON Y. APPLETON Attorney and Arbitrator	69 →	◯
	ROBERTA RALPH Attorney/Law Instructor	70 →	◯

| Judge of the Superior Court Office No. 37 **Vote for One** | BONNIE LEE MARTIN
Incumbent Judge of the Superior Court of Los Angeles County | 71 → | ◯ |

Judge of the Superior Court Office No. 40 **Vote for One**	DAVID J. AISENSON Judge, Municipal Court, Los Angeles Judicial District	73 →	◯
	NATHAN AXEL Judge of the Municipal Court, Los Angeles Judicial District	74 →	◯
	ROBERT M. TAKASUGI Incumbent Judge, Superior Court	75 →	◯

Chapter 11

The Role of Court Personnel and Some Recommended Changes in the Judicial Process

It is often said that our nation is one of laws and not of men. In fact, of course, it is the human element that breathes life into our laws. After all, it is people who create the laws, enforce them, and interpret their meaning. Thus, laws are often only the agencies of those human beings who establish and apply them. We must therefore examine the actors in the system if we are to understand the process of American criminal justice.

The actors who perform within the judicial function of the criminal justice system are motivated by the same fears of crime, the same desires for ego satisfaction, the same attitudes toward certain characteristics of the people who appear before them as any of us might be. Social psychologists have pointed out that our perceptions of persons and things are often environmentally dependent; that is, such factors as early childhood experiences, background, educational attainment, and other circumstances shape our perceptions of what is good or bad, threatening or nonthreatening, meaningful or meaningless.

Although it is beyond the limits of this introductory text to examine these factors, it is nevertheless important that the student be aware of these conditions and of the important impact that the perceptions of actors in the justice system have upon the administration of justice in the American courtroom. A mere description of the functions of such courtroom actors as the judge, prosecutor, defense counsel, and jury conceals the fact that they are not passive agents in the process, but fellow human beings with the same weaknesses as you and I. This we must live with and accept. However, when the criminal justice process attracts and retains those with questionable qualities and even provides the setting where their imperfections carry significant consequences for society, we should be alarmed. In this chapter, we will, in addition to examining the

respective roles of the actors in the judicial process, look at some other considerations that are important in how justice is administered in our criminal courts.

THE JUDGE

To most citizens, the judge is the most visible and the ultimate dispenser of
criminal justice. Although the police may, in fact, be more visible agents of
criminal justice, they can be thought of as initiating the process rather than
serving as the final arbiter of justice. It could well be that because of their
ultimate role, most citizens accord judges (other than those at the lowest level of
the judiciary) the highest status among all the actors in the criminal justice
process.

The role (and usually the prestige) of judges is often *institutional in nature;*
that is, the status of the court in the judicial hierarchy as well as the level of
government in which the court is located are important. For example, justices of
the peace and judges in local courts are usually accorded less status than judges
who preside over state courts of general jurisdiction. By the same token, federal
judges are accorded greater prestige than state judges on comparable judicial
levels.

The role that judges play in the administration of justice is a very broad and
meaningful one. The judges of our criminal courts are advisers and guardians of
the accused's legal rights. Every person who is arrested is brought before the
judge to be advised of his rights. The judge will inquire into the circumstances
of the arrest to ensure that the police have not infringed upon the individual's
rights. Judges also have discretion over whether or not the individual will be released either by the posting of bail or on his own recognizance. The judge hears
and rules on pretrial motions of the accused and the state. At the arraignment, a
judge hears the defendant's plea, and if the accused pleads guilty, the judge is
responsible for examining the understanding and basis for the plea. In a jury
trial, the judge interprets the law and determines the admissibility of evidence.
In a nonjury trial, the judge rules not only on issues of law, but on issues of fact
and determines the defendant's guilt or innocence. When guilt has been determined after the trial or when the defendant voluntarily enters a guilty plea, the
judge is responsible for deciding the proper sentence.

Another important, but less visible, role that judges perform is that of a
manager. The judge is often responsible for the management of the court and
courtroom. This includes the selection and training of court clerks, the supervision of court records, which grow to voluminous proportions in many courts,
and the recruitment and supervision of probation officers. The scheduling of
cases is often at least indirectly the responsibility of the judge, as is the appointment and supervision of the court bailiff in many jurisdictions. In larger
jurisdictions, these administrative tasks are the responsibility of the senior

presiding judge. In recent years, professionally trained court administrators have been employed by a growing number of the larger state court systems so that the judges can concentrate on their strictly judicial responsibilities.

Constraints on Judges

Although it would appear that judges have a great many opportunities to exert a decisive influence on the administration of justice, they are, in fact, constrained by a number of factors. The process of setting bail, for example, is governed by the criminal code of the state. The state codes and indeed the Eighth Amendment prohibit excessive bail. The criminal codes also limit the discretion of the judge in rendering sentence for an offense by prescribing, in most cases, the statutory maximum and minimum sentence that can be imposed. Judges are also constrained by their relationship with other actors in the administration of criminal justice. Since the judiciary must rely on the executive branch in the person of the police and the prosecutor to bring cases before them, these individuals can significantly determine the workload of the court. Judges also are hampered in their role in criminal cases by lack of knowledge of the facts which have been developed through prearrest and pretrial investigation. In most instances, the judge is completely unfamiliar with the case until the testimony begins to unfold during the trial.

This absence of independent and complete information is certainly visible in the area of plea bargaining. This practice, sometimes referred to as plea negotiation or "copping a plea," is quite common in the administration of criminal justice. Although a prosecutor plays a more significant role than the judge in these negotiations, the judge does become involved in a number of ways and is often constrained as a result. Plea bargaining amounts to an accommodation between the state (the prosecutor and, to a lesser extent, the judge) and the defendant. This accommodation may take one of several forms. Most typically, the defendant agrees to plead guilty if the state will agree to charge the accused with a lesser offense. For example, someone charged with burglary might agree to plead guilty if the charge were reduced to larceny. Many courts have developed informal working agreements whereby judges will accept the prosecutor's recommendations once such deals have been made. Since the judge may not have all the facts in a particular case, he or she often defers to the prosecutor's judgment regarding the propriety and wisdom of a negotiated plea.

Another form of plea bargaining occurs when the defendant is assured that if he pleads guilty, he will be treated leniently (for example, placed on probation or sentenced to the minimum prison term). When a defendant has been charged with multiple offenses, the prosecutor may agree to charge him only with the most serious and drop the others if he will plead guilty. Or, if the individual pleads guilty to multiple offenses, the judge may agree to impose sentences that run concurrently rather than consecutively.

To one degree or another, then, this accommodation process must often involve the judge, particularly if the bargain demands some leniency in sentencing. In such cases the prosecutor cannot act independently; he must consult with the judge and obtain his or her approval and assurance that the sentence will in fact be lenient. Whatever their origins, then—the prosecutor's indirect action or the direct involvement of the judge—these bargainings which occur outside the courtroom reduce the judge's flexibility. Instead of exposing the truth through the exacting scrutiny of the trial and the weight of evidence, these arrangements make concessions that constrain not only judicial behavior but the criminal justice system itself.

The judge is also constrained by the suggestions made by probation officers in their presentence investigation reports.[1] Usually the judge requests that these reports contain the dispositional recommendations of the officer who conducted the background investigation of the accused. If the judge trusts the probation officer's wisdom, these recommendations will probably be adopted. How much this approach constrains the judge we do not know, for a second set of factors may be operating. The probation officer may often accommodate his or her recommendation to the judge, rather than vice versa. For example, through experience with a particular judge, the probation officer may recommend a disposition that he or she thinks the judge wants or will accept.

The backlog of cases in the lower criminal courts in many urban areas severely limits the role of judges. Although the judge is supposed to serve as an adviser and guardian of the legal rights of the accused, this important function often does not receive the attention it should. Preliminary and bail hearings and hearings on motions and arraignments are typically conducted on an assembly-line basis, lasting no more than a minute or so per case in these trial courts.[2] In bail hearings, for instance, judges typically do not consider the facts surrounding the commission of the crime or the characteristics of the accused. What they concentrate on instead is the particular offense charged and the prior record of the defendant. Using these factors as guidelines, they rely on a bail bond schedule or accept the suggestion of the prosecutor or arresting police officers.

These constraints on judges and the gulf that separates the ideal from the actual vary from city to city and court to court. In those courts in which the workload is smaller, the judge may find greater time to exercise the proper judicial role. The judge may also, in smaller communities, develop closer relationships and understanding with the local prosecutor and defense attorneys that will provide a better insight into the cases that come before the bench. In larger cities, where the judge must deal with hundreds of attorneys from the prosecutor's office, private law firms, and public defender's offices, the situation is far different.

The judges that sit on the U.S. district court benches probably approach most closely the ideal, in terms of what citizens perceive the role of judges to be. Because the federal trial courts are relatively well staffed with supportive personnel, federal judges have more time to exercise a strictly judicial function.

The cases that come before them are not the routine, minor criminal cases which glut the lower state courts, and they therefore require greater legal expertise and judgment. Federal trial judges also have greater access to legal research personnel to help them interpret and apply the law. The Administrative Office of the United States Courts and the Federal Judicial Center assist them in their administrative duties, and the center also carries on research and conducts training programs for judges and other court personnel. Finally, in recent years there have been some significant efforts to reduce plea bargaining in the federal courts. As a consequence, more cases now go to trial on their merits, and federal judges can spend less time acquiescing to the judgments and recommendations of others and more time performing their unique responsibilities.

The Issue of Judicial Selection

Many students of the American judiciary have been concerned about the methods that are used to select judges. Their concern is that in many cases selection processes impede the appointment of the most qualified people to judgeships, These concerned groups have included the American Bar Association, the American Judicature Society, state and local bar associations, and numerous civic organizations. Over the years, these groups have been instrumental in producing needed reforms in a number of states.

The states employ a variety of methods to select state court judges. Nearly one-half of the states still rely on partisan elections. In these states, a disproportionate number of which are in the South, individuals are popularly elected after receiving their party's nomination at a political convention or after winning a primary election. The next most frequent method is the nonpartisan election, in which the individual is popularly elected on a ballot that does not specify any affiliation with a political party. In fourteen states, mostly in the Northeast, judges are selected by the chief executive of the jurisdiction. This method is similar to the procedure used in the federal system, where judges are appointed by the president with the advice and consent of the Senate. A few states still retain the system that was so popular in the early years of our nation's history in which the legislative body selects judges. For the most part, however, this form of selection is only for judgeships in the courts of limited and special jurisdiction, Table 11-1 indicates the methods used by states in selecting trial court judges.

The method of selecting judges in the United States is far different from the process in Great Britain and many West European countries. In England, the lord chancellor is the principal judicial officer. Vacancies in the High Court of Justice are filled on the recommendation of the lord chancellor, as are vacancies in the fifty-six county courts of England and certain local courts in London. The lord chancellor is appointed by the crown on the recommendation of the prime minister. Although the reader may think that this system would infuse the judiciary of England with the same political considerations so often denounced

TABLE 11-1 Methods of Selecting Trial Court Judges by States*

Partisan Election	Nonpartisan Election	Executive Appointment	Selection by Legislative Body	Appointment by Other Judges	Merit Selection
ALABAMA	Arizona	ALABAMA (some juvenile judges)	COLORADO (municipal judges)	ALASKA (magistrates)	ALASKA
Arkansas	California	Delaware	CONNECTICUT	HAWAII	COLORADO
CONNECTICUT (probate)	Florida	GEORGIA (county and municipal judges)	IOWA (police judges)	IDAHO (magistrates)	IOWA
GEORGIA	IDAHO	HAWAII	MARYLAND (people's court, Montgomery county)	ILLINOIS (associate judges)	MISSOURI (St. Louis and Kansas City)
ILLINOIS	IOWA (municipal judges)	INDIANA (some municipal judges)	MISSISSIPPI	SOUTH DAKOTA	NEBRASKA
INDIANA	Kansas	MAINE	(municipal police judges)	(justices of the peace)	UTAH
KENTUCKY	KENTUCKY (circuit judges)	MARYLAND	MONTANA	VIRGINIA (many minor judgeships)	VERMONT
Louisiana	MARYLAND (Baltimore city court)	Massachusetts	(some police judges)		
MAINE (probate)	Michigan	New Hampshire	NEW JERSEY		
MISSISSIPPI	Minnesota	NEW JERSEY	(some magistrates)		
MISSOURI	MONTANA	NEW YORK	OKLAHOMA		
NEBRASKA (magistrates)	Nevada	(municipal judges)	(municipal judges)		
New Mexico	North Dakota	RHODE ISLAND	OREGON		
NEW YORK	Ohio	SOUTH CAROLINA	(municipal judges)		
North Carolina	OKLAHOMA	(municipal judges	RHODE ISLAND		
Pennsylvania	OREGON	and magistrates)	(municipal judges)		
SOUTH CAROLINA	SOUTH DAKOTA	WASHINGTON	SOUTH CAROLINA		
(probate, some county judges)	WASHINGTON	(municipal judges)	VIRGINIA		
Tennessee	Wisconsin	FEDERAL DISTRICT COURTS			
UTAH (municipal judges, justices of the peace)	WYOMING				
VERMONT (probate judges, justices of the peace)					
West Virginia					
WYOMING					

*States appearing in capital letters use several methods of judicial selection.

Sources: Council of State Governments, *State Court Systems* (Lexington, Ky., 1970), pp. 10–14; Law Enforcement Assistance Administration, *National Survey of Court Organization* (Washington, D.C.: October 6, 1973).

in the United States, those who have examined the English judiciary point out that such is not the case. Stason, for example, says:

> The traditions of the Bench and Bar in England are such that the Lord Chancellor's appointments to the Bench can be said to be uniformly nonpolitical in character. Tradition is a powerful sanction, and tradition commands that when an appointment is to be made to the British Bench, only the best in the way of judicial ability will be accepted, and once the appointment is made, the independence of the judge is assured.[3]

In France and many other West European countries, the judiciary is entirely separate from the practice of law. When students complete law school, they choose to go into either the practice of law or the magistrature. If they decide upon the latter, they must pass competitive examinations; thereafter, as vacancies arise, they enter upon their judicial duties and do so at a fairly early age. They spend their lives in public service, starting at the lower court levels and progressing according to their experience and ability. If a vacancy occurs in a higher court, a highly qualified judiciary commission submits the names of three carefully screened candidates, and the minister of justice appoints the best qualified.[4]

In recent years, there have been increasing efforts to reform the traditional methods of selecting judges in the United States. The best-known reform idea has been the Missouri Plan of merit selection. Since it was first adopted in that state in 1940, six other states have adopted similar systems. Under the Missouri Plan, a nonpartisan nominating commission, consisting of three attorneys selected by the Missouri Bar Association, three lay persons appointed by the governor, and the chief justice of the state supreme court, sends to the governor the names of three qualified individuals for the vacant judgeship. From this nominating list, the governor appoints one person. The newly appointed judge serves for a one-year probationary period, and then must win approval of the voters by running unopposed on a separate nonpartisan judicial ballot. The only question appearing on the ballot is: "Shall _____ be elected to the office for the term prescribed by law?" If there is a majority of affirmative votes, the individual is elected to the full term of office. A few other states have adopted the idea of separate nominating commissions or, as they are sometimes called, merit commissions or judicial qualifications commissions. For the most part, however, they nominate judges only for certain state or city courts.[5]

The President's Commission on Law Enforcement and Administration of Justice has expressed some grave concerns over the methods most states use to select judges. The commission is concerned by the fact that politics plays such an important role in the selection of judges (and what this may mean for the administration of criminal justice) and, secondly, by the fact that political selection in no way ensures that top-notch people will be elected or even

M. Licht/Stockmarket, Los Angeles

consent to run because of the politicization of the office. Regarding the role of politics in the selection of judges, the commission says:

> In our largely urban society where only a small portion of the electorate knows anything about the operation of the courts, it is usually impossible to make an intelligent choice among relatively unknown candidates for the bench. The inevitable result is that in partisan elections the voters tend to follow their party's nominations without any serious attempt to evaluate the relative merits of the candidates. In normally Democratic or Republican districts, designation as the majority party's nominee ordinarily assumes election.[6]

Under this system, the leaders of the dominant party select the judges. This selection process takes place in closed meetings in which compromises and bargaining strategies are carried on in an effort to reward party supporters;

under these circumstances, too little attention is given to the abilities of the party's nominees.

In an effort to avoid such situations, many people advocate nonpartisan elections of judges. Although this method may have some appeal to those who would diminish the impact of partisan politics, it also has some evils associated with it. Winters and Allard question this method on the following grounds:

> It nullifies whatever responsibility political parties feel to the voters to provide competent candidates and thereby closes one of the avenues which may be open to voter pressure for good judicial candidates. Indeed, experience indicates that where appeal to the voters on political grounds is made impossible. . . . other considerations equally irrelevant to a candidate's qualifications for judicial office are injected into the election. . . .[7]

The President's Commission on Law Enforcement and Administration of Justice is a strong advocate of the merit selection plan because it provides a more appropriate and rational approach than relying upon popular election. The commission recommends that nonpartisan nominating boards be supplied with professional staffs and be made permanent agencies. It further recommends that the states direct intensive efforts toward developing standards that the nonpartisan nominating committee can employ in the selection of qualified potential jurists. Some states are now moving in that direction.

THE PROSECUTOR

The office of the prosecutor is known by various names in different states. In some states, the office is referred to as the district attorney, the county solicitor, or the state's attorney. At the federal level, the prosecutor is known as the U.S. attorney. The prosecutor plays perhaps the most crucial role in the administration of criminal justice because the office occupies a central and very important position between the police and the courts. In fact, the prosecutor is the "traffic cop" of the criminal justice process. The decisions that the prosecutor makes determine how cases that are brought by the police will be disposed of. For example, the prosecutor may decide to "nolle pros" (*nolle prosequi*) a case, that is to decline prosecution, or he or she may decide to reduce the charge through plea bargaining or for some other consideration. In a number of jurisdictions, warrants of arrest must be approved by the prosecutor before the court will issue the warrant. In many of these instances, the screening by the prosecutor results in the court merely rubber stamping the petition for a warrant that the prosecutor brings before the court.

The prosecutor is the central figure in the process of plea bargaining. Although judges are involved to varying degrees in the process, it is the prosecutor who plays a direct role in negotiation with the accused and his defense attorney.

Where possible sentencing alternatives are involved, the judge will play a direct role; in other cases, the judge's involvement will be less direct.

Much plea bargaining reflects the heavy workload of the prosecutor's office and of the court itself; but there is a certain amount of "gamesmanship" involved as well. If the prosecutor feels that the evidence is sufficient to convict the accused for the crime charged, there is little incentive for the prosecutor to negotiate. If, on the other hand, there is a probable chance of acquittal for the accused, the situation changes. The prosecutor, in order to obtain a conviction (prosecutors are often judged by the number of convictions they obtain), may be predisposed to bargain with the defendant. Defense attorneys can often use this set of circumstances to their advantage.

Also, experienced criminal defense lawyers and defendants often feel, perhaps rightly, that a defendant who is found guilty will receive a harsher sentence than one who has his plea bargained. Many defendants with records of arrest and conviction will in fact take the initiative in asking their defense lawyers to try to "cop a plea." They know that there is a better than even chance that the prosecution will win if the case goes to trial and that their past record will have an important influence on the sentence they receive.

How prevalent is plea bargaining in our criminal courts? Nobody really knows. We can, however, get some idea of its extent from the number of criminal court cases that are settled by pleas of guilty and, therefore, never go to trial. Newman found, in his examination of criminal court cases in Wisconsin, that 93.8 percent of all cases in that state during the period studied were disposed of by a guilty plea without trial.[8] The President's Commission on Law Enforcement and Administration of Justice examined the number of criminal cases that were disposed of by guilty pleas in the federal courts and the courts of eight states and the District of Columbia and found that an average of 87 percent of all defendants in those areas entered pleas of guilty. Table 11-2 shows the results of the study.

Of course, the extent of plea bargaining depends in part upon the willingness of the prosecutor and the judges to engage in this tactic. Locale also seems to be a factor. Cole points out that the courts of the primarily rural state of Maine, without the backlog of cases of our major metropolitan areas, infrequently engage in plea bargaining.[9] On the other hand, he points out that some major metropolitan cities such as Philadelphia and Pittsburgh use the negotiated settlement in less than one-third of the cases.[10] In these cities, a system of expedited trials has reduced the administrative pressures for bargaining, and the police and prosecutor more carefully screen the cases.[11]

Probably, the most well-developed system of plea bargaining exists in recorder's court in Detroit, where a "bargaining prosecutor" is available to consult with defense attorneys, who line up for consultation. Near the prosecutor's office is the "bullpen" where prisoners awaiting arraignment or trial are located. A steady stream of lawyers can be seen marching back and forth

TABLE 11-2   Guilty Plea Convictions in Ten Jurisdictions*

Jurisdiction	Total Convictions	Guilty Pleas Number	Guilty Pleas Percentage
California (1965)	30,840	22,817	74.0
Connecticut	1,596	1,494	93.9
Hawaii	393	360	91.5
Illinois	5,591	4,768	85.2
Kansas	3,025	2,727	90.2
Massachusetts (1963)	7,790	6,642	85.2
Minnesota (1965)	1,567	1,437	91.7
New York	17,249	16,464	95.5
Washington, D.C.	1,515	817	73.5
U.S. district courts	29,170	26,273	90.2
Average			87.0

*1964 data unless otherwise indicated.
Source: President's Commission on Law Enforcement and Administration of Justice, *Task Force Report: The Courts* (Washington, D.C.: U.S. Government Printing Office, 1967), p. 9.

between these holding cells and the prosecutor's office, trying to negotiate a plea when the defendant appears for trial.[12]

The prosecutor also controls the grand jury. In those states in which cases must first be presented to the grand jury, the prosecutor plays a crucial role in determining whether the accused will be indicted. Since the grand jury hearing is an ex-parte proceeding, the prosecutor has almost unlimited discretion in producing evidence, interviewing witnesses, etc. Since the prosecutor is the only attorney present during the grand jury hearings, his or her legal opinions and judgments will obviously carry a great deal of weight with the citizens who constitute the grand jury. The prosecutor also has the authority to control and direct the investigative powers of the grand jury and often selects the particular activities that the grand jury will examine. An excellent example of this can be seen in the attempt of a New Orleans prosecutor, Jim Garrison, to use the grand jury of that parish (county) to overturn the findings of the Warren Commission in the assassination of John F. Kennedy. Garrison single-handedly convinced the grand jury that a leading businessman in that city conspired to kill Kennedy. The accused was eventually exonerated at the trial, but his business and reputation were destroyed in the process. Such is the awesome power of the prosecutor.

Prosecutors are also investigators and initiators of the criminal process in other ways. As the chief law enforcement official of the jurisdiction, the prosecutor often works closely with the police on important investigations; in many cases dealing with complex and technical matters such as fraud, organized crime, homicide, and the corruption of public officials, the prosecutor even supervises the police investigation. In larger cities, the office is usually assigned a special staff of investigators; in many instances, they are police detectives temporarily detailed to this office, but, in some instances, they may be an independent group of investigative personnel.

Of course, since the prosecutor has the responsibility of presenting the government's case in court, he or she needs to fulfill the role of a skillful trial attorney. In fact, the role of the prosecutor is a very broad one that is sometimes very difficult to grasp. For example, one noted legal expert has this to say about the role of the prosecutor:

> Appraisal of the role of the prosecutor is made difficult because that role is inevitably more ambiguous than that of the police or the trial court. It is clear that the police are concerned with the detection of crime and the identification and apprehension of offenders; it is likewise apparent that courts must decide the issue of guilt or innocence. A prosecutor, however, may conceive of his principal responsibility in a number of different ways. He may serve primarily as trial counsel for the police department, reflecting the views of the department in his court representation. Or, he may serve as a sort of ''house counsel'' for the police, giving legal advice to the department on how to develop enforcement practices which will withstand challenge in court. On the other hand, the prosecutor may consider himself primarily a representative of the court, with the responsibility of enforcing rules designed to control police practices and perhaps otherwise acting for the benefit of persons who are proceeded against. Another possibility is that the prosecutor, as an elected official . . . will try primarily to reflect community opinion in the making of decisions as to whether to prosecute. The uncertainty as to whether the prosecutor is responsible for all these tasks and as to which is his primary responsibility creates difficult problems in current administration.[13]

Selection and Jurisdiction

Because of the immense power that this office has, it is very attractive to some attorneys who have political ambitions. With the possible exception of the mayor's office, no other local official probably has such opportunities for public exposure through the media. The important trials they prosecute, the investigations they conduct, and their public statements are often given widespread publicity. The important political value of this publicity can be seen in the fact that with the exception of three states, the prosecutor is a local official. In forty-five states, the office is an *elective* one with all but one state using a partisan ballot. In the remaining five states, the prosecutor is an appointed official. The prosecutor is elected on a county basis in twenty-nine states, by judicial district in twelve states, and from both county and judicial district in four states.[14] In thirty-eight states, the prosecutor has both criminal and civil responsibilities; in only twelve states does the prosecutor handle criminal cases only.[15] The Advisory Commission on Intergovernmental Relations classified the prosecutor systems of the states into nine categories as follows:

1. State prosecutor systems: Alaska, Delaware and Rhode Island;

2. State-appointed local prosecutors: Connecticut and New Jersey;

3. Local (judicial district) prosecutors with criminal and appeals responsibilities: Georgia and Massachusetts;

4. Local (judicial district) prosecutors with solely criminal responsibilities: Arkansas, Colorado, Indiana, New Mexico, North Carolina and Tennessee;

5. Local (judicial district) prosecutors with civil and criminal responsibilities, but no appeals duties: Alabama, Louisiana, Oklahoma, South Carolina;

6. Local (county) prosecutor with criminal and appellate responsibilities: Hawaii, Illinois, Kansas, Michigan, Minnesota, New York, North Dakota, Ohio, Oregon, Pennsylvania, Vermont and Washington;

7. Local (county) prosecutors with solely criminal responsibilities: Missouri and Texas;

8. Local (county) prosecutors with criminal and civil, but not appellate responsibilities: Arizona, California, Idaho, Iowa, Maine, Maryland, Montana, Nevada, Nebraska, New Hampshire, South Dakota, Virginia, West Virginia, Wisconsin, Wyoming; and

9. Overlapping county-judicial district prosecutors: Florida, Kentucky, Mississippi and Utah.[16]

Most of the more than 2,900 state prosecutors serve in very small offices with just one or two assistants. Although in the largest cities this office may consist of several hundred personnel made up of assistant prosecutors and various staff assistants, most prosecutors lack the assistance and facilities that they need. Many prosecutors serve only part-time and rely upon their outside private law practices to support them. In 1966, the National District Attorneys Association conducted a survey of all state and local prosecutors in the nation and found that the average annual salary for a prosecutor was less than $4,000.[17] Of course, salaries are much better today, but it is by no means a lucrative post.

Characteristics

The prosecutor's office has seemed to attract two kinds of individuals. In the smaller communities, where the salary of the prosecutor is low, young attorneys who are financially struggling and relatively inexperienced are most likely to be attracted to the office. They often seek the position of prosecutor because they want public exposure and the opportunity to build up a clientele for their private practice and to acquire trial experience. The second type of seeker for this office comes from the lower or middle ranks of the legal profession and is someone who has become interested in politics to further his or her career. Such individuals are most likely to be found in larger cities and are often more experienced attorneys of middle age who hope that the office and the publicity that this office has at its disposal can propel them into a judgeship or some higher state political office. They are aware that the office of the prosecuting attorney is an excellent steppingstone for such political ambitions.

Consequently, the turnover in most prosecutor's offices is quite high, with the average tenure rarely exceeding two four-year terms.[18] In most cities, prosecutors also select a high proportion of their assistants primarily on the basis of party affiliation and the recommendations of ward leaders and elected officials.[19] These factors create many foreseeable conflicts of interest. As the attorney for the state, the prosecutor is supposed to vigorously and impartially prosecute the crimes which come to the attention of this office. Yet, since the prosecutor is usually very politically sensitive and must rely on informal accommodations with other attorneys and with private clients, it is very questionable whether he or she can, in fact, be impartial.

Another major characteristic of state prosecutors is the absence of supervision by the states. The prosecutor is virtually unrestrained in his or her conduct or in the management of the office and the cases handled. Even the state attorney general's office has virtually no control over prosecutors. A few states have attempted to remedy this by giving the attorney general's office the right to inquire into the operations of local prosecutors, but this legislation has had little supervisory effect.

This set of circumstances does not exist at the federal level. The term of office for U.S. attorneys is four years. Although U.S. attorneys are politically appointed, the Department of Justice chooses the nominees for the position and maintains continuous contact and supervision over the U.S. attorneys situated throughout the country. All U.S. attorneys are provided with specific guidelines from the Department of Justice which they are expected to follow. In the event that the U.S. attorney is dealing with a particularly important or sensitive criminal case, the case must often be referred to Washington for review and instructions on how it should be handled. In recent years, the Department of Justice has taken a special interest in the handling of organized crime investigations and prosecutorial action by the U.S. attorneys in the field. In many of these cases, Washington delegates a special strike force of attorneys and investigators to assist, coordinate, and supervise the efforts of the particular U.S. attorney in the field.

Training

Many attorneys become prosecutors without any meaningful experience in the criminal justice process and only a rudimentary knowledge of criminal law. Part of this problem stems from the lack of preparation that law schools provide in the area of criminal law. Most law schools require only one course in criminal law during the entire three-year course of study. The National District Attorneys Association survey mentioned earlier found that the typical assistant prosecutor is hired after very limited experience in practice and that most of that experience was in civil law. Even the prosecutor who is elected to office often lacks substantial criminal law experience.[20]

This lack of experience and knowledge of criminal law has some strange consequences. More often than is generally known, the fledgling prosecutor relies upon veteran police detectives for assistance in coping with the intricate nature of criminal law and the criminal law process. Since almost no jurisdictions provide any form of training for new prosecutors, they have to learn by doing. In larger offices which employ assistant prosecutors, a young assistant will often be assigned to the traffic court or the complaint bureau. The idea is to give him or her experience in handling minor cases so that if errors are made they will not be important ones. Then, after gaining experience and demonstrating ability, the assistant can progress to handling more important cases. Although there certainly may be some advantages to such on-the-job training, there are some less visible problems as well. Many times, young and inexperienced prosecutors who are assigned the complaint bureau become advocates of the police. They may tend to become overly reliant upon the police officer's judgment in determining what complaints should be filed rather than acting as impartial legal experts who screen complaints based upon their merit.[21]

Even in our largest cities, there is no training other than on an informal basis through interaction with the more experienced attorneys on the prosecutor's staff. In some cases, the new assistant is provided with a manual or written policy guidelines, but these form directives do not explain how to handle the many situations that confront a prosecutor. Occasionally, the new assistant is exposed to staff meetings and discussions about certain policies or cases with which the office must deal, but for the most part, staff meetings deal with office procedures and details.

THE CRIMINAL DEFENSE ATTORNEY

Most people have a very distorted view of the practice of criminal law. The electronic media would have us believe that the private practice of criminal law is a stimulating challenge, in which the skillful art of criminal trial advocacy is pitted against the legal adversary of the state in the cause of triumphant justice. This popular TV image depicts the defense counsel as a tireless and thorough investigator, a skillful legal adversary, and the champion of justice. The fact of the matter is that the practice of criminal law is often not nearly so stimulating or intellectually challenging, and criminal defense lawyers are certainly not the superhuman heroes popularized in fictional accounts.

The defense counsel plays an important role in our system of law and justice. Theoretically at least, our legal system is an adversarial one, the idea being that circumstances and indeed the truth or falsity of legal issues can be made known by submitting them to the test of advocacy in which one side is pitted against the other. Since the law is complex and the accused is unskilled in its intricacies, that individual needs assistance in the preparation and defense of his case. Thus, the defendant almost by necessity must obtain legal counsel in cases where the possible penalty is serious.

The primary responsibility of the defense attorney is to *represent* the client. This implies that the defense attorney is responsibile for preparing the case and for selecting the strategy of defense. This further assumes that mutual confidence and cooperation must exist between attorney and client. Without this relationship, the lawyer (and indeed the client) cannot effectively function under our system of trial advocacy.

Many people wonder why a defense lawyer consents to defend a guilty client. They feel that this is a perversion of justice and that under the circumstances the accused should not be entitled to legal assistance. Similarly, many law-abiding citizens are upset when they hear of a defendant who by the skillful manueverings of his lawyer is able to "beat a rap" on a legal technicality. Again, they feel that this certainly is a perversion of justice.

Admittedly, this is very difficult for many of us to accept. However, you must understand the theory of law in America and the responsibilities the adversary system of criminal justice entails. Since it is an adversary system, our laws recognize that those accused of crime have every right to use the skill and resources at their disposal to gain the ultimate goal of winning. In fact, the code of the legal profession demands that the attorney represent the client with all the resources and legal skills at his or her command. This is true in spite of the defendant's guilt or innocence. To do otherwise would violate the principles of American jurisprudence. The doctrine of fairness also plays a role here. The resources of the state are quite formidable, and the defendant must be entitled to use whatever resources he has at his disposal. If this means that a case is dismissed because of a technical error on the part of the police, this is the price that we must pay to ensure that the scales of justice remain in balance between the power of the state on the one hand and the rights of the individual on the other. In this way, we also maintain that delicate system of governmental checks and balances between the executive branch (in this case the police) and the judiciary. Without such checks and balances we could not enjoy those fundamental liberties that are uniquely ours in the United States.

Characteristics

How then does the practice of criminal law square with the popular image and how far does it depart from the ideal? In the first place, the practice of criminal law and the professional competence of many of its practitioners leave a great deal to be desired. Many criminal attorneys who practice regularly in our criminal courts are members of what has been called "the courthouse gang." In the District of Columbia, they are called the "Fifth Streeters," and in Detroit they are referred to as the "Clinton Street Bar Group." In most large cities, certain criminal attorneys have their offices conveniently situated near the building that houses the criminal courts and are often found prowling the courts searching for clients who can pay a modest fee.[22] As Blumberg so well describes them, these criminal defense lawyers, whom he refers to as "regulars," are:

> highly visible in the major urban centers of the nation; their offices—at times shared with bail bondsmen—line the back streets near courthouses. They are also visible politically, with clubhouse ties reaching into judicial chambers and the prosecutor's office. The regulars make no effort to conceal their dependence upon the police, bondsmen, jail personnel, as well as bailiffs, stenographers, prosecutors and judges.[23]

The average criminal trial lawyer is certainly no F. Lee Bailey or Edward Bennett Williams, who enjoy national reputations as criminal defense lawyers. These individuals are at the pinnacle of their profession and usually accept only the most sensational and dramatic cases or those that assure them sizable fees. Many criminal legal specialists just manage to eke out a modest living. Defending criminals, except in a few celebrated cases, is certainly not a financially rewarding undertaking. Many defendants are not well off and they can scarcely afford to pay high fees to their legal counsel. Attorneys who practice this type of law soon realize this fact. Oftentimes, criminal trial attorneys have contacts with pawnbrokers, used-car and used-furniture outlets, or similar places of business which will dispose of the property of the defendant so that the attorney can be assured of receiving something in the way of a fee. In other cases, the attorney will make every effort to either obtain money in advance or somehow work out a financial obligation that will bind the family of the accused to paying the fee.

> "The lawyer goes out and tries to squeeze money from the defendant's mother or an aunt," explains Judge Charles W. Halleck, of the local trial court in Washington, D.C. "Sometimes, he asks a jailed defendant, 'You got $15 or $25? Here let me hold it for you,' and, later that becomes part of the fee."[24]

This situation is very different from that found in civil trial practice, where the attorney may take part of the settlement as the legal fee or may work on a contingency basis. As a consequence, criminal trial attorneys are most likely to be the strongest advocates of plea bargaining. They thus avoid the expense and work of a trial for a client who cannot pay.

Much of their success depends upon their sociability and contacts rather than their legal skills. For example, many criminal attorneys spend a great deal of their time trying to develop contacts with the police for possible referral of clients, with bailbondsmen for leads, and with the prosecutor's office and the judges for plea-bargaining considerations. If they get the reputation for too zealously defending their clients, particularly in more serious crimes, they will alienate the judges, prosecutors, and the police. This is especially true if the attorney is able to gain acquittals based on legal technicalities. Judges, prosecutors, and the police do not like to look foolish when their cases are overturned by the higher courts or when their investigative and arrest procedures are brought into question or receive publicity.

Because of these characteristics of criminal trial practice, the legal profession holds the average criminal trial lawyer in lower regard than most other specialists in the profession. Cole describes the status of the criminal trial attorney within the legal profession as follows:

> The membership of the urban bar appears to be divided into three parts. First, there is an inner circle which handles the work of banks, utilities and commercial concerns; another circle includes lawyers representing interests opposed to those of the inner circle; and finally, an outer group scrapes out an existence by "haunting" the courts in the hope of picking up crumbs from the judicial table. With the exception of a highly proficient few who have made a reputation by winning acquittals in difficult, highly publicized cases, most of the lawyers dealing with criminal justice belong to this periphery.[25]

Consequently, many attorneys either avoid the practice of criminal law altogether or, even worse, do not prepare themselves adequately for the cases they do defend. In a study of the criminal courts of Virginia, over 40 percent of the criminal appeals which were heard by the Virginia Supreme Court of Appeals during the 1970 term affirmed the decision of the lower court without consideration of the constitutional issues involved because during the trial the defense attorneys failed to make proper and timely objections.[26]

This picture of criminal trial practice is more typical of large urban areas; in smaller cities and communities, the practice of criminal law is usually more respectable, and there are, of course, conscientious, dedicated, and honest criminal trial lawyers practicing their specialties throughout the criminal courts of our nation. However, it does remain an unfortunate fact of our society that criminal law practice is generally held in low esteem. The tragedy of this situation is that the practice of criminal law has the potential for being one of the most challenging undertakings of the entire legal system. However, until there is a significant overhaul of the machinery of criminal justice, the practice of criminal law will still be relegated to the making of deals in the back rooms of police stations, the recesses of the criminal court corridors, or the prosecutor's office.

Defense of Indigents

Studies have indicated that in some of our major cities as many as 75 percent of all defendants in criminal cases are unable to afford the cost of hiring an attorney to defend them.[27] The Supreme Court, in the 1963 case of *Gideon v. Wainright*, ruled that defendants in felony trials are constitutionally entitled to be represented by publicly provided attorneys if they are unable to afford to retain counsel.[28] In 1972, the Supreme Court extended this right by holding that no person could be imprisoned as the result of a criminal prosecution in which he was not accorded the right to public representation, thus, effectively expanding the right to almost all criminal cases.[29] Although the Court required the appointment of counsel in these cases, it did not set standards for indigency. As a consequence, jurisdictions throughout the country have established different standards.

Throughout the United States, there are basically three systems by which indigent defendants are provided defense counsel. These are (1) *the assigned-counsel system,* (2) *the voluntary defender program,* and (3) *the public defender system.* Each of these programs features different characteristics which are worth examination.

The Assigned-Counsel System

In this system, the judge after determining that the accused cannot afford to retain his own lawyer will provide a court-assigned attorney. Attorneys are usually assigned from a list which the court maintains of attorneys who have registered with the court and indicated their willingness to defend indigents. The vast majority of states use this method. There are a number of drawbacks associated with the assigned-counsel system. In the first place, those lawyers who voluntarily place their names on this list are most likely to be young and inexperienced lawyers relatively fresh out of law school who have not established a practice nor had much trial experience. They place their names on the assigned-counsel list to obtain the experience they require. Obviously, an established criminal trial lawyer who is successful and has clients need not resort to this approach.[30]

Another problem is that in many instances the attorney is appointed so late in the proceedings that he or she does not have the chance to really study the facts of the case, conduct the required investigations, and prepare the defense. As a result, the attorney often has to ask for a postponement of the case, which can be a particular hardship for the accused, particularly if he is in jail and cannot make bond. Even where a defendant is free on bond, the mental anguish associated with the postponement of the trial date can be severe for many defendants and their families.

A further disadvantage is that many jurisdictions pay for the services of a court-appointed attorney on a sliding-fee basis, and the fees are too low for the attorney to spend a great deal of time in preparing the case or taking it to trial, for that matter. Instead, the attorney is likely to persuade the indigent client to plea bargain. However, since so many inexperienced attorneys are represented by this system, they are perhaps more prone to take the case to trial if for no other reason than for the trial experience this will provide. Furthermore, since they do not have a long list of clients awaiting their services, they can prolong their services through a trial proceeding and thus obtain additional remuneration.

The Voluntary Defender Program

This program is offered by private law offices usually affiliated with a Legal Aid Society, which specializes in providing legal assistance to the poor, and by legal aid bureaus associated with various charitable organizations. Until the 1960s, these programs existed in only a few metropolitan areas. Since the mid-1960s, however, the federal government has provided a great deal of additional funding, and today such programs have assumed a major role in providing legal services to the poor. Originally funded by the Office of Economic Opportunity, they are now largely funded by the Legal Services Corporation, which came into existence in 1974 after OEO was disbanded and the federal government passed the Legal Services Act. In addition, Legal Aid societies receive portions of their budgets from local charities such as the United Way, various grants-in-aid such as federal revenue sharing, and local bar associations. Although current figures are not available, a study done in 1968 indicated that the federal government in that year funded 299 such programs at a cost of $30.4 million and that approximately 1,800 full-time attorneys handled nearly 900,000 cases and served 300,000 clients.[31]

These programs suffer from a number of weaknesses. The major weakness is the uncertainty of continued financial support that always hovers as a threat, particularly if an agency must rely to a significant extent on charitable contributions to sustain itself. There is also some evidence that private agencies are less willing than government-financed agencies to bring their cases to court.[32] Such agencies also receive varying degrees of resistance from local bar associations and judges who view these organizations as competitors for fees that they or members of their profession might otherwise obtain.[33] Although this is a very questionable basis for rejection since many of the clients they serve could hardly pay for private legal counsel, this problem does exist. Finally, there is the very simple yet real problem of trying to cover all the courts in a metropolitan area or servicing the numbers of poor that could use their legal assistance.

The Public Defender System

The first public defender office was created in Los Angeles County in 1914. Since that time, public defender offices have been created in quite a few areas. Although there are some who criticize public defender programs as not going "all out" for their clients, this cannot be taken as an across-the-board condemnation of these programs.[34] All factors considered, it is probably the best method that exists for providing legal assistance to indigent defendants. The public defender system operates on public funds, and thus the attorney's staff and office have a relatively stable base of financial support. Many public defenders are experienced trial attorneys and are often given civil service status at fairly decent salaries. Moreover, defender offices, particularly in larger communities, have some funds available for investigative purposes and sometimes even have their own investigative staff. Studies have shown that the public defender system is no more expensive to operate than are assigned-counsel systems due to the economies of scale present in such operations.[35] Since the income of the public defender continues regardless of whether or not the case goes to trial, there is less likelihood that the attorney will plea bargain an otherwise meritorious case away or engage in delaying tactics so as to frustrate the prosecution into a bargaining position.

One of the problems this office has always faced is lack of adequate public support. Many citizens are hostile to this agency because they feel that criminals do not deserve to be defended by their tax dollars. Although the same argument could be raised for the assigned-counsel system and the voluntary defender program, which in part often rely on public tax support, the operations of these systems and agencies are not quite so visible to the public, nor does the public understand as fully·their method of financing. Some people criticize the public defender system because it does not really provide the indigent defendant with a choice of attorneys since in most instances, the accused is assigned an attorney. However, most public defender offices do have provisions for reassigning staff members if there is an obvious conflict between an attorney and a client.

The Involvement of Law Students in Criminal Defense Practice

Although most law schools do not emphasize criminal law in their curricula, a few efforts to involve students in the practice of criminal law should be mentioned. The Roxbury Defender Project, sponsored by the Boston University Law School, involves thirty third-year law students, who, after an intensive classroom exposure to criminal procedure and trial practice, are assigned to defend indigent misdemeanants in the misdemeanor courts of the Roxbury District of Boston.[36] Harvard University Law School operates a similar program in other Boston courts.

Duke University Law School has in the past sponsored a unique program in which selected law students spend the summer working with U.S. attorneys in North Carolina. This program has been very successful, and most of the prosecutors and students involved openly commended the program for giving them a new perspective on the practice of criminal trial work, provided by the close working relationships and mutual exchange of ideas.[37]

One of the most ambitious projects is that of Northwestern University Law School, which was one of the first to recognize the need to strengthen the criminal law offerings in the school's curriculum. Beginning in 1965, a special internship was instituted in which the course of study for students interested in criminal law was divided between academic learning and field experience.

During the first year of law school residency, each student participating in the program completes ten semester hours in criminal law courses and submits a master's thesis on a subject related to police work. Along with this first-year course work, the student observes closely the operations of the Chicago Police Department. During the second year, the student is assigned as a legal adviser to a metropolitan police department. The program director supervises closely the progress and the performance of the student. Several times each year, the student returns to the law school to participate in seminars which the school conducts for police legal advisers throughout the nation.[38] Although this program is not specifically designed to produce criminal defense lawyers, it provides the student with a greater knowledge and appreciation for the administration of criminal justice which would serve him or her well in a career as a criminal defense attorney.

JURIES

The use of juries today is far different from the use for which they first came into being. The reader will recall that the original jury system, which developed in England during the Middle Ages, was for the purpose of compelling testimony in trials. These early jurors were not unbiased citizens of the community or a representative sample of peers, but witnesses who were brought before the courts of the crown and compelled to relate what they knew about the crime and the accused. The present use of the jury originated in the major concession forced upon King John in the Magna Carta that henceforth noblemen were granted the right to a trial by their peers.[39]

Trial juries play a crucial role in the administration of criminal justice. It is the decision that they render which usually terminates the trial, for in most states a finding of not guilty in criminal cases cannot be overturned by subsequent appeals, and a ruling of guilty can be overturned through the appellate process only very infrequently.

Composition

It is a well-recognized fact that what decision a jury renders depends a great deal on who makes up the jury and how they were chosen. It is true that most juries are composed of ordinary citizens, but they are often not representative of a true cross-section of the community. For the most part, they operate without any guidelines from their fellow citizens. In fact, the entire deliberative process of the jury is so designed by its secretiveness and its seclusion to eliminate the impact of community attitudes upon the members' judgment. As Jacob puts it: "They are selected by chance to *serve* their community rather than *represent* it."[40]

Exploring this question of community representation a little further, let's consider a few facts: Although in theory every citizen should have an equal chance to be selected for jury duty, this does not occur. Statutes usually prescribe that jurors be chosen from voter registration lists, which is the first means employed to discriminate. All citizens who are not qualified to vote, such as convicted felons and citizens who have not been in the community long enough to satisfy residency requirement, are automatically excluded. In studying voting behavior, political scientists have often found that the poor and members of minority groups, which are too often synonymous, are not registered voters and, therefore, automatically excluded.

Common practice excludes still others from jury lists. Juries are selected in some communities by jury commissioners who are required twice a year to furnish the court with a list of names. They obtain these names by asking their friends, service clubs, and others to volunteer. In a few instances, jury service is used as a low-level form of patronage to retirees or others who are unemployed. Often, when jury selection depends upon such factors, only persons known to the commissioner will be called.

In too many instances, working people are also excluded from jury service along with certain professionals such as doctors and lawyers. Working people are excluded in some jurisdictions when they can claim financial hardship and attest that they cannot afford to miss work and lose their pay, which is substantially more than the pay for serving on a jury. This bar to jury service is now slowly disappearing in areas where union contracts provide for some compensation during jury service, and many firms encourage participation by making up the difference in pay that a person would lose by jury service.[41]

Studies conducted in Baltimore, Los Angeles, and Milwaukee indicated that housewives, retirees, professionals, managers, and proprietors are overrepresented on juries, while working-class citizens are underrepresented.[42] In Baltimore, for example, people in the occupational classifications of manager, professional, or proprietor made up 40.2 percent of the jurors, but constituted only 18.7 percent of the general population. On the other hand, while 41.3 percent of the population consisted of working-class people, only 13.4 percent of blue-collar workers were found on the juries studied.[43]

Similarly, many studies have documented the fact that discrimination seems to run along racial lines. A study in Virginia indicated that adult blacks, although constituting an average of 14 percent of the population of the jurisdictions studied, constituted only slightly less than 2 percent of the jurors empaneled in those particular districts.[44]

Deliberations

Research conducted using simulated and real juries has provided some interesting insights into this normally secret process. It seems, from the research, that juries are far less deliberative in criminal cases than might be imagined. A University of Chicago research group, after conducting extensive interviews of criminal trial jurors in New York and Chicago, found that almost all juries voted as soon as they retired to their chambers. In 30 percent of the cases, it took only one vote among the jurors to reach a consensus and to return a unanimous verdict. In those cases where the first vote was not unanimous, the eventual vote ended up unanimous 90 percent of the time. The striking fact was that in these 90 percent of the cases, the original vote, if it was a majority one, was the way the final vote ended up. It would seem that peer-group pressure was enough to change the minds of the dissenters. Under these circumstances, the instance of a single individual holding out and not voting in accord with the majority so as to have a hung jury is very rare indeed.[45]

In a later study by this same research group, some further interesting facts were uncovered. As might be imagined, the juror's occupation and biases seemed to play an important role. Jurors let occupational identification, that is, respect for, or interest in, the defendant's choice of vocation influence their estimate of his worth. In criminal cases, racial prejudice by jurors from a variety of occupational backgrounds seemed to influence their decisions concerning defendants who were members of minority groups.[46]

Videotape simulations of jury deliberations have indicated that there are some obvious decision-making dynamics that occur in jury deliberations. Women play a far more passive role than men in these deliberations.[47] The more formal education a juror had, the more likely that individual was to particate openly and frequently in the discussions and deliberations.[48] Most of the discussion in the jury room centered on the procedure that they should use in conducting their deliberations and exchanging examples from their own personal experiences which they felt were appropriate to help them make decisions in the cases before them. There was far less discussion of the testimony during the trial or the instructions that they had received from the judge than might be imagined.[49]

The nationality of the jury members seemed to play an important role in determining whether the accused would be found guilty or not. Jurors of German, Scandinavian, and English ancestry were much more likely to vote for the state, while jurors of Negro or East European background were much more likely to side with the defense.[50]

An extensive study of juries by Kalvern and Zeisel also provided some interesting insights into the jury system. It was found that judges agreed with the decision of juries in about two-thirds of all cases. In those cases in which the judge did not agree with the jury, it was usually because the jury was perceived as being too lenient. Many of the disagreements between the judge and the jury also centered on such factors as the jury's belief that the punishment for the crime was too severe since the defendant had already suffered as a result of his crime and need not be further punished. Juries were also more sensitive to improper police methods and to defendants who were charged with crimes occurring in subcultures where norms differed from those of the jury members themselves. Finally, juries tended to weigh more heavily than the judges the contributory fault of the victim in rape and assault cases.[51]

Although the use of trial juries is under attack by certain reform groups who would abolish them, history and the lack of a viable substitute would seem to indicate that juries will continue to play an important role in the administration of criminal justice. If the future should indicate any changes in the traditional jury system, it is likely to occur only in the manner of selection and composition and the number of jurors used—outright abolition of their function does not seem indicated nor even perhaps warranted.

WITNESSES

Witnesses in criminal trials are classified into two categories: (1) the lay or ordinary witness and (2) the expert witness.

The lay or ordinary witness is a person who has some personal knowledge of the facts of the case and who has been called upon to relate this information in court. Police officers usually fall within this category. The lay witness is permitted to testify about facts only and may not state an opinion concerning matters before the court except in a few limited instances when this is permitted by the judge.[52] Lay witnesses are permitted to testify only to what they perceived through their five senses that is relevant to the case.

With the great advance of science and with the wide variety of skilled occupations, juries are often called upon to pass judgment on many matters about which the jurors have no personal knowledge. The services of the expert witness have been developed to assist them. The function of the expert witness is to give the jury the benefit of his or her knowledge of a particular science or skill. Expert witnesses are permitted to express their opinions concerning a particular set of facts or circumstances or about some examination of evidence made by them. Of course, the jury may or may not accept their opinions.

Before one can be an expert witness, two fundamental rules have to be satisfied: First, the subject matter to which the expert witness will testify must be a field in which the average person would have little or no knowledge. Second, the witness must have the qualifications that are necessary to make him or her an expert in the field. A voir dire examination is conducted by both the prosecutor and defense counsel to ascertain whether the individual has the qualifications that would make him or her an expert in a particular field. The final decision, however, as to whether someone qualifies as an expert witness is made by the trial judge. Even though the trial judge rules that the individual is indeed an expert witness, the opposing counsel can cross-examine the expert in an effort to destroy his or her credibility to the jury.

THE BAILIFF

The bailiff is an officer of the court. The idea for this office evolved from the Statute of Winchester in 1285, by which King Edward I tried to establish a uniform system of law enforcement in England. The original responsibility of this official was to keep under surveillance persons who were traveling about town streets after dark and to periodically check on all known and observed strangers.

As we have seen, today the bailiff is responsible for keeping order in the court and protecting the security of jury deliberations and court property. At the county level, the bailiff is often a member of the sheriff's department who, as a uniformed officer, is assigned to the court. Many municipal courts rely on a form of political patronage to fill this position, and the bailiff is appointed by the judge to serve in a particular court.

THE COURT CLERK

The office of court clerk is normally attached to the main trial court of the county or municipality. In most states, the court clerk is a popularly elected official. In some states, this position is considered a patronage appointment for the party represented by the senior judge on the bench or by the party which is represented by the majority of judges in the court. The court clerk collects fines, forfeitures, penalties, and court costs in criminal cases, is usually responsible for keeping the records of the court proceedings and actions, and may be empowered to prepare formal writs and process papers issued by the court. Court clerks usually are salaried officials, but in some states they are still paid on a fee basis. In several states, the position of court clerk is combined with that of the elected county clerk, who records legal papers in the county as well as handling the administrative and clerical responsibilities of the court.

THE COURT REPORTER

Court reporters are employed to record and transcribe trial or other court proceedings. In the past, the court reporter normally used shorthand, but most now use stenotype machines. In the last few years, courts, in an effort to become more cost effective, are increasingly turning to tape recorders. One of the problems of using tape recorders is the difficulty of editing the tape to remove objectionable comments. In most cases, the court reporter is salaried and is also paid an additional sum, usually by the page, for the transcribing and preparation of the court record in cases of appeal. In some instances, the court reporter is responsible for the care and security of the physical evidence introduced during the trial if it is not the express responsibility of the bailiff to do so. However, this responsibility extends only to the time that the evidence is in the courtroom; permanent responsibility for the maintenance of the evidence during the trial is usually the task of the court clerk or, in the case of the state's evidence, the police in certain circumstances.

THE CORONER

The office of coroner, although not a judicial office in the strictest sense, does perform quasi-judicial functions. The first mention of this official is recorded in 1194 during the reign of King Richard I of England. Unfortunately, little is known of his specific responsibilities other than that he was a representative of the crown assigned to perform ministerial tasks at the county level.

The present-day function of the coroner seems to date from 1275, when under Edward I his responsibilities were expanded to include the specific task of conducting investigations into unnatural and sudden deaths. He was also charged with the duties of overseeing the criminal prosecutions which involved the forfeiture of the accused's property to the crown, the collection of taxes, and the levying and collection of fines.

Today, the coroner in the majority of states is an elected county official whose chief function is to investigate the cause of death which occurs in the absence of witnesses, under suspicious circumstances, or where there is evidence of possible violence. The coroner is authorized to conduct *inquests* concerning suspicious deaths. These are quasi-judicial hearings that have some of the same characteristics as a trial. The coroner usually has the authority to subpoena witnesses and documents, cross-examine witnesses under oath, introduce evidence, and receive testimony. Most states do not require that the inquest follow the exacting rules of criminal procedure that govern trials. In most instances, the coroner is authorized after conduct of the hearing to issue warrants of arrest or at least require the prosecutor to initiate the obtaining of such a warrant.

One of the major criticisms of this office has been the lack of qualifications required of the coroner. Since, in many cases, coroners have no background in medicine or law, they cannot perform their obligations satisfactorily. As a result of this, a number of states have abolished the office of coroner and substituted the office of *medical examiner* in its place. The medical examiner must be a licensed physician and in some instances must also be a qualified specialist in pathology. Many states, such as Massachusetts, which was the first to adopt this idea in 1877, have vested the legal responsibilities in the office of the county prosecutor and the medical responsibilities in the appointed medical examiner. A few states have appointed medical examiners who operate out of a central state agency.

RECOMMENDED REFORMS OF THE JUDICIAL PROCESS

Whereas law enforcement and corrections have made some important strides in recent years to adopt reform strategies and programs, the courts continue to lag far behind. So serious has the situation become that a special National Conference on the Judiciary was held in Williamsburg, Virginia, in 1971, which brought together the president, the chief justice of the U.S. Supreme Court, the U.S. attorney general, and the chief justices of nearly all the states to discuss ways to solve the crisis facing the courts.

Although it is not possible to review all the current suggestions for court reforms, some of the more useful will be highlighted in the remainder of this chapter. Many of these recommendations can be found in the publications of the American Bar Association Project on Standards for Criminal Justice, the American Judicature Society, National Council on Crime and Delinquency, National Advisory Commission on Criminal Justice Standards and Goals, and the President's Commission on Law Enforcement and Administration of Justice. The student who is interested in examining court reform more extensively should consult these sources for more comprehensive and definitive recommendations.

Changes in the Pretrial Process

Screening and Diversion from the Judicial Process

The rationale behind screening and diversion from the judicial process is twofold: First, the sheer numbers of cases that burden the courts must be reduced, and secondly, there may be more appropriate ways to deal with offenders than by invoking the trial process. This is not a suggestion for leniency—it merely recognizes that in terms of both financial costs and more intangible costs to society, it may be more practicable to consider alternatives. The idea behind the recommendations for pretrial screening is to reduce the number of cases that the criminal courts deal with so that our prosecutorial and judicial officials can concentrate more of their attention on those cases which deserve the time and expense of adjudication.

The pivotal figure in the pretrial screening and diversion process is the prosecutor. The implementation of an effective screening and diversion procedure would require that the prosecutor establish certain criteria to determine whether it is in the best interests of the accused to subject him to trial. For example, under a pretrial screening and diversion philosophy, prosecutors would have to examine many factors of the particular case as well as the accused much more closely than they now routinely do. They would have to develop certain decisional guidelines as to whether a trial is in the best interests of society, the courts, and the accused. Some considerations might be the sufficiency of the evidence against the defendant, which would indicate whether a conviction was likely and whether the conviction, once obtained, could be sustained on appeal. The more difficult, but no less meaningful, questions that the prosecutor would also have to consider before invoking the trial process concern the value of prosecuting the individual in terms of preventing future criminal behavior by the accused and by others. What impact would the use of diversion measures have on society in terms of its concerns for safety and security? The prosecutor would also have to consider the impact of further proceedings upon the accused and his family and how the trial and possible incarceration of the accused might seriously disrupt family ties, create severe financial hardship, and expose the accused to an experience that would produce a more embittered and nonsocialized individual more prone to criminal tendencies than when he entered the criminal justice system.

Abolition of Plea Bargaining

As mentioned, in many courts the vast majority of criminal convictions are obtained by the defendant entering a guilty plea, often as the result of plea-bargaining agreements between the prosecutor and the defense counsel. This is a particularly pernicious practice that destroys the basic concept of justice.[53] It is harmful to society because it results in leniency that reduces the deterrent impact of the law, and it is harmful to the accused who by engaging in it forfeits those rights which have been incorporated into the trial process for his protection.

Invariably, one of the major recommendations that comes up in the discussion of court reform is to abolish this practice. Prosecutors and judges justify its existence on the grounds that if it did not occur the courts would break down from the workload. Probably, it would not be practical to abolish plea bargaining altogether. What is immediately needed is meaningful reform. The first task is for the court to take a larger role in the process. In too many cases, judges merely acquiesce in the bargain which the prosecutor and defense counsel have struck. Judges should examine all the facts of the case and require of prosecutors written explanations for their decisions. Judges should also make certain that the accused fully understands the consequences of the bargain and his guilty plea and that he is aware that he is forfeiting all rights to a trial. In too many cases, the accused is at the mercy of his defense counsel and must rely upon that individual for the appropriate legal advice. If judges would take a larger role in the plea-bargaining process and refuse to accept settlements when there were questions of impropriety, there would be less criticism of this practice.

Abolition of the Grand Jury

The grand jury has for all intent and purpose outlived its usefulness in the majority of criminal proceedings. Great Britan realized this and in 1933 abolished it outright, although the right to be indicted by a grand jury had existed in that country since the fourteenth century. Willoughby puts the entire issue of the grand jury into perspective when he says:

A grand jury is in the nature of a fifth wheel; that real responsibility for the bringing of criminal charges is, in fact, exercised by the prosecuting attorney, the grand jury doing little or nothing more than following his suggestions; that it entails delay . . . ; that it renders prosecution more difficult through important witnesses getting beyond the jurisdiction . . . or through memory of facts becoming weakened by lapse of time; that it entails unneccessary expense to the government; and that it imposes a great burden on the citizen called upon to render jury service.[54]

Grand juries are extremely costly to empanel, service, and maintain. Although the grand jury was originally conceived as a screening device to protect the accused from false accusations, it no longer serves this objective. For example, a study of the operations of the grand jury in Baltimore during 1967 indicated that this grand jury returned indictments in 98.18 percent of those cases it heard, only to have 42 percent of these indictments later dismissed before trial because of insufficient evidence or some technicality that made prosecution impossible.[55]

The use of grand juries also has another dysfunctional consequence for the administration of justice. In some cases, their legal intricacies of empaneling, conduct, and deliberations have actually thwarted justice. Individuals who may have been guilty have been able to have charges against them dismissed because of legal irregularities in the grand jury process which a skilled defense attorney has been able to use advantagously.

However, the continued use of the investigatory grand jury is recommended by most legal reform groups. The grand jury which is routinely used in the processing of criminal cases is the hearing grand jury. The investigatory grand jury is a special type of grand jury which is convened to inquire into particular areas such as organized crime or official corruption in the community. These investigatory grand juries should be retained as a watchdog. In some politically sensitive areas, where the police or the prosecutor are reluctant to conduct the necessary investigations, these special grand juries can perform an important role in the investigation and accusation that leads to the prosecution of crime.[56]

It should be pointed out, however, that investigatory grand juries also pose some serious problems for the administration of justice. History is replete with examples of the unscrupulous use of such an instrument for personal and political interests. For example, during Lincoln's administration they were used against those who did not support the Union's cause. During Roosevelt and Truman's administration they were used to silence Bolshevik and Nazi sympathizers. Later they were used by Senator Joseph McCarthy and Representative Richard Nixon during the red-baiting scare of the 1950s.[57]

Although the investigatory grand jury can be used effectively to weed out local corruption and organized crime, they must be controlled very carefully if they are in fact to serve as effective instruments of justice and not tools of oppression against certain minority interests.

Timely Processing of Criminal Cases

One of the immediate goals of court reform is to shorten the time between arrest and the beginning of trial. Every state should require that, at least in felony cases, an arrestee be brought before a magistrate within six hours of his arrest for an initial appearance. This initial appearance would be used to advise the individual of his constitutional rights and to inquire into the police conduct in this area. In addition, the accused should be advised of the charges against him, and the appropriate bail should be determined.

Once this has occurred, states should require that where the individual is jailed and cannot make bond, a preliminary hearing should be conducted within at least ten days. Individuals who are incarcerated should receive priority in scheduling preliminary hearings. In those cases where the individual is out on bond, provisions should be made to conduct the preliminary hearing within two weeks of the arrest.

According to the recommendations of the National Advisory Commission, the entire process from arrest to trial should take no longer than sixty days. This proposal would require a number of things: First, pretrial motions and conferences would necessarily have to be conducted within certain frames of time, say within ten days after the preliminary hearing. For example, defense attorneys would have to file their motions within ten days after the preliminary hearing. Prosecutors would have to file their countermotions within seven days of the filing of the motion by the defense attorney, and the judge would have to rule on the motion within the following five days. Similar time frames would have to be adopted for the scheduling of the arraignment and the grand jury where it is used.

Reforms in scheduling of court trials should deal with the problems associated with continuances. In many jurisdictions, the granting of continuances often unnecessarily prolongs the time required to get the case to trial. Defense counsels are particularly notorious for using delaying tactics. Many times, they will ask the judge for a continuance on the grounds that they need additional time to prepare the defense. In some cases, this may be a meritorious request; other times it is used to frustrate the prosecution, the state's witnesses, or the complaining victim or to cover up the fact that they have as yet made no effort to prepare the defense case. Judges should be more careful in granting such continuances and insist upon a definite showing of need.

Jury Size and Unanimity

Requiring less than twelve jurors is often recommended as a reform proposal. About twenty states have enacted statutes to the effect that there can be six jurors in certain courts of limited jurisdiction, and other states are considering such legislation. In the 1970 case of *Williams* v. *Florida*, the U.S. Supreme Court held that Florida's use of a six-man jury did not violate the defendant's

Sixth and Fourteenth Amendment rights to trial by jury. The Court held that the important factor was not the size of the jury, but whether the group was "large enough to promote group deliberation, free from outside attempts at intimidation and to provide a fair possibility for obtaining a representative cross-section of the community."[58]

In light of the ruling of the Supreme Court, the National Advisory Commission recommends that "juries in criminal prosecutions for offenses not punishable by life imprisonment should be composed of less than 12, but at least 6 persons."[59] A jury of less than twelve persons can still provide the required group deliberation and resistance to outside influences and can reflect a representative cross-section of the community as easily as a jury of twelve individuals. The six-person jury would be far less costly to empanel and maintain, particularly in cases involving sensational crimes, where it becomes exceedingly difficult to empanel twelve persons acceptable to the prosecution and the defense.

Another question that is relevant to the use of juries concerns the unanimity required before a jury can convict. It has been argued, for example, that "the unanimity of a verdict in a criminal case is inextricably interwoven with the required measure of proof."[60] In other words, a unanimous verdict is required to prove the individual guilty beyond a reasonable doubt. Most state constitutions require that there can be no conviction except by unanimous verdict. A few states permit conviction by less than a unanimous verdict for crimes.[61] As mentioned earlier, Oregon, for example, provides that ten votes can convict except in first-degree murder cases.

However, there are those who adamantly maintain that unanimity be required. Probably the most succinct argument for the retention of the unanimous requirement has been expressed by Holtzoff, who says:

> Unanimity is important and vital for two reasons: first, it leads to a more thorough consideration of the questions at issue and a more careful deliberation in the jury room than might otherwise be the case, since debate and discussion must continue until a unanimous verdict is reached; and second, the fact that the verdict is unanimous is in itself strong assurance of its fairness and justice. The only possible drawback to the requirement of unanimity is that occasionally it leads to a deadlock and, thereby, requires re-trial before another jury. The percentage of cases in which this happens in jurisdictions in which the common law system still prevails is, however, not sufficiently large to constitute an important factor.[62]

In spite of this, the American Bar Association, in examining the research on the question of jury deliberations as well as the legal considerations involved, concluded that the requirement for unanimity serves no useful purpose. Its Advisory Committee stated that "the minimum standards should recognize the propriety of less than unanimous verdicts as now permitted in six states."[63]

Upgrading the Prosecutor

Another area of concern among those who would improve the judicial process is the need for change in the present selection, retention, and training of prosecutors and their legal assistants. There is a recognized need to improve the caliber of persons attracted to this office and to retain them as careerists. It has been suggested that selection of prosecutors be based upon their qualifications similar to the selection of judges under the Missouri Plan. In addition, there is a need to drastically increase their salaries and those of their assistants to retain them in this very important position. The National Advisory Commission recommends that prosecutors receive the same remuneration as the presiding judge of the trial court of general jurisdiction.[64] Once this has been accomplished, it would be possible to prohibit them from engaging in the private practice of law, which inevitably leads to conflict of interest.

Likewise, the salaries for assistant prosecutors should be commensurate with salaries paid to attorney associates in private law firms in the area. In addition, there is the real need to provide prosecutors and assistant prosecutors with extensive training in the criminal law and trial practice and with an adequate legal research capability. In medium-sized cities, the prosecutor's staff should have at least one researcher to help research the necessary case and statutory laws. In smaller jurisdictions where this may not be practicable, the prosecutor should at least have access to an adequate legal library.

Improving Defense Services for the Indigent Defendant

States need to improve the system of defense counsel to indigent defendants. This would require, as a minimum, the appointment of a full-time public defender at a salary commensurate with the job's responsibilities plus provision of the necessary facilities and staff. Applicants for this position should be nominated and approved by a select body of responsible citizens, who would send a list of three qualified nominees to the governor, who would then appoint the individual. The public defender would be a salaried employee of the state, appointed for at least a four-year term and removed from office by a special judicial commission which would also have the authority to investigate and remove judges for cause.

Like the prosecutor, the public defender should be provided with legal research capabilities and funds for investigative facilities needed to prepare the client's defense as well as funds to employ such experts as psychiatrists, forensic pathologists, and criminal investigators when necessary.

Videotaping of Criminal Trials

A relatively recent development which seems to promise to eliminate many unnecessary delays in criminal trials needs to be mentioned. In the last six years, videotaping of trials has produced some astonishing findings. Although it has been used to date almost exclusively in civil cases, a number of pilot projects are examining how it can be adapted to criminal trials.

McCrystal describes the technique that has been employed in civil cases and the results of using videotaping equipment in a particular case:

> All proceedings, except the empaneling of the jury, opening statements and closing statements, had been recorded previously out of the presence of the jury on videotaping equipment. The tape was then edited by the judge and all inadmissible evidence, objections and rulings on matters of law eliminated. Each attorney then made an opening statement to the jury which was also videotaped and shown on a screen. After this was accomplished and the jurors had seen the videotaped opening statements and trial, the lawyers each made ''live'' closing arguments before the jury who then retired to deliberate. The initial taping of the testimony and the opening statements required a full day. After the tape was edited, it took only two hours and 40 minutes, and the entire process of reviewing the opening statements and the trial on videotape, the live closing statements and the jury deliberations and verdict took less than seven hours. The advantages of this included the following:
>
> 1. The trial moved rapidly and without distracting interruptions, since all delays or interruptions in the presentation of the evidence were edited out.
>
> 2. Jurors were not prejudiced by, or asked to disregard questions or answers ruled to be improper and were thus able to base their judgment solely on proper evidence.
>
> 3. The use of a chart by a doctor was more effective because the camera could zoom in for closer examination.
>
> 4. It was less confusing to jurors not to have to hear comments or exchanges between opposing counsels when evidence was offered.
>
> 5. Some of the witnesses interviewed said they were more at ease giving their testimony in the presence of the two attorneys and the camera operator than they would have been in the courtroom in the presence of the judge and jury.[65]

Systems Analysis in the Management of Criminal Cases

Another major innovation that promises to bring badly needed reform to the judicial process is the introduction of new technological advances in the prosecution of criminal cases. Such a systems model, known as the Prosecutors Management Information System (PROMIS), has been operating in Washinton, D.C. since 1971.[66]

Essentially, PROMIS makes available to the prosecutor's office a wealth of computerized information on each case, as well as reports and analyses of all case data so that priority areas can be identified and the prosecutor's legal staff can more meaningfully control their workload.

This is accomplished by computerizing a great deal of information about persons arrested and scheduled to appear for trial. Also included is extensive information concerning the circumstances surrounding their crimes. For example, the PROMIS system provides the prosecuting attorney's office with the following information:

Information about the defendant, including name, alias, sex, race, date of birth, address, facts about prior arrests and convictions, employment status, and alcohol or drug abuse.

Information about the crime, including the date, time, and place of the crime, the number of persons involved, and information about the gravity of the crime in terms of the amount and degree of personal injury, property loss, or damage.

Information about the time, date, and place of arrest; the type of arrest; and the identity of the arresting officer.

Information about criminal charges including the charges originally placed by the police, and the charges actually filed in court, and the reasons for changes in the charges by the prosecutor.

The dates of every court event in a case from preliminary hearing through arraignment, motion hearing, continuance hearing, and final disposition to sentencing; the names of the principals involved in each event, including the defense and prosecution attorneys and the judge; the outcomes of the events; and the reasons for these outcomes.

The names and addresses of all witnesses and victims, the prosecutor's assessment of whether each witness is essential to the case or not, any indications of reluctance to testify on the part of the witness, and other witness characteristics, such as whether he or she is related to the victim or defendant.[67]

As might be imagined, this PROMIS-generated information is of major assistance in helping the prosecutor prepare and manage his or her caseload. For example, since the establishment of this system, prosecutors have been able to concentrate their attention on the more serious cases, which can be identified by means of the information provided. Also, potential problem areas can be identified and handled prior to the trial date. The system automatically prepares a list of witnesses and their addresses so that subpoena lists can be compiled. In addition, the system compiles a workload report so that the court can monitor the progress of cases and pinpoint any unusual delays.

Although at this time this sophisticated case management program exists only in Washington, D.C., it is being refined and developed so that it can eventually be used as a prototype for widespread application in other congested urban courts throughout the country.

The Court Administrator

States are realizing that the responsibility for the management of the courts can no longer properly rest with the judiciary. If the court process is to be speeded up and judges are to devote their time to adjudicating cases, reviewing plea-bargaining agreements, and generally improving the legal process, they must be relieved of the responsibilities of court management.

Although Connecticut is credited with the first state use of a court administrator in 1932, the model that has served as an impetus to develop the concept at the state level has been the Federal Judicial Center. This center, created in 1967, has been given the responsibility to develop and apply relevant management techniques to the administration of the federal courts. Among its important accomplishments are the application of systems analysis and design to reorder the case calendaring systems in metropolitan district courts, a feasibility study of the use of circuit law clerks, an examination of the impact of specific types of litigation on the resources and workload of the courts, the use of computers for case scheduling, and the conduct of training sessions for judges and other court personnel.[68]

At the state level, the court administrator is often appointed by the chief justice or presiding judge of the state's highest appellate court. The responsibilities of this office are to establish across-the-board policies and guidelines for the management and operations of all state courts. This includes (1) the development of a general budget for the operation of all state courts for submission to the state legislature; (2) the establishing of uniform personnel practices in recruitment, hiring, removal, compensation, and training of all nonjudicial employees of the courts; (3) the compilation of statistical summaries on court operations; (4) complete fiscal management responsibilities such as purchasing, disbursement, accounting, and auditing for the entire state court system; (5) training programs for judicial and nonjudicial personnel assigned to the courts; and (6) judicial assignment under the auspices of the presiding or chief justice in order to ensure that judges will be assigned to those jurisdictions where they are needed.[69]

Because of this recent interest in court administration, new career opportunities and programs are developing for individuals interested in court management as a vocation. One such program, the Institute for Court Management at the University of Denver, has been duplicated by other universities throughout the nation that have begun to develop at the graduate level special degree programs in court management. Usually these programs apply public and business management to court operations and include courses in the legal process, budgeting and fiscal management, personnel, and computer applications. From all indications, this career field will grow substantially in the years ahead.

SUMMARY

The judge, prosecuting attorney, defense counsel, and jury play extremely important roles in the administration of justice—roles which are often very different from those commonly portrayed on TV or in the movies. In practice their roles are often modified by circumstances not apparent to the average citizen. For example, judges, prosecutors, and defense lawyers often interact in a process of mutual accommodation to each other which imposes restraints on how they can individually operate. These role relationships and interdependencies often produce effects which work at cross-purposes to the idealized image of justice that exists in the minds of many. Plea bargaining, practices of criminal defense attorneys, and the awesome power of the prosecutor affect the manner in which justice is dispensed.

Jurisdictions have adopted one of three programs to provide legal defense services to the defendant who is unable to afford to retain his own defense counsel: the assigned-counsel system, the voluntary defender program, and the public defender system. Each has its own peculiar characteristics and strengths and weaknesses.

The judicial system is in drastic need of major reform. Some of the more frequently suggested modifications are increased screening and diversion from the judicial process, abolition of plea bargaining, the abolition of the hearing grand jury, additional efforts to process criminal cases move expeditiously, reduction in jury size and elimination of requirements for unanimity, upgrading the office of the prosecutor and prosecutorial personnel, the use of videotapes in criminal trials, and wider adoption of the use of court administrators.

Suggested Additional Readings

Advisory Commission on Intergovernmental Relations. *Court Reform.* Washington, D.C.: U.S. Government Printing Office, 1971.

American Bar Association Project on Standards for Criminal Justice: *Standards Relating to the Prosecution Function: Approved Draft.* Chicago: American Bar Association, 1970.

Frank, Jerome. *Courts on Trial.* New York: Atheneum, 1969.

Friesen, Ernest, Edward C. Gallas, and Nesta M. Gallas. *Managing the Courts.* Indianapolis: Bobbs-Merrill, 1971.

James, Howard. *Crisis in the Courts.* New York: McKay, 1971.

Jones, Harry, ed. *The Courts, the Public, and the Law Explosion.* Englewood Cliffs, N.J.: Prentice-Hall, 1965.

Mileski, Maureen. "Courtroom Encounters: An Observation Study of a Lower Criminal Court." *Law and Society Review* 5 (1971): 473-538.

Suffet, Frederic. "Bail Setting: A Study of Courtroom Interaction." *Crime and Delinquency* 12 (1966): 318-331.

Skolnick, Jerome. "Guilty Plea Bargaining: Compromises by Prosecutors to Secure Guilty Pleas." *University of Pennsylvania Law Review* 112 (1964): 865-885.

Vera Institute of Justice. *Programs in Criminal Justice Reform.* New York: Vera Institute of Justice, 1972.

Watson, Richard A., and Rondal G. Downing. *The Politics of the Bench and Bar: Judicial Selection under the Missouri Nonpartisan Court Plan.* New York: Wiley, 1969.

Notes

1. For example, see Marvin E. Frankel, *Criminal Sentences: Law without Order* (New York: Hill & Wang, 1973).

2. Maureen Mileski, "Courtroom Encounters: An Observation Study of a Lower Criminal Court," *Law and Society Review,* 5 (1971): 473-538.

3 E. Blythe Stason, "Judicial Selection around the World," in Glenn R. Winters (ed.), *Judicial Selection and Tenure* (Chicago: American Judicative Society, 1973), pp. 45-52.

4. Ibid., p. 48.

5. For example, see Glenn R. Winters, "The Merit Plan for Judicial Selection and Tenure: Its Historical Development," in Winters (ed.), op. cit., pp. 29-44.

6. President's Commission on Law Enforcement and Administration of Justice, *Task Force Report: The Courts* (Washington, D.C.: U.S. Government Printing Office, 1967), p. 66.

7. Glenn R. Winters and Raymond Allard, "Judicial Selection and Tenure in the United States in American Assembly," *The Courts, the Public and the Law Explosion* (Englewood Cliffs, N.J.: Prentice-Hall, 1965), pp. 142-144.

8. Donald J. Newman, "Pleading Guilty for Considerations: A Study of Bargain Justice," *Journal of Criminal Law, Criminology and Police Science* 46 (March-April 1956) 780-790.

9. George F. Cole, *The American System of Criminal Justice* (North Scituate, Mass.: Duxbury Press, 1975), p. 297.

10. Albert N. Alschuler, "The Prosecutor's Role in Plea Bargaining," *University of Chicago Law Review,* 61 (1968).

11. Cole, loc. cit.

12. Ibid.

13. Wayne R. LaFave, *Arrest: The Decision to Take a Suspect into Custody* (Boston: Little, Brown, 1965), p. 515.

14. Advisory Commission on Intergovernmental Relations, *State-Local Relations in the Criminal Justice System* (Washington, D.C.: U.S. Government Printing Office, 1971), pp. 113-114.

15. Yong Hyo Cho, *Public Policy and Urban Crime* (Cambridge, Mass.: Ballinger, 1974), p. 57.

16. Advisory Commission, op. cit., p. 113.

17. National District Attorneys Association, *The Prosecuting Attorneys of the United States* (Chicago: NDAA, 1966), pp. 193-195.

18. Richard L. Enstrom, "Political Ambitions and the Prosecutorial Office," *Journal of Politics,* 33 (1971): 190-194.

19. President's Commission, op. cit., p. 73.

20. National District Attorneys Association, op. cit., p. 194.

21. H. R. Wildermann, "The Process of Socialization in the Role of the Prosecutor," *Journal of Social Interaction,* 2 (Spring 1965): 26-35.

22. Cole, op. cit., p. 257.

23. Abraham S. Blumberg, "Lawyers with Convictions," *Transaction,* 4 (July 1967): 18.

24. As quoted in Leonard Downie, Jr., *Justice Denied* (New York: Praeger, 1971), p. 173; and Cole, op. cit., p. 263.

25. Cole, op. cit., p. 260.

26. Board of Governors, Criminal Law Section, Virginia State Bar, *Report to the Governor and the General Assembly of Virginia; A Study of the Defense of Indigents in Virginia* (Annapolis, Va., 1971).

27. J. Edward Lumbard, "Better Lawyers for Our Criminal Courts," *Atlantic Monthly* (June 1964): 86.

28. 372 U.S. 335 (1963).

29. *Argersinger v. Hamlin,* 407 U.S. 25 (1972).

30. Bertram F. Wilcox and Edward J. Bloustein, "Account of a Field Study in a Rural Area of the Representation of Indigents Accused of a Crime," *Columbia Law Review,* 59 (April 1959): 551-583.

31. Harry P. Stumpf and Robert J. Janowitz, "Judges and the Poor: Bench Response to Federally Financed Legal Services," *Stanford Law Review* 221 (1969): 1059.

32. Harry P. Stumpf, "Law and Poverty: A Political Perspective," *Wisconsin Law Review* (1968): 698-699.

33. Ibid., p. 699.

34. For example, see Dallin H. Oaks and Warren Lehman, *Criminal Justice System and the Indigent* (Chicago: University of Chicago Press, 1968); and Michael Moore, "The Right to Counsel for Indigents in Oregon," *Oregon Law Review,* 44 (Spring 1965).

35. For example, see "Representation of Indigents in California: A Field Study of the Public Defender and Assigned-Counsel Systems," *Stanford Law Review* 13 (1961): 522-565.

36. R. Spangenberg, "The Boston University Roxbury Defender Project," *Journal of Legal Education,* 17 (1965): 311.

37. T. E. Purver, "Operation of the United States Attorney's Student Assistant Program," *American Criminal Law Quarterly 2 (1964): 175.*

38. President's Commission, op. cit., p. 63.

39. Herbert Jacob, *Justice in America* (Boston: Little, Brown, 1972), p. 121.

40. Ibid. p. 122.

41. Ibid., p. 123.

42. Edwin S. Mills, "Statistical Study of Occupation of Jurors in a U.S. District Court," *Maryland Law Review,* 22 (1962): 205-216; W. S. Robinson, "Bias, Probability and Trial by Jury," *American Sociological Review,* 15 (1950): 73-78; Marvin R. Summer, "Comparative Study of Qualifications of State and Federal Jurors," *Wisconsin Bar Bulletin,* 34 (1961): 35-39.

43. Mills, op. cit., p. 208.

44. S. W. Tucker, "Racial Discrimination in Jury Selection in Virginia," *Virginia Law Review,* 52 (1966): 749.

45. Dale W. Broeder, "University of Chicago Jury Project," *Nebraska Law Review,* 38 (1959): 746-747.

46. Broeder, "Occupational Expertise and Bias as Affecting Juror Behavior: A Preliminary Look," *New York University Law Review,* 40 (1965): 1079-1100.

47. *Fred L. Strodtbeck, et al., "Social Status in Jury Deliberations," American Sociological Review,* 22 (1957): 713-719.

48. Rita M. James, "Status and Competence of Jurors," *American Journal of Sociology,* 64 (1959): 563-570.

49. Ibid.

50. Broeder, op. cit., pp. 748-749.

51. Harry Kalvern, Jr., and Hans Zeisel, *The American Jury* (Boston: Little, Brown, 1966).

52. Gilbert B. Stuckey, *Evidence for the Law Enforcement Officer* (New York: McGraw-Hill, 1968), p. 61.

53. It should be pointed out that some observers feel that plea bargaining is absolutely indispensable to true justice. See Arthur Rosett and Donald R. Cressey, *Justice by Consent* (Philadelphia: Lippincott, 1976).

54. W. F. Willoughby, "Principles of Judicial Administration," in James M. Burns and Jack W. Peltason (eds.) *Government by the People* (Englewood Cliffs, N.J.: Prentice-Hall, 1963), p. 202.

55. National Advisory Commission, op. cit., p. 75.

56. For example, see the recommendations in Committee for Economic Development, *Reducing Crime and Assuring Justice* (New York: CED, June 1972), chap. 3.

57. See Richard Harris, "Annals of Law, Taking the Fifth-Part III," *New Yorker* (Apr. 19, 1976): 42-97.

58. 399 U.S. 78, 100 (1970).

59. National Advisory Commission, op. cit., p. 101.

60. *Hidbon v. U.S.* 204 F. 2d 834 (6th Cir. 1953).

61. For example, Montana; two-thirds; Oklahoma and Texas; three-fourths; and Idaho; five-sixths.

62. *R. Holtzoff, "Modern Trends in Trial by Jury, Washington & Lee Law Review,* 27 (1959): 27-28

63. American Bar Association Project on Standards for Criminal Justice, *Standards Relating to Trial by Jury* (New York: Institute of Judicial Administration, 1968), p. 28.

64. National Advisory Commission, op. cit., p. 229.

65. James L. McCrystal, "The Videotape Jury Trial," *The Judges' Journal,* 2 (July 1972).

66. See Sidney Brounstein and William Hamilton, "Analysis of the Criminal Justice System with the Prosecutors Management Information System (PROMIS)," in Leonard Oberlander, ed. *Quantitative Tools for Criminal Justice Planning* (Washington, D.C.: U.S. Government Printing Office, 1975):91-111.

67. Ibid., p. 97.

68. Joseph D. Tydings, "The Courts and Congress, *Public Administration Review,* 31 March-April 1971): 116-117

69. See National Advisory Commission, op. cit., chap. 9.

Part 4

CORRECTIONS

Chapter 12

Corrections: Historical Perspective

THE QUEST FOR PHILOSOPHICAL IDEALS

The development of corrections mirrors our changing attitudes toward the proper response of society to the deviant behavior of the offender and the developments and modification of the criminal law. The correctional alternative of imprisonment, as we perceive it today, is a very recent societal response to deviancy. History does not tell us a great deal about how societies dealt with criminal behavior, particularly cultures outside Western Europe. We do know that as people began to form into groups for collective safety certain customs and habits became established mores. In primitive times, individuals sought redress from those who wronged them by any means they saw fit. Later, when group customs and mores developed, individual retribution was somewhat supplanted by group retribution. Even later, as states were formed and custom began to develop into law, the state became the instrument of punishment in place of the individual, the tribe, or kinfolk. Table 12-1 shows the general transformation of punishment, social relationships, and sanctions throughout Western history.

The student must realize that, fundamentally, correctional systems do not exist apart from the influence of society. Society determines how the correctional process is to be defined and develops the broad policy guidelines it expects corrections to adhere to. In the more heterogeneous and pluralistic societies and cultures of the Western world—particularly the United States— definitive guidelines as to the proper disposition and handling of the offender are more varied, as different attitudes prevail among society and find expression in the policy-making process. An excellent example of this is the issue of capital punishment. In more homogeneous societies where there is a greater similarity of attitudes based upon common culture and mores, it is possible to define more clearly and with greater social consensus both the seriousness of different acts of criminal behavior and the proper disposition of those who offend against the defined legal code.

TABLE 12-1 Historical Development of Law and Punishment

	Ca. 500,000–200,000 B.C.: Appearance of Genus Homo	Ca. 200,000–25,000 B.C.: Appearance of Early Modern Man	Ca. 25,000–3500 B.C.: Development of Rudimentary Religion	Ca. 3500–400 B.C. Development of First Criminal Codes	Ca. 400 B.C.–A.D. 500 Development of Roman Law	Ca. 500–1750: Medieval and Feudal Justice	Ca. 1750 to Present
Period							
Nature of Social Relationship							
	Pretribal	Incipient group and tribal	Intermediate group and tribal	Intermediate group and tribal	Advanced group and tribal; incipient organized state	Feudal and intermediate organized state	Advanced organized state
Sanctions							
	?	Incipient customs and mores	Intermediate customs and mores	Customs and mores; incipient laws	Customs and rudimentary laws	Customs and common law	Statutory laws
Form of Punishment							
	Personal retribution	Personal retribution; group and tribal retribution	Personal retribution; group and tribal retribution	Personal retribution; group and tribal retribution; state retribution	State retribution; group and tribal retribution; personal retribution	State and ecclesiastical retribution	State retribution, reformation, rehabilitation, and reintegration
	Injury, torture, death			Torture, injury, death, banishment, forfeiture		Torture, forfeiture, injury, death, excommunication, banishment	Fine, supervision, incarceration, death

Philosophical Bases for Corrections

Punishment

Over the centuries, corrections has been synonymous with punishment. Even today, this attitude is held by a sizable segment of the American public, particularly in cases involving more serious crimes. If basic attitudes toward punishment have not changed, at least the means of employing punishment have. Today, we use more ''humane'' techniques, and society has been given the responsibility to act as the agent of punishment in behalf of the victim rather than permitting the private settling of feuds. The response of punishment has, in some cases, been defended as permitting the offender the feeling of having atoned for his actions while reaffirming among the law-abiding members of society the appropriateness of their noncriminal behavior.

Deterrence

Next in importance as a meaningful principle of corrections is deterrence, that is, the concept that the imposition of some form of punishment will diminish the incidence of criminal behavior in a society. This idea of deterrence arose in Italy and England during the latter part of the eighteenth century. Judges at that time had very broad discretion to render retributive punishments to offenders, and sentences and forms of punishment were often completely out of proportion to the seriousness of crimes.[1] The proponents of what we now refer to as the classical school of criminology were outraged by these excessive punishments. It was their belief that the ultimate objective of punishment was not punishment for the mere sake of punishment, but to deter criminal behavior, and therefore penalties should be no greater than to prevent the occurrence of crime. In this vein, Jeremy Bentham (1748-1832), an English judge, philosopher, and prolific writer, introduced the concept of the ''hedonistic calculus,'' whereby punishment would be rendered in proportion to the seriousness of the crime. It was his belief that criminal behavior would be effectively deterred by punishing an offender to the point where the pain of punishment was slightly greater than the pleasure received by the one committing the offense. The same pleasure-pain principle would also deter those who were merely potential offenders.

Isolation

Society has also subscribed to the idea that offenders should be isolated from lawful members of society in order not to contaminate the law-abiding and in an effort to protect society from those who by their criminal acts would prey upon others. This was the major impetus behind exile and transportation as ways of dealing with the offender. Even after the curtailment of exile and transportation, this purpose of corrections remained and was expressed in the fortresslike structure and security precautions characteristic of many early prisons. This same attitude often prevails today and is openly expressed in the hostility many communities have shown toward the establishment of correctional institutions or community treatment programs for offenders and narcotic addicts in their areas.

Rehabilitation

Another philosophical goal of corrections which has received a great deal of emphasis in recent years due to the efforts of the "new penology" is rehabilitation. This goal links criminal behavior with abnormality or some form of deficiency in the criminal. It assumes that human behavior is the product of antecedent causes. The goal then is to identify these antecedent conditions and in so doing to understand the inadequacy, be it physical, moral, mental, social, vocational, or academic. Once the offender's problems are diagnosed and classified for treatment, the offender can be corrected by appropriate psychological or physical therapy, counseling, education, or vocational training. Unfortunately, it is now being recognized that the goal of rehabilitation, regardless of how laudable it may sound and how it appeals to our more humane instincts, suffers from a number of weaknesses which make it very elusive.

First, in many cases we are unable to identify what these particular antecedent conditions are and how they possibly interact in causing criminal behavior. For example, how can we say with any assurance that poverty and lack of education were the causes for the criminal behavior of an offender when there are many well-to-do citizens with high levels of education who also commit crimes of various types and, conversely, poor people with little formal education who are noncriminal? How then can we measure in any meaningful way whether the treatment program we devise is really correcting the problem? Secondly, the rehabilitative philosophy assumes the characteristic of a medical model which implies that the offender is somehow "sick" in that he cannot adjust to society. This is fallacious reasoning. He may be well aware of what he is doing and completely rational in deciding for himself that involvement in crime has a higher personal payoff than legitimate behavior. The rehabilitative model also assumes that the one being treated must accept or learn to accept the values of those treating him even though their backgrounds, perceptions, and attitudes may be completely different. This is a particularly questionable assumption in prisons today where increasingly larger percentages of inmates are expressing open hostility to the assumptions of the rehabilitative model. They perceive themselves as de facto political prisoners·or as victims of society's capricious system of laws and justice which operates under a dual standard for the poor and well-to-do.[2] In these instances, rehabilitative personnel are seen as agents of the establishment who are trying to brainwash them into accepting their view of society.[3]

Many critics of this model also claim that the rehabilitative ideal, which says that it is therapeutic in nature, takes on a punitive harshness in application. They point to the rehabilitative ideals underlying the founding of the juvenile courts and sexual psychopath laws as examples of rehabilitative ideals gone awry.[4] The report on the experiences of the Attica prison rebellion pointed out the hard fact that rehabilitation and reform are often no more than a facade. In the words of the official commission's report:

> Prison administrators throughout the country have continued pledging their dedication to the concept of rehabilitation while continuing to run prisons constructed in the style and operated in the manner of the 19th century walled fortresses. "Security" has continued to be the dominant theme: The fantasy of reform legitimatized, but the functionalism of custody has perpetuated them.[5]

Reintegration

The newest philosophical basis for corrections is reintegration of the offender into the free community. This model is a more realistic extension of the rehabilitative philosophy and tries to compensate for the weaknesses of that approach while adopting some of its more acceptable ideas. It sees the cause of crime and the functions of corrective efforts along two dimensions. Like the rehabilitative model, it views the offender as needing some help and at the same time recognizes that criminal behavior is often a result of disjunction between the offender and society. It is this characteristic which separates it from the rehabilitative model. In the rehabilitation model, emphasis is focused on treating the offender as an isolated entity and looking for the cause of behavior as emanating from within the individual. The reintegrative model realizes that society and the individual are inseparable considerations, and so the offender's environment is also emphasized. If the individual is to be helped, this must be accomplished by assisting him to cope with the forces of the everyday environment to which he will return upon his release from prison rather than isolating and trying to "treat" him in the highly structured and artificial world of a penitentiary or other similar institution.

This approach stresses community-based institutional treatment where the individual can be assisted in a more "natural" environment so that when he is eventually released from custody, he can adjust better to postinstitutional life. In this philosophy of corrections, contact and interaction with positive elements of the free society are an important part of the overall treatment program. This appears to be the direction that corrections has been moving in the past few years and probably will continue to increasingly emphasize in the future.

Courtesy of the Salem Witch Museum, Salem, Massachusetts

HISTORICAL DEVELOPMENT OF CORRECTIONAL RESPONSES

The European Heritage

Fleeing social and legal injustices and seeking a land where they could worship God as they saw fit, the Pilgrims came to America with the heritage of their English customs, laws, and institutions for dealing with the criminal. Part of this heritage was a repressive criminal code and the use of gaols for the incarceration of offenders.

However, the gaols of that period served different purposes than the jails we are now accustomed to. During the Middle Ages and up until the time of American colonization, imprisonment had three purposes: temporary detention awaiting trial, a means of exerting pressure for payment of fines, and temporary confinement before being placed into servitude.[6] This concept of the purposes of jails came with the early colonists to America. Punishment for various offenses still called for death, mutilation, public whippings, or placing the offender in the stocks. The idea of separate jails or prisons explicitly for the purpose of the long-term incarceration of offenders was practically unknown. Instead, gatehouses, towers, cellars, and barracks became temporary detention facilities which held the offender until he was disposed of in some manner.

Operated by private keepers for the sake of personal profit and populated by the ill, by felons, misdemeanants, and debtors, by men, women, and children—all of whom were congregated together totally unsegregated—these gaols had developed a notorious reputation for their wanton depravity and the spread of pestilence.[7] Since the private keepers relied on profit, a fee system developed by which inmates were charged for better meals, service of prostitutes, removal to better quarters, admission and discharge service, and a host of other considerations, all of which were made available for the right price. Without the resources to pay these fees, however, the majority of the inmates were left to suffer in the filth of these unsupervised and disorderly cesspools. It was this legacy that the early English and European colonists brought with them to the New World.

Early American Institutions

The colonies of Massachusetts and Pennsylvania share the credit for the first colonial attempts to develop an alternative to the corporal and capital punishments that were dispensed under the king's justice as the only means to deal with offenders. The idea began to form that long-term incarceration might be an effective and more enlightened substitute. In 1632, Boston became the site of a small wooden building that might be called the first prison in the colonies. It served for six years as the only such institution in the Massachusetts Bay Colony. In 1638, a second and even smaller institution was established in New Plymouth. By 1655, the general court of the Massachusetts Bay Colony felt that there was a growing need for institutions to house petty offenders, drunkards, and debtors. It was proposed that such institutions should be established in each county, and the counties were authorized to build such facilities. Although it would be many years before such an institutional arrangement would become a reality, a few counties did establish such institutions at that time.

In 1784, Massachusetts established the first known centralized institution in North America for housing offenders sentenced to long-term incarceration. Unlike its predecessors in Boston and New Plymouth, it accepted prisoners from throughout the colony rather than just local offenders. The facility was located on Castle Island in Boston Harbor and received prisoners who were sentenced to long terms or for life at hard labor. However, the state felt that the Boston Harbor facility was not secure enough to house long-term desperate offenders, and it was abandoned in 1800 in favor of a maximum-security prison which had just been built at Charlestown.[8]

The Development of the Pennsylvania System

The early colonists in Pennsylvania were members of the Society of Friends or, as they came to be known, the Quakers. On grounds of religion and humanitarianism, they were opposed to what they perceived as a harsh and barbaric code of criminal justice that was embodied in the English law that had prevailed in the colony since its founding. In 1682, William Penn's first assembly passed "The Great Law," which incorporated the Quaker criminal code and was much more humane than the English criminal law. However, the king of England did not look favorably upon this attempt to repeal the English law. He saw it as another attempt by the colonists to question his country's right of sovereignty over the colonies. Threatening direct military intervention, he forced the Quakers to repeal their newly enacted criminal code.

Up to the outbreak of the American Revolution, the Quakers continued to protest the harshness of the English code and constantly sought to reform it. By 1762, they had succeeded in having the list of capital offenses reduced to first-degree murder and had instituted fines and imprisonment in lieu of death or torture for many offenses. After the American Revolution, the Quakers turned their attention to prison reform and began to formulate ideas on better ways to handle and reform criminals. In May 1787, a group of Quakers formed the Philadelphia Society for Alleviating the Miseries of Public Prisons and set about immediately to redress the shocking conditions found in Philadelphia's Walnut Street Jail. This society, consisting of many of the leading citizens of the city, sought legislative approval for transforming the Walnut Street Jail into a prison. Approval for the conversion was granted, and this facility is recognized by penal historians as the first true prison in America.

The members of the Philadelphia Society were committed to the following ideas: First, the control of prisons should be by voluntary citizens who would make up an unpaid board of inspectors. This was considered a means by which more efficient, less costly, and more humane treatment could be given the prisoners. Second, public labor by prisoners should be abolished and "more private or even solitary labor" should be substituted.[9] Third, reformation would occur through an individual offender's being subject to solitude, where he could "reflect" on his past offenses and atone for his actions.

The Pennsylvania legislature passed a law authorizing all county courts, at their discretion, to send to the Walnut Street Jail convicts sentenced to hard labor for terms of more than one year.[10] For the more hardened offenders, there were sixteen solitary cells in a specially constructed "penitentiary house" adjacent to the Walnut Street Jail. These cells each measured 6 feet wide, 8 feet long, and 9 feet high. In addition, six similar cells were constructed on the ground floor of one of the workshops where convicts could labor in total solitude.

Offenders convicted of more serious crimes were confined in the solitary cells. These prisoners were not permitted to have visitors or any contact with the outside world except for an occasional visit by a clergyman. They performed no labor, but were to spend their solitary existence contemplating their sins and atoning for their crime. Each of the cells had double doors and a small hatch that covered the single tiny window which was locked from the outside. In this way, the convict was exposed to almost total darkness even during the day. The prisoner was fed a daily diet of maize and molasses. For a primitive toilet, a large uncovered leaden pipe in the floor of each cell led to an outside sewer in the prison courtyard. The only heat was provided by a totally inadequate, small stove in the common corridor of the cell block.

Offenders who were considered more tractable or who had been sentenced for less serious crimes lived together in eight rooms where they worked together at carpentry, shoemaking, weaving, and nail making. The unskilled prisoners were given more menial tasks to perform. The few women sent to the Walnut Street Jail lived together in other quarters and were employed spinning cotton, carding wool, preparing flax and hemp, washing, and mending. Unlike the male prisoners, the women were permitted to engage in conversation in the shops and during meals. The men were forced to work in total silence, but some conversation was permitted prior to retiring at night. Each of the male prisoners was credited with roughly the prevailing wage for the particular work he performed. Out of this was deducted the cost of his maintenance, his trial and his fine. If he still owed money for his maintenance when his sentence expired, he was held in confinement until the debt was fully paid. If, on the other hand, he had money coming to him for his labors, he was given it in full. During the period of confinement, special emphasis was placed upon the value of religious services and the development of Christian ideals.[11]

Under such leadership and organization, the Walnut Street Jail became, in the words of its founders, "the happy reformation of the penal system. The prison is no longer a scene of debauchery, idleness and profanity; an epitome of human wretchedness; a seminary of crimes destructive to society; but a school of reformation and a place of public labor."[12] However, this success was short-lived. Increasingly, larger numbers of more serious offenders were sent to the Walnut Street Jail for longer sentences, and it soon was so crowded that it became a mere warehouse of humanity. The original unpaid, supervisory board of citizen-inspectors was supplanted by Philadelphia politicians, who took over the operation and management of the institution. As a result, after 1800 the Philadelphia Society became a force of opposition and campaigned bitterly for the reenactment of their form of penal system.

The principles governing the Pennsylvania system advocated by the Quakers were well expressed by Robert Vaux in his *Letter on the Penitentiary System of Pennsylvania* in 1827:

1. Prisoners should not be treated with revenge; but rather in a manner to convince them that the way of the transgressor is hard and by selective forms of suffering they can be made to amend their lives.

2. To prevent the experience of imprisonment becoming a corrupting experience, prisoners should be kept in solitary confinement.

3. Solitary confinement and the seclusion it affords will give the offender the opportunity for deep reflection and moral guidance so that he may repent for his transgressions.

4. Solitary confinement offers the same variety of discipline as any other mode affords. It is particularly punishing to man, who by his very nature is a social animal.

5. Solitary confinement is more economical since prisoners will; a) not have to be sentenced for such long periods of time for the required penitential experience, b) fewer keepers will be required, c) expenditures for clothing will be diminished.[13]

In 1818, the Commonwealth of Pennsylvania began construction of the Western Penitentiary at Pittsburgh on the principles of the Pennsylvania system. One hundred ninety solitary cells, measuring 7 by 9 feet each, were constructed in a semicircle around the central prison yard. However, this arrangement quickly proved to be inappropriate, as effective solitary isolation was not provided and the cells were too small to permit solitary labor. As a result, by 1833 the board of managers recommended the demolition of the prison because it was unsuitable for the purposes for which it was originally designed.[14]

The Development of the Auburn Plan

Thomas Eddy, a Quaker philanthropist from New York became impressed with the work of the Philadelphia Society and how it had transformed the Walnut Street Jail into a prison. He also fell under the spell of Cesare Beccaria, who in 1764 published his very influential *Essay on Crime and Punishments*. The purpose of this monumental essay was to call attention to the need to make punishment less arbitrary and severe than it had been, and it argued quite eloquently for the need to eliminate the excessive reliance on capital punishment.[15] Under Eddy's guidance, Newgate Prison opened near New York City in 1797, and he became the first warden. Newgate consisted of fifty-four rooms and was constructed as a *congregate prison;* that is, convicts were lodged together in large rooms with eight prisoners to a room. A rather extensive system of prison industries employed the inmates, and as in the early days of the Walnut Street Jail, the prisoners were paid the prevailing wage for their work less the cost of their maintenance and trial. Immediate problems arose with the system of congregate lodging, and politicians began to meddle in the operation of the institution and eventually took over the management and control of the prison itself. In a short time, overcrowding aggravated moral contamination and created disorder. Mass pardons favored obedient prisoners over penitent and reformed criminals, and as a result, Eddy resigned in 1803.[16]

This "failure" of the Newgate Prison led to what has been called the Auburn plan of prison program and design. It was recognized that there was a certain

value to permitting prisoners to work together at congregate labor as Newgate
had done and which the Pennsylvania system with its emphasis on solitary
confinement did not effectively provide for. However, the experiences at Newgate also indicated the disadvantages of congregate work and housing facilities
in terms of the potential for disorder. Somehow, the best features of both
Newgate and the Pennsylvania system would have to be incorporated.

In 1816, New York began the construction of a new prison at Auburn. In
1819, the prison opened with a master carpenter as the warden and a hatter as his
assistant. Originally, the prison was to have been constructed after the model
provided by the Pennsylvania system, with its emphasis on solitary confinement. However, it was felt that the cost of constructing separate solitary cells
would be prohibitive, and so only a few such cells were built to meet the
requirements of the law as to solitary confinement and to provide a solitary
cellblock for disciplinary cases. As a result, most of the prisoners were housed
in large, congregate night rooms.

In the first few years of operation, an experiment was conducted in which a
classification or grading system was devised. The most incorrigible offenders
were placed in solitary cells without labor in order to test the relative merits of
the Pennsylvania system over the congregate system in terms of reformative
effects. In the second category, less recalcitrant prisoners were also placed in
solitary confinement with labor being provided as a form of recreation and
reward. In the third category were the most tractable offenders and those who
appeared to have the best chance of reforming. In this grade, the prisoners
worked together as a group during the day and were secluded at night.[17] The
experiment was abandoned in 1823 as a failure. Particularly obvious was the
terrible impact of idleness and solitary confinement on the minds of inmates. A
large number of those confined to solitary went insane and horribly mutilated
themselves or committed suicide. In addition, solitary confinement without
labor had deleterious effects on the physical health of men, and most of them
were severely impaired for life. As a result, the governor in 1823 pardoned most
of the inmates who had been confined to solitary cells.

However, in the open-congregate system, problems of control, discipline,
contraband smuggling, and inmate corruption similar to the experience of
Newgate began to develop. As a result, a compromise plan was adopted which
became known as the Auburn system. Under this system, instead of mingling
freely in the yard, workrooms, and congregate sleeping quarters, prisoners
were permitted to associate with each other only during the day in order to
permit maximum industrial production. This association, however, was conducted in strict silence, and the rule of total and perpetual silence was harshly
enforced. Nor was the prisoner permitted to communicate with anyone on the
outside except under the most unusual circumstances. At night, the prisoners
were separated totally. This was felt to be necessary in order to eliminate the
corruption of prisoners by their fellow inmates and to reduce the opportunity for
inmates to develop plans that would be disruptive to the administration of the

institution. Another characteristic of the Auburn system was the emphasis placed on hard manual labor as a reformative tool and as a means of economic self-sufficiency for the prison. Warden Elam Lynds believed that adult convicts were hopelessly incorrigible and that industrial efficiency was the overriding purpose of the prison.[18] Finally, a great deal of emphasis was placed on the use of corporal punishment to maintain absolute discipline and obedience. Warden Lynds is reported to have said:

> I consider the chastisement by the whip the most efficient and at the same time the most humane which exists; it never injures health and obliges the prisoners to lead a life essentially healthy. Solitary confinement, on the contrary, is often insufficient and always dangerous. I have seen many prisoners in my life whom it was impossible to subdue in this manner and who only left the solitary cell to go to the hospital. I consider it impossible to govern a large prison without a whip. Those who know human nature from books only may say the contrary.[19]

The Controversy over the Pennsylvania and Auburn Systems

A hot controversy arose over the relative merits of the Pennsylvania and Auburn plans. The Philadelphia Society pushed for the adoption of the Pennsylvania system, while the Boston Society for the Improvement of Prison Discipline and the Reformation of Juvenile Offenders supported the Auburn plan.[20] Both societies were convinced of the merits of their plans, and both groups were zealous crusaders for reform as well as completely unscrupulous in their use of statistics to prove their arguments. The controversy even spilled over into other nations that were developing prisons modeled after America's system. In addition, famous international figures became involved in the controversy. Charles Dickens, after a visit to America, extensively criticized the Pennsylvania system in his *American Notes*. However, Beaumont and de Tocqueville praised it quite highly.[21] In fact, most European countries were in favor of the Pennsylvania system and adopted it in a modified form.

The single, most instrumental spokesman for the Auburn system was Reverend Louis Dwight, who, as secretary of the Boston Society, traveled extensively to proselytize the merits of the Auburn system. He became the best-known American prison expert during the first half of the nineteenth century and was particularly influential in convincing the states to adopt the Auburn system. His arguments focused attention on the economics of each system. Under the Auburn system, prison construction costs were less because of the reduced emphasis on total solitary confinement. Also, the use of congregate inmate labor had definite revenue-producing advantages. As a result, the Auburn system was adopted by all the states except Pennsylvania and New Jersey. In a short time, even these two states abandoned the Pennsylvania solitary system because overcrowding forced the placing of two men in a cell. All this controversy and the attention it focused on prisons was responsible, however,

TABLE 12-2   Early American Prisons, 1790–1835

State	Name and Location of Prison	Years of Receiving First Prisoner
Pennsylvania	Walnut Street Jail, Philadelphia	1790
New York	Newgate Prison, New York City	1797
New Jersey	State Penitentiary, Lamberton	1798
Kentucky	State Penitentiary, Frankfort	1800
Virginia	State Penitentiary, Richmond	1800
Massachusetts	State Prison, Charlestown	1805
Vermont	State Prison, Windsor	1809
Maryland	State Penitentiary, Baltimore	1812
New Hampshire	State Prison, Concord	1812
Ohio	State Penitentiary, Columbus	1816
Georgia	State Penitentiary, Milledgeville	1817
New York	Auburn Prison, Auburn	1819
Tennessee	State Prison, Nashville	1831
Illinois	State Penitentiary, Alton	1833
Louisiana	State Penitentiary, Baton Rouge	1835

Source: Wayne Morse (ed.), *The Attorney General's Survey of Release Procedures* Washington, D.C.: U.S. Government Printing Office, 1940).

for the creation in America, by 1835, of the first genuine penal system in the world. The development of this system is summarized in Table 12-2.

EARLY BRITISH ADVANCES IN PENOLOGY

During the seventeenth century, as mentioned, the criminal code in England was quite harsh, with over 200 offenses calling for the death penalty. Historians give several explanations for this emphasis on capital punishment as an appropriate response to criminal behavior. First, the British government did not feel that long-term incarceration or transporting offenders to penal colonies served as an effective deterrent to criminal acts. Nor did the government have any faith in gaols or gaol keepers as being able to bring about the required repentance on the part of the offender. Furthermore, many English people opposed creating a centralized police force and prison system because of their fear that these could easily become tools of monarchical and political oppression. Government was committed to the ideas that property rights of the middle and upper class must be protected against the criminal "rabble" and that order maintenance was a primary function of government. Disregarding the social conditions facing the lower class which spawned these property offenses, the government increasingly passed legislation authorizing the imposition of the death sentence for more and more property crimes.

Nonetheless, it was recognized that convicted offenders could serve the crown by being transported to the New World to labor in such remote places as Virginia, Georgia, and the West Indies. When the use of black slaves grew, the

Courtesy of the Federal Bureau of Prisons

need for penal labor diminished in the colonies, and the practice of transporting convicts came to an abrupt halt when the American colonies declared their independence. The problem now became one of finding a place to house prisoners and providing some useful activity during their period of incarceration. In 1776, the practice was adopted of employing prisoners to clean the Thames and to build docks.[22]

To accomplish this, the convicts were quartered in old ships that were anchored in the Thames and later moved to Gibraltar. Serious epidemics were a frequent occurrence aboard these hulks, and Parliament, afraid of the spread of contagion, passed the Hard Labor Act in 1779, which called for the construction of two permanent, long-term penitentiaries. These prisons, however, were not built. Captain Cook's discovery of Australia in 1770 focused the attention of Parliament on this remote and barren colony as a possible dumping ground for the convicts now quartered in the hulks.

The first contingent of felons departed from Spithead, England, on May 13, 1787, in a flotilla of eleven vessels, nine of which carried convicts. Altogether, there were 552 male and 190 female prisoners, some of whom were pregnant. The voyage lasted eight months. The ships were supposed to have enough supplies to last two years, but because of dockside pilferage and the fact that many necessary items were simply forgotten, there was no clothing for the women, many of whom were nearly nude, and no medicine or ammunition even for the marines guarding the prisoners, and even they mutinied because of the terrible conditions.

These ships became known as "floating hells" because of the corruption among the shipowners and crews, who starved the prisoners and overloaded the ships in order to maximize their profits. The ships' crews often drew lots for the female felons aboard, many of whom were glad to escape from the fetid compartments below deck in which they were chained.

Reform Efforts

While these practices were occurring, reform groups were developing in England which would have a significant impact on the future of British penology. Influenced by the philosophies and practices of such individuals as Cesare Beccaria, Jeremy Bentham, Samuel Romilly, James Mackintosh, and Sir Robert Peel, increasing pressure was being applied to Parliament to mitigate the harshness of the criminal law. Frequent debate in the House of Commons raged over the retention or abolition of the death penalty for the commission of many offenses. It was particularly through Romilly's efforts that Parliament appointed, in 1819, a Committee of Inquiry into the Criminal Laws. This committee's report called for the modification of the harsh criminal code and focused further attention on the need to reform existing means of dealing with offenders.

John Howard

Certainly one of the most influential reformers of this period was John Howard, whose publication of *State of Prisons* in 1777 made him the focus for prison reform movements. His contributions to prison management and reform had a significant impact not only in Great Britain, but in continental Europe and America as well. Howard became the high sheriff of Bedfordshire in 1773, and in his official capacity saw abuses in prison which he had never dreamed existed. In 1775, he left England and traveled across the continent of Europe, visiting prisons and jails. It was from these journeys that he gathered the data for his later publication. He proposed a number of "correct principles" that should guide penal administration and the handling of convicts, which in the years ahead were widely adopted. Some of these principles were:

1. Women offenders should be segregated from males and young offenders from old and hardened criminals.
2. Gaolers should be honest, active and humane . . . and should have salaries proportioned to the trust and trouble.
3. No prisoner should be subject to any demand for fees. The gaoler should have a salary in lieu of having to rely on fees.
4. There should be provisions for an infirmary, a chaplain and a proper diet of wholesome food.
5. Separate cells for each prisoner should be provided as well as linen and bedding and stoves to warm the day-room in winter.[23]

Sir Robert Peel

Another notable penal reformer was Sir Robert Peel. In 1821, Peel was appointed as home secretary, and he immediately set about to reform the criminal code and to apply Howard's principles to local prisons. As a result, capital statutes were revised and consolidated, reducing the number of capital offenses from 200 to 14. In addition, a statutory framework for an effective prison system was created which included requirements for proper health and sanitation facilities, the humane treatment of prisoners, and the segregation of sexes. The severity of punishment for minor offenses was also reduced. Nonetheless, prisoners were still treated far differently than they are today. Prisoners were required to wear masks in the corridors and during the exercise period, sat in separated pigeonholes in chapel, and worked a crank in solitary cells to earn meals.[24]

Alexander Maconochie

In 1840, Alexander Maconochie, a captain in the Royal Navy, began four years of command at a penal colony known as Norfolk Island off the coast of Australia. He was one of the most astute and progressive administrators ever known to penology. It was his firm belief that brutality and cruelty debase the prisoner as well as the society that would tolerate such treatment, and he was committed to the idea that a prisoner should be treated in such a manner that he would be fit to return to society completely devoid of the hostility and criminality that had made him an offender.

He developed a plan for the administration of the penal colony which he called his "apparatus." This plan called for the following provisions:

1. Sentences should not be for a period of time, but for the performance of a specified and determined quantity of labor; in brief, time sentences should be abolished and task sentences substituted;

2. The quantity of labor a prisoner must perform should be expressed in a number of "marks" which he must earn by improvement of conduct, frugality of living and habits of industry before he can be released;

3. While in prison, he should earn everything he receives; all sustenance and indulgences should be added to his debt of marks;

4. When qualified by discipline to do so, he should work in association with a small number of other prisoners, forming a group of six or seven, and the whole group should be answerable for the conduct and labor of each member of it;

5. In the final stage, a prisoner while still obligated to earn his daily tally of marks, should be financially compensated for his labor and be subject to a less rigorous discipline in order to prepare him for his release and return to society.[25]

Maconochie tried to restore some semblance of dignity to the convicts' lives. He abolished the use of flogging or chains as disciplinary measures except in extreme cases. By being compensated for their labor, prisoners could obtain the financial means to arrange for their families to join them. To encourage the development of responsibility among the inmates, a system was established by which an inmate could become a work foreman. In addition, the first form of inmate governance was developed which permitted certain convicts to participate in making decisions about the operations of the penal colony.

Unfortunately, as is often the case, Maconochie was a man far ahead of his time whose actions were misunderstood. The board of overseers of the Australian penal colonies, as well as the guards at the Norfolk colony, were bitterly opposed to his methods and openly resented the innovations. The guards particularly were used to compelling obedience through corporal punishment and did not accept or understand the value of alternative methods. In addition, many of the prisoners were the most intractable ones who were prior offenders and had been sentenced to Norfolk Island as a last resort.[26] In 1844, the board of overseers relieved Maconochie of command, charging that the "wholesale and invigorating influence of a firm and resolute discipline had disappeared without promised improvements in moral character." The real reason was that Maconochie's "apparatus" had increased operational expenses.[27]

The Tickets of Leave

England, in 1857, passed the Penal Servitude Act, which ended the transportation of offenders. Now it became necessary to find some other method for handling those offenders who in the past had been shipped off to the penal colonies and forgotten. Parliament was very reluctant to spend the money necessary to build institutions for long-term incarceration. Instead, in order to reduce the numbers of prisoners serving sentences, legislation was passed establishing a ticket-of-leave system whereby prisoners who had served a year of congregate labor could earn, by hard work and good conduct, a conditional release and thus be permitted to return to their homes before the completion of their sentences. The only conditions that they had to adhere to were that they must abstain from crime and find legitimate employment. This ticket-of-leave system had originated earlier in the Australian penal colonies. However, as Johnson points out:

> Half measures did not alleviate prison conditions. The Prisons Act of 1857 transferred ownership and control of all municipal prisons to the national government. Imprisonment which had become the major penal tool, after playing a secondary role to the gallows and transportation to penal colonies, did not signal the triumph of humanitarianism over repression as attitudes and behavior still fluctuated from retribution and repression to less harsh methods.[28]

Finally, in the second half of the nineteenth century the English government recognized that it was necessary to build prisons to house convicts sentenced to long terms of imprisonment, and construction began.

Crofton and the Irish System

The prisons in Ireland, like those in England, were not producing the reformed prisoners required for the effective use of tickets of leave. Additional punishment of the inmates only seemed to worsen the situation. In 1854, Sir Walter Crofton was appointed chairman of the board of directors of the Irish prisons. Within a few years, he became convinced that prisoners must be trained "naturally to a state of reformation for without the required reformation, the public would never accept the released prisoner."[29] To accomplish this, he abandoned the more flagrant forms of corporal punishment and reserved the use of such physical punishment to extreme cases only. He also instituted a policy whereby the inmates were to be treated as "men" and not as "convicts."

To achieve this objective, he introduced a system of incarceration, consisting of three stages which, in time, became known as the Irish system. In the first stage, the inmate was confined in a semisolitary situation at the prison at Mountjay, Dublin, under close discipline. For the first four months, the prisoner was on a restricted diet and performed menial tasks. During the second four months, the experienced tailors and shoemakers were put to work at their trades, providing their services to the maintenance of the prison. One hour of schooling was provided daily to all but the most intractable offenders, who were segregated and kept in chains on a reduced diet. For the most part, this schooling consisted of only the most elementary form of subject matter, and particular emphasis was placed on familiarizing the student with the mark system and the ticket of leaves.

If the prisoner warranted consideration, he was transferred after eight months to Spike Island Prison to labor on the military and penal fortifications in the area. A system of four conduct classes was implemented at this stage which required that he display the proper demeanor and industriousness at work and that he successively engage in the schooling that was provided at this institution. He earned marks for his satisfactory behavior, and each step required the accumulation of a certain number of marks. In addition, small wages were paid according to the conduct class the inmate was in.

Those that indicated promise and reformation were transferred to the third stage, which consisted of a number of small prison units of less than 100 inmates who labored on projects such as harbor and land reclamation under the supervision of only a few unarmed guards under working conditions similar to those found in the outside world. As a consequence, the inmate's behavior could be observed under less enforced discipline, and this stage would serve as a period of transition from imprisonment to eventual conditional release. It was Crofton's feeling that this display of trust was important to the inmate, as well as being necessary to convince the public that prisoners could be trusted. Special emphasis at this stage was upon lectures which stressed the advantages of leading a law-abiding life, maintaining regular employment, and avoiding evil companions.[30] The moral instructor, J. P. Organ, was active in seeking employment for those released on tickets of leave and continued to visit the released offender and supervise his conduct after he returned to free society.[31]

The Irish system seemed to be working well. Through Crofton's efforts, prison populations were reduced, tickets of leave were more frequently given, and fewer released prisoners were being returned to prison for new crimes. Reformers felt that he was on the right track, but in 1862 a general increase in crime in Great Britain resulted in a backlash of public and legislative anger. Special legislation was passed by members of Parliament who favored long sentences and more severe and restrictive policies. In addition, increased political and bureaucratic centralization of the prison system destroyed any chances for innovative programs. In this setting, the Irish system was abandoned in favor of more "traditional" responses.

This then is the legacy of today's correctional systems. In the chapters on corrections which follow, we will examine some of the other traditional methods of dealing with offenders, prison systems as they exist today, and innovative ways to deal with offenders.

SUMMARY

For most of human history the only disposition available to one who violated the legal norms of society was punishment, and only in the past 200 years has imprisonment replaced physical torture, enslavery, or mutilation as the method of punishment. Since the advent of the twentieth century, society has become concerned about the rehabilitation and reintegration of offenders.

In the United States two approaches to corrections competed in the nineteenth century: the Pennsylvania system of solitary confinement and the Auburn plan of congregate forced labor. The economic advantages of the Auburn plan led to its wide adoption.

In Great Britain, a few individuals such as Howard, Maconochie, and Crofton questioned the traditional approaches to corrections, and their principles provided the foundation for modern corrections.

Suggested Additional Readings

Barnes, Harry Elmer. *The Story of Punishment*. Boston: Stratford, 1930.
Burns, Henry, Jr. *Corrections: Organization and Administration*. St. Paul, Minn.: West, 1975.

Conrad, John. *Crime and Its Correction*. Berkeley: University of California Press, 1965.

Heath, James. *Eighteenth-Century Penal Theory*. London: Oxford University Press, 1963.

Honderich, Ted. *Punishment: The Supposed Justifications*. Middlesex, England: Penguin, 1969.

Ives, George. *A History of Penal Methods*. London: Stanley Paul, 1914.

Jones, Howard. "Punishment and Social Values." In Grygier Tadeusz, Howard Jones, and John C. Spencer, eds., *Criminology in Transition*. London: Tavistock, 1965, pp. 1-23.

Lewis, Orlando F. *The Development of American Prisons and Prison Customs, 1776-1845*. Albany, N.Y.: Prison Association of New York, 1922.

Menninger, Karl. *The Crime of Punishment*. New York: Viking, 1968.

Rusche, George, and O. Kirchheimer. *Punishment and Social Structure*. New York: Columbia University Press, 1939.

Sellin, Thorsten. "A Look at Prison History." *Federal Probation*, 18 (September 1967).

Sutherland, Edwin. *Criminology*. Philadelphia: Lippincott, 1924.

Teeters, Negley K. *They Were in Prison*. Philadelphia: Winston, 1937

———— and John D. Shearer. *The Prison at Philadelphia: Cherry Hill*. New York: Columbia University Press, 1957.

Notes

1. Paul W. Tappan, *Crime, Justice and Correction* (New York: McGraw-Hill, 1960), p. 243.

2. James W. L. Park, "What Is a Political Prisoner?" *American Journal of Corrections* (November/December 1972): 22–23.

3. Notes from a discussion with inmates of Southern Michigan Prison, Jackson, Mich. during a series of meetings in 1975.

4. Francis A. Allen, "Criminal Justice, Legal Values and the Rehabilitative Ideal," *The Journal of Criminal Law, Criminology and Police Science*, 50 (September-October 1959): 226–232.

5. New York State Special Commission on Attica, *Attica* (New York: Bantam, 1972), p. 2.

6. Elmer H. Johnson, *Crime, Correction and Society*, rev. ed. (Homewood, Ill: Dorsey, 1968), p. 477.

7. Lionel W. Fox, *The English Prison and Borstal System* (London: Routledge, 1952), pp. 20-21.

8. American Correctional Association, *Manual of Correctional Standards* (Washington, D.C.: American Correctional Association, 1966), p. 3.

9. Thorsten Sellin, "The Origin of the Pennsylvania System of Prison Discipline," *Prison Journal* 50 (Spring-Summer 1970): 14.

10. Ibid.

11. Orlando F. Lewis, *The Development of American Prisons and Prison Customs, 1776-1845* (Albany: Prison Association of New York, 1922), pp. 26-28.

12. Francis C. Gray, *Prison Discipline in America* (London: J. Murray, 1848) p. 22.

13. Sellin, op. cit., pp. 15-17.

14. Lewis, op. cit., pp. 43-57.

15. Cesare Beccaria, *An Essay on Crimes and Punishment* (London: Almon, 1967).

16. Johnson, op. cit., p. 485.

17. Lewis, op. cit., p. 80.

18. Ibid., pp. 86-95.

19. Gustave de Beaumont and Alexis de Tocqueville, *On the Penitentiary System in the United States and Its Application in France* (Carbondale: Southern Illinois University Press, 1964), p. 201.

20. See Steward H. Holbrook, *Dreamers of the American Dream* (New York: Doubleday, 1957), pp. 240-244.

21. Beaumont and de Tocqueville, op. cit., pp. 57-58.

22. William Branch-Johnson, *The English Prison Hulks* (London: Christoper Johnson, 1957), p. 3.

23. John Howard, *State of Prisons, 1777,* in George G. Killinger and Pual F. Cromwell, Jr. (eds.), *Penology* (St. Paul, Minn.: West, 1973), pp. 5-11.

24. George Ives, *A History of Penal Methods* (London: Stanley Paul, 1944), pp. 182-186.

25. Quoted by John V. Barry in "Captain Alexander Maconochie," *The Victorian Historical Magazine,* 27 (2) (June 1957): 5.

26. Ibid., p. 79.

27. Ibid., p. 147.

28. Johnson, op. cit., pp. 492-493.

29. Ibid., p. 492.

30. Robert A. Terrell, *History of the Irish Prisons* (London: Trafalgar, 1929), p. 49.

Chapter 13

The Jail and Temporary Detention Facilities

Jails are local facilities usually used to house misdemeanants after they have been convicted and persons accused of crimes who have not yet appeared in court to answer the charges against them. Jails are also used for other purposes. A person found guilty of a felony is often remanded to the custody of the local jail while the court decides the appropriate sentence. Many jurisdictions authorize the courts to remand a material witness to a crime to jail if it appears that the individual's safety is jeopardized and he or she needs custodial protection or if there is reason to believe that the witness will flee the jurisdiction and therefore not be available to testify in court. In most cases, however, material witnesses are placed under protective custody in their own homes, with relatives in another city, or in a hotel rather than being confined in jail.

Thus, jails serve primarily as pretrial detention facilities for persons arrested for felonies and misdemeanors and as posttrial places of incarceration for convicted misdemeanants. If the arrestee cannot post bond, he will remain in the custody of the jail until the completion of his trial. If the accused is found guilty of a misdemeanor, which usually carries a sentence of one year or less, he will often be remanded to the jail to serve out the court-imposed sentence.

Jails are usually operated on a county basis under the authority of the county sheriff. In some larger cities, jails are operated at the municipal level and are under the administration of the local police. Although many smaller police departments have a cell or two for temporarily holding arrested persons, strictly speaking, these are not jails, but lockups. Those arrested for certain minor offenses, such as public drunkenness or driving under the influence, are detained in lockups until the next day or so, when they appear before the city magistrate to stand trial. The Law Enforcement Assistance Administration of the U.S. Department of Justice considers a jail to be a local place of confinement where inmates are confined for forty-eight hours or more.[1]

The *1970 National Jail Census* reported that there exist in the United States 4,037 locally administered jails with the authority to detain prisoners for forty-eight hours or longer. This number does not include jails in Delaware, Connecticut, and Rhode Island, where the local jails are administered and controlled by the state correctional departments. At the time the survey was taken in March 1970, these jails held 160,863 inmates, which included 7,800 juveniles.[2] More than half (52 percent) of the adults in these jails at the time of the survey had not as yet been convicted by the courts, and nearly two-thirds (66.1 percent) of the juveniles were similarly awaiting a formal hearing. Technically, these individuals were still innocent.

HISTORY OF JAILS: A SHAMEFUL LEGACY

The jail is the oldest institution for incarcerating offenders. American jails trace their ancestry to England, where gaols developed in the tenth century.[3] At that time the shire or county was a very important locus of government authority. Although the modern nation-state was developing, the state did not provide the local services and institutions required by people. As a consequence, a great deal of power and autonomy came to rest with counties, and jails became a part of the machinery of county government. The desire for local autonomy was particularly strong at that time. Some citizens unhappy with the power of counties wanted even greater autonomy in their political destinies and formed town governments. Along with the creation of town government arose town jails. Thus, county and municipal jails developed side by side.

By the late sixteenth and seventeenth centuries there existed two hundred "common jails" in England.[4] They were provided, owned, and administered by several different authorities. Responsibility for maintaining the county jail rested with the sheriff. Towns had their own jails under the jurisdiction of their own officials. Burns points out that practically every municipal corporation during this time, however small, might have its own jail.[5] Private jails were also established by various ecclesiastical orders, members of the church hierarchy, and high-ranking noblemen, who operated them on a profit basis.[6] In theory, each of these jails was the property of the crown, and those who operated them were responsible to the monarch as keepers of common jails.

As mentioned in the previous chapter, these early gaols had little resemblance to what we think of as a jail today. The sheriff was authorized to repair or rebuild with county funds any county gaol "presented" by the grand jury as insufficient or inconvenient.[7] (This same responsibility for the periodic investigation by the grand jury of the county jail still exists in a number of states today.) By law the grand jury could levy a sum known as the "county bread" for providing food to poor prisoners. Although the sheriff was considered the caretaker of the gaol, he infrequently exercised direct custodial control over its operations. His position was one of importance and influence, and he contracted to a keeper the actual duties of caring for the gaol and its occupants.[8]

Usually the keeper was paid no salary. He was paid by a system of fees which made gaol keeping a very lucrative occupation. In fact, the job of keeper was usually sold by the sheriff to the highest bidder. Under the supervision of the keeper were turnkeys, who were paid from the fees collected by the keeper. He had no obligation to the prisoners themselves, other than to see that they did not escape.[9]

Inmates had to support themselves. To do so, they were allowed to beg. Sometimes relatives and friends helped them when they could or charitable persons donated food and clothing. Some limited work was also available. In some gaols, inmates were permitted to work at producing nets, laces, and purses, which were sold outside the jail. Frequently the inmates could be seen in front of the gaol tied to each end of a chain running through a staple fixed to the outside wall from which they pleaded with passersby to purchase their wares.[10]

Not until the beginning of the nineteenth century did England's gaols begin to assume functions more characteristic of modern jail administration. Up to this time the gaols were not special institutions designed to house prisoners for short-term periods of incarceration. Instead, they were mere temporary holding or security facilities to which convicted offenders were sent for very brief periods of incarceration prior to being placed in the stocks, executed, subjected to branding or some form of mutilation for their misdeeds, or, in the seventeenth and eighteenth centuries, transported to penal colonies. Only in the case of debtors, who were kept imprisoned until they paid their creditors, were these early gaols used for any form of long-term imprisonment. By the nineteenth century, some parts of the criminal code had been modified and gaols began to house those who had been convicted of minor offenses. About this time imprisonment for debt began to disappear and the gaols began to receive both accused and convicted criminals on a regular basis.[11]

Jail Development in the United States

The English gaol tradition came with the colonists to the New World. The oldest jail system in America was established in Virginia at the time of the founding of the Jamestown colony. In 1626 Virginia prescribed that the marshal's fee for admission and discharge of prisoners was 2 pounds of tobacco.[12] Five years later the Virginia general assembly raised and restructured the fee schedule so that the marshal would receive 10 pounds of tobacco for arresting an individual, 10 pounds for admitting him to jail, and another 10 pounds for his discharge.[13]

In 1634 the Virginia colony was divided into eight shires and a sheriff was appointed for each. In 1642 the general assembly of that colony passed the first laws dealing with the erection and maintenance of jails. It stipulated that jails were to be built in each county by the county commissioners and were to house those arrested and waiting trial. The sheriff was to maintain custody of the jail and its prisoners. Payment for food and lodging was to be provided by the prisoners themselves. The cost was to be determined by mutual agreement between the sheriff and the inmates.[14]

The counties were slow to comply with these laws and continued to use the back rooms of taverns as jails. It was not until the general assembly enacted a penalty against the counties for noncompliance in the form of a fine of 5,000 pounds of tobacco and liability for the escape of any prisoners that the counties started to build the required jails.

During this time, Pennsylvania was also developing a jail system, a process that passed through three stages. The typical English jail system was established under the laws of the Duke of York in 1676.[15] By 1682 this system was replaced by the adoption of the Quaker workhouse or house of correction, which became the basis of the colony's jail system for about thirty years.[16] When the criminal code was modified in 1718, corporal punishment was substituted for imprisonment and in most cases, this led to less emphasis on the workhouse as a place of confinement. Instead, whippings, branding, and other forms of physical punishment were meted out. In other cases fines were established as substitutes for imprisonment.

The first law creating a county jail in Pennsylvania was passed on March 20, 1725.[17] The legislation authorizing a county jail system later became a model for other states. The law provided for the appointment of a board of five special county commissioners or trustees, who were authorized to purchase the land for the jail site and to estimate its cost. Each county was to follow this procedure and was required to establish a county jail. The administrative control of each county jail was to rest with the sheriff. The five commissioners were responsible for maintaining the facility and were authorized to assess taxes for its support. The sheriff had the authority to appoint an undersheriff or keeper to run the day-to-day operations of the facility.

The customary extortion and other forms of abuse associated with the English jail system were present in the early jails of Pennsylvania (the engraving shows Philadelphia's famous Walnut Street Jail).[18] The sheriff was able to demand exorbitant fees from those confined. Sometimes prisoners were able for the proper price to live in taverns or even the sheriff's own house. Wealthy prisoners could escape from the degradation of jail confinement entirely by simply bribing the sheriff to permit them to live in private homes with little or no control or surveillance.[19] Normally, no pretense was made of feeding or clothing the inmates, who were compelled to provide for their own needs. Whereas wealthy inmates might live quite comfortably, it was not unknown for prisoners who had no resources to die of starvation.[20]

Beginning about 1730, attempts were made to eliminate some of these abuses. The sheriff was prohibited from selling intoxicating spirits to the prisoners. However, all this accomplished was to provide a middle-man's profit to the sheriff, who now would merely send out for liquor or food at the request of the prisoner and charge him a "handling fee" for this service. Laws were also passed which prohibited a sheriff from holding office for more than three

Courtesy of the Federal Bureau of Prisons

successive years, after which time he would not be able to hold the office again until three years had passed. This resulted in attempts to gouge the prisoners even more during the time that the sheriff was in office. In many instances this law was circumvented by having the sheriff and the undersheriff "trade off" official positions. When the incumbent sheriff's three years were up, his undersheriff would be appointed as sheriff and he in turn would be appointed as the undersheriff. In this manner they traded the office back and forth.[21]

This then was the heritage that was passed on from Virginia and Pennsylvania to other colonies and later states. The idea of the jail was adopted by Massachusetts in 1699, New Jersey in 1754, South Carolina in 1770, and Georgia in 1791.[22]

THE JAIL IN THE CRIMINAL JUSTICE SYSTEM

The jail is an integral part of the criminal justice system. Although it might be considered a subsystem of the corrections component, it plays a role far more important than this classification would suggest. Since it is a subsystem of a larger system, it must coordinate its efforts in cooperative arrangements with other parts of the criminal justice process. Like the human body, the criminal justice system will not function well if any of its parts are operating below acceptable standards. As we shall see, the jail has traditionally operated below standard.

The jail serves as the portal to the criminal justice system. It is important as an indicator of the interest and concern with justice, punishment, and rehabilitation expressed by society and the local community. The person who is awaiting trial or serving a sentence experiences first-hand and with varying degrees of intensity what it is like to be exposed to the values of society as they are related to crime and punishment.

A stay in jail is the most widely experienced form of incarceration. Only the police and the courts represent the justice system more directly as determined by numbers of citizen contacts. There are no exact figures on the number of people arrested and detained in jails throughout the nation, but the President's Crime Commission survey found that of the 2 million persons committed to institutions in 1965, two-thirds were confined in jails and workhouses. This figure did not include those persons in jail awaiting trial, which would have made the number significantly larger. During this period it was estimated that there were about 5 million misdemeanant arrests. Under these circumstances, the influence of the jail in terms of the number of persons who experience confinement in some form is considerable.

The Jail and the Police

The jail is not only of strategic importance in terms of the number of persons that come in contact with it and the influence it has on them, it also performs a service function for the other agencies within the system. The relationship of the jail to the police is one of accommodation and necessary cooperation. The jail has the responsibility to accept any prisoner who is legally arrested and can be legally received and detained by the jail. Not all persons arrested by the police can be legally received and detained. For example, in some jurisdictions juvenile arrestees have to be detained in special juvenile facilities.[23] Initially, the jail plays a passive role in the justice system, and to some extent the jail population reflects this. If the community and therefore the police are particularly concerned with enforcing laws against drunks or vagrants, the jail will contain a large number of such people. If it is the policy of police department personnel to "rough up" certain individuals they arrest, those arrested are likely to become more recalcitrant and provide further problems for the jail personnel. The important point is that community and police policy affects the jail. The jail then is not an independent and isolated institution within the community. It is a part of a larger system, and what the rest of that system does will affect it directly. By the same token, the way the jail operates will also affect the community and the criminal justice system.

Since the jail holds the accused until the formal machinery of criminal justice begins to move, jail personnel and the police have to work together. For example, if accomplices must be kept separated, the police will request jail personnel to do this. When a long-term investigation is required, the police and the jail may need to coordinate their efforts in scheduling investigative interviews or in making the accused available to the police, the prosecuting attorney, and defense counsel. This need for coordination and information exchange is also necessary and important when the jail is holding a material witness for the police or prosecutor.

The Jail and the Courts

The jail and the courts must also cooperate very closely if the work of both is to be accomplished. The court both influences the jail's activity and in turn is dependent on the jail's successful handling of the court-imposed workload. Unlike the passive role it plays in its relationship with the police, the jail takes a much more active role in scheduling and coordination in its relationship with the court—so much so in fact, that it almost seems that the jail in many instances is a department of the courts.

The extent of this interdependence between the court and the jail can be demonstrated by examining the sentencing decision rendered by the court. The courts can sentence an individual to jail, modify his sentence before completion, place an offender on probation, and in some instances sentence him to a work release program. These decisions will influence the jail population, its composition, and the extent to which the jail must be involved in alternative programs. For example, the court may authorize work release and order the jail to provide such a program. The jail must then make the necessary arrangements for handling such a program. If misdemeanants are sentenced to the jail rather than to workhouses or work farms, this increases the number of prisoners that the jail must deal with. And setting aside arrests for public drunkenness clearly has an impact on jail populations. In other cases the courts may decide that the jail should serve only as a temporary detention facility before trial and all sentenced offenders might be sent to a county correctional institution, which would reduce the jail population.

The jail functions as the distributor in the criminal justice system. It serves as the transfer point for prisoners who have been sentenced to the workhouse, county farm, or a penal institution. In some cases, it also transfers individuals to the federal corrections system.

Until recently, the jail served a passive role in bail proceedings, which are court-supervised even though in some cases the matter is routine. The accused either made bail and was released or was unable to make it and was held for trial. Some new bail projects have now expanded the roles of the jail. In a few jurisdictions today, jail authorities are now involved in selecting persons for release on their own recognizance. In some cases this may be done by jail personnel themselves, although in most cases it is handled by the probation department or by joint agreement and consultation among the courts, probation personnel, and jail officials.

Because of the need for close coordination between the court and the jail, jail facilities have been developed which are in close proximity to the court. The idea has been that this will make it easier to transport offenders to the court and limit the problems of security when prisoners are transferred. In recent years, jail consultants and progressive jail administrators have increasingly recommended that jails be built on the outskirts of cities, particularly in larger cities that must house a sizable number of prisoners.[24] Admittedly, this has created some problems because the courts and police headquarters are situated downtown. However, the advantages of situating the jail on the outskirts of the city would seem to far outweigh the disadvantages. The use of downtown jails limits jail programming. With no facilities available for recreational and similar programs, prisoners are confined to the internal recesses of the jail and their activities are quite limited. In these situations, pent-up frustrations and crowding can lead to serious jail disruptions and rioting, as witnessed in jail facilities in New York, Washington, D.C., and other cities. It would seem that the inconvenience of locating such facilities away from the central city would be more than compensated for by the increased opportunities this presents for the development of a wider range of programs for prisoners.

The Jail and Corrections

Many view the jail as having primarily a law enforcement function because of the nature of many of its operations and because the chief administrator of the jail is usually a law enforcement officer. However, the jail does not have specific law enforcement functions. It does not serve as a base of operations for criminal detention or apprehension although it may be in a department where these activities go on. Jail personnel may be sheriff's deputies or police officers; however, their specific duties while working in the jail are not in the area of law enforcement.

Jails are part of the overall corrections program. They are, in fact, penal institutions. Like other correctional institutions, they hold many prisoners who are serving sentences, and they have a responsibility for their care. In the past, the emphasis of most jails was merely on detention. In recent years this traditional role has been redefined and made much more encompassing. Now, the courts and the community in some locales are demanding of their jails a correctional effort. This means that these institutions will be required to develop correctional programs and rehabilitative efforts for those inmates serving out their sentences in these local institutions.

The jail, in many cases, has a particular advantage over other correctional institutions in that it is located in the community and can coordinate those community resources to develop effective programs. Additionally, it deals mainly with misdemeanants, who may be more tractable and amenable to various programs than are felons. It is particularly with the misdemeanant that rehabilitative efforts should be developed before the offender reaches the point where his actions or attitudes require long-term incarceration. The argument for the role of the jail in the overall correctional process has been well stated by the President's Commission on Law Enforcement and Administration of Justice:

> On the correctional continuum, jails are the beginning of the penal or institutional segment. They are, in fact, the reception units for a greater variety and number of offenders than will be found in any other segment of the correctional process, and it is at this point that the greatest opportunity is offered to make sound decisions on the offender's next step in the correctional process. Indeed, the availability of qualified services at this point could result in promptly removing many from the correctional process who have been swept in unnoticed and undetected and who are more in need of protective, medical and dental care from welfare and health agencies than they are in need of custodial care in penal and correctional institutions. In a broad sense, the jails and local, institutions are reception centers for the major institutions.[25]

In addition to its own correctional function, the jail must develop close and effective coordination with the state correctional program so that both can learn from the experiences of the other. Since the jail typically has too few personnel and resources to develop a training program, the state department of corrections can be of important assistance in providing training opportunities. The state can also share its acquired knowledge with jail personnel, particularly in terms of program implementation and rehabilitative techniques that have proved successful and can be adopted by local jails. The jail system is also important as a focus of research efforts and data gathering that can aid state correctional efforts in program evaluation, particularly as states move into the area of developing community-based treatment alternatives.

THE JAIL TODAY: MAJOR PROBLEMS AND AREAS OF NEGLECT

The harsh reality is that most jails remain a serious problem in the system of American justice. For years, criminologists, study commissions, interested citizen groups, and some governmental officials have deplored the conditions existing in many of our nation's jails. The ill and the healthy, the old and the young, petty offender and the hardened criminals, the mentally defective, the psychotic and sociopathic, the vagrant and the alcoholic, the habitual offender who is serving a life sentence in short installments—all continue to populate our jails in an indiscriminate mass of human neglect. Since there are some 4,000 local jails in the United States, they are shaped by characteristics as varied as the social fabric of the communities where they are found.

Certain negative characteristics associated with our jails almost defy improvement. Often, one or more of these characteristics affect the other characteristics, so that any overall solution is that much more difficult to attain. These negative characteristics are:

1. The heterogeneity of the offenders that inhabit our jails
2. The problems of local control and politics
3. Demeaning physical facilities
4. Inadequate personnel
5. Inept administration
6. Failure to adopt alternative programs and dispositions

Heterogeneity of Offenders

The heterogeneous nature of the offenders in our jails presents a problem in terms of program development and rehabilitative strategies. When jails must deal with such a broad range of offenders and individual needs, it is not easy to tailor appropriate programs. Lack of available resources further complicates the problem.

Jail inmates do, however, share certain socioeconomic characteristics. Inmates are typically poor, have low levels of educational attainment, and have histories of chronic unemployment. A relatively high percentage of them are members of minority races. Unfortunately, these characteristics are most likely the reasons they languish in jail to begin with. This is particularly true among pretrial detainees. Those who are employed or have the means to post bond escape incarceration.

Although inmates might be similar in financial status, race, and other characteristics, they are completely dissimilar in needs. The petty thief, the alcoholic, the narcotics user, the child beater, and the wife deserter are, to one degree or the other, all in need of different programs of help or treatment.

Local Control and Politics

The fact that jails are local institutions is another of the major problems. Many communities are without the leadership, insight, or resources to bring about change. Having to rely primarily on property taxes for a financial base, local communities facing higher operating costs and demands for educational support, roads and streets, capital improvement, and a host of other considerations cannot give priority to jail services without forgoing needs in other areas. Since jail improvement has a low priority for most citizens, money to finance a jail or to provide the most rudimentary correctional program is usually absent.

Local politics has also played an important role. Of all the jails in the United States, 73.3 percent are administered by the sheriff.[26] In many states, the sheriff is an elected officer whose responsibilities for maintaining the local jail are clearly spelled out in the state constitution. Thus, the sheriff is free to operate with almost no control by the state. Even in fiscal appropriations, this officer is relatively unsupervised. Monies are usually appropriated by the

county legislative authority in accordance with constitutional or statutory declarations that the county government must provide monies for the maintenance of
the jail. In many cases where the states have tried to extend some supervisory
control over the jail, individual sheriffs and their state political associations
have been able to rebuff these attempts.

Another problem that makes it more difficult to wrestle control of jails away
from the county sheriff is the encroachment of municipal and separate county
police forces into the enforcement responsibilities of the sheriff's departments.
As these functions are reduced, the county jails become a larger share of each
sheriff's vested interest and, thus, a function that sheriffs are less willing to
relinquish.

Strangely enough, studies have shown that the population of a jail is not
directly related to the size of the population in the jurisdiction it serves. The
Nebraska Commission on Law Enforcement and Criminal Justice recently did a
study of its jails and the counties they serve. It found that the jail populations, in
this state at least, reflect the particular sentencing policies of the local courts and
the policies of law enforcement practices more than the absolute population of
the county itself.[27] Much of this is, of course, due to the existence or nonexis-
tence of alternative dispositions and institutions, such as detoxification centers
and state misdemeanant institutions. Since it is usually the larger urban centers
which have alternative programs and institutions, relative numbers of prisoners
in urban jails are reduced.

Although many inmates are in jail only temporarily until they come to trial,
the "temporariness" of this period of incarceration can be quite lengthy. An
Illinois survey found that pretrial detention, in some cases, can run into years,
depending upon the legal maneuvers in the courts brought about by the prosecution and defense postponing or continuing cases, unavailability of witness,
etc.[28] Although such lengthy delays are not typical, since court decisions
and statutory pronouncements are designed to avoid such occurrences, this
problem does exist to various degrees in many jurisdictions. As a consequence,
many jails find themselves having to accommodate two to three times the
number they were designed to hold. Crowding of men and women into these
institutions in forced idleness as they await delayed trails creates potentially
explosive situations.

Demeaning Physical Facilities

A recent study of the District of Columbia jail points out the terrible state of
affairs in many of America's jails today. One wonders if even the best programs
available would make any difference in such squalor. The report gives us an
insight into the jail conditions that exist in the capital of the nation that prides
itself on its humanitarian concerns and position of leadership in the Western
world. In the words of the report:

The District of Columbia jail is a filthy example of man's inhumanity to man. It is a case study in cruel and unusual punishment, in the denial of due process, in the failure of justice.

The jail is a century-old and crumbling. It is overcrowded. It offers inferior medical attention to its inmates, when it offers any at all. It chains sick men to beds. It allows—forces—men to live in crowded cells with rodents and roaches, vomit and excreta. It is the scene of arbitrary and capricious punishment and discipline. While there is little evidence of racial discrimination (the jail "serves" the male population of the District of Columbia and is, therefore, virtually an all-Black institution), there are some categories of prisoners who receive better treatment than others.

The eating and living conditions would not be tolerated anywhere else. The staff seems, at best, indifferent to the horror over which it presides. This, they say, is the job society wants them to do. The facilities and amounts of time available for recreation and exercise are limited, sometimes by a guard's whim. Except for a few privileged prisoners on various details, there is no means by which an inmate may combat idleness—certainly nothing that could be called education, counseling or self-help.[29]

The President's Commission on Law Enforcement and Administration of Justice reports that 35 percent of the cells being used by jails across the country are at least fifty years old and that some of them were built in the nineteenth century.[30] Table 13-1 indicates the distribution by age of jails in the United States as of 1966. The President's Commission reported that one New England state had four jails having a total of 899 cells without any sanitary facilities. Since the construction of many of these institutions predates inside plumbing and electricity, they still use slop buckets, and unshaded electric bulbs dangle from exposed fixtures. Inmates are kept in large unsegregated bullpens rather than in individual cells. One New England state was reported to have three jails that were over 160 years old; a state in the Midwest reported to the commission that many of its jails are over 100 years old.[31]

The National Advisory Commission on Criminal Justice Standards and Goals points out how jail facilities normally get into such disrepair depending upon the manner in which they are used. Those jails that hold few prisoners tend to be neglected, and those that are constantly overcrowded are forced to push their equipment and fixtures beyond the breaking point.[32] Under either set of circumstances, the jail's physical plant soon finds itself badly in need of repairs.

The *1970 National Jail Census* also found that 5 percent of the jails included in its study were significantly overcrowded. Ironically, the larger the jail and its capacity to house prisoners, the more likely it was to be overcrowded.[33] At the same time, studies in some areas report that a large percentage of available jail space is unoccupied. For example, surveys of Idaho's jail population at different times showed that the jails in that state were operating at only 55 to 65 percent of their design capacity.[34] This indicates first that little thought or consideration goes into the planning or renovation of existing jail physical

TABLE 13-1   Distribution of Ages of Jails by Percentage (1966)

Age	Percentage
Less than 10 years	24
10–24 years	11
25–50 years	30
Over 50 years	35
Total	100

Source: President's Commission on Law Enforcement and Administration of Justice, *Task Force Report: Corrections* (Washington, D.C.: U.S. Government Printing Office, 1967), p. 166.

plants and second that the problem will not be solved merely by building new and more appropriately sized jail facilities; the entire system of detention and delivery must be examined more closely if we are not to continue to perpetuate past mistakes.

One of the major problems associated with the demeaning nature of jails, even in new facilities, is the traditional way jails are constructed. In order to provide maximum security at minimum cost, certain standard construction characteristics have been developed. Glaser gives us a picture of the typical jail:

> In nearly all jails, the available space is divided into inflexible cells or cage-like day rooms. Rows of cells compose self-contained cellblocks that face a large cage or "bullpen." The arrangement is designed so that a relatively small number of staff can insure the secure confinement of a comparatively large number of inmates. Items are passed into the bullpens through slotted doors, largely preventing contact between staff and inmates.
>
> Many jail cells have neither toilets nor wash basins. The majority of inmates have access to shower facilities less than once a day. These inadequacies, combined with the short supply or complete lack of such items as soap, towels, toothbrushes, safety razors, clean bedding and toilet paper, create a clear health problem, not to mention the depressing psychological effects on inmates.[35]

Given the fact that even basic sanitary facilities are often missing, it should come as no surprise that other facilities such as a dining room, recreation area, chapel, classrooms, or a place for inmates to enjoy some solitude other than the dreariness of their cells are also absent in many jails.

Inadequate Personnel

The neglect of local jails is as obvious in the caliber of staff personnel as it is in dismal physical facilities. Jail employees almost invariably are untrained, too few in number, and underpaid. They are second-level victims of the societal arrangements that perpetuate the jail.[36]

**TABLE 13-2   Minimum Educational Requirements by Percentage of
Local and State Institutions (1966)**

| | Minimum Educational Requirement, percent | | | |
Position	None	High School or Equivalent	College	Graduate Study
Superintendent, head jailer, etc.	53	39	8	
Custodial officer	53	46	1	
Social worker	9	41	44	6

Source: President's Commission on Law Enforcement and Administration of Justice, *Task Force Report: Corrections* (Washington D.C.: U.S. Government Printing Office, 1967), p. 165.

In 1975, the Law Enforcement Assistance Administration released a report on a 1972 survey of local jails in the United States. Of the approximately 4,000 jails operating throughout the nation at the time of this survey, it was found that less than 4 percent had professional staff in such areas as social work, psychology, psychiatry, or other treatment specialties.[37] This is not much of an improvement over earlier findings. For example, in 1966 the National Council on Crime and Delinquency conducted a similar survey of jails throughout the country and found that approximately 3 percent of the nation's jail facilities had such personnel.[38] Even though the federal government substantially increased expenditures for local criminal justice programs between 1966 and 1972, when these surveys were taken, it appears that little was done to add treatment personnel to the staffs of local jail facilities.

The National Council on Crime and Delinquency and the President's Commission also examined the types and qualifications of personnel who supervise local jail facilities. The majority of personnel (78 percent) were merely custodial guards. For the position of superintendent, warden, or head jailer, 53 percent of the institutions called for no specific minimum educational requirement, 39 percent required a high school education, and only 8 percent required the jail administrator to have a college degree. As might be imagined, the requirements for a custodial officer or jail guard were even less. In over one-half of the institutions surveyed, there was no educational requirement whatsoever.[39] Table 13-2 indicates the minimum educational requirements for some categories of personnel found in our jails. Although the data reflect 1966 figures, there probably has been little overall improvement during the intervening years, with the possible exception that a few social workers on jail staffs must now have college degrees.

As for preservice training of jail personnel, only 8 percent of local jails required any form of training. Only 38 percent of the institutions surveyed offered any kind of in-service or formal on-the-job training for their staff. Where they did require some in-service training, it usually consisted of how to handle firearms, techniques of physical restraint, training in riots and disorders, and how to supervise correspondence.[40] Most of the local jails surveyed provided no merit system or merit incentive programs for jail employees, which indicates that well-functioning systems of personnel management and development were practically nonexistent.[41]

The President's Commission also examined existing salary ranges for personnel employed in our nation's jails. Unfortunately, these data are for 1966 and have not been updated; nevertheless we can get some idea of the relatively meager salaries we pay jail personnel. For example, the average salary of the chief administrator of a jail facility was less than $7,000 per year, and custodial personnel received an average annual salary of less than $4,000.

In local jails, law enforcement personnel are traditionally used as custodial officers. Even in California, which probably is one of the more advanced and professionalized states in the area of jail management, a large percentage of sworn law enforcement personnel are engaged in custodial tasks. A 1970 jail survey in that state found that over 25 percent of the deputies in fifty-eight county sheriff's offices were engaged in custodial activities.[42] In other states the figure would probably be even higher. Law enforcement personnel have enough trouble enforcing the law and keeping the peace, and under the circumstances we should not expect them to be either expert or very much interested in managing local jails. In addition, the psychological role-set of a law enforcement officer is to arrest offenders and to see to it that they get into jail; the role of a correctional worker should be more rehabilitative and should prepare an inmate to get out of jail and return to the community as a law-abiding citizen. However, the use of low-paid custodians to relieve law enforcement personnel is no solution to this problem. In many cases, such individuals are even less qualified and competent to perform the responsibilities than are the law enforcement officers they replace.

Nationally, there were 3.2 inmates for each custodial officer in our nation's jails in 1972. This number varied from state to state and ranged from 1.3 to 11.4.[43] On the surface, this might appear adequate. However, this figure includes part-time custodial personnel, and the typical custodial person is also involved in administrative tasks, such as records keeping, booking, and other forms of paperwork. In addition, jails must be manned twenty-four hours a day every day of the year. Thus, the effective ratio of jail personnel to inmates shrinks to 1:23. Given the conditions that exist in many jails, this does not even permit the custodial officer to effectively supervise the inmates in terms of security, let alone become a participating member in alternative programs that might be developed. The Nebraska study indicated that staff personnel could not observe all prisoners from their assigned stations.[44] In the Idaho research, how serious this problem is, especially at night, was pointed up when the study group found that only 32 percent of the jails in that state had a full-time staff member present during the night.[45]

Administrative Problems

One of the major impediments to change in our jails is the quality of administrative leadership. There is adequate documentation attesting to the fact that many sheriffs and police chiefs are not even effective administrators of law enforcement let alone having the managerial abilities associated with maintaining a jail facility. Many sheriffs are particularly poor administrators. For the most part, they are politicians who are primarily interested in developing and maintaining the necessary political connections to ensure their tenure in office.

If they have to demonstrate any managerial competency, it is in the law enforcement function since citizens are much more likely to demand high levels of police service than they are to concern themselves with jail operations. The only time most citizens are apt to question the managerial competence of the jail operation is when disorders or escapes occur.

Furthermore, since most of the citizens who are politically powerful in a community are those least likely to find themselves incarcerated in the jail, they have no first-hand knowledge of the conditions that exist. Even if arrested, they are most likely to make bond and not have to be subjected to anything worse than the slight inconvenience of being booked and having to contact their attorney or a bondsman.

Given these circumstances, most sheriffs or police chiefs with responsibility for maintaining detention facilities are concerned primarily with security and next with ensuring that riots and disorders do not occur. They wish to avoid the negative publicity that is often associated with escapes and disorders. The guiding dictum then becomes "to keep it quiet" and to quell quickly any outbursts that are likely to come to public attention. Third, jail administrators are concerned that they appear to be servicing the courts properly. This means developing operating policies that ensure that inmates will be present before the court on their trial date and that court orders are carried out. Finally, jail administrators are concerned with keeping operating costs for the jail at a minimum to avoid inquiries and citizen concern. This is not meant to imply that these should not be important concerns; however, in too many instances these are the *only* concerns.

All in all, the emphasis seems to be on maintaining a high degree of anonymity in terms of the operation of the jail. The objective appears to be to keep the entire operation removed as far as possible from contact with the public, and in those instances when public contact is unavoidable, to make that exposure as brief as possible, and to make it appear at least superficially that the agency and its chief administrator are competent.

The overriding concern for security has manifest itself in some strange accommodations in the operating policies of many jails. Given limited manpower, custodial personnel have often knowingly or unwittingly turned over the internal maintenance of the jail to the inmates themselves. In this way, they rely on the inmates (or at least the inmate leaders) to maintain order. The ramifications of this policy are far-reaching. Inmate leaders become exploiters, not only of other prisoners, but even of the jailors themselves. They begin to make innocent demands upon the custodial staff for certain concessions. As they win concessions, they strengthen their power base and become more demanding.[46] As the power cliques develop, disastrous consequences can ensue. A study of the Philadelphia jail pointed out that development of certain leadership cliques in that facility led to "mass intimidation" and sexual assaults upon other inmates. Even the jail administrators themselves were forced to acknowledge that virtually every slightly built young man committed by the courts is sexually approached within a day or so after he is admitted. Many of the young men were repeatedly raped by gangs of prisoners.[47]

Lack of Alternative Programs and Dispositions

The *1970 National Jail Census* indicated that 86 percent of all jails had no recreational facilities and 89 percent had no educational programs.[48] The follow-up survey conducted in 1972 showed that only 12 percent of all jails have any kind of vocational program or programs that in some way would help prisoners obtain employment or employment-related counseling.[49] In fact, the 1972 survey indicated that over two-thirds of all the jails had no general re-habilitative programs whatsoever, not even group counseling, remedial educa-tion, or alcoholic or drug-related programs.[50]

As a consequence, most inmates face a daily routine of boredom and idle-ness. Card playing, conversation, and occasional television viewing are the only pastimes available. Even though community resources in both programs and personnel are usually available, they are seldom used or even solicited. The problems associated with this type of idleness are well stated by Glaser, who says of this condition:

> The major costs to society from jail conditions probably stem not from the clear violations of moral norms that the inmates suffer there, but rather from the prolonged idleness of the inmates in highly diverse groups cut off from much communication with outsiders. In this inactivity and crowdedness, day after day, those inmates most committed to crime "brainwash" the inexperienced to con-vert initial feelings of guilt or shame into smug rationalizations for crime. Also, jail prisoners become extremely habituated to "killing time," especially during pretrial confinement. Thus, deficiencies of ability to support themselves in legitimate employment, which may have contributed to their criminality, are enhanced at their release. While reformatories and prisons are often called "schools for crime," it is a far more fitting label for the typical urban jail.[51]

These then are some of the negative features that have come to be associated with American jails, They are, indeed, formidable obstacles to change and a monument to our lack of concern for other human beings. The next section will examine some of the changes in our usual method of dealing with misdemean-ants that either are occurring or have been recommended. Although a great deal remains to be done, it is encouraging to see that at least in a few instances improvements are being sought.

NEW MEANS OF DEALING WITH MISDEMEANANTS AND RESTRUCTURING JAILS

Diversionary Measures

One of the major recommendations for reform is to divert those accused of misdemeanor crimes and many adjudicated offenders from the process of incarceration. The development of diversionary programs has been recommended by the President's Commission on Law Enforcement and Administration of Justice, the American Bar Association Commission on Correctional Facilities and Services, several federal agencies which have studied the problem, and a variety of individuals, including judges, legislators, correctional workers, police, prosecuting attorneys, and defense lawyers.[52]

It needs to be pointed out that although diversion is more and more being described as a proved, successful reform policy, many basic questions about it remain unanswered and, in fact, may never have been raised or debated. What programs qualify as diversion programs? What reforms are encompassed by diversion? How do diversion programs function? What are their objectives? How successful have they been?

Since alternative diversionary programs are, for the most part, new ventures, little has been done to evaluate their impact, and programs that have been evaluated have often been evaluated improperly.[53] As a consequence, most of our knowledge about their success or failure must be impressionistic. Fortunately, more rigorous evaluative techniques are being applied to these programs which will give us a better insight into their relative merits in the near future.

Some of the more notable diversionary techniques are the following:

Citation in Lieu of Arrest

Any strategy for minimizing the detention of persons not yet convicted of a criminal offense should be directed at the point of first contact with the criminal justice system, that is, at the point of arrest. Just as the police are authorized to issue citations for traffic violations, it has been recommended that they also have the authority to issue citations for certain categories of offenses under prescribed conditions. The citation would indicate the time and place that the accused was to appear in court to answer the charges. No physical arrest would be made.

Statutory and administrative guidelines would be needed first to authorize the police to deal with offenders in this manner and secondly to prescribe the criteria that must be met before this could be done. Usually, the issuance of the citation in lieu of an arrest would be warranted in the following instances:

1. The offense is a misdemeanor where there is no danger of physical harm involved. This could also be applied to some felonies in certain situations.

2. The accused is identified and a member of the local community.

3. The police officer has reason to believe that the continued liberty of the accused does not constitute an unreasonable risk of bodily injury to himself or others.

4. There is no reason to believe that the accused will flee from the jurisdiction or not appear at his trial at the appointed place or time.

The implementation of such a program would require that police departments develop certain administrative procedures. For example, it would be necessary to give police officers on the street the necessary discretionary authority to do this. This would require special training and the availability of certain departmental resources, such as access to a communications and records system that could verify the identity of the accused in order to satisfy the above criteria. A number of police agencies are now experimenting with this approach. Oakland, California, implemented its Police Citation Program in 1970. Under this program, police officers are authorized to issue summonses rather than making formal arrests for misdemeanors. The accused is instructed where to appear for booking and charging. If the officer in the field decides to take the individual into custody, the desk supervisor on duty can authorize a release on a citation if he or she feels it is warranted. When the program was first initiated, there was a high rate of failure to appear for booking or trial, but a year later the rate was appreciably less.

A number of other cities are using a stationhouse release procedure. An individual who is arrested is taken to the police station, booked, and then released with a citation to appear for trial. In New York, this has developed into the Manhattan Summons Project, and the citation program of the Sunnyvale, California, police department operates in this manner. In the Sunnyvale program, almost 50 percent of those arrested are released under this program without having to post bond or be incarcerated in the jail. The failure-to-appear rate, under this program, has been approximately 7 percent.[54]

In the Manhattan project, 36,917 summonses were issued in the first two years of the program's existence. The failure-to-appear rate was only 5.3 percent, and a number of these "no shows" resulted from such factors as hospitalization or the fact that the defendant was being held in detention by another jurisdiction. Estimates are that in the first two years of the program's existence, the New York City police department saved over 368,000 police work-hours, which saved the taxpayers of that city an estimated $2.5 million in police services alone.[55]

Alternatives to Traditional Bail

One way to divert many offenders from our jails is to make possible their release without the necessity of posting a surety bond through a bail bondsman.

Although it is not necessary to use the services of a bail bondsman if the arrestee has the money (or in some cases tangible collateral) to satisfy the court, often those arrested do not have the financial resources to post their own bond and must turn to the bail bondsman. A bail bondsman's fee is typically 10 percent of the bond posted and many arrestees are unable to pay this fee. As a consequence, they are committed to jail, pending their trial, while defendants who can afford to post their own bond or pay the fee of a bail bondsman are released.

One of the most publicized endeavors to correct this practice is the Manhattan Bail Project. This program was initiated by the Vera Foundation of the New York University School of Law and the Institute of Judicial Administration in October 1961.[56] It was originally staffed by law students from the New York University School of Law, who worked under the supervision of the Vera Foundation. These students interviewed defendants and did an investigation of the offense and the accused's background. They examined such factors as length of residence, current employment status, local relatives with whom the arrestee had contact, and prior criminal record. In consultation with other staff members, they would carefully review these facts. If the Vera staff decided to recommend probation, this information was forwarded to the court. The court then determined, from the facts and recommendations, whether the individual was entitled to pretrial release without having to post bond.

Excluded from consideration were those individuals charged with or having a previous record of narcotics offenses, homicide, forcible rape, sodomy involving a minor, corrupting the morals of a child, carnal abuse, and assault on a police officer.[57] The success of this program is indicated by the 1964 report of the work of the Vera Foundation:

> The results of the Vera Foundation's operation show that from October 16, 1961 through April 8, 1964, out of 13,000 total defendants, 3,000 fell into the excluded offense category, 10,000 were interviewed, 4,000 were recommended and 2,195 were paroled. Only 15 of these failed to show up in court, a default rate of less than 7/10 of 1 percent. Over the years, Vera's recommendation policy has become increasingly liberal. In the beginning, it urged release for only 28 percent of defendants interviewed; that figure has gradually increased to 65 percent. At the same time, the rate of judicial acceptance of recommendations has risen from 55 percent to 70 percent. Significantly, the District Attorney's office, which originally concurred in only about half of Vera's recommendations, today agrees with almost 80 percent. Since October 1963, an average of 65 defendants per week have been granted parole on Vera's recommendations.[58]

Philadelphia and San Francisco have adopted the features of the Manhattan Bail Project. The Philadelphia program, known as the Philadelphia Common Pleas and Municipal Court Release on Recognizance Program, is available to all felons and misdemeanants arrested in that city. Its purpose, like that of the Manhattan Bail Project, is to eliminate the necessity for posting money bond in those cases of indigent defendants whom it appears will remain in the city and appear at the time of their trial. If the arrestee qualifies for the program, he is released on his own recognizance. The National Advisory Commission on Criminal Justice Standards and Goals describes the procedure and the performance of this program:

> Arrested persons are interviewed at the police station by the staff of a pretrial services program, who obtain and verify information regarding the accused. The information sought includes residence, family ties, employment, and prior record. The interviewer submits copies of his report to the court, the district attorney, the public defender, and the ROR [release on own recognizance] program agency. A point system which places values on ties to the community is applied to each accused, and from that system a recommendation is made to the court as to whether the accused qualifies for ROR. The judge at arraignment can then either accept or reject the recommendation.
>
> The ROR investigators verify more thoroughly the information concerning defendants who are detained after arraignment. Further interviews may also be conducted. Where warranted, the interviewer may recommend that a petition be filed on behalf of the defendant, requesting the court either grant ROR or reduce bail. The pretrial services staff also follows up on persons released on ROR. Each released defendant is obligated to report by telephone to the ROR main office. ROR staff also contact defendants to remind them of their court date.
>
> In the first year of the program, ROR staff interviewed 36,252 arrested persons and initially recommended ROR for 17,175, or 47.4 percent. The court granted ROR to 13,041 of those recommended for such release and not otherwise discharged from custody.
>
> During the same year, ROR defendants had a total of 24,790 court appearances scheduled and only 7.4 percent failed to appear, of which 5.6 percent were willful failures.[59]

Illinois has also modified the traditional bail bond practice in an effort to cut down on the number of pretrial detainees in that state's local jails and to avoid the discriminatory practices associated with conventional bail bond provisions. In 1963, the Illinois state legislature passed a bill authorizing a 10 percent cash bond program. Under this system, the accused is required to post only 10 percent of the bail set by the court or prescribed for the offense in the bail schedule. If the defendant appears in court, 90 percent of the required 10 percent is refunded to him. In essence, the defendant pays 1 percent to the state for the administrative paperwork involved rather than 10 percent required by private bail bondsmen under conventional bail statutes.

A number of studies have been made in an effort to determine the feasibility of this program. The clerk of courts for the criminal division of the circuit court in Chicago reported that in 1964, 600 conventional surety bonds and 686 10 percent bonds were issued. The forfeiture rate for failure to appear in court was 6.3 percent for those individuals posting the conventional bonds and only 5.4 percent for those posting the 10 percent bonds.[60] A more recent study has indicated that this same similar relationship exists. Blankenship found that the forfeiture rate in Chicago's courts for those who post the 10 percent bond was 6.1 percent in 1969.[61]

Jail Regionalization

Another recommendation for the improvement of the jail system in America calls for transferring control and responsibility for maintaining them to the state and for developing jails and lockups on a regional basis under the control of correctional authorities who can develop the needed program services.[62]

In terms of cost-benefit analysis, particularly when the "costs" of not being able to provide the necessary services to inmates housed in local detention facilities are included, the arguments for jail consolidation are impressive. What now exists is an ugly tapestry of small, local jails scattered about. Regionalization would consolidate existing facilities by means of cooperative agreements between governmental jurisdictions. For example, designating one county as the site of a jail to serve the adjacent two to three counties is one proposal. The county that served as the jail site would maintain the facility under its jurisdictional control and the other counties would send their arrestees to it under a contractual agreement that stipulates that the host county receive so much money per inmate. Such an arrangement exists in Liberty County, Georgia.

Another proposal that combines the advantages of the regional jail concept with better programming is for the states to enact legislation that would turn these facilities over to the state department of corrections. Since the states have more highly developed correctional systems, including more highly trained correctional and treatment specialists, and more sound fiscal bases, they could incorporate the existing jail systems into statewide systems of misdemeanant institutions. In this manner, reception and classification programs could be developed, alternative community-based programs implemented, and more effective research and evaluative data gathered. Although only a couple of states have adopted this proposal, a number of states are presently looking into the feasibility of such an approach.

It should be pointed out, however, that regionalizing jail systems has some drawbacks. It may not be practicable to house pretrial detainees in these facilities, particularly if the various courts that the facility serves are widely dispersed. Such an arrangement may make it difficult to transport defendants back and forth from the courts as well as making it difficult for attorneys to consult with their clients. It may be better under the circumstances to detain prisoners *temporarily* in local detention facilities *for no longer than twenty-four hours*. Local courts would have to be administered to ensure that the accused is brought before the court within that period. Such provisions already apply at the federal level in felony cases.[63] The states, however, have usually not adhered to this requirement.

A second problem with the regionalization of jails is that this removes the accused from his family. Often, an indigent defendant's family will not be able to afford the expense of traveling to visit him. This maintenance of family ties is considered by all penologists to be an important factor in any meaningful program of rehabilitation. In addition, the site of a regional jail facility may be such that it does not provide opportunities for work or academic release. All these factors must be carefully considered in determining the feasibility of adopting such a concept.

State Supervision of Local Jail Facilities

When the President's Commission released its report in 1967, only about 40 percent of the states had set any standards for the operations of jails or local institutions, and what standards they did set focused almost exclusively on construction and health standards. Even the U.S. Bureau of Prisons, which has for a number of years had its own jail inspection teams which travel around to local jails to certify them as temporary detention facilities for federal prisoners, is usually only concerned with the jail's construction and security characteristics and health-related matters.

In the last few years, however, the states have taken a more meaningful role in supervising local jail facilities. Michigan, as an example, passed legislation in 1973 which authorized the creation of the Office of Jail Services within the Michigan Department of Corrections. This agency is empowered to make inspections of all local jail facilities in the state. All jails are required to provide adequate security; mail and visitation privileges; special programs for inmates; and the segregation of offenders by age and crimes committed; as well as the usual concerns for facilities and health. Failure to comply as noted by the Office of Jail Services results in the matter going to the state attorney general, who can then seek court-ordered compliance.

In addition, the Michigan Office of Jail Services provides training and programming assistance to the local jails, utilizing the experienced personnel available within the Michigan Department of Corrections. At first, there was a great deal of concern from the sheriffs and police officials in that state that the passage of such legislation and the creation of this special unit would result in a state takeover of local jails. However, these fears did not materialize, and now most of the law enforcement officials in that state who are responsible for maintaining the jails welcome the assistance provided.

The Use of Jail Volunteers

There has been some recent interest in the use of volunteers in rehabilitative programs in jails. However, few jails have tried to establish such programs. The use of volunteers inside the jail has several advantages, one being that it reduces the public's ignorance of how bad the situation is. Conditions considered to be tolerable by the jail administration may seem completely intolerable to the volunteer. For example, few if any volunteers would accept a total lack of medical service as a condition of incarceration in even the smallest jail. In addition to their usefulness as providers of supplementary services in the jail, volunteers are thus a source of public information and of public demands for improved jail conditions.[64]

One of the leading jail volunteer programs in the country has been established at the Ingham County Jail outside of Lansing, Michigan. This institution has a broad rehabilitative program, offering services designed to meet the vocational, academic, social, and personal needs of inmates. An outstanding component of the rehabilitation plan at the jail is its volunteer involvement. In the first two years of the program, the fresh and innovative thinking of volunteers was instrumental in establishing programs in auto mechanics, blueprint reading, math, physics, arts and crafts, and accounting.

Work Release, Educational Programs, and Counseling Services

A number of jails and misdemeanant institutions have established work-release programs for their inmates. Such programs exist in Birmingham, Alabama; Cincinnati, Ohio; Denver, Colorado; Honolulu, Hawaii; Phoenix, Arizona; Multnomah County, Oregon; and Seattle, Washington.[65] Santa Clara, California, has administered a work-release program since 1957. All inmates in that county's Elmwood Rehabilitation Center, which houses 600 sentenced felons and misdemeanants, are eligible for the program. Approximately one-third of the population is out on work release on any one day. A follow-up study, comparing a sample of inmates who participated in the program with a sample that did not, indicated that participants remained free in the community following release longer than did nonparticipants.[66]

These work-release programs are of two types. In the more typical program, the inmate works at his place of employment during the day and returns to the jail facility after working hours. The second type permits the offender to work and live at home during the week and to serve his jail sentence on the weekends.

At the Cook County Jail in Chicago, a nonprofit organization provided an educational program for inmates. In order to assess the program's effectiveness, a group of inmates exposed to the educational program were compared with a group which was not. It was found that the inmates who had participated in the educational program encountered less difficulty in seeking and obtaining employment after their release, had higher employment aspirations, worked longer, and experienced fewer arrests. With an average of 5.4 months spent in the educational program, the average gain was 1.1 grade levels. As the amount of time spent in the program increased, so did the level of overall academic achievement. There was a significant relationship between overall academic achievement and success upon release.[67]

The last programming area to be discussed is the development of counseling services within jail systems. One of the most unfortunate consequences of our misdemeanant justice system is that inmates tend to pass through the system repeatedly, often returning for the same kind of offense. Generally they receive little or no help with personal problems that may be the major contributor to their behavior. It is imperative that these persons receive help in the redirection of their lives. Many times, if these individuals can be helped at this stage, they can be turned around.

Every institution for misdemeanants should have sufficient counseling services, staffed by competent, trained personnel. Unfortunately, jails do not provide these services. The National Council on Crime and Delinquency's survey indicated that jails have trained counselors or social workers in the ratio of 1 for every 846 inmates.[68] In addition, group interaction programs with trained discussion leaders are also notably absent. Although some jails do provide these services, they are still few and far between.[69] In their place, the inmates often develop their own "group interaction programs," where the counseling emphasis is often on how to commit crimes and escape justice. It is time that such dialogues were supplanted by more appropriate and positive counseling services.

The road to jail reform has often been a slow, tortuous path of deep resistance and frustration. Even today, with the exception of the few isolated examples presented in this chapter, the picture is dismal. It has taken us over three centuries to progress this far. Whether in our lifetimes our jails will adopt some of the modern concepts of penology is uncertain—the only thing that history has taught us is that it has taught us little or nothing.

SUMMARY

The jail serves as the gateway to the criminal justice process. The history of jails in both England and later America is a story of neglect, brutality, and debasement. Although jails have improved substantially in the twentieth century, they still are operated in a manner that we as a nation cannot be proud of.

The major problems confronting our jails are interrelated and complex. In the first place, the sheer number and variety of offenders create difficult problems for devising any meaningful programs to assist the offender to become a law-abiding citizen. The problem is made more difficult by the fact that jails are under local control and jail administrators are often local politicians with law enforcement interests. Many jails are totally inadequate in terms of physical facilities and personnel and are hampered by having inept administrators. Finally, and as a result of the above factors, we have failed to adopt meaningful alternative programs and dispositions for the hundreds of thousands of individuals who each year end up serving some period of time in jail.

In the past few years, a number of changes have been proposed and adopted in some scattered jurisdictions throughout the country. For example, an increasing emphasis is being placed on diverting the offender through such programs as citations in lieu of arrest and reforms in the bail bond system. Other suggested reforms are jail regionalization, state supervisory authority over local jails, and the increased use of volunteers and support programs in jails.

Suggested Additional Readings

Alexander, Myrl: *Jail Administration*. Springfield, Ill.: Charles C Thomas, 1957.

Allen, Harry E., and Clifford E. Simonsen: *Corrections in America: An Introduction*. Beverly Hills, Calif.: Glencoe Press, 1975.

Amir, Menachem: "Sociological Study of the House of Correction," *American Journal of Corrections*, 29 (2) (March-April 1967): 36-41.

Fishman, Joseph F.: *Crucibles of Crime: A Shocking Story of American Jails*. New York: Cosmopolitan Press, 1923.

Flynn, Edith E.: *Prisoners in American*. Englewood Cliffs, N.J.: Prentice-Hall, 1973.

Glaser, Daniel: "Some Notes on Urban Jails," in Daniel Glaser (ed.), *Crime in the City*. New York: Harper & Row, 1970.

Goldfarb, Ronald: *Jails: The Ultimate Ghetto*. Garden City, N.Y.: Anchor, 1975.

Law Enforcement Assistance Administration: *1970 National Jail Census*. Washington, D.C.: U.S. Government Printing Office, 1971.

Mattick, Hans. "The Contemporary Jails of the United States," in Daniel Glaser (ed.), *Handbook on Criminology*. Chicago: Rand McNally, 1974.

———. and Ronald P. Sweet: *Illinois Jails: Challenge and Opportunity for the 1970's*. Washington, D.C.: U.S. Government Printing Office, 1970.

McGee, Richard A. "Our Sick Jails," *Federal Probation* 35 (March 1971): 3-8.

National Sheriff's Association. *Manual of Jail Administration*. Washington, D.C.: National Sheriff's Association, 1970.

Webb, Sidney, and Beatrice Webb. *English Prisons under Local Government*. Hamden, Conn.: Archon, 1963. (Originally published in 1906.)

Notes

1. Law Enforcement Assistance Administration, *Local Jails* (Washington, D.C.: U.S. Government Printing Office, 1973), p. 1.

2. Law Enforcement Assistance Administration, *1970 National Jail Census* (Washington, D.C.: U.S. Government Printing Office, 1971), p. 19.

3. Frederick Pollack and Frederick W. Maitland, *History of the English Law* (Cambridge: Cambridge University Press, 1952), p. 516.

4. Sidney Webb and Beatrice Webb, *English Prisons under Local Government* (Hamden, Conn.: Shoe String, 1963), p. 3.

5. Henry Burns, Jr., *Origin and Development of Jails in America* (monograph) (Carbondale: Southern Illinois University Press,), p. 2.

6. See John Howard, *The State of the Prisons* (London: Dent, 1929).

7. E. M. Leonard, *History of English Poor Relief* (Cambridge: Cambridge University Press, 1900), pp. 220-221.

8. H. E. Barnes and N. K. Teeters, *New Horizons in Criminology* (Englewood Cliffs, N.J.: Prentice-Hall, 1949), p. 389.

9. Burns, op. cit., p. 4.

10. Ibid.

11. Ibid. p. 6.

12. Ibid., p. 8.

13. Ibid.

14. Oliver P. Chitwood, *Justice in Colonial Virginia,* vol. XXIII (Baltimore: Johns Hopkins, 1905), pp. 111-112.

15. Louis N. Robinson, *Penology in the United States* (Philadelphia: Winston, 1922), p. 37.

16. Burns, op. cit., p. 11.

17. Harry E. Barnes, *The Evolution of Penology in Pennsylvania* (Indianapolis: Bobbs-Merrill, 1927), pp. 58-63.

18. Ibid., pp. 63-65.

19. Burns, op. cit., p. 13.

20. Harry E. Barnes, *The Story of Punishment* (Boston: Stratford, 1930), p. 192.

21. Robert T. Treymine, *Early Colonial Jails* (New York: Meinster, 1899), pp. 111-113.

22. Robinson, op. cit., pp. 36-37.

23. A number of federal courts are now ruling that the confinement of a juvenile in a county jail for adults is in violation of the provision against "cruel and unusual punishment" of the Eighth Amendment; see Bureau of National Affairs, Inc., *The Criminal Law Reporter,* 16 (Dec. 18, 1974): 1045.

24. Public Management Consultants, *Recommended Changes for Jail Management in Atlanta, Georgia* (Atlanta, Ga.: 1969).

25. President's Commission on Law Enforcement and Administration of Justice, *Task Force Report: Corrections* (Washington, D.C.: U.S. Government Printing Office, 1967), pp. 162-163.

26. Richard A. McGee, "Our Sick Jails," *Federal Probation* 35 (March 1971): 5.

27. Nebraska Commission on Law Enforcement and Criminal Justice, *For Better or for Worse? Nebraska's Misdemeanant Correctional System* (Lincoln: 1970), pp. 97-105.

28. Hans W. Mattick and Ronald Sweet, *Illinois Jails: Challenge and Opportunity for the 1970s* (Washington, D.C.: U.S. Government Printing Office, 1970), p. 49.

29. American Civil Liberties Union, *The Seeds of Anguish: An ACLU Study of the D.C. Jail* (Washington, D.C.: ACLU, 1973), pp. 3, 5.

30. President's Commission, op. cit., p. 166.

31. Ibid.

32. National Advisory Commission on Criminal Justice Standards and Goals, *Corrections* (Washington, D.C.: U.S. Government Printing Office, 1973), p. 275.

33. Law Enforcement Assistance Administration, *Local Jails,* pp. 4-5.

34. Idaho Law Enforcement Planning Commission, *State of Idaho Jail Survey of City and County Law Enforcement Agencies* (Boise: 1969), pp. 12-13.

35. Daniel Glaser, *Crime in the City* (Harper & Row, 1971), p. 238.

36. Mattick and Sweet, op. cit., p. 368.

37. Law Enforcement Assistance Administration, *The Nation's Jails* (Washington, D.C.: U.S. Government Printing Office, May 1975).

38. National Council on Crime and Delinquency, *Corrections in the United States* (New York: National Council on Crime and Deliquency, 1967).

39. Henry Burns, Jr., "American Jail in Perspective," *Crime and Delinquency* 17 (October 1971): 451-452.

40. President's Commission, op. cit., p. 165.

41. Ibid., p. 455.

42. California Board of Corrections, *A Study of California County Jails* (California Council on Criminal Justice, 1970), p. 102.

43. Law Enforcement Assistance Administration, *The Nation's Jails,* p. 9.

44. Nebraska Commission on Law Enforcement, op. cit., p. 27.

45. Idaho Law Enforcement Planning Commission, op. cit., p. 9.

46. For an excellent portrayal of how this occurs and the results of such power shifts, see Greshan M. Sykes, *A Society of Captives* (New York: Atheneum, 1970), especially chap. 3.

47. Allen J. Davis, "Sexual Assaults in the Philadelphia Prison Systems and Sheriff's Vans," *Trans-Action* 6 (1968): 9.

48. Law Enforcement Assistance Administration, *1970 National Jail Census,* p. 191.

49. Law Enforcement Assistance Administration, *The Nation's Jails,* p. 39.

50. Ibid., p. 41.

51. Glaser, op. cit., p. 241.

52. Raymond T. Nimmer, *Diversion: The Search for Alternative Forms of Prosecution* (Chicago: American Bar Foundation, 1974), p. 3.

53. Nancy Goldberg, "Pre-Trial Diversion: Bilk or Bargain?" *NLADA Briefcase,* 31 (1974): 490.

54. *Handbook for Expansion of Pretrial Release in the San Francisco Bay Area* (Berkeley, Calif.: Association of Bay Area Governments, 1971).

55. *The Manhattan Summons Project,* (New York: Criminal Justice Coordinating Council of New York City, 1970), p. 2.

56. For an excellent review of the Manhattan Bail Project, see Charles E. Ares, Anne Rankin, and Herbert Sturz, "The Manhattan Bail Project: An Interim Report on the Use of Pre-trial Parole," *New York University Law Review* 38 (January 1963): 67-92.

57. Ibid., p. 68.

58. Daniel Freed and Patricia Wald, *Bail in the United States: 1964,* working paper for the National Conference on Bail and Criminal Justice (New York: Vera Institute of Justice and U.S. Department of Justice), pp. 62-63.

59. National Advisory Commission, op. cit., p. 109.

60. Charles Bowman, "The Illinois Ten Percent Bail Deposit Provision," *University of Illinois Law Forum* (1965): 35.

61. Robert K. Blankenship, "Indigent Bail Provisions in Cook County Illinois," unpublished master's thesis (Ann Arbor: University of Michigan, 1970), p. 37.

62. President's Commission, op. cit., p. 79.

63. See 18 U.S.C. 3501, and *United States v. Keeble,* 495 F.2d 757 (8th Cir. 1972).

64. Tully L. McCrea and Don F. Gottfredson, *A Guide to Improved Handling of Misdemeanant Offenders* (Washington, D.C.: U.S. Government Printing Office, 1974), pp. 28-29.

65. Sharron Lee, "Comparisons and Considerations for Social Services in Local Jails," (Seattle, Wash.: Seattle-King County Corrections Development Project, 1972), pp. 15-18.

66. A. Rudoff, T. C. Esselstyn, and George L. Kirkham, "Evaluating Work Furlough," *Federal Probation* 35 (March 1971): 34-39.

67. Paul S. Venezia and Stephen D. Gottfredson, "The PACE Institute: A Limited Assessment of Its Effectiveness," (Davis, Calif.: National Council on Crime and Delinquency Research Center, 1972).

68. National Council on Crime and Delinquency, op. cit., p. 142.

69. See Edith E. Flynn, "Jails and Criminal Justice," in Lloyd Ohlin, ed., *Prisoners in America* (Englewood Cliffs, N.J.: Prentice-Hall, 1973), p. 75.

Chapter 14

Corrections in the United States

The correctional system in the United States is one of extreme diversity in which a broad range of institutions, theories, programs, and operating strategies prevail. The problems associated with institutional and program diversity are compounded by the diversity of offenders with which the system must deal. A number of offenders are hardened recidivists who are irrevocably committed to criminal careers; others subscribe to more conventional values; still others are aimless individuals who are committed to neither socially appropriate nor socially inappropriate behavior. Among offenders are those who are severely disturbed emotionally and psychologically, narcotic addicts, sex deviates, alcoholics, and sociopathic offenders, and all must be handled by appropriate casework techniques as well as security considerations.

IMPEDIMENTS TO CORRECTIONAL REFORM

The National Advisory Commission on Criminal Justice Standards and Goals identifies six problems which make correctional reform difficult to achieve:

1. Fragmentation of corrections
2. Overuse of corrections
3. Overemphasis on custody
4. Ambivalence of the community
5. Lack of financial support
6. Lack of knowledge base for planning[1]

Fragmentation of Corrections

Corrections, like all the other agencies of criminal justice, is structured and administered on the concept of political federalism in which the maintenance of correctional institutions and programs is fragmented among different jurisdictions at the federal, state, county, and municipal levels of government. This fragmentation has produced semiautonomous responsibility for dealing with convicted offenders among a multiplicity of programs and jurisdictions. The result has been the poor utilization of resources, inequities in financial support for program improvement, lack of effective supervisory control, duplication and waste in institutional construction and program implementation, and the influence of local politics in the administration of these programs and facilities.

In the past, there may have been a need to maintain local correctional facilities because of the problems associated with inadequate transportation and communication networks, but this is certainly not the case in our modern urbanized society. Today, the trend in modern penological thinking is toward the consolidated administrative control of all correctional programs and institutions in the state.

There are a number of sound arguments for consolidation. In the first place, the taxing resources of states have a number of advantages not available to local or county governments. Thus, program support for the purchase of required resources for a statewide correctional system would be better. Consolidation would also provide for a more equitable distribution of taxes required to support correctional institutions. Statewide systems could also develop standardized policies and procedures which would ensure higher standards of program performance and efficiency.

A centralized administrative authority would also have other positive benefits. For example, a large agency would have the political leverage to compete better for scarce appropriations. Career opportunities, training, salaries, and a host of other personnel considerations would conceivably also improve.

Lastly, with the present trend of corrections toward community-based programs and specialized institutions tailored to the particular needs of offenders, it is almost mandatory that the states assume responsibility, for local and county governments are not capable of providing such facilities and programs.

Whether consolidation can ever become a reality is open to some doubt. The political partisanship and desire for local autonomy which has always been a characteristic of American political institutions and interests must be overcome. It has been a major obstacle to correctional reform in the past and a significant contributor to the failure of our correctional programs to be more effective. Until this impediment to change can be overcome, we will continue to be frustrated in our attempts at more meaningful correctional strategies.

Overuse of Corrections

Our response to criminal behavior has been based on the two ideas of punishment as a deterrent and punishment for the sole purpose of punishment. Since the inception of American corrections and the growth of our urban society, we have increasingly turned to the law and the use of penal institutions as means of social control. Neither approach has been very effective. The criminal laws, particularly those dealing with victimless crimes, have been violated with impunity. Institutionalization of offenders has also been a failure in terms of deterrence as indicated by the high percentage of offenders who upon release commit new crimes and are returned to prison.

Perhaps in the past when there were no alternatives available for dealing with the offender, there was some justification for incarcerating law breakers, at least on the grounds of protecting society. Although some classes of offenders do pose a real threat to society by their freedom, a great many of the individuals who are now housed in our prisons could be handled much more meaningfully outside the walls of our institutions. Many progressive prison administrators are now saying that our correctional systems should exist primarily to deal with those offenders who can be helped only by intensive institutional care and supervision and with those individuals whose freedom is a clear threat to the safety of society.[2] This argument calls for greater consideration of alternative methods of dealing with offenders. As long as we continue to invoke laws that are made to be broken and indiscriminately sentence offenders to our penal institutions, we saddle our correctional systems with an impossible task.

Overemphasis on Custody

The security of any facility is determined by the most dangerous inmate in the prison population. Although any institution may have only a few such individuals scattered among the hundreds that populate the facility, security precautions must be guided by the possible actions of these few. Because of the public concern that is often associated with prison escapes, wardens and other administrators risk their careers if they manage institutions where such occurrences are frequent. Under these circumstances, the primary concern expressed by prison administrators for maintaining tight security is quite understandable.

However, this emphasis on security works against the development of effective treatment programs within institutions. For example, the massive fortresslike structures which for years dominated prison design were completely unsuitable for vocational programs, recreational facilities, and more diversified prison industries programs. Security in an institution that has treatment programs is more difficult to maintain because of the movement of inmates within the institution as they attend classes, counseling sessions, and vocational training programs.

This overemphasis on custody can also be seen in the proliferation of jails, juvenile detention homes, and large institutions for adult and juvenile offenders. The National Advisory Commission commented on the results of years of emphasis on custody in prison design and programming:

> The mega-institution, holding more than a thousand adult inmates, has been built in larger number and variety in this country than anywhere else in the world.

Large institutions for young offenders have also proliferated here. In such surroundings, inmates become faceless people, living out routine and meaningless lives. And, where institutions are racially skewed and filled with a disproportionate number of ill-educated and vocationally inept persons, they magnify tensions already existing in our society.[3]

Lack of Financial Support

Considering the number of inmates to be supervised and the facilities that must be maintained, the corrections component, including probation and parole, does not seem to receive its fair share of the revenues going to the agencies of criminal justice. Table 14-1 indicates the percentage of expenditures for all the agencies of justice by level of government for fiscal 1969.

TABLE 14-1   Costs of Administration of Criminal Justice (1969)

Level of Government	Courts	Prosecution and Defense	Police	Corrections	Total
National	1.4	1.8	6.7	1.0	10.9
State	3.2	1.1	8.5	12.4	25.2
Local	9.0	3.2	45.2	6.5	63.9
Total	13.6	6.1	60.4	19.9	100.0

Percentage of Expenditures

Source: Committee for Economic Development, *Reducing Crime and Assuring Justice,* © 1972, p. 84. Reprinted by permission.

Although the courts and prosecution and defense services receive less money for their functions than do corrections, these agencies and actors in the criminal justice process are not responsible for the maintenance of the nearly 1,600,000 individuals that were under correctional control in 1971.[4] In an effort to reduce this disparity somewhat, laws passed in 1973 require that at least 20 percent of the federal funds disbursed by the Law Enforcement Assistance Administration to the states to aid crime control be allocated specifically to corrections.

Attitude of the Community

Nearby communities often tolerate the presence of correctional institutions, inasmuch as larger institutions often provide jobs for local residents. However, this tolerance is usually a conditional one. It exists as long as inmates are locked up and out of sight; the surrounding communities feel reasonably safe, provided the convicts are maintained behind massive walls and elaborate security precautions exist to prevent escapes. When these conditions don't exist, the neighboring communities are far less likely to accept a penal institution on their doorstep. In the past few years, as correctional institutions and programs have tried to ''breakout'' from behind walls and start alternative community-based programs, furious opposition has come from neighborhood citizen groups, fighting the establishment of community residential facilities for inmates. These groups feel that such programs jeopardize their security.

Part of the blame for such attitudes must rest with prison administrators of the past, who were only too quick to isolate corrections from the general public by high walls and locked doors. Unfortunately, they failed to realize that the antidote to intolerance of convicted offenders is the active involvement of wide segments of the community in support of correctional processes.

Lack of Knowledge Base for Planning

One of the major obstacles to correctional reform lies in our failure to develop a knowledge base through research and data-gathering activities that would give us the ability to determine which correctional practices are effective with which types of offenders.

We need to know a great deal more about crime and delinquency and how to prevent it and how to treat individuals who engage in criminal behavior. Without such information, the whole policy formulation process breaks down. Today, correctional administrators have little research data to guide them in choosing among various alternatives. Consequently, administrators rely on experience or intuitive hunches as a basis for planning. When we consider the possible consequences of such seat-of-the-pants decision making, it becomes very apparent why traditional correctional programs can boast of very little success.

THE FEDERAL PRISON SYSTEM

In 1776, the Continental Congress provided that persons convicted of violating federal laws be confined in colonial and local institutions. These institutions would be paid a fee on the basis of the cost for housing each prisoner. During the late eighteenth and most of the nineteenth centuries, there were relatively few federal prisoners because the law enforcement authority of the federal government was confined to the offenses of counterfeiting and piracy and other felonies committed on the high seas. As Congress began to extend the enforcement powers of the federal government, federal prisoners began to populate local and state prisons. The states did not object to boarding federal prisoners as long as they were permitted to sell their labor to private individuals. Many abuses resulted from this practice, and in 1887, Congress prohibited the employment of federal prisoners by contract or lease. As a result of this, the states began to charge the federal government the then exorbitant rate of 25 to 35 cents a day per prisoner for board. Some states refused to accept any federal prisoners because they could no longer sell their services for profit.

As the numbers of federal offenders increased, the problem of their custody became more acute. In 1891, federal commitments to penitentiaries numbered 1,600, and it was recognized that something had to be done.

The First Federal Prisons

At the urging of the Department of Justice, Congress authorized the purchase of three sites for federal penitentiaries in 1889. It was decided to construct one in the South, one in the North, and one in the far West; however, no money was appropriated for their construction. In 1895, Congress transferred the military prison at Fort Leavenworth, Kansas, to the Department of Justice for the confinement of federal civilian prisoners. In a few short years, this facility proved to be much too small, and the Department of Justice finally convinced Congress that it was completely inadequate. Congress then appropriated funds for a federal penitentiary to be built on an 800-acre site adjacent to Fort Leavenworth. Using prison labor, the 1,200-capacity institution was first oc-cupied in 1906, but it was not completely finished until 1927. After the prison-ers were transferred to the new institution, the old Fort Leavenworth facility was returned to the War Department for the use of military prisoners.

The number of federal prisoners grew rapidly. In June 1895, there were 2,500 prisoners; a year later, 3,000. In 1899, Congress appropriated funds for a federal penitentiary at Atlanta, Georgia. Construction began in 1900, and in 1902 a group of 350 prisoners first occupied the institution. The Atlanta penitentiary was completed in 1921.

The penitentiary slated for the West was eventually located at McNeil Is-land, Washington, a 7-mile stretch of territory lying in Puget Sound. The federal government first established a small territorial jail at this site in 1875. It offered to donate this jail to the new state of Washington in 1889, but the offer was declined. Although the Department of Justice urged that this territorial jail and its site be abandoned on a number of occasions, it remained federal prop-erty. In 1903, Congress voted funds to convert the jail into a penitentiary.

The Development of Additional Federal Institutions

Women prisoners continued to board in institutions operated by the states. By the early 1920s, the number of female prisoners had increased to the point where a special facility for women became a necessity. The assistant attorney general of the United States at this time was a woman, and with the aid of a number of women's organizations, Congress was persuaded to construct an independent reformatory for women. In 1924, Congress appropriated the necessary funds, and in 1927 a 500-inmate institution was opened at Alderson, West Virginia.

In 1925, Congress authorized the purchase of an institution for male offenders between the ages of seventeen and thirty, and as a result, the federal reformatory at Chillicothe, Ohio, was opened in 1926 at the site of an old World War I training facility. In 1929, the federal government purchased a garage near the Hudson River docks in New York City and converted it into a jail facility for federal prisoners awaiting trial.

The Creation of the U.S. Bureau of Prisons

On May 14, 1930, President Hoover signed an act of Congress creating the Bureau of Prisons. The original authorization creating the bureau stated:

> That there is hereby established in the Department of Justice a Bureau of Prisons responsible for the safekeeping, care, protection, instruction and discipline of all persons charged with or convicted of offenses against the United States. The control and management of said institution shall be vested in the Attorney General, the said institutions to be so planned and limited in size as to facilitate the development of an integrated Federal penal and correctional system which will assure the proper classification and segregation of Federal prisoners according to their character, the nature of their crime, their mental condition and such factors as should be taken into consideration in providing an individualized system of discipline, care and treatment.[5]

To relieve overcrowding in federal prisons, the bureau was authorized to transfer prisoners to open camps, a move which set the stage for similar programs by the states. Congress approved additional construction of yet another penitentiary, a reformatory, a medical center, and several institutions for short-term offenders. It directed the U.S. Public Health Service to furnish medical personnel and services to all the institutions. It placed the small U.S. Probation Service within the bureau's organization and established an independent three-man Board of Parole to replace the old system of separate boards at each individual institution. New legislation authorized diversified industrial employment within the institutions of the federal system.

In the years since its inception, the Federal Bureau of Prisons has grown rapidly, adding new institutions and programs to the point where it now is the acknowledged leader in American correctional systems. As of 1969, the Bureau of Prisons operated an integrated system of thirty-five facilities covering eight correctional categories:

Youth and juvenile institutions

Young adult institutions

Adult penitentiaries

Adult correctional institutions

Short-term camps

Female institutions

Community treatment centers

A medical treatment center, used for treatment of inmates with medical or psychiatric problems[6]

ADMINISTRATION OF CORRECTIONS

State Administration

Until the beginning of the twentieth century, prisons in the various states operated almost as independent fiefdoms. The wardens and superintendents of these institutions reported directly to the governor or the legislature. This was a period of political patronage, and prison administrators and custodial staff held their jobs by virtue of political connections. It was not unusual for newly appointed governors to engage in large-scale dismissal of prison personnel, replacing them with their own political followers. During this period, the governor or the legislature did the hiring, the purchasing, and the budgetmaking for the prisons within the state. After the Civil War, some of the states attempted to bring their prisons under some sort of administrative control by appointing boards of charities or corrections, which were the forerunners of present state departments of correction.

Today, every state has a centralized department of corrections. It may be an autonomous agency or a unit within a department of human resources or similar body. The corrections department supervises all state-run correctional institutions for adults, youthful offenders, and juveniles. In addition, this agency is responsible for all state-sponsored community-based correctional institutions and programs. In many states, parole services including all parole officers and, in some instances, the parole board, are also under the department of corrections. In recent years, additional responsibilities have been given to various state departments of correction. For example, some are now responsible for inspecting local jails, lockups, and other misdemeanant institutions. Michigan and Ohio are also beginning to incorporate probation services within the department of correction.

The head of the state department of corrections is usually referred to as the director of corrections. In most states, this officer is appointed by the governor with approval of the legislature. In recent years, states are turning more and more to the appointment of a qualified and experienced penologist for this position. No longer are political considerations as important as they once were in the selection of this administrative head. The responsibilities of this individual are enormous. In those states where the department of corrections is an autonomous state agency, the director is responsible for administration of the entire system, which includes the presentation of the budget to the chief executive and its defense before the state legislature. Besides being a knowledgeable penologist and administrator, the director must be skilled in the art of politics so as to represent the agency effectively before the legislature and obtain the required program authorizations and appropriations.

Institutional Administration

The head of the prison is known by various titles, usually warden, superintendent, or director. The responsibilities of this individual are to manage the institution and to present the institution's budget to the director of corrections or some fiscal agent of the executive department. In some instances, the warden may also be required to defend budget requests before the executive fiscal agency or even the state legislature or one of its committees.

In larger institutions, the warden is usually assisted by one or more associate wardens. Many states and the Federal Bureau of Prisons have adopted the organizational recommendations developed by the American Correctional Association which call for two associate wardens in medium to large prisons. One of these associate wardens is directly responsible for custody, which includes the custodial guard force, and the other associate warden is responsible for the classification and treatment maintained by the institution. Custody and treatment are the major operating units within most prisons. Directly under the associate warden for custody is the captain of the guard force, who is the commanding officer of the custodial line personnel. This custody section also consists of a number of watch lieutenants and sergeants and a large number of correctional officers or guards. Contrary to popular belief, the custodial officer's main job is not preventing escape from the prison; perimeter security devices such as high walls and guard towers take care of this function fairly easily. The main responsibility of the custodial officer is to maintain control within the prison to assure the safety of both inmates and prison employees. The custodial line personnel are in daily contact with the inmates and can make an important contribution to the efforts of the treatment personnel.[7]

Depending upon the institution, its budget, and the prevailing philosophy, the treatment unit may consist of such professional personnel as psychiatrists, psychologists, social caseworkers, medical personnel, chaplain, counselors, and teachers of academic and vocational programs. In addition, there may be a prison industries manager, who is responsible for the industrial production enterprises of the prison; a business manager, who is responsible for accounting, procurement, payroll, and supplies; and a medical services manager, who is responsible for the medical, dental, and other health-related facilities within the prison. Figure 14-1 shows an organizational chart for a medium-sized prison for men.

The management of a prison is no small task, rivaling that of many large industries in its complexity of administative functions. The large inmate population with the special problems associated with the prison environment makes

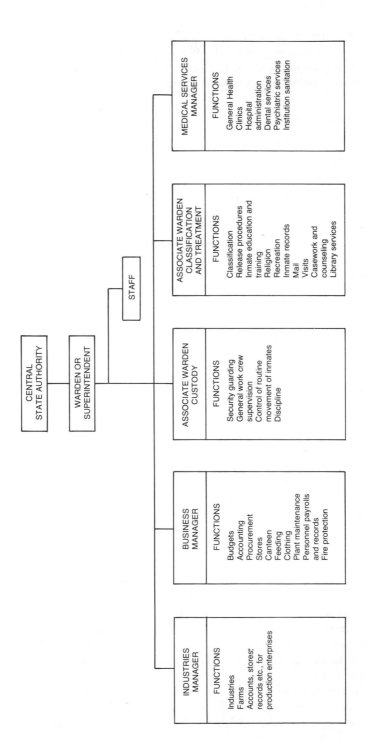

Figure 14-1 Organizational Arrangement for an Adult Male Institution of Less than 2,000 Inmates

Reprinted (with change in title) with permission of The American Correctional Association from the *Manual of Correctional Standards*, 1966 ed., p. 319.

it even more difficult to manage. Under these circumstances, the management of prisons may indeed be one of the most complex and demanding tasks facing any public administrator. It certainly requires the most capable managers to be found anywhere in the public service today.

Prison Programs

Penal institutions have varied programs, depending upon the age, sex, prior criminal record, education, and medical and psychiatric needs of inmates. Since it is not possible to review all the specialized programs that exist, emphasis will be placed upon those programs that typically are found in most adult prisons today.

Classification

Classification attempts to match the needs of the offender with the particular program that can best help him. In the not too distant past, judges had the authority to sentence convicted offenders to any institution within the state. Usually this provided no means to match the individual needs of the offender with appropriate treatment programs which existed in different institutions. Beginning in the 1930s, a few correctional systems in the United States began to adopt the classification concept, and other states have now followed suit. Under this system, the department of corrections has the authority to assign inmates to those institutions where they can receive the treatment they need. The only exception to this is that in some instances in the case of less serious crimes, the judge can sentence someone on a short-term basis to a local facility or work-house.

Out of the classification concept have arisen reception and diagnostic programs and facilities. The first of these was the diagnostic depot at the Joliet, Illinois, prison. Where such programs exist, all inmates sentenced to a state correctional system are first sent to a special centralized facility for extensive testing and evaluation. The objectives of these facilities are typically:

1. Diagnosis of case problems
2. Prescription of classification to specific programs to meet diagnosed problems
3. Induction and orientation of inmates to the correctional system
4. Medical examination, quarantine, and treatment of new inmates.[8]

At the reception and diagnostic center, the new inmate is interviewed by specialized clinical personnel, such as psychologists, psychiatrists, physicians, dentists, and a chaplain. Often, a presentence report gathered by probation or parole authorities accompanies the individual to the center and provides background information which guides the clinical personnel in their evaluation.

Frequently, letters of inquiry are also sent to the inmate's immediate family and to previous employers and schools in an effort to obtain better information on the individual's background. Many times, the center will question social welfare agencies in his former locale that may have had prior contact with him.

After all this information has been gathered, a social history is prepared. The staff of the center then meets to classify the inmate in terms of his particular needs and potential security risk. For example, the individual might be found to be in need of intensive psychiatric help, alcoholic or drug-related rehabilitation, group therapy, educational programs, or some combination of these. Once these needs are determined, he is then sent to the particular institution that has the necessary programs. Although these centers perform a very important function, knowledgeable observers point out that they tend to drain the institutions themselves of professional personnel, thus placing a premium on diagnosis rather than on treatment.[9]

In states without a centralized reception and diagnostic facility, individual institutions have developed their own classification committees. The committees vary somewhat in composition, but usually consist of the associate warden for classification and treatment or the associate warden's immediate subordinate, a high-ranking custodial officer, and the counselor, psychologist, or social worker who prepared the social history. This classification committee meets with the inmate and makes an appropriate program assignment on the basis of the social history report and discussion with the inmate.

A more recent development in classification is the treatment-team concept developed at the federal correctional institution in Ashland, Kentucky, and the Air Force Retraining Facility at Amarillo, Texas. In the team approach, a counselor, a custodial officer, and a teacher from the institution's academic program work together and are jointly assigned to individual inmates. The same team may be assigned all the men in a particular dormitory or cell block. In addition to being responsible for the original classification, they also handle all disciplinary problems among their assignees. This approach relieves the classification committee of its very time-consuming disciplinary function and provides some continuity in supervision. It also makes custodial and academic staff more treatment-oriented by virtue of their involvement in the correctional treatment process.

Health

Most prisons of any size have a health and medical program. In those states without centralized reception and diagnostic facilities, the prison medical facility quarantines all inmates for a week or ten days. The medical services unit is responsible for maintaining proper sanitary conditions in the physical plant and in the food service area. Hospitals are usually maintained in most of the larger prisons and are staffed by a physician, nurses, and other health-related personnel. All but the largest prisons contract for the services of an optician and dentist, who make periodic visits to the institution. In some of the largest institutions, prison hospitals are reasonably well-equipped, even for major surgery. When necessary, nearby hospitals are used. Psychiatric services are very limited. A 1965 survey of prisons in the United States indicated that less than 1 percent of all adult institutions provided psychiatric services.[10]

Academic Programs

Academic programs in prisons range all the way from courses for illiterates to college extension courses. Most prisons have a prison school of sorts with a director of education in charge. Unfortunately, in some adult institutions, academic instruction is provided mainly by inmate teachers. Many of them lack a college education, and some have not even completed high school. Invariably, these inmate teachers are pressured by their students to make the classes effortless and to complete false reports on student progress. Inmate teachers are also susceptible to bribes from their students for good grades and reports. Prisons are also typically short on classroom facilities and teaching aids.

In too many instances, civilian teachers at correctional institutions tend to be rejects from public school systems. Like many of the inmates, the instructors are primarily interested in putting in their time with a minimum of work. Little effort is exerted to make the classroom sessions more meaningful or to employ teaching techniques that could be of more benefit to the inmates.

Vocational Training

Many American prisons have developed a variety of vocational training programs for inmates. With passage of the 1965 amendments to the Vocational Rehabilitation Act, significant vocational training opportunities became available to inmates as correctional institutions were able to acquire the necessary equipment and trained instructors. Such shops as automobile repair and maintenance, radio and television repair, welding, sheetmetal work, and woodworking are now rather common. The well-organized shops have civilian vocational instructors, a place to do the shop work, and space to conduct the necessary instruction. This situation is far different from that which existed just a few short years ago, when the usual vocational activity consisted of making license plates, doing laundry, or producing brooms and twine.

One of the recurring problems that prisons face in developing meaningful vocational training programs is finding appropriate jobs for former offenders who have acquired a skill while in prison. It is often difficult for a released offender to acquire a job as a mason, carpenter, or other skilled worker because of the reluctance of unions to permit them to join. Often, regardless of the man's skill, he will be relegated to an apprenticeship, since the unions do not consider his experience in prison-sponsored vocational training programs as qualifying him for a journeyman's level.

Libraries

Most prisons have some kind of library. These usually vary from very bad to mediocre in terms of reading materials available. The major problem in trying to develop adequate libraries is the cost involved. Since very few institutions have specific money set aside in their operating budget to purchase up-to-date library materials, they must rely on books donated from outside sources, which are often out-dated and not of general interest to the inmates.

Of special concern to some inmates is access to legal books within prison libraries. Many inmates spend a great deal of their time filing legal petitions with the courts for relief by way of habeas corpus writs. In California, the question of whether prison administrators are required to furnish law libraries to inmates has been answered in the affirmative. In the case of *Gilmore v. Lynch*, a statewide regulation which severely restricted titles of law books which could be placed in a prison library was held unconstitutional. The court in this case noted that the adequate filing of petitions for habeas corpus writs by inmates required that prisons maintain sufficient legal holdings so that inmates could obtain the information they needed.[11]

A number of good libraries are maintained by the Federal Bureau of Prisons. Some have professional librarians to operate the libraries and to supervise the prisoners who act as attendants or helpers in the library. An excellent example of an institutional library can be found in the federal government's Kennedy

Youth Center in Morgantown, West Virginia. The library at this facility is impressively large, with many excellent holdings as well as audiovisual and other learning aids. In this institution, a special committee with inmate representatives selects the materials that the library acquires.

Prison Industries

The subject of prison industries has an interesting history. Prison industries have been based on the so-called sheltered and open-market systems. Today, prison industries are based on the state-use system and the public-works-and-ways system, both considered sheltered-market systems.[12] The state-use system produces goods and renders services for agencies of the state or its political subdivisions. Thus, prison industries manufacture goods that are not sold on the open market, but only to other state or local governmental jurisdictions. Public-works-and-ways systems involve road construction and repair, reforestation, soil-erosion control activities, and the like on public property only.[13]

Such was not always the case. During the nineteenth century, prison industries sold their goods and services on the open market in competition with private industry. Labor unions and employers associations became very upset by this competition and applied a great deal of pressure on Congress and state legislatures to prohibit the sale of inmate-produced goods or inmate services on the open market. In 1929, Congress passed the Hawes-Cooper Act, which deprived prison-made goods of their interstate character and made them subject to state law. The Ashurst-Summers Act of 1953 prohibited transportation of goods into states forbidding their entry and required the labeling of prison-made goods shipped in interstate commerce. By 1940, every state had passed legislation prohibiting the sale of inmate-produced goods on the open market.[14]

The inmates engaged in prison industries in any institution are usually only a small percentage of the prison's total inmate population. Many inmates are assigned to kitchen or mess duties, the laundry, maintenance work, and unskilled tasks such as pushing a broom or cleaning windows.

Prison wages are very nominal in American prisons. In the mid-1960s, a married prisoner might earn 8 cents an hour for working a 40-hour week; half of this would be sent to his family and half would go to his account (one-quarter for use in the prison commissary and one-quarter for going-home money).[15] Even today, the average prevailing pay in state institutions is still probably less than 50 cents an hour. Some federal institutions are paying their inmate labor more, based upon the skill involved in performing the specified job.

Several renowned penologists have suggested that prisons pay their inmate labor the prevailing wage for the particular work they perform and then charge them for their maintenance and care after taking out an appropriate share of the individual's earnings for his family's support. However, this scheme has very little chance of becoming a reality in view of the prevailing attitude which demands that as part of his punishment, the prisoner be legally, socially, and economically disabled.[16]

Recreation Programs

Almost all prisons have developed a recreation and leisure-time program for their inmates. The major sports of football, basketball, and baseball are participated in by intramural teams, and some prisons even have extramural teams that compete with teams from the outside community. Some prisons with funds to hire a director of recreation and purchase materials and equipment have developed fairly broad recreation programs. Some institutions even have gymnasiums for their inmates, weight-training programs, and a host of other athletic sports. For those inmates who do not engage in the very active sports, most prisons provide alternative forms of recreation. Arts and crafts are often available, as are organized chess matches, debating teams, music groups. Even dramatic groups have been formed in some places. Movies are provided on a routine basis, as are TV-viewing rooms, and many institutions permit radios in individual cells or dormitories. Some institutions permit outside entertainers to perform in the institution periodically as well as permitting inmates with special entertainment skills to perform on the outside.

TYPES OF INSTITUTIONS

General Classifications

There are several types of institutions among prison systems today. These institutions are usually designated by the type of security they afford and the characteristics of the offenders in them.

Maximum-Security Institutions

The more hardened and dangerous offenders are found in maximum-security prisons. A typical maximum-security prison is usually enclosed by massive concrete or stone walls from 18 to 25 feet high or by a series of double or triple perimeter fences topped with barbed wire and spaced 15 to 20 feet apart. On the outer-perimeter walls are located well-protected towers strategically placed so that the guards have an open field of fire and can observe the external and internal sections of all the surrounding walls and the prison yard. Electronic sensing devices are employed as perimeter security measures in more and more institutions today.

The internal security considerations are just as formidable. The inmates are housed in interior cell blocks, each of which has its own self-contained security enclosure. The cell blocks are partitioned off from each other by a series of enclosures that limit internal movement. The idea behind this type of construction is to create a series of miniature prisons within a prison so that in the event of riots or escapes, each section can be sealed off from the others. Thus, any prisoner seeking to break out would first have to penetrate the internal security system before he could challenge the external wall and perimeter security devices.

In recent years, the trend has been away from the construction of these types of institutions, particularly ones with massive stone walls surrounding them, because of their prohibitive cost. New maximum-security institutions often use technological intrusion and security devices, such as infrared sensors and closed-circuit TV for security, which permits the facility to have a more campuslike appearance.

Medium-Security Institutions

These institutions house inmates who, although not as dangerous to society and their fellow inmates as those confined in maximum-security prisons, do pose a threat of escape and often have served prior sentences. Normally, they are not massive fortresslike structures so prevalent in maximum-security prisons. In most instances, a series of fences or enclosures surround the perimeter. Many of these institutions are constructed on a block arrangement in which inmates live together in designated units. Less emphasis is placed upon controlling the internal movement of prisoners. These facilities often have dormitories, honor units, or some similar form of housing for inmates that have earned the privilege of living in such quarters. There is usually a special maximum-security unit for inmates who pose a threat to the security of the institution or to other inmates. Often such inmates will be transferred to a maximum-security prison until they demonstrate the appropriate conduct or are released at the expiration of their sentence.

Minimum-Security Institutions

These prisons do not utilize fixed observation posts for armed guards on the perimeter. In fact, depending upon where they are situated and the type of offenders they contain, there may be no perimeter fence. Inmates in minimum-security institutions are generally housed in private or semiprivate rooms or in dormitories. Although housing inmates in individual rooms has certain advantages, such facilities are often too costly to construct, and thus most inmates live in small dormitories accommodating from ten to twenty inmates. Recent years

have seen a large growth in the number of minimum-security facilities. The President's Commission found that of the 350 state institutions surveyed, 55 were maximum-security, 124 were medium-security facilities, 103 were classified as minimum-security; and the remaining 68 were mixed-security institutions. [17]

The minimum-security institution, of course, houses less dangerous offenders. In many instances, offenders with relatively short sentences and/or without extensive criminal records are housed in these facilities. Since these institutions offer greater freedom to the inmate, many correctional departments transfer inmates to them from medium-security institutions when they have demonstrated by their conduct that they have earned this privilege. Often, the minimum-security institution provides an adjustment stage prior to release. For example, inmates of more closely guarded institutions who have a year or so left to serve may be transferred to one of these facilities to help them adjust to less controlled discipline so that they are better prepared for their ultimate release.

Prison Camps

These are a form of minimum-security institution that developed in the Midwest, the West, and the South. In the Midwest and the West, they are usually used as farming and forestry camps. Pennsylvania, Maryland, California, Oregon, Ohio, Wisconsin, and Washington have used these arrangements extensively. Placement of inmates in prison camps provides useful and instructive work for inmates in a more favorable environment than is normally found within traditional institutions and enables prisoners of various types to be separated, thus reducing the possibility of contamination of attitudes. Use of work camps relieves the problem of overcrowding in institutions and is less costly than maintaining traditional prisons.

Until recent years, Southern prison camps had a very poor reputation. First begun during the period of reconstruction following the Civil War, they were operated under a lease system. Private bidders would contract with the state for the use of inmate labor and then lease the inmates to private individuals, who used them in lumbering, quarrying, and turpentine operations. When the federal courts began to prohibit the leasing of prisoners, this practice disappeared and the Southern states turned to using their inmate labor on road crews and chain gangs, which labored under brutal conditions. In recent years, however, the Southern states have abolished their road gangs and have developed various camp institutions devoted to farming and forestry. In some cases these camps are among the best such programs in the nation.

Special Institutions

Some specialized institutions have developed for handling certain categories of offenders. For example, the California camp or ranch system, which operates under county authority but is partially subsidized by the state, provides special facilities for the rehabilitation of juvenile offenders. The California Youth Authority also has a number of camps for youthful offenders, which permits that state to separate young offenders by age, crime, and individual needs so that younger first-time offenders do not associate with more criminally sophisticated and intractable youths.

A few states and the federal government have developed special facilities for those inmates who need intensive medical and psychiatric help not normally available in other institutions. Among these are the California Medical Facility at Vacaville and the United States Medical Center at Springfield, Missouri. States have also developed special institutions and programs for the criminally insane; Michigan constructed the first such facility in 1885. Special institutions and programs are also available for women offenders, for example, the state institute at Clinton, New Jersey, and the federal one at Alderson, West Virginia. Today, the various types of special institutions and programs offer a wide choice of alternatives for meeting the particular needs of offenders.

Classifying Institutions By Program Emphasis

It's not enough to classify penal institutions by the degree of security they offer or by the age and type of offenders they contain. These categories need further definition, which is provided by the administrative characteristics of the particular institution. Administratively, prisons may follow either the *traditional* model or the *collaborative* model.

The Traditional Model

The traditional institution is administered with the idea that security is of paramount importance in order to protect the institutional staff as well as the community. To accomplish this, high walls are constructed, mechanical security devices and armed guards are employed, and inmate searches and body counts are made frequently. However, it is not necessary that all the physical aspects of gun towers, fences, and other obvious displays of security be present for an institution to be a traditional type. Administratively contrived security precautions, such as frequent searches and "shake-downs," head counts, disciplinary segregation, and other forms of control less visible to the outside world can prevail even in institutions that are not bounded by high walls or fences.

Traditional institutions adhere to the idea that deterrence requires strict discipline, regimentation, and punishment, all in an atmosphere of impersonality and quasi-military rigidity. Mail is censored, visitation privileges are closely controlled, privacy is virtually nonexistent, and inmates march in groups and are identified by number.

Certain operational policies characterize such institutions. Particular emphasis is placed upon maintaining staff and inmate "distance." The inmates are required to defer to the status of custodial and staff personnel by addressing them as "mister" or by their appropriate rank. Disciplinary infractions are dealt with summarily; guards, for example, are required to "write up" any offensive conduct or failure to obey these rules by an inmate. Failure to do so brings an immediate reprimand from the guard's superior.

This impersonality and social distance is maintained by mass handling of prisoners. Inmates, for example, are often marched in groups to meals, to work, to recreation, and to the commissary. As a consequence, inmates and staff have very little opportunity for personal interaction. This massive impersonality of the traditional institutions can be seen in Sykes's study of a maximum-security institution in New Jersey. Each inmate coming into that institution is issued a *Handbook for Inmates* which states, among other things, the following:

> Form by twos when passing through the Center. Keep your place in line unless you are ordered to step out.
>
> When walking in a line, maintain a good posture. Face forward and keep your hands out of your pockets.

When the bell rings for meals, work, or other assignment, turn out your light, see that your water is turned off, and step out of your cell promptly.

On returning to your Wing, go directly to your cell, open the door, step in, and close the door without slamming it.

Gambling in any form is not allowed.

Do not speak or make gestures to persons who are visiting the institution.[18]

A number of observers who have studied the patterns of interaction in a traditional prison have pointed out that this distance and impersonality actually breaks down. It is not possible for custodial people to maintain their authority over inmates because prisoners do not perceive the authority of the guards as legitimate and thus they do not feel compelled to obey. Also, the officials cannot distribute meaningful rewards or sanctions which might provide them with control over the inmates. First, with increasing rapidity today, the courts are forbidding use of many of the usual forms of discipline that correctional officials relied upon in their attempts to control prisoners, and secondly, what may be intended by officials as a punishment, such as solitary or segregated confinement, is actually a "reward." The individual receives greater prestige in the eyes of the inmates for ignoring the rules and being punished.

Within most traditional prisons, the pressures that prison officials apply have been shown to increase the rapid growth and development of an inmate subculture. Such prison subcultures present an interesting view of human behavior under conditions of enforced control and confinement.

The most obvious manifestation of such subcultures is the formation of *inmate groups*. These groups are fostered by the stresses and deprivations associated with imprisonment. Since inmates spend extensive time together under the circumscribed environment of regimentation and confinement, they are drawn together on the basis of similar experiences which develop into common perceptions and interests. These prisoner groups provide meaningful rewards to their members since they offer protection from the actions of the prison officials and other inmates. The group in turn exerts influence over its members as well as restraining nonmembers. The leader's knowledge of prison life is used to manipulate official policies and custodial personnel so that they can be used for the benefit of the group. The "old con" instructs the new inmate. Through membership, the individual inmate gains access to special privileges and "grapevine" communication, which is particularly important when officials restrict communication. In return for conforming to the demands of the inmate group, the inmate gains satisfaction from membership among persons who understand him, and he enjoys the greater physical security which the group provides.

Certain mechanisms maintain the inmate groups. Newcomers are screened for membership qualifications, and once accepted, they are taught certain values and attitudes which have been transmitted through generations of prisoners. In addition, a novice is taught certain argot or slang expressions which are part of the inmate subculture. This argot permits the inmate to classify his perceptions of others into some sort of role framework. In the free world, we speak of Mr. Smith, the attorney, or of Mr. White, the engineer. Thus, some role-sets develop, according to the occupation of the individual. In prison, almost everybody is just another "con"; in order to differentiate and identify individuals by role-sets, such expressions as a "real man," "fag," "wolf," or "ball buster" are applied. Thus, the newcomer learns that his fellow inmates are as varied as people in the outside world. Some are okay; others are dangerous and should be avoided. Group ties are supported by sanctions ranging from gossip and ostracism to violence. Inmate commitment to these groups is encouraged by the basic split between officials and inmates, the emphasis on custody, and the inmate's hostility against officials.[19]

In order for an individual to become a member of an inmate group, the novice must first be accepted for membership and then must be willing to accommodate himself to the values and customs of the inmate group. Clemmer calls this the process of "prisonization," which is the taking on by the inmate "in a greater or less degree, the folkways, mores, customs, and general culture of the penitentiary." The newcomer adapts to the life of the prison, accepting the humble role of prisoner, new habits of eating and sleeping, and a new language. He makes the values of the inmate group his own. [20]

Sykes and Messinger have examined the values and general culture that prisoners within custodial-oriented institutions adopt as a part of the inmate society. They refer to these values as the "inmate social code," which is similar to Clemmer's idea of prisonization. This social code admonishes inmates to:

1. Not interfere with other inmate's interests
2. Never rat on another con to the prison officials
3. Don't be nosy; don't have a loose lip; keep off a man's back
4. Be loyal to your class—the cons
5. Don't exploit other inmates. This means breaking your word, selling favors, being a racketeer or welshing on debts
6. Play it cool—do your own time
7. Don't be a sucker—guards are hacks or screws and aren't to be trusted
8. Be tough—don't suck around; don't whine or cop out.[21]

A number of researchers have examined how inmates become socialized to the values of the inmate subculture over time. Wheeler set about to see the degree to which prisoners identified with the values of the institutional staff as compared with the values of the inmate code. He found that the period of time a prisoner spends inside the institution affects the way he identifies with the values of the staff or the values of other inmates. For the first six months of incarceration, the attitudes and values of the inmates are more similar to those of the prison staff. After six months of imprisonment, the inmate begins to identify more and more with the other inmates and the prison social code. When it comes near the time for his release from prison (less than six months to serve), the inmate becomes more accepting once again of staff values and influence.[22]

Another study of prisoners in a maximum-security institution, conducted by Garabedian, confirmed Wheeler's findings and found that inmates in the early phases are twice as likely to conform to staff norms as inmates in the middle period. This trend suggests that there may be a steady absorption of the prison culture similar to the process of prisonization, but that this process is reversed as the inmate comes to the end of his prison career. [23]

The Collaborative Model

In recent years, the administration of prisons has been undergoing some significant changes. Increased emphasis is being placed upon the development of a collaborative model that would offset the negative consequences of authoritarian programming in the traditional model. The collaborative model rests on the idea that inmate rehabilitation and reintegration can be better accomplished through closer interpersonal relationships between inmates and the institutional staff and through use of the full range of community resources. Increased contact with noncriminal ways of life is expected to lead to the assimilation of more appropriate values on the part of the inmate.

This model stresses the need to reduce mass treatment and depersonalization. A number of prisons have implemented certain policies in this regard. Under certain circumstances, inmates are allowed to express their individuality by wearing civilian attire rather than the traditional prison garb. Some freedom is also permitted in hair styles or the growth of a beard, sideburns, or mustache. The old policy of requiring inmates to march to the dining hall and to sit in silence on one side of long, narrow tables is giving way to the use of small, scattered, informal dining rooms, where the inmates sit around a conventional table and are able to converse with each other.

Greater emphasis is placed on decreasing the size of residential units. In medium and minimum-security institutions, many states are constructing small dormitories or individual rooms. In fact, in spite of the cost, some institutions are being constructed so that it is physically impossible to house a second person in the room. Hygiene facilities, such as toilets, washrooms, and showers, are being partitioned for greater privacy.

Many institutions are also making their schedules more flexible, with the inmates given greater latitude to determine their own schedules for waking up, eating, working, and retiring and their use of leisure time or recreational facilities. Such a policy exists under the differential treatment program at the Robert F. Kennedy Youth Center at Morgantown, West Virginia. This institution, which houses federal violators up to age twenty-three, permits inmates to have alarm clocks so that they can wake early to study academic subjects and thus earn incentive points.

One of the most important and imaginative features of the collaborative model is its emphasis upon a coordinative endeavor for purposes of inmate rehabilitation.[24] One such promising program is the *integrated treatment team concept*. This arrangement may prove to be the single most meaningful contribution of the collaborative approach. In the traditional model, custodial personnel were often suspicious of treatment personnel and vice versa; inmates were often distrustful of both and would play one off against the other. Although line personnel were in much more frequent contact with inmates than were members of the treatment staff, they were often downgraded by the treatment personnel for their preoccupation with security rather than treatment. By the same token, the treatment staff was often criticized by custodial people for not understanding the necessity for security and for being "bleeding hearts."

The integrated treatment team approach recognizes that for purposes of rehabilitation, certain conditions and attitudes must prevail. It is based on the belief that:

1. Effective communications must exist between treatment and custodial personnel and between these groups and the inmates.

2. Custodial personnel have a very important role to play in treatment and rehabilitation because of their daily contact with inmates.

3. The experience of custodial people can be of importance to the rehabilitative objectives of the treatment staff.

4. Treatment personnel can be of assistance to the custodial force in helping them to recognize certain behavioral manifestations of inmates and to diagnose and deal with inmate problems.

5. Any program of meaningful change must involve the inmate in the program.

Out of the recognition of these factors, staff teams were developed initially in juvenile training schools and in several federal correctional institutions. Although some problems did develop in implementing such programs, there were some significant contributions as well: Custodial personnel were given the opportunity to become active and functioning members of an overall treatment approach. They were developed into paraprofessionals and were trained in counseling and other rehabilitative techniques. No longer were they merely turn-keys or guards; now they joined with treatment personnel in performing casework and classification services for inmates assigned to their custody. These staff teams, in collaboration with the inmates, developed special programs, monitored the progress of the inmates under their care, and functioned as a unified whole.

This development is in sharp contrast with the classification and counseling practices that usually prevail in traditional institutions. In these, a single classification committee, presided over by senior custodial personnel, is concerned primarily with security classification of inmates and their work assignments. Caseworkers present information regarding an inmate to this committee and make recommendations for educational and vocational training and work assignments. Rarely are members of the custodial force consulted, nor is the inmate significantly involved. Consequently, the custodial staff feel no obligation to participate in the inmate's program and to oversee his progress. The social caseworkers usually have so many prisoners to counsel that counseling sessions are nothing more than a few minutes' discussion with the inmate. The social caseworkers have no idea of how well inmates are doing because they lack contact with the custodial personnel assigned to the cell block or work area. Only in serious disciplinary cases is the caseworker even aware of any particular problems the inmate may be having, and by the time the case becomes serious, what might have been prevented has already occurred. By the same token, the inmate, unable to receive any help from his infrequent counseling sessions with the caseworker and ignored by custodial personnel, turns to his fellow inmates for support.

The collaborative model and communications. As might be imagined, the collaborative model has contributed to the growth of communication among treatment staff, custodial personnel, and the inmates themselves. Custodial personnel, in most instances, have found that inmate morale and cooperation are more directly related to the manner in which inmates are treated than to how strictly discipline, security, and other control measures are imposed. This should come as no surprise. Most inmates who have had some meaningful input into the decisions made about them are likely to react more favorably to their particular programs and be more interested in proving that their ideas are correct than are inmates who are given little or no opportunity to express themselves.

Inmate expression is very important to the concept of the collaborative model, and therefore group counseling is used extensively to foster communication. Group counseling sessions, involving treatment and custodial people and inmates, are held periodically. Although most of these sessions center on the concerns of the inmate, they provide the treatment and custodial personnel the opportunity to understand the range of problems and attitudes associated with prison life and to express themselves and explain their actions to the inmates as well.

In these counseling sessions, a primarily nondirective method is employed by both treatment and custodial staff. The custodial staff is trained by counseling specialists in how best to develop their own counseling techniques. Many of these sessions are quite frank and open discussions. Although a number of the inmates often use these sessions to blame the police, the correctional personnel, or others for their problems, they do provide the custodial and treatment personnel some insight into who might be potential troublemakers and they give inmates a chance to express their feelings. Without these sessions, the institutional personnel might never know who these individuals are and how to deal with their negative attitudes, and without the opportunities for mutual discussion, an inmate is likely to express his negative attitudes in disruptive behavior within the institution, which heightens tension and could conceivably lead to serious problems of disorder within the prison.

The collaborative model and participatory decision making. Another significant feature of the collaborative model is the utilization of inmate representatives in the institutional policymaking process. This inmate representation has two purposes:

1. To enable inmates to have some advisory input into the management policies and decisions of the institution.

2. To assist the administration in the actual day-to-day management of the institution by offering alternative mechanisms to solve inmate grievances and to improve discipline.

The idea of inmate councils or a form of inmate self-government is not new. In the 1860s, the Detroit House of Correction, under the leadership of its director, Zebulon Brockway, established a policy whereby selected prisoners were assigned to custodial and monotorial duties.[25] In 1888, the warden of the Michigan State Prison in Jackson formed the Mutual Aid League of Michigan in which he appointed nine prisoners to serve as an advisory board for the purpose of preserving "good order."[26] The individual most responsible for the development of inmate governance was Thomas M. Osborne, who, beginning in the first quarter of the present century, established inmate governments at the Auburn and Sing Sing prisons in New York and at the naval prison at Portsmouth, New Hampshire. Inmate governance councils based on the system developed by Osborne, were then adopted by a number of other prisons in the eastern United States.

Inmate governance councils generally have certain features in common. Inmate representatives are chosen by the inmates themselves. These representatives then meet at periodic intervals with institutional representatives to discuss rules and regulations that guide the policies of the institutional staff in their handling of the prison population. This affords the inmates some input into the regulatory process. In some cases, these inmate councils serve as adjudicatory boards to handle inmate grievances and discipline. For example, an inmate court can be established to determine appropriate disciplinary measures for the violation of certain regulations by inmates. Instead of the prison administration unilaterally deciding what disciplinary action to impose, the matter is turned over to the inmate council for disposition.

Inmate governance councils can also keep the prison administration aware of certain grievance areas that threaten the stability of the institution. The problems associated with racism are a particularly sensitive area within many prisons today. One of the major difficulties in combating this phenomenon is the absence of dialogue between prison staff and inmate groups which might alleviate the underlying causes of the friction. Without this dialogue, attitudes are often expressed in aggression and violence, inmate strikes, and a further polarization between inmate groups as well as between inmates and prison officials. The importance of opening up channels of communication through inmate participation in decision making can be seen by the following report of the South Carolina Department of Corrections:

> One way in which to head off confrontation is the use of the concept of maximum feasible participation. This term means little more than the notion that those who are allowed a voice in the rule-making process are more likely to obey such rules. It does not mean that the prisons would be run by a town meeting of the cell blocks or even that there would be any real power given to inmates to control the prisons. All that is implied by the notion is that at some point along the line, the inmate (either individually or through a representative) is allowed to make a meaningful input into the decision-making process that surrounds him with rules. One means of accomplishing this goal would be the establishment of an inmate council with elected representatives. Such a council should be able to present questions to the administration concerning various rules and practices of the institution and receive a straightforward answer. The inmate council would then be able to accept the explanation or suggest alternatives for the consideration of the administrators. Through a series of long-range dialogues between inmates and administrators, many of the problems which plague our prisons could be worked out.[27]

It must be pointed out that shared decisionmaking through the development of inmate councils has not enjoyed a great deal of success in the past. Typically, a number of problems have arisen. In the first place, correctional officials have been very reluctant to share any of their prerogatives with inmates. This has led to situations where inmate councils have little legitimacy with the prison officials and, as a result, even less legitimacy with the inmate population. Thus, rather than advising on problems that are meaningfully connected with institution management, they are often given less sensitive tasks, such as organizing inmate recreation and cultural activities, athletic contests, talent shows, and art and craft projects.

A great deal of the opposition that prison officials express toward creation of these shared decision-making programs has been brought about by the negative experiences they have had with such programs in the past. Sometimes, inmate cliques have controlled elections to councils or have put pressures on those elected to reduce their orientation to staff objectives. Often these advisory groups are oriented primarily to articulating and exaggerating inmate complaints and presenting the prison officials with their demands without addressing the merits of the complaints objectively. In some instances, inmate council members have used their position on the council to extort special considerations from other inmates. In a few institutions where these councils do exist in any meaningful way, the trend in recent years has been to actively engage them in some more important areas of mutual concern, such as food service, housekeeping, and safety, but retain key management decision making by prison officials.

CURRENT STATUS OF CORRECTIONS

Although corrections has made definite progress in recent years, hard questions are being raised as to how meaningful this progress has really been. A great deal of concern is being expressed over whether prisons, even with the employment of innovative programs, will ever succeed in reforming a significant number of inmates. Many knowledgeable penologists feel that because of the very nature of the environment within prisons, even the best devised programs will, at most, achieve only a limited success by almost any standard.

Today the situation is somewhat paradoxical. On the one hand, we are developing more and better programs and personnel to operate them; on the other hand, problems within prisons are also accelerating. In face of mounting fiscal problems, states are unable to allocate the necessary resources to operate correctional systems; at the same time, more and more offenders are being sentenced to institutions that are often unable to accommodate them. With greater use of probation and other diversionary measures, our prison populations are increasingly becoming populated with the more hardened and intractable offender. Racial problems, drugs, violence, and a multitude of other concerns face prison managers. Society continues to subsidize this failure in ever more costly ways. It has been estimated that it costs the taxpayers between $6,000 and $7,000 annually to keep an unmarried man in prison and approximately $11,000 to imprison a married man when we include the cost of public welfare support which goes to his family during his absence.[28] When we measure our "product" by these cost factors, it is obvious that we should seriously examine some possible alternative solutions.

One final comment should be made. This need for more meaningful alternatives is not meant to imply, as some would recommend, that we abolish prisons completely—such suggestions are ludicrous. A certain percentage of offenders pose a threat to the safety of society and must be imprisoned. However, there are many prisoners in our penal institutions today who would be more effectively dealt with by means other than imprisonment. Assuming these prisoners can be identified, the question then becomes: Are we, as a society, more interested in merely punishment through incarceration or do we really want to forsake punishment so that we can improve the chances of having offenders lead a noncriminal life? The next chapter will examine some new correctional programs which are attempting to accomplish just that.

SUMMARY

The corrections component of the criminal justice system in the United States is a checkerboard affair of various programs, philosophies, and institutions. Overall, it suffers from a number of weaknesses: It is overly fragmented;

it has been overused; it has traditionally emphasized custody; and it suffers from citizen apathy, lack of financial support and lack of an effective means to evaluate its work.

Prison programming generally includes vocational and academic training, health programs, libraries, recreational programs, prison industries, and some form of classification procedure. Prisons may be classified by the degree of security they provide and by their program emphasis. While the traditional model emphasizes an authoritarian environment, the collaborative model emphasizes integrating treatment and custodial personnel in a team approach that includes the inmate in the operations of the institution and in his own program.

Suggested Additional Readings

Clark, Ramsey. "Prisons: Factories of Crime." In David M. Petersen and Charles W. Thomas, eds., *Corrections: Problems and Prospects.* Englewood Cliffs, N.J.: Prentice-Hall, 1975.

Cohn, Alvin W. "Contemporary Correctional Practice: Science or Art?" *Federal Probation* 34 (September 1970).

Dinitz, Simon, and Walter C. Reckless, eds., *Critical Issues in the Study of Crime.* Boston: Little, Brown, 1968.

Geis, Golbety. "Recruitment and Retention of Correctional Personnel." *Crime and Delinquency* 12 (July 1966).

Gill, Howard B. "A New Prison Discipline." *Federal Probation* 34 (June 1970).

Glaser, Daniel. "Politicization of Prisoners: A New Challenge to American Penology." *American Journal of Correction* 33 (November–December, 1971): 6–9.

Goldfarb, Ronald, and Linda Singer. "Disaster Road: The American Prison System." *Intellectual Digest* 2 (December 1971).

Martlin, M., ed. "Corrections in the United States." *Crime and Delinquency* (January 1967).

Megathlin, William L., and Sherman R. Day. "The Line Staff as Agents of Control and Change." *American Journal of Corrections* 34 (May–June 1972).

National Council on Crime and Delinquency. *Coordinating California Corrections: Institutions.* Sacramento, Calif.: NCCD, July 1971.

Piven, Herman, and Abraham Alcabes. *The Crises of Qualified Manpower for Criminal Justice: An Analytic Assessment with Guidelines for New Policy.* Vol. 1. Washington, D.C.: U.S. Government Printing Office, 1969.

Teeters, Negley K. "State of Prisons in the United States: 1870–1970." *Federal Probation* 33 (December 1969).

Notes

1. National Advisory Commission on Criminal Justice Standards and Goals, *Corrections* (Washington, D.C.: U.S. Government Printing Office, 1973), pp. 10–14.

2. See Michael S. Serrill, "Profile—Minnesota," *Corrections Magazine* 1 (3) (January–February 1975): 3–28.

3. National Advisory Commission, op. cit., p. 1.

4. Committee for Economic Development, *Reducing Crime and Assuring Justice* (New York: Committee for Economic Development, 1972), p. 39.

5. Federal Bureau of Prisons, *Thirty Years of Prison Progress* (Washington, D.C.: U.S. Government Printing Office, n.d.).

6. Federal Bureau of Prisons, *Annual Report, 1969* (Washington, D.C.: U.S. Printing Office, 1969).

7. Louis P. Carney, *Introduction to Correctional Science* (New York: McGraw-Hill, 1974), p. 128.

8. Michigan Governor's Committee on Corrections, *Committee on Corrections Report* (Lansing, Mich.: 1972), p. 12.

9. Vernon Fox, *Introduction to Corrections* (Englewood Cliffs, N.J.: Prentice-Hall, 1972), p. 174.

10. President's Commission on Law Enforcement and Administration of Justice, *Task Force Report: Corrections* (Washington, D.C.: U.S. Government Printing Office, 1967), p. 51.

11. *Gilmore v. Lynch,* 400 F.2d 228 (9th Cir. 1968) aff'd *Younger v. Gilmore,* 404 U.S. 15, 92 S.Ct. 250, 30 L. Ed. 2d 142 (1971).

12. Elmer H. Johnson, *Crime Correction and Society* (Homewood, Ill.: Dorsey, 1968), p. 560.

13. Ibid.

14. Ibid., p. 562.

15. Walter C. Reckless, *The Crime Problem* (New York: Appleton Century Crofts, 1967), p. 705.

16. Ibid., p. 706.

17. President's Commission, op. cit., pp. 179–180.

18. Gresham M. Sykes, *A Society of Captives* (New York: Atheneum, 1970), p. 23.

19. George H. Grosser, "The Role of Informal Inmate Groups in Change of Values," *Children* 5 (January–February 1958): 26.

20. Donald Clemmer, *The Prison Community* (New York: Holt, Rinehart & Winston, 1958), pp. 298–300.

21. Gresham Sykes and Sheldon I. Messinger, "The Inmate Social Code," in Norman Johnston, et al., eds., *The Sociology of Punishment and Correction* (New York: Wiley, 1970), pp. 401–408.

22. Stanton Wheeler, "Socialization in Correctional Communities," *American Sociological Review* 26 (October 1961): 699–700.

23. Peter G. Garabedian, "Social Roles and Processes of Socialization in the Prison Community," *Social Problems* 11 (Fall 1963): 145.

24. For example, see Robert B. Levinson and Roy E. Gerard, "Functional Units: A Different Correctional Approach," *Federal Probation* 37 (December 1973): 8–15.

25. Zebulon R. Brockway, *Fifty Years of Prison Service* (New York: Charities Publication Committee, 1912), pp. 96–97.

26. Harold M. Helfman, "Antecedents of Thomas Mott Osborne's 'Mutual Welfare League' in Michigan," *Journal of Criminal Law, Criminology and Police Science* 40 (January–February 1950): 597–600.

27. South Carolina Department of Corrections, *The Emerging Rights of the Confined* (Columbia, S.C.: 1972), p. 94.

28. N. C. Chamelin, V. B. Fox, P. M. Whisenand, *Introduction to Criminal Justice* (Englewood Cliffs, N.J.: Prentice-Hall, 1975), p. 396.

Chapter 15

Community-Based Corrections: Programs, Facilities, and Future Trends

In the past few years, corrections has increasingly sought alternatives to traditional forms of imprisonment and to prisons themselves. This change of thinking is seen in three current trends in corrections. First, offenders who require institutionalization are increasingly being commited to a growing number of smaller penal institutions near urban areas. Prison administrators are realizing that massive and isolated prisons do not provide the best setting for prison programs; institutional programs and inmates must interact more with the programs, resources, and positive influences available in society. As a result, states are increasingly using their correctional resources to establish and maintain smaller urban facilities rather than continuing to construct additional isolated institutions in rural areas. Second, with the creation of institutions, increasing emphasis is being placed on developing special programs that have in some cases been specifically designed for such community-based institutions. Third, probation and parole are now more often used as alternatives to incarceration. In this chapter we shall look at some of the special programs and institutions that are developing under the community-based model.

BASIS FOR COMMUNITY BASED-CORRECTIONS: DIVERSION

The basic rationale behind community-based corrections is diversion; that is, directing offenders away from the criminal justice system itself when possible and, failing that, away from the usual processes of corrections. The growth of diversion is due to three important factors.

Failure of Traditional Methods

The usual means of handling offenders has been an abysmal failure which more than likely contributes to the incidence of crime rather than deterring or preventing it. For example, even the U.S. Bureau of Prisons, which is probably our most progressive penal system, was elated to find in a recent study that two years following release from that system only one-third of the released offenders were recidivists.[1] Many penologists would put the actual rate of recidivism much higher, around 50 to 60 percent. Since it is likely that many released offenders commit additional crimes but are never caught, the picture is even more bleak.

Impact of the Community on Behavior

The idea that social forces in the community have the potential for impacting favorably or unfavorably upon the individual is by no means new. Studies conducted in the late 1920s and the early 1930s, as the result of a notable group of sociologists at the University of Chicago, pointed out that community disorganization contributed significantly to criminal behavior. Out of this research developed the famous Chicago Area Projects, which focused on providing casework assistance to gangs and neighborhood youths to prevent crime and to interest the youths in noncriminal activities.[2] These early projects provide the theoretical underpinning for ideas that have developed into formalized community-based corrections. Since that time, other cities have developed similar programs.[3]

Although the community can have both negative and positive effects, placing an offender in a prison often strengthens the negative influences. Separated from the positive influence of noncriminal elements of the community, the offender falls back on the influences of fellow inmates. Through the documented process of inmate socialization, he is often likely to become even more procriminal and less willing and able to identify with more appropriate noncriminal references in the outside world upon his release. Under these circumstances, he is most likely, upon release, to seek out associations in the community that have attitudes and characteristics that he became accustomed to while in the prison. The community-based correctional concept realizes that the offender must be encouraged to identify and maintain whatever ties he has with law-abiding members of society which incarceration usually severs, while at the same time being given appropriate supervision and help in order to limit his exposure to and association with those who encourage continued criminal behavior.

Growing Demands of Interest Groups

Interested citizens both within and outside the criminal justice system are becoming increasingly alarmed at the failure of our traditional correctional institutions to ''correct'' and are waging an effective campaign to encourage the adoption of alternative means for dealing with offenders. A corollary development may, in the long run, be even more effective than the influence of these groups alone. In the past decade, a large number of Americans have become disaffected with our governmental system in terms of how it operates. Much of this disenchantment results from citizens' feeling that they are merely acted upon, rather than actors in the process of government. Although one would be hard pressed to equate this general disenchantment with the operations of government with demand for correctional reform at the grass-roots level, it may well be serving to encourage already existing advocates of penal reform to focus more intensely on correctional operations as an immediate example of the need for more governmental responsiveness to citizen-initiated changes. This general disenchantment with corrections may be indicated by a recent attitude survey among Americans which found that 69 percent of the citizens surveyed had lost confidence in the ability of prisons to rehabilitate offenders.[4]

Diversion as an Alternative

These three factors—the failure of our criminal justice process and institutionalization to deter crime or prevent its recurrence, recognition that the community has a significant impact upon behavior, and the growing involvement of interest groups in penal reform—are modifying our traditional responses to crime and channeling our efforts in the direction of diversion with its emphasis on movement away from the justice system.[5] In the years ahead, we will probably see increasing growth of community-based programs in which established agencies of justice relinquish their traditionally unilateral handling and responses to deviant behavior in favor of joint programs involving the total community.[6]

Diversion focuses upon the development of specific alternatives to processing offenders in criminal justice system. Specifically, it recommends two approaches: In the first instance, special emphasis is placed upon developing more effective preventive strategies to divert offenders from criminal behavior so that they will not come in contact with the justice system to begin with. This approach—most common in dealing with juveniles—relies on attempts of parents, police, schools, neighborhoods, and peers to address social problems and thus minimize referral to or entry into the governmental agencies designated to handle those manifesting deviant behavior.[7]

However, preventive strategies do not always work—many individuals will still commit criminal offenses and be arrested. In these cases, the approach is to divert individuals from the usual processes for handling offenders. This approach is the subject of this chapter. Specifically examined will be alternative programs and strategies employed by corrections in diverting offenders from the usual forms of incarceration and the negative influences of the traditional prison and its programs.

The Relationship of Diversion to Reintegration

The long-range goal of diversion programs is the successful reintegration of the offender back into community life as a law-abiding citizen. To achieve this, the concept of community-based corrections is guided by three considerations:

1. *More realistic adaptation of institutional life to realities of life in the community*
   Prisons, jails, and juvenile institutions need to introduce changes which will make conditions in them more similar to conditions in free society.

2. *Link to other community agencies*
   There are a large number of organizations, public and private, offering services to a wide variety of distressed people. Examples are vocational rehabilitation, mental health, family counseling, and drug user programs. Correctional agencies need to make more successful links to these services so that they can be used to help the offender.

3. *Civic engagement and participation*
   Both by means of formal organizations and through the assistance of individuals, there is increasing recognition that volunteer citizen participation offers tremendous potential for working with offender reintegration problems. Traditionally, this civic participation has come from established religious, social service and employer groups. The correctional field needs to learn more effective methods of engaging these resources and applying their help.[8]

COMMUNITY-BASED PROGRAMS

Work-Release Programs

Under work-release programs, selected inmates are released from the institution during the day to continue their regular jobs in the community while spending daily after-work hours and weekends in confinement. Vermont is credited with establishing the first work-release program in 1906. The legislature of that state enacted a law providing for extramural civilian employment and authorized county sheriffs to set their prisoners to work outside the jail. Sheriff Frank H. Tracey, of Montpelier, rebuffed in his efforts to find employers, hired some of his prisoners to work on his own farm at prevailing rates paid civilian laborers. Part of the prisoners' earnings were paid to the state, and the remainder was retained by Sheriff Tracey and given to them when they finished their jail sentence. This early form of work release contained most, if not all, of the basic elements found in today's work-release programs.[9]

Although Vermont is credited with the original idea, the Huber Act passed by Wisconsin in 1913 is the model act upon which modern work-release programs are based. The Huber Act provided that county jail inmates, with the permission of the court, could be enrolled in work-release programs under the supervision of the sheriff. In 1957, a North Carolina statute extended work release to offenders in state institutions, but only certain misdemeanants recommended for work release by sentencing judges were eligible. In 1959, North Carolina passed new provisions which extended for the first time, eligibility to certain classes of felony offenders. By 1971, forty-one states and the District of Columbia had adopted work-release programs. The Prisoner Rehabilitation Act passed by Congress in 1965, authorized the U.S. Bureau of Prisons to use work-release programs.[10] In Europe, Sweden passed similar legislation in 1945, followed by Scotland in 1947. During the 1950s, Norway, Great Britain, and France also authorized similar programs. [11]

States that have implemented work-release programs usually follow one of two established approaches or a combination of the two. In the older approach, prisoners work in the community while living in the penal institution itself. This arrangement has caused some problems for both prison officials and inmates participating in the program. The work releasees are often harassed and intimi-dated by nonparticipating inmates, who accuse them of being "privileged characters." This has sometimes led to situations where qualified inmates have refused to participate in such programs. Another problem is controlling the flow of contraband smuggled back into the prison by work releasees either volun-tarily or because of inmate intimidation and threat. A third problem is that many prisons are situated in relatively remote areas where job opportunities in neighboring communities are very limited.

The second approach, which is gaining in popularity, is to use a special small facility situated near an urban center as a residential unit for inmates on work release. This arrangement seems to have overcome many of the problems associated with trying to administer a program from the prison institution itself.

Advantages and Limitations of Work Release

Work-release programs have advantages for the inmate and for the state. These programs permit the inmate to develop contacts and work experience not usually available within the prison. In this way, the individual prepares himself for eventual release. By establishing himself in a job while still in prison, the offender has immediate employment upon release and does not face the prob-lem of trying to find legitimate work with the associated stigma of being an exconvict. Work experiences can also be beneficial to many inmates who have failed to develop appropriate work habits throughout their lives. Unable to accustom themselves to the routine and the demands that a worker be at work at a certain time, do the job properly, and get along with supervisors and fellow workers, they often have preprison histories that show a pattern of failure. Prison industries have not been shown to be very effective in developing appro-priate work habits, but work-release programs can help overcome some of these problems.[12]

The second major advantage is economic. As pointed out in the previous chapter, it is very costly to keep an offender in prison, especially a married man.

In work release, the inmate is required to pay for his own room and board and provide support for his family. A prescribed portion of his earnings is taken out by prison officials for these purposes. A small sum is retained by the inmate in order to purchase necessities. Any remainder is put into a special fund which the offender receives upon release.

A number of studies have been conducted to determine the effectiveness of work-release programs. One of the largest and most intensive studies was made of work releasees in Santa Clara County, California, from 1967 to 1971. Data were gathered from the postinstitutional adjustment records of 991 inmates who had been on work release and compared with those of 1,369 prisoners who had not. The inmates in the sample had been released from the institution during the period from 1957 to 1967.[13] Among other things, the study indicated that inmates who had participated in work-release programs felt closer ties to their families and that their families were more predisposed to accept them, whereas families of nonparticipating inmates were more likely to reject them. Work releasees displayed slightly greater hostility toward the criminal justice system. The researchers felt that the reason for this was that individuals in the work-release program were less likely to perceive themselves as criminals and thus, were more resentful toward the police, courts, and corrections for their incarceration. The work releasees also were more successful in maintaining jobs during the period after their release. Finally, the work releasees were less likely to be rearrested and convicted for the commission of additional crimes after their release.[14]

Work release also has some problems associated with it. One of the major problems is that the unnatural restrictions placed on the work releasee have some psychological consequences. The individual is prohibited from participating in certain conduct. For example, he cannot stop on the way home after work for a drink with his fellow workers, regardless of how they might implore him to "have a beer" with them. By the same token, he must refrain from the use of any narcotic. Although a well-adjusted member of society could ignore these temptations, many offenders show a psychological predisposition toward lack of self-control. As a result, these temptations may be too much for the individual to handle. Many administrators of work-release programs go to great lengths to control such behavior, such as requiring that all individuals participating in the program take Antabuse, a substance that induces nausea if one drinks alcoholic beverages. Likewise, periodic urine specimens are taken to determine if the work releasee has taken narcotics.

Another negative consequence of work release is that these programs often compete directly with prison industries. If a prison system uses the work-release plan intensively, many well-motivated and skilled workers are diverted from prison industry programs. Also, unscrupulous private employers may exploit the individual on work release because of his vulnerability. Program administrators must constantly be alert to these consequences.

Academic-Pass Programs

Academic-pass or study-release programs are similar to work-release programs in that inmates are permitted to leave the institution to attend school and return to the prison or community facility after class. Most academic-pass programs utilize nearby educational institutions, such as vocational-trade institutes, junior and community colleges, and universities. In a few instances, correctional authorities also use nearby high schools, but generally high-school classes are taught within the institution. The release of an inmate to attend a high school presents some problems with inmate and student peer interactions not normally found at the college level. The Michigan Department of Corrections contracts with that state's regional network of community colleges to provide degree programs both inside the penal facility and at the community college. All costs for tuition, books, and other supplies are paid for by the state. One of the most extensive such programs is the cooperative program between Jackson Community College and Southern Michigan Penitentiary. It is not unusual in that program to find correctional employees and inmates sitting in the same classroom with regular students, exchanging and sharing viewpoints and gaining new perspectives through dialogue.

One interesting program, which had its beginnings in Oregon, is the New Gate Project. This project is now being sponsored by the National Council on Crime and Delinquency. This program is designed to offer inmates the opportunity to obtain an on-campus university education. In conjunction with cooperating universities, inmates are enrolled in academic programs and live like other students in university residence halls or dormitories. They must refrain from use of alcoholic beverages or narcotics and must report to supervising counselors in their dormitories at least once a week. The cost of this program is about the same as maintaining an unmarried prisoner in the traditional penitentiary.[15]

The purpose of academic-pass programs is, of course, to enable deserving interested inmates to obtain the education and job skills necessary to lead legitimate and productive lives upon their return to society. Through education, it is hoped that they can assimilate more appropriate values and become contributing members of society.

Conjugal and Family Visitation Programs

Conjugal visitation is a program by which the wife and in some cases the children of an inmate are permitted to visit with him in a special private facility of the prison. Usually, a separate section of the prison or small cottages are made available. Here, the inmate and his wife may have privacy and engage in the physical phase of the conjugal relationship. Advocates of conjugal visitation programs contend that these programs help the inmate maintain meaningful ties with his wife and children and that it reduces the incidence of homosexuality among inmates. Those opposed to such programs argue that (1) they are incompatible with existing mores since they emphasize mostly the physical satisfaction of sex; (2) married inmates who participate in these programs are those individuals who can best adjust to prison life anyway; (3) those inmates who present the greatest sexual problems, i.e., homosexuals and other sex deviates, are least likely to benefit from conjugal visits; (4) such programs offer no solution to the sexual tensions of single male or female prisoners; (5) wives may become pregnant, creating further problems for the state and the inmates; and (6) the maintenance of these separate, private facilities is too costly.[16]

Conjugal visits were first established in the United States at the Parchman Prison farm in Mississippi in 1918. At this institution, a "little red house" was set aside for the use of inmates and their wives. More recently, the California State Prison at Tehachapi instituted a somewhat similar program. At Tehachapi, housing which was previously occupied by staff has been set up to accommodate family visits. Eligible inmates are permitted the use of this facility for a two or three-day period, during the prerelease phase of their sentence. This situation more closely resembles the full family setting. Facilities for cooking and recreation are provided, and the children are included.

The Latin American countries and a number of West European nations have for many years sanctioned conjugal visits for their inmates. Many Latin American countries do not restrict their programs to male inmates; in certain cases, female inmates are permitted conjugal visits with their husbands. Some Latin American nations even permit male prisoners to engage the service of prostitutes, who are brought into the penitentiary for the men.[17]

The value of conjugal or family visiting programs is unclear. There is some evidence that the fears of those who argue against them have not been realized. On the other hand, there also exists no well-documented evidence that such programs have been very successful in meeting the objectives of their proponents.

Michael Serill, writing for *Corrections Magazine*, describes the operation of the family visiting program at California's San Quentin Penitentiary in the article quoted below.[18]

Family Visiting at San Quentin

Richard Schwerdtfeger pulled his station wagon up to the gate of San Quentin prison and began unloading box after box of groceries. The boxes, along with several pieces of luggage, were searched by a guard and transferred to an electric cart inside the prison gate. Schwerdtfeger, his wife, and his daughter, Joanna, piled into the cart themselves and chugged off to the main prison several hundred yards away. The cart passed through an electric gate leading to a triangular patch of grass enclosed by a high fence topped with barbed wire. Forming two sides of the triangle were the walls of two of San Quentin's giant cellblocks. The third side was a cliff leading down to San Francisco Bay.

Within the enclosure were three 2-bedroom house trailers, each twelve by sixty feet. They were recently purchased by the California Department of Corrections for $6,000 each. The Schwerdtfegers, very excited, began moving their luggage and boxes of groceries into one of the trailers. Suddenly, a young man appeared—their son, Michael. Michael, twenty-nine, has been a resident of San Quentin for six and a half years. His crimes: murder, kidnapping, and robbery. His sentence: death, commuted four years ago to life without possibility of parole.

The Schwerdtfegers had been a very tightly knit family, they said, and had come to visit Michael frequently. But this was their first opportunity to see him privately, thanks to the Department of Corrections' "family visiting program." The program was "outstanding," according to the elder Schwerdtfeger, a heavy-set, jolly man with a bushy gray mustache. Just to be able to sit down and eat a meal with his son, to sit comfortably and talk, to watch television—it would be so much more "normal," he said, than the crowded atmosphere in the San Quentin visiting room. The family had been granted a nineteen-hour visit.

California's family visiting program has been in operation seven years now and Department of Corrections officials are as enthusiastic about it as they ever were. Twelve of the departments's thirteen institutions permitted 9,000 private visits with wives, parents, and other relatives through the program last year and the department has plans to expand it to perhaps double that size.

The visits last either nineteen or forty-three hours, and take place in the privacy of prison outbuildings and furnished trailers purchased for that purpose. New trailers, like those at San Quentin, have been installed within the security areas of several institutions so that all inmates except those in maximum security will have a chance to participate.

At San Quentin the man in charge of the program is Sergeant Hal Brown, a sixteen-year veteran of the prison. In June, about 150 of the prison's 2,400 inmates were enrolled in the program, Brown said, and many more qualify. Medium-security inmates, like Michael Schwerdtfeger, have their visits in the trailers inside the walls, while minimum-security men occupy seven apartments in two houses outside the walls.

Though inmates' wives are the most frequent visitors, Brown said, to call the program "conjugal visiting" would be a misnomer. To prove his point, Brown noted that in April there were 114 visits and 267 visitors; in May there were 87 visits and 174 visitors—meaning that many children and other relatives also come.

To qualify for the program, inmates must have twelve months "clean time," must never have been caught introducing contraband into the prison, and cannot be designated as a "mentally disordered sex offender." Wives must bring their marriage licenses with them to be admitted. The program operates six days a week, and visitors must supply all the food for the visits.

Correction officers are not permitted inside the apartments and trailers while a visit is going on; inmates are instructed to appear outside at certain hours of the day for the regular count.

Inmates can generally get a nineteen-hour-visit about every twenty days, Brown said, and a forty-three-hour visit about every forty days. In mid-June, the forty-three-hour visits were booked until September 29. "A nucleus of people get twice as many visits as anyone else," Brown said, because when there is a last minute cancellation there are a few wives who live near the prison and can be there within thirty minutes.

Brown, who handles the entire program alone, is well liked by both the visitors and inmates. The visitors greet him by his first name and give him kisses. He is the only staff member ever to have gotten a "certificate of appreciation" from the Black Muslims inside the prison for his "courtesy, fairness and helpful manner." Brown explained his popularity by saying that he is "flexible" in running the program. "It's not a normal thing to go to a state prison for a family visit, so you've got to give a little bit."

Despite the fact that he is heavily overworked, spending up to five hours a day of his own time on the program, Brown says that "Not one inmate is going to suffer. No visitor is going to suffer. . . . I'm going to do it [alone] to the best of my ability because I believe in it."

The sergeant says the family visiting program has been a "tremendous boost to morale in this institution. . . . The thing that really impresses me is that we're saving families. If we're saving families we're saving inmates, and we're saving kids." Brown contends that the initial opposition to the program by the line staff has largely dissipated.

Officials in other states largely oppose conjugal or family visiting within institutions, partly on the grounds that the same objective could be better accomplished through home furloughs. But Sergeant Brown pointed out that the great majority of inmates at San Quentin and other California institutions will never have a chance for furloughs, and said that the family visiting program is a viable alternative.

It has also been charged that conjugal visiting is degrading to both the inmate and his wife. But all Brown sees is "tremendous joy, happiness. People have the desire to be together and they don't [care] where. . . . [Furthermore] I don't think these guys are hunting for sex alone. The drive is to be with the people they love, to be with their families."

While the Schwerdtfegers were moving into their trailer in the medium-security visiting area, another group of people, and a swarm of children, were unpacking their groceries and making coffee in the two family visiting houses outside the walls.

George 2X Jackson and his wife Cynthia 2X, sat down in the living room of the "pink house" to talk to a visitor, while their two-year-old son George, Jr. romped happily on the rug. Jackson, doing one-to-fourteen years for forgery, said the family visiting program is "the best thing that ever happened" to California prisoners.

Jackson said he has been receiving visits since November, 1973, when he was classified minimum custody, and has had two or three a month ever since.

Jackson said he was married once before when he started another term in prison in 1968. He snapped his fingers, indicating that the marriage immediately broke up. "No contact," he said. "Across the table [in the visiting room] it's not real. There is no contact. You've got to be able to touch to maintain romantic love."

Asked whether he thought the program was degrading, Jackson bristled and escorted his visitor to his family's living quarters, which consisted of one large room with a bed, other furniture, and a private bath. "Is this degrading?" he asked. "We are Muslims. We respect our women. If I thought this degraded her, I would never do it."

To those who say that the family visiting program is more than any criminal deserves, Jackson replies: "Though we have broken the rules, we're still human. We still breathe and eat and love."

Home Furlough Programs

In the place of the conjugal visit, a growing number of states are experimenting with home furlough programs. These should be distinguished from emergency release programs in which an inmate is allowed to return home temporarily because of a serious situation in his immediate family, such as a death or grave illness, and is often accompanied by a supervising custodial officer. In home furlough programs, the inmate returns home for a few days without supervision.

In 1918, Mississippi was the first state to introduce furlough programs; these were ten-day holiday leaves for minimum-custody inmates. Arkansas followed in 1922; Louisiana was next in 1964. The U.S. Bureau of Prisons, North Carolina, Utah, and the District of Columbia introduced these programs into their systems in 1965. By 1972, twenty-nine states had home furlough programs for adult offenders.[19] Most had similar criteria for determining what type of inmate was eligible for home furlough. Usually, the factors considered were the security risk—the adjustment the individual had made while in prison and type of crime for which he was sentenced—and the time remaining to serve, and in many instances he had to be serving the remainder of his sentence under minimum-security conditions. Sex offenders were almost always excluded.[20]

A survey conducted in 1974 indicated that all but eleven states had adopted home furlough programs for adult offenders and that all but five states authorized home furloughs for juvenile offenders. Table 15-1 indicates inmate furlough programs by states for both adult and juvenile inmates.

Today, more than 350,000 furloughs are now granted annually to adult inmates in America's prisons. Once adult furlough programs were initiated, they grew with incredible speed. In Oregon, the first such program was approved in 1967 and nine furloughs were granted the following year; during 1974, a total of 27,000 such leaves were granted. Florida alone granted over 42,000 furloughs between July 1974 and April 1975; however, all but 12,000 of these went to residents of Florida's network of community correctional centers. By the same token, the vast majority of furloughs in Oregon were to residents in work-release centers.

The corrections directors in Connecticut, Illinois, Michigan, and other states with large furlough programs all say that furloughs are only one part of an overall program designed to build up a solid base of community and family support for an inmate *before* he walks out the front gate of the prison. Another benefit of furloughs, they say, is that they improve morale in institutions and

TABLE 15-1   Inmate Furlough Programs by States (1974)

	NUMBER OF FURLOUGHS			
	Adults		Juveniles	
	Per Month	Fiscal 1974	Per Month	Fiscal 1974
ALABAMA	90	1,805	NA[a]	NA
ALASKA	NA	NA	NA	NA
ARIZONA	NA	77[b]	NA	NA
ARKANSAS	14[c]	170[c]	NA	NA
CALIFORNIA	93[c]	1,121[c]	25	960
COLORADO	190	2,300	150	1,800
CONNECTICUT	550	6,600	235	2,800
DELAWARE	25	450	75-80	800-1,000
D.C.	3,000[d]	38,000[d]	NA	NA
FLORIDA	4,388[e]	53,000	84	1,011
GEORGIA	230	2,800	137	1,643
HAWAII	Not permitted		27	499
IDAHO	21	200	43	300
ILLINOIS	375[c]	4,500[c]	1,400	16,300
INDIANA	38	425[f]	110	1,300
IOWA	186	2,238	NA	NA
KANSAS	25	302	122	1,346
KENTUCKY	45	500	7	78
LOUISIANA	NA	1,671	NA	NA
MAINE	78	935	64	767
MARYLAND	500-700	5,000	210	2,100
MASSACHUSETTS	651[e]	8,115	No juvenile institutions	
MICHIGAN	400-500	5,282	45	500
MINNESOTA	33	393	NA	600
MISSISSIPPI	40	490	60-75	800-900
MISSOURI	NA	934	Not permitted	
MONTANA	Not permitted		34	402
NEBRASKA	194	2,322	Included in adult figures	
NEVADA	Furlough program just approved		1-2	8-10
NEW HAMPSHIRE	Furlough program just approved		100	1,200
NEW JERSEY	8,352	696	NA	NA
NEW MEXICO	NA	135	Included in adult figures	
NEW YORK	1,352	16,226	188	2,250
NORTH CAROLINA	2,918	35,020	130[g]	1,560
NORTH DAKOTA	6	29	7	168
OHIO	Furlough program just approved		200-300	3,160
OKLAHOMA	Not permitted		106	1,282
OREGON	3,716	27,000	NA	NA
PENNSYLVANIA	350	1,506	1,500	18,000
RHODE ISLAND	Furlough program just approved		150	1,800
SOUTH CAROLINA	753	9,877	Not permitted	
SOUTH DAKOTA	1	10	Included in adult figures	
TENNESSEE	105	1,300	459	5,508

TABLE 15-1   Inmate Furlough Programs by States (1974)

| | NUMBER OF FURLOUGHS | | | |
| | Adults | | Juveniles | |
	Per Month	Fiscal 1974	Per Month	Fiscal 1974
TEXAS	Not permitted		200	2,400
UTAH	45	540	25-40	350-
VERMONT	778	9,340	50	700
VIRGINIA	NA	4,500	127[h]	2,000
WASHINGTON	239	2,865	86	1,040
WEST VIRGINIA	Not permitted		Not permitted	
WISCONSIN	Not permitted		NA	NA
WYOMING	Not permitted		Not permitted	
FEDERAL SYSTEM	1,450	17,400	No juvenile institutions	

NA =Figures not available.
[a] From December 1974 through April 1975.
[b] Excludes furloughs from work release centers.
[c] Includes some work and study release.
[d] Program recently cut back sharply.
[e] For April 1975.
[f] From July 1974, through May 1975.
[g] From January 1975, through May 1975.
[h] For May 1975.

Reprinted with permission from the July/August 1975 issue of *Corrections Magazine,* published by the Correctional Information Service, Inc., 801 Second Avenue, New York, NY 10017.

give parole boards something tangible to look at when deciding whether an offender should be released.

One of the most controversial furlough programs in the country is in Massachusetts. This state has a program by which inmates serving life sentences for murder can ultimately participate in furlough programs. Some such offenders are now participating in the program. Massachusetts, like other states, has had to overcome tremendous public and political hostility to the adoption of such programs, and running battles over the feasibility of furloughs have been generated by the media, the legislature, the governor, and citizen opposition and support groups in that state.

The most typical criticism is that furlough releasees will commit new crimes during their period of freedom from institutional surveillance. Unfortunately, in a few instances, this has happened and has heightened the controversy. Another frequently expressed fear is that releasees will flee. Finally, there are those who contend that such programs increase the risk that additional children will be born to "problem families."[21] Society faces similar hazards from inmates released on parole and in many respects, furlough releasees are less likely to get into trouble than parolees. In the first place, since fewer individuals are released on furlough, correction officials can examine all the factors and be much more selective in whom they permit to participate in these programs. Secondly, the criteria for participation in such a program are much more stringent than those for parole eligibility. Since correctional officials will be blamed if an individual on furlough does get into trouble, they are very careful in their selection of home furlough releasees.

There are some sound arguments for the careful use of home furlough programs. An inmate's behavior and adjustment during temporary release gives correctional officers an opportunity to gauge the suitability of the individual for eventual release to parole. Home furlough allows outside facilities and resources to be utilized more fully, thus reducing the need to build, staff, equip, and supply certain institutional programs. For example, certain prerelease activities, such as mock job interviews could be replaced by direct "real" experience, and the family's home could be used rather than special facilities constructed within the institution for family visits. Such programs would also militate against the general trend of family dissolution, which is often a result of extended incarceration in prison.[22] Prison officials also point out that experience with home furlough programs makes the inmates more cooperative, more willing to obey orders from correctional guards, and more willing to participate in prison programs.[23]

Like other community-based institutional programs, home furlough programs will undoubtedly continue to be increasingly used as an alternative to long-standing correctional practices. The immediate need is to develop extensive research capabilities and analysis of its successes and failures so that guidelines can be developed for the future use of such programs.

COMMUNITY-BASED INSTITUTIONS

The Prerelease Guidance Center

Prerelease guidance centers are facilities where inmates are sent usually three to twelve months before their release on parole.[24] They are usually located near urban areas. Their purpose is to facilitate the adjustment of inmates from institutional life to free society by gradually exposing them to fewer controls. To offset the dependency syndrome that often accompanies extended incarceration, inmates in these settings are encouraged to be more independent in a positive sense.

The U.S. Bureau of Prisons began in 1961 to gradually establish a network of these centers in major urban areas throughout the United States. When a deserving inmate is within a few months of release, he is sent to one of these centers, ideally, in his home city. Each center closely supervises about twenty federal prisoners.

Inmates wear civilian clothes at the center. Following orientation sessions, they are encouraged to go out into the community and obtain employment. Gradually, as time passes and they begin to show that they are adjusting, they arre given more freedom. As their parole date approaches, some may even be permitted to move out of the center, although they are still required to return for counseling sessions and conferences several times a week.[25]

These centers are often staffed by specialists in counseling therapy who are rotated from regular institutional staff. Several of these programs utilize carefully screened college students in the behavioral sciences who work with youthful offenders as paraprofessional counselors. They often also assist the regular staff by providing coverage during the late night hours and weekends.[26] An important feature of this concept is the active involvement of federal parole officers in the counseling sessions. Thus, the parole officer who will assume the individual counseling responsibility when the inmate is placed upon parole has the opportunity to interact with the inmate before his release. Killinger and Cromwell give us some insight into how the program functions:

> When an individual returns from a temporary release to home, work or school, his experience can be discussed with him by staff, to try to assess his probable adjustment and to note incipient problems. Many difficulties can be anticipated in this way. The inmate's anxieties can be relieved by discussion, and discussion may also help him develop realistic plans for coping with prospective problems. When persistent or serious misbehavior occurs, sanctions are available to staff, ranging from restriction of further leaves or temporary incarceration to renewed institutionalization, with recommendation to the parole board that the date of parole be deferred.[27]

In recent years, a number of states have developed similar prerelease centers, and cooperative arrangements have been made between the U.S. Bureau of Prisons and some states in the development and utilization of such programs. For example, federal prerelease guidance centers in Detroit and Kansas City receive state inmates, and in a number of states the federal prison system sends its prisoners to state centers prior to their release. In this manner, duplication of facilities is avoided through cooperative correctional programming.

Halfway Houses

A recent movement in community-based corrections has been the development of halfway houses. In fact, the prerelease guidance center is a form of halfway house since it can be considered a "halfway-out" facility. Other programs are considered "halfway-in." The concept of the halfway house is not a new one. A special study commission in 1820 recommended that Massachusetts establish such programs.[28] In 1864, Boston opened a halfway house for women released from that state's prison system. In a few years, religious and volunteer groups opened similar facilities in Philadelphia, New York, Chicago, and New Orleans. All these operations were privately supported and managed. One well-intentioned group opened a halfway house for exconvicts in New York in 1896. This facility, known as Hope Hall, was run by a husband-and-wife team who, because of their action, suffered such police intimidation and harassment that they appealed to the president of the United States to intercede in their behalf and to restrain the police.[29]

The purpose of these early halfway houses was similar to their use today. They were founded to provide exconvicts a temporary place of shelter, food, clothing, advice, and aid in obtaining gainful employment.[30] The founders of these early halfway houses were the pioneers of community-based treatment centers. Unfortunately, they were often scorned and held in contempt by professional correctional workers. They also often met with a great deal of hostility and resentment from citizens in the communities where they were located as well as from public officials and law enforcement officers.

In the 1950s interest in the halfway house concept was renewed. Like their earlier counterparts, these modern halfway house facilities were also privately sponsored by interested citizens or religious organizations. In the last few years, there has been increasing interest in halfway houses supported by public monies and managed by professional correctional personnel. Recently, federal legislation was passed authorizing the use of halfway houses for federal parolees who are having difficulty making adjustment to their life in free society and appear to be running the risk of parole revocation. Rather than waiting for failure and having to recommit the individual to prison, the alternative is to send him to a community treatment center for additional intensive treatment, counseling, and supervision.

The federal government has also been developing what we can refer to as "halfway-in" programs. In October 1971, Congress authorized the federal courts to direct a probationer to reside or participate in the program of a community treatment center as a condition of probation and as an alternative to prison incarceration. As of 1972, the U.S. Bureau of Prisons was maintaining fourteen such institutions throughout the United States which were supervising a total of 350 offenders.[31]

A similar program, known as Probationed Offenders Rehabilitation and Training (PORT), has been established on a multicounty basis in Minnesota. This program provides an alternative for male offenders who require a greater change in their life style than probation can accomplish and yet do not belong in prison. The program provides for a live-in residence facility on the grounds of a state hospital. Both felons and misdemeanants are sentenced to this institution by the courts in the sponsoring three-county area. The program is supervised by a corporate board of directors, which consists of citizens in the area as well as local and county law enforcement and probation officials. Special efforts are made to enroll the offenders in educational institutions in the community, to find work for them, and to expose them to professional treatment and interaction with lay volunteers made up of interested citizens and students in nearby colleges.[32]

It would appear that the use of halfway houses will continue to grow in the years ahead and that these facilities will play new and important roles. For example, they probably will increasingly be used for individuals with special difficulties, such as drug abuse, alcoholism, and psychiatric problems. In an effort to serve these target groups, halfway houses will require a larger share of the correctional manpower and resources now being applied to the maintenance of traditional prisons. It has also been recommended that halfway houses serve still another important function. With the advent of bail reform, individuals who can meet certain criteria are being released on their own recognizance. One of the usual requirements is that the individual have roots in the community in which he stands accused. This would include family, friends, a job, etc. Many accused individuals, however, have poor family ties and poor work histories, which are often the result of educational and cultural deprivation. Not meeting some of the basic criteria, they are excluded from the use of recognizance bond and must await final disposition in jail. The halfway house could provide services to an individual, enabling him to become eligible for recognizance bond. At a minimum, this would include providing shelter and supervision prior to final disposition. Whether the accused is found guilty or not, he is usually in need of a range of services which the halfway house is often in a position to provide, directly or indirectly, such as medical, dental, psychological, and psychiatric services, individual and group counseling, and employment placement services. The delays which occur between the time of arrest and final disposition are often lengthy, in some cases six months or more. Even if the process is speeded up and the time from arrest to final disposition is reduced to two or three months, much can still be accomplished during this time.[33]

The Minnesota Restitution Center

In 1972, corrections officials of Minnesota approved the creation of the Minnesota Restitution Center. This pioneering corrections project operates under the theory that offenders should pay for their crimes by working and paying back their victims, not by sitting in a prison cell. As of 1975, seventy-one men had been released to it from the state prisons at Stillwater and St. Cloud. As the first program of its kind in the country, the center has attracted considerable attention among corrections professionals and the national media.

Most of the funding for the program has come from the Federal Law Enforcement Assistance Administration. This agency was so impressed with the concept that it has funded five other restitution centers, four in Georgia and one in Iowa. Several other states are considering similar programs. After visiting the Minnesota Restitution Center, a group of Canadian correctional officials began developing similar programs in that country. One of the advantages of the restitution center is that it has demonstrated itself to be a politically acceptable program, which would tend to encourage its establishment in other states.

Minnesota corrections administrators feel that the primary advantage of the program is that it finally focuses attention on the victim, who has long been neglected by the criminal justice system. It also significantly reduces costs to the taxpayers. On the average, it costs Minnesota between $16 and $25 a day to keep an inmate in a state prison, while the estimated daily cost of offender maintenance in a restitution center is only $14.50. At the same time, the inmates in the center are working, paying taxes, supporting families who might otherwise be on welfare, and of course, paying back their victims.

To be eligible for the program, an offender must meet certain conditions. For example, he must reside in the seven-county Twin Cities metropolitan region (which contains about two-thirds of the state's population); the crime that he was sentenced for must not have involved the use of violence or weapons; the offender must not have been arrested for a violent or weapons offense for the five preceding years; the offender's earning ability has to be compatible with the amount of restitution and the time he has remaining on parole; and he must not be a professional criminal.

The individuals chosen to participate in the program serve approximately four months in prison. Before they are released from prison, they must sign a contract with the parole board and the department of corrections by which they agree to abide by the rules of the restitution center and the conditions of the special parole that they are receiving. The conditions are that they obtain and hold a job and use a part of their earnings to make regular payments to their victims. They must also agree to pay $12.50 a week for room and board while staying at the center and to participate in both center and outside therapy programs if they have psychiatric, alcohol, or drug problems. If an offender fails to abide by these conditions, the center can petition the parole board to revoke his parole, and he will be returned to prison.

One feature of the program is that the potential candidate for the restitution center must meet with his victim. This is a unique experience for most offenders and often seems to make a strong impression on them.

The Community Corrections Center

A number of states are developing community-based correctional institutions in carefully selected city neighborhoods in an effort to reduce the isolation of offenders from community services and other resources. Most of these centers require that the individual live in. He may be released for short periods to work or visit with his family, but must return to the center at night. Others are centers for released offenders, such as individuals on parole. Special services and programs are available to help the released offender. If he is having a difficult time adjusting to release, he is encouraged to come into the center for assistance and counseling. As an extension of parole or postrelease services, such a center can draw upon the medical, social work, psychiatric, educational, and employment resources of correctional agencies and the community and can involve community, neighborhood residents, and family members in offender rehabilitation and reintegration.

At the present time, there appears to be no single model for the facilities or program design of a community corrections center. However, one of the most promising proposals has resulted from a recent project undertaken by the Institute for the Study of Crime and Delinquency. This project was designed to develop conceptual, operating, and architectural designs for correctional practice, and it resulted in the proposal for a community-based program for young adult offenders.[34] This so-called youth correctional center calls for three residential units located in the high-delinquency areas from which the young adult felon population is drawn. In Phase I, the offender would be housed in a medium-security residential unit, where he would be strictly confined at all times under close security. This phase would usually last for one month. In Phase II the offender would live in a less custody-oriented unit and would be given limited access to the outside community for work, school, or other activities. This period would last approximately three months. In Phase III the offender would reside in the community and return to the unit once a week or more often for group meetings and special services. This phase would last about twenty months.[35]

CORRECTIONAL ISSUES AND TRENDS IN THE FUTURE

Although it is dangerous to try to predict the changes that will possibly occur in corrections in the last quarter of the twentieth century, some observations should be given. Some definite trends seem to be developing today that might be useful for predicting the future issues, programs, and focus of corrections. Some of the more important trends will be examined in this section.

Judicial Expansion of Inmate Rights

In recent years, the courts, particularly those at the federal level, have been applying broad constitutional standards to the operations of penal institutions. The courts are beginning to insist that prisoners have certain rights which are no different from the rights of a free citizen. This is a fundamental reinterpretation of the law. In the past, an offender, as a matter of law, was considered to have forfeited virtually all rights upon conviction and to have retained only those rights which were expressly granted him by statute or the correctional authority.[36] The offender was considered a noncitizen and excluded from the constitutional protections afforded free members of society.

The National Advisory Commission on Criminal Justice Standards and Goals succinctly points out the former status of convicted offenders and the attitudes of the courts:

> The courts refused for the most part to intervene. Judges felt that correctional administration was a technical matter to be left to experts rather than to courts, which were deemed ill-equipped to make appropriate evaluations. And, to the extent that courts believed the offenders' complaints involved privileges rather than rights, there was no special necessity to confront correctional practices, even when they infringed on basic notions of human rights and dignity protected for other groups by constitutional doctrine.[37]

This attitude existed because society cared very little about corrections and even less about convicts themselves. The changes have occurred because society itself has become more concerned. The closer scrutiny of correctional practices was just one result of society's more sweeping concern for individual rights and governmental accountability, particularly of the executive branch, of which corrections is a part. This concern had its beginnings with the civil rights movement and was reflected in such areas as juvenile justice, public welfare, mental institutions, and military justice. Part of the growth of reform in correctional institutions and policies arose from the fact that corrections for the first time was being scrutinized and experienced by large segments of society who formerly had no contact with the system of justice and corrections in particular. The correctional experiences of dissenting groups, many of whom came from middle-class backgrounds, acted as a catalyst for change upon the entire justice process.

Finally, the questionable effectiveness of correctional systems as rehabilitative instruments, combined with the unbelievable conditions existing in many penal institutions, could no longer be ignored by the courts. As the courts began to examine the operations of correctional institutions and systems more carefully, they began to redefine the legal framework of corrections. They placed binding legal restrictions on correctional administrators and required that correctional systems measure up to externally imposed criteria rather than permitting them to police themselves, which had usually been the policy before.

As the courts started exerting more supervisory control over correctional operations, many aggrieved inmates saw that the courts were now for the first time being receptive to their claims. As a consequence, offenders flooded the courts with petitions for judicial relief, and the courts addressed themselves to the petitions. For example, in the 1971–1972 term of the U.S. Supreme Court this highest tribunal in the nation decided no less than eight cases dealing with convicted offenders and a few others which were at least related. In each of them the Supreme Court ruled in favor of the offender, and in five of the eight cases the decision was unanimous.

Some of the more significant Supreme Court rulings in the area of corrections have been that a formal procedure must be held in order to revoke one's parole,[38] that institutionalized offenders are entitled to access to legal materials,[39] that a sentencing judge cannot use unconstitutionally obtained convictions as a basis for sentencing an offender,[40] and that indefinite commitment of one who is not mentally competent to stand trial for a criminal offense violates due process of law.[41]

The National Advisory Commission on Criminal Justice Standards and Goals has proposed that states take the following immediate steps to ensure that their correctional systems comply with the changes occurring in the adjudicated rights of prisoners:

1. Each correctional agency should immediately develop and implement policies and procedures to ensure that those in custody have the right to immediate access to the courts (a) to challenge the legality of their confinement or conviction; (b) to seek redress for illegal conditions or treatment while in custody; (c) to pursue remedies in existing civil legal problems; and (d) to assert their constitutional rights when violated by correctional or governmental authority.

2. Each correctional agency should immediately develop and implement policies and procedures to ensure that offenders have access to legal assistance through counsel or a chosen substitute with problems or proceedings relating to their custody control management or legal affairs while under correctional authority. This would include counsel at: (1) post conviction proceedings testing the legality of conviction or confinement; (2) proceedings challenging conditions or treatment under confinement or other correctional supervision; (3) probation revocation and parole grant and revocation proceedings; (4) disciplinary proceedings in a correctional facility that impose major penalties and deprivations.

3. Each correctional agency should establish immediately policies and procedures to fulfill the right of offenders to be free from personal abuse by correctional staff or other offenders. The following should be prohibited: (1) corporal punishment; (2) the use of physical force by correctional staff except in extreme cases for self-defense, etc.; (3) any deprivation of clothing, bed and bedding, light, ventilation, heat, exercise, balanced diet or hygenic necessities; (4) infliction of mental distress, degradation or humiliation.[42]

The effects of these changes are being felt throughout correctional systems in the United States. The expansion of offenders' rights is the most recent indication that corrections is moving from a punitive strategy to a strategy of reintegration which requires that we acknowledge that 99 percent of all prisoners will someday return to free society. Without doubt, these judicial pronouncements have created difficulties for correctional administrators, as the suddenness of these changes found many prison officials unable to cope with them. In the long run, however, just as the pronouncements of the Supreme Court in the 1960s contributed significantly to increased professionalism among the police, so can they serve a similar role in corrections.

Improvements and Developments in Correctional Manpower Requirements

As corrections moves ahead, one of the first concerns must be for the continued development of professional management capabilities among correctional administrators. In the past, corrections has been characterized by a virtual absence of professionally trained managers. Just as in the police service, advancement was often up through the ranks with little thought given to the more difficult demands placed upon those in higher levels of management. When corrections saw its role as merely to maintain security and custody of offenders, the demands upon correctional administrators were far less demanding. Today, the problems of administration have grown tremendously as corrections is becoming increasingly involved in a wide range of programs, types of institutions, and policy decisions that are being imposed by the courts, legislative directives, and important reform groups.

Correctional systems are beginning to realize that the management of an institution or treatment center or any of the new programs requires expert managerial skills. A modern-day correctional administrator must be able to cope with such concerns as inmates' rights, employee-management relations, treatment programs, fiscal management, and the administration of the physical plant.

A number of state correctional systems are implementing programs of career development for middle- and upper-level management personnel. Young, college-educated men and women are being brought in and given experience in the various phases of the correctional system. As they mature and indicate their potential, they are encouraged to obtain advanced degrees in the area of management, such as public or business administration, or in their specialist areas, such as psychology, social work, or sociology.

Manpower skills are also being developed among personnel in the lower levels of correctional institutions. This is being brought about by some major organizational changes in a number of correctional institutions. In the past, most large correctional institutions were organized on the basis of two major operating units: custody and treatment. As we have seen, custody personnel are primarily concerned with maintaining discipline and security within the institutions, and the treatment staff consists of such personnel as psychiatrists, psychologists, educators, social workers and correctional counselors. Today, more and more institutions are being organized into small, relatively self-contained functional units or those which employ the correctional team concept.[43] For example, 50 to 100 inmates are housed together as a unit and work in a close, intensive treatment relationship with a multidisciplinary, relatively permanent team of staff members whose offices are located in the unit. Inmates assigned to one unit may have a history of narcotics abuse, another unit may be for inmates involved in academic or vocational programs, and another unit may be for inmates who present special security problems or have emotional problems that need intensive scrutiny.

As we saw in Chapter 14, the team approach, in which custodial and treatment personnel work together, recognizes that custodial personnel play a very important role in the programs the institution has established, and they are given additional training in order to carry out their responsibilities.

The Development of Correctional Alternatives

Diversion and community-based programs will almost certainly continue to grow as alternatives to the usual ways of handling offenders, and greater emphasis will be placed on the development and testing of these alternatives. A number of pilot programs are now being developed under the sponsorship of the federal government, and there are indications that the number of such programs is growing rapidly. Such programs as detoxification centers for alcoholics and offenders with related problems are being established in many parts of the country. Community programs for youth who are drifting away from parental control, community psychiatric programs, and services for those with chronic problems of unemployment are examples of the types of programs that are needed and are beginning to appear.[44]

The emphasis is on preventive services rather than on waiting until the problems of crime and delinquency have manifested themselves and then reacting through the very expensive process of incarceration. Increasingly, it would seem that incarceration will be used only when other alternatives have failed and for those individuals who demonstrate that because of their danger to society they must be locked up. In order to implement such preventive and diversionary strategy, however, we must develop better predictive or early warning systems that give us a clue that certain individuals are moving toward the correctional system. This strategy should reduce the workload of corrections and focus its attention more sharply upon those whose problems cannot be met more appropriately by other agencies.[45]

Changes in the Organization and Delivery of Correctional Services

The reader will recall that one of the obstacles to correctional reform is the fragmentation of correctional systems among various levels of government. Although the immediate future will not see all correctional programs and institutions centralized at the federal level or even at the state level, there will be less correctional fragmentation among political units than exists today. New programs and the associated involvement of the courts, law enforcement, and mental health and social welfare agencies will facilitate greater communication, resource exchange, and information sharing and conceivably reduce the multiplicity of correctional agencies among these levels of government.

Although the autonomous governmental control of correctional programs will be less, many more types of programs will be available. The Joint Commission on Correctional Manpower and Training sees the relationship between centralized administrative control and decentralized programming in the following way:

> The correctional system of the future will have a configuration of numerous, quite autonomous subsystems operating to maximize cooperation and interchange . . . [and] we ought not to expect a monolithic correctional apparatus for the United States in the future. But remedies must and will be found for the present problems of fragmentation. They will take the form, we predict, of a large repertoire of reciprocal arrangements between the parts of the total system. These new arrangements will be used flexibly and with much less reverence for the sanctity of organizational and governmental boundaries than is evident today.
>
> Offenders with special requirements will be sent to specialized facilities capable of meeting their needs, regardless of the jurisdictional niceties involved. Offenders whose primary requirement is to reestablish themselves in their home communities will be routed there and supervised by local authorities. The federal and state governments will facilitate the efforts of local governments to develop strong community-based programs and will backstop them with resources they cannot provide; for example, a fully staffed center for screening and diagnosis of offenders or an institution for mentally ill offenders.
>
> The administrators of a cooperative correctional system would need to understand the national network of services of which their particular program would be an integral part. They would need to be aware of the laws, policies, and procedures through which cross-jurisdictional cooperation could be implemented. They would need to participate in those public and private organizations which address the problems of coordinating correctional efforts across the country and carry out planning and information-gathering activities. In sum, they would need to be outwardly directed, rather than concerned only with local activities. They would need to work with the totality of corrections-related activities rather than with the happenings of their own organizational enclave.[46]

Changes in Crime and the Offender Population

Many of the so-called victimless crimes will probably receive less emphasis than they have in the past. These ''crimes,'' which often indicate some form of personal maladjustment rather than constituting a direct threat to the well-being of society, will probably either be decriminalized through less strict enforcement or will be handled outside the formal process of criminal justice by diversionary programs or the use of civil penalties in lieu of criminal charges.

We may well see some changes in the types of offenders who come under correctional supervision in the years ahead. The noted criminologist Daniel Glaser, in a very insightful paper on the future of corrections, sees some meaningful changes occurring in the types of offenders dealt with by corrections in the years ahead.[47] He contends that offenders as a group will tend to take on characteristics similar to those of the general population, with the exception that correctional clients will probably be increasingly younger in age if greater correctional effort is directed at prevention rather than acting after the crime has occurred.

Today, the typical prison population includes disproportionate numbers of males, young offenders, racial and ethnic minorities, and the poor, under-employed, and uneducated residents of large central city neighborhoods. Glaser feels that those committed to corrections will come to include more affluent, more white, and more female offenders. A larger proportion will not suffer the social disadvantages of many of those in our correctional systems today. He believes that these changes will occur because poverty among certain disadvantaged segments of our population will be lessened, and they will enjoy greater economic and social opportunities than they have in the past.[48]

Although Glaser does not address this possibility, we may see increasing enforcement of white-collar crime in the United States in the years ahead. Such offenses as tax fraud, corporate price fixing and other typical white-collar crimes may, under pressure for equal enforcement of the criminal law and through the urgings of consumer advocate and reform groups, become more important concerns of the criminal justice system. If this occurs, the composition of offender groups will change accordingly.

Glaser believes that the increase of females in the offender group will come about from the same dynamics which have produced the women's liberation movement. With the emancipation of the female from sex-segregated roles, women may become increasingly involved in traditional masculine roles, including various forms of criminal behavior. This would mean a change from the more passive crime-related behavior of the female in the past (e.g., prostitution, check passing, and shoplifting) to more aggressive acts, such as robbery, burglary, confidence games, and more violent types of crime.

It would seem that some of the trends Glaser discusses are now occurring. For example, women are increasingly making up a larger percentage of offenders appearing in criminal courts and being sentenced to correctional programs. If correctional statistics were available on the numbers of offenders being handled by *all* existing correctional programs, we probably would see some slight changes in the composition of the offender population. However, within institutions a disproportionate number of offenders are still the disadvantaged, and in future years those less-advantaged than others will still probably make up more of the correctional population.

Research Efforts

Although there still is not a great deal of research which would help improve the corrections process, more work has probably been done in the past ten years than in all the preceding years. During the 1960s, a number of university centers for research were instituted to conduct research directly applicable to corrections. In addition, such agencies as the Ford Foundation, the Law Enforcement Assistance Administration, the National Probation and Parole Institutes, the Joint Commission on Correctional Manpower and Training, and the National Institute of Mental Health have initiated research into correctional programs and the broad areas of crime and delinquency.

The efforts of these groups and others have been to help corrections develop better programs and gain insights in dealing with offenders. An information base is being created and will certainly grow in the future as research efforts are expanded. Regarding this expanding base of correctional research, Carter, McGee, and Nelson say:

> We predict by the year 2000 that there will be an on-going and reasonably effective informational network which will tie practitioners together with correctional researchers and facilitate their communications with each other. It seems probable that the Federal government will play a leading role in funding and maintaining this network.[49]

The National Institute of Corrections

Since the above statement was written, the federal government has taken major steps to encourage research and information dissemination in corrections. In 1974, Congress approved the creation of the National Institute of Corrections within the U.S. Bureau of Prisons. This new agency was authorized by Congress to make a significant effort to improve the administration of corrections in the United States. Among its specific responsibilities were:

- To receive and make grants that would improve corrections;
- Serve as a clearinghouse and information center for corrections;
- Provide consultant services to Federal, State and local criminal justice agencies;
- Assist Federal, State and local agencies and private organizations in developing and implementing improved corrections programs;
- Conduct seminars, workshops and training programs for all types of criminal justice personnel associated with the rehabilitation of offenders;
- Conduct, encourage and coordinate correctional research;
- Formulate and disseminate correctional policy, goals and standards;
- Conduct programs evaluating the effectiveness of new correctional approaches, techniques, systems, programs and devices.[50]

This agency views its role as bringing organization, direction, and leadership to the corrections community. In the first year of its operation, it focused primarily on the development of more effective personnel in corrections, including correctional administrators, researchers, criminal justice educators in colleges and universities, general correctional personnel, and volunteers in corrections.

In the years ahead, it sees its responsibilities in three areas. The first responsibility of the institute is *research and evaluation*. It plans to conduct, encourage, and coordinate research relating to corrections, including the causes, prevention, diagnoses, and treatment of criminal offenders. It also plans to conduct evaluation programs to study the effectiveness of new approaches, techniques, systems, programs, and devices employed to improve the corrections system. The second area of major effort will be *policy formulation and implementation*. This includes formulating and disseminating correctional policy, goals, standards, and recommendations for federal, state and local correctional agencies, organizations, institutions, and personnel. Third, it is to serve as a *clearinghouse and information center* for the collection, preparation, and dissemination of information on corrections, including such areas of concern as programs for prevention of crime and recidivism, training of correction personnel, and rehabilitation and treatment of criminal and juvenile offenders.

These then, are some of the developing ideas, trends, and programs which corrections seems to have charted out for itself during the last quarter of the twentieth century. In spite of a deep skepticism many seem to hold about the general efficacy of reform efforts in corrections, we must remember that we have progressed a great deal in the last 200 years when we look at the total history of how we have dealt with offenders. Although a great deal remains to be accomplished, the pace of change seems to be accelerating rapidly. Certainly, the troubled enterprise of corrections in America warrants our continued concern and efforts.

SUMMARY

Community-based correctional programs provide an alternative to traditional methods of handling offenders. The idea behind comunity-based programs is *diversion*—to limit the exposure of the offender to the negative experiences of imprisonment. Some of the more popular community-based institutions and programs are work release, community corrections centers, academic pass, prerelease guidance centers, halfway houses, conjugal and family visitations, home furloughs, and the restitution center.

Current trends which will shape the future of corrections include the judicial expansion of inmate rights, improvements in correctional personnel, the development of correctional alternatives based upon preventive strategies, changes in the organization and delivery of correctional services, changes in the nature of crime and offender population, and increased research efforts.

Suggested Additional Readings

Frank, Benjamin. *Contemporary Corrections: A Concept in Search of Content.* Reston, Va.: Reston Publishing, 1973.

Griggs, Bertram S., and Gary R. McCune. "Community-based Correctional Programs: A Survey and Analysis." *Federal Probation* (June 1972).

Harlow, Eleanor, Robert J. Webber, and Leslie T. Wilkins. *Community-based Correctional Programs: Models and Practices.* Washington, D.C.: U.S. Government Printing Office, 1971.

Hickey, William L. "Strategies for Decreasing Jail Populations." *Crime and Delinquency Literature* 3 (1971):76–94.

Hood, Roger, and Richard Sparks. *Key Issues in Criminology.* New York: McGraw-Hill, 1970.

Keller, Oliver J., and Benedict S. Alper. *Halfway Houses: Community Centered Corrections and Treatment.* Lexington, Mass.: Raytheon/Heath, 1970.

McCartt, John M., and Thomas Mangogna. *Guidelines and Standards for Halfway Houses and Community Treatment Centers.* Washington, D.C.: Law Enforcement Assistance Administration, May 1973.

Milton, Luger. "Utilizing the Ex-Offender as a Staff Member: Community Attitudes and Acceptance." In *Offenders as a Correctional Manpower Resource.* Washington, D.C.: Joint Commission on Correctional Manpower and Training, 1968.

Moyer, Frederic D. *Guidelines for the Planning and Design of Regional and Community Correctional Centers for Adults.* Urbana: University of Illinois, 1971.

Schwartz, Richard D., and Jerome H. Skolnick. "The Stigma of 'Ex-Con' and the Problem of Reintegration." *Social Problems* 10 (Fall 1962):133–42.

Turner, Merfyn. "The Lessons of Norman House." *Annals of the American Academy of Political and Social Science* (January 1969).

Notes

1. U.S. Department of Justice, Bureau of Prisons, "Success and Failure of Federal Offenders Released in 1970," mimeo (Apr. 11, 1974), p. 1.

2. Solomon Kobrin, "The Chicago Area Project—A 25-Year Assessment," *The Annals of the American Academy of Political and Social Science* 322 (March 1959): 19–29.

3. Walter B. Miller, "Preventive Work with Street Corner Groups," *The Annals of the American Academy of Political and Social Science* 322 (March 1959): 97–106.

4. *The New York Times,* Nov. 30, 1973, sec. II, p. 2, col. 1.

5. It should be pointed out, however, that an opposite trend toward a "get tough" policy with offenders may be developing. Popular sentiment is calling for stricter laws and their enforcement. At this time, it is too early to gauge the effect of such attitudes on corrections.

6. For example, see George Killinger and Paul F. Cromwell, *Corrections in the Community* (St. Paul, Minn.: West, 1974).

7. Ibid., p. 6.

8. Law Enforcement Assistance Administration–National Institute of Law Enforcement and Criminal Justice, *Reintegration of the Offender into the Community* (Washington, D.C.: U.S. Government Printing Office, 1973), p. 5.

9. Walter H. Busher, *Ordering Time to Serve Prisoner* (Washington, D.C.: U.S. Government Printing Office, June 1973), p. 3.

10. Ibid., pp. 3–4.

11. Stanley E. Grupp, "Work Release and Misdemeanants," *Federal Probation* 29 (June 1965): 7.

12. See Daniel Glaser, *The Effectiveness of a Prison and Parole System* (Indiana: Bobbs-Merrill, 1969), especially chap. 10.

13. Alvin Rudoff and T. C. Esselstyn, "Evaluating Work Furlough: A Follow-Up," *Federal Probation* 37 (June 1973): 48–53.

14. Ibid., pp. 50–53.

15. N. C. Chamelin, V. B. Fox, and P. M. Whisenand, *Introduction to the Criminal Justice System* (Englewood Cliffs, N.J.: Prentice-Hall, 1975), p. 397.

16. Columbus B. Hopper, "The Conjugal Visit," *Journal of Criminal Law, Criminology and Police Science* 53 (September 1962): 340–343.

17. For example, see Norman E. Hayner, "Attitudes toward Conjugal Visits for Prisoners," *Federal Probation* 36 (March 1972): 43–49.

18. Source: Michael S. Serrill, "Family Visiting at San Quentin. Reprinted with permission from the July/August 1975 issue of *Corrections Magazine,* published by the Correctional Information Service, Inc., 801 Second Avenue, New York, NY 10017.

19. Carson W. Markley, "Furlough Programs and Conjugal Visiting in Adult Correctional Institutions," *Federal Probation* 37 (March 1973): 19–26.

20. Ibid., pp. 22–24.

21. Donald R. Johns, "Alternatives to Conjugal Visiting," *Federal Probation* 35 (March 1971): 48–51.

22. Ibid.

23. Serill, op. cit., p. 12.

24. Chamelin, Fox, and Whisenand, op. cit., p. 397.

25. Killinger and Cromwell, op. cit., p. 68.

26. Ibid.

27. Ibid., p. 69.

28. Oliver J. Keller and Benedict S. Alper, *Halfway Houses* (Boston: Heath, 1963), p. 7.

29. Ibid.

30. Killinger and Cromwell, op. cit., p. 78.

31. Bertram S. Griggs and Gary R. McCune, "Community-based Correctional Programs: A Survey and Analysis," *Federal Probation* 36 (June 1972): 10.

32. Kenneth F. Schoen, "PORT: A New Concept of Community-based Correction," *Federal Probation* 36 (September 1972): 35–40.

33. John M. McCartt and Thomas Mangogna, *Guidelines and Standards for Halfway Houses and Community Treatment Centers* (Washington, D.C.: U.S. Government Printing Office, June 1973), pp. 17–18.

34. H. B. Bradley, "Community-based Treatment for Young Adult Offenders," *Crime and Delinquency* 15 (1969): 359–370.

35. E. Harlow, R. Weber, and L. T. Wilkins, "Community-based Correctional Programs," in E. Eldefonso (ed.), *Issues in Corrections* (Beverly Hills, Calif.: Glencoe Press, 1974), p. 367.

36. National Advisory Commission on Criminal Justice Standards and Goals, *Corrections* (Washington, D.C.: U.S. Government Printing Office, 1973), p. 18.

37. Ibid.

38. *Morrissey v. Brewer,* 408 U.S. 471 (1972).

39. *Younger v. Gilmore,* 404 U.S. 15 (1971).

40. *United States v. Tucker,* 404 U.S. 443 (1972).

41. *Jackson v. Indiana,* 406 U.S. 715 (1972).

42. National Advisory Commission, op. cit., pp. 23–31.

43. See Robert B. Levinson and Roy E. Gerard, "Functional Units: A Different Correctional Approach," *Federal Probation* 37 (December 1973): 8–15.

44. Robert M. Carter, Richard A. McGee, and E. Kim Nelson, *Corrections in America* (Philadelphia: Lippincott, 1975), p. 375.

45. Ibid., p. 376.

46. Elmer K. Nelson, Jr., and Catherine H. Lovell, *Developing Correctional Administrators* (Washington, D.C.: Joint Commission on Correctional Manpower and Training, November 1969), p. 15.

47. Daniel Glaser, "Changes in Corrections during the Next 20 Years," paper presented before the American Justice Institute, Mar. 2, 1972.

48. For another interesting viewpoint, see Edward C. Banfield, *The Unheavenly City* (Boston: Little, Brown, 1970).

49. Carter, McGee, and Nelson, op. cit., p. 395.

50. National Institute of Corrections, *Status Report* (Washington, D.C.: U.S. Government Printing Office, October 1975), pp. 2–3.

GET READY
FOR TOMORROW

Chapter 16

Parole and Probation

PAROLE

Parole is the conditional release of an individual from a correctional institution—the offender may return to the community, but he must abide by certain rules of conduct which are specified by the paroling authority and enforced by a parole officer. These rules are in effect until the expiration of his sentence. If the parolee breaks a rule, parole may be revoked and he will be returned to a correctional facility.

Historical Background

The history of parole reflects the changing philosophy on how to deal with the offender. The reader will recall that in the late eighteenth and early nineteenth centuries, the philosophy that guided the development of corrections shifted from simple punishment to reformation. This shift in emphasis contributed to the development of parole. As reformers of that period were able to modify the criminal codes and sentencing practices which called for execution, corporal punishment, branding, mutilation, or transportation to long-term imprisonment as a response to criminal behavior, certain changes had to be made.

Correctional reformers wanted prisons to be places of meditation, repentance, and expiation, where the convicted criminal could atone for his transgressions. They also recognized that not all imprisoned offenders would atone and that society would have to be protected from less repentant criminals after their release (a problem that did not arise when offenders were executed). Parole, as a means of protecting society while helping the offender readjust to life in the community, was the logical solution—but it was preceded by several developments that were, in some cases, less than satisfactory alternatives, but that are considered to have provided the foundation for modern parole: (1) conditional pardons, (2) apprenticeship by indenture, (3) transportation to Australia, (4) tickets of leave, and (5) indeterminate sentences.

Conditional Pardons

As early as 1597, England passed an Act of Banishment which provided that criminals and rogues be sent to the colonies to labor in the king's service. By the early eighteenth century, the new American colonies desperately needed workers to clear land and build settlements and military strongholds— particularly in the South, where Spanish military forces threatened the security of the colonies. For England, the transportation of criminal offenders provided a partial answer to its economic problems, which included widespread un- employment and a sharp increase in taxes required by the enactment of poor relief laws.[1]

To ensure that physically able felons would be sent to the colonies, offenders were selected for transportation from lists compiled by court officials. Upon the recommendation of the courts, the king authorized the home secretary to grant stays of execution for the chosen offenders in his name. These offenders were then asked if they would agree to be sent to the colonies and remain there to work in the service of the king. Of course, many agreed to this alternative. If they agreed, they were immediately given an unconditional pardon. However, some of the offenders who were granted these unconditional pardons did not depart for the colonies as they had agreed and others who had gone to the colonies returned to England before their period of service was completed. Therefore, a law was enacted which made all pardons conditional; in order to receive the pardon an offender had to complete a period of service in the colonies for a prescribed period of years. In many cases, he could never return to England, or the pardon would be revoked.

Apprenticeship by Indenture

When transportation was first instituted, the government paid a small fee to the contractor (shipmaster) for each prisoner he transported to the colonies. In 1717, this practice was changed by the passage of a new law which gave the contractor "property in the service" of the prisoner until he had completed the full term of his sentence. The offender literally *belonged* to the contractor, and the government took no further interest in his welfare or conduct unless he escaped from the contractor or returned to England in violation of his pardon.

When the contractor arrived in the colonies, he sold each prisoner's services to the highest bidder for the duration of the sentence and transferred his warrant authorizing his "property in the service" to the purchaser. The prisoner then ceased, technically, to be a criminal and became an indentured servant. In- dentured service, dating from the Statute of Artifices passed in 1562, originally meant apprenticeships for training in a specialized trade. Both apprentice and master were bound by a contract which specified their rights and respon- sibilities, though in fact most of the "rights" belonged to the master and most of the "responsibilities" were borne by the apprentice.

The indenture concept is very similar to the procedure used by parole boards in each state today. A prisoner conditionally released on parole, like the indentured apprentice, agrees in writing to accept and abide by the conditions specified on the release form. Once this agreement is accepted, the parole board and the individual sign the form—the *conditions of parole*. New Jersey's requirements, representative of those in others states, read as follows:

State of New Jersey
Conditions of Parole

1. From the date of your release on parole and until the expiration of the maximum of your sentence(s), unless sooner discharged from parole, you shall continue to be in the legal custody of the Chief Executive Officer of the Institution from which you are released and under the supervision of the Bureau of Parole of the Department of Institutions and Agencies.
2. You shall be required to abide by the rules and regulations formulated by the State Parole Board for the supervision of persons on parole.
3. As a condition of your being on parole, you are required to:
   a. Conduct yourself in society in compliance with all laws and ordinances;
   b. Conduct yourself with due regard to moral standards;
   c. Demonstrate that your conduct on parole has been good at all times;
   d. Demonstrate that you are a fit person to be at liberty;
   e. Make restitution for your crime, when required; .
   f. Contribute to the support of your dependents;
   g. Abstain from the use or sale of narcotics and the excessive use of intoxicating beverages;
   h. Refrain from association with persons of bad character or those who are considered by the Parole District Supervisor or his designated representative to be undesirable companions;
   i. Refrain from conduct while on parole which shall give reasonable cause to believe that you have resumed, or are about to resume, criminal conduct or associations;
   j. Reside in a place approved by the Bureau of Parole;
   k. Seek employment diligently and render to your employer the best service of which you are capable;
   l. Report to or notify your Parole District Supervisor or his designated representative:
      (1) As soon as possible but in any event within forty-eight hours after your release on parole from the institution;
      (2) Whenever you are in any kind of trouble or in need of advice;
      (3) As soon as possible after an arrest on any new charge;
      (4) Whenever you are instructed to report by the Parole District Supervisor, his designated representative, or other competent authority;
      (5) Before paying any fine or attempting to obtain bail;
   m. Obtain permission from your Parole District Supervisor or his designated representative:

(1) Before marrying or applying for a divorce;
(2) Before purchasing a motor vehicle, obtaining a learner's permit, a driver's license, or applying for a motor vehicle registration;
(3) Before entering any form of conditional sales agreement or borrowing money or articles of substantial value;
(4) Before entering any business, changing your place of residence, or changing your employment;
(5) Before leaving the State of your approved residence;
(6) Before applying for a permit to carry a firearm, securing a hunting license, or carrying a firearm for any purpose.

4. This parole may be revoked without notice:
   a.   If you violate any of the conditions of your parole, other than by subsequent conviction of crime, you shall be required to serve the time remaining on your sentence(s), to be computed from the date you are declared delinquent, unless said revocation is rescinded or unless reparoled.
   b.   If you are convicted of a crime while on parole, or commit an offense on parole which subsequently results in a conviction of a crime, you shall be required to serve the time remaining on your sentence(s) to be computed from the date of your release on parole, unless said revocation is rescinded or unless reparoled.

NOTE: In cases where the prisoner is paroled from a county penitentiary, the term "Chief Probation Officer" shall be substituted for the term "District Parole Supervisor" in the above conditions of parole.

SPECIAL CONDITION(S)

In consideration of the action of the State Parole Board in paroling me, I hereby accept this parole and such State Parole Board action and I hereby agree to be bound by the foregoing conditions which shall constitute my parole contract with the State of New Jersey. Any violation of any condition hereof shall be sufficient cause for revocation of my parole.

Dated _____ 19 _____

Witness:

_____   _____

                                                          Signature

Transportation to Australia

After the Revolutionary War, transportation of prisoners to America came to an end. England did not repeal its transportation laws, however, and judges continued to impose sentences of transportation. As a result, the temporary detention facilities built to house prisoners before they were sent to the colonies were soon overflowing. In an attempt to relieve this overcrowding, the crown began to offer pardons freely, but a serious outbreak of crime resulted, and the public demanded that the prisoners be transported again.

Under William Pitt, a conservative prime minister, the government had little interest in the rehabilitation of criminals. But the public clamor for removal of the prisoners, plus a growing fear that epidemics would break out if the temporary detention facilities were not emptied, necessitated some action. A few years earlier, Captain Cook had discovered Australia, and the Pitt government felt that this remote colony would be an ideal place to deposit convicted felons. In 1787, the king approved the idea, and the first detachment sailed in that year.

In 1790, the power to pardon felons was bestowed on the governor of the Australian colony. At first, these pardons granted to prisoners with good work and behavior records were unconditional. But, problems arose (as they had before), conditions were added, and the pardons became known as tickets of leave. They were declarations signed by the governor that released a prisoner from the penal colony on condition that he would lawfully support himself and would seek and maintain employment within a specified district. Unlike modern parole, the ticket of leave did not provide for government supervision of the released prisoner; it simply stated the conditions of the pardon:

> It is His Excellency, the Governor's pleasure to dispense with the government work of . . . tried at . . . convicted of . . . and to permit . . . to employ . . . (off government stores) in any lawful occupation with the district of . . . for his own advantage during good behavior or until His Excellency's further pleasure shall be made known.[2]

Under the original plan, the period of time a prisoner need serve before becoming eligible was left entirely to the governor's discretion. Later, the policy was changed to provide that those sentenced to seven years could obtain a ticket of leave after serving four years, those sentenced to fourteen years were eligible after service of six years, and those who carried life sentences were eligible after eight years.[3]

These rules were the forerunners of the "good-time" laws which now exist in all states. Under these laws, the amount of time before the convicted offender is eligible for parole is automatically reduced for good behavior. For example, many states have passed one-fourth good-time laws, under which an offender is eligible for parole after serving three-fourths of his minimum sentence. Thus an individual who is sentenced to two to five years, is eligible for parole after serving eighteen months. In some states, good-time laws do not apply to someone sentenced to life imprisonment unless a "lifer" law prevails. Usually, this statute provides that someone sentenced to life on a charge other than first-degree murder must serve a minimum of ten years before he is eligible for parole consideration.

An inmate serving a life sentence for first-degree murder can be paroled only if the governor first commutes the sentence to a term of years. In most instances, the parole decision-making authority will serve as an advisory board to the governor on commutation. In Michigan, for example, the parole board will not consider recommending commutation to the governor until the "lifer" has served about fifteen years, but will conduct an initial interview with the inmate after ten years. On the average, Michigan inmates whose life sentences are commuted serve for about twenty-five years.[4]

The English and Irish Experience with Tickets of Leave

By 1817, Australia and even America had experimented with the ticket-of-leave system, but the English were slow to follow—in part perhaps because the English had an abiding faith in transportation as a solution to the problem. In 1857, however, England passed the Penal Servitude Act, which ended transportation and substituted imprisonment, providing for a ticket-of-leave system and specifying the length of time prisoners had to serve before becoming eligible for conditional release.

Those whose sentences were longer than seven years but not more than ten years became eligible for tickets of leave after serving four to six years. Prisoners whose sentences were longer than ten years but less than fifteen were eligible after six to eight years, and those with sentences of fifteen years or more were eligible after six to ten years. Thus, the act not only served as the legal foundation for the ticket-of-leave system, it also introduced the idea of the indeterminate sentence.

The following conditions were endorsed on the license that was given to each prisoner released under the ticket of leave:

1. The power of revoking or altering the license of a convict will most certainly be exercised in the case of misconduct.

2. If, therefore, he wishes to retain the privilege, which by his good behavior under penal discipline he has obtained, he must prove by his subsequent conduct that he is really worthy of Her Majesty's clemency.

3. To produce a forfeiture of the license, it is by no means necessary that the holder should be convicted of a new offense. If he associates with notoriously bad characters, leads an idle or dissolute life, or has no visible means of obtaining an honest livelihood, etc., it will be assumed that he is about to relapse into crime, and he will be at once apprehended and recommitted to prison under his original sentence.[5]

In theory, the government was to select with care those prisoners who could most benefit from this form of conditional release. But England failed to learn from Australia's problems with unsupervised ticket-of-leave holders and experienced a serious crime wave as a result. When angry citizens called for repeal of the Penal Servitude Act, the queen was forced to convene a special royal commission to study the problem. This commission suggested that the prisoners granted tickets of leave be supervised by the police to ensure more uniform and systematic enforcement of the ticket-of-leave provisions, and the queen agreed.

As we have seen, Sir Walter Crofton, leader of Ireland's prison reform movement, was instrumental in developing the Irish ticket-of-leave program. The Irish ticket of leave, which was slightly different from the one used in England, imposed the following conditions:

1. The holder shall preserve this license and produce it when called upon to do so by a magistrate or police officer.
2. He shall abstain from any violation of the law.
3. He shall not habitually associate with notoriously bad characters, such as reported thieves and prostitutes.
4. He shall not lead an idle and dissolute life, without means of obtaining an honest livelihood.

If the license is forfeited or revoked in consequence of a conviction of any felony, he will be liable to undergo a term of penal servitude equal to that portion of his term of . . . years, which remains unexpired when his license was granted, viz., the term of . . . years . . . months.[6]

Ticket-of-leave men residing in rural districts were supervised entirely by the police, but those who lived in Dublin were supervised by a civilian employee, the inspector of released prisoners. It was his responsibility to obtain employment for the ticket-of-leave men, report violations to the police, and generally see to it that his men lived up to the terms of their tickets of leave. To accomplish this objective, he was required to have the released offenders report to him at stated intervals, to visit their homes every two weeks, and to verify their employment. It appears that the ticket-of-leave holders were not hounded by the police during their period of supervision. They were, however, required to inform employers of their status; failure to do so could result in revocation of the privilege. The supervision plan built into the Irish system prevented the kind of problems encountered by England; as a result, the Irish system inspired more public confidence.

Prison Reform in America and the Indeterminate Sentence

The development of parole in the United States was based on three underlying concepts: (1) shortened imprisonment as a reward for good conduct, (2) the indeterminate sentence, and (3) supervision.[7] The idea of shortening the term of sentence gained statutory recognition in 1817 when New York passed the first good-time law. In 1869, Michigan adopted the first indeterminate-sentence law. However, it was in New York that the indeterminate sentence became a reality. Zebulon Brockway, first warden of New York's Elmira Reformatory, was familiar with ticket-of-leave policies (particularly Ireland's). He convinced New York officials that the length of an inmate's sentence should be flexible, depending on his conduct. He campaigned for the use of the indeterminate sentence for inmates sentenced to Elmira, and in 1876 New York passed the necessary authorizing legislation. Under the provisions of the indeterminate sentence, the offender was to be released at a time when his conduct demonstrated that he was ready to be returned to society. Since the offender was released before the expiration of his sentence, special provisions were made to provide him with community supervision, and parole became a reality. In this way, parole became an indispensable partner of the indeterminate sentence. Brockway's reforms, as practiced at Elmira, are credited with establishing the concept of parole in the United States.

At first, responsibility for supervising the paroled offender was assumed primarily by private reform groups. Later, a few states appointed agents to help released offenders obtain employment. But only in the first two decades of the twentieth century did the states finally adopt the idea of professionally trained public employees—parole officers—to carry out the task of supervision.

The Functions of Parole

Parole can be considered as an extension of the *rehabilitative (and now, reintegrative) program of the prison*. Although parole is often considered as a form of leniency by its critics, it is in fact an extension of assistance and rehabilitation begun in the prison which seeks to release the inmate at a time when he is most able to benefit by release and return to society to lead a law-abiding life. If prisons are, in fact, to be concerned with modifying criminal behavior so that the offender can eventually be reintegrated into society, parole is also supposed to provide the supervision and assistance that makes successful reintegration possible. Finally, parole is a means to protect society. By careful selection and community supervision, parole should afford an element of protection not available if the offender were simply released at the expiration of his sentence.

The Organization of State Paroling Authorities

The states vary somewhat in the way they organize their adult parole authority and the responsibilities the parole agency has. Most states have separate parole authorities for adults and for juveniles. Juvenile parole is often operated on an institutional basis in which full-time institutional personnel who are in close contact with the child determine the appropriate time and conditions of parole, whereas parole of adults is often the responsibility of a separate and independent agency. In addition to hearing and granting applications for parole, the adult paroling authority in a number of states also has additional responsibilities. A study by the National Council on Crime and Delinquency of adult parole authorities throughout the country found that a number of state parole boards were also responsible for:

Conducting clemency hearings
Commuting sentences
Appointment of parole supervisors
Administration of parole services
Granting of parole from local institutions
Granting or revoking "good time"
Supervision of probation services
Determining standards for "good time"
Granting of pardons[8]

The Institutional Model

Although there is a great variety in the organizational makeup of adult paroling authorities, the National Advisory Commission on Criminal Justice Standards and Goals has tried to develop a three fold classification into which most adult paroling authorities can be grouped.[9] The first of these is the institutional model. This model is based on the idea that parole should be carefully linked with institutional programs. In this way, the decision whether or not to release an individual rests with the staff of the correctional institution itself. Behind this model is the theory that institutional staff members are in the best position to carefully judge the suitability of the inmate for parole and that the parole decision itself can be more appropriately coordinated with the overall institutional program devised for the particular offender.

Those who argue against this arrangement contend that institutional factors may play a major role in deciding whether or not the inmate should be paroled. An institution faced with problems of overcrowding may tend to release individuals prematurely. Prison officials may also use the threat of not granting parole as a means to keep inmates in line and to enforce strict rules and regulations. Because of such abuses, some years ago reformers sought to remove decision-making authority from institutional officials. So effective was this reform movement that today the purely institutional model for dealing with adult offenders does not exist in any state.

The Independent Model

Reformers advocated that independent parole boards should make the ultimate decision on granting parole. Although it may be argued that this model is more objective than the institutional model, it too suffers from a number of weaknesses: The first problem is that independent parole boards often do not understand the programs carried on by the institutions and the role they play in the overall treatment plan once an individual is released. Independent boards are also criticized for relying too much on inappropriate considerations, such as the feelings of the local police chief. Occasionally, these independent boards are tainted with scandals of political corruption, such as those which occurred a few years ago in Georgia in which it was alleged that unscrupulous interests paid members of the parole board to act favorably toward parole requests of certain prison inmates. Another frequent criticism is that members of independent parole boards are often appointed for strictly political reasons and lack the necessary training or experience in corrections.

This lack of knowledge about the correctional process and correctional programming may be the single most important argument against this type of organizational arrangement. With the increased use of release programs, half-way houses, and other community-based alternatives, overall programs must be linked very closely with institutional efforts for parole considerations. This requires that parole board members have a broad knowledge of corrections and develop a close working relationship with correctional institutions.

The Consolidated Model

The consolidated model, which more and more states are now adopting, combines the best features of the institutional and independent models while diminishing the negative features of both. This arrangement consolidates all correctional programs within a state under a department of correctional services which is divided into institutional and field programs (parole services). For example, in 1974, Kansas established a department of corrections with one division responsible for facility and jail standards and another for parole. Under this arrangement, institutions and parole services are within one department, yet both possess independent powers. About 60 percent of the states have now adopted this approach.[10] Many of these states provide that the director of corrections or a designated staff officer has the authority to sit on the parole board as a decision-making member.

Advocates of the consolidated model argue that there is increased concern for the entire correctional process in departments where parole releasing authority is part of a unified system. They claim that sensitivity to institutional programs seems more pronounced in consolidated systems than in completely autonomous ones. They also contend that removal of parole decision making from the immediate control of specific correctional institutions tends to give greater weight to a broader set of considerations, a number of which are outside direct institutional concerns.[11]

The primary organizational concerns of parole would seem to require that states foster a close coordination between parole decision makers and the increasingly complex set of programs now being developed in many correctional systems, while at the same time preserving the autonomy that permits parole boards to serve as checks on the overall system. At the present time, the consolidated authority seems to be the means best devised to accomplish this task.

The Organization and Responsibilities of the U.S. Board of Parole

In order to see how a parole board system might operate, let's examine the federal system. The responsibility of the U.S. Board of Parole is to consider parole applications of inmates in federal prisons.[12] The U. S. Board of Parole was created by Congress in 1930 and consists of eight full-time members appointed by the president with the advice and consent of the Senate. Members serve overlapping six-year terms and can be reappointed. The attorney general of the United States appoints one member of the board to be chairman and three members to serve as members of the Youth Correction Division, which considers cases of youthful offenders in federal institutions.

At the board's headquarters in Washington are additional support and specialist personnel to assist the board. These include a staff director, legal counsel, program executives for the adult and youth corrections division, eight hearing examiners, and clerical staff. In addition, the board is assisted by the caseworkers and administrative personnel of the various federal correctional institutions and by the probation officers who are employed by the various federal district courts and who provide both probation and parole supervision to federal offenders.

The Board of Parole has broad jurisdictional authority over all federal prisoners serving over six months in a federal prison. Federal statutes give the Board of Parole supervisory power over adults who have violated the laws of the United States, youthful offenders committed under the Youth Corrections Act, juvenile delinquents who have been sentenced in federal courts under the Juvenile Procedures Act, and individuals committed under the Narcotic Addict Rehabilitation Act. The explicit major powers of the board include authority:

1. To determine the date of parole eligibility for adults committed under the "indeterminate sentencing statutes"
2. To grant parole at its discretion
3. To prescribe terms and conditions governing the prisoner while on parole or mandatory release
4. To issue warrants to recommit parole and mandatory release violators
5. To revoke parole and mandatory release and to modify the conditions of supervision
6. To reparole or rerelease on mandatory release

A federal prisoner sentenced to a term of at least 181 days becomes eligible for parole according to the type of commitment he received from court. The most commonly used commitments are adult regular and adult indeterminate commitments, Youth Corrections Act commitments, Federal Juvenile Delinquency Act commitments, and Narcotic Addict Rehabilitation Act commitments. Under the adult regular sentences, parole may be granted after the offender has served one-third of the maximum sentence specified by the court.

Parole may be granted at any time to individuals sentenced on adult indeterminate commitments. Individuals committed under the Youth Corrections Act may be paroled at any time, but not later than two years before expiration of the maximum term imposed. Parole may be granted to Federal Juvenile Delinquency Act commitments at any time. Persons committed under the Narcotic Addict Rehabilitation Act may be paroled to an aftercare program after six months of institutional treatment.

At least one personal hearing is conducted by the board with each prisoner in a federal institution serving a term of more than one year. This hearing occurs either near the time he becomes eligible for parole if he applies or at the time of the initial hearing, which usually takes place within two months after commitment. In some cases, the decision regarding parole is made on the basis of the initial hearing, but more often than not at least two hearings are held for each prisoner. Because the Bureau of Prisons maintains institutions throughout the country, it is not practical to have members of the board conduct all these hearings. Instead, special legislation was enacted to permit the board to use hearing examiners to conduct parole hearings and to recommend to the board whether the individual should or should not be paroled.

Bimonthly visits to each federal institution are made by members or hearing examiners to conduct personal hearings with prisoners who recently have been committed, are eligible for parole, are scheduled for a review hearing, or are entitled to a revocation hearing. Upon return to headquarters, the parole board member or the hearing examiner meets with other members to further consider the file and to vote for parole, for continuation of incarceration to a specified date, or for continuation to expiration of sentence, less good-time credits.

Generally, the board does not sit as a group to vote, but rather each member votes on an individual basis. Each official decision requires concurrence of at least two members. There are some situtations, however, in which it is deemed necessary for a larger group of members to consider parole, for instance, when the following conditions exist:

1. National security is involved.
2. The prisoner was involved to a major degree in organized crime.
3. There is national or other unusual interest in the offender or his victim.
4. Major violence has been perpetrated or there is evidence it may occur.
5. The sentence is for forty-five years or more.

Any parole board member may request that the board meet en banc to deliberate on a case. At such proceedings, a member of the board's staff presents an oral summary of the case and members discuss its elements before arriving at a decision. A majority of members must be present to constitute a quorum for the consideration and the resulting decision.

Reviews of the board's decisions are not automatic, but these are scheduled by the board at times when it may wish "to determine progress in reaching institutional goals, to evaluate adjustment to confinement, to ascertain changes in attitude, or to reappraise plans for community living after release.''[13] Reconsiderations may also be initiated by the prisoner or his family, friends, or other interested persons. In addition, special interviews may be granted a prisoner with a sentence of 40 years or more if requested by either the warden or one of the board members.

Prisoners serving regular adult or juvenile sentences who are not paroled may be released before the end of their sentences by earning good-time credits. They earn a specified number of days according to a formula contained in the statutes, and they may earn extra good time through exceptionally meritorious behavior or by receiving assignment to a prison industries job or to a minimum-security camp. The number of such credits varies according to the maximum term imposed by the court, but, in long-term cases, as many as ten days may be earned for each month served. Inmates released on the basis of good-time credits are called mandatory releasees and come under the board jurisdiction as if on parole. For example, an inmate sentenced to twenty years may earn enough good-time credits to be released after sixteen years. During the last four years of his unexpired sentence, he must abide by the same conditions as parolees and is subject to revocation and return to the institution. The only exception is that the last 180 days of an adult mandatory releasee's term are dropped from his supervision period. A releasee who has fewer than 180 days remaining on his term, does not receive community supervision, but is considered to have been released at expiration of his sentence. A juvenile's term is not so shortened. An offender committed under the Youth Corrections Act is not mandatorily released, but by law must be paroled no later than two years before the end of his sentence. He remains under the jurisdiction of the Youth Corrections Division for his entire term unless discharged earlier by the division.

Decisions Upon Which Parole Is Based

Most parole boards base their decisions on whether or not an inmate should be granted parole on a number of factors.

Prior Record

Since an extensive criminal record is one of the better predictors of further criminality, this factor weighs very heavily. Since first offenders have the best prospects for parole success, most paroling authorities will give special consideration to such offenders. Also often considered for early parole are situational offenders, that is, individuals who acted under impulse and the situation of the moment in committing the crime and do not have a past history of law violations.

The habitual offender, particularly if he is a chronic sex offender or armed robber, shows a history of assaultive crimes, or has previously demonstrated little or no response to incarceration and to institutional programs, must usually show a significant change before parole boards will favorably consider his parole request. Parole boards also consider professional criminals to be bad risks. Many such offenders consider the risk of imprisonment as a cost of doing business and almost invariably return to their former life styles upon release.

Seriousness and Nature of Current Offense

A second very important consideration is the offense for which the individual is currently incarcerated. Normally, the criminal code and the sentencing judge will have set the prison term so as to take the seriousness of the offense into account. However, since the type of offense has predictive value with respect to the commission of further crimes, parole boards will also consider this factor, especially where the current offense is part of a pattern of behavior which is deemed likely to continue. Studies have shown that larceny, burglary, forgery, and auto theft seem to be the most likely to be repeated.[14] Similarly, persons who are serving sentences for escapes have been demonstrated to be poor parole risks.[15] Parole boards must also consider with great care paroling those persons whose offense if repeated would be a serious threat to the safety of the public.

Circumstances of the Offense

While the sentencing court will have considered the personal and social circumstances surrounding the offense, these may be relevant to the parole decision as well, since the board must consider the likelihood of recurrence of such circumstances or situations. For example, the individual whose crimes are related to alcoholism or the support of a narcotics habit may be in a higher-risk group than an individual serving for the same offense without these aggravating factors. Circumstances which either extenuate or aggravate the offense can be useful in predicting whether there will be a repetition.

The Placement Situation

The board must also review and consider the situation into which the individual will go if paroled. A person returning to a stable, intact marriage has a higher chance of successful adjustment than one not so situated. The prospects for employment are important for the same reasons. The better the release plan, the better the prospects for success. Often parole boards will set special conditions of parole with respect to situations or behaviors which the offender must avoid because they would decrease his chances for remaining law-abiding.

Institutional Record

The board will review the individual's record while incarcerated. A failure to behave responsibly in the institution does not forecast well for a successful return to the community. The individual who is assaultive, who cannot get along with people, or who cannot work responsibly will face problems in these same areas upon release. On the other hand, if the person has involved himself in programs relevant to his particular problem and seems to be making a sincere effort, this offers at least some additional hope for the future. These factors must be carefully weighed, however, since some individuals conform well in prison, but do not do well in the community. In a number of more progressive states, parole boards are working with institutional administrators to make prison programs more relevant and better tests of future community adjustment than they have been in the past.

The Development and Use of Prediction Methods

In the last two decades, there has been a great deal of interest among researchers in developing prediction criteria which could help parole boards make a decision on whether an individual should be released on parole.[16] The object of these researchers has been to gather data on successful and unsuccessful parolees in an effort to identify the specific characteristics that are associated with success and failure. With the increasing adoption of computer technology with its storage and retrieval capabilities, the future would seem to hold some promise for more "scientifically" enlightened decisions by parole boards. However, current prediction methods still suffer from a number of weaknesses: First, researchers have not been able to identify all the factors that may have led an individual to commit a crime in the first place nor all the factors that may cause him to commit further offenses once he is released. The second problem is one of reliability. It has not been sufficiently demonstrated that particular characteristics that seem to be associated with the failure of one individual on parole will also be associated with the failure of another individual who has the same characteristics. For example, two parolees who have been imprisoned for drug-related offenses, come from unstable backgrounds, and are of the same age when released will not necessarily both commit new crimes. Upon release, one may lead a law-abiding life and the other return to crime. For a predictive measure to be reliable, it must be able to predict with a higher degree of accuracy than most prediction devices now do.

U.S. Board of Parole Severity Scale

The U.S. Board of Parole has been working on the development of some uniform guidelines to assist hearing examiners and parole board members in making decisions. One of these guidelines is a severity scale which considers two factors that research conducted by the Bureau of prisons has shown to be particularly important: (1) the length of sentence served and (2) the type of offense for which the inmate is imprisoned. Table 16-1 depicts this severity scale.

**TABLE 16-1   U.S. Board of Parole Severity Scale
for Decision Making**

OFFENSE CHARACTERISTICS: Severity of Offense Behavior (Examples)	OFFENDER CHARACTERISTICS: Parole Prognosis (Salient Factor Score)			
	Very Good (11–9)	Good (8–6)	Fair (5–4)	Poor (3–0)
	Average Total Time Served Before Release (Including Jail Time)			
LOW Immigration law violations Minor theft (includes larceny and simple possession of stolen property, less than $1,000) Walkaway	6–10 months	8–12 months	10–14 months	12–16 months
LOW MODERATE Alcohol law violations Counterfeit currency (passing/possession, less than $1,000) Drugs: Marijuana, possession (less than $500) Firearms Act, possession/purchase/sale, single weapon not altered or machine gun Forgery fraud (less than $1,000) Income tax evasion (less than $3,000) Selective Service Act violations Theft from mail (less than $1,000)	8–12 months	12–16 months	16–20 months	20–25 months
MODERATE Bribery of public officials Counterfeit currency (passing/possession $1,000–$19,999) Drugs: "Hard drugs," possession by drug user (less than $500) Marijuana, possession ($500 or more) Marijuana, sale (less than $5,000) "Soft drugs," possession (less than $5,000) "Soft drugs," sale (less than $500) Embezzlement (less than $20,000) Explosives, possession/transportation Firearms Act, possession/purchase/sale, altered weapon(s), machine gun(s), or multiple weapons Income tax evasion ($3,000–$50,000) Interstate transportation of stolen/forged securities (less than $20,000) Mailing threatening communications	12–16 months	16–20 months	20–24 months	24–30 months

OFFENSE CHARACTERISTICS: Severity of Offense Behavior (Examples)	OFFENDER CHARACTERISTICS: Parole Prognosis (Salient Factor Score)			
	Very Good (11–9)	*Good* (8–6)	*Fair* (5–4)	*Poor* (3–0)
	Average Total Time Served Before Release (Including Jail Time)			
Receiving stolen property with intent to resell (less than $20,000) Smuggler of aliens Theft, forgery/fraud ($1,000–$19,999) Theft of motor vehicle (not multiple theft or for resale)				
HIGH Burglary or larceny (other than embezzlement) from bank or post office Counterfeit currency (passing/possession, $20,000 or more) Counterfeiting (manufacturing) Drugs: "Hard drugs," possession by drug-dependent user ($500 or more) "Hard drugs," sale to support own habit Marijuana, sale ($5,000 or more) "Soft drugs," possession ($5,000 or more) "Soft drugs," sale ($500–$5,000) Embezzlement ($20,000–$100,000) Interstate transportation of stolen/forged securities ($20,000–$100,000) Mann Act violation (no force—commercial purposes) Organized vehicle theft Receiving stolen property ($20,000–$100,000) Robbery (no weapon or injury) Theft, forgery/fraud ($20,000–$100,000)	16–20 months	20–26 months	26–32 months	32–38 months
VERY HIGH Robbery (weapon) Drugs: "Hard drugs," possession by non-drug-dependent user ($500 or more) or by nonuser (any quantity) "Hard drugs," sale for profit (no prior conviction for sale of "hard drugs") "Soft drugs," sale (more than $5000) Extortion Mann Act violation (force) Sexual act (force)	26–36 months	36–45 months	45–55 months	55–65 months

OFFENSE CHARACTERISTICS: Severity of Offense Behavior (Examples)	OFFENDER CHARACTERISTICS: Parole Prognosis (Salient Factor Score)			
	Very Good (11–9)	Good (8–6)	Fair (5–4)	Poor (3–0)
	Average Total Time Served Before Release (Including Jail Time)			
GREATEST Aggravated felony (e.g., robbery, sexual act, assault), weapon fired or serious injury Aircraft hijacking Drugs: "Hard drugs," sale for profit (prior conviction(s) for sale of "hard drugs") Espionage Explosives (detonation) Kidnapping Willful homicide	(Greater than above—however, specific ranges are not given due to the limited number of cases and the extreme variations in severity possible within the category)			

NOTES: 1. If an offense is not listed above, the proper category may be obtained by comparing the severity of the offense behavior with those of similar offenses listed.

2. If an offense behavior can be classified under more than one category, the most serious applicable category is to be used.

3. If an offense behavior involved multiple separate offenses, the severity level may be increased.

4. If a continuance is to be given, allow 30 days (1 month) for release program provision.

5. These guidelines are predicated upon good institutional conduct and program performance.

6. "Hard drugs" include heroin, cocaine, morphine or opiate derivatives, and synthetic opiate substitutes.

Source: Peter B. Hoffman and Lucille K. DeGostin, "Parole Decision-Making: Structuring Discretion," *Federal Probation* (December 1974): 7–15. Reprinted by permission.

The scale ranks crimes according to their seriousness and relates this information to the amount of time the inmate has served in prison. It has been demonstrated that an inmate imprisoned for a particular offense has a better chance of success on parole if his period of incarceration is not too lengthy. For example, in Figure 16-1, someone who has committed a burglary would have the best prognosis for parole success if released after serving sixteen to twenty months. Beyond that time, the prognosis for successful parole declines. The severity scale is just one of the guidelines that the U.S. Board of Parole uses in making parole decisions.

Resistance by State Parole Boards

Although the federal government uses prediction methods rather extensively, the states lag far behind in their development and use. Hayner has examined why state parole boards are reluctant to use such devices, and he believes there are several reasons:[17] First, parole board members are extremely sensitive to public opinion and therefore are reluctant to parole individuals that the public would object to even though these individuals might possess all the predictive characteristics of being able to successfully return to society, as many murderers do. Second, parole boards want to encourage constructive use of prison time. As progress is made in the administration of correctional institutions, increasing opportunities for self-improvement are available to inmates. Boards want to facilitate the work of prison staffs by rewarding prisoners who take advantage of their opportunities. The majority of prediction instruments give little weight to institutional factors which many parole boards rely on heavily in making their determinations. The reason researchers do not include institutional behavior and adjustment factors is that these factors are recognized as having little validity. An individual's adjustment in the institution is very often not meaningfully related to his behavior after he leaves prison. Many inmates soon learn to "play the game" and engage in those activities which the parole board will look upon favorably. Their involvement in these programs then has little or no positive effect. Third, parole board members share the conviction that each case is unique. Although they may act on the basis of hunches about uniformities in prisoner backgrounds, they hesitate to admit the hunches. The idea is strongly entrenched that there is no substitute for careful study of the individual case.

Another problem is that many states have imposed legal restrictions which make it impossible for a parole board to release a man when it appears that he will be able to avoid involvement in further offenses. For example, a number of states have adopted deadly weapon statutes that make certain sentences mandatory when the offender has been convicted of using a firearm in the commission of the crime. These statutes usually prohibit parole until a fixed proportion of the sentence has been served. Finally, there is the problem of overcoming traditional ways of thinking. Many parole board members refuse to accept that prediction studies have any merit and rely instead on their intuitive hunches and common sense to guide their decisions.

Characteristics Associated with Parole Success/Failure

Probably the most comprehensive research on the postrelease success of inmates is the encyclopedic work of Glaser.[18] In a 5½-year study of the rehabilitative effects of parole and prison agencies of the Bureau of Prisons, Glaser followed the postrelease successes and failures of inmates and was able to develop a number of important associations between certain characteristics and success or failure. Some of the conclusions he reached were:

- The older a man is when released from prison, the less likely he is to return to crime.
- The younger a person is when first arrested, convicted, or confined for any crime, the more likely he is to continue in crime.
- Drug offenders and individuals committed for economic-related offenses such as auto theft, burglary, larceny, and check forgery are most likely to recidivate. Those convicted of robbery, kidnapping, and violation of liquor laws have intermediate levels of recidivism. The best chances for parole success are for persons convicted of homicide, rape, embezzlement, and income tax fraud.
- One's race is not related in any meaningful way to parole success or failure.
- The more prior felony sentences an individual has, the more likely he is to continue in crime.
- Most parolees seek noncriminal careers. When they fail, it is because of a complex set of social, economic, and personal relationships.

Although Glaser and other researchers have begun to make some headway in examining factors related to success or failure on parole, these scholars would be the first to admit that, like other predictive criteria, they need much more extensive and intensive examination. There is an immediate need for more extensive *cohort analysis,* in which a large selected group of offenders are tracked from the moment they are arrested until perhaps five years after their release from prison or until they recidivate. An important component of this analysis would be an examination of prearrest factors, such as the individual's environment, psychological characteristics, and other factors that might have a relationship to his criminal behavior. Associated with this is the need to study the effects of processing the individual through the criminal justice system, the impact of institutionalization, and finally the factors which are instrumental in bringing about criminal or noncriminal behavior after his release. Whether these factors can ever be identified and related with any predictive validity to parole success or failure is questionable. Today, social science is just not up to this task, but research of this nature is necessary to develop techniques for beginning to answer these questions.

Interstate Compacts for Parole and Probation

Years ago, there was no means by which a parolee or probationer could be supervised outside the state where he was convicted. As a consequence, an offender who committed a crime in a state other than his home state could not return home while on parole or probation—even though the offender might stand the best chance of success with his family. In 1936, Congress passed the

Crime Control Consent Act, which permitted states to enter into mutual agreement to supervise probationers and parolees for each other. By the early 1950s, interstate compacts for the supervision of parolees and probationers were part of the laws of all states. A few years later, similar interstate compacts on juveniles were adopted by the states.

The compacts identify a "sending state" and a "receiving state." The sending state is the state of conviction, and the receiving state is the state to which the parolee or probationer returns. The offender must satisfy certain residency requirements before the receiving state will agree to accept him. Usually, the offender must be a citizen of the state or have relatives or employment there. The receiving state agrees to accept the offender and give him the same supervision as it would one of its own parolees or probationers. The offender who obtains the benefits of out-of-state supervision waives extradition (technically referred to as rendition). Thus, the sending state may enter the receiving state and take custody of the parolee or probationer who has violated the terms of his release without going through extradition proceedings. A supplementary agreement permits the violator to be incarcerated in the receiving state at the expense of the sending state.[19]

State parole boards usually designate one member of the board to be the interstate compact administrator. This person arranges the supervision of parolees who are either sent out of the state for supervision or received into the state after conviction in another state. Since probation is often administered at the local level, the compact arrangements do not work as smoothly for probation supervision as for parole supervision; however, some probation exchanges are usually worked out between the states.[20]

Parolees' Rights

In the past fifty years, states have developed certain procedures for returning a parole violator to prison. Before a parolee can have his parole revoked, most states now require that a revocation hearing be held. Until the late 1960s, however, the "hearing" was often nothing more than a request by the parole agent or his parole supervisor that the parole board revoke an individual's parole, a request which usually was automatically complied with. In too many instances, parolees were sent back to prison for such ambiguous and undefined reasons as "poor attitude" or allegations of "failure to cooperate."

It was generally felt that since the parolee was on parole by grant of this privilege, there was little need for parole boards to concern themselves with questions of the parolee's right of due process, the right to a hearing and review, and matters of proof.

A study of parole board revocations in 1964 indicated that there was no hearing at all in at least seven states. Even in those states which did provide for a revocation hearing, the individual was immediately returned to prison, and often it would be weeks before any type of hearing was held.[21] When the parole board did get around to conducting a revocation hearing, it was usually so superficial and one-sided as to make it meaningless anyway.

Only in a very few cases did the parole board conduct a meaningful hearing, and in even fewer cases was the warrant canceled and the inmate again released to parole. Even if the warrant was withdrawn, the parolee had already suffered a disruptive experience, and family relationships and his employment were already disturbed. During these revocation hearings, it was almost unheard of to permit the parolee to be represented by counsel, to cross-examine the witnesses against him, to demand proof, or to introduce witnesses in his own behalf. In those rare instances when counsel was permitted, the states would not assign an attorney to indigent parolees, which was the category many fell into.

Court Rulings

Beginning in the 1960s, the appellate courts have become increasingly concerned with the parole practices employed by the states. Although the entire parole process has come under a great deal of scrutiny in recent years, parole revocation practices have come under the closest examination. The courts have been developing a distinctive theme in the law that if a privilege such as parole is to be denied, it can be done more readily before rather than after it is granted.

The courts have taken a rather zigzag approach in dealing with the legal questions surrounding parole revocation. At first, the courts held that parole revocations were entirely within the discretion of parole boards and that as a consequence, there was no justification for making the hearing an adversarial process in which the parolee had the right to counsel, to be confronted by his accusers, and to cross-examination of witnesses. However, in the last decade, the courts have been chipping away at the idea that the parolee has no right to invoke certain requirements from the parole board. In 1967, in the case of *Mempa v. Rhay*, the Supreme Court addressed itself to this question in the case of a probationer who had his probation revoked and was sentenced to an institution.[22] The Supreme Court held, in this case, that a state probationer had the right to a hearing and to counsel when it was alleged that a probationer had violated his probation and was to be sentenced to an institution. As a result of this decision, many states began adopting this rule not only for probationers, but for parolees as well.[23]

The application of the Mempa case to the states meant that drastic changes were called for, not only in long-standing legal positions, but in the procedures required to revoke the parolee's or probationer's privilege as well. For example, the New York Court of Appeals, basing its decision on the Mempa case, reversed its former position and required the parole board of that state to permit parolees to be represented by counsel at revocation hearings. The changing philosophy of the courts in their concern for procedural due process is quite well expressed in *Murray v. Page* [429 F.2d 1359 (10th Cir. 1970)]:

> Therefore, while a prisoner does not have a constitutional right to parole, once paroled he cannot be deprived of his freedom to be informed of the charges and the nature of the evidence against him, and the right to appear and be heard at the revocation hearing is inviolate. Statutory deprivation of this right is manifestly inconsistent with due process and is unconstitutional; nor can such right be lost by the subjective determination of the executive that the case for revocation is "clear."[24]

Generally, parole boards have resisted these court orders, regarding them as an arbitrary encroachment by the courts into their area of authority. Many parole board members feel that the adoption of an adversarial format will cause the fact-finding mission of the hearing to be lost in legal argument and maneuvering.

On June 29, 1972, the U.S. Supreme Court rendered a landmark decision which is having a significant impact upon parole boards throughout the nation. In the case of *Morrissey v. Brewer,*[25] two parolees petitioned the Supreme Court on the grounds that their paroles had been revoked without a hearing, which was in violation of their rights to due process. The Court stated that the question was not whether parole was a "right" or a "privilege" but whether by the actions of a governmental agency (parole board), the individual can be made to suffer a "grievous loss." Although the Court admitted that the parolee is not entitled to the full range of rights due a defendant in a criminal proceeding, it did rule that due process requires that a parolee be given a two-stage hearing. A preliminary examination was to be conducted promptly by a hearing officer soon after the arrest or alleged violation. The purpose of this hearing is to determine if there is probable cause to believe that the parolee has committed a parole violation. At this preliminary hearing, the parolee may appear and speak in his own behalf and may bring whatever documents and witnesses are necessary to support his case. The parolee is further entitled to receive advance notice of the hearing, its purpose, and the alleged violation.

If the parolee desires a subsequent hearing prior to the final decision, he must be afforded this right. In this hearing, he has certain fundamental rights, among which are (1) the right to receive written notice of the conditions of parole he allegedly violated, (2) the right to be informed of all evidence against him, (3) the opportunity to be heard in person and to present evidence in his behalf, (4) the right to confront and cross-examine adverse witnesses unless the hearing examiner or parole board considers it in the best interests of the witness not to have his identity disclosed, and (5) the right to receive a written statement by the board or the factfinders as to the specific evidence relied upon to revoke parole.

Developing Trends in Parole

The Development of Parole Teams

In most instances, an individual parolee is arbitrarily assigned to an individual parole officer who has a vacancy in his or her case load. This traditional pairing up is being modified in a number of parole offices throughout the United States today. In its place, a team approach is being employed in which a team of parole officers assumes collective responsibility for a parolee group as large as their combined former case loads. Under this system, parolees are assigned to parole officers who are best able to relate to and supervise them. For example, if certain parole officers seem to have better success with drug-related offenders, then parolees with this type of history are assigned to them.

This team approach is a much more prudent use of the organizational talent and manpower available in parole agencies. It also facilitates the use of paraprofessionals and volunteers, which is becoming increasingly popular as a means to assist parole officers and parolees. Often the use of carefully selected volunteers has proved to be very beneficial, as it provides a means to match parolees with individuals who can understand their particular problems of adjustment and, as a consequence, relate in more meaningful ways.

In some parts of the country, volunteer groups have developed to help prisoners even before their release. In the state of Washington, concerned citizens developed a volunteer sponsors group to visit men in prison, particularly those who had infrequent contacts with anyone from the outside. Their goal was to establish a human contact in which there is real commitment and to follow it up with specific help when the inmate is paroled. This program now numbers over 500 volunteers.[26] In California, a program using volunteer parole aides, some of whom are exconvicts, has begun. One of the most interesting developments is the National Parole Aid Program begun by the American Bar Association. This program was started as a result of the feeling that the citizen volunteer movement, although very popular in probation, was not being utilized to its fullest potential in parole. The program operates by enlisting attorney volunteers to act as parole officers for a single offender under the general supervision of an experienced parole officer.[27]

The Parole Contract Plan

A few states, such as Florida, Georgia, Michigan, North Carolina, and Minnesota, have implemented parole contract plans as an innovative means to make institutional programs more effective. Under the parole contract plan, an inmate meets with counseling specialists when he or she first arrives at the prison. Together, these counseling specialists and the inmate devise a mutually satisfactory plan that the individual will engage in during the period of incarceration. For example, the inmate may be in need of further education and express a willingness to obtain a high school diploma and then go on to complete a vocational trade program. The counseling staff will then draw up a contract agreement with the inmate. The contract specifies that the department of corrections agrees to provide the inmate with the opportunity to obtain a high school diploma and to participate in a vocational training program; the inmate agrees to fulfill these goals by a certain date; and the parole board agrees to parole the inmate upon fulfillment of the contractual obligation.

The basic elements of the parole contract plan are the following:

> A written, legally enforceable contract between the inmate, his institution, and the parole authority;
> A target date, which becomes the parole date if all contract provisions are met by the inmate;
> Face-to-face negotiations between the inmate (often helped by an advocate), the institution, and the parole authority;
> The involvement of an outside party who independently determines whether the contract has been fulfilled;
> Contract provisions spelling out measurable goals for inmates in the areas of education, training, counseling, and institutional behavior, and a guarantee from the correctional system that programs and services to fulfill these goals will be available as needed.[28]

Inmates enter into the contracts voluntarily. If the inmate withdraws from the program or fails to meet the contract terms, he reverts to the regular parole process. Some states permit inmates to renegotiate their contracts if they cannot live up to the agreement. In some states, as many as half of all inmates with parole contracts fail to complete them.[29] In Michigan, a study done by that state's department of corrections indicated that in the first year of the parole contract program, 20 percent of the 202 inmates participating in the program had their contracts terminated.[30] No doubt more would have their contracts revoked as the program continued.

The advocates of the plan cite a number of advantages for such programs: First, the correctional authorities are forced to examine the programs within the system and in the community that can be developed and used and to account for their availability and effectiveness. The contract also forces a parole board to define its criteria for release. The contract plan should also result in reduced tension in prison, increased inmate motivation, lower costs resulting from less time served in institutions, better program coordination, fewer parole hearings, and immediate input from the parole board regarding an offender's program while he is incarcerated.[31]

Another major advantage is that the program places the responsibility on the inmate. Rather than fostering dependency as prison life usually does, since all meaningful decisions are made by prison officials, it encourages goal setting and accomplishment on the part of the inmate. These attitudes, if properly channeled, increase the inmate's ability to cope with the problems of the free

MICHIGAN DEPARTMENT OF CORRECTIONS

CONTRACT SERVICE PROGRAM AGREEMENT

CSO-250A REV.10/74

This agreement made this day between __John Q. Resident__ , no. __A-222111__ , the Bureau of Correctional Facilities, the Bureau of Field Services and the Michigan Parole Board, upon all parties hereto being fully and completely informed in the particulars, the parties do hereby contract and agree as follows:

PART I — RESIDENT

I, __John Q. Resident__ , no. __A-222111__ , understand and agree to successfully complete* the objectives as they are specifically outlined in Part IV below in consideration for a specific date of parole. I understand that programs offered at Bureau of Correctional Facilities institutions outlined in Part IV must be completed before I may take part in programming offered by the Bureau of Field Services. I understand that, at any time, I may submit a request to my assigned counselor for renegotiation of this contract. I will to the best of my ability carry out the objectives of this contract, and realize that failure to do so will cancel and negate the contract.

PART II — BUREAU OF CORRECTIONAL FACILITIES/BUREAU OF FIELD SERVICES

I, __Wayne Monroe__ , representing the Bureau of Correctional Facilities, agree to provide the necessary programs and services at institutions within the Bureau of Correctional Facilities as specified in Part IV below in sufficient time to enable __John Q. Resident__ , no. __A-222111__ , to successfully perform and complete the objectives of this contract.

I, __Leslie Mason__ , representing the Bureau of Field Services, agree to provide the necessary programs and services associated with work release, work study and/or community residential placement as specified in Part IV below in sufficient time to enable __John Q. Resident__ , no. __A-222111__ , to perform and successfully complete the objectives of this contract.

PART III — PAROLE BOARD

We, __Alger Kent__ , __Emmet St. Clair__ and __Crawford Calhoun__ , of the Michigan Parole Board agree to order a parole for the above named resident on or before __August 22 , 1977__ , contingent upon his successful completion of the objectives mentioned in Part IV below.

PART IV — OBJECTIVES (List and number each separately.)

1. By August 1975, I will enroll in the high school program on a full-time basis so that I graduate from high school by January 1976.

2. By January 1976, I will enroll in college programming so that I complete a minimum of one college class per semester until my release.

3. By September 1975, I will begin regular participation in group counseling attending a minimum of 80% of the meetings so that I earn average or better reports regarding progress in group counseling for at least six months.

4. By May 1977, I will be screened for transfer to a corrections center; if eligible, I will be placed in a corrections center until my release.

5. While at the corrections center I will secure home placement and employment for my release.

Figure 16-1   Parole Contract Agreement

world upon release. Figure 16-1 shows the parole contract agreement used by Michigan. At the present time, this plan is for the most part being used for first-time offenders and those sentenced for less serious crimes. Those states using it, however, are already studying its impact to see if it can be expanded.

MICHIGAN DEPARTMENT OF CORRECTIONS

CONTRACT SERVICE PROGRAM AGREEMENT — Page 2

CSO-250B

PART IV — CONTINUED   John Q. Resident, A-222111

6. Upon completion of my high school programming outlined above I will participate on a routine institutional work assignm ent and earn average or better reports regarding adjustment and per- formance on the assignment until my release.

7. While on the work assignment I will maintain a savings in my resident account equal to a minimum of 10% of my wages earned for my release.

8. Prior to my release I will secure dental treatment.

PART V — CONDITIONS UNDER WHICH THE CONTRACT MAY BE VOIDED

1. I understand that, during the course of this agreement, should I commit an act which, if dealt with in a court of law, could result in conviction for a criminal offense (felony or misdemeanor), this agreement is subject to renegotiation or termination.
2. I understand that if I commit more than one infraction of rules and regulations promulgated by the Department of Corrections regarding resident behavior in any thirty day period or any act of serious insubordination, attempt to escape or escape this contract is subject to review. The terms may be renegotiated or the agreement terminated.
3. I understand that it is my responsibility to protect that level of custody to which I am assigned after transfer from the Reception and Guidance Center. Should this agreement call for a reduction in custody, (for example, a transfer to a community residential placement), it is my responsibility to assure that I continue to be eligible for a transfer to that reduced custody status. I further understand that should I fail to progress to reduced custody status, or should I transfer to an increased custody status, this agreement is subject to review. The terms may be renegotiated or the agreement can be terminated.
4. I understand that should I commit an act which may be considered a breach of contract under paragraphs 1 thru 3 above, before the effective date of parole in Part III, the Parole Board may suspend the order of parole pending the outcome of an administrative hearing regarding the possible breach of contract.
5. If previously unknown information regarding pending felony prosecution or detainers from other jurisdictions become available, this agreement is subject to review and the terms may be renegotiated or the agreement may be declared null and void. I understand that should a detainer be lodged against me by another jurisdiction, the commitment to parole in Part III above shall be subject to that detainer.

SIGNATURE RESIDENT	DATE	MEMBER — PAROLE BOARD	DATE
John Q. Resident	6/19/75	Alger Kent	
CORR. FAC. REPRESENTATIVE	DATE	MEMBER — PAROLE BOARD	DATE
Wayne Monroe		Emmet St. Clair	
FIELD SERVICES REPRESENTATIVE	DATE	MEMBER — PAROLE BOARD	DATE
Leslie Mason		Crawford Calhoun	

*Successfully completed for the purpose of this contract means completed with a passing grade or evaluation of satisfactory within the reasonable capabilities of the resident, for the specific program or service objective being evaluated by the responsible staff member assigned to the individual program or service objective.

The Need to Attract Qualified Parole Board Members

A few states are slowly beginning to realize the need to attract qualified individuals to serve on parole boards. Very few states require any specific qualifications for appointment to the boards—nor does the federal government. Table 16-2 indicates the methods by which adult parole board members were appointed in 1972.

TABLE 16-2   Method of Selection of Parole Board Members (1972)

Appointing Officer or Agency	Number of States
Governor	35
State official	7
Special boards	4
Civil service	4

Source: American Correctional Association, *Parole* (College Park, Md.: American Correctional Association, 1972).

In some jurisdictions, highly competent individuals have been appointed to parole boards and some have gained experience through years of service on the parole board. But in 1972, parole board members in forty-two states were serving terms of six years or less. It is not unusual to have new parole board members appointed whenever there is a change in a state administration. Under these circumstances, politics is too often a more important consideration than the appointee's qualifications.

In an effort to curb this practice, Colorado, Michigan, Ohio, and Wisconsin have placed the parole board under the civil service merit system. In addition, Colorado, Michigan, and Wisconsin require appropriate college degrees and experience in corrections or closely related areas. Many of the parole board members in these states have extensive experience in responsible positions in corrections before joining the parole board. Florida requires that appointees pass a special examination in penology and criminal justice which is administered by a special examining board of specialists in these areas.

As more complex and diverse institutional programs develop, states must begin to realize that parole board members must be trained professionals in the field of corrections. Since parole is an integral part of the overall corrections process, parole board members must be trained and dedicated professionals who have an understanding of criminal behavior, institutional programs, and the complex set of relationships upon which better parole decisions must ultimately be based.

Abolition of the Indeterminate Sentence and Parole?

Since 1869, when Michigan enacted the first indeterminate-sentence law, it has been widely held that the indeterminate sentence is the best way to facilitate rehabilitation among inmates. Since an indeterminate sentence prescribes both minimum and maximum periods of incarceration, parole boards and correctional staff can release early those inmates who demonstrate that they have been rehabilitated. At the same time the indeterminate sentence can also be used to keep in prisons those offenders who have not been rehabilitated and who would be a threat to the safety of society if released. Indeterminate-sentence laws were enacted by every state.

Closely associated with the indeterminate sentence is the idea of parole. Since under the indeterminate sentence an inmate could be released before the expiration of his sentence, there had to be some provisions for continued supervision in the community upon release. As a consequence of this, the adoption and development of parole proceeded hand in hand with the adoption of the indeterminate sentence.

However, use of the indeterminate sentence and parole has come under criticism in recent years. In too many instances, the indeterminate sentence has been used as a means to control the conduct of inmates, rather than for the purposes for which it was designed. Correctional administrators have been accused of using it as a means to force compliance from inmates by threatening to keep an individual in prison under the provisions of the indeterminate sentence if he doesn't "behave." In addition, the uncertainty of the release date has created a great deal of anxiety among inmates, who have come to hate such sentences.[32]

The reexamination of indeterminate sentences and parole is having a tremendous impact on correctional philosophy and practices that we have been paying homage to for the past 100 years.

The Maine Criminal Code

In 1975, Maine became the first state to pass legislation discarding the indeterminate sentence and parole.[33] Other states, such as Minnesota and California, are also considering major changes in these areas. Under Maine's new criminal code, judges must sentence offenders to flat terms, in other words, for a set period of time. There is no parole, although that state's bureau of corrections may allow an inmate to return to his or her community under work-release or academic-release programs. Judges are still given discretion to choose the terms and conditions of sentences. They may select imprisonment, restitution to the victim, fines, probation, or any combination of these penalties.

Closely tied in with the flat sentence requirement are revisions in the sentencing provisions of the new criminal code. The new code does not classify crimes into felonies or misdemeanors. Instead, each crime is assigned to one of five categories; the sentencing judge must set a definite term of incarceration within the limits of the category. The maximum term for a class A crime (e.g., armed robbery) is twenty years; for a B crime (e.g., arson), ten years; a C crime (e.g., burglary), five years; a D crime (e.g., possession of LSD), less than one year; and a class E crime (e.g., public indecency), six months. Under the new code, the possession of a small amount of marijuana is now considered a civil rather than a criminal offense with a maximum penalty of a $200 fine. Criminal homicide in the first degree carries a mandatory life sentence, while criminal homicide in the second degree requires a minimum sentence of twenty years. In order to permit some flexibility in the new flat sentences, good-time provisions remain.

The ideas behind imposing the definite sentence and abolishing parole in Maine are expressed in that state's new criminal code. It was felt that this policy would, among other things, give fair warning of the type of sentence that might be imposed for the commission of a particular crime, eliminate discrepancies in sentences given by judges, and relieve the uncertainty among inmates as to when they would be released.

A number of factors led Maine to abolish the indeterminate sentence and parole. Correctional administrators recognized that use of the indeterminate sentence and parole forced many inmates to volunteer for rehabilitative programs in which they had no interest in order to "look good" to the parole board. Also, the legislature's Criminal Code Revision Commission, which wrote the new law, seemed to be particularly upset by public protests that the state parole board was releasing inmates from prison too soon. (In the past, the board had granted parole to 97 percent of those coming up for first hearings.)

The new law has created considerable controversy. Prison reform groups, which are generally in agreement with the idea of flat sentences, say the maximum terms are too long. The governor's own Task Force on Corrections recommended that in most crimes a maximum five-year sentence is warranted. The Criminal Code Revision Commission also pointed out that although one of the goals of the new criminal code was to reduce sentence disparities, the sentencing judge still has discretion within the range specified and that disparities in sentencing will therefore continue to exist. One judge may sentence an individual to twenty years for robbery, while another judge imposes a ten-year sentence for the same crime.

Although it is still too early to tell what will occur in other states in the years ahead, the provisions of the new legislation in Maine are receiving a great deal of attention from other states and professional groups in corrections. The Maine code may well usher in some drastic revisions in correctional practices and modify this aspect of the criminal justice process substantially.

PROBATION

Whereas parole is the conditional release of an offender after he has served a period of incarceration in prison, probation is the conditional release of an individual by the court after he has been found guilty of the crime charged. In the case of probation then, the individual has not been sentenced to prison, although he may, in fact, have been incarcerated in jail following his arrest and while awaiting trial. In the case of parole, the decision is made by a parole

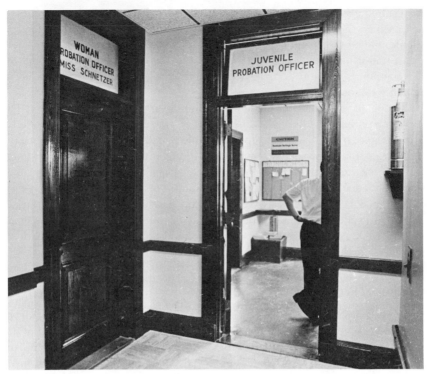

board; in probation, the decision is made by the sentencing judge. The judge, at his discretion, may place the individual on probation, where he is supervised by a probation officer and is subject to court-imposed guidelines of behavior. If the probationer violates the conditions of probation, his freedom in the community may be revoked by the judge, and he may be sentenced to a period of incarceration as prescribed by the particular statute he violated.

Like parole, many critics of probation consider it a form of leniency. Compared with the alternative of incarceration, it might be. Nonetheless, probation is, in fact, a sentence and not a dismissal of the charges. The court will specify the conditions of this form of sentence, which might be to obtain or remain in gainful employment, to make restitution to the victim, to abstain from the use of alcoholic beverages, to remain in the jurisdiction of the court, or other conditions. The probationer agrees to these conditions and agrees to be supervised by the probation department until he successfully completes his period of probation and is discharged from the sentence.

A sentence of probation is imposed by a judge in one of two ways: The judge may impose a prison sentence as determined by the statute violated and then suspend its execution and place the offender on probation, or the judge may defer sentencing and place the individual directly on probation. If the offender should violate the conditions of probation in the first instance, his period of incarceration has already been determined. If in the second instance he violates the conditions of probation, he will be brought back to the court to have sentence imposed.

In most jurisdictions, the judge's discretion in granting the time an offender serves on probation is limited by the period of time that the sentence specifies. For example, if the statute calls for a possible period of incarceration of one to three years, the judge cannot sentence the offender to probation for more than the three-year maximum. However, in some states, the length of the probated term may exceed the term that the defendant would be required to serve if incarcerated.[34] Many states also specify that in the case of more serious crimes, probation is not an alternative. In a few jurisdictions, a jury may recommend probation and the judge must follow the recommendation; in most jurisdictions, however, the decision rests solely with the judge.

Origins of Probation

Modern probation stems from early common law practices which developed as methods of avoiding the severity of criminal laws. During the period of its widespread temporal power, the Roman Catholic Church demanded the right of immunity from secular law for clericals.[35] This immunity was known as *benefit of clergy*. Later, *rights of sanctuary* developed by which those accused of crimes were granted immunity from the civil authorities by seeking the protection of the church.

Probation is primarily an American development. The father of probation is John Augustus. In 1841, while a spectator in the Boston Police Court, he requested that the judge permit him to be the sponsor for an offender about to be sentenced. The court agreed to his request, and the convicted offender was sentenced to his custody. Augustus continued his efforts and developed several of the features that often characterize probation today. First, he selected offenders who were charged with their first offense and appeared amenable. Second, he assumed responsibility for an offender only after a careful examination of the facts of the case and of the history and character of the defendant. Third, he agreed to send the offender to school or to see that he obtained employment and housing. Finally, he developed a system of making impartial reports to the court on the status of those committed to his supervision and of maintaining a careful register of his probationers.

In 1878, the Massachusetts legislature approved of the idea that the mayor of Boston should appoint a probation officer as part of the police force. From Boston, the idea spread slowly across the United States. At first, most probation officers handled only juvenile cases, but as the years passed, courts were increasingly inclined to extend this service to adult offenders. The idea of using probation as an alternative to incarceration spread to other countries as well. The first countries to adopt it outside of the United States were Australia and New Zealand. When England adopted the Probation of Offenders' Act in 1907, the idea soon spread to the Continent, where it was eventually adopted.

The Growth and Use of Probation

Probation is the largest community-based program for handling offenders and is being increasingly used for individuals who are not considered persistent professional or dangerous offenders. For example, in Indiana in 1972, of those persons convicted of an offense for which imprisonment was an alternative, 56 percent received probation.[36] The success of probation is well-documented by statistics. In Michigan, the department of corrections studied 2,411 cases placed on probation in 1968. These probationers were studied for three years, and it was found that 79.1 percent of the offenders were successful under probation. Of the 20.9 percent that failed, 15.3 percent had their probation revoked for technical violations, while only 5.6 percent committed new offenses.[37]

The Organization of State Probation Agencies

State probation departments are organized in diverse ways. They may be a part of the executive or the judicial branch, and they are administered by both state and local governments. For example, in Michigan, certain probation departments are administered by local courts while others are under the control of the state department of corrections, which is an agency of the executive branch. In Ohio, juvenile probation is a local function of that state's courts which deal with juvenile matters, while adult probation is handled in some cases under the administrative authority of the local courts and in other cases by an agency located in the executive branch of state government. In New York, the state division of probation is in the executive branch, as are all local probation agencies except those in New York City, which are in the judicial branch.[38]

There has been a great deal of argument over which administrative arrangement is best. Although the National Advisory Commission on Criminal Justice Standards and Goals advocates placing all state probation services under a unified state correctional system, many argue that this function should be retained by the local courts. The arguments for both sides have been summed up as follows:

Arguments for Having Probation Services Administered by Local Courts

Under this arrangement, probation would be more responsive to court direction. Throughout the probation process, the court could provide guidance to probation workers and take corrective action when policies were not followed or proved ineffective.

This arrangement would provide the judiciary with an automatic feedback mechanism on effectiveness of dispositions through reports filed by probation staff. Judges would place more trust in reports from their own staff than in those compiled by an outside agency.

Courts have a greater awareness of needed resources and may become advocates for their staffs in obtaining better services.

Increased use of pretrial diversion may be furthered by placing probation services under the auspices of the courts. Since courts have not been inclined to delegate their authority to persons not connected with the judiciary or its staff, it is likely that probation services which are not under the court will have less discretion in employing diversionary measures.[39]

Arguments for Having Probation Services Administered by a Central State Executive Agency

When probation services are attached to the courts, judges frequently become the administrators of probation in their jurisdictions—a role for which they are usually ill-equipped. Judges cannot effectively divide their time between administering probation services and yet perform their judicial functions.

When probation is within the judicial system, the probation staff is likely to give priority to services for the courts such as issuing summonses, serving subpoenas, etc., rather than providing services to probationers.

Since the criminal courts in particular are adjudicatory and regulatory rather than service-oriented organizations, probation services that are attached to courts will not develop a professional identity of [their] own.

The executive branch contains the allied human service agencies, including social and rehabilitative services, medical services, employment services, and housing, which can be used to develop more coordinated cooperative and comprehensive program efforts with probation agencies.[40]

Probation Work as a Career

Like the other agencies of criminal justice, probation suffers from a lack of qualified and well-trained personnel and supporting financial resources. In 1970, the National Council on Crime and Delinquency indicated that there were 24,758 officers engaged in federal, state, and local probation and parole services in the United States. It is not possible to break these figures down in order to provide a more accurate picture of the number of probation officers because some jurisdictions combine the functions of parole officer and probation officer. In addition, some probation officers handle only juveniles, and some supervise only adults. Data are not available that would differentiate these categories. Only a few states, such as Wisconsin, have combined all adult and juvenile probation cases, whether felon or misdemeanant, in a single bureau of probation and parole in an attempt to centralize services at the state level.

Probation services and departments range from small, rural offices in which the chief probation officer is the entire staff to highly complex and specialized organizations, such as the Los Angeles County Probation Department, which employs over 4,000 staff members, about 2,200 of which perform professional probation services as deputy probation officers and supervisors.

Qualifications

The American Correctional Association, in its *Manual of Correctional Standards,* suggests that individuals preparing to become probation officers complete two years of graduate study in social work, thereby earning a master's degree in social work, or two years of work in a comparable behavioral science with at least one year of graduate study. In addition, probation officers should possess highly developed skills in casework, counseling, interpersonal communications, and leadership.[41] Carney believes that these criteria are unrealistic because of the critical shortage of probation officers across the nation and because higher education offered in corrections is inadequate.[42] He bases his argument on the fact that most schools of social work offer very few courses in the specialized field of corrections and its particular problems. Consequently, students in traditional social work programs are not being adequately prepared for the unique problems that they will face in working with offenders. Many young probation officers indicate that they would be more successful if they had acquired more knowledge of the system of criminal justice before beginning their careers.

Most academic programs are also woefully inadequate in training social work students in the process of decision making, yet probation officers must make countless decisions—not to take action, to delay action, or to take one form of action in lieu of another. Cohen has said that the only "legally relevant" issue in probation and parole is that which "involves authoritative decision-makers exercising a vast discretion."[43] Immediate work needs to be done to understand how best to reach appropriate probational decisions. This will be no easy task, as the vast majority of probation officers' decisions are unrecorded; indeed the vast percentage of them are not normally even thought of as decisions. Furthermore, these decisions are not simply a function of an offender's behavior, but rather reflect the interrelationship of many factors, some of which are explicit, such as the operating procedures of the probation office, and some of which are considerably more complex and subtle and include the probation officer and the social and political system in which he or she operates.[44]

Functions

Probation officers are responsible for the management and supervision of offenders who make up their case loads. For a number of years now, the recommended case load has been established at fifty units. The American Correctional Association and the President's Commission on Law Enforcement and Administration of Justice recommend fifty-unit and thirty-five-unit case loads, respectively, with the provision that each presentence investigation and report that the probation officer is required to compile should count as five supervised cases. Both of these arbitrary figures seem to be without any meaningful justification. The usual rationale for smaller case loads is that the fewer individuals the probation or parole officer has to supervise, the more effective the supervision will be. However, research has indicated that there appears to be no relationship between size of case load and success or failure of a probationer or parolee. Adams conducted detailed reviews of case-load size research in which he summarized the findings of a dozen case load studies conducted in the federal system and in California in which case loads ranged from only 12 offenders to 210. He could find no evidence which indicated that offenders in the smaller case loads did any better than offenders who were part of much larger case loads.[45]

A probation officer does far more than merely supervise a case load of probationers. In addition to providing counseling, employment assistance, and other related services, a probation officer must be an investigator and a diagnostician of the needs of the probationer and must be able to develop, coordinate, and implement the special casework services needed. Probation officers also perform another unique role, the importance of which often goes unrecognized. A probation officer often serves in a quasi-judicial function, especially where judges more or less automatically impose the sentence recommended in the probation officer's presentence report. Various studies have shown a very high relationship between probation officers' recommendations and dispositions made by judges. Carter and Wilkins have pointed out that judges follow probation officers' recommendations in better than 95 percent of the cases.[46] Part of this might be attributable to the probation officer anticipating what sentence the judge is predisposed to give and then recommending it, but there are probably many instances where the judge goes along with the recommended sentence on the assumption that the probation officer, having conducted the presentence investigation, has the most complete facts.

Unless prevented by statute, the court has the power to set the specific conditions of probation for adult offenders. Often the judge imposes the specific requirements on the probationer that the probation department recommends. The probation officer is also responsible for initiating revocation of probation, although it is the judge who actually revokes probation. Most probation revocation statutes are so vaguely worded that it is not difficult for the probation officer who wishes to do so to find cause to invoke the revocation process, usually on the basis of some technical violation. Finally, the probation officer has the ability to render punishment under the guise of rehabilitation, for example, by demanding that the probationer not live in or frequent certain areas, not engage in certain employment, and not associate with certain people.[47]

Shock Probation

One of the suggested methods of handling offenders is to incarcerate the offender for a brief part of his sentence, suspend the remainder, and place him on probation. This approach, called shock probation, attempts to avoid the long-term prison commitment and its effects on the attitudes of the offender. Those who advocate the use of shock probation contend (1) that short-term institutionalization may be to the inmate's advantage since the period of incarceration can provide probation agencies the opportunity to evaluate the needs of the offender in more detail so that they are in a better position to help him and (2) that it will jolt the individual into a realization of the realities of prison life and thereby serve as a more meaningful deterrent to future criminal behavior than probation alone.[48]

This technique is so new that there have been very few evaluative studies of the success or failure of shock probation as a sentencing alternative. There is one notable exception to this. In 1965, the general assembly of Ohio passed the first shock probation act, and in 1972 a group of researchers compared the program in its first year of existence (1966) with its use in 1970. The study showed that the success rate for releases in 1966 was about 85 percent and about 92 percent for those released in 1970.[49] However, since those released in 1970 had served only two years on probation at the time of the study, the long-term impact of the program has not been established. Table 16-3 shows the percentage of failures and success of the two groups in the study.

TABLE 16-3   Disposition of Shock Probation Cases of Males and Females Released From Three Ohio Prisons in 1966 and 1970

Sex and Year	Successes		Failures	
	N	Percent	N	Percent
Males, 1966	46	85.2	8	14.8
Females, 1966	6	85.7	1	14.3
Males, 1970	12	90.0	44	10.0
Females, 1970	1	93.2	3	6.8
TOTAL	65		56	

Source: Paul C. Friday, David H. Petersen, and Harry E. Allen, "Shock Probation: A New Approach to Crime Control," in David M. Petersen and Charles W. Thomas, *Corrections* (Englewood Cliffs, N.J.: Prentice-Hall, 1975), p. 251.

Probation Subsidy Programs

A few states, notably Michigan and California, recently developed a probation subsidy program in which the state offers to pay counties that administer probation services to *keep juvenile offenders out of state institutions*. The concept of the subsidy program is closely linked with ideas generated by modern correctional philosophy that strives to keep delinquents out of institutions that often further educate them in crime and at the same time stigmatize them. The most highly developed program is in California, where the program was inaugurated on a trial basis in 1965. By 1973, forty-five of California's fifty-eight counties were participating.

Juveniles in California, who without the provisions of the program would be sentenced to one of the California Youth Authority institutions, are eligible for the program which the authority manages. Under the subsidy plan, the participating counties are paid as much as $4,000 per year for each probation case that they retain. Most of the cases come from the juvenile courts; however, a few serious cases of youthful offenders found guilty by the general criminal courts have also been involved in the program. As of 1971, a fraction over 20 percent were removed from the program because they had in some way violated the conditions of probation.[50]

Los Angeles County, the most populous county in the state, received over $5 million in subsidies during the 1968-1969 fiscal year. By 1971, subsidies to the participating counties amounted to nearly $20 million. Although this is a great deal of money, it is far less than the state would have to pay for the institutionalization of these offenders had not such an incentive program existed.

The program has helped California cut back drastically on its costs of institutionalization and the need to expand institutional facilities and programs during a period of critical budget cuts. The program has also enabled the counties to develop outstanding probation departments and to expand their staffs and attract many qualified professionals. Although some claim that overall it has been a demonstrated success and others claim that the program is too lenient and does not serve as a deterrent to crime, it is still too early for any conclusive argument to be made concerning its success or failure.

Use of Indigenous Paraprofessionals

In the past ten years, there has been a growing trend among probation departments to recruit auxiliary personnel from the same social class as the probationers. Such persons are referred to as *indigenous paraprofessionals*. Many probation officers agree that their clientele are often alienated from the mainstream of society by virtue of their norms, values, and life styles. Frequently, these probationers are referred to as hard to reach, unmotivated, mistrustful, and resentful of authority. As Beless and others have said: "There exists a marked *social distance* between many middle-class professional corrections workers and a large segment of their lower-class clientele."[51]

As a consequence of this, a number of probation departments are experimenting with the use of indigenous paraprofessionals to assist probation officers. These people bring to their staff positions valuable qualities: an understanding of lower-class life, the knowledge of the urban slum, and the ability to communicate with and be accepted by the ethnic poor. Grosser sees the local resident worker as a bridge between the lower-class client and the middle-class professional worker.[52]

A logical extension of using indigenous paraprofessionals in probation work is to use former offenders in this role. A number of probation agencies are now doing this. This idea draws upon the experience of such groups as Alcoholics Anonymous and Synanon, which operate on the idea that those who have experienced and overcome a problem have a unique capacity to help others with similar problems. Riesman characterized this phenomenon as the helper therapy principle and concluded:

> Perhaps, then, social work's strategy ought to be to devise ways of creating more helpers! Or, to be more exact, to find ways to transform *recipients* of help into *dispensers* of help, thus reversing their roles, and to structure the situation so that recipients of help will be placed in roles requiring the giving of assistance.[53]

One such program is the Chicago-based Probation Officer Case Aide (POCA). This program uses indigenous paraprofessionals for federal probation and parole, with some being former offenders. Applicants for probation officer assistant (POA) are recruited primarily from neighborhoods having high proportions of offender clients. The majority of applicants come to the project by way of recommendations of probation staff officers, referrals from local social service agencies, and self-referrals. In establishing the program, the crucial issue was the selection criteria. It was finally decided that applicants would be chosen by a selection committee of the project staff. Once selected, the POA attends orientation and training sessions and is then assigned to a probation officer who supervises ten POAs.

It has been found that these indigenous paraprofessionals are interested, available, and able to work well under professional supervision. It also has been demonstrated that they provide a productive and effective service to professional probation officers. They are frequently able to intervene in cases where probation staff officers might encounter problems.[54]

Another interesting variation of this idea has been proposed by the National Council on Crime and Delinquency, which not only recommends the use of former offenders to assist in probation work, but even suggests using carefully selected probationers to work with other probationers. In this way, an individual, while helping others, would be contributing to his own self-help and improvement and would be developing skills that might help him become a probation officer or other social service employee.[55]

Something similar to this has already occurred in the Chicago POCA project. One former offender in the program joined the POCA project and began attending classes at a local junior college. He was later admitted to the criminal justice program in a major university and was hired by the Illinois Department of Corrections as an adult parole officer. Another man, after serving as a POA, obtained employment with the Illinois Department of Social Services as a youth supervisor.

Probation will probably continue to be used extensively as a means to divert offenders from institutions, and use of probation volunteers and indigenous paraprofessionals will probably increase. The future of parole seems to be somewhat uncertain. If, indeed, states begin enacting legislation that permits the courts to sentence offenders to definite periods of imprisonment after which the offender is released without community supervision, parole services as we know them today will be drastically reduced. At this time, however, it is too early to tell whether such trends will develop extensively in the future.

SUMMARY

Parole is the conditional release of an offender who has served a period of time in prison, while probation is the conditional release of an individual who has been found guilty in court. Parole has its roots in such practices as conditional pardons, indenture, tickets of leave, and indeterminate sentences. Modern parole originated at the Elmira Reformatory. Parole is not a form of leniency but rather an extension of the rehabilitative and reintegrative program begun in the institution. States have traditionally organized adult paroling authority around three models—the institutional, the independent, and the consolidated. In recent years, the consolidated model has been adopted by most states. Just as each state has its own parole authority, so does the federal government. Decisions of parole boards are usually based upon the seriousness and nature of the current offense, the circumstances of the crime, the placement situation, and the offender's institutional record. In recent years, some states and the federal government have been developing prediction methods to assist parole boards in making their decisions.

Among some of the changes occurring in parole in recent years have been the increased legal rights of the parolee, the development of parole teams, the parole contract plan, and improvements in the selection of parole board members. In spite of the advances in parole, there is some indication that in the years ahead parole, along with the indeterminate sentence, may cease to exist. Both are being closely examined by some states.

Probation services are also undergoing changes. One is the movement toward providing adult probation services through a centralized state authority rather than on a strictly local basis. Other innovations are probation subsidy programs, shock probations, and use of volunteers, indigenous paraprofessionals, and former offenders as probation aides. Probation will probably continue to be used extensively as a diversionary practice.

Suggested Additional Readings

American Bar Association Project on Minimum Standards for Criminal Justice. *Standards Relating to Pretrial Release.* New York: Institute of Judicial Administration, 1968.

————: *Standards Relating to Probation*. New York: Institute of Judicial Administration, 1970.

Bates, Sanford. "When Is Probation Not Probation?" *Federal Probation* 24: 13–20.

Campbell, W. J. *Probation and Parole: Selected Readings*. New York: Wiley, 1960.

Dressler, D. *Practice and Theory of Probation and Parole*. New York: Columbia University Press, 1960.

Empey, Lamar T. *Alternatives to Incarceration*. Washington, D.C.: U.S. Government Printing Office, 1967.

England, R. "What Is Responsible for Satisfactory Probation and Post-Probation Outcome?" *Journal of Criminal Law, Criminology and Police Science* 47 (1957):667–676.

Friday, Paul C., David M. Petersen, and Harry E. Allen. "Shock Probation: A New Approach to Crime Control." *Georgia Journal of Corrections* 1 (July 1973):1–13.

Glaser, Daniel, and V. O'Leary. *Personal Characteristics of Parole Outcome*. Washington, D.C.: U.S. Government Printing Office, 1966.

Meiners, R. C. "A Halfway House for Parolees." *Federal Probation* 29 (June 1965):47–52.

Pigeon, Helen D. *Probation and Parole in Theory and Practice*. New York: National Probation and Parole Association, 1942.

Smith, Robert L. *A Quiet Revolution–Probation Subsidy*. Washington, D.C.: U.S. Department of Health, Education, and Welfare, 1972.

Notes

1. William Parker, *Parole: Origins, Development, Current Practices and Statutes* (College Park, Md.: American Correctional Association, May 1972) p. 10.

2. Charles L. Newman, *Sourcebook on Probation, Paroles and Pardons* (Springfield, Ill.: Charles C. Thomas, 1970), p. 23.

3. Parker, op. cit., p. 13.

4. Michigan Department of Corrections, "Operation and Philosophy of the Michigan Parole Board," mimeo (Feb. 10, 1975), p. 6.

5. Newman, op. cit., p. 26.

6. Ibid., pp. 30–31.

7. Parker, op. cit., p. 17.

8. National Council on Crime and Delinquency, *Corrections in the United States* (New York: NCCD, 1967), p. 217.

9. National Advisory Commission on Criminal Justice Standards and Goals, *Corrections* (Washington, D.C.: U.S. Government Printing Office, 1973), pp. 395–397.

10. National Probation and Parole Institutes, *The Organization of Parole Systems for Felony Offenders in the United States*, 2d ed. (Hackensack, N.J.: National Council on Crime and Delinquency. 1972).

11. National Advisory Commission, op. cit., pp. 396–397.

12. This section is adapted from U.S. Department of Justice, *The Utilization of Experience in Parole Decision-Making–Summary Report* (Washington, D.C.: U.S. Government Printing Office, November 1974), pp. 3–5.

13. U.S. Board of Parole, *Biennial Report 1968*–70 (Washington, D.C.: U.S. Department of Justice, 1970), p. 17.

14. Daniel Glaser, *Effectiveness of a Prison and Parole System* (Indianapolis: Bobbs-Merrill, 1959), p. 23.

15. Michigan Department of Corrections, op. cit., p. 3.

16. For example see Don F. Gottfredson, "A Shorthand Formula for Base Expectancies," California Department of Corrections, Research Division, *Research Report No. 5* (Sacramento, July 1962); P. G. Ward, "Validating Prediction Scales," *British Journal of Criminology* 7 (1967): 36–44; Peter B. Hoffman and James L. Beck, "Parole Decision-Making: A Salient Factor Score," *Journal of Criminal Justice* (Winter 1974): 195–206.

17. Norman S. Hayner, "Parole Boards' Attitudes toward Predictive Devices," in Norman Johnson et al., eds., *The Sociology of Punishment and Correction* (New York: Wiley, 1970), pp. 839–843.

18. Glaser, op. cit.

19. Hazel B. Kerper and Janeen Kerper, *Legal Rights of the Convicted* (St. Paul, Minn.: West, 1974), p. 509.

20. Ibid.

21. Robert Sklar, "Law and Practice in Probation and Parole Revocation Hearings," *Journal of Criminal Law, Criminology and Police Science* 55 (1964): 75.

22. 389 U.S. 128 (1967).

23. National Advisory Commission, op. cit., p. 405.

24. Quoted in ibid, pp. 405–406.

25. 408 U.S. 471 (1972).

26. "A New Helping Hand for Prison Inmates," *Readers Digest,* 97 (August 1970): 147–150.

27. Louis P. Carney, *Introduction to Correctional Science* (New York: McGraw-Hill 1974), p. 327.

28. Steve Gettinger, "Parole Contracts: A New Way Out," *Corrections Magazine* 2 (1) (September/October 1975): 4.

29. Ibid.

30. Michigan Department of Corrections, "Contract Service Program Pilot Phase," mimeo (1975), p. 4.

31. Gettinger, op. cit., p. 5.

32. For example, see American Friends Service Committee, *Struggle for Justice: A Report of Crime and Punishment in America* (New York: Hill and Wang, 1971); Jessica Mitford, *Kind and Unusual Punishment: The Prison Business* (New York: Knopf, 1973).

33. The following discussion of the new provisions in Maine is based on Steve Gettinger, "Profile: Maine," *Corrections Magazine* 1 (6) (July-August 1975): 13–26.

34. Kerper and Kerper, op. cit., p. 251.

35. Elmer H. Johnson, *Crime, Correction and Society* (Homewood, Ill.: Dorsey, 1968), p. 666.

36. State of Indiana, *Report to the Citizens Council on Probation* (1973), p. 2.

37. State of Michigan, Department of Correction, *Criminal Statistics* (Lansing, 1972), p. 9.

38. National Advisory Commission, op. cit., p. 313.

39. Ibid.

40. Ibid. p. 314.

41. American Correctional Association, *Manual of Correctional Standards* (College Park, Md.: American Correctional Association, 1971), p. 98.

42. Louis P. Carney, *Introduction to Correctional Science* (New York: McGraw-Hill, 1974), p. 303.

43. Fred Cohen, "The Legal Challenge to Corrections," *Joint Commission on Correctional Manpower and Training* (Washington, D.C.: March 1969), pp. 26–27.

44. Robert M. Carter et al., *Corrections in America* (Philadelphia: Lippincott, 1975), p. 194.

45. See Stuart Adams, "Some Findings from Correctional Case-load Research," *Federal Probation* 31 (December 1967): 55.

46. Robert M. Carter and Leslie T. Wilkins, "Some Factors in Sentencing Policy," *Journal of Criminal Law, Criminology and Police Science* 58 (4) (1967): 503–504.

47. Eugene H. Czajkoski, "Exposing the Quasi-Judicial Role of the Probation Officer," *Federal Probation* 37 (September 1973): 9–13.

48. See I. R. Kaufman, "Enlightened Sentences through Improved Technique," *Federal Probation* 26 (1962):3–10; Irving W. Jayne, "The Purpose of the Sentence," *National Probation and Parole Association Journal* 2 (1956): 315–319.

49. P. C. Friday, D. M. Petersen, and H. E. Allen, "Shock Probation: A New Approach to Crime Control," *Georgia Journal of Corrections* 1 (July 1973): 1–13.

50. California Youth Authority, *Probation Subsidy Evaluation* (Sacramento, Calif: May 1972).

51. Donald W. Beless, William S. Pilcher, and Ellen Jo Ryan, "Use of Indigenous Nonprofessionals in Probation and Parole," *Federal Probation* 36 (March 1972): 11.

52. C. F. Grosser, "Local Residents as Mediators between Middle-Class Professional Workers and Lower-Class Clients," *Social Service Review* 40 (1) (March 1966): 56–63.

53. F. Riesman, "The 'Helper' Therapy Principle," *Social Work* 10 (April 1965): 28.

54. Beless et al., op. cit., p. 15.

55. See National Council on Crime and Delinquency, *Team Management in Probation and Parole* (Paramus, N.J.: NCCD, 1972).

THE JUVENILE JUSTICE PROCESS

Chapter 17

The Juvenile Justice System

JUVENILE DELINQUENCY TRENDS

Although the proportion of youth in the population of the United States has declined from the all-time high of the late 1950s and 1960s, their contribution to the total number of arrests continues to grow at an unprecedented rate. The number of cases of delinquency handled by the juvenile courts in 1973 increased by more than 3 percent over the 1972 figure while at the same time the population aged ten through seventeen increased less than 1 percent.[1] In most years of the past decade the increase in delinquency cases exceeded the increase in the juvenile population. Between 1960 and 1973, the number of delinquency cases more than doubled (124 percent increase) while the number of children aged ten through seventeen increased by only 32 percent.[2] Figure 17-1 shows this trend for the years 1957–1973. In 1973, juveniles age seventeen and under were involved in nearly 56 percent of the arrests for auto theft, 35 percent of the arrests for armed robbery, and 55 percent of the arrests for burglary.[3] These data reflect some interesting trends. Although auto theft is normally a crime committed by juveniles, FBI data show an overall decline for arrests for juveniles in this category from 1970 to 1973. On the other hand, arrest data show that youths of seventeen and under are being arrested in increasing numbers for violent crimes. What these statistics do not reveal, of course, is the relative percentage of crimes being committed by juveniles which do not come to the attention of the police and as a consequence never end up in the statistical compilations of the *Uniform Crime Reports*. Nor do they show the many cases of delinquency that are handled informally by the police and the family without involving the courts. Because of the wide discretion that the police have in handling many cases of delinquency, the juvenile justice system often does not

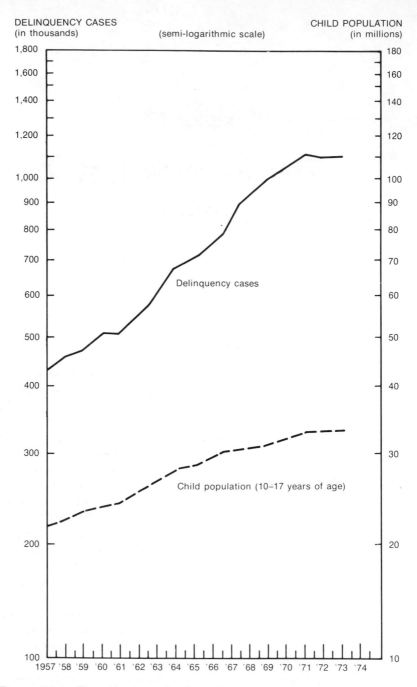

DELINQUENCY CASES
(in thousands)

(semi-logarithmic scale)

CHILD POPULATION
(in millions)

Delinquency cases

Child population (10–17 years of age)

1957 '58 '59 '60 '61 '62 '63 '64 '65 '66 '67 '68 '69 '70 '71 '72 '73 '74

Figure 17-1   Trend in Juvenile Court Delinquency Cases and Child
Population 10–17 Years of Age, 1957–1973

Source: Department of Health, Education and Welfare, *Juvenile Court Statistics —1973* (Washington: U.S. Government Printing Office, March 1975) p. 9.

become involved. For example, a 1965 study by the Chicago Police Department's Youth Division indicated that 66.1 percent of all official police contacts with juveniles in that city were adjusted by the police without referral to the juvenile court.[4]

Delinquency Among Girls

Delinquency remains a problem primarily of male youth, but the disparity between the number of boys' and girls' delinquency court cases is narrowing. For many years, boys were referred to court for delinquency about four times as often as girls. In the past few years the rapid increase of referral of girls' cases has reduced this ratio to about three to one. There is some evidence that this ratio is still slowly declining.[5] For example, in 1973 girls' cases increased at the rate of slightly over 4 percent compared with only 2 percent for boys' cases. Data gathered by the Office of Youth Development of the U.S. Department of Health, Education, and Welfare indicate that juvenile courts in rural areas are particularly increasing the number of youthful female offenders that they handle. This may be a reflection of less tolerant attitudes of officials in these areas toward girls' delinquent behavior that tends to be overlooked in urban areas. However, even in urban areas the juvenile courts are handling more and more female delinquency cases.

Not only are girls being referred to the juvenile court in ever-growing numbers, but the juvenile courts are also adjudicating them as delinquents at a rate faster than that for boys. Between 1965 and 1973 the number of girls formally adjudicated as delinquent increased by 110 percent, whereas the number of boys' cases increased by 52 percent.

Police arrest data also indicate that girls are participating in delinquent acts at a faster rate than boys. Between 1960 and 1973 arrests of girls under eighteen years of age increased by nearly 400 percent for violent crimes and over 300 percent for property crimes; for boys under eighteen the percentage increases for these crimes were a little over 200 percent and 82 percent, respectively.[6] Specialists in the study of delinquency have attributed the rise in delinquency among girls to two factors. First, society has modified its protective attitude toward women. Second, women are rejecting some of their traditional, passive roles and are becoming more aggressive and independent. This combination of factors encourages change in the role perceptions held by society and women themselves. As women become more assertive in their new roles, society and the agencies of criminal justice relax their traditional protective tolerance and handle women offenders more like male offenders. This less inhibited behavior pattern of women probably contributed in various ways to the exploding delinquency rate among girls, which includes large increases in the number of girl runaways and drug users (who often turn to shoplifting, robbery, prostitution, etc. to support their "habits").[7]

THE JUVENILE COURT

In the United States, a special tribunal has been created and given the specific responsibility and authority to adjudicate matters involving young people. In addition to delinquency cases, juvenile courts in most jurisdictions handle cases involving neglected and dependent children as well as children who are considered in the law to be "wayward." A "wayward child" is typically defined as "a child between seven and seventeen years of age who habitually associates with vicious or immoral persons, or who is growing up in circumstances exposing him to lead an immoral, vicious or criminal life."[8]

Juvenile courts often adjudicate offenses committed by an adult upon a child, such as child abuse or contribution to the delinquency of a minor. In large urban areas, juvenile courts also are often responsible for the maintenance of detention facilities. Usually these detention facilities are for the temporary housing of children who come to the attention of the court either as delinquents or as neglected or dependent children. A child charged with a serious criminal offense is usually transferred to a state juvenile institution after adjudication by the court. The court usually tries to have neglected or dependent children transferred to special foster homes or child welfare facilities.

The juvenile court has original jurisdiction over all children under a specific age, usually seventeen. In some states juvenile courts share jurisdiction with the general trial courts under youthful offender statutes which raise the age limit to twenty-one or twenty-three for offenders with no prior criminal record.

In about forty states the juvenile courts have some flexibility in exercising their original jurisdiction and thus can waive jurisdiction over a minor, who will then be transferred to the adult criminal court for trial. These waiver laws vary greatly. In about one-half of the states which permit this practice, the juvenile court alone decides whether the child should be transferred to the adult court. In about one-third of these states waiver is authorized for any offense but usually only when the child is above the age of fifteen or sixteen. Some states permit waiver when the child commits another crime while under court supervision. In other states the authority for the juvenile court to transfer a minor to the general trial courts is determined by both the offender's age and the type of crime committed.[9] For example, the juvenile code of Michigan provides that:

> In any case where a child over the age of 15 years is accused of any act the nature of which constitutes a felony, the judge of probate of the county wherein the offense is alleged to have been committed may after investigation and examination, including notice to parents if address is known, and upon motion of the prosecuting attorney, waive jurisdiction; whereupon it shall be lawful to try such child in the court having general criminal jurisdiction of such offense.[10]

Although many states have this type of authorizing legislation, juveniles are rarely turned over to the adult criminal courts for trial. What few exceptions are made are cases of a particularly heinous nature, such as homicide and/or rape, where the offender is at least sixteen or seventeen years old and has a long history of serious criminal offenses.

Organization

Typically, juvenile courts follow two patterns of organization: In most areas they are a specialized function of a probate court, court of domestic relations, or family court. As such they are merely appendages of courts whose main responsibility is to deal with wills and estates, divorces, and similar legal proceedings, and there may or may not be a specially designated judge who handles juvenile cases. It is not unusual, for example for a judge on a probate court to devote most of his or her time to probate matters and to look upon juvenile matters as an irritating sideline. In densely populated areas, a practice is to rotate the job of juvenile court judge among the several jurists serving the court. Sometimes a particular judge who has indicated a preference or expertise in juvenile matters is assigned to concentrate on these cases.

In large metropolitan areas, the juvenile court is often an entirely separate court of general jurisdiction. This type of arrangement establishes the juvenile court as a respected judicial entity on a par with courts of similar importance in the state.

Problems

Overall, juvenile courts suffer from a number of weaknesses. In the first place, the diversity of the juvenile court's role often creates problems. Although it is expected to extend a benevolent helping hand to wayward children, it is also expected to protect the community from offenders who are often as dangerous to society as those individuals with whom the adult criminal courts must deal.

Another source of difficulty which isn't always obvious is the inferior position the juvenile court usually has in the court hierarchy. Since few jurisdictions have made it a separate court on a level with other courts of general jurisdiction, it is held in low regard by lawyers, judges, and the police. The court by its very organizational characteristics must rely greatly on local government, local organizations, and often the local voters for funds and support. This dependence makes it very vulnerable to criticism of its operation, programs, and methods of disposing of cases. Its lack of independence further complicates the typical juvenile court's already intricate relationships with other organizations. Increasingly the juvenile court has been looked upon as a provider of the social services to which local government has become more and more committed. To carry out even a portion of these obligations, it must not only curtail its own activities, particularly its judicial responsibilities, but also rely heavily on the goodwill and assistance of many local groups, among them the police, schools, and welfare agencies. This reliance often creates cross-pressures, such as the police demanding that the court deal more strictly with delinquents while another agency urges greater leniency. Consequently the juvenile court has often found itself embroiled in local conflicts between the police and school officials over the handling of arrests made during school hours and on school property for marijuana use and other offenses.

Underlying and intensifying all these difficulties is the court's lack of resources. Procedures for gathering and recording information and other essential tasks are cumbersome and antiquated. The struggle to carry out service functions with inadequate staff and facilities detracts from judicial responsibilities so that in the final analysis neither is fully performed.

ORIGINS OF THE JUVENILE JUSTICE SYSTEM

Scholars and historians are unable to agree on the legal foundation for the present-day juvenile court. Some argue that its beginnings can be traced to the English feudal courts of high chancery. Under the English laws of equity, the courts of high chancery were given the responsibility by the crown to serve as *parens patriae* (in place of the parent) to protect the interest of the child whose property was in jeopardy. Later these courts extended their protection to other areas of general child welfare and incorporated the neglected and dependent child within their jurisdiction. There is no indication, however, that these courts exercised any jurisdiction over the delinquent child.

The other viewpoint is that juvenile courts sprang from the common law of crimes. Under the common law, a child under seven years of age was considered incapable of developing the required criminal intent, and a child between the ages of seven and fourteen was also deemed incapable of developing the required intent unless it could be shown by his maturity and understanding that he was aware of the consequences of his actions. Because of this and because adult criminal courts were unable to deal effectively with youthful offenders, special quasi-judicial tribunals began to develop and formulate administrative and procedural guidelines for dealing with children. Eventually these became commonly accepted policies which were then institutionalized into practice as a way to deal with delinquent youth.

Until about 1825 there were no special provisions for handling delinquents in America. The common law and customary practice of dealing with youthful offenders was to assume that children accused of misbehavior and crimes were guilty as charged. Possible innocence was not considered: the jury's responsibility was to determine whether children understood their offenses. Juries were often reluctant to sentence children to jail and often acquitted them after a brief trial, finding "lack of knowledge" the reason for the crime.[11]

By the early nineteenth century this method of handling delinquents had become unsatisfactory for two major reasons: First, despite courtroom partiality toward youths, increasing numbers were being convicted and sent to jails, where it was commonly believed that they were schooled in crime by adult offenders. Second, and more important, some children gained acquittal by appealing to the jury's sympathy—an equally unsatisfactory disposition because it allowed them to escape the consequences of their actions.[12]

Early Juvenile Reformatories

These shortcomings in the criminal justice system prompted concerned reform groups in Boston, New York, and Philadelphia to concentrate on creating special institutions for juveniles. The first refuge was founded in New York in 1824 by members of the Society for the Reformation of Juvenile Delinquents. In 1826 following the recommendation of Boston's mayor, the Boston City Council founded the House of Reformation for juvenile offenders. At the same time, a group of Philadelphia's leading citizens received a charter to form a house of refuge, which opened in 1828. The New York and Philadelphia refuges were privately managed although they did receive public sanction and financial aid; the Boston House of Reformation was a municipal institution. These three institutions were the only organized efforts to reform juvenile delinquents until 1847, when state institutions were opened in Massachusetts and New York.[13]

The guiding premise of these early reformatories was that children should be punished not cruelly, but correctly. Thus a regimen of work, study, and imposed discipline was adopted in which children would be taught the habits of piety, honesty, sobriety, and hard work.[14] These early reformatories were required by their charters to receive destitute and orphaned children as well as those convicted of crimes—crimes sometimes no greater than vagrancy, idleness or stubbornness.[15]

Although their initial purpose of reform must be admired, the refuges did not live up to the glowing expectations of their founders. These institutions were soon criticized for their apparent inability to halt juvenile delinquency or to prevent the spread of violent activities by gangs of youth who roamed the streets of our major cities after the Civil War. Although one cannot blame these reformatories completely for the growing upsurge in delinquency since they could not possibly handle all the children coming before the court, they can be directly blamed for failing to deal effectively with those under their care.

These early institutions were immediately faced with the problem of overcrowding and having to deal with large numbers of children without adequate financial support. To make ends meet, they began entering into contractual agreements with private businessmen to provide child labor. This soon led to scandalous instances of brutality and neglect by private entrepreneurs who exploited the children. Although education was an initial purpose of these refuges, the children were soon seen as merely laborers who could produce a profit for the businessman as well as maintain the financial stability of the institution; thus time devoted to schooling was not justified on economic grounds.

Another problem that contributed to the failure of the refuges was the indiscriminate grouping of serious offenders with children who were not delinquents or had committed only minor offenses. Under these circumstances, the inevitable happened—the recalcitrant and serious youthful offenders began exerting their influence, and the refuges became miniature schools of crime.[16]

The Development of Juvenile Courts

Developing along with the idea that juveniles should be institutionalized apart from adult offenders was the idea that children should be separated from adults before and during the trial. In 1861 the mayor of Chicago was authorized to appoint a special commission to hear and decide cases involving boys from ages six to seventeen who were charged with committing minor offenses. In 1867 this commission was given the power to place the delinquents who came before it on probation or to sentence them to a special institution for delinquent children. In 1869 a Massachusetts law permitted the employment of a state agent who would be available for counsel and guidance to the court and would locate and report on foster homes that the court might use in disposing of the children who came before it.[17] Boston passed a law in 1870 which required that children's cases should be heard separately and that an authorized state agent should be appointed to investigate cases, attend trials, and protect children's interest.[18] A few years later Massachusetts passed additional legislation which specified that in juvenile cases, the courts were to hold separate sessions, schedule juvenile cases by a special docket, and maintain a separate records system.

Chicago is credited with the first true juvenile court in the United States. In the last decade of the nineteenth century a group of prominent and dedicated reformers consisting of some Chicago jurists, the Illinois Bar Association, civic groups, and a small yet zealous group of social scientists and social workers began concerted efforts to persuade the Illinois state legislature to enact laws dealing with children and to vest the authority for applying these laws in a court that would be designated specifically for this purpose. In April 1899, the legislature passed the Act to Regulate Treatment and Control of Dependent, Neglected and Delinquent Children, and on July 1, 1899, the Juvenile Court of Cook County was established in Chicago. For the first time, one specific court had responsibility for dependent, neglected, and delinquent children. The specific philosophy which guided the original legislation, and which is still an important part of present-day thinking, was that the juvenile should be protected and that this protection was a responsibility of the court. The delinquent child was not to be treated as a criminal, but as a person in need of help and reform.[19] To accomplish this, some changes were made in juvenile courts. In place of the adversarial proceedings which typify the adult criminal trial, informal hearings were conducted in an atmosphere more conducive to treatment than to adjudicating guilt or fixing blame. In this informal atmosphere, the judge assumed the role of a fatherly and sympathetic figure while remaining a symbol of authority. Special emphasis was placed on investigating, diagnosing, and prescribing treatment. The individual's background was more important than the facts of a given incident; specific conduct was regarded more as symptomatic of the need for the court to apply its resources and to help rather than as a prerequisite for jurisdiction.

Because the ostensible purpose of the juvenile court was to treat and help rather than adjudicate guilt or innocence, the court was empowered to act in ways inconsistent with many of the procedural safeguards available to adults in the regular courts. For example, since the hearing was not an adversarial process, there was no need for defense lawyers or a prosecutor to be present. Trials by juries were dispensed with for the same reason. Other basic rights, such as the right to cross-examine and to be confronted with the witnesses against the accused, were seldom practiced in these courts. By the same token, the child who was found guilty of a delinquent act had no right to appeal his case to a higher state court for review.

In place of these legal guarantees and rights, the courts employed behavioral scientists, particularly social workers, psychologists, and psychiatrists, because delinquency was considered a disease which needed expert diagnosis and treatment. This use of treatment personnel has been a unique characteristic of the entire juvenile justice process since its inception. Along with this emphasis, a new legal vocabulary developed that was adopted by the juvenile court. Instead of a complaint, there was a petition; a summons was used in place of a warrant; instead of a preliminary hearing, there was an intake interview; in place of am arraignment, there was a hearing or inquiry; finding of involvement replaced a conviction; and there was a disposition instead of sentence.

Another characteristic of juvenile courts which has developed over the years is the extension of their authority over forms of behavior which if committed by an adult would not be a crime, but under the provisions of state juvenile codes places the child under the authority of the court. For example, the Michigan Probate Code vests jurisdiction in the juvenile division of that state's probate court over a child:

1. Who has violated any municipal ordinance or law of the state or of the United States
2. Who has deserted his home without sufficient cause or who is repeatedly disobedient to the reasonable and lawful commands of his parents, guardian or other custodian
3. Who repeatedly associates with immoral persons or who is leading an immoral life; or is found on premises occupied or used for illegal purposes
4. Who being required by law to attend school, willfully and repeatedly absents himself therefrom, or repeatedly violates rules and regulations thereof

5. Who habitually idles away his or her time

6. Who repeatedly patronizes or frequents any tavern or place where the principal purpose of the business conducted is the sale of alcoholic liquors.[20]

By 1911 a dozen states had followed the example of Illinois, and by 1925 all but two states had instituted juvenile courts. Today there is a juvenile court act in all fifty states and the District of Columbia, with approximately 2,700 courts responsible for hearing cases involving children.[21] Although juvenile courts vary greatly in their organization and staffing, generally the states adopted the basic philosophy and principles of the Chicago court and the Illinois act as well as many of the legal features associated with these pioneer efforts.

THE JUVENILE JUSTICE PROCESS

The vast majority of juveniles who appear in juvenile court are referred there by the police who have arrested them. In some cases private citizens or the child's parents can refer the child to the jurisdiction of the court. Just as the arrest of an adult must be accompanied by an arrest warrant, a legal instrument called a petition must be filed with the juvenile court to convey to the court the authority to intervene in the matter. Like an arrest warrant, a petition must specify the particular statutory violation, and it usually includes such additional information as the name, age, and residence of the child, the names and residences of his parents or guardians and a brief description of the circumstances surrounding the commission of the offense.

The Intake Interview

The next step is the intake interview. If the child is in custody, most states require that the intake interview take place within a specified time after arrest. The intake interview is a preliminary examination of the facts conducted by the court. Usually this intake process is presided over by a referee. Although not a judge, the referee usually has a background in social work or the behavioral sciences and in a few instances may also be an attorney. Many times the referee is a probation officer assigned to the juvenile court. The functions of the intake interview are to protect the interests of the child and to dispose of those cases which do not warrant the time and expense of court adjudication. This preliminary inquiry may vary from a brief examination of the facts to an in-depth investigation of all the factors involved in the juvenile's case, including a background investigation of the child's family, interviews with school officials, psychological or psychiatric testing, and health examination. Most states also provide that relevant witnesses can be summoned by the court at the intake interview and be forced to appear and give testimony under penalty of law. If the interview is a formal one, the child, his parents, and an attorney can be present. Depending upon the referee's judgment as to the sufficiency of evidence, the need for court intervention, and the basis for legal jurisdiction of the court, the referee can dismiss the case, authorize a hearing before the juvenile court judge, or make an informal adjustment. If the referee chooses the latter course, he or she can exercise some limited discretion in properly disposing of the case. In many juvenile courts approximately one-half of the cases are informally adjusted by referral to another agency, by continuation on informal probation, or in some other way. For example, in the 1973 survey of juvenile courts in the United States conducted by the Office of Youth Development of the Department of Health, Education, and Welfare, 54 percent of delinquency cases received nonjudicial dispositions.[22]

The referee or intake officer also determines whether a child should be detained pending court action. In some jurisdictions the child does not have the statutory right to bail as do most adults accused of crimes. In most jurisdictions which do not extend the right of bail to the juvenile there are provisions for the child to be released to his parents unless it can be demonstrated that the release of the child poses a threat to the safety and well-being of the community or himself. When detention is warranted, the referee usually has the right to place the child into detention but only limited authority to hold him there. If more extended detention pending the formal appearance of the child before the court is warranted, this must be authorized by the juvenile court judge.

The Adjudication Inquiry and Adjudication Hearing

If the referee or intake officer determines that the court should formally intervene in the case, the juvenile then appears before the judge for the arraignment. This step is usually called an *adjudication inquiry*, a *judicial hearing*, or, in some courts, a *formal appearance*. At this stage the juvenile court judge examines the facts of the case to determine if the facts and the nature of the child's behavior warrant an adjudication hearing by the court. In recent years provisions have been made to notify the juvenile at this stage of the charges against him and to advise him of his constitutional rights and his right to an attorney.

At the adjudication inquiry, the judge can dispose of the case or order a formal adjudication hearing, depending upon the seriousness of the case. If it is a case of serious misbehavior or if the child indicates that he or she wants a hearing or wants to hire an attorney, the judge will schedule an adjudication hearing.

The adjudication hearing in the juvenile process is considerably different from the trial process involving an adult accused of a crime. In order to keep the process more informal and less adversarial in nature, rules of evidence are often not strictly adhered to, and unsworn and hearsay testimony are often received and considered. The standard of proof is supposed to be guilt beyond a reasonable doubt, but this requirement is not always adhered to. Most juvenile courts have no provisions for jury trials, and the state is not usually represented by the prosecutor. Instead, the prosecution of the case may fall upon a probation officer or a police officer. In this latter case the police officer testifies to the facts of the case as he is aware of them. The probation officer acts not so much as a legal inquisitor but as an individual who is present to relate to the court what the investigation of the child and his alleged offense has uncovered.

Since their objective is to protect and help the child, juvenile courts usually attempt to exclude from these proceedings all persons except those who have relevant and material testimony to present. In determining its disposition of the juvenile, the court places a great deal of reliance on the clinical and social report prepared by the probation officer and the diagnostic staff. This report is very similar to the presentence investigation which is conducted in the adult criminal court, with the possible exception of its greater emphasis on diagnostic testing.

Disposition

Most states give juvenile court judges very broad discretion to dispose of cases. The judge has the power to dismiss the case, give the juvenile a warning, fine him, place him on probation, arrange for restitution, refer him to an agency or treatment facility, or commit him to an institution. A child sentenced to an institution usually receives an indeterminate sentence not to exceed his twenty-first birthday. If the child's crime or the community's protection warrants a longer period of incarceration, at age twenty-one he will be transferred to an institution that handles adult offenders. Under these circumstances, a juvenile might be committed to an extended period of incarceration in both juvenile and adult institutions. The Children's Bureau of the Department of Health, Education, and Welfare is very critical of this practice and recommends that in most cases the child not be committed for more than three years unless the threat to the community or the possibility for harm to the child necessitates he remain in protective custody.[23] Figure 17-2 indicates the basic juvenile justice process.

There is as much variation in the structure and organization of agencies administering services and facilities for delinquent children as there is in the structure of the courts. As a result of this, responsibility for the child often shifts back and forth among courts and a variety of public and private agencies, both state and local. A number of states are now trying to incorporate all public agencies dealing with the child into a single unified state agency. In Michigan, a proposed department of children and youth services would have the following responsibilities:

1. To provide all State institutional, probation and aftercare services to children committed to the Department by the juvenile court.

2. To set minimum standards for all State, local, private and public institutions including probation and aftercare programs for neglected, dependent and delinquent juveniles.

3. The operation of any public institutional program, probation and aftercare services that do not meet the minimum standards as set forth by the Department.[24]

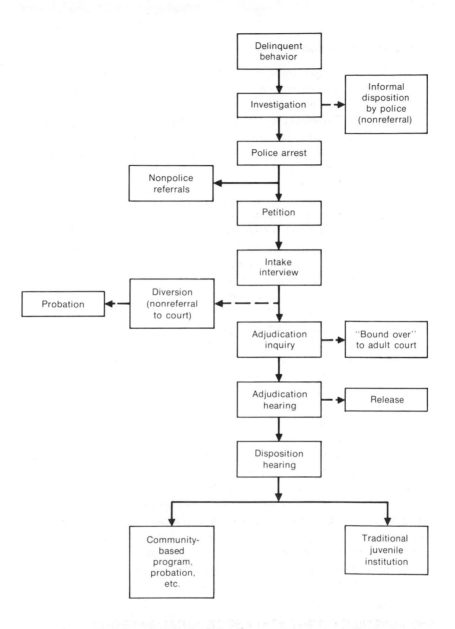

Figure 17.2   Basic Juvenile Justice Process

*Note: In a number of states the filing of the petition follows the intake interviews. In those states if the referee or similar official concludes that the facts of the case warrant the formal intervention of the court, a petition will be issued which binds the child over to the jurisdiction of the court. In other states, a petition must be signed before the formal process (beginning with intake) can be initiated.

Role of the Probation Officer

One of the most important members of the juvenile court team is the juvenile probation officer. The function of the juvenile probation officer is to combine individualized, rehabilitative diagnosis and treatment with effective community supervision. Probation officers investigate the juvenile's all-important social history and establish a link between the court and behavioral scientists such as psychologists or psychiatrists who diagnose the treatment required by the child. The probation officer is required to make factual and objective reports to the court as well as recommendations and suggestions for the proper treatment and disposition of the juvenile. As a legal representative of the court, the probation officer is also responsible for developing the probation plan. The probation plan is both a study of the child and a recommended course of action for the court in dealing with the child. It is based on a social study of the child which comes from such sources as the delinquent himself, his parents or relatives, school officials, the police, social agencies, and the diagnostic services of behavioral scientists who have examined the child. The plan specifies whether the child needs the services of the court, whether it is more feasible to treat him in the community under a supervising probation officer, or whether institutionalization is warranted. If the investigation indicates that the child does not need the services of the court since other agencies are available in the community to meet his needs, the probation officer then must see that the delinquent is willing to accept the referral and must provide the agency with the information needed to work effectively with the child. If the probation plan does not call for institutionalization and if the child is placed under supervision in the community, the probation officer is also responsible for seeing that the child adheres to the probation plan and the limitations set down by the court.

It is generally agreed that the most appropriate role for the juvenile probation officer is that of a correctional social worker rather than that of a law enforcement officer. Thus the probation officer is expected to provide treatment consistent with the philosophy of social work as practiced today. To accomplish this, the juvenile probation officer must know how to use and interpret findings from psychological testing and psychiatric examinations. The probation officer also guides and counsels the child about problems that may have played an important role in his past delinquencies.

THE JUVENILE COURT AND PROCEDURAL SAFEGUARDS

Throughout its history the juvenile court in America has maintained that since its function was to protect the child, it was not appropriate for that tribunal to engage in the adversarial tactics that mark the adult criminal trial. This philosophy has had a tremendous impact on how the juvenile court has operated. From its inception wide differences have been tolerated—indeed insisted upon—between the procedural rights accorded to adults and those of juveniles. As a consequence almost all jurisdictions until recently did not grant to juveniles the basic constitutional rights that are afforded adults charged with a crime. Although the U.S. Supreme Court has extended a number of constitutional rights to juveniles being handled by the juvenile courts, the child still does not have the right to bail, to indictment by grand jury, to a public trial, or to trial by jury. Rules governing the arrest and interrogation of adults by the police are frequently not observed in the case of juveniles.[25]

According to Shears, since the child should be made "to feel that he is the object of the state's care and solicitude" and not that he is under arrest or on trial, the rules of criminal procedure which govern our criminal trials are considered by many to be inappropriate to juvenile court proceedings. The right of the state to deny to the child procedural rights available to his elders is based on the assertion that a child, unlike an adult, has a right "not to liberty, but to custody." He can be made to obey his parents, to go to school, etc. If the parents of the child do not provide the proper supervision and care of the child —that is, if the child is delinquent—the state may intervene. When the court intervenes, it does not deprive the child of any rights, because he has none. It merely provides the custody to which the child is entitled.[26]

Attitudes such as these and the absence of basic constitutional rights in juvenile court proceedings prompted Roscol Pound, a former dean of the Harvard Law School, to say of the juvenile court:

> The powers of the Star Chamber [medieval site of torture used to extract a confession from an accused] were a trifle in comparison with those of our juvenile courts. . . . The absence of substantive standards has not necessarily meant the child receives compassionate and individualized treatment. The absence of procedural rules based upon constitutional principles have not always produced fair, efficient and effective procedures. Departures from established principles of due process have frequently resulted not in enlightened procedure, but in arbitrariness.[27]

Supreme Court Decisions

Beginning in the late 1960s the Supreme Court began to examine the question of whether the juvenile offender was entitled to the same constitutional guarantees as an adult would have in our criminal court system. The first major case of importance was *Kent v. United States,* which was decided in 1966.[28]

Morris A. Kent, Jr., age sixteen, was arrested by the Washington, D.C., police in 1961 and charged with housebreaking, robbery, and rape. Kent had a rather extensive juvenile record for housebreaking and purse snatching dating back to 1959 and was on probation for earlier offenses at the time of his arrest. Upon being apprehended, Kent was taken to police headquarters and interrogated for seven hours, during which time he confessed to other acts of housebreaking, robbery, and rape. After making the confession, Kent was detained at the juvenile receiving home for almost a week without any examination by a judicial officer as to the legality of the arrest and detention.

The juvenile court then waived jurisdiction over Kent, and he was turned over to the adult criminal court to stand trial on the charges. The District of Columbia juvenile court was permitted to turn a juvenile over to the adult courts after completing a "full investigation" of the facts in a case. In the Kent case, this "full investigation" consisted of the judge reviewing the probation report and social service file maintained on Kent by the court's probation staff. The Supreme Court did not determine the propriety of the waiver or consider the other questionable issues of the validity of the confession or detention without an appropriate judicial hearing. What the Court did was send the case back to the juvenile court to determine whether review of a probation file, maintained in regard to the defendant for a prior offense, satisfied the requisite of a full investigation.

The significance of this case lay not so much in the decision as in the indication it gave of the general attitude of the Supreme Court. The Court was putting the juvenile justice system on notice that these courts could not be afforded the luxury of procedural arbitrariness and it questioned the efficacy of the *parens patriae* philosophy. In the words of the Court:

> There is evidence, in fact, that there may be grounds for concern that the child receives the worst of both worlds; that he gets neither the protection accorded to adults nor the solicitous care and regenerative treatment postulated for children.[29]

The warning of the Court in the Kent case exploded like a bombshell in 1967, when the U.S. Supreme Court proclaimed in the landmark decision of *In re Gault* that children handled by the juvenile courts were entitled to many of the due process guarantees afforded adults.[30] Gerald Gault was a fifteen-year-old boy who had been committed as a juvenile delinquent to the state industrial school by the juvenile court of Gila County, Arizona. Like Kent, Gault was already subject to an earlier juvenile court probation order, based on his having been along with another boy when a woman's purse was taken. In the case involving Gault which the U.S. Supreme Court heard, a neighbor had charged that Gault and another boy had made an obscene telephone call to her. The police arrested Gault. Gault's parents were at work at the time, and apparently no efforts were made to contact them after their son was taken into custody; they seem to have first learned of their son's detention that evening through the parents of the other boy about whom the neighbor had complained. After hearing of his arrest, Gerald's parents went to the detention home, where they were informed of the reason for their son being in detention and were told that a hearing would be held the following day.

The next day the police officer in charge of the case filed a petition for the hearing to be held that same day. No copy of the petition was served on the boy's parents. The petition contained only legal allegations and recited no facts. The hearing was conducted in the judge's chambers without the complainant being present, and no sworn testimony was given. The court made no effort to make any record of the proceedings so that the only information concerning the hearing was in the record of a habeas corpus proceeding brought after the juvenile court hearings had been concluded.

Gerald was released from custody two days after the initial hearing, and on that day the police left a note for Mrs. Gault to inform her that there would be another hearing three days later. At the second hearing the judge apparently relied on admissions that the police had obtained from Gerald after he had been arrested. The arresting officer indicated that Gerald had admitted to making the phone call in question. At the beginning of the second hearing Mrs. Gault asked the court to compel the complainant to attend. The judge ruled that her attendance was not necessary; her version was reported in court on the basis of a telephone conversation that the investigating officer had conducted with her. A probation "referral report" was in the judge's hands, but it was not shown to Gerald or to his parents. At the conclusion of the hearing the judge committed the boy to the state industrial training school "for the period of his minority, unless sooner discharged by due process of law." Since Gerald was fifteen at the time, he would thus have been subject to custodial control until his twenty-first birthday. Interestingly, the same offense if committed by an adult would have constituted only a misdemeanor under Arizona law.

Arizona did not have a law which provided for a juvenile to appeal his case from a juvenile court to a higher state appellate court. Under the circumstances the Gaults could only file a habeas corpus writ with the Arizona Supreme Court, which was done a few months later. The Arizona Supreme Court ordered a hearing to be held on the writ in the Superior Court; the latter court denied the writ on the ground that there was no denial of either constitutional or statutory rights in the juvenile court hearing, and the Arizona Supreme Court concurred. On review, the U.S. Supreme Court reversed the decision of the Arizona Supreme Court, finding that Gault had been denied his fundamental rights to due process. In doing so, it imposed a far-reaching set of standards upon the thousands of juvenile courts throughout the nation. Specifically, the Court imposed the following procedural safeguards in delinquency cases and thus decreed a new direction in the juvenile court practice.

1. Under the due process clause it is constitutionally mandated that there be notice of charges given to the juvenile himself and to his parents. This notice must be in writing and must contain the specific charge or allegations of fact on which the proceeding is to be based. The notice must be given as early as possible and "in any event sufficiently in advance of the hearing to permit preparation."[31]

2. In delinquency proceedings which may result in commitment to an institution, the child and his parent must be notified of the child's right to be represented by counsel. If they are indigent, the court must appoint defense counsel.[32]

3. The juvenile has the right to be confronted with the witnesses against him.

4. The juvenile must be advised of his right against self-incrimination.

The U.S. Supreme Court did not specifically decide in the Gault case whether there is a right to appellate review or whether juvenile courts are required to provide a transcript of the hearings for review. Nor did it answer the question of whether the juvenile offender is entitled to trial by jury or what should be the burden of the state in proving its case against a youth accused of a crime. These issues have been addressed by the Supreme Court in more recent cases. *In re Winship* [397 U.S. 358 (1970)], the Court reversed the conviction of a twelve-year-old boy who had been declared delinquent after having been accused of stealing $112. The burden of proof used in the delinquency proceeding was a "preponderance of the evidence." The Court held that the correct standard is "proof beyond a reasonable doubt" and that anything less is a violation of the due process requirements of the Fourteenth Amendment.

In the case of *McKeiver v. Pennsylvania* [403 U.S. 528 (1971)] the Supreme Court declined to rule that a juvenile facing delinquency proceedings has a constitutional right to a jury trial. The Court felt:

> If the jury trial were to be injected into the juvenile court system as a matter of right, it would bring with it into that system the traditional delay, the formality, and the clamor of the adversary system and, possibly, the public trial.[33]

Although many students of the juvenile justice process believed that the mandates of the Court would spell the end of the traditional philosophy of the juvenile court, this has not happened. Research on the impact of the Court's pronouncements indicates that a number of things have occurred. In the first place, the requirements issued by the Court have not been uniformly adopted by the states. Some researchers believe that the juvenile courts have made only minimal changes in procedure in reaction to Supreme Court decisions.[34] Certainly there was no overnight rush to comply, and the courts have been able to retain their basic philosophy while slowly phasing in the adjustments that the Supreme Court ordered.

Undoubtedly, the overall impact of the Gault case has been to increase legal fact finding. Probably the greatest change has occurred from the growing use of defense lawyers which seems to have decreased the number of cases which reach adjudication and disposition.[35] From 1957 to 1973, there was a steady decline in the number of cases handled judicially and a steady increase in the number of cases disposed of by nonjudicial means.[36] This may very well indicate that because of more legalistic screening more cases are being diverted from the formal process of the adjudication hearing.

In the final analysis, it would seem that procedural due process for juveniles does not conflict with the benevolent philosophy of the court as many juvenile court advocates thought it would as a result of the changes brought about by the Gault case. The juvenile courts have accommodated themselves to change in ways not disruptive of traditional practices, beliefs, and operating procedures.

DELINQUENCY DIVERSION PROGRAMS

Recent years have seen the juvenile justice system and related agencies begin to concentrate more of their attention and resources on providing alternatives for dealing with delinquent youth. The major emphasis today is on diverting youth before they are adjudicated and labeled "deviant" or "undesirable."

Evidence cited by the President's Commission in 1967 suggests that a child's chances of becoming a chronic and serious delinquent are increased once he enters the criminal justice system and is officially labeled "delinquent."[37] In spite of the supposedly benevolent intent of juvenile statutes and the juvenile court, the fact that the child is processed and judged under them imposes a stigma that is difficult for the child to overcome. Models of delinquency diversion seek to avoid this social-psychological phenomenon of labeling or stigmatizing youth.

Stigmas received by youth assume greater importance when one realizes that many children are referred to juvenile court for acts which although symptomatic of behavioral problems do not really constitute a crime in the strictest sense. Such acts as running away from home, frequenting an undesirable place, associating with undesirable companions, truancy, ungovernability, and curfew violations bring juveniles to the attention of the juvenile courts in most jurisdictions. Once in court, they are defined as "delinquent" with all of the undesirable connotations such labeling attaches. This stigma affects the child's self-concept, as well as the attitude of his parents, teachers, peers, and other community members with whom he interacts.

By now it should be evident that youth coming under the jurisdiction of juvenile courts may be classified into two categories. First are those who have committed acts which would be crimes if committed by adults, and second are those who have committed noncriminal offenses—who have broken no law but are designated as "beyond control," "runaways," or "minors in need of supervision." When the two categories are given equal dispositions, children who have not engaged in criminal conduct find themselves drawn into the correctional system.

The idea that legal systems may themselves contribute to the very problems that they were established to correct is given detailed examination by Sheridan. He says:

> The label of "delinquent" sets a youngster apart from his peers—in his own estimation and by the community in general. Through forced association with others similarly labeled, this feeling is reinforced. He begins to think of himself as a delinquent and acts accordingly.
>
> Placing of such children in correctional institutions exposes them to association with more sophisticated delinquents who have committed serious offenses and developed a pattern of delinquent conduct. . . . Despite all measures, statutory or otherwise, to protect from stigma the youngster who is a product of the

correction system, it is well known that such stigma exists to almost as great a degree as in the adult field.[38]

Upon examining the way juvenile courts typically handle their referrals, one finds that a large percentage—54 percent in 1973—are "adjusted" short of appearance before a judge.[39] This does not mean that the child was not in fact guilty of the particular delinquent act; it merely means that the court intake officer for any number of reasons felt that the behavior did not necessitate an appearance before the judge, and as a consequence the statutorily sanctioned authority of the judge was not invoked. In a large court, one-half to three-fourths of all complaints received may be handled in this way. It is certainly not unusual for a young offender to have his case "adjusted" two, three, four, or more times before being taken before the judge.

If such a large number of delinquency complaints can be handled in this way, it is conceivable that many of them could have been diverted without ever being referred to court at all. As a consequence, advocates of diversionary measures argue that delinquency rates could become more realistic, courts could be freed to concentrate on more difficult chronic offenders, and children could in many cases avoid the stigma of official labeling.

Although it is not practicable to review all the diversion models that have been developed, the beginning student in criminal justice should be aware of some of the more notable programs. These programs can be classified into four different types: (1) school-related, (2) court-related, (3) police-related, and (4) community-related models.[40]

School-Related Delinquency Diversion Programs

The school-related programs recognize that the school plays an important role in delinquency prevention. It is often in the school that the first indications of delinquency-prone conduct are observable. It is also recognized that youth who drop out of school prematurely commit more crimes than youth who stay in school and finish their education. In an effort to combat this problem a number of school-related delinquency diversion programs have been implemented in recent years.

The Collegefields Group Educational Center

This center provided a specialized educationally based rehabilitation program for delinquent and predelinquent boys ages fourteen and fifteen who were perceived by Newark, New Jersey, school and juvenile court authorities as potential dropouts. The boys were also identified on the basis of behavior suggesting delinquency-prone attitudes. The boys were exposed to intensive guided group interaction techniques to rehabilitate them and to guide them toward more prosocial attitudes and school performance. They were also given the opportunity to gain work experience along with their usual academic studies. The Family Service Bureau of Newark provided casework services to the families of the boys in the program to minimize the impact of negative family influences.[41]

Providence Educational Center

This is a very recent program funded by the Law Enforcement Assistance Administration, which focuses on and identifies outstanding criminal justice projects with the hope that through careful program analysis and research these projects can be adopted by other communities throughout the nation. This program is being developed in St. Louis among inner-city youth. After adjudicating a child as either neglected or delinquent, the juvenile court has the alternative of sending the child to the Providence Educational Center, a non-residential school and resocialization center for boys twelve to sixteen years of age with learning problems. Over 62 percent of the referrals have committed serious crimes, such as stealing, armed robbery, destruction of property, attempted rape, and attempted homicide.

By improving classroom performance and reversing negative attitudes, the program aims to help juveniles hold down jobs or successfully reenter high school after leaving the program. The approach of the program is to combine an emphasis on counseling and treatment with individualized instruction and supported learning. A special counseling office charts each student's progress on an individualized treatment plan. The classes are geared to help the child through remedial education and consist of no more than twelve students who are supervised by two master teachers and a full-time social worker. Individual counseling, "rap" sessions, and regular lessons proceed side by side so that the emotional problems which often underlie learning problems can be treated as they arise.

The child remains in the project until he has attained an eighth-grade reading level and his social skills and behavior have shown similar progress. Continual monitoring and evaluation help school officials decide whether the child is capable of making it on the outside without resorting to criminal behavior. The average length of stay is nine months.

To ensure that the growth and improvement which occurs at the school continues after the child returns to the community, the center has initiated an aftercare program offering essentially the same counseling services provided to the individual while he was in the school. The aftercare staff begins working with a student several months prior to his anticipated release. Together with the boy's classroom teachers, the staff reading specialist, and juvenile court officers, the aftercare staff discusses the student's options and outside goals. The child may choose to return to public school for a high school diploma, to work, or to enter a work program or vocational school. The aftercare staff maintains liaison with his teachers in the public schools, his employer, or the youth's supervisors in a vocational program until a successful transition is made.

Preliminary analysis of the program seems to indicate a much higher degree of success than that of traditional programs for dealing with delinquents. In standardized tests administered to students who have been at the school from two to seven months, the average reading achievement score increased from 4.4 to 4.8 and the average math score from 3.6 to 4.5. These are important increases in view of the fact that the center's students are "problem learners."

Similarly, while 28.1 percent of the school's students committed offenses while enrolled in the school or during the six-month aftercare period, some 70 percent of the youths released on conventional probation in St. Louis and 50 percent of those assigned to conventional residential institutions committed further offenses.[42]

Court-Related Delinquency Diversion Programs

The emphasis of court-related diversionary programs is on diverting youthful offenders before adjudication of the child as a delinquent. After a preliminary examination of the facts indicates guilt, the courts may postpone finding the child delinquent until he or she has completed a designated program or committed another offense while in the program.

Maryland's Intake Services Law

Under a statutory revision of Maryland's juvenile code, a child coming before the juvenile courts in that state may at the option of the court undergo informal disposition. As part of this informal disposition, "adjustment services" may be provided for up to forty-five days. These services include counseling with the child or his family or referral to appropriate community agencies. This action can be taken only after all conditions are explained to the parties concerned and there is voluntary agreement to accept the conditions of the service. Once the decision has been made to follow the informal procedure, the court agrees not to file the petition unless a new complaint has been received. On a statewide basis, approximately 50 percent of all complaints are disposed of in this manner.[43]

Project Crossroads

This federally funded project is designed to test the feasibility of using extensive professional and volunteer sources to develop remedial education programs, job placement opportunities, and counseling for delinquent offenders. The program enlists the support of the juvenile courts and the police for a pretrial diversion program in which the child receives ninety days of rehabilitative services prior to the court hearing. The court can extend this period up to sixteen months. At the conclusion of the service period the child's case is reviewed, and the court decides whether the child warrants its further attention.[44]

Other court-related services include probation volunteers; court-sponsored group homes for children who are not yet delinquent but who have prodelinquent attitudes or behavioral problems; volunteer interpreters to explain to non-English-speaking families the process of the juvenile court and availability of services; employment aides to help the court obtain employment for youth; and educational aides to help the child obtain remedial education or entry into appropriate vocational training programs.

Police-Related Delinquency Diversion Programs

Many police agencies also recognize that they have an important role to play in diverting potential delinquents from the juvenile justice system. This is no new role for the police. For many years police agencies have been involved in varying degrees with prevention activities such as sponsoring athletic teams, maintaining day-camp programs, and other activities. In recent years, however, some police agencies have become much more involved in delinquency prevention programs.

Police-School Liaison Programs

A sizable number of police agencies have police-school programs. Generally the programs are little more than periodic visits by the police to the schools in the community where the latest police gadgetry is displayed and the children are allowed to turn on the siren of the police automobile. Other police agencies, however, have initiated much more meaningful programs. Los Angeles, as an example, has a program in which officers are permanently assigned to schools. The officers in this program have college degrees, often in education, and conduct courses in the social sciences and help students familiarize themselves with the system of criminal justice. These police officers also perform counseling functions and thus are in frequent contact with students.

Police Department Social Service Unit

The city of Wheaton, Illinois, participated in a three-year action research project with the University of Illinois Graduate School of Social Work to demonstrate that the combined efforts of law enforcement and social work would be more effective than separate and independent efforts. Social workers worked with the police to provide direct treatment and crisis-intervention service twenty-four hours a day. In addition, they handled nonviolent clients referred by the police department and referred individuals to appropriate community agencies. Although not directed specifically at juveniles, the project dealt extensively with problems of youth that bring them into contact with the police, such as drug abuse, running away, and other offenses. The primary purpose of the project was to reduce the number of cases referred to the criminal justice system for disposition. Of course, one of the important priorities of the project was to develop interprofessional relationships built around a police-social worker team, which may become a more acceptable organizational model for some police agencies of the future.[45]

Many other recommendations have been made that the police increase their diversionary efforts in dealing with potential delinquents. One of these recommendations is that the police develop and encourage the creation of *neighborhood citizen action programs* in which groups of citizens who have a greater understanding of the area's crime and delinquency problems bring them to the attention of the police. Another proposal is for the establishment of volunteer *block mothers programs,* in which the police with the help of social workers train a group of responsible women to care for and supervise children and to interview and work with adolescents and older youth. Establishment of *police youth councils* is another recommendation. Since the police and youth often interact only in negative circumstances, there is a need to involve both groups in less conflict-laden situations. The average teenager has little understanding of the problems and responsibilities of the police, but police youth councils with broad representation from all types of youth could meet periodically with police representatives to discuss student and police attitudes and activities. Such a council might also explore alternatives to existing police methods for dealing with youth and delinquents.[46]

Community-Related Delinquency Diversion Programs

These programs and school- and court-related diversion programs often overlap. Community-related programs may take numerous forms, including group homes, halfway houses, day-care centers, youth treatment centers, citizen volunteer programs, youth service bureaus, community health and recreation programs, church projects, and others.

Criswell House: An Alternative to Institutionalization

Criswell House in Tallahassee, Florida, is a demonstration project designed to serve as an alternative to the training school. The program, operated by the Florida Division of Youth Services, helps youngsters who need something less than incarceration but more than remaining at home. The boys referred to Criswell House live in residence and attend local public schools during the day. The program is designed around a somewhat unstructured setting in which decisions by staff members are kept at a minimum so that the child must develop responsibility for making decisions affecting his own life and those with whom he lives. This is not meant to imply that the youth has free rein; although staff members consciously try to avoid making the child dependent upon them for decisions, they are readily available for counsel and guidance.[47]

Homeward Bound Program

This program has received a great deal of publicity because of its unusual approach to treating delinquents. It utilizes the lure of adventure and challenge and recognizes that delinquent boys often have a strong need to express manliness. The program entails a strenuous physical regimen conducted along the rugged terrain of the Appalachian Trail in Massachusetts. Long overland hikes of 90 to 100 miles, rappelling exercises down cliffs, and other challenges seem to particularly appeal to many of the delinquent youth participating in the program. The emphasis of the program is on challenging youths and altering many of their personal characteristics. The following description of the program indicates how this might be accomplished:

> The need to pace oneself, and the requirements of persistence in the morning run and dip, the circuit training, and the 90- to 100-mile overland expeditions challenge the delinquent's impulsivity and endurance.
>
> The necessity of safety rules and climbing regulations in rappelling, sea expeditions, and search and rescue operations, causes him to question his previous concept that laws and regulations are to be ignored or treated lightly.
>
> The placing of larger measures of responsibility on him as he holds the safety line of a peer who is rappelling, or assumes leadership of his brigade in stressful situations, forces him to re-evaluate his worth in relationship to his peers.
>
> His dependence on his brigade leader and peers for success, safety and well-being cause him not only to re-examine his attitude towards authority, but also to understand and attempt the strength and weaknesses of himself and others.
>
> Lastly, the sobering experience of the solo causes him to think deeply and long about his accomplishments, and consider what brought him to Homeward Bound, and where and how he is going from here.[48]

Youth Service Bureau (YSB)

This approach is currently one of the most promising community-based delinquency programs being developed. A youth service bureau is basically an independent public delinquency-prevention agency established to divert children and youth from the juvenile justice system by (1) mobilizing community resources to solve youth problems, (2) strengthening existing youth resources and developing new ones, and (3) promoting positive programs to remedy delinquency-breeding conditions.

The primary target of the youth service bureau is children between the ages of seven and eighteen who have been referred to the justice system but for whom the authority of the court is not necessary. The bureau also seeks to help children with problems which might eventually bring them into conflict with the law, and it works to improve and strengthen other agencies and resources that may unwittingly be contributing to delinquency-producing conditions.

The bureau can be organized on a town, city, or county basis, and it operates independently of other agencies or systems. Its organization is structured around a policy-making board of citizen leaders drawn from the power structure of the community and from high-delinquency neighborhoods. The bureau may have branches, each with its own neighborhood board, professional advisory council, working citizen committees, and youth service workers.

Sources of referral to the youth service bureau are quite broad and include parents, schools, social agencies, and youth themselves. The National Council on Crime and Delinquency recommends that the bureau accept referrals from the juvenile justice system only on the condition that these authoritative agencies close such cases and that the bureau not refer a juvenile to these agencies if service is refused or if the child or his family is uncooperative. An "open-door" policy is always maintained so that the youth can refer himself back to the bureau.

The entire thrust of the program can be seen in the principles by which the bureaus operate. These are:

1. Involves citizens, youth, and professionals in the neighborhood as well as persons in a position of social, economic, and political power to perform YSB functions through active volunteer working committees, giving them a decision-making voice on the YSB citizen board.

2. Promotes relationship of confidence and trust between the YSB and its clients as a cornerstone of all the activities and operations of the bureau; strives to avoid any trace of stigma to children referred to the bureau on the part of staff, citizen aides, or the community.

3. Involves the client in identifying problems underlying behavior and draws on a variety of resources in solving them.

4. Does not intervene in the lives of children and their families if its services are not wanted but always leaves the door open.

5. Documents gaps in community services for youth and seeks to have them filled through citizen action but resists the temptation to fill service gaps with its own staff in long term direct service programs.

6. Seeks to strengthen existing agencies by assisting them with problems of hard-to-reach youth; demonstrates innovative programs.

7. From its inception, builds in evaluation under the supervision of a qualified research agency to keep operation in line with goals.[49]

These then are some of the delinquency diversion programs being developed to handle youth outside the juvenile justice system.

THE JUVENILE JUSTICE AND DELINQUENCY
PREVENTION ACT OF 1974

The process and institutions of the juvenile justice system are in need of reexamination. The system cannot continue its policy of acting in isolation from the other agencies of justice, from public and private social agencies, and from meaningful programs of research. A major legislative attempt to curtail this isolationism and the "shotgun" approach to delinquency prevention was made by Congress in 1974. The Juvenile Justice and Delinquency Prevention Act established the Office of Juvenile Justice and Delinquency Prevention within the Law Enforcement Assistance Administration of the U.S. Department of Justice. This new office was given legislative authority over a wide range of programs involving the juvenile justice system, such as prevention, diversion, training of juvenile justice personnel, treatment, rehabilitation, evaluation and research, and other areas which might improve the juvenile justice system of the United States. Specifically, the purposes of the act were as follows:

1. To develop an agency which would provide for the thorough and prompt evaluation of all federally assisted juvenile delinquency programs.

2. To provide technical assistance to public and private agencies, institutions and individuals in developing and implementing juvenile delinquency programs.

3. To establish training programs for persons including professionals, para-professionals and volunteers who work with delinquents.

4. To establish a centralized research effort on the problems of juvenile delin-quency including an information clearinghouse to disseminate research findings.

5. To develop and encourage the implementation of national standards for the administration of juvenile justice, including recommendations for adminis-trative, budgetary and legislative actions at the Federal, state and local levels to facilitate the adoption of such standards.

6. To assist states and local communities with resources to develop and imple-ment programs to keep students in elementary and secondary schools and to prevent unwarranted and arbitrary suspensions and expulsions.

7. To establish a Federal assistance program to deal with the problems of runa-way youth.[50]

To help this office accomplish its important coordinative undertaking at the federal level, a special Coordinating Council was established consisting of heads of federal departments whose agencies are involved in delinquency-related programs. Such officials as the attorney general, the secretary of labor, the secretary of health, education, and welfare, and the director of the Special Action Office for Drug Abuse and Prevention serve on this council. To give professional advice to the council, a special National Advisory Committee for

Juvenile Justice and Delinquency Prevention was also created. This committee, appointed by the president, consists of twenty-one advisers representing juvenile or family court judges, juvenile probation and correctional personnel, law enforcement agencies, private and voluntary organizations, and community-based programs.

The Office of Juvenile Justice and Delinquency Prevention is authorized to provide grants and contracts to agencies of state and local government as well as private institutions and individuals to assist in the development of delinquency-related programs. The major emphasis of these programs, however, must be on the development of advanced programming techniques. In fact, 75 percent of all monies spent by this office must be specifically earmarked to develop and maintain advanced programs. The following categories are to receive special emphasis:

1. Community-based programs to work with youth (development of foster care and shelter care, group homes, halfway houses, home health services, etc.)

2. Community-based programs to work with parents in order to strengthen the family unit

3. Youth service bureaus

4. Comprehensive programs of drug and alcohol abuse

5. Educational programs or supportive services designed to keep delinquents and other youth in schools

6. Expanded use of probation; recruitment and training of probation officers and other professionals and volunteers

7. Youth-initiated programs such as Outreach, which tries to involve those juveniles most alienated or removed from the positive influences of society

8. Probation subsidy programs

9. Research and evaluation

10. Monitoring of jails and detention facilities to ensure that proper procedures and facilities are available and that juveniles are not incarcerated along with adults

For the first time we are organizing our human and physical resources to investigate the national problem of delinquency in a concerted and coordinative manner. Although this is a significant step, it will be many years before any significant and wide-ranging solutions are uncovered. In the meantime we as a nation are going to experience continued frustration and disappointment with the limited success of many of our program efforts.

SUMMARY

Juvenile delinquency is increasing at an alarming rate, especially among females. The juvenile court is a twentieth-century response to the problems of dealing with children who are law violators or who need society's protection.

The procedure in juvenile courts is much different from the procedure in adult courts because juvenile courts were founded on the philosophy that the function of the court was to treat and help. In recent years the operations of the juvenile court have received a great deal of criticism, and a number of important Supreme Court decisions have dealt with the rights of juveniles.

The major emphasis of the juvenile justice system today is on diversion and treatment rather than adjudication and incarceration. Diversion programs can be classified into school-related, court-related, police-related, and community-related models. In 1974, Congress established a special federal office to coordinate the efforts of the juvenile justice system at the federal, state, and local levels.

Suggested Additional Readings

Amos, William E., and R. L. Manella. *Delinquent Children in Juvenile Correctional Institutions*. Springfield, Ill.: Charles C. Thomas, 1966.

Finklestein, M. Marvin. *Prosecution in the Juvenile Courts: Guidelines for the Future*. Washington, D.C.: U.S. Government Printing Office, December 1973.

Garabedian, Peter C., and Don C. Gibbons. *Becoming Delinquent: Young Offenders and the Correctional System*. Chicago: Aldine, 1970.

Gula, Martin. *Agency-Operated Group Homes*. Washington, D.C.: U.S. Government Printing Office, 1964.

The Institute of Criminal Justice and Criminology, University of Maryland. *New Approaches to Diversion and Treatment of Juvenile Offenders*. Washington, D.C.: U.S. Government Printing Office, June 1973.

Mack, Julian. "The Juvenile Court." *Harvard Law Review* 23 (1909).

Management and Behavioral Sciences Center, Wharton School, University of Pennsylvania. *Planning and Designing for Juvenile Justice*. Washington, D.C.: Law Enforcement Assistance Administration, 1972.

McNeil, F. "A Halfway-House Program for Delinquents." *Crime and Delinquency* 13 (October 1967):538–544.

Rubin, Ted, and Jack F. Smith. *The Future of the Juvenile Court: Implication for Correctional Manpower and Training*. Washington, D.C.: U.S. Government Printing Office, 1968.

U.S. Department of Health, Education, and Welfare, Youth Development and Delinquency Prevention Administration. *State Responsibility for Juvenile Detention Care*. Washington, D.C.: U.S. Government Printing Office, 1970.

Notes

1. U.S. Department of Health, Education, and Welfare, *Juvenile Court Statistics– 1973* (Washington, D.C.: U.S. Government Printing Office, March 1975), p. 1.
2. Ibid.
3. Federal Bureau of Investigation, *Uniform Crime Reports, 1973* (Washington, D.C.: U.S. Government Printing Office, 1974).
4. Chicago Police Department, "1965 Youth Division Offense/Offender Data Sheet" (unpublished).
5. U.S. Department of Health, Education, and Welfare, op. cit., p. 2.
6. Federal Bureau of Investigation, op. cit., p. 126.
7. Address by Professor Robert C. Trojanowicz to the Michigan Juvenile Judges Conference, Lansing, Mich., May 1976.
8. Mass. Gen. Laws Ann., ch. 119, §52 (1969).
9. President's Commission on Law Enforcement and Administration of Justice, *Task Force Report: Juvenile Delinquency and Youth Crime* (Washington, D.C.: U.S. Government Printing Office, 1967), p. 4.

10. Michigan Probate Code, § 712A.4 (1968).

11. Anthony Platt, *The Child Savers* (Chicago: University of Chicago Press, 1969), p. 202.

12. Robert M. Mennel, "Origins of the Juvenile Court," *Crime and Delinquency* (January 1972): 70.

13. Ibid., pp. 70–71.

14. New York Society for the Reformation of Juvenile Delinquents, *Annual Report* (New York: 1827), pp. 3–4.

15. Mennel, op. cit., p. 71.

16. James Lieby, *Charities and Corrections in New Jersey* (New Brunswick, N.J.: Rutgers University Press, 1967), p. 82.

17. President's Commission, op. cit., p. 3.

18. Ibid.

19. See *Commonwealth v. Fisher,* 213 Pa. St. 48, 62 A. 198 (1905).

20. Michigan Probate Code, chap. XII-A, § 712A.2.

21. President's Commission, op. cit., p. 3.

22. U.S. Department of Health, Education, and Welfare, op. cit., p. 11.

23. U.S. Department of Health, Education, and Welfare, *Standards for Juvenile and Family Courts* (Washington, D.C.: U.S. Government Printing Office, 1966), p. 84.

24. Michigan Advisory Council on Criminal Justice, *Criminal Justice Goals and Standards for the State of Michigan* (Lansing, Mich.: MACCJ, 1975), p. 46.

25. F. W. Miller, R. O. Dawson, G. E. Dix, and R. I. Parnas, *The Juvenile Justice Process* (Mineola, N.Y.: Foundation Press, 1971), p. 1162.

26. Robert Shears, "Legal Problems Peculiar to Children's Courts," *American Bar Association Journal* 48 (1962): 720.

27. Foreword to Pauline V. Young, *Social Treatment in Probation and Delinquency* (New York: McGraw-Hill, 1973), p. xxvii.

28. 383 U.S. 541 (1966).

29. 383 U.S. at 556.

30. 387 U.S. 1 (1967).

31. 387 U.S. at 33.

32. 387 U.S. at 41.

33. Frederick L. Faust and Paul J. Brantingham, *Juvenile Justice Philosophy* (St. Paul, Minn: West, 1974), p. 537.

34. See Norman Lefstein, Vaughan Stapelton, and Lee Teitelbaum. "In Search of Juvenile Justice: Gault and Its Implementation," *Law and Society Review* 491 (1969).

35. Charles E. Reasons, "Gault: Procedural Change and Substantive Effect," *Crime and Delinquency* 16 (April 1970): 163–171.

36. See U.S. Department of Health, Education, and Welfare, *Juvenile Court Statistics—1973*, p.11.

37. President's Commission, op. cit., p. 417.

38. William H. Sheridan, "Juveniles Who Commit Non-Criminal Acts: Why Treat in a Correctional System?" *Federal Probation* (March 1967): 26–27.

39. U.S. Department of Health, Education and Welfare, *Juvenile Court Statistics– 1973*, p. 11.

40. This typology of delinquency diversion models is taken from Institute of Government, Corrections Division, *Models for Delinquency Diversion* (Athens, Ga.: University of Georgia, October 1971).

41. Saul Pilnich, "Collegefields Group Educational Center," United Community Fund and Council of Essex and West Hudson Counties, New Jersey (Grant No. 65015).

42. Law Enforcement Assistance Administration, *Providence Educational Center: A Program for Juvenile Delinquents* (Washington, D.C.: U.S. Government Printing Office, 1975).

43. Institute of Government. op. cit., p. 33.

44. The National Committee for Children and Youth, *Project Crossroads: Final Report, Phase I* (Washington, D.C.: U.S. Department of Health, Education, and Welfare, 1970).

45. See Institute of Judicial Administration, *Criminal Justice Newsletter* 2 (Aug. 9, 1971).

46. See National Council on Crime and Delinquency, *Citizen-Action to Crime and Delinquency* (Paramus, N.J.: NCCD, 1968), p. 18.

47. John M. Flackett, "Criswell House: An Alternative to Institutional Commitment for Juvenile Offenders," *Federal Probation* 34 (December 1970): 30–37.

48. Herb C. Willman, Jr., and Ron Y. F. Chun, "Homeward Bound: An Alternative to the Institutionalization of Adjudicated Juvenile Offenders," *Federal Probation* 37 (September 1973): 56.

49. National Council on Crime and Delinquency, "What Is a Youth Service Bureau?" mimeo (1971), p. 3.

50. "The Juvenile Justice and Delinquency Prevention Act of 1974," *The Criminal Law Reporter* 15 (Sept. 11, 1974).

Index